Russia's Far East

THE NATIONAL BUREAU OF ASIAN RESEARCH

The National Bureau of Asian Research (NBR) is a nonprofit, nonpartisan institution that conducts advanced research on policy-relevant issues in Asia. It also serves as the global clearinghouse for Asia research conducted by specialists and institutions worldwide. NBR is uniquely positioned to promote informed and effective U.S. policy toward the region.

- NBR sponsors projects that examine the economic, political, and strategic questions affecting U.S. relations with East Asia, South Asia, and the former Soviet Union.

- NBR efficiently draws upon the world's premier specialists to develop and carry out its research agenda.

- Through its advisory board, programs, and print and electronic publications, NBR integrates its research into the policymaking communities of the United States and Asia.

NBR's operations are governed by its Board of Directors, a nationally prominent group of leaders with long-term interests in Asia. NBR's research agenda is developed in consultation with its Board of Advisors, which consists of experts from research centers, universities, and corporations, and of more than sixty U.S. Senators and Representatives. Guidance is also provided by leading American companies through NBR's Corporate Council.

Russia's Far East: A Region at Risk

Edited by

Judith Thornton and
Charles E. Ziegler

 NBR The National Bureau of Asian Research

in association with

University of Washington Press
Seattle and London

Library of Congress Cataloging-in-Publication Data

Russia's Far East : a region at risk / edited by Judith Thornton and Charles E. Ziegler.
    p. cm.
    Includes index.
    ISBN 0-295-98235-7 (alk. paper)
    1. Russian Far East (Russia)—Politics and government—20th century.
2. Russian Far East (Russia)—Economic conditions—20th century.   3. Russia (Federation)—Foreign relations—Pacific Area. 4. Pacific Area—Foreign relations—Russia (Federation). 5. Pacific Area—Economic conditions—20th century.
I. Thornton, Judith. II. Ziegler, Charles E.
    DK771.D3 R86 2002
    330.957'086—dc21   2002002118

The paper used in this publication meets the minimum requirements of American National Standard for Information Sciences—Permanence of Paper for Printed Library Materials, ANSI Z39.48-1984.

Contents

INTERNATIONAL RELATIONS:
PROSPECTS FOR COOPERATION

Acknowledgments

This book emerged from an eighteen-month project developed by The National Bureau of Asian Research (NBR) on the impact of post–Cold War economic and political reform on stability and security in the Russian Far East, Russia as a whole, and the Northeast Asian region. In order to thoroughly assess the factors contributing to, or impeding, transition, we enlisted participants from Russia, China, Japan, Korea, and the United States to contribute papers, make presentations at project meetings, and participate in an email discussion forum.

A great deal of institutional cooperation and coordination contributed to the success and rich findings of the project. Most significantly, the efforts of Dr. Pavel Minakir, Ms. Valentina Buldakova, and the staff at the Economic Research Institute in Khabarovsk must be commended. They skillfully and gracefully organized the Khabarovsk project meeting and field research trips throughout the Russian Far East in October 1999 and efficiently handled all of our planned and last-minute needs. Closer to home, we are also grateful to the Russian, East European, and Central Asian Studies Center at the University of Washington's Henry M. Jackson School of International Studies for collaboration on a one-day symposium held in Seattle in May 2000.

The editors thank the authors for their contributions to the project and for their willingness to revise their chapters. In addition, we are indebted to Akihiro Iwashita, Gao Zhongyi, and Vladimir Popov for their participation in the project. For their contributions as able discussants, we owe a debt of thanks to Tsuneo Akaha, Greg Brock, Steve Blank, John Hardt, Robert Stuart, and Tom Wuchte. We also sincerely thank former Ambassador to the USSR Jack F. Matlock, Jr., for making a keynote dinner address during the project's final meeting, and Carol Vipperman, president of the Foundation for Russian American Economic Cooperation, for a special presentation at the final conference.

The chapters in this volume have been extensively revised based on a series of interactive research meetings and an email discussion forum involving academics, businesspeople, and policymakers with expertise in the Russian Far East. Earlier versions of the chapters by Clay Moltz, Sergey Sevastyanov, and Rajan Menon and Charles Ziegler appeared in December 2000 issues of the *NBR Analysis*. In addition, summary articles by Tony Allison, Jennifer Duncan and Michelle Ruetsche, Nadezhda Mikheeva, Pavel Minakir, Vladimir Popov, and Judith Thornton were published in a special issue of *Comparative Economic Studies* in Winter 2001.

We are indebted to a number of people at NBR. Without them, the project would have remained an idea and the production of a book would have been impossible. We thank Richard Ellings, NBR president, and Herbert Ellison, former director of NBR's Eurasia Policy Studies Program, for their support of the project; and Erica Johnson, who helped to formulate and administer the project and worked diligently with the editors and contributors to coordinate the preparation of the manuscript and ensure its timely publication. At various stages, other NBR staff lent valuable assistance, particularly Jonathan Carver, Jen Linder, Meira Meek, Jocelyn Roberts, and Loren Runyon. We also thank Bruce Acker, who helped conceive of the project and served as copyeditor for the volume.

We are deeply appreciative of Michael Duckworth and his colleagues at the University of Washington Press for their patience while we went through drafts and solved the typical problems associated with producing an edited volume.

Finally, we gratefully acknowledge the Carnegie Corporation of New York, the United States–Japan Foundation, Center for Nonproliferation Studies at the Monterey Institute for International Studies, and the Henry M. Jackson Foundation for their generous financial support, without which whatever good the findings will serve would not have been possible.

Judith Thornton, Seattle, Washington

Charles E. Ziegler, Louisville, Kentucky

INTRODUCTION

1

The Russian Far East in Perspective

Judith Thornton and Charles E. Ziegler

REGION AT RISK

The past decade has brought remarkable changes to the post–Cold War world. Nowhere is the alteration of the economic and military balance larger than in Northeast Asia, where four geopolitical giants—the United States, Japan, Russia, and China—face each other on the Pacific Rim. The future of their economic and strategic relationship is contingent on choices that have yet to be made. A future based on economic openness and capital market integration could link Russian energy and raw materials with Japanese capital, U.S. food, technology, and know-how, and Chinese labor in the transformation of what is potentially the most dynamic region of the world economy. But in an alternative future, Northeast Asia could also become a major trouble spot in which criminal groups and corrupt officials compete for control of Russia's resources, unemployed North Korean and Chinese workers flood into Russia's fertile Amur River Valley, and Russian military producers in Khabarovsk and Primorye provide the ships, aircraft, submarines, and missiles to modernize an expanding Chinese military force.

This study of the security implications of economic and political issues in the Russian Far East (RFE) highlights the risks of change in one of Russia's most remote and troubled regions. In its policy responses, the Russian government faces conflicting goals. Russia's leaders want to seize the benefits of open markets and investment while retaining political powers founded on strong administrative control. They want to gain access to world technologies while protecting their loss-making domestic producers. Economic forces from the world market, however, challenge the old administrative methods of Russia's federal and regional governments and present them with new and difficult sources of uncertainty.

TRANSITION AND THE ROLE OF THE SOVIET LEGACY

A huge area, the Russian Far East (excluding the Republic of Sakha) is one-third the size of the United States, with less than 3 percent of its population.[1] Although in many respects the Russian drive to explore and develop the Far East parallels America's drive westward, nothing in the region even vaguely compares to Silicon Valley, Los Angeles, or Seattle. While much of the U.S. West Coast is overcrowded, the tsars and the Soviets had to entice settlers to the Far East with high wages and expensive subsidies. When that did not work, they resorted to prison labor.

In the Soviet era, the RFE maintained a gigantic military-industrial complex and served as a tightly controlled playground for the Russian military. With the breakup of the Soviet Union, regional institutions unraveled under the pressure of collapsing federal military budgets and fierce, violent competition for ownership and control of the region's ports, enterprises, and resource wealth. A decade after the collapse of the Soviet Union, towns built around military production still depend on foreign and domestic military orders for their subsistence, and unemployed workers turn to informal, private markets or criminal activities. Ten percent of the region's Soviet population of eight million has migrated away, notably from the Far North, yet unemployment remains high, and over 40 percent of the population subsists at less than the official poverty rate. Although Russian President Vladimir Putin and certain regional officials have pledged to reverse this trend, few Russians can be expected to move eastward in the near future.

During seventy years of Soviet rule, the RFE served primarily as a frontier outpost and raw-materials base for the rest of the country. Located thousands of miles from Moscow and the more populated European Russia, this region was considered vulnerable, and with some justification. Soviet and Japanese troops exchanged fire several times along the Manchurian border before the two countries signed a nonaggression pact in 1940. America's military presence in Japan and Korea after World War II, together with its forward-deployed forces throughout the western Pacific, posed a significant military challenge to the USSR's eastern littoral. Chinese hostility during the Cultural Revolution, together with a longstanding dispute over territory along the Amur River and in Primorye, led to armed clashes on Damanskii Island in 1969 in which several hundred soldiers died.

In response to threats real and perceived, by the early 1980s Moscow had stationed nearly half a million troops in the region. The Soviet military deployed hundreds of intercontinental and intermediate-range nuclear missiles in Siberia and the Far East, complemented by over 200 strategic bombers and thousands of fighter aircraft. Under the leadership of Admiral Sergei Gorshkov, the Soviet Pacific Fleet expanded dramatically—in the late 1980s the Fleet had some 160,000 naval personnel operating 120 submarines and nearly 200 surface combatant ships.[2] Soviet border guards, the *pogranichniki*, were responsible for patrolling the extensive frontiers to prevent spies and saboteurs from infiltrating the USSR, and of course to prevent malcontents from leaving. Prior to 1992, a large portion of the area was closed to foreigners and to Soviets lacking the required residential permit.

The Soviet leadership paid only sporadic attention to the Russian Far East. Under Stalin it served as the center for some of the country's worst labor camps, which were tasked with mining gold and logging, and as the location of a frontier cult glorifying the achievements of socialism in a distant, inhospitable territory. Leonid Brezhnev's regime also stressed the frontier ethos, pouring resources into the Baikal-Amur rail line (called the "project of the century" and known by the Russian acronym BAM) and manufacturing heroes out of border guards and miners. Early in his tenure, Mikhail Gorbachev proposed opening up the Russian Far East to international development, and in 1987 he pushed the Long-Term Program for the Comprehensive Development of the Far Eastern Economic Region through the Politburo. But as with so many grandiose Soviet projects, nothing came of the 232-billion-ruble, fourteen-year plan, which was to make the region self-sufficient in energy by the year 2000.

Despite Moscow's best efforts to maintain a tight rein over this vital region, a regional consciousness and frontier spirit often intruded. Lenin's idea of a Far Eastern Republic (1920–22) to serve as a buffer state in the early years of the Russian Revolution was resurrected following the breakup of the USSR. This may have been largely a political ploy by regional politicians to win concessions from a weakened Moscow, but it indicates the enduring appeal of separatism in the post-Soviet era. For those living in the RFE, the capital and European Russia are geographically and psychologically distant. In Soviet times, the center (the political power eminating from the Kremlin) was generous in compensating the region's inhabitants for living and working in such a remote and inhospitable place, but the investments and subsidies are now long gone, and Soviet central planning left the Russian Far East ill-prepared for the twenty-first century.

As a result of the command system, the RFE entered the reform era with a distorted structure of costs and production. Its economy, dominated by the primary industries of fishing, military equipment, timber, nonferrous metals, and diamonds, had been linked to the western Soviet Union in a pattern of forced integration, which imposed high real transport costs on the region's links to the outside world. The Russian Far East was the terminus of the Trans-Siberian and Baikal-Amur railroads connecting Europe and Asia. However, the region was highly dependent on imports from outside for its subsistence. Value-added production in the region accounted for only one-third of regional output. Transportation costs accounted for another third. More than half of the food, consumer goods, and energy used in the region were shipped in from elsewhere in the Soviet Union. In spite of its high level of dependence on outside supply, relatively little exchange took place in the foreign market. Eighty percent of imports came from elsewhere in the Soviet Union. Ninety percent of exports were sent to other regions of the USSR.

The structure of domestic prices was distorted relative to the world market as well. The RFE bought energy and sold raw materials at low domestic prices, buying consumer goods and industrial equipment at high relative prices, much as if it faced implicit import tariffs on manufactures and implicit export taxes on its raw materials exports. Exporting firms received not world prices but low domestic prices for their goods.

The prospect of opening its economy to the world market and adopting a structure of prices close to those on the world market confronted the region with a daunting situation. At world terms of trade, the region's raw materials had far greater value relative to manufactured goods outside rather than inside the country. With access to the world market, raw materials could be sold more profitably to Japan than to Moscow.

However, many of the region's manufacturing firms faced a more difficult alternative. When assessed at world prices, the value of the final products they produced would not cover the raw materials costs alone of producing them, even if the charges for existing labor and capital stock were zero. These industries exhibited negative value-added at world market prices. They would be bankrupt once the regional economy opened to the world market unless they could improve their underlying technology.

In a 1996 study, Judith Thornton estimated apparent competitiveness of each industrial sector at world prices and identified four sectors of the Russian Far East—food processing (fishing), forest products, light industry, and the chemical industry—as negative value-added sectors at world prices. Three additional sectors—agriculture, ferrous metals, and coal—were unprofitable—that is, could not cover existing wages at world prices.[3] The implications of these estimates were serious for the region, for two of the region's main export sectors, fishing and timber, would become unprofitable once they paid the full price for energy. Further, the precipitous drop in domestic demand for military equipment after the collapse of the

Soviet Union reduced regional machinery production to a fraction of its former level. Without central subsidies, the region's traditional industries would have to downsize, and it was uncertain what new economic activities could take up the slack.

Russia's leadership is once again promising to revive the Russian Far East. En route to the July 2000 meeting of the G-8 in Okinawa, Japan, President Vladimir Putin stopped off in Blagoveshchensk, a quaint Russian port city of 230,000 on the Chinese border. There he warned, "If we don't make a real effort to develop Russia's far east, then in the next few decades, the Russian population will be speaking mainly Japanese, Chinese, and Korean."[4] Putin reassured governors from the Russian Far East and the neighboring Transbaikal regions that the survival of Pacific Russia ranked high in his priorities. Attributing the RFE's problems to its "colossal distance and alienation from the center," Putin admitted that of 14 billion rubles ($513 million) allocated to the region in the 1999 Russian Federation budget, only 1.5 billion ($53 million) was actually spent for the region's benefit.

Yet, it would take more than an overnight visit to the region for Putin's new administration in Moscow to familiarize itself with the real problems besetting Pacific Russia. During almost a decade of economic reform, the Russian Federation and its unruly regions have yet to agree to a clear framework of rights and responsibilities between the center, the territories, and the municipalities. While a fragmented federal government struggled with political deadlock, budget deficits, and growing federal debt, regional administrations picked up almost 90 percent of the costs of healthcare, welfare, and education. Long before the August 1998 financial crash left Russia without a functioning banking system, the regional enterprises and administrations were already returning to the practices of the central planning era, using barter payments, arrears, and tax offsets to acquire inputs, compensate workers, and subsidize the unpaid fuel and energy costs of federal agencies in their regions. Lacking most of the federal support they once enjoyed, military facilities declined into decrepitude, while once-busy military producers sought foreign orders or delivered crop harvesters on credit to the local collective farms.

In 2001, new friendship treaties with China and North Korea promise increased attention to Russian energy exports to China and an expansion of rail links between the RFE and Pyongyang. The RFE territories are actively preparing an ambitious new regional development program premised on federal support for energy infrastructure, military investment, and the region's physical infrastructure. However, regional observers ask whether new programs, like many past promises, will fail to be implemented.

When contributors to this National Bureau of Asian Research project visited the Russian Far East during the fall of 1999 and winter of 2000, they discovered that both the RFE's economic problems and the solutions to them were defined differently in Moscow than in the regions. Regional administrators complained that local communities received little benefit from local resources, whose profits flowed to Moscow in the form of taxes, or offshore. They argued that the federal government responded to any increase in direct funding of local public services by reducing federal transfers to the region.[5] And they noted that they lacked the authority to counterbalance confiscatory taxes, tariffs, and regulations in a political structure in which the local regulatory personnel of thirty different federal agencies outnumbered local bureaucrats several-fold. Some local authorities sought greater autonomy in managing public policies; others lobbied for larger federal support to fund public expenditures and the cost of federal agencies.

At the same time, federal authorities countered that territorial governors often exercised semifeudal powers within territorial networks, transferring ownership of enterprises to regional elites, gaining tax exemptions for regional firms, allocating budget funds and subsidized energy to favored constituencies, raising protectionist barriers to shield local producers from outside competition, and intimidating local media and political competitors. Even so, federal agencies in the regions depended on in-kind subsidies and housing from the regional government to survive, as federal payments and wages fell further and further into arrears. Meanwhile, in Moscow, central authorities blamed economic disorganization—falling tax revenues, the informal economy, capital flight, demonitization of economic links, and economic disintegration—on regional separatism. They claimed that local elites plundered former state enterprises, and they sought to increase central authority— reestablishing vertical chains of command between the center and the regions and recentralizing tax revenues in the federal treasury.

ECONOMIC REFORM AND ECONOMIC GROWTH

The election of Vladimir Putin on March 26, 2000, signaled a revival of the processes of economic and political reform in an environment in which a compliant Duma is prepared to give the president much of what he asks. In late 1999, then– Prime Minister Putin appointed a St. Petersburg colleague, German Gref, to head a team tasked with preparation of a program of economic reform for Russia. The resulting lengthy document, submitted to the government on May 22, 2000, is liberal in its goals and in its support for private enterprise and market processes. What is still uncertain is how much of the Gref program will actually be implemented in practice. For, at the same time that he brought his new social contract to the table, Putin also began a process of "streamlining" the administrative structure of the Russian government, and the administrative changes seem to contradict Gref's ambitious program of market-supporting reforms. In April 2001, President

Putin's annual address to the Federal Assembly reaffirmed his support for building the institutional infrastructure of a market economy but described a more interventionist strategy for building state capacity and fostering economic growth.[6]

During 2000 and 2001, the environment for economic reform was more favorable than it had been in several years. At long last, after a decade of stagnation, several forces combined to set the Russian economy on the path of renewed economic growth. Lower inflation kept the ruble exchange rate low in spite of rising hard currency reserves (although price pressures emerged in 2001). The low ruble exchange rate bolstered import-substituting production and enhanced the profitability of exports. High oil prices and renewed growth in Russia's main export markets allowed the federal government to raise export tariffs on oil, petroleum products, and minerals. Rising tax collection brought federal budget revenues to 17 percent of GDP for 2000, bringing the federal budget surplus to 2.5 percent of GDP, even after payment of current debt obligations to the Paris Club in January 2001.

Economic data for the year 2000 were impressive. Real gross domestic product increased 7.7 percent compared with 1999, industrial output 9.6 percent, and total investment 17.7 percent compared with 1999.[7] In 2000, Russia enjoyed a trade surplus of $61 billion and a current account surplus of $46 billion, equal to 19 percent of GDP. The revenues from export tariffs on energy and minerals gave the federal budget a surplus equal to 2.5 percent of GDP. Estimated unemployment fell to 10 percent of working population.

Still, recovery was fragile. Exports accounted for almost one-fourth of GDP, and 36 percent of the Russian population earned real income below the subsistence level. Data compiled by Nadezhda Mikheeva in this volume show that, taking into account real costs of living, the shares of the population living in poverty were higher in all RFE regions than the Russian Federation average.

Reform of capital markets moves slowly.[8] The Agency for Restructuring Credit Organizations (ARCO) has few resources and faces major political constraints. In the May 2000 issue of *Russian Economic Trends*, Knut Eggenberger wrote, "The authorities' lack of a clear strategy for how to deal with the banks, the nontransparency with which some well-connected banks were provided cash infusions by the Central Bank, and worst of all, the ease with which assets could be stripped from insolvent banks without recourse from authorities have taught prospective bankers a lesson: You can rip off your creditors (depositors and foreign investors) with impunity."[9] Sberbank, the state bank, holds 90 percent of household and 25 percent of corporate deposits, although a transparent accounting would probably show that it, too, is insolvent according to international accounting standards.

In the first half of 2001, real economic growth continued, fueled by a revival of domestic demand. There were signs of a modest recovery in fixed investment as well, funded from enterprises' own resources. However, in the Russian Far East, the rising cost of food imports combined with declining exports to Japan resulted in a measured decline in real income. For example, Khabarovsk reported a 3 percent decline in real standard of living in spite of growing exports of military hardware to China.[10]

IMPLEMENTING ECONOMIC REFORM

In 2001 the prospects for future economic reform are mixed. German Gref's "Strategy of Russia's Development to the Year 2010" aspires to create a new social contract between the Russian government and its citizens. Gref's program goes much beyond earlier goals in seeking to rekindle growth and raise standards of living. Some of the specific steps he promises to take are to:

- Introduce measures protecting private property rights, including increased ownership of land and real estate and improved protection of stockholder rights;
- Provide equal conditions for competition by increasing transparency and reducing monopoly power and regulatory protectionism;
- Reduce regulatory burdens and reform customs legislation and procedures;
- Reform taxes;
- Balance government expenditures in line with tax revenue;
- Shift to a "subsidiary state model," focusing state assistance on those in need; and
- Build an effective government that supports civil society by providing reform of courts and law enforcement, reform of the civil service, strengthening federalism, and introducing a gradual decentralization of the fiscal system.

Passage of the second part of the tax code by the State Duma and Federation Council in summer 2000 was a first step in carrying out one of these reforms. The new package of tax laws, which took effect in 2001, includes a flat 13 percent income tax, a unified social tax set at 35.6 percent for annual income less than 100,000 rubles, with declining marginal rates for higher amounts, a 20 percent value-added tax (VAT) assigned exclusively to the federal government, and a reduction in turnover tax. Other planned measures include removing tax loopholes, ending special fiscal arrangements between the federal budget and autonomous regions, increasing state spending on education, healthcare, and defense, and bringing all budget funds under control of the federal treasury.

When the Duma adjourned in July, it had succeeded in passing amendments to lower the corporate profit tax to 24 percent and passing (in two readings) a Land

Code, which establishes private ownership of urban land but not agricultural land. The Duma also passed the first reading of labor laws, pension reforms, and bills to reduce administrative obstacles facing businesses.[11]

Most important for the RFE were legislative changes defining the tax regime of natural resources. A draft chapter of the Tax Code sets a unified tax on natural resource production to replace excise duties, royalties, and payments for resource extraction. Calculated on sales revenues, the basic tax rates are 8 percent on nonferrous metals and gemstones, 6 percent on gold, and 16.5 percent on natural gas and oil. New tax rates on hydrocarbons become effective in 2005. Revenues from taxation of oil and natural gas would go 80 percent to federal and 20 percent to regional budgets.[12]

Still, there has been little progress in defining a clear legislative framework for production-sharing agreements (PSAs). In September 2000, President Putin gave German Gref and the Ministry of Trade and Economic Development the responsibility for coordinating PSA legislation. A year later, many forces impede this goal. The Ministries of Fuel and Energy and Finance oppose proposed changes. Politicians in the Duma and Federation Council who play a key role in adding projects to the PSA list oppose measures giving preferential treatment to a few territories. Domestic oil companies, which have profited from high export prices, have little interest in supporting legislative changes that would bring in increased competition from foreign multinational companies.

THE ECONOMIC SITUATION IN THE RUSSIAN FAR EAST

Chapters in this volume document that although there is considerable diversity among territories, the standard of living in the RFE is substantially more depressed than the all-Russian average. Although GDP per capita for the RFE was close to the all-Russian level, per capita real income was well below the Russian average in all regions of the RFE except the Republic of Sakha.

In chapter 4, "Social and Economic Differentiation in the Russian Far East," Nadezhda Mikheeva estimates the impact of these large-scale changes on the well-being of the populations in the individual territories of the RFE. She observes that the territories of the RFE underwent drastic drops in industrial production and real income. In response, there was a large out-migration of population during the 1990s. The region's recovery in 2000 was modest, in part due to weak consumer sectors and distance from European Russia.

In 1998, per capita real income in most regions of the RFE was about 60 percent of the 1993 level. Estimates of the size of the informal economy varied widely from 15 to 63 percent of official income, and the extent of economic decline varied widely as well. By 1998, real per capita earnings in Sakha were five times higher than in the Jewish autonomous *oblast*. In Chukotka autonomous *okrug*, which experienced a massive outflow of population, average real income was only 95 percent of the estimated subsistence minimum. Although Sakhalinskaia oblast received a substantial flow of foreign investment into its oil and gas industry, 39 percent of its population also earned less than subsistence.

RFE budget revenues declined apace with production. Federal public investment in the regions fell to 15 percent of pre-reform levels, but federal transfers were substantial in the poorest regions: the Jewish autonomous oblast (48 percent of budget revenues), Chukotka (28 percent), and Koriak autonomous okrug (40 percent).

Mikheeva's regressions seeking to identify determinants of decline in real income confirm observations that much of the difference in rates of decline could be attributed to the initial structures of the individual regions. In the northern regions, a higher share of agriculture was associated with greater decline of income. In the southern territories, a large share of transport services moderated the collapse of production. Higher federal and territorial investment also moderated the observed decline. Federal spending was directed to compensate for declining income, thus providing an implicit social safety net.

A detailed assessment of the region's natural resource potential by a group of scholars from the Khabarovsk-based Economic Research Institute of the Russian Academy of Sciences raises both hopes and concerns. The region's territory, accounting for 36 percent of Russia's total land area, is valuable for its strategic location on the Pacific and for its vast stocks of resource wealth. Some of these stocks, such as forest resources and fisheries, have been harvested at high rates, so the region's long-term health depends on increased attention to long-term sustainability. Other resources—minerals, oil and gas, hydroelectric potential—are largely untapped. Currently, extraction costs are high, and political uncertainty hinders access to cost-reducing investment.[13]

Still, continued rapid growth in Asia, notably in China and Korea, and renewed expansion in Japan will generate rising demand for energy and raw materials, especially a rising demand for the natural gas of Siberia and the RFE. Energy multinationals Royal Dutch/Shell, ExxonMobil, and BP-Amoco are poised to undertake investment in delivering the hydrocarbons of the Sakhalin shelf to Asia and to Russia.[14] If current plans are implemented, then Sakhalin oil and liquefied natural gas would be transported to Japan, Korea, Taiwan, and the rapidly growing southern provinces of China. Further, if a secure framework can be established for multilateral investment in the production and distribution of Russia's natural gas, then the next decade could see the beginnings of a network of natural gas pipelines linking Sakhalin, Sakha, Irkutsk, and Krasnoyarsk with the expanding economies of Northeast Asia. China, the two Koreas, and Japan would enjoy environmental benefits and falling energy costs, while the RFE would enjoy both lower energy costs and greater regional income.

Yet, data on employment in natural resource extraction and estimates of possible new development of agriculture in the southern RFE provided by Alexander Sheingauz and his colleagues in chapter 5 show that resource development alone would be insufficient to support the more than seven million people presently living in the RFE. Thus, the region's future will depend as well on whether it can establish a secure environment for investment and whether it is able to enhance economic links with its neighbors in Asia. It would be inefficient for a growth-oriented Russian government to direct the majority of high-technology resources to military purposes when other investment needs are so great.

THE PERFORMANCE AND PROSPECTS OF INDIVIDUAL ECONOMIC SECTORS

While the prospects for individual economic sectors vary, all civilian branches of Pacific Russia's economy are influenced by the same forces—investor perceptions of political and economic risk, property rights, taxes, regulatory regimes for access to assets and natural resources, and state capacity to govern at the center and in the regions.

Nowhere is the lack of private property rights more harmful than in the case of agricultural land. Ownership of tiny, poorly located private plots is widespread. These minute parcels account for a majority of local vegetable production in a sector whose technology (pails and shovels) is almost medieval. Transformation of local collective farms into joint stock companies has given collective farm members few effective ownership rights, since control rights remain in the hands of farm managers and local government officials.

Jennifer Duncan and Michelle Ruetschle's "Agrarian Reform and Agricultural Productivity in the Russian Far East" (chapter 8), which is based on interviews with territorial officials, collective farm managers, and small peasant farmers, shows the dire situation of the agricultural sector, even in the geographically favorable regions of Amur and Primorye. Agricultural reform is only partly implemented, and the state-owned land redistribution fund holds much of the land out of productive use. Even when land is nominally privatized by distribution of land shares, former collective farm managers continue to use the land for free.

Duncan and Ruetschle observe that there is no market for agricultural land. Moreover, farms face an undeveloped food processing industry, restricted market access, and few workers with agricultural skills. Little credit is available for new equipment. Many large farms have had their bank accounts frozen for back taxes, forcing them to operate almost completely through barter. Legally, individuals own the land of former collective farms in common, but, in practice, the farmer contributes the land to the farm unit, which uses the land without compensating the farmer in any way. Without central subsidies, agricultural output is down 25 percent, and the region depends on foreign imports for most of its consumption.

The fishing industry, at first glance, appears to be in a much stronger position. Fishing enterprises were able to go to the international market to get credit for the acquisition of enormous trawler-processors and to outfit older ships with modern technology. Nevertheless, as Tony Allison writes in chapter 6, "While Moscow has struggled with the federation subjects (and they with each other) for control of the resource, the most important commercial stocks, king crab and pollock, have been sharply reduced in many areas through overfishing and ineffective management."

The fishing industry has critical importance to the RFE, as Allison points out. If unrecorded high-seas shipments are included, the fishing industry accounts for one-half of regional exports. Huge modern trawlers, built in the shipyards of Spain, Norway, and Germany and financed through long-term bare boat charters, have appeared in the North Pacific.[15] Yet because of corruption and illegal activity in Russia, the Russian fleet relies on foreign ports for repairs, servicing, and transshipment of products, leaving Russian ports decaying.

More seriously, overfishing has led to declining catches. Local territories fight with each other over declining quotas. Meanwhile, investors are withdrawing from the industry, frightened by the decline in stocks, the unpredictability of the resource allocation system, and the larger uncertainties of the business environment.

Allison argues that overfishing is not the only problem: so is the inability to set and enforce any rational rules. The Putin government says it will establish rule of law, including in the fishing industry, but the danger is that a more complex regulatory regime may make things worse, not better. There is a risk that antiforeign regulation will reduce efficiency and industry revenue. One litmus test of reform will be whether Russia is able to attract the Russian fleet back to Russian ports.

Out of all regional sectors, oil and gas provide the most promise. On the eve of a visit to Sakhalin Island in September 2000, Vladimir Putin named a working group headed by Minister of Trade and Economic Development German Gref and instructed its members to identify legislation that will be required in order to allow new energy projects in Siberia to move forward.[16] The most important change is the elaboration of production-sharing legislation that removes inconsistencies with other preexisting laws and offers production-sharing agreements to a longer list of projects. Further legislation is needed to enforce the existing exemption of energy equipment from VAT, clarify customs procedures, define reimbursable costs, and simplify the process for receipt of environmental approvals and other regulatory documents. Yet, in 2001, little progress has been made in defining a secure regime for investment in oil and gas.

In chapter 7, "Sakhalin Energy: Problems and Prospects," Judith Thornton argues that development of Russia's oil and gas resources could provide immense benefits to all the countries of Northeast Asia. A network of natural gas pipelines linking Russia's eastern regions with Northeast Asia would lower energy costs and provide environmental benefits for all, while yielding income and employment in Pacific Russia to reverse the region's economic decline. Challenges remain in developing a secure framework for multilateral investment in the production and distribution of natural gas. Production and delivery of pipeline gas require large specific investments in both producing and consuming countries, and the scale of a pipeline project must be very large in order to reap the benefits of scale economies. Yet the huge up-front investment confronts both sides of the market with a risk of expropriation or default by the other party.

Thornton investigates the strategic mechanisms applied by Russia, the host country, and western multinational corporations in order to reduce the risks of outright or creeping expropriation. She argues that western multinationals have reduced the costs and risks of expropriation by involving a group of complementary firms and international banks in each project to spread the risk. They have tried to set up "self-enforcing arrangements" that in effect hold each other's assets hostage. They have committed resources gradually so that a host-country's short-run incentives to expropriate would be offset by the long-term incentives to gain access to future finance, technology, and know-how. They have tried to retain the ability to punish defection from the agreement. And they have designed their projects to assure a steady flow of benefits to the local government in each period, even before production begins. These strategies have allowed Royal Dutch/Shell to move ahead with offshore oil extraction and a proposed $8 billion liquefied natural gas facility on Sakhalin and have encouraged ExxonMobil to finalize contracts for engineering and design of onshore and offshore drilling, processing, and pipeline systems on Sakhalin.

BANKING IN THE RUSSIAN FAR EAST

Banking is just one part of a modern capital market, but it is an essential part. Without the ability to carry out simple payments functions, businesses are reduced to carrying stacks of cash around in a suitcase. (This is, in fact, what some western businesses were forced to do in the wake of Russia's financial crisis in August 1998.)

According to Pavel Minakir's account of the influence of the 1998 financial crisis on the RFE economy (chapter 3), the regional banking system remains underdeveloped. Presently, firms rely primarily on Sberbank, the Russian savings bank, for settlement activities. Regional banks have low liquidity and little diversification. With the disappearance of the federal bills market, they have shifted away from treasury bills (GKOs) to investment in firms and other banks. However, the main bank activity is currency exchange, since banks are unable to assure the return of credits.

In the wake of financial crisis, the Central Bank attempted a reconstruction of the payments system based on about 200 core banks. Regional governments could determine which regional banks would be refinanced by ARCO, the bank restructuring agency. The Central Bank divided regions into three categories, with some RFE territories falling into each category. The first was a small group of 22 regions with healthy banks (including Kamchatskaia oblast in the RFE). Second, there were 26 regions where banks were to be refinanced by the Central Bank (including Sakha, Khabarovsk, Primorye, and Amur). Third, in 29 regions (including Magadan and Sakhalin) banks were to be refinanced with local resources.

Local banks that have survived were allowed to pay off their debts to local creditors in exchange for an equally large debt to the Central Bank. Strict requirements are imposed on banks receiving refinancing by ARCO. Under the initial Central Bank refinancing program, each territory would form a pool of three or more banks that would receive credits from the local branches of the Central Bank and from the local administration. ARCO would provide credits collateralized by a large share of each bank's stock. This plan was intended to make the banks the property of the federal government, a development opposed by the territorial administrations.

In addition to ownership of core commercial banks, the Central Bank also restored the territorial network of Central Bank branches to process payments flow. Alpha Bank was allowed to set up ten regional branches for this purpose. So the Central Bank's regional policy is to manage financial flows from the center. Territorial authorities had alternative plans. They wanted to give regional banks the maximum independence from the center—transferring property rights to the local administrations (which would make these core commercial banks governmental in either case). Since the financial crisis, local administrations have used a variety of mechanisms to control local financial flows. They have introduced direct control over interbudgetary currency flows (in Khabarovsk) or established regional treasuries (Sakha, Magadan, and Irkutsk). Sometimes, regional governments own bank stock or manage banks in trust. In this way, banks survive based on their rights to serve regional budget accounts, their tax breaks, or other preferential arrangements. By creating local payments systems, by issuing local promissory notes for territorial use, and by directing bank credits to local firms, the territorial administrations have created a set of highly inefficient, segmented local markets. These measures allowed regional commerce to continue after a total breakdown of the central financial system, but they are inadequate to support a market system. However, refinancing left the core banks under effective government ownership or control.

In the future, Russia will need commercial banks operating on commercial principals. If it can succeed in attracting foreign commercial banks, then their presence would gradually allow an expansion of credit and encourage investment.

The breakdown of state capacity and weakening of institutional infrastructure accompanying the Russian transition have merely intensified the existing isolation of the Russian economy from the economic activity of the growing Pacific market. Today, Russia is still near the bottom on any ranking of economic and political risk. The deficiencies of its government institutions are a primary source of the weakness of its economy, and its economic weakness leaves it vulnerable to instability and unrest.

If President Putin's reforms strengthen property rights and rule of law, thus creating an incentive-compatible regime of taxes and regulations, then Russia's short-term, resource-based growth may turn into long-term, productive structural change. But if a recentralization of control rights and cash flow rights in Moscow creates a persistent conflict of interest between Russia's center and its regions, then tax evasion, rule breaking, disorganization, and disorder could persist in the Russian Far East, creating one more source of instability in an already wobbly part of the world.

POLITICAL AND SECURITY ISSUES

President Putin's model for federal relations seemed clear shortly after his election. Centralization was embedded in the Russian genes, he confided to journalists. A week later he announced the creation of seven super-districts, each headed by a presidential representative who would have authority over federal agencies in his *guberniia*. Five of the seven representatives were recruited from the security services and military. In May 2001, Putin named them representatives to the Security Council, increasing their authority.

While new economic measures and recent economic performance are hopeful, Putin's plans for political reform are troubling. They fail to address, and may even worsen, the sources of regional inefficiency. Putin's establishment of seven new federal districts is intended to impose greater uniformity on the policies of federal agents and allow increased central monitoring of local practices, but it will also separate bureaucratic decision-making from information about local circumstances and local priorities. It will deprive local voters of the ability to hold local elected officials accountable for the performance of local government and limit the ability of local governments to provide growth-enhancing public services and foster investment. As long as centrally determined taxes and regulations are not linked to local benefits, state capacity to govern will still lack basic incentive compatibility. Even more than in the past, governors will be evaluated on their ability to influence central allocations, subsidies, and exemptions for their regions. Local authorities will have little ability to influence whether federal police and law enforcement agencies provide security of persons and property in their territory.

Presidential representatives have responsibility for the use of federal subsidies, the implementation of federal programs, and the performance of federally owned enterprises. They coordinate the work of thirty to forty federal agencies in the regions with a total staff of 460,000. Deputy Prime Minister Viktor Khristenko announced that important staff appointments in the regions must receive approval from the presidential representatives.[17] The federal interagency collegia currently operating in each oblast and republic would have to be reorganized at the district level and councils of governors would be established.

In May 2000, the prosecutor-general formed an office in each of the seven districts. The Ministries of Justice and Interior and the Federal Tax Police are to be restructured similarly. The Ministry of Justice is to monitor territorial legislation in order to bring subnational laws into conformity with those of the Russian Federation. Under Putin's proposed new laws, the president would gain the right to dismiss governors, mayors, and regional Duma members who violate federal laws.

Putin named Lieutenant General Konstantin Pulikovskii, who grew up in Ussuriisk, Primorye, and previously served as deputy commander of federal troops in Chechnya, to be the presidential envoy for the Far Eastern district. In June 2000, Pulikovskii arrived in Khabarovsk, the district headquarters, while the press speculated on whether he would devote his time to enforcing central directives in the regions or, instead, to lobbying for regional interests at the center.

Observers ask how the district leader will exercise authority vis-à-vis the territorial budgets. Although the office of the Presidential Envoy has acquired considerable control over budget expenditures and appointments, difficulties persist in defining federal and territorial authority. In the past, the federal government often enforced its authority by playing one oblast or *krai* against another, which kept the territories divided and unable to exert unified pressure on the center for greater autonomy. But, with conflicts resolved at the district level, will the federal authorities find themselves facing the united opposition of a group of governors? Moreover, if a district administration proves effective in providing missing institutional infrastructure, will this framework create a new, united demand for regional autonomy where none had existed before?

During the spring and summer of 2000, Putin forced through major parliamentary reforms as well. Changes provide that territorial governors and legislative chairmen who currently sit in the Federation Council will lose their positions in the Council at the end of their terms, or no later than January 1, 2002. Each oblast or krai will send two representatives to the Federation Council, one nominated by the governor, the other appointed by the territorial legislature. Putin proposed establishment of a State Council staffed by territorial governors, which would be a consultative body in the executive, rather than legislative, branch of government. These legislative changes, then, will mean a major reduction in the power of the regional governors to influence the ultimate form of Russia's federalism.

Russian observers also point out that the proposed administrative changes entail difficult tradeoffs. Abel Aganbegyan, rector of the Russian Federation Academy of the National Economy, argues that the regional branches of federal agencies, such as the Ministry of Interior, Federal Security Service, tax inspectorate, and tax police, have not been under the effective control of either local or central authorities. "Moscow cannot take care of everything. It is simply deluged by the volumes of incoming information and top-priority issues." Presidential representatives may monitor and increase the accountability of federal agencies. Moreover, he argues that a presidential representative can coordinate interregional sharing of railroads, transport facilities, ports, fuel, and energy networks. On the other hand, he observes, central subsidies breed parasitism and unwillingness to mobilize resources because of the loss of future subsidies. In addition, he finds it harmful that resources generated in the regions are drawn inevitably to the center. "How is it possible that the living standards of a Moscow resident are three times higher than the national average in Russia.... If you take regions with similar conditions, such as Moscow and Ivanovo, for example, the difference in income is fully ten times."[18]

The dismissal of Primorskii krai's authoritarian governor Yevgenii Nazdratenko in February 2001 provides insight into how the federalism may evolve under Putin. Using the pretext of continuing energy shortages in the krai, and working through his representative Konstantin Pulikovskii, Putin secured the governor's resignation. However, within a few weeks Nazdratenko was appointed chairman of the State Fisheries Committee, a powerful sinecure, over the objections of German Gref, Prime Minister Mikhail Kasianov, and other leading officials. (Moscow was unable to block the election of Sergei Darkin, a local executive, over the candidate preferred by the center, First Deputy Presidential Envoy Gennadii Apanisenko.)

Nazdratenko was in essence rewarded for his "loyalty," a trait highly valued by Putin, in resigning his office and promising not to run for governor again. The process was dominated by the usual Kremlin personalistic politics, and suggests that Vladimir Putin may prove quite effective at reining in Russia's maverick governors. It also casts doubt on Russia's evolution toward a genuine federal system based on constitutional principles.

THE RUSSIAN FAR EAST MILITARY-INDUSTRIAL COMPLEX

A smaller defense establishment and declining demand for military hardware explain much of the economic decline of the RFE. In "Security Implications of Defense Conversion in the Russian Far East" (chapter 11), Katherine Burns argues that the burden of defense spending significantly retarded economic growth in the Soviet Union. She estimates that between nine and fourteen million Soviet workers were employed in defense enterprises in the 1980s, compared with fewer than two million employed in similar enterprises in the United States at that time. Yet, her survey of individual defense facilities in the RFE leads her to conclude that attempts to convert the region's thirty-two largest defense plants to civilian production have had very limited success. She sees these firms' physical isolation, their separation from research and development facilities in Moscow and St. Petersburg, and their lack of access to new investment as barriers to conversion. Specific firms, such as Dalzavod in Primorye, developed coping strategies that combined new civilian products with attempts to expand foreign sales. Military sales, particularly to so-called rogue states and to China, raise concerns in the West.

China has taken advantage of the availability of Russian military equipment at low prices to expand and upgrade its force structure, while China's neighbors in Asia view its military modernization with considerable concern. China's growing economic and military strength already constrains Russian options, but in Russia's calculus of the benefits and costs of military sales, the short-term survival of its producers outweighs the prospects of future external threats.

Sergey Sevastyanov is more upbeat about the RFE military-industrial complex than Burns. In chapter 9, he addresses both the current status of the Far East's military-industrial sector and Russia's security concerns in Asia. Looking at domestic issues first, he argues that Russia's most serious sources of insecurity arise from domestic threats: endemic corruption, drug trafficking, environmental pollution, technological breakdowns, shortages of energy and food, and civil violence.

In the Soviet era, half of RFE industrial output was defense related, although military demand began to decline after 1989. The first years of reform, 1991–94, saw a huge decline in demand for military products, for example, at Dalzavod, which produced ships, and Zvezda, which built submarines. Other large military producers are surviving on sales to the foreign market and on modest civilian production. For example, Progress, the helicopter producer, became a member of a large consortium organized by Kamov (helicopter design). Its Ka-50 Black Shark and Ka-52 Alligator helicopters have gone to Turkey and South Korea. Now they have received renewed Russian state orders as well. They are also selling civilian helicopters and have fabricated 700 containers for Japan. Zvezda and

Eastern Shipyard, a ship-repair facility, are building small and medium-sized fishing boats. Electronics producer Izumrud has received orders from the Vladivostok telephone company and from the electric power producer Vladenergo.

The Asian financial crisis cut into Russia's military exports to the region. In 1997 foreign military sales fell to $2.5 billion dollars. There has been some recovery since then, as well as a considerable increase in domestic demand for military hardware in 2000. In 1999 Russia sold $4.8 billion in weaponry abroad, nearly twice the $2.6 billion posted in the previous year, but still well below the American figure of $11.8 billion in weapons exports.[19]

In chapter 10, James Clay Moltz explores the nuclear-proliferation and environmental risks presented by funding cuts and the resulting disorganization in managing nuclear facilities and materials. He considers several scenarios under which command and control of Russian nuclear facilities and fissile material might break down, and provides documentation of past incidents.

Although some of the Moltz scenarios might appear unlikely before the fact, the explosion and sinking of the Kursk nuclear submarine, with a tragic loss of life, documents the importance of taking safety measures against what appear to be (ex ante) low-probability, high-cost events. Higher federal revenues in 2000 will allow the federal government to reverse some of the decline in its military sector. However, the Putin administration needs to reevaluate the size and structure of its current military establishment and ask whether an immense and dilapidated military sector, on balance, increases or decreases its domestic security.

REGIONAL TIES

Conducting foreign policy toward the Asia Pacific region proved more problematic as Russia became increasingly decentralized. In chapter 12, "The Regional Dynamic in Russia's Asia Policy in the 1990s," Elizabeth Wishnick identifies two competing visions of Russia's place in the Pacific. Moscow has focused on developing an economic and strategic partnership with Beijing, while the Russian Far East has viewed collaboration with the United States, Japan, and South Korea as having greater potential. From the perspective of Russia's national interests, China is a logical counterweight to U.S. hegemony and a ready market for Russian weaponry. Beijing's leaders likewise value Russian support for their Taiwan policy, opposition to the U.S. missile defense program, and general antipathy to Washington's hegemonic position in the western Pacific.

Russian officials in the Far East share a much more jaundiced view of the Chinese. They know that China does not have the investment capital needed to transform its economy, and the influx of shoddy merchandise into Russia in the early 1990s still rankles. The threat of large-scale Chinese immigration is more immediate for the Russian Far East than it is for European Russia. By contrast, Japan and South Korea do not pose any demographic threat to the RFE, and they are far wealthier and more willing to invest than are the Chinese.[20] They, together with the United States, are key to the Russian Far East's successful integration into the Asia Pacific economy. Such issues as missile defense and American hegemony of the post–Cold War world mean little to the Russian Far East. Far more important to the region is U.S. investment in oil and gas, timber, telecommunications, fishing, and consumer goods production.

Mikhail Alexseev makes a persuasive argument in chapter 13 that the fear of massive Chinese immigration into the Russian Far East is unwarranted. Politicians and journalists have pushed the "yellow peril" argument since the region opened up in 1993, with some of the more irresponsible claiming that 400,000 to 2 million illegal migrants had settled in the RFE, largely in Primorskii krai. Concentrating on Primorye, Alexseev finds these figures to be greatly exaggerated. In 1997, for example, a total of 52,000 Chinese visited Primorye, of which 39,000 did not have visas. However, only 468 of these failed to return to the PRC, and 2,100 were forcibly deported. In addition, Alexseev suggests that the flow of migrants from the PRC is increasingly rule-based and controlled by the authorities.

However, as he rightly points out, the reality of low migration numbers does not preclude the use of a "Chinese threat" by local politicians as a weapon in their struggle for power. Russia's Far East contains potentially explosive ingredients for ethnic conflict. These include a huge, sparsely populated territory that is losing population and has extensive borders; readily identifiable ethnic minorities that can easily be "constructed" as adversaries by nationalist politicians, Cossacks, and communists; the absence of strong democratic institutions and a political culture of trust and tolerance; ongoing disputes between Moscow and the periphery; and lingering uncertainties about the borders. Regional fears of Chinese immigration indicates a genuine security concern with maintaining control of borders, and more broadly with keeping control of the process of economic and political change.

Sergei Chugrov addresses the political aspects of regionalism in the Russian Far East in chapter 14, using data from the 1993, 1995, and 1999 parliamentary elections. Chugrov presents a somewhat surprising hypothesis—that electoral politics in the RFE have not really divided into a contest between reformers and conservatives. Rather, voters tend to group parties together as those of the establishment (old or new—the *nomenklatura* parties) and those on the outside. In the 1993 and 1995 elections, for example, Chugrov suggests that parties outside the establishment—the ultranationalist Liberal Democratic Party of Russia (LDPR) and the reformist party Yabloko—received a proportion of the vote above the national average for quite different reasons. A vote for the LDPR represented an emotional reaction to the loss of superpower status, while a Yabloko vote indicated support for Russia's openness to the outside world. Chugrov also finds that in 1995, regions with lower average incomes tended to vote for the *nomenklatura* parties (the Communist Party of the Russian Federation and Our Home is Russia), while more prosperous regions backed the challengers (Yabloko and the LDPR).

The December 1999 parliamentary elections may indicate a shift away from previous voting patterns in the Russian Far East. The "party of power," in this election the Unity bloc of Sergei Shoigu and Vladimir Putin, did far better than the parties of power in either of the previous elections. In seven of ten territories, Unity garnered votes at higher proportions than its national average. Chugrov suggests this vote may reflect a new willingness to rebuild ties with the center, since a central plank of Unity's platform was reestablishing order in Russia and strengthening control over the regions. He also notes that Unity was associated with new ideas and uncorrupted newcomers to politics, a pattern that has appealed to residents of the Far East.

Although relations with the other neighboring states are important, China is the key regional actor for Russia in the Asia Pacific, and, in chapter 15, Ni Xiaoquan finds that China and Russia have common interests and perceptions on many international political and economic issues. Both countries favor a multipolar world, oppose American missile defense plans, share concerns about terrorism and drug smuggling in Central Asia, and hope to expand trade. While the national governments speak encouragingly of a "strategic partnership," misunderstandings and tensions impact relations at the local level. Acute sources of tension include familiar issues like boundary demarcation and illegal immigration, along with "new" security issues along the Sino-Russian border. Governors Nazdratenko of Primorye and Viktor Ishaev of Khabarovsk resisted territorial concessions by the national government along the Amur River, using nationalist reactions for political ends. The new security issues of drug smuggling, illegal weapons sales, and criminal gang activity are potentially destabilizing, but also provide a basis for cooperation along the 4,300-kilometer border. By far the most significant efforts to deal with these problems have taken place in national-level discussions, bilateral summits, and multinational fora.

China, Ni observes, has no clear or comprehensive policy toward the Russian Far East. China's policies toward Russia are state to state, reflecting Beijing's *realpolitik* view of international relations. A top priority of China's policy is halting the American national and theater missile defense programs, which could effectively neutralize China's strategic deterrent and would definitely limit Beijing's flexibility vis-à-vis Taiwan. Russia provides valuable diplomatic support for the one-China policy and preservation of the Anti-Ballistic Missile Treaty in its present form. Ni expects that the Putin administration will continue to pursue close ties with China, while following a more pragmatic approach than his predecessor in developing economic relations with the West. Putin, like Yeltsin, is not interested in forming a political or military alliance with China, but Ni expects the Russian president to place greater emphasis on Sino-Russian economic cooperation and to adopt more effective measures to address cross-border problems.

The RFE plays a large part in Sino-Russian economic relations, with the RFE accounting for about one-third of total bilateral trade in 1999. Chinese-Russian economic relations, however, have not lived up to expectations. For years, national leaders have envisioned trade expanding to $20 billion dollars. Instead, total turn-over has generally fluctuated between $5 billion and $7 billion per year. As with Japan, much of the cross-border trade—small-scale and primarily involving con-sumer goods—is not included in official figures. Chinese investment in the Rus-sian Far East is miniscule, and Russian fears of being overwhelmed by Chinese immigrants makes Chinese entrepreneurs and investors suspect. The absence of economic and tax laws on both sides of the border are a further obstacle to regional economic cooperation. Putin's positive approach to China, together with China's and Russia's accession to the World Trade Organization, would help the two na-tions resolve the obstacles to more fruitful economic ties.

Russia and South Korea have approached their relationship from widely varying motives. For Russia, the end of the Cold War provided new opportunities for trade with and investment from one of East Asia's vibrant tigers. Seoul was more interested in the political side of the relationship, using Russia's declining leverage on the Korean Peninsula to achieve a breakthrough in its policy toward Pyongyang. A few Korean firms have pursued opportunities in the Russian Far East, with the focus primarily on natural resources and short-term gains. As Yong-Chool Ha demonstrates in chapter 16, Russia and South Korea started the 1990s with expec-tations that were not borne out. Both countries found themselves in unfamiliar situations: one coping with the loss of superpower status and trying to build productive ties with former enemies; the other a new democracy trying to break out of the stereotypes of the Cold War while venturing onto the regional stage.

As Ha notes, misperceptions and inexperience led to wild oscillations in Rus-sian–South Korean relations. Early optimism was dashed when Russia proved unable to repay a $3 billion loan extended late in the Gorbachev era. Conservatives and nationalists in the Russian Duma excoriated Foreign Minister Andrei Kozyrev and the Yeltsin administration for abandoning the North; after Yevgenii Primakov was appointed Minister of Foreign Affairs in 1996, the pendulum swung back toward a more balanced approach to the two Koreas. Moscow has tried to portray itself as a major player in inter-Korean relations, but its declining military and political presence and the marginal position of the Russian Far East in the Asia Pacific economy limit Russia's role on the Korean Peninsula. Reunification of the two Korea's, however, would have significant advantages for the recovery of the Russian Far East economic situation and for Russia's role as a diplomatic power in Northeast Asia, notably removing a major barrier to delivery of pipeline gas to Northeast Asia.

Logically, integration of the Russian Far East into the Asia Pacific economy presumes a close and constructive relationship with Asia's powerhouse, Japan. However, as Kunio Okada notes in chapter 17, Japan's overall trade with Russia is considerably lower than it was with the Soviet Union. Japanese-Russian trade dropped off significantly in the 1990s, with Japanese exports accounting for much of the decline. Officially, Russia accounted for only .11 percent of Japan's exports in 1999 and just 1.22 percent of its imports. However, the statistics do not account for the large unofficial trade (such as third country re-exports and shuttle trade) that have characterized the postcommunist period, nor do they take into account major projects in the developmental stage. Japanese exports to Russia follow a pattern similar to that in Soviet times, with Japan providing machinery, equipment, and financing in exchange for future deliveries of raw materials.

Okada states that the dispute over the Northern Territories is not a fundamental obstacle to better economic cooperation. There are far deeper structural problems that constrain trade, while Russia's uncertain political environment, complicated tax system, and poor industrial infrastructure discourage serious Japanese investors.

Seung-Ho Joo's analysis of Russian–Korean economic ties (chapter 18) is likewise a study in frustrated expectations. Trade increased dramatically after the 1990 normalization of diplomatic ties, but even at its highest point in 1996 did not reach four billion dollars. As Joo indicates, Russia accounts for about 1 percent of South Korea's total trade, while Korea's share in Russian trade is only 2 percent. Moreover, trade is not diffuse but rather is highly specific. Electronic products comprised well over half of South Korea's exports to Russia in 1995; steel and metal products constituted over half of Russian exports to South Korea. Just seven of Korea's giant *chaebol* account for 90 percent of trade with Russia, in distinct contrast to the dominance of small and medium-sized enterprises active in Russia-China trade. South Korean foreign direct investment (FDI) in Russia amounts to only 1.4 percent of total Korean FDI and accounts for only 0.5 percent of total FDI in Russia. Much of South Korea's investment is concentrated in the Russian Far East, particularly in Primorskii krai, and in hotels, the food industry, mining, and metallurgy.

Like Japan and China, South Korea is keenly interested in obtaining oil and natural gas from Russia, and the Korean Gas Corporation is participating in the Kovyktinsk field feasibility study. If successful, this project will not only lower the price of natural gas in South Korea, it could also provide a stimulus to North-South reconciliation. Russian–South Korean cooperation in the stalled Tumen River Area Development project is similarly valued for political reasons. South Korean officials expect long-term multinational development projects in the region will help draw Pyongyang out of its isolation and stabilize the peninsula. If Russia resolves its debt problem and continues to play a balanced and constructive role on the Korean Peninsula, Joo argues, it can be a positive factor for security in Northeast Asia.

Gradually, Asia is gaining attention in U.S. foreign policy, reflecting its growing weight in the world. However, uncertainty about the U.S. role in the region remains. Washington's policy has been to engage Russia as a responsible power, encouraging democratization and integration of the Russian Far East into the world economy, working with Russia to stem the flow of illegal drugs and weapons, and preventing the reemergence of a conventional Russian threat in the region. In chapter 2, Rajan Menon and Charles Ziegler analyze U.S. foreign policy interests and regional security on two levels—a traditional balance of power approach and a new security approach—and argue that both are necessary to understand dynamic processes in this part of the world.

Moreover, while foreign policymakers in Russia, the United States, and China continue to view regional politics using the traditional realist paradigm, the new regionalism has become increasingly important to Northeast Asia and the Russian Far East. In Russia and China, the center's control over the periphery seems to be eroding. Russia's regional authorities are closely involved in developing new transportation corridors and establishing direct business contacts with firms and organizations in Korea, Japan, and the U.S. West Coast. Recognizing that economic integration is vital to the RFE's future, local officials have, with Moscow's imprimatur, solicited foreign investment, established missions abroad, and exchanged trade delegations with neighboring countries. Governmental and nongovernmental organizations are also coordinating responses to the RFE's serious environmental problems at the regional level. Coordination, or lack thereof, between Moscow and the Russian Far East, and the effectiveness of local and national efforts at coping with population migration, drug smuggling, and control of nuclear materials, are clearly of great importance to Russia's security.

ECONOMIC, POLITICAL, AND SECURITY BARRIERS
TO INTEGRATION

Economic prosperity is the key to regional stability. Yet, the region's resource base in marine products, timber, and agriculture can employ, at most, a fraction of the region's population. Access to timber cutting rights and fishing quotas remains subject to political bureaucracies in Moscow and in the regions. Thus, any change in political leadership presents an important source of economic uncertainty, leading to a brief time horizon and rapid depletion of resource stocks.

This collection details many problems that impede Russian integration into the Pacific economy. Despite its abundant natural resources and its proximity to trading partners in the Asia Pacific, the official economy of the Russian Far East has experienced falling output, employment, and real wages over the past decade. Foreign and domestic investment is low and declining, causing capital stocks to depreciate. Chaotic, corrupt systems for allocation and enforcement of fishing quotas, timber, and mineral rights have generated a deterioration of resource stocks.

Although the precipitous fall in the value of the ruble in 1998 lowered the dollar costs of Russian products, the prospects for a revival of investment and economic recovery are limited by Russia's outmoded technology, lack of economic infrastructure, and weak institutional base. Investors cite many problems: absence of property rights, weak financial markets, an inadequate legal system, lack of rule of law, expropriatory taxes, and burdensome regulations. These problems constitute significant barriers to investment, placing Russia near the bottom of most assessments of political risk.

Development of Far Eastern and Siberian oil and natural gas could play a vital role in fueling Asian growth in the coming decades and is the best prospect for linking the RFE to the Asia Pacific economy. Production of oil from the Sakhalin shelf and planned construction of pipelines and a facility to manufacture liquefied natural gas are a promising start. However, construction of infrastructure for pipelines and development of natural gas from Sakhalin, Sakha, and Kovyktinsk will require long-term distribution contracts between suppliers and users, providing the commitment to justify the billions of dollars of foreign investment in dedicated energy networks. Proposed construction of a liquefied natural gas plant on Sakhalin Island will provide a bellwether for all of Russia's future international projects.

Future prosperity is also contingent on the prospects of former military enterprises in the region. To date, only a fraction of the defense plants that dominate the RFE economy have been successfully converted to civilian production. In the wake of ruble devaluation, some of these firms are making a successful transition to the production of equipment for the energy and agricultural sectors. Most, however, still depend on expanding domestic and international military sales, notably to the modernizing Chinese military. Federal plans now being drafted would revive the region's military industrial capacity to deliver military hardware to "rogue states."

An effective development program for the region will need to address the problem of converting the militarized economy and labor force to civilian production. Revival of coastal support for the fishing fleet and creation of support services for the energy sector will require major changes in the domestic economic environment.

Inability to create a working structure of fiscal federalism between the Russian Federation and its territories remains a key source of insecurity. Territorial administrations have filled the void left by decentralization in the post-Soviet era. Despite Putin's establishment of federal districts, the regional governors have an extremely large measure of authority through discretionary allocation of budgets, powers of appointment, and allocation of housing and services subject to administrative control. Still, it is important to remember that, for many categories of social protection, the roles of territorial and local (or municipal) governments have been crucial. RFE governors use the Association for the Far East and Baikal to make their joint case for greater federal expenditure in the region, but, because of the great heterogeneity among the territories, their ability to pursue common policies is limited by interregional competition over federal resources.

Political insecurity in Russia's Far East greatly complicates regional security. Russia's nuclear facilities present risks of nuclear proliferation and environmental damage, while the press cites alleged links between Russia's military and organized crime, such as the use of submarines to run drugs. Sergey Sevastyanov, in this volume, terms these risks a "Comprehensive Insecurity Syndrome," which ranges "from endemic corruption to drug trafficking; from environmental pollution to technological breakdowns; from energy and food supply shortages to the violent outbreaks of separatism."

Superpower security during the Cold War was premised on accumulating military power to deter aggression from clearly identifiable opponents. In the era of globalization, the rules have changed. Russia and the United States no longer consider each other implacable enemies, yet each continues to maintain large force structures configured offensively. Policymakers in both countries acknowledge the radically changed nature of the post–Cold War world, yet security planners have had great difficulty adjusting to new threats. Of course, simple bureaucratic inertia accounts for much of this old thinking. All bureaucracies resist change, and military bureaucracies are more conservative than most. It is equally difficult, however, to change perceptions among officials and security experts, whose view of the world is dominated by realist conceptions of power and national interest.

Several major transnational challenges and opportunities to Russian and regional security are manifested in the Russian Far East. The first is the demand for energy. The growth in East Asian consumption is outpacing the rest of the world's, and the Russian Far East has significant reserves of oil and natural gas that could help meet the needs of China, Japan, and South Korea—if the investment capital is available to develop these supplies. A second issue is the threat of radioactive contamination and the diversion of radioactive materials—from nuclear accidents, theft, unauthorized dumping, or improper disposal of wastes. Instances of nuclear smuggling from the former Soviet Union have so far been limited in scope, but could expand in the future.[21] The residual concentration of nuclear facilities in the Russian Far East makes this a particularly acute regional problem, and one with obvious security implications. Third is the issue of illegal population migration, a potentially major problem given the proximity of China, with its huge number of poor citizens and increasingly open borders. Fourth is the possibility that the Russian Far East might become a major transit point for narcotics and weapons. The concentration of organized gangs in Russia's Wild East makes transnational criminal activities a significant problem.

Russia's efforts to come to grips with the new security milieu have proceeded incrementally. President Vladimir Putin's announcement in November 2000 that the armed forces would be trimmed by 600,000 and restructured to enhance efficiency may be the first step in a broad, effective military reform. However, military thinking in Russia continues to emphasize the deployment of huge numbers of troops and weaponry, despite the country's inability to fund this massive burden or to employ it effectively, as demonstrated in Chechnya. Serious military reductions are resisted as undermining the nation's prestige. As seasoned defense observer Pavel Felgengauer suggested of the Russian military brass, "they still maintain the old imperial strategy of confronting the entire world."[22]

The continued poverty of the Russian Far East, the pervasiveness of organized crime, and weak state authority provide a fertile breeding ground for illicit activities that can prove harmful to Russia's neighbors in the Asia Pacific and the United States. In a the current environment, free trade and more open borders also facilitate drug and weapons smuggling, illegal immigration, the movement of terrorists, and the spread of disease. In this milieu, maintaining national security will require adopting creative approaches that go beyond the traditional and increasingly inadequate methods of border control. As Stephen Flynn notes, properly confronting these threats will require a paradigm shift in guarding national borders.[23] Moreover, just as relatively safe, stable nations will be increasingly hard-pressed to isolate themselves from international problems, domestic troubles in unstable countries like Russia will not be easily contained within their ever more porous borders. The benefits of integrating Russia's

Far East into the Asia Pacific will be tempered by new dangers to the region's neighbors, including the United States. A cooperative international approach, rather than isolation or neglect, will be crucial in restoring political stability and economic health to the Russian Far East. These goals are clearly consonant with U.S. foreign policy and security interests.

Official Washington has not done a good job of recognizing or responding to the risks of a rapidly changing balance of power in Northeast Asia. One might ask, does it matter? These difficulties seem remote from Moscow, and equally distant, if not more so, from Washington, D.C. Yet, repeatedly in the twentieth century, the U.S. policy process was caught off-guard by unanticipated developments in Northeast Asia. The turbulent changes underway in all the major societies in the region—Japan, China, Russia, and the two Koreas—remind us that there are likely to be major surprises ahead in this region once more.

A new U.S. administration is seeking to create incentives for cooperation in its dealings with both Russia and China. The United States and Russia already are working together to dismantle nuclear submarines, expand trade, and stem environmental damage in the Far East. But the two countries could do more to strengthen their tenuous partnership in the region. Cooperation in this troubled part of the federation might encourage Russia to be more forthcoming in other areas that are of greater immediate significance for U.S. security, such as NATO enlargement, the Balkans, Central Asia, and arms control. And collaboration in solving the Russian Far East's pressing problems could help maintain Russian stability overall, which is obviously in America's national interest.

Astute observers of these issues now make an important point that in this new security environment it is critical to move from a deterrence posture to one of reassurance. All the major nations—the United States, Russia, China, Japan, and India—are responsible for promoting an evolution in thinking, but the United States, as the motive force and leading beneficiary of globalization, has a special responsibility for transforming global security. Washington, however, still has not fully accepted this responsibility. Washington's plans for national and theater missile defenses, for example, threaten to undermine Russia's and China's deterrent capabilities, and as envisioned do not adequately address these nations' security concerns. Far-sighted programs intended to reassure Russian leaders were enacted over the past decade, most notably the Nunn-Lugar program for dismantling nuclear weapons and the Materials Control, Protection, and Accounting Program to ensure control over nuclear materials and guarantee their safe disposal. Further cooperation in transforming Russia's heavily militarized, poor, and disorderly Far East would improve the security of Russia, the United States, and Northeast Asia, as contributors to this volume emphasize.

THE IMPACT OF GLOBALIZATION

Nations are still important in world politics, but the separate national economies are giving way to the interdependence of globalization. The same processes that contribute to more open markets and communications, and facilitate movement of people and goods, also make it harder to control illegal or harmful activities. These activities, which include environmental pollution, drugs and arms smuggling, illegal immigration, the spread of infectious diseases such as tuberculosis and HIV, and the proliferation of weapons of mass destruction, are taking place on a transnational scale. These problems are especially acute in the Russian Far East, and are beginning to impact the security and well-being of Russia's Pacific neighbors, including the United States.

Much of the Russian Far East's future depends on the economic interests, political perceptions, and security concerns of the regional powers. The major actors in East Asia hold widely varying notions of what sovereignty is and is not in the twenty-first century. The United States appears committed to the "open international society" of globalization, but significant segments of public opinion, and quite a few members of Congress, are suspicious of more porous borders. China maintains a traditional Westphalian view of sovereignty, and Beijing will brook no interference in its internal affairs—whether over human rights, Tibet, or Taiwan—by the United States or any other country.

Russia, preoccupied with a rebellious Chechnya and disturbed by NATO's willingness to enforce peace in the Balkans, shares China's view that sovereignty should be sacrosanct and resents U.S. meddling in other countries' internal affairs. Yet virtually all of Russia's more thoughtful and influential leaders realize that the country can only emerge from its deep economic crisis by preserving an open society and welcoming globalization. Nowhere is this more clear than in the Russian Far East, where links to the Asian regional economy are far more important than economic ties to European Russia. As evidence, an improvement of Russian relations with China has allowed border cities like Blagoveshchensk and Heihe to develop as trading centers. An expected increase in trade has fostered much new investment on the Chinese side, but relatively little on the Russian side. Great benefits are to be reaped from cross-border cooperation once more of the region's leaders recognize the importance of integration with their East Asian neighbors.

Closer ties with China are currently being pursued in arms contracts, and China hopes to accomplish a major military modernization cheaply by purchasing Russian military equipment and gaining access to military-related processes, technologies, and designs. In the short-run, Chinese demand contributes to the survival of regional military producers, but, in the long-run, Chinese military strength could be threatening to Russian interests.

Japan, the largest economic power in Northeast Asia, has played a small role in Russia. Japan's aversion to the high levels of economic risk in Russia is as important as the northern islands dispute in accounting for Japan's lack of involvement. Japan has benefited greatly from the global economy, but that country's decade-long recession will likely drag on as long as Japan fails to address the mammoth burden of nonperforming debt in its banking system and is unable to open its domestic economy to greater competition. Nevertheless, Japan will continue to be the largest potential customer for the resources of the RFE—fish, timber, ferrous and non-ferrous metals, and, especially, energy.

On the Korean Peninsula, the attitudes toward greater integration with Russia's eastern territories are mixed. With a large share of heavy industry and medium-level technologies, South Korea is well positioned to provide an offshore home for the Russian fishing fleet and to expand its economic interaction with Russia. Because of the high levels of risk in Russia, South Korea initially focused on projects with low capital requirements, such as foodprocessing and consumer manufactures, but there are many other potential economic links in sectors such as shipbuilding and energy.

North Korea would be a major beneficiary of economic integration and the development of energy resources. Yet in mid-2001, North Korea seemed to be backing away from expanded contacts with South Korea again. In August 2001, upon Kim Jong Il's return from a two-week visit to Moscow, the North Korean press announced the government's unwillingness to resume discussions with the United States if preconditions were attached, indicating that their foreign minister would not attend the ASEAN Regional Forum where informal discussions might have occurred.

Security in the modern world involves much more than having strong military capabilities. It also means having a healthy economy where people can be productive; government capacity to provide institutional infrastructure and rule of law; and a workable social consensus. The global market places constraints on national policies, and, as a result, governments with poor policies and weak state capacity will lose access to foreign investment and technology.

Operating in the global market confronts governments with new sources of risk. Openness requires a higher level of sophistication and a stronger commitment to transparency in implementing fiscal, monetary, and exchange rate policy. However, trade regimes and capital market policies are important determinants of economic growth. It is crucial that protectionist barriers be reduced and that capital markets be liberalized to allow foreign investors to participate and local investors to diversify their portfolios.

The new sources of uncertainty introduced by globalization require domestic institutions and domestic policies that are flexible and can adjust to unanticipated shocks. Policymakers must respond to unanticipated opportunities, such as North Korea's tentative opening, or unanticipated threats, such as heroin smuggling. The potential opportunities and risks in Pacific Asia present the need for multilateral consultation to consider the consequences of alternative contingencies and to respond with policies that foster growth.

Security today is both more complex and more interdependent than in the Cold War era. As an expanding China and declining Russia alter the economic and geopolitical balance in Asia, military issues remain, but in the more open world of the twenty-first century, they are increasingly edged out by the more immediate, and in many ways more intractable new challenges to national well-being. In developing their security plans for an interdependent world, policymakers need to pay increased attention to lessons of economic development in Northeast Asia—a region at risk.

NOTES

1. Russian convention distinguishes the Russian Far East from eastern, central, and western Siberia. The Far Eastern Federal District includes ten territories: the Republic of Sakha; Primorskii and Khabarovskii krais; Sakhalinskaia, Kamchatskaia, Magadanskaia, Amurskaia oblasts; the Jewish autonomous oblast; and Chukotskii and Koriakskii autonomous okrugs. The Russian Far East's largest city, Vladivostok, is the capital of Primorskii krai (also called Primorye). All told there are eighty-nine subjects of the Russian Federation, including republics, krais, oblasts, autonomous oblasts, and autonomous okrugs.

2. International Institute for Strategic Studies, *The Military Balance 1989–1990* (London: IISS, 1989), 42.

3. Judith Thornton, "Structural Change in the Russian Far East: The Implications for Trade and Factor Markets," *Atlantic Economic Journal* 24, no. 3 (September 1996): 208–27.

4. "Putin Alarmist about Fate of Russian Far East," *RFE–RL Security Watch,* vol. 1, no. 2 (July 31, 2000).

5. Ekaterina Zhuravskaya estimates that each ruble of increase in direct local taxation results in a decline in federal transfers of 0.9 rubles. See "Incentives to Provide Local Public Goods: Fiscal Federalism, Russian Style," EERC Working Paper 99–15E, <www.EERC.ru>.

6. "Putin's Address to the Federal Assembly," BBC Monitoring Service, April 3, 2001, in Johnson's Russia List #5184, April 4, 2001.

7. All data from Bank of Finland, "Russian and Baltic Economies: The Week in Review," Issue 52 (2000)–Issue 15 (2001).

8. See Pavel Minakir, "Influence of the 1998 Financial Crisis on the Russian Far East Economy," chapter 3 in this volume.

9. Russian-European Centre for Economic Policy, "Has Russia Turned the Corner?" *Russian Economic Trends*, May 16, 2000, 8.

10. American Russian Center, University of Alaska, Anchorage, *Russian Far East News*, July 2001 <www.arc.uaa.alaska.edu/arc/>.

11. Bank of Finland, *Russian and Baltic Economies: Week in Review*, no. 30 (July 27, 2001), 1.

12. Russian-European Center for Economic Policy, *Russian Economic Trends*, July 30, 2001, 5.

13. See Alexander S. Sheingauz, Victor D. Kalashnikov, Natalia V. Lomakina, and Grigorii I. Sukhomirov, "The Russian Far East's Competitive Position in Northeast Asian Markets," chapter 5 of this volume.

14. See Judith Thornton, "Sakhalin Energy: Problems and Prospects," chapter 7 of this volume.

15. A bare boat charter is a contract in which an operating company leases the ship without the associated fishing equipment and infrastructure. The operating company then bears the cost of fitting out the ship.

16. "Federal Commission to Identify Needed Reforms for Expansion of PSA," *Gubernskie Vedomosti*, August 17, 2000.

17. *Rossiiskaia gazeta*, August 22, 2000, as cited in East-West Institute, *Russian Regional Report* 5, no 31 (August 30, 2000) <rrr@iews.org>.

18. Abel Aganbegyan, "General Laws Do Not Breed Bribery. It Is Bred by Exclusive Rights," *Rossiiskaia gazeta*, June 7, 2000, 1.

19. Steven Lee Myers, "Global Arms Sales Swell to $30 Billion," *New York Times*, August 21, 2000, 9.

20. There was some concern that Koreans from Central Asia would flock back to the Russian Far East, but reportedly only 2,000–3,000 have resettled in the region around Lake Khasan.

21. Rensselaer W. Lee and James L. Ford, "Nuclear Smuggling," in Maryann K. Cusimano, ed., *Beyond Sovereignty: Issues for a Global Agenda* (Boston: Bedford/St. Martin's, 2000).

22. Vladimir Isachenkov, "Putin Risks Alienating Military with Painful Cuts," Associated Press, November 10, 2000.

23. Stephen E. Flynn, "Beyond Border Control," *Foreign Affairs* 79, no. 6 (November/December 2000): 57–68.

2

The Balance of Power and U.S. Foreign
Policy Interests in the Russian Far East

Rajan Menon and Charles E. Ziegler

The Russian Far East is of great significance to the economic well-being and security of Northeast Asia. The region has an area of 6.2 million square kilometers—well over one-fourth of the Russian Federation's total area and three-fourths the size of the contiguous United States. By contrast, its population, at less than eight million, comprises just over five percent of the Russian Federation's total population. It lies nine time zones to the east of Moscow and is connected to the Russian heartland by communications links that are long, few in number, and vulnerable, yet its wealth in energy and various industrial raw materials is abundant. It is located next to China, a rising power, and the Korean Peninsula, a potential flashpoint, and it overlooks Japan, the world's second largest economy.

The size, remoteness, and strategic salience of the Russian Far East raise the question of Moscow's ability to control and defend this region, the more so given a Russian government so hobbled by economic and military weakness that the security of the provinces is called into question. Vladimir Putin's success in ousting Primorye governor Yevgenii Nazdratenko demonstrates Moscow still can exercise a form of control over the regions, but one that bears little resemblance to the rule of law. Under these circumstances, the fate of the Russian Far East is of great concern to Moscow.[1] For their part, residents of the Russian Far East tend to believe that Moscow has little to offer them, and that its priorities and concerns are becoming progressively disassociated from theirs.

What will be the denouement? One possibility is heightened tensions between Moscow and the Russian Far East, with Moscow seeking—ineffectually—to retain control but unable to offer incentives to obey or disincentives against disobeying by virtue of its economic and military weakness. Another possible outcome is that leaders in the Russian Far East, facing pressure from Moscow, increased immigration from China, and growing Chinese power, may conclude that ties to the central government in Moscow and to the rest of Russia are critical in order to counterbalance Chinese hegemony and territorial claims. In addition to looking to the central government as a counterbalance, political leaders in the Russian Far East could seek to fan Russian nationalism, both in response to the perceived threat from China and as a means of promoting their political legitimacy. A third possible outcome is that the growth of Chinese military and economic power, combined with the decline and disunity of Russia, may lead the Russian Far East to be absorbed into a Chinese sphere of influence. De jure, it would remain part of the Russian Federation; de facto, it would become an extension of China—economically, militarily, and demographically.

A fourth future would have various constituent parts of the Russian Far East mutate into a balance-of-power system within a fragmenting Russia. Outside powers (China, Japan, and South Korea—or a unified Korea) would compete for the statelets' allegiance and resources, transforming what had once been sovereign Russian territory into Northeast Asia's newest zone of great-power competition. The fault lines within the Russian Far East—an area that is often spoken of (and sometimes written about) as if it were a uniform zone—would ease the intrusion and jockeying of outside powers and their quest to carve out spheres of predominance.[2] The United States could play a key role under these conditions, perhaps one analogous to Britain's in the eighteenth and nineteenth centuries as a balancer determining the outcome of rivalries, or perhaps as a participant in the scramble for advantage.

Whether or not one accepts any of these possibilities as a probable outcome is less important than the broader point that the relationship the Russian Far East has had with Moscow and the states of Northeast Asia for the last fifty years has changed and is almost certain to metamorphose further. Because of the size and location of this vast area, the geostrategic consequences of this transformation will be significant for the United States and its allies and for the future balance of power in Northeast Asia. Meanwhile, U.S. foreign policy planning has only begun to address the radically altered security environment in the Russian Far East and the implications of such changes.

U.S. foreign policy has been slow to adapt to changing conditions in the Western Pacific, the region adjacent to the Russian Far East. Although this area of the world is vitally important for the United States, Washington's policy since the end of the Cold War has suffered from an absence of long-range planning. The strategic environment in this region has changed dramatically over the past decade, in large part due to the collapse of the Soviet Union and the often chaotic transformation of the Russian Far East. Consequently, a new concept of U.S. interests and priorities needs to be developed.

Our analysis proceeds on two levels. We first adopt a traditional, state-to-state approach, focusing on the decline of one regional power (Russia), the ascendance of a second (China), the uncertain status of two others (the United States and Japan), and the possible reconfiguration of a critical subregion, the Korean Peninsula. We then examine regionalism and center-periphery relations in Russia. These are not two distinct and watertight levels of analysis. Rather, traditional security dynamics affect the context for regional issues such as population movements or energy development, and vice versa.

SHIFTING POWER ALIGNMENTS

For better or worse, the United States is now a hegemonic power in world politics, including in the Asia Pacific region. Throughout the twentieth century, the grand strategy of the United States was designed to preserve access to markets, to keep open the lines of communication at sea, and to prevent any alignment of hostile and superior forces capable of threatening the security of the United States or its principal allies. As part of this policy following World War II, Washington built a network of alliances to contain Soviet power. In East Asia, bipolar confrontation in the 1950s and 1960s gave way to trilateral competition in the 1970s and 1980s, with the enmity between once-erstwhile allies the USSR and China being the principal catalyst for change. At the dawn of the twenty-first century, the region's balance of power is again in flux.

Washington may be the hegemon, but it is an uncertain one. There are doubts about its staying power; its China policy seems to lurch from a focus on human rights to a pragmatic approach driven by economic and strategic logic; and its alliances and bases seem to rest on the logic of a Cold War competition. The Asia policy of the Clinton administration reflected these contradictions and uncertainties. For example, President Clinton's decision to visit Beijing in June 1998 without a stopover in either Japan or South Korea humiliated and discomfited these states, which Washington continues to identify as key allies. Similarly, Clinton rejected a Chinese offer on trade in early 1999, but the administration subsequently made frantic efforts to secure a comparable deal before the November 1999 World Trade Organization meeting in Seattle. Likewise, the political, economic, and ecological problems of the vast Russian Far East are of great consequence for reform and democracy in Russia, but there has been nothing approaching a coherent U.S. policy aimed at addressing them, least of all one that creates a commonality of purpose and a synergy of resources among America's key allies. There has been talk about a regional security system for Northeast Asia on occasion, but not much by way of action.

Officially, Washington has viewed Russia as one partner among many in the Asia Pacific region. Walter Slocombe, under secretary of defense in the Clinton administration, listed six U.S. goals regarding Russia: (1) to prevent the redeployment of a conventional threat to the Asia Pacific region resulting from changes in Russian capabilities or intentions; (2) to develop bilateral and multilateral channels responsive to U.S. goals and influence; (3) to promote the development of democratic free-market societies; (4) to promote regional stability, thereby permitting international access to emerging markets and resources; (5) to prevent the proliferation of weapons of mass destruction and the means for their delivery; and (6) to encourage Russia to play a constructive role in the region.[3]

While these are unobjectionable goals, the key issue is how they should be realized. In this regard, one of the weaknesses of America's position has been the perception, not entirely without merit, that the United States relies almost exclusively on military power as an instrument of foreign policy, while neglecting skillful diplomacy and other nonlethal methods of persuasion.[4] Congress has been notably reluctant to support the State Department and suspicious of the utility of such international organizations as the United Nations, International Monetary Fund, and WTO. Supporting the U.S. military resonates much better with voters, even if armed force is less cost-effective than foreign aid or diplomacy in securing U.S. interests abroad. Leaders in the executive branch appreciate the utility of raw force, but they need to have a better understanding of what Joseph Nye has called "soft power"—trade, investment, culture, and information flows. These are the elements of globalization, a multifaceted process that the rest of the world sees (some with admiration, others with apprehension) as Americanization.[5]

Russia and China are at the same time attracted and repelled by globalization. The two countries share a nineteenth-century vision of sovereignty as being absolute. Consequently, they reject the international community's new willingness to restrict a country's freedom to handle its national minorities as it deems appropriate. Both wish to take advantage of globalization's benefits—technology, foreign investment, and the information revolution. Yet they also seek to avoid limits on their political autonomy and domestic maneuverability, and they fear cultural penetration or contamination at a time when the new bases of national legitimacy and social solidarity are at issue in both countries. This helps explain

Beijing's and Moscow's adamant opposition to the bombing of Yugoslavia by NATO, western criticism on Chechnya, or the emphasis on human rights that shapes, however intermittently, U.S. foreign policy. China and Russia face challenges to central control from their border provinces—Tibet and Xinjiang in the case of the former, Chechnya and Dagestan in the latter. Acknowledging the right of multilateral organizations to intervene to protect human rights is distasteful to both Moscow and Beijing, the more so when multilateral responses appear to be choreographed by the United States.

Therein lies the opposition to a unipolar world voiced so stridently by Moscow and Beijing. Both countries view unipolarity and, in some respects its spinoff, globalization, as conferring an undue advantage on the United States. Russia and China are also disturbed by what they see as Washington's arrogant approach to foreign affairs. Indeed, this convergence of perspective has led them to describe their relationship as a "strategic partnership" in support of a multipolar world. This relationship is not a full-blown alliance, but neither is it merely an ad hoc and fitful meeting of the minds.[6] It results from an intersection of interests and will likely prove durable (although hardly trouble-free). A common concern about U.S. dominance and the desire for leverage against Washington has facilitated it, but it is also the result of a fundamentally new bilateral relationship that began to take shape in 1988. That, in turn, is the outcome of several developments: the delimitation of the lengthy (4,300 kilometers) and long-disputed border, expanding (yet still paltry) trade, Russian arms sales, and a regular flurry of visits by top leaders from both countries.

Yet complexity and ambivalence lie just beneath the surface of camaraderie. Both Russia and China understand that neither can offer the other the investment and technology that each needs in order to attain the levels of power and prosperity required for success in the twenty-first century. Indeed, insofar as foreign investment and trade are concerned, the two countries are competitors for the attention of the West and the developed economies of the Asia Pacific. Talk about a strategic partnership and the flow of its arms to China notwithstanding, Russia realizes that China could surpass it economically and militarily. As a result, it could face a state that, while it may not be an immediate military threat, would begin dealing with a weak Russia from a position of condescension and strength. China, for its part, understands that despite the verbal solidarity between Moscow and Beijing, Russia's myriad problems make it incapable of tangibly adding to Chinese power. If the Soviet Union was a threat to China by virtue of its strength, post-Soviet Russia is a problem on account of its weakness, as manifested, for example, by its unsafe nuclear reactors and arsenal, pervasive organized crime, epidemics, and instability.

Russia's proximity makes it a source of danger to China—but in a wholly different way than was true during the Cold War.

As for economic cooperation, questions about Russia's political and economic prospects cast doubt on a future of mutual investments, rising bilateral trade, and increasing reliance by an energy-starved China on Russian oil and natural gas. Indeed, at the beginning of the twenty-first century, the hopes aroused during the Gorbachev years for increasing mutually beneficial economic cooperation remain unrequited, with recrimination between China and Russia as to who is principally to blame.[7] Even more specific plans have failed to pan out, as witnessed by the commitment made by Moscow and Beijing in April 1996 to increase Russian-Chinese trade to $20 billion by 2000. In actuality, trade turnover is a mere $6 billion. For China's northeastern provinces (Heilongjiang, Jilin, and Liaoning), and particularly for its dynamic southeastern ones (particularly Zhejiang, Fujian, and Guangdong), the far more promising economic orientation appears to be toward Japan, South Korea, and the United States. These states have the capital, technology, and managerial knowledge that Russia manifestly does not have—and is unlikely to have within any reasonable span of time.[8] If regional preferences have an increasing effect on Chinese foreign policy, it follows that multifaceted strategic cooperation between Russia and China—which on China's side would be driven by its northeastern provinces—may encounter early limits.

The other major shift in Northeast Asia will occur on the Korean Peninsula, and the odds are that it will eventually lead to Korean unification. The only uncertainty is whether it will take the form of a hard landing (a North Korean collapse that generates various instabilities ranging from violence to massive population movements) or a soft landing (a negotiated unification which, while imposing major economic burdens on South Korea, involves minimal violence and upheaval). The reunification of Korea will have several consequences for Russian security in general and for the Russian Far East in particular. If it involves a violent implosion in North Korea, streams of refugees could head into the Russian Far East across the Tumen River. This outcome would generate ethnic tensions, which are already at play given the sizeable Chinese migration into the area, and burden the already hard-pressed local economies. And a South Korea preoccupied with and weighed down by the integration of North Korea would not be likely to spare resources to invest in the Russian Far East's economy. Sensing the impending change on the Korean Peninsula, Russia has sought to retain influence in North Korea, even though, since the Gorbachev years, it has tried to engage South Korea. If Korean unification is inevitable, Russia naturally wants it to occur in a manner that reduces the danger to the Russian Far East. There is also a long-term calculation at work. Russia realizes that a unified Korea aligned with China to balance a resurgent Japan could increase the leverage that China might exert against a Russia in decline. An upsurge in Japanese nationalism, or increased Japanese militarism, could result from rising Chinese power and declining Japanese confidence in the alliance with the United States.[9] It is for these reasons that Moscow, even though it recognizes the greater strategic significance of South Korea and has ended the Soviet-era military alliance with Pyongyang, continues to supply Pyongyang with arms and maintains a limited economic relationship with North Korea.[10]

Were a unified Korea to align with an increasingly powerful China, Russia would face several choices: adjust to Chinese hegemony, form a coalition with Japan against China, or join with Japan and the United States to balance China. Each choice would consign Russia to a position of weakness, or the role of a junior partner, and would entail other difficult choices. For instance, any dramatic change in relations with Japan would require a solution to the dispute over Habomai, Shikotan, Etorofu, and Kunashiri Islands—in Japan's parlance "the Northern Territories," in Russia's, "the South Kuriles." Since Russia now controls them, it would, perforce, be the side that would have to yield territory, or at least agree to do so at some future date. Former Russian President Boris Yeltsin and former Japanese Prime Minister Ryutaro Hashimoto pledged in 1997 to settle the territorial dispute and conclude a peace treaty by the year 2000, but there has been no breakthrough because neither country has a government with the political strength needed to make the difficult concessions.[11]

As another example of the unpalatable choices Russia would have to make in the face of rising Chinese power, consider the costs of accommodating China. Such a course of action would almost certainly reduce Moscow's influence in the Russian Far East, because the region's transactions with, and dependence upon, China would increase, and Moscow's capacity to defend itself would decrease. More ominously, because of the demographic imbalance between the Russian Far East and China's northeast provinces and China's determined quest for reliable sources of energy, the Russian Far East could, over a long period of time, be detached from the Russian Federation. This would emasculate Russian power in general and reduce to near insignificance its role in the Northeast Asian balance of power.

As the preceding discussion makes clear, Washington confronts a new and uncertain environment in the Western Pacific/Northeast Asia. The United States has been deeply engaged—economically, politically, and militarily—in this region, and this is not likely to change given the logic of geography, the influence of history, and the existing patterns of U.S. trade with and investment in East Asia. What has changed, and will continue to do so, is the balance-of-power patterns. The post–Cold War era creates uncertainties aplenty.[12] Will the Russian Federation remain viable, with the center exercising effective control over the provinces? If not, what will be the consequences for the Russian Far East, and how will its future orientation (instability, a Chinese sphere of influence, an arena for great-power competition, a region economically energized by steady integration with the dynamic Asia Pacific economies) shape the regional balance? Will the growth in China's power transform it into a hegemon, and if so, will regional states respond through resistance, manifested in the form of countervailing coalitions, or through appeasement, and what will be the consequences for U.S. interests in either case? Or will China's progressive integration into the global economy generate internal changes that would render it a cooperative partner for the states of the region?

The future of the Korean Peninsula is another prominent question mark. Can we expect the status quo to be maintained with minimal variation, or might we expect upheavals in North Korea that would lead to the collapse of the regime in Pyongyang and a slow, turbulent, and, for Seoul, costly reunification? Will a unified Korea become a democratic, prosperous, and significant player in the regional balance of power within a short period of time, or will the process take much longer? Will the bilateral alliances that the United States forged with Japan and South Korea during the Cold War endure after unification, or will they be regarded in Washington, Tokyo, and Seoul as increasingly irrelevant to the challenges of the post–Cold War era? If these alliances do erode, how will Japan and a unified Korea function in the regional balance—independently (and with greater military power), in concert with states with whom they share convergent interests, or as junior partners of China? Will the competition among Russia, China, Japan, and a unified Korea be unregulated and unpredictable, or will it be rendered more predictable—and thus less volatile—thanks to growing economic interdependence, a preoccupation with economic growth in each of these countries, and the creation of a multilateral security regime?

Much of the uncertainty in this changed regional environment is connected to the fluctuating relations between the center and periphery within Russia and to the emergence of new regional alignments in Northeast Asia. These factors must be considered in tandem with the more traditional concepts of national security.

REGIONALISM, FEDERALISM, AND SECURITY

Federal polities around the world have, in an age of globalization and growing interdependence, experienced a trend toward greater participation by subnational units in foreign policy. Even centralized unitary systems are not immune to this process. States, provinces, regions, and locales establish permanent offices in foreign capitals, create special economic zones, hold trade shows, compete for foreign investment, and participate in international organizations and conferences.[13] Cities, states, and provinces in ever-greater numbers are establishing world trade centers to promote their integration into the world economy.

This decentralization presents new challenges to central governments still operating on traditional principles of Westphalian sovereignty.[14] National elites may fear that subnational initiatives will fragment foreign policy, making it chaotic and unfocused. Inexperienced local elites may violate diplomatic protocol or inadvertently work at cross-purposes with the national government's goals. Direct contacts between regional units and foreign powers may circumvent the sovereign powers of the national government. International initiatives launched by a country's states and provinces may contravene constitutional provisions that reserve foreign policy prerogatives for the central government.[15] This regionalization of international relations makes it problematic for states to conduct coherent, unified foreign policies. While this process is not entirely new, the currents of globalization are bound to accentuate it.

As one of the world's more decentralized countries, the United States is particularly susceptible to fragmentation in its foreign policy. The U.S. Congress, buffeted by various lobbying groups, regularly confronts the executive branch on foreign affairs. States and cities often seek to influence other countries through selective purchasing laws or other trade restrictions, as in the boycotts of firms operating in apartheid-era South Africa. In June 2000 the U.S. Supreme Court struck down a Massachusetts law prohibiting companies with business interests in Burma from bidding on state contracts. Even in a decentralized United States, where courts have increasingly ruled in favor of state prerogatives, this ruling reaffirms the federal government's supremacy in foreign affairs.[16]

While the trend in the United States over the past two decades has been toward gradual decentralization in many areas of domestic and foreign affairs, in Russia the provinces were abruptly presented with far broader powers of self-government as the Soviet Union collapsed. However, the provinces had very little idea, and even less judicial guidance, as to how to use these powers. Russia's new federalism is still a work in progress. The 1993 Constitution of the Russian Federation allocates foreign policy and security predominantly to Moscow's purview. In practice, however, the emasculation of state power and the center's virtual neglect of the provinces have encouraged regional authorities, most notably the powerful governors, to act independently while continuing to press Moscow for Soviet-style subsidies.

Russia's Far Eastern provinces are the most logical candidates for autonomous development and decentralized governance. The Russian Far East is far closer geographically and perceptually to East Asia than to European Russia. While political separatism may not be a tenable option for the Far Eastern provinces, it is apparent that European Russia lacks the necessary resources to develop the East's transportation infrastructure or to invest in modernizing industry or the extractive industries. The region's economic future depends on cooperation with the states of Asia and the Pacific, including the United States.

Emerging Regional Linkages

One example of such regional cooperation is the "East by West Corridor," a project being developed by regional authorities in Russia, China, and the United States. The corridor would utilize the Russian ports of Vladivostok, Vostochnyi, and Nakhodka to ferry goods from the industrial centers of Northeast China to California, Oregon, Washington, and Alaska. Northeast Chinese manufacturers of clothing, furniture, and cement who currently supply the U.S. West Coast could reduce shipping costs by using this more direct route, avoiding the southern port of Dalian. In turn, U.S. exports, which now consist primarily of cotton, petroleum, machinery, and chemicals, would reach China's northeast quicker via Primorskii krai's ports. Russia's regional port authorities are expected to contribute to the project by constructing a modern highway from the ports to the Chinese borders.[17]

There are other regional links between the Russian Far East and the United States. The State of Washington established a trade office in Vladivostok in 1995 to promote its products and services, to assist businesses, and to facilitate cultural exchanges.[18] The American Business Center on Sakhalin, established under the auspices of the U.S. Department of Commerce, assists American business ventures in the Russian Far East. U.S. shippers from the West Coast provided the impetus for another program, Clear-Pac, which, together with Russian administrators and customs officials, was established under the auspices of the Gore-Chernomyrdin Commission in 1995. This venture lowers shipping and storage costs by expediting documentation of cargo entering Vladivostok, cutting the average customs clearance times from nine days to two.[19] These and other cooperative ventures have been coordinated through the Seattle-based Foundation for Russian American Economic Cooperation, which serves as a hub to promote connections among grass-roots organizations, the private sector, regional officials, and federal decision-makers.[20]

Russia's Far Eastern regions also are working directly with their counterparts from China, Japan, and South Korea on a variety of economic and cultural projects. For example, in late 1999 Beijing Mayor Liu Qi hosted a delegation of Russian regional leaders, headed by Governor Valentin Tsvetkov of Magadan, seeking opportunities for cooperation.[21] Japan has targeted its assistance toward the Russian Far East in the form of financing for reconstruction of the Zarubino port and creation of a venture fund to encourage the development of small and medium-sized enterprises in the Russian Far East and Siberia. The Primorye government has established working ties with such Japanese prefectures as Hokkaido and Niigata that border the Japan Sea and is working with the Japanese business organization Keidanren on a variety of projects. The Far Eastern regions and South Korea established an Association of Businesses, chaired by Yevgenii Nazdratenko, the former governor of Primorskii krai, to facilitate regional cooperation.[22]

Putin and Regionalism

Maintaining the territorial integrity of the Russian Federation has become a vital security concern for Russian politicians across the political spectrum, and the increasing assertiveness of the Russian Far East no doubt adds to the sense of urgency. Moscow's brutal campaigns against a breakaway Chechnya in 1994–96 and 1999–2000 signal its readiness to deal harshly with threats to the Russian Federation's territory. Outright secession, however, does not seem likely in the case of Russia's Far Eastern provinces. There are no strong cultural or ethnic pressures for separation from the Russian homeland. Local elites advance separatist agendas more as bargaining ploys to enhance their political positions and extract resources from the center than as serious options.[23] The Russian Far East could benefit significantly from greater integration with the Asia Pacific economies without the necessity of a formal divorce from the Federation, especially as separation might reduce its security with respect to other Northeast Asian powers, particularly China.

Attempts by regional governors, legislators, and other officials to engage with the outside world have posed foreign policy challenges for the Kremlin. Moscow has allowed the regions to establish missions in other countries, to conduct foreign trade and solicit foreign investment, and to send delegations abroad, providing these actions do not infringe on the constitutionally protected spheres of the federal government. However, President Vladimir Putin has stressed his determination to reassert Moscow's control over the regions. Given Putin's determination to crush Chechen separatism and his goal of rebuilding the Russian state, a period of recentralization is likely. The question is how this may be accomplished without negatively impacting Russia's fragile democracy. The means by which Nazdratenko was eased from power—the threat of possible criminal prosecution combined with the inducement of a lucrative sinecure as head of the State Fisheries Committee—signals that Russia is far from consolidating a law-based federal system. It also suggests that Russia's president may indeed prove successful in reasserting central control over the regions.

Putin has emphasized the importance of traditional values in rebuilding the Russian state. These include enhancing patriotism and national pride, building a strong and effective state apparatus, achieving social consensus on a reform strategy, and reestablishing Russia as a great power in the modern world.[24] The president has undertaken a series of measures to reunify the Russian Federation, from associating himself with the political bloc Unity (*Edinstvo*) for the 1999 parliamentary elections, to forming seven super-regions headed by appointed governor-generals responsible for enforcing Moscow's edicts throughout the country. The Russian president secured overwhelming support from the Duma for his plan to curtail the power base of regional officials in the Federation Council. As of this writing, Putin has proven to be quite effective in his attempt to consolidate control over the Russian lands. However, it remains unclear whether the erosion of the central government's power and the leeway seized by the provinces has proceeded so far that any radical centralization will prove impossible or, worse, set off greater instability.

During the Yeltsin era, provincial elites such as Yevgenii Nazdratenko entered the realm of foreign policy in ways that challenged Moscow's authority. Nazdratenko, for example, used the threat of separatism to extract greater resources from Moscow. He also opposed the Ministry of Foreign Affairs on the implementation of the territorial agreement signed with China in 1991 that returned 1,500 hectares of territory near Lake Khanka to China. Nazdratenko claimed that granting China coastal territory would allow the Chinese to construct a port on the Sea of Japan and destroy Primorskii krai's economy, and he encouraged Primorskii's Cossacks and other nationalist forces to rally against the planned transfer. Yet Nazdratenko's skillful manipulation of the Chinese factor and Russian nationalism in Primorye did not preclude his developing a pragmatic working relationship with Chinese authorities. Such pragmatism benefited his province, while it also shored up his power base in the regional business community. This, in turn, helped him defeat local opponents like former Vladivostok Mayor Viktor Cherepkov, as well as central authorities like former presidential envoy Viktor Kondratov. However, Nazdratenko's luck ran out when Kondratev's successor, Kontantin Pulikovskii, backed by a determined president, engineered his resignation.

In Khabarovskii krai, Governor Viktor Ishaev also played the China card to enhance his authority, albeit with less skill than Nazdratenko. Ishaev argued that the 1991 territorial agreement with China would endanger Russian security by allowing Chinese military vessels to navigate the Amur River.[25] Curiously, he has focused much of his regional diplomacy on strengthening Khabarovsk's ties with Malaysia. He attended the November 1998 APEC summit in Kuala Lumpur, at which Russia was admitted to membership, and hosted a visit to Khabarovsk by Prime Minister Mahathir in September 1999. At the end of 1999 there was only one Malaysian firm operating a timber concession in the krai, but Ishaev pushed the potential for further development of timber resources and possible cooperation on aircraft and ship production.[26] Ishaev has also practiced regional diplomacy in Japan, calling for the establishment of a six-nation Northeast Asian Development Bank to finance transportation and energy infrastructure projects.[27]

Regional leaders in the Russian Far East have more complex attitudes toward China than do their counterparts in Moscow. Russia's national elite hold a nineteenth-century geostrategic perspective—they are interested in courting China as a counterweight to U.S. hegemony in regional and world affairs and are aware of China's increasing influence on the world economy. They understand that supplying China with advanced weaponry may be a mistake over the long term, but at present the economic benefits from arms sales eclipse the more distant security concerns.[28]

Short-term economic interests likewise motivate Russia's Far Eastern leaders. They realize that it is the United States, Japan, and South Korea who can offer needed capital and technology, not Moscow or European Russia. China is less attractive economically to the Russian Far East. Chinese entrepreneurs may create small or medium-sized joint ventures in the region, but they do not have the capital needed to develop the Russian Far East's energy and transportation infrastructure. There is also a popular perception, laced with racial overtones, that China poses an immediate demographic threat. Distant Moscow and European Russia, by contrast, seem much less preoccupied with the issue of Chinese migration.[29]

Another problem in developing economic ties between China and the Russian Far East is Moscow's bureaucratic regulations and economic disincentives. For example, Blagoveshchensk has the potential to develop closer links with rapidly growing Heihe, just across the Amur River in China, but Moscow has imposed visa and transportation restrictions. Discussions have been held on constructing a bridge over the Amur to facilitate commerce, but Russian authorities claimed they could not afford to pay half the cost. When Chinese authorities offered to pay the full cost of the bridge, the Russian side stubbornly refused to cooperate.[30] Without stronger support from the center, the border provinces will continue to stagnate.

Control over military resources has also become an arena for contention between the center and the regions. In the heavily militarized Russian Far East, local authorities have resisted assuming the burden of feeding and housing soldiers and subsidizing the utility bills of military facilities. The center has not provided Russia's armed forces with the resources to adequately clothe, feed, and shelter the troops, much less to maintain their fighting capabilities, so military units have become increasingly dependent on local authorities for their basic needs. Local and regional elites in turn resent having to spend their already strained budgets to cover Moscow's debts. In some cases regional officials have developed close ties with military units stationed in their territories, a trend that calls into question the extent to which central military authorities exercise full control over the army.

These informal civil-military alliances could become destabilizing over the long run if Moscow continues to be unresponsive to local government and military needs.[31] According to a 1998 military reform program, Russia plans to consolidate its eight military districts into six zones, while devolving command and control and enhancing overall coordination. But neither the current districts nor the planned zones coincide geographically with regional administrative boundaries.[32] Yet military demands have focused more on improving living standards and restoring morale than in exercising political power. This suggests that localized, military-based separatism is not likely in the near future.

Far East Separatism?

The Russian Federation is at present a very weak state, but the existence of a weak state does not necessarily translate into the potential for disintegration. Of the relatively homogeneous states (and the Russian Federation, which is 82 percent Russian, falls under this rubric), the United States is the only country in the past 200 years that has come close to breaking up from domestic pressures.[33] The regions of the Russian Far East are heavily Slavic, so the ethnic incentive toward separatism that resulted in the breakup of the Soviet Union is not present. Moreover, despite the formation of loose regional economic associations, Russia's regions have proved unable to develop close working relationships with each other. The vertical ties that dominated under Soviet politics still prevail to a large extent. Thus, secession in the Russian Far East, should it come about, may be less the product of ethnic nationalism (à la Chechnya) than the result of a progressive fraying of the bonds that hold this part of Russia to the Federation. And that, in turn, may have more to do with the erosion of the power of the central government than with willful separatism in the Russian Far East.

But pressures for disintegration could also come from outside the Russian Federation. Nations may encourage separatism as a means of weakening a powerful or threatening neighbor. Japan is determined to secure the return of the Northern Territories, and its foreign policy has sought to weaken the four islands' ties to Russia. Short of fuel, battered by earthquakes, and neglected by Moscow, the islanders have at times contemplated placing themselves under Japanese authority. Despite the symbolic importance of these islands, their defection from Russia would hardly be analogous to the first domino that sets off the fragmentation of the other eastern territories of Russia. Nor is the separation of the Northern Territories likely to come about short of a major confrontation between Russia and Japan, which neither is inclined to risk.

China is the one external power that could possibly exploit Russia's internal weaknesses. This could be done deliberately, as part of a policy to recover territories across the Amur River conceded in the unequal treaties of the past. But Moscow and Beijing have reached agreement on virtually the entire eastern border and, for now, are drawn together by military ties and a shared determination to counter the hegemony of the United States. In the distant future, a powerful and rich China might seek to rectify the historical injustices of the nineteenth century.[34] A more immediate source of concern for Russia is China's demographic pressures, which, if left unchecked, could drastically alter the ethnic balance in certain regions of the Russian Far East and provide a motive for separation. Heilongjiang, Jilin, and Liaoning Provinces have a combined population of 105 million, fifteen times the entire population of the Russian Far East.[35] Although this is far less than the inaccurate figure of 300 million often cited by more alarmist publications, it is nevertheless an imbalance—and one that exists at a time when a power transition is underway between Russia and China. To date, the number of Chinese who have entered Russia illegally or have overstayed their visas is very small.[36] But the question is whether pressures within China, and continuing weaknesses in Russia, will increase the rate of migration.

A scenario under which China swallows up the Russian Far East seems far-fetched for the foreseeable future. China is preoccupied with internal reform and will be for some time. Chinese foreign policy is focused on securing the return of Taiwan and dealing with the challenges posed by the United States in the Asia Pacific. China is above all interested in preserving regional stability. The collapse of the Soviet Union was deeply disturbing to Beijing's leaders; further turmoil on China's northern borders would not be welcomed, and an aggressive move into the Russian Far East would alarm China's neighbors in East Asia, entrench the United States in the region, and create major complications between Beijing and Washington.

Yet nationalistic Russians do worry about the possibility of ceding control over time of their Far Eastern economy to Chinese immigrants. As one Russian scholar has noted, transplanted Chinese control a large portion of the financial capital of Southeast Asia. Although making up only 3.5 percent of Indonesia's population, Chinese controlled nearly 80 percent of that country's 300 largest companies in 1993 and nine out of ten of Indonesia's biggest financial and industrial groups. Chinese occupy similar positions of economic power in Malaysia, Thailand, and the Philippines.[37] Anti-Chinese sentiment, based on resentment of Chinese wealth, has occasioned violence in Indonesia and other countries in Southeast Asia. Given the typical Russian resistance to foreign ownership and investment, combined with mistrust of the Chinese in the Russian Far East, ethnic tensions would be unavoidable. However, while Chinese immigrants could conceivably establish a comparable dominant position in the Russian Far East economy, it would take several generations for this to occur, and is not likely until the business environment improves markedly.

New Security Threats

In Russia, as in the United States, the transportation and sale of illegal narcotics are now being described as a security threat. The Russian Far East, geographically proximate to North Korea and the drug routes of Central and Southeast Asia (Afghanistan and the Golden Triangle), is particularly susceptible. The drug trade poses a danger to Russia itself and to the surrounding countries. Primorye is one of the leading distribution centers in Russia for illegal drugs. Unemployment and poverty make drugs a popular escape as well as an attractive source of income, and the number of known addicts in the krai is increasing.[38] Japan's government is concerned that North Korean heroin and Iranian drug dealers are making their way to Japan via the Russian Far East.[39] The South Korean government also views the North Korea–China–Russian Far East narcotics connection as a new form of security threat.[40] All countries in the region, with the exception of North Korea, could benefit through cooperation to control the illegal narcotics trade.

Another of the "new security" threats is environmental degradation. There are several examples of environmental cooperation among government and nongovernmental organizations in the Russian Far East and Asia Pacific. One of the most vital is the dismantlement of Russian nuclear submarines and safe disposal of radioactive waste off the Pacific coast. The Pentagon's Defense Threat Reduction Agency, under the provisions of the Strategic Arms Reduction Treaty, is assisting Russia in eliminating 480 submarine-launched ballistic missile (SLBM) launchers and 31 ballistic missile submarines. Fourteen Delta and Yankee class submarines are to be dismantled at the Zvezda shipyard in Bolshoi Kamen, south of Vladivostok. Japan has provided funding to construct a liquid radioactive waste treatment facility on a barge to prevent the sort of radioactive waste dumping that occurred in 1993. However, progress is slow, and one of the contractors, McDermott International of New Orleans, has charged Zvezda with intentional delays to drive up costs and bring more revenue into depressed Bolshoi Kamen.[41]

Another example of environmental cooperation is the Phoenix Fund, an NGO founded late in 1997 by experts from Russia and the United States that is working with the Global Survival Network and Primorskii krai's State Committee for Environmental Protection. The Phoenix Fund is dedicated to protecting the endangered Siberian tiger, assisting with biodiversity and conservation projects in the Russian Far East, and promoting environmental education in the schools and among the public.[42] Among Russia's Asian neighbors, Japan has been the most active in pressing environmental causes. Friends of the Earth-Japan, with the support of Japanese and western donors and the Japanese government, operates a Russian Far East Environmental Hotspots project, the goal of which is to reform environmentally destructive Japanese-Russian trade practices and to reduce the wasteful consumption of wood products.[43]

In short, the greatest threats to Russian security in the Asia Pacific region are presented by internal problems, a point noted in Russia's National Security Concept of January 2000.[44] The Russian Far East, while it has great potential, is awash in such problems and is not blessed with particularly competent or far-sighted leadership. The region is being pulled in two seemingly opposite directions, resulting from the dual pressures of a difficult transition from communism and the impact of globalization. The pull of the Asia Pacific's economic power and the circumstances of geography force the area's political leaders and business entrepreneurs to think and act regionally, especially given that the rest of Russia cannot be relied upon for economic development and that autarky is not an option. Regional economic integration, however difficult for some provinces, is vital to the region's future. Conversely, the pressures for political identification with the Russian Federation are powerful, even without Moscow's recent efforts to rein in local autonomy, and secession is not in the cards. Underpopulated, poor, and demographically vulnerable, the Russian Far East needs Moscow's protection. A more robust form of federalism (through economic association or a regional caucus in the Federation Council) is possible, but Russia's sovereignty and strength are important guarantees for the Russian Far East and will not be challenged lightly. Moreover, China's looming power has strengthened Russian national awareness in the Far East.

POLICY IMPLICATIONS

The Russian Far East has yet to figure prominently in Washington's security calculations or in those of its key allies in the Western Pacific. China and Taiwan, Japan, and the Korean Peninsula have absorbed the bulk of U.S. attention in East Asia—and for understandable reasons. Yet Russia and the Russian Far East play an important, albeit latent, role in the security calculations of the region's powers. The role that Russia can play in the Northeast Asian balance of power depends heavily on whether stability prevails in the Russian Far East and on the nature of Moscow's relationship with this distant area. The United States stands to gain from a Russia that is stable and united by a federal arrangement that accommodates the provincial desire for autonomy while maintaining the unity of the federation. Of the scenarios sketched earlier in the chapter, the most undesirable are the first (a fragmenting Russia, with the Russian Far East becoming a gaggle of vulnerable statelets) and the second (a Chinese sphere of influence over the Russian Far East).

Multilateral initiatives can help reduce the probability that either scenario will become reality. If such initiatives are to be realized, a working assumption must be that Russia's Far East is an integral part of any effort that seeks to increase the likelihood of a Russia that is united, democratic, and moving toward economic prosperity. With this in mind, the United States should take the lead in organizing its allies in the Western Pacific to develop a long-term plan to address the economic and ecological problems that plague the Russian Far East. Outside assistance is no panacea, and the resources of the United States and its allies are limited and needed for other purposes at home and abroad. That said, a multilateral effort based on a carefully planned division of labor can make a difference, and it can lend a post–Cold War rationale for cooperation between the United States and its allies in Northeast Asia. A multilateral initiative aimed at the Russian Far East would not only contribute to the economic development of the region, it could also address important security concerns. For example, if the Russian Far East's small population and out-migration caused by economic hardship aggravate the demographic imbalance favoring China, then creating economic opportunities that convince people to stay and that, in the long run, attract others, serves both an economic and a security purpose.

Similarly, the lack of progress in defense conversion (in an area heavily dependent on military industries) reduces the likelihood that demobilized soldiers will find employment at a time when a demoralized military is a source of potential instability in the Russian Far East, as elsewhere in Russia.[45] A cooperative regional program focused on accelerating defense conversion would promote stability and allow this outpost of Russia to escape from an economy and psychology anchored in a military definition of security. Likewise, regional cooperation on energy development enhances overall regional security. China's increasing dependence on far-flung sources of foreign oil increases its sense of vulnerability, and Japan's heavy dependence on the Persian Gulf for its energy imports has the same effect in Tokyo. Multilateral efforts to develop Siberian gas and Sakhalin oil will contribute to regional security by easing the energy predicaments of China and Japan and by initiating the cooperative development of Russia's energy resources, and it will also benefit the economy of the Russian Far East.[46] However, foreign oil companies are often perceived as exploitative by Russians, and with good reason. Exxon Corporation, for example, received a negative environmental impact assessment in connection with the Sakhalin-1 project, and in 1999 was ordered by the Russian Supreme Court to refrain from discharging toxic wastes into the sea.[47] Modest investments by the oil companies—in orphanages, drug treatment centers, or projects to restore the environment—could do much to alleviate the suspicions of the local inhabitants, but few seem interested in being good global citizens.

This regional economic effort can be complemented by a multilateral security regime that includes Russia and China, who are still left out of existing regional security arrangements held over from the Cold War. The focus of a regional security dialogue and, ultimately, of a regional security regime, should be on military-to-military exchanges, arms control and confidence-building measures (particularly on the Korean Peninsula), nuclear safety and proliferation, terrorism, environmental cooperation, and a common policy toward the ravages of AIDs, organized crime, and drugs. The purposes of such a multilateral security effort range from a simple alteration of the climate of mistrust to the more ambitious task of tackling common problems.

Alas, efforts to develop multilateral cooperation in the realms of economics and security have to date proved only marginally successful, and early indications suggested that the Bush administration would to give up on them altogether. U.S. foreign policy in Northeast Asia is still derivative of the attitudes and institutions of the Cold War. The Clinton administration paid only sporadic attention to the region, dealing with regional crises on an ad hoc basis and neglecting a long-term policy. A new, more comprehensive framework for thought and action is in order. A sustained attempt to deal with the problems of the Russian Far East should be included as an important component of a broader U.S. policy toward Northeast Asia. The process of stabilizing this distant Russian frontier will not prove easy—there will be expenses involved, and the benefits will be realized only slowly, but the stakes are compelling enough to make the undertaking worthwhile.

NOTES

1. See, for example, Tsuneo Akaha, ed., *Politics and Economics in the Russian Far East: Changing Ties with the Asia-Pacific* (London: Routledge, 1997), especially the chapters by Vladimir Ivanov.

2. These divisions stem from deep rivalries among the federation subjects and the varying relationships with and attitudes toward Moscow. See Gilbert Rozman, "Troubled Choices for the Russian Far East: Decentralization, Open Regionalism, and Internationalism," *Journal of East Asian Studies* 11, no. 2 (Summer/Fall 1997):541–49; and Rozman, "The Crisis of the Russian Far East: Who is to Blame?" *Problems of Post-Communism* 44, no. 5 (September–October 1997):3–12.

3. *Tradition and Transformation: U.S. Security Interests in Asia*, Hearing before the Subcommittee on Asia and the Pacific, U.S. House of Representatives, May 7, 1998, 67.

4. Francois Heisbourg, "American Hegemony? Perceptions of the U.S. Abroad," *Survival* 41, no. 4 (Winter 1999–2000):5–19.

5. Joseph S. Nye, Jr., *Bound to Lead: The Changing Nature of American Power* (New York: Basic Books, 1990).

6. For details, see Rajan Menon, "The Strategic Convergence Between Russia and

China," *Survival* 39, no. 2 (Summer 1997):101–25.

7. See Gilbert Rozman, "Northeast China: Waiting for Regionalism," *Problems of Post-Communism* 45, no. 4 (July–August, 1998):3–13; and Rozman, "Troubled Choices for the Russian Far East," 549–61.

8. On trends in Russo-Chinese trade and China's doubts about the economic value of Russia, see Gilbert Rozman, "The Strategic Quadrangle and the Northeastern Region," in Rouben Azizian, ed., *Strategic and Economic Dynamics of Northeast Asia: Global, Regional and New Zealand Perspectives* (Auckland: University of Auckland, Centre for Strategic Studies, 1999), 10, 15–16.

9. As Gilbert Rozman notes, "increasing numbers of Japanese are doubting that their national interests are identical with those in the United States and that the United States in the absence of the Soviet enemy will be as steadfast in the containment of rival powers." Ibid., 13.

10. Hai Su Youn, "Changes in DPRK-Russia Relations 1989–1999: Before and after Kim Jong-Il," *Journal of East Asian Affairs* 13, no. 2 (Fall/Winter 1999):434–61.

11. For a comprehensive discussion of the obstacles, see Gilbert Rozman, ed., *Japan and Russia: The Tortuous Path to Normalization, 1949–1999* (New York: St. Martin's Press, 2000); and Charles E. Ziegler, "Russo-Japanese Relations: A New Start for the Twenty-First Century?" *Problems of Post-Communism* 46, no. 3 (May–June 1999):15–25.

12. These are discussed in Rajan Menon and S. Enders Wimbush, "Asia in the Twenty-First Century," *The National Interest*, no. 59 (Spring 2000):78–86.

13. Ivo Duchacek, "Perforated Sovereignties: Towards a Typology of New Actors in International Relations," in Hans J. Michelmann and Panayotis Soldatos, eds., *Federalism and International Relations: The Role of Subnational Units* (Oxford: Oxford University Press, 1990), 14–15.

14. One should not, however, exaggerate the extent of the Westphalian state's sovereignty. See Stephen D. Krasner, *Sovereignty: Organized Hypocrisy* (Princeton, N.J.: Princeton University Press, 1999).

15. Duchacek, "Perforated Sovereignties," 28.

16. The case was *Crosby v. National Foreign Trade Council*. See "Justices Overturn a State Law on Myanmar," *New York Times*, June 20, 2000. On the foreign policy implications of this case, see Brannon P. Denning and Jack H. McCall, "States' Rights and Foreign Policy," *Foreign Affairs* 79, no. 1 (January/February 2000):9–14.

17. John Helmer, "'East by West' Corridor Expected by Year's End," *Journal of Commerce*, July 19, 1999, 9.

18. Charles Ziegler interview with Olga Romanyuk, director, Washington State Trade Office, Vladivostok, March 13, 2000.

19. John Helmer, "Adding Ports to Speed Process," *Journal of Commerce*, August 12, 1999, 1.

20. Information on the Foundation for Russian American Economic Cooperation can be found on its web site at <www.fraec.org>.

21. Xinhua News Agency, from BBC Monitoring (Asia Pacific-Political), November 30, 1999, downloaded from <www.monitor.bbc.co.uk/newsline.htm>.

22. Charles Ziegler interview with Vladimir Alekseevich Stegnii, vice governor, Primorskii krai, March 14, 2000. It is unclear whether Nazdratenko retained his chairmanship of this organization after his resignation as governor.

23. Mikhail A. Alexseev and Tamara Troyakova, "A Mirage of the 'Amur California': Regional Identity and Economic Incentives for Political Separatism in Primorskiy Kray," in Alexseev, ed., *Center-Periphery Conflict in Post-Soviet Russia* (New York: St. Martin's Press, 1999).

24. "Vladimir Putin: Rossiia na rubezhe tysiachiletiia," *Rossiiskaia gazeta*, December 31, 1999, 4. Putin emphasized that a strong state should not be equated with a totalitarian one, and that great-power status would be indicated by technological and economic advances and not through military force.

25. Alexander Lukin, "The Image of China in Russian Border Regions," *Asian Survey* 38, no. 9 (September 1998):826–27.

26. "Khabarovsk Keen on Establishing Closer Ties," *New Straits Times*, November 15, 1998, 5; Hardev Kaur, "A New and Alternative Market," *New Straits Times*, September 22, 1999, 5.

27. The six nations were Russia, China, Japan, Mongolia, and the two Koreas. Eiji Furukawa, "Russian Far East Seeks Closer Ties," *Nikkei Weekly*, January 31, 2000, 23.

28. For a good analysis of different Russian attitudes toward China and how these relate to Russian foreign policy, see Alexander Lukin, "Russia's Image of China and Russian-Chinese Relations," *East Asia: An International Quarterly* 17, no. 1 (Spring 1999):5–39.

29. Elizabeth Wishnick, "One Asia Policy or Two? Moscow and the Russian Far East Debate Russia's Engagement in Asia," IREX/Huang Hsing Foundation Hsueh Chun-tu Lecture Series, February 24, 2000. See also Mikhail Alexseev, "Chinese Migration in the Russian Far East: Security Threats and Incentives for Cooperation in Primorskii Krai," chapter 13 in this volume.

30. Charles Ziegler interview with Michael Scanlan, U.S. Consulate, Vladivostok, March 13, 2000.

31. Martin Nicholson, "Towards a Russia of the Regions," *Adelphi Paper 330* (September 1999), 70.

32. Ibid., 68.

33. Thomas E. Graham, "The Prospect of Disintegration is Low," paper presented to the conference "Federalism in Russia: Is It Working?" Washington, DC, December 19, 1998.

34. For additional information on China's relations to the Russian Far East, see Ni Xiaoquan, "China's Threat Perceptions and Policies toward the Russian Far East," chapter 15 in this volume.

35. *China Statistical Yearbook* (Beijing: China Statistical Publishing House, 1998), 107. We are grateful to Mark Frazier for calling our attention to this source.

36. Charles Ziegler interview with Sergei Grigorevich Pushkarev, head of the Federal Migration Service for Primorskii krai, Vladivostok, March 13, 2000.

37. Vilia Gelbras, "Kitaiskii faktor vnutrennei i vneshnei politiki Rossii," in G.

Vitkovskii and D. Trenin, eds., *Perspektivy Dalnevostochnogo regiona: Mezhstranovye vzaimodeistviia* (Moskva: Tsentr Karnegi, 1999).

38. "Narkotika: Mestnaia i zaboznaia zapolonila krai," *Vladivostok*, March 15, 2000.

39. Charles Ziegler interview with Yasumasa Iidzima, Political Counselor, Japanese Consulate, Vladivostok, March 13, 2000.

40. Charles Ziegler interview with Young Hoon Kang, Political Counselor, Consulate of the Republic of Korea, Vladivostok, March 14, 2000.

41. Russell Working, "Nuclear Waste Project Drags on at Bolshoi Kamen," *Vladivostok News*, January 14, 2000, available at <vn.vladnews.ru/2000/iss207/text/biz1.html>.

42. For more information on the Phoenix Fund, see its web site at <www.phoenix.vl.ru/about.htm>.

43. For more information on Friends of the Earth-Japan, see its web site at <www.foejapan.org/en/siberia/hotspots.html>.

44. "Kontseptsiia natsionalnoi bezopastnosti Rossiskoi Federatsii," *Nezavisimoe voennoe obozrenie*, January 14, 2000.

45. For more on defense conversion, see Katherine Burns, "Security Implications of Defense Conversion in the Russian Far East," chapter 11 in this volume.

46. However, at peak production the Russian Far East will be able to supply only a fraction of Asia's total demand for oil and natural gas. See Judith Thornton, "Sakhalin Energy: Problems and Prospects," chapter 7 in this volume.

47. The Supreme Court invalidated a decree by former Prime Minister Sergei Stepashin that would have allowed Exxon to discharge wastes into the Sea of Okhotsk and the Beiring Sea. Environment News Service, October 12, 1999.

ECONOMIC OUTCOMES
OF MARKET REFORMS

3

Influence of the 1998 Financial
Crisis on the Russian Far East Economy

Pavel Minakir

BACKGROUND AND REASONS FOR THE FINANCIAL CRISIS

The financial crisis of 1998 was in essence a currency crisis, since a policy of inflation control and noninflationary budget deficit financing—which was in discord with actual exchange rates—was its basis. After a currency corridor was imposed in 1995, inflation decreased from 6 percent monthly to 6 percent annually before August 1998. This was largely a factor of the relative growth of treasury bills (GKOs) in budget deficit financing. At the same time, the decreased inflation meant a progressive revaluation of the national currency. Sustaining the dollar's fixed exchange rate over a long period of time brought about fiscal stabilization with low inflation rates. Yet this excluded monetary stabilization, which is usually characterized by a quicker decline of the ruble exchange rate than the rate of domestic inflation, and thus, due to the growth of money surplus in the economy, leads to the increase of effective and aggregate demand and a rise in national supply. At the same time export would be expected to grow due to the decline of the ruble exchange rate. Instead, the actual revaluation of the ruble caused a loss of competitiveness not only by exporters but also by investors in the Russian market. According to Vladimir Popov, by 1996 the Russian-American price ratio was 70 percent, as compared to 40 percent in 1994.[1] Naturally, this made investment projects even less attractive. The domestic rate of return was enormously high because of high interest rates in commercial banks and high risks for foreign investors in Russia. Besides, and this is the main aspect for a future crisis, the growth of exports started to slump: from 69 percent in 1994 and 120 percent in 1995, to 9 percent in 1996, -0.3 percent in 1997, and -19.4 percent in 1998. And imports increased steadily due to the ruble revaluation: up 114 percent in 1994, 120.6 percent in 1995, 113 percent in 1996, and 107 percent in 1997. After the drop in oil prices, this trend finally caused a current account deficit in the first half of 1998. In addition, world oil prices dropped another 52 percent in the second half of 1998 and 1999. This downward trend was partially reversed in 2000, as oil prices continued to rise. Although not a direct cause of the crisis, the current account deficit was an indicator of troubles in the currency sphere and became the basis of foreign capital outflow from Russia. The value of capital invested in GKOs and stocks of Russian companies fell almost tenfold from October 1997 through June 1998. Short-term foreign capital in the GKO market was valued at $20 billion by mid-1998, which exceeded the Central Bank's currency reserves. Together, these factors indicated the prelude of a currency crisis of the Mexican type.[2]

Reasons for the prolonged high ruble exchange rate include:

- political liabilities inside the country and the desire to uphold a national image in international financial institutions;
- insurance for foreign investments in GKOs through forward contract liabilities of commercial banks;
- stimulating investors inside the country to invest in GKOs rather than in hard currency; and
- striving to maintain high purchasing power inside the country to imitate stability in the national standard of living.[3]

On the whole, the economic and financial situation was extremely difficult by August 1998. Domestic government debt was about 390 billion rubles, and more than 50 percent of GDP in current prices of that period. By the beginning of August, currency liabilities were $26 billion, including $15.2 billion in liabilities on fixed-date contracts for currency supplies to foreign residents. In six weeks during the summer of 1999, the outflow of private deposits made up about 10 percent of total deposits. This made the stability of the banking system questionable. Ruble assets of companies in the banking sector dropped by almost 6 percent, and output correspondingly fell by 6.3 percent.[4]

The decisions of August 17, 1998, which formally meant admission of failure on the previous currency and financial policies, turned out to be a unique phenomenon of stabilization. The government decided to:

- freeze internal debt payments;
- expand the currency corridor (i.e., a step toward a floating exchange rate); and
- place a moratorium on private-sector payments of external debts.[5]

Each of these decisions separately had precedent in international practice, but implementing this entire complex was unprecedented. Benefits were obvious for most exporters, who had a net currency surplus, and for commercial banks, which managed to convert their assets into currency without liabilities on debt repayments.

Devaluation led to the quick growth of net exports (in ruble terms) without revitalization of investment, strong pressure on consumer expenses, and very low levels of government spending (until August 1999). Thus the continuation of GDP growth observed from the fourth quarter of 1998 (if we take quarterly sequential indices instead of indices based on 1997) depends considerably on the trade balance.

The crisis had a debt character, though it differed from the Mexican and Korean crises because it hinged on domestic rather than international borrowing, which, moreover, was covered partially by outside loans. A big part of the problem could have been solved if after May 1998 the government and the Central Bank had initiated a smooth devaluation of the ruble.[6] This would not have solved all problems, since a considerable share of external debt on GKOs was to be paid back in foreign currency, not in rubles. But on the whole, the amount of borrowing could have been reduced as a result of devaluation, especially as total debt was no more than 60 percent of GDP, which is not an indicator of an international crisis of trust in governmental liabilities. Probably the government made a decision to announce a default, which caused dramatic and uncontrolled ruble devaluation, because of the turmoil in the largest banks, which had borrowed large amounts of foreign currency, rather than because the government could not cover short-term debts.

As is generally known, ruble devaluation took three steps:

(1) 50 percent in August 1998 according to a decision of the government and the Central Bank;
(2) 100 percent between August and December 1998; and
(3) 35 percent from January through September 1999.

Total devaluation was 400 percent, half of which was provoked by default directly.

The new government introduced a new financial policy in October 1998. Its separate decisions and measures included:

- introduction of a flexible exchange rate with strict administrative control;
- wide currency emission, controlled by the Central Bank;
- attempts to change tax regulations; and
- selective support of the banking system.

Generally, the financial policy, full of contradictions, was carried out by the Central Bank. Although the Central Bank, forced by balance-of-payment conditions, gave up the principle of maintaining the exchange rate as the anchor of inflation, it returned to strict regulation of the exchange rate by the end of the year, without absolute control of money supply.

On the whole, during 1998 consumer prices increased by 84.5 percent, compared to 11 percent in 1997. However, producer prices grew by only 23.2 percent, which formed the basis of the revitalization of market conditions and had a deflationary effect in import-substitution sectors. In 1998 the total decline of real GDP was 4.6 percent, and industrial production declined by 5.2 percent. Agriculture has shown the worst results.

The government began to realize the positive effects of devaluation, which were reinforced by the subsequent ruble depreciation. These effects—which were true for the Far East as well as for the whole country—included:

- Price competitiveness of Russian products on the world market strengthened.
- Foreign goods lost their price competitiveness on the Russian market, which has led to a partial substitution of imported goods and services, and, naturally, to an increase in aggregate demand, which in turn has caused an improvement in market conditions.
- The money supply situation improved due to the increased inflow of export profits converted into rubles. But this effect has turned out to be weaker than had been expected, as a considerable share of currency profits was not converted into rubles but spent on technology imports and payments on currency liabilities. In fact, a major part of the extra money was supplied by emission of the Central Bank, rather than by foreign currency, which was being sold at the end of 1998. However, over 80 percent of this emission was aimed at supporting the liquidity of a group of commercial banks rather than at the productive sectors of the economy.
- Cash payments in taxation and commerce increased, leading to higher tax revenues and the formation of a higher level of stable demand expectations, which by itself is able to improve market conditions.[7]

At the same time a number of negative effects and limits did not allow some opportunities to be realized. First, the technological level of most Russian companies, especially in extracting fields, as well as the current state of production equipment, does not allow for a satisfactory substitution of imports without considerable additional investment and prevents producers from using the benefits of scales of production. In addition, opportunities to increase exports of raw materials are limited by the low price elasticity of these exports. Moreover, a substantial increase in raw materials exports, for example oil exports, could collapse world prices, which in turn could lead to losses in external trade. Inflationary processes that started with the devaluation are substantially narrowing the possible reach of devaluation effects. Inflation on the domestic market leads to a loss of price competitiveness. As quality is also questionable, import substitution becomes problematic in some sectors, which in turn increases inflationary expectations. Finally, the steady growth of demand under the influence of devaluation is connected with growth in the money supply, which means an increase of real exchange rates. As a result, interest rates declined, aggregate demand grew, and the economy expanded overall. However, in Russia's case, interest rates did not fall and no significant changes in the level of monetary supply has been noted since the beginning of 1999. Therefore, the stabilization of the economy—which failed to result in economic growth (GDP growth rate in 1999 was 3.5 percent and 7.6 percent in 2000)—is due exclusively to the external market.

ECONOMIC CONSEQUENCES OF THE FINANCIAL CRISIS

The combined influence of positive and negative effects of the ruble's depreciation has revealed itself in the general economic, and even more in the overall industrial, dynamics since the end of 1998. Growth in several branches of industry had already started by November 1998. Unlike light industry, which has never recuperated from the substantial decrease of demand, the food and electric energy industries and export-oriented branches of extracting industries had almost fully restored their levels of production by December 1999.

The improvement of market conditions continued in 1999, and was reflected in the 7 percent increase in GDP in the first nine months of the year. Since this increase is compared to the first nine months of 1998, it needs to be corrected according to the sharp decline of September 1998. Such a correction makes for a much less optimistic evaluation of a statistically pleasing picture of growth in the first three quarters of 1999. The problem is the fact that most of the main factors of economic growth—except for pure exports, which total the value of exports minus the value of imports—are still inactive and do not participate in the forming of the perspectives of the domestic market.[8]

Already by the fourth quarter of 1998, both industrial output and GDP had started to grow and had almost reached the pre-crisis level by the end of the year, which to a large extent was due to import substitution. The reasons for this growth, however, were connected with a considerable improvement in the economy resulting from the partial devaluation of the ruble. At the same time this growth made fundamental problems with the base macro- and microeconomic parameters more evident. These problems resulted from the same devaluation. Indeed, no correction of the economic system has occurred and there are no signs of even a hysteresis equilibrium. This allows us to speak not only about evident achievements in the restoration of general economic dynamics, but also about the existence of serious problems in sustaining the positive growth of macroeconomic indicators.

The situation in the Russian Far East has been developing according to a similar scenario, with some deviations, since in the Far East it is more difficult to use the advantages of devaluation to spur economic growth than in Russia as a whole. In the RFE, consumer product industries occupy a much smaller niche in the structure of production, which means that the effect of internal demand growth caused by the loss of price competitiveness of imported products is much weaker in the region; and the main stimulus is thought to be the increase of hard currency's share in profits rather than the regeneration of internal markets through import substitution. Also, credit debts in the region consist largely of debts to energy producers, most of whom are situated outside of the region, and therefore the growth of the money supply resulting from the increase in export income is distributed among external creditors without producing noticeably strong monetary impulses inside the Far Eastern region. Moreover, most of the exports of the Russian Far East are transported in large volumes, and since transport and freight processing tariffs are collected in hard currency, the share of transportation costs is high even after the devaluation of ruble. Also, natural resource companies of the Russian Far East receive equipment and technology inputs almost entirely through imports: therefore this part of the costs also has not changed after the devaluation.

By the end of 1998, the decrease in production in the Russian Far East compared to 1997 amounted to 1.9 percent, and production fell an additional 1.1 percent in the first half of 1999. During 1998 production decreased in almost all branches of industry. Export volumes shrank by 37 percent. Growth in exporting branches could have been more significant, but unlike the rest of Russia, which benefited from high oil prices, the Far Eastern region has faced a new wave of decline in world prices for its exported raw materials. As a result, the real value of exports has gone down by 27 percent while ruble incomes from exports were increasing.

However, by the third quarter of 1999 the situation had already improved compared to the same quarter of 1998 (again, we must keep in mind the decline of the third quarter of 1998). The total increase in the region's industrial production over nine months of 1999 was around 7 percent, and even higher in certain federation subjects (Khabarovskii krai—10.5 percent; Sakhalinskaia oblast—14 percent).

Two main factors enabled the growth of industrial production in 1999, while other branches of the economy did not experience any significant change (GDP growth totaled only 3 percent). First, deprecation of the ruble has sharply increased the volume of rubles in the Russian money supply as a result of export revenues being converted to domestic currency. This was also accompanied by the sustained growth in world prices for energy resources, which in turn has contributed to the growth of the rubles supply. At the same time, forecasts of expanded exports due to the depreciation of the national currency did not come true. The raw materials-oriented structure of Russia's exports prevented the economy from using the effect of growth of external trade competitiveness: a sharp increase in raw materials exports could have brought world prices down. Meanwhile, export-oriented expansion of processing industries was obstructed by the low technological level and lack of developed market infrastructure. Import volumes have shrunk due to the sharp price increases for imports on the domestic market. As a result, in 1999 the overall Russian external trade balance had achieved a positive value of more than $36.3 billion and $60.6 billion in 2000, compared to $15 billion in 1998. The Russian Far East has also experienced a sharp decrease of exports due to the contraction of military contracts with China. The region's foreign trade decreased by 33 percent compared to 1998 (See Figure 3.1).

Figure 3.1 Foreign Trade Growth Rates
(as a percent of the 1992 base level)

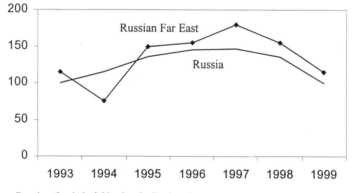

Source: Russian Statistical Yearbook, Regional Statistical Offices.

The growth of the money supply has contributed to the improvement in payments in Russia's economy. If in August 1998 the share of goods paid for with real money in all of the economy was only 35 percent, by November 1999 this share had gone up to 52 percent. Yet this did not lead to the decrease in the absolute volume of arrears, which grew from 1.16 trillion rubles in August 1998 to 1.42 trillion in November 1999. The share of credit arrears in GDP also has gone up, to 31.7 percent by the end of 1999 as compared to 26.7 percent in 1998. The level of GDP monetarization grew by only 1 percentage point from 1998 to 1999, amounting to 14.8 percent in 1999, which is still extremely low for the Russian economy. Yet this factor, too, has demonstrated low elasticity to the revitalization of market conditions.

Overdue credit arrears of large and medium-sized companies in the Russian Far East by the middle of 1999 exceeded 104 billion rubles, compared to 94 billion rubles of regional industrial production. Therefore, the share of overdue credit arrears in the gross regional product (GRP) exceeds 75 percent—still much higher than the Russian average. This gives further evidence of the difficulties experienced by the region in using the effects of devaluation to its advantage, and of the real disparity of world prices for export products of the Far Eastern region compared with the rest of Russia.

Second, dynamics of consumer incomes, and therefore real demand, appeared extremely sluggish compared to the revitalization of industry. Consumer prices in the Far East grew by an average of 84 percent in 1999 compared to 1998 and 34 percent in 2000 compared to 1999. At the same time, the average wage in the region grew only 33.8 percent. As a result, real consumer incomes in the region decreased, averaging only 84 percent of the 1998 level.

The decrease in real incomes led to the consolidation in 1999 of a change in consumer behavior that originated right after the crisis of August 1998. Alarmed by the shrinking real incomes and the expectation of high inflation, people have sharply decreased consumption of goods and services, giving more preference to increasing their savings. Private savings were growing not only in the form of dollar assets, but also in the form of deposits in Sberbank (recently the only bank with at least some level of household trust). The increase in Sberbank deposits is explained by the fact that the high dollar exchange rate often prevents leftover income from being used to purchase foreign currency. In mid-1999 the proportion of consumer spending to aggregate monetary consumer income in federation subjects of the Far East was fluctuating between 39 and 85 percent (Russian average = 80 percent).

As a result, sales of consumer goods after nine months of 1999 amounted to only 86.5 percent of their 1998 level. Agricultural production was also influenced by this situation. Except for the slight growth (2 percent in nine months) in the Republic of Sakha and the Jewish autonomous oblast, all other territories in the region experienced a decline of agricultural production, ranging from 32 percent on Kamchatka to 6 percent in Amurskaia oblast.[9]

Taking into account that increases in output were low, entrepreneurs could afford to disregard the current limitations of consumer demand, since the increase in the stock of finished products at the given level of output was also relatively small. At the same time, it is becoming increasingly evident that the low level of real demand has already become a significant factor limiting growth, and in the future its role as a macroeconomic barrier may become even stronger.

Table 3.1 Consumer/Producer Prices
1998–2000 as a percent of Fourth Quarter of 1999

Quarters	Consumer price index	Industrial producer price index
1998		
First quarter	37.8	48.5
Second quarter	38.1	48.5
Third quarter	58.0	58.7
Fourth quarter	72.9	72.7
1999		
First quarter	85.2	87.6
Second quarter	91.3	92.0
Third quarter	96.3	97.9
Fourth quarter	100.0	100.0
2000		
First quarter	103.5	100.6
Second quarter	108.7	103.9
Third quarter	112.2	110.9
Fourth quarter	118.1	117.6

Source: Review of the Russian Economy. Main Tendencies of Development. 2001: 85.

Another important factor that may seriously obstruct the restoration of economic activity is a continued threat of inflation. As Table 3.1 shows, the correlation of consumer and producer prices, characteristic of 1992–94 when rapidly growing producer prices were the main inflation factor, was restored again in 1999.

The situation in the Far East is not as straightforward as it is in Russia in general. However, in this region also, according to the data available for the first nine months of 1999, the growth rate of producer prices exceeds that of consumer prices in the Republic of Sakha, Khabarovskii krai, and Magadanskaia and Kamchatskaia oblasts. The situation in some provinces of the Far East is better, since the share of consumer goods imported from other regions is quite high, and therefore the high consumer price index reflects the high indices of producer prices in exporting regions and countries rather than an advantageous situation with production costs in these territories.

Revitalization of investment activity somewhat compensated for the limitations of real consumer demand in 1999. The all-Russian volume of investments in main assets in 1999 totaled 101 percent of the 1998 level. In the most economically developed territories of the RFE (except the Sakha Republic) these investments decreased from January through September 1999. However, by the end of the fourth quarter, the level of investment activity in the region stabilized—the long stretch of shrinking investments in main assets appears to have come to an end (see Figure 3.2).

The Russian Far East's prospects for economic growth are largely connected with the realization of Sakhalin oil and gas projects, and especially with the start of Sakhalin-1 and Sakhalin-3 projects. The launch of these projects should solve the problem of gas supply to Primorskii and Khabarovskii krais. Along with stimulating economic growth on Sakhalin, these projects may also present impulses for investment activity in Primorye and Khabarovsk due to the need for construction of natural gas pipelines and power plants.

In Khabarovskii krai, work has already started on the first stage of a Komsomolsk-na-Amure-Khabarovsk pipeline, which caused noticeable growth in investment in 1999. The start of such projects can significantly increase entrepreneurial expectations in the Far East, since it leads to the growth of expectations that goods produced in the region will become more competitive as the cost of electricity is reduced. Similarly, the construction of the Buriiskaia hydroelectric power station in Amurskaia oblast in 1999 may positively affect gross investment through a related increase in contracts with machine-building and construction companies in the southern territories of the Russian Far East.

The increase of state purchases of defense products secured in the 2000 federal budget also has the potential to contribute to the growth of industrial production in the Far East, and especially in Primorskii and Khabarovskii krais.

In general, it is important to point out that for the first time since the start of the radical economic reforms, the Russian Far East's prospects for restoring its economy are based not on external factors but on domestic growth in aggregate demand. Yet the presence of numerous and not always rational barriers to market entry, ambiguous and unstable business policies, discrimination against investors, and the exceptional fiscal character of economic policy result in the reluctance of domestic entrepreneurs to take risks, in particular in making long-term investments to help create and develop market demand.

Figure 3.2 Dynamics of Investment in Main Assets
(as a percent of 1990 base level)

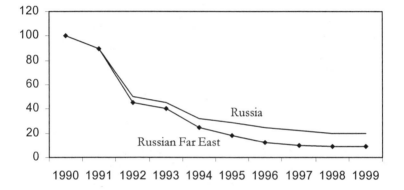

Source: Regional Statistical Offices, Russian Statistical Yearbook, Regiony Rossii.

The focus of regional elites on concentrating political power—and through doing so, gaining full control over the economy—has become a strong factor obstructing improvement in the conditions necessary for economic growth. In this connection, the discussion of Putin's strategic objectives concerning changes in the existing structure of power, including the relations between federal authorities and regional elites, could play a key role in evaluating the prospects not only for political transformation but also for the country's economic revival.

FINANCIAL CRISIS AND THE REGIONAL BANKING SYSTEM

The general financial crisis was most damaging to the banking sector, which is still focused on financial speculation rather than traditional operations of commercial banks. Until mid-1998, the main tendencies of the banking system's development were defined on the one hand by the exaggerated scale of operation on financial markets (mainly on the state's debt market), and on the other by the active enlistment of international financial resources for these purposes. By August 1998, an exceedingly large volume of hard currency obligations to nonresident banks had been accumulated. By the beginning of August, these obligations amounted to $26 billion (including $15.1 billion in immediate operations and $11.2 billion in bank deposits and credits).

Leading up to what was obviously going to be a crisis, banks could not (or maybe did not want to) change their strategy, and continued to use considerable amounts of capital in the extremely narrow—and extremely risky—market of state obligations, which eventually led to their financial crash. Therefore, underestimation of risk, inadequate economic behavior in a complex situation, and perhaps lack of professional knowledge on the part of a large number of commercial bank employees were some of the true causes of the crisis.

Another reason for the financial catastrophe was the loss of Central Bank control over certain financial markets, which allowed credit institutions to execute extremely risky operations. Most large banks had taken up the hedging of hard currency risks of nonresident investors in short-term government securities, GKOs and OFZs, by signing immediate contracts with the foreign investors for supplying foreign currency. At the same time, these contracts were not included in the calculation of the normative capital sufficiency. Only post factum—by the middle of 1999—over balance and immediate positions started to be a part of calculations during the battle for control of banks' activity.

A third reason for the banking system's vulnerability has to do with its institutional structure, which was drawn up during the reform period. The correlation between large and small credit-monetary institutions—between Moscow-centered and regional banks—which had evolved by 1998, has largely predetermined a catastrophic situation under crisis conditions. The system of credit institutions being formed in Russia was supposed to solve a problem of utmost importance to any bank organization—the problem of capitalization. Since banks cannot perform their functions without their own assets, stimulating the processes of forming and concentrating bank capital was thought to be the solution. This process included several factors.

First, considerable advantages were granted to the commercial banks to allow them to accumulate resources. For example, budget funds were injected into the commercial banks. All state-funded organizations had to transfer their accounts to commercial banks. The entire system, therefore, was built on money from the state budget. Commercial credit to state enterprises and the government, as well as acquisition of property rights during the privatization, were carried out with money from the federal budget.

Second, the concentration of capital in a limited group of banks was actively stimulated—these banks were granted means for quickly increasing capital. This was supposed to solve the problem of initial capital accumulation and was largely successful. The financial sector was growing at mind-boggling rates. This process was not spontaneous—it was an important part of the reform strategy. Accumulation of financial assets in a limited number of select credit institutions allowed the latter to enter international capital markets as borrowers and to become constant creditors to the government. Moreover, these banks were serving market-making functions for state debts and corporate stocks, as well as for the currency market.

Under conditions of low capitalization, it was impossible to solve all these problems without transferring financial resources from the regions to trusted, Moscow-centered banks. This resulted in the formation of a highly polarized economic system, where up to 80 percent of all financial resources were held in a limited number of Moscow banks, while numerous regional credit institutions had extremely low resource endowments.

This model of development became one of the main reasons for the financial catastrophe. For large national banks that had significant shares in GKOs and no less significant hard currency debts, four-fold devaluation of the ruble accompanied by the state's refusal to pay its debts became deadly—putting giant "holes" in their balances.

After the crisis, RFE banks were relatively untouched by the common illness of the payments system. Throughout the rest of Russia, the task of restoring the payments system was also quickly resolved. Immediately after the August 1998 default, the amount of assets remaining in corresponding accounts of commercial banks in the Bank of Russia fell to 10 billion rubles compared to 20 billion in the first quarter of 1998. This was due to the redirection of funds to hard currency in the face of the expected ruble devaluation and factual bankruptcy of many large multibranch banks, which seized their clients' assets.[10]

This crisis was overcome partially through the identification of defaulter-banks by the rest of the credit community and by directing client assets past these "black holes." But the main instrument for overcoming this crisis was handled by the Central Bank of Russia, which first restored the clearing system of payments in the Moscow region and then (after the ruble's devaluation) sharply increased the liquidity of the banking system by lowering reserve requirements and purchasing hard currency on the market.

The changes in the capital flows of banks in the Russian Far East were more evident. From 1997 to 1999, the number of credit institutions in the Russian Far

East gradually decreased, as it did throughout Russia. At the same time, the rate of decrease was somewhat slower than throughout Russia. The total share of credit institutions with headquarters in another region rose by an average of 20 percent by the end of 1999 as compared to the beginning of 1998, and remained stable at 88 percent, which allows us to conclude that there was a growing and absolute dominance of extraregional banks in the region. By mid-1999, the RFE banking system had lost twenty-one banks and seventeen branches; sixty-nine branches of extraregional banks also ceased to exist.

In the first half of 1999, assets of banks in the Far East were growing faster than total assets of the Russian banking system (134.1 percent and 126.3 percent, respectively). As a result, the share of Far Eastern banks slowly began to grow again after a sharp decline by October 1998—and in July 1999 amounted to 0.7 percent of total bank assets in Russia.

The aggregate share of resources of credit institutions in 1998 and 1999 fell by 2.3 percent, and recently amounted to 16.5 percent of total assets. At the same time, there has been growth in the share of resources deposited by enterprises and households. Private deposits recently amounted to about 40 percent of the shrinking assets of credit institutions. The assets of commercial banks and the federal government, which usually appear in the "other" part of the balance sheets, play an insignificant role in the formation of the resources of credit institutions.[11]

In general, before and after the crisis, deposited assets exceeded the banks' own resources five-fold. This situation was the result of the general shrinkage of credit institutions' profits as well as the reluctance to reissue stocks, which was conditioned by the wish to limit access to control and to sustain the earnings yield of securities (see Table 3.2).

In the post-crisis period, the structure of resource allocation by credit institutions has experienced significant shifts toward operations with hard currency, resulting in a 14 percent decrease in the share of credit operations and a 3 percent decrease in securities operations.

At the same time, by April 1999 the value of bank resources in securities neared that of January 1998, leading to the conclusion that the portfolio of regional banks includes a small share of state liabilities (see Table 3.3). The increase in currency operations is a result of the growing amount of U.S. dollars being circulated in the country and the shrinkage in the assortment of bank services, which forced credit institutions to focus on one of the least risky and most stable market segments.

Changes in the structure of resource allocation of banks were naturally followed by changes in the profit structure. As a result of the general decrease in the share of credit operations, the percent of bank profits from these activities fell from 47.5 in January 1998 to 16.8 percent in April 1999. No less significant changes have occurred with income from securities operations: their share in the respective period has dropped 19.3 percent to 6.2 percent of total income (as registered on the last day of the survey "Bulletin of Bank Statistics"). The banks have compensated for this by increasing the volume of hard currency operations. By April 1999, the share of these operations in total income was roughly two and one-half times greater than in January 1998 (see Table 3.3).

Table 3.2 Dynamics and Structure of the Resources of Credit Institutions (percent)

	January 1998	July 1998	January 1999	April 1999
Own assets	18.8	14.9	16.7	16.5
Corporate assets	29.5	38.8	32.9	33.0
Private deposits	42.3	41.6	40.6	40.2
Other assets	9.4	4.7	9.8	10.3
Ratio of own to borrowed assets	4.3	5.7	5.0	5.1

Source: Calculated from *Bulletin of Bank Statistics*, no. 10 (1997); no. 5 (1998); and no. 10 (1999).

The amount of credits issued by independent banks and branches of extraregional credit institutions has decreased by 229 million and 48 million rubles, respectively, demonstrating a stable level of resources diverted from credit operations (lending) during the increase in the volume of hard currency operations. The total amount of resources lent by banks shows that hard currency trading, which is generally considered to be a main direction of banks' activity, is not considered to be so by the Far Eastern credit institutions.

Corporate credits occupy the largest place in the general structure of credits issued by commercial banks, accounting for about 90 percent of all allocated resources. Throughout the survey period, this number slowly decreased from 91.3 percent to 87.7 percent. Second in importance in the credit portfolios of regional banks is interbank credit operations: their amount has grown from 4.7 percent to

12.2 percent—thereby shrinking the amount of resources allocated to households from January to April 1999 by 6.3 percent. The amount of corporate credits is three times more than the amount of corporate deposits, but the amount of household credits is five times less than the amount of household deposits.[12]

Table 3.3 Dynamics and Structure of Resource Allocation of Banks
(percent)

	January 1998	January 1999	April 1999
Credits	37.8	23.3	23.2
Securities	23.6	14.4	20.9
Hard currency	7.3	20.3	18.4
Other	31.3	42.0	37.5

Source: Calculated from *Bulletin of Bank Statistics*, no. 10 (1997); no. 5 (1998); and no. 10 (1999).

The changes in the credit policies of commercial banks are demonstrated by the decreasing amount of credits that can be issued by a single credit institution. This value for the Russian Far East amounted to 35.5 million rubles at the beginning of 1999 (12 percent of the average level throughout Russia), including 26 million rubles issued to enterprises and organizations (13 percent of the Russian average), and 4.8 million rubles to households (including private entrepreneurs), the latter constituting 35 percent of the Russian average.[13]

Investments in state securities by banks in the Far East is much lower than generally throughout Russia, but this is compensated for by the allocation of funds to stocks and participation in associated and subordinate public companies (Table 3.4).

The amount of credits issued by regional banks was growing faster than investment in state securities throughout Russia (the share of investments in federal debt obligations from July to December 1998 decreased 0.9 percent) and slower in the Far East (increased by 10.7 percent). By the middle of the year this correlation had somewhat improved to 7.8:1 (the Russian average remained unchanged). At the same time, assets withdrawn from the stock market are not directed into the real sector of economy, and in general, as noted, the credit base in the Russian Far East is rapidly shrinking. The situation is worsened by the growth of indebtedness on ruble and hard currency credits.

Table 3.4 The Structure of the Credit Portfolio of Credit Institutions
(percent)

	July 1998		January 1999	
	Russia	Far East	Russia	Far East
Total investments in debt obligations, excluding state liabilities	7.3	0.6	7.8	19.2
State liabilities	86.3	76.5	84.9	68.6
Stocks	3.6	19.2	3.6	9.7
Participation in associated and subordinate public companies	1.4	0.6	2.8	1.0
Other participation	1.4	3.1	0.9	1.5
Total	100.0	100.0	100.0	100.0

Source: Bulletin of Bank Statistics, no. 10 (1999).

The following statements describe the general situation of banks in the Russian Far East.

(1) Private deposits constitute the main part of resources of regional banks, but their share has somewhat decreased in the post-crisis period.
(2) The main focus of regional banking activity after the financial crisis has shifted to hard currency operations, which have substituted for operations with state securities. This change was determined not only by the attitude of bank management, but also by the greatly increased demand for foreign currency by households and companies. The concentration of banking operations on the currency market demonstrates the lack of will or ability of regional banks to serve as instruments for effective accumulation and redistribution of deposited resources.
(3) The structure of banks' investment portfolios also has shifted from investment in state securities to investment in fund instruments of enterprises, organizations, and banks, but the total amount of issued credits is extremely small compared to the sums involved in currency operations and does not correspond to the demand for borrowed capital.

(4) Regional banks are characterized by low liquidity, compounded by a low level of diversification.

Immediately after the financial crisis of 1998, work began on several strategies for restructuring the banking system. The federal strategy—as proposed by the Central Bank—views the regional constituent of the banking system as the central point of restructuring. This is due to the fact that the ultimate goal of bank restructuring—construction of an effective system of payments—is impossible to achieve without building a regional network of banks which would be large enough to supply at least a minimum of bank services. In accordance with the Central Bank's plan, a system of about 190–200 reliable regional banks should be developed. These banks have to be chosen with input from regional governments and must receive support provided by special plans of financial revitalization. Execution of the technical part of this task is bestowed upon the Agency for Restructuring Credit Organizations (ARCO).

The Central Bank has proposed a general division of all regions into three categories:

Category one includes those federation subjects that will be first to receive funds for the restructuring of the bank system. Banks based on existing financially secure organizations will be created. Of the 26 regions identified by the Central Bank in this category, 4 are in the Far East: the Republic of Sakha, Khabarovskii and Primorskii krais, and Amurskaia oblast.[14]

The second category consists of regions where "foundation" banks, or leading banks, will be built from existing banks that are experiencing problems and cannot independently overcome financial difficulties. In working with these banks, the federal government plans to enlist resources of local administrations and bank stockholders to minimize the expense to the national budget. In practical terms, this means that regional authorities must rescue these banks on their own. This category includes 29 territories, 2 of which are in the Far East: Magadanskaia and Sakhalinskaia oblasts.

The third category consists of those regions (22) that do not need a system of basic banks since they are already supplied by all necessary banking services. The Far East is represented here by Kamchatskaia oblast.

Therefore, the Central Bank has identified 79 banks in 69 regions as the basis for the future banking system, and 55 regions were identified as prospects for foundation or leading banks. According to preliminary calculations, restructuring these banks will require five billion rubles of budget money for refinancing and six billion for sustaining liquidity.

ARCO demands that banks comply with certain requirements in order to be considered a foundation bank and to enter the program of restructuring. First, the amount of deposited resources of households and institutions must account for no less than 10 percent of total assets enlisted in the region. The banks with good connections with local administration obviously have a head start here, since they are usually handling the budget accounts. Second, credits issued to producers by the applying bank must constitute not less than 30 percent of a bank's total assets. Here also, the advantage belongs to banks that are close to local administrations, since they are processing credits to local producers. Third, the bank must be able to pay all currently applicable taxes, although it can be granted a deferral of overdue payments. It is also advisable that the local administration holds a large share of the bank's stock (at least 25 percent), gives guarantees for ARCO funds received by the bank, or helps to develop and strengthen the client banks (including through budget flows).

Therefore, the Central Bank's plan is in accord with the wishes of federation subject governments to support banks that identify themselves as being close to the administration. In reality, regional administrations receive a chance to restructure "their" banks using money from the federal budget, while the federal government—represented by ARCO—plans to use the administrative tools of the regions. Ideally this should lead to the creation of an efficient banking system—and one that will be satisfactory for regional needs.

Yet, restructuring implies ARCO's ability to influence the decisions made by banks in various ways, including through a controlling share of stock. This means that the bank would become a property of the federal government, which is unlikely to be suitable to local authorities.

Aside from restructuring, the Central Bank is also planning to restore a regional network of Central Bank branches to process financial flows. The necessity of this is substantiated by the fact that regional banks have a very low level of technology. In ARCO's opinion, the creation of new banks in regions most hurt by the financial crisis will cost twice as much as setting up a network of Central Bank branches. ARCO's program includes the creation of branches of the large-capital Alpha Bank in ten regions that in its judgement have no active banks that could serve as foundation banks. Alpha Bank has already received a one billion ruble credit from ARCO (10 percent of all funds allocated for restructuring) for this purpose.

Despite the overall orderliness and technical simplicity of the Central Bank's strategy, it still has two serious shortfalls. First, ARCO has very limited resources—10 billion rubles (about 400 million dollars) is obviously not enough for the restructuring of even one large bank. For example, 46 billion rubles would be necessary to drag a bank like SBS-Agro out of the financial pit. Second, the Central Bank's strategy is reconstructing the previous layout—evaluating strictly regional banks according to the criteria of being manageable from the center.

The obvious tendency to strengthen federal control over regional banks is very unsettling for the regional elites. They justly point out that the restoration of a system in which 80 percent of Russia's financial resources were concentrated in Moscow banks (which eventually led to the general financial crisis) is not the best way of solving existing problems.

Therefore, regional authorities are working on alternative schemes of restructuring the credit-monetary system. These are oriented toward giving regional banks the maximum possible independence from the center and, where possible, transferring the property rights (full or partial) of these banks to local administrations. Many regions have already expressed their refusal to follow the Central Bank's plan.

The central idea of the regional strategy to restructure the banking system is to gain control over financial flows. Proposals for realizing this idea range from introducing direct control over inter-budgetary currency flows by concentrating all collected taxes within the region to forming regional gold and currency treasuries. Regional authorities see their second task as the creation of so-called governor's (*gubernskie*) banks that are fully controlled by regional administrations and the creation of regional payments pools. This means not only transferring regional budget accounts to these banks but also mandatory requirements for enterprises to use the services of these banks.[15]

Currently, many regional administrations are actively regulating bank activity by buying stock shares or executing their trust management. The Khabarovskii krai administration has taken the first path: it is a founder of the two largest banks in the krai—Dalkombank and Regiobank. The second path was taken by Sverdlovskaia oblast and Saint Petersburg, where administrations have accepted management of controlling shares in several large banks, in return granting these banks tax preferences and the right to handle budget accounts.

The third means of participation by regional administrations in the restructuring of regional banks is to lobby for their interests at the Central Bank. Issues of sustaining or withdrawing licenses and customizing standard financial requirements for certain regional banks have become questions of top priority for administrations.

By creating regional banking groups under their control, regional authorities solve several tasks. First, they create local payments systems. Second, they stimulate credits for local enterprises. Third, they receive a chance to incorporate regional money substitutes (emitted by administrations and controlled banks) in territorial circulation, therefore stimulating regional economic development without spending actual money.

However, there also exist certain negative consequences. The main niche in the bank system would be given to small and medium-sized banks. This would considerably decrease the overall effectiveness of financial services. These banks would have difficulty servicing large clients. They may fall short of necessary resources, technologies, connections, experience, or personnel. In addition, these banks would experience problems in providing services to a large number of small clients and households. Therefore, the problem of restructuring regional banks cannot be solved by focusing on small and medium-sized banks, since the task of finding sources of financing is no less difficult than in the Central Bank's strategy.

In addition to these matters, there are questions about the role of foreign banks in restructuring the Russian banking system. The possibility of enlisting foreign capital in the Russian banking sector has been discussed continually since the start of the reform period. Potential advantages of foreign banks are well known and are actively propagated by the advocates of their participation in the Russian bank system.

Interest in this problem has increased in recent years. Immediately after his appointment as prime minister, Yevgenii Primakov voiced support for opening the credit market to foreign banks, grounding this approach on the need to receive new banking technologies and improve competition and effectiveness in the banking system. Another important reason for the increased attention to this subject is the lack of a clear understanding of where to find the resources to restructure the banking system and overcome its crisis.

Opportunities for developing depository services for households, which according to some estimates hold between $40 and $70 billion, present a serious argument in favor of foreign bank participation in the Russian banking sector. It is thought that people would be more willing to entrust their savings to outsider banks than to Russian ones, which have compromised their trust on a multitude of occasions.

In order to make the Russian market more attractive for foreign banks, they have been promised an opportunity to convert debts of Russian banks to their own capital. In this case, foreign banks receive a right not to write off the debts of Russian credit institutions as costs and receive additional opportunities to conduct operations on Russian fund markets.

As of July 1, 1998, nonresidents were participating in the capital (through establishing joint banks or purchasing shares of Russian banks) of 146 credit institutions registered on Russia's territory (by year-end, this number had dropped to 142). At the same time, as of February 1999, 19 credit institutions were fully owned by nonresidents, and 13 other credit institutions had nonresidents who owned more than half of their founding capital.

The structure of enlisted resources of foreign banks significantly differs from general Russian standards: the share of current accounts of clients in the enlisted resources was less than 14 percent (22 percent for Russian banks), and deposits accounted for around 3 percent (38 percent for Russian banks). Main assets were enlisted from banking institutions. Thus foreign banks are not really oriented toward enlisting financial resources from Russia's economy. The main part of foreign bank operations has traditionally been concentrated on currency. Less than 1.5 percent of credits issued by foreign banks to nonfinancial enterprises was denominated in rubles, compared to 58 percent for the Russian banks in general. This means that foreign banks in Russia never were universal credit institutions aiming to give their clients the full range of services. Therefore, the idea of substituting stagnating Russian banks with prosperous foreign ones would seem overly optimistic.

Moreover, a whole series of institutional barriers to the diversification of banking services exists on both the Russian and foreign sides. Foreign banks operating in Russia usually do not have the right to make independent management decisions—all strategic, and often even tactical issues, have to be confirmed by the parent bank in accordance with internal procedures and regulations. Although this is a natural attitude for a parent bank that is trying to consolidate information, decision-making, and control over risk, from the perspective of a Russian client, this signals an inability of foreign banks to react quickly to demands and problems and an extreme lack of flexibility in making even routine decisions.

Another considerable limitation to foreign banks' ability to work with Russian clients is the lack of substantial owned assets, a relatively small amount of the foreign capital. This shortfall is especially evident when servicing the largest Russian companies, whose financing needs exceed the aggregate possibilities of the banking system. We must also not forget that current Russian supervisory norms are largely tied to the amount of a bank's capital, and therefore limit the scale of the bank's expansion.

An absolute institutional limitation on the activity of foreign banks in Russia is their lack of developed regional and branch networks, which is necessary for servicing clients, especially private ones.

Another important limitation to the expansion of the foreign banking business from the Russian side is the requirement that foreign participation be limited to 12 percent. Foreign banks have experienced increased problems with this limit after the devaluation of ruble, since hard currency denomination of the founding capital of Russian banks had shrunk. However, Central Bank President Viktor Geraschenko indicated that the government is ready to change or even cancel this limitation, but it has not done so yet.

In general, foreign banks have suffered considerable losses in the wake of the financial crisis. According to some estimates, the aggregate capital of foreign banks by fall 1998 had turned into a negative value. This fact made them freeze all new projects in Russia and rethink their previous expansion strategies.

However, there are certain positive processes going for the foreign banks. First, many Russians in September–August 1998 hurried to transfer all or part of their funds to foreign banks. This led to a 150 percent increase in the share of ruble accounts held in foreign banks—from 2.2 percent in mid-1998 to 3.3 percent by December 1998. The foreign banks' share in hard currency accounts also grew from 6.5 percent to 9 percent in the same period. Still, these positive phenomena are obviously too insignificant quantitatively and are not having much influence on foreign credit organizations.

In sum, foreign banks do not receive significant incentives to expand in the Russian market and at the same time face several substantial barriers. They will not be interested in building their presence in the Russian market in the near future, and cannot directly aid in solving the internal problems of the Russian banking system.

STEPS FORWARD FOR THE REGIONAL BANKING SYSTEM

For the Russian Far East, the possibility of applying either one of the existing strategies depends on the ability to solve the most pressing problems of the regional banking system.

Causes of the bank crisis in the Far East can be divided into three large groups: macroeconomic factors, regional problems, and internal bank problems. A major problem exists in the banking system's lack of assets. Many banks were created with the minimum possible founding capital, which thereafter could have been increased only from profits. However, profits were often used for current consumption or invested in passive assets. The capital values of many banks were actually "air balloons" and the crisis has only revealed their true nature.

Moreover, as a result of the crisis, the bank sector lost many of its assets. Devaluation of the ruble, which has led to the multifold growth of the ruble valuation of hard currency liabilities and a significant outflow of previously enlisted resources, has created a very complicated situation for all credit institutions. According to different estimations, the banks have lost 30–60 percent of their aggregate ruble capital, or 55–80 percent of that capital in dollars. This particular result of the crisis is attracting a lot of attention, but the government still has not determined its approaches to solving the problem. As a result, some banks are being held above water by substituting their indebtedness to clients with indebtedness to the Central Bank of Russia. Some banks have started negotiations to try to place part of their losses on the shoulders of their creditors. Others, having lost all hope, are simply waiting for their turn in line for liquidation procedures.

Another important step toward shoring up the RFE's banking system is improving the territorial system of bank supervision by strengthening the role and functions of agencies of the Central Bank. To date, neither the scope of the parameters of bank development nor the instruments of the Central Bank's influence in the regions allows the Bank to monitor the ongoing processes and manage them in the case of dangerous fluctuations. This applies particularly to the branches of banks from outside the region.

Underestimation and underwriting of risks have taken on a widespread character and have led to significant distortion of bank accounting and statistics. Development of financial markets and their instruments in Russia has proceeded at such a high pace that Russian banks have quickly acquired all the new technologies for falsification of accounting. Without the development of systems for territorial bank supervision, the existing practices may become chronic and will only further weaken the stability of credit-monetary institutions.

At the same time, two serious problems exist with perfecting the banking legislation in the Russian Far East. This legislation cannot be created independently from the existing banking system: a country cannot just borrow its neighbor's system of rules and requirements. In Russia, the creation of such a system is complicated by vast territorial distances accompanied by a high level of diversification of regional development.

NOTES

1. Vladimir Popov, "Uroki valiutnogo krizisa dlia Rossii i drugykh stran," *Voprosy ekonomiki,* no. 6 (1999).

2. Manuel F. Montes and Vladimir V. Popov, *Valiutnye krizisy: Gollandskaia bolezn ili aziatskii virus?* (Singapore: Institute of Southeast Asian Studies, 1999).

3. A. Illarionov, "Kak byl organizovan rossiiskii finansovyi krizis," *Voprosy ekonomiki,* no. 11–12 (1998).

4. *Sotsialno-ekonomicheskoe polozhenie Rossii* (Moskva: 1999); and Popov, "Uroki valiutnogo krizisa dlia Rossii i drugykh stran."

5. Montes and Popov, *Valiutnye krizisy: Gollandskaia bolezn ili aziatskii virus?*

6. A. Illarionov, "Mify i uroki avgustovskogo krizisa," *Voprosy ekonomiki,* no. 10–11 (1999); Montes and Popov, *Valiutnye krizisy: Gollandskaia bolezn ili aziatskii virus?*; and Popov, "Uroki valiutnogo krizisa dlia Rossii i drugykh stran."

7. P. A. Minakir, ed., *Ekonomicheskaia politika na Dalnem Vostoke Rossii* (Khabarovsk: DVO RAN, 1999).

8. *Sotsialno-ekonomicheskoe polozhenie Rossii.*

9. Minakir, *Ekonomicheskaia politika na Dalnem Vostoke Rossii.*

10. O. M. Renzin, "Dalnevostochnaia bankovskaia sistema: Masshtaby i struktura," in *Dalnii Vostok Rossii: Ekonomichseskii potentsial* (Vladivostok: Dalnauka, 1999).

11. Ibid.

12. O. M. Renzin, "Finansovye instrumenty v rossiiskoi ekonomike i restrukturizatsiia

bankovskoi sistemy," in *Banki na Dalnem Vostoke i v Sibiri: Istoriia, sovremennaia situatsiia i problemy razvitiia* (Khabarovsk: 1999); and Renzin, "Dalnevostochnaia bankovskaia sistema."

13. Renzin, "Finansovye instrumenty v rossiiskoi ekonomike."

14. Ibid.

15. Minakir, *Ekonomicheskaia politika na Dalnem Vostoke Rossii;* and Renzin, "Dalnevostochnaia bankovskaia sistema."

4

Social and Economic Differentiation in the Russian Far East

Nadezhda Mikheeva

The economic systems of Russia's regions are greatly differentiated, and the process of interregional stratification has been significantly intensified in the course of reforms. The social and economic position of particular regions under crisis conditions proved to be affected by many factors associated with the pace and specific features of reforms. By the late 1980s, interregional parity of production levels, living standards, and some of the well-established interregional ratios broke down, and groups of relatively rich and poor regions started to develop.

An example from the Russian Far East is fairly illustrative. In the pre-reform period, the region had one of the country's highest levels of income per capita, which was intended to compensate for unfavorable living conditions and shortages of social infrastructure. Throughout almost the entire Soviet period, the development of the region was based on extensive transfer of funds from the central government. With the onset of reforms, the region quickly lost the advantages it had by virtue of its specific economic and security significance and took the lead in the decline of production, investment, the share of unprofitable businesses, and so forth.

A specific feature of the subjects of the Russian Federation in the Far East is that, contrary to the older regions with their historical specialization and social infrastructure, the development of land and migration to the RFE were associated with the necessity to solve problems facing the nation in general, for example in defense and natural-resource extraction. The regions of the Far East were a vivid example of how a planned-economy approach to development was realized. The regional production structure was dictated from the viewpoint of "the efficiency of the national economy." More accurately, the criteria for location of economic activity and population were political, military, strategic—anything but economic. Due to a number of factors, the Russian Far East turned out to be the most expensive region in Russia.

In spite of the common problems facing the component regions, the Russian Far East has never been an integral unit in terms of economics and, especially, politics. According to the state structure of the Russian Federation, the Russian Far East comprises ten equal and independent—but economically greatly differentiated—federation subjects, each of which has its own bodies of state management that directly interact with the central authorities in Moscow. These ten federation subjects are united into the "Interregional Association of the Far East and Trans-Baikal," but this is nothing more than a coordination agency.

This chapter examines the economic aspects of the differentiation process in the subjects of the Russian Federation in the Far East in the years of reform and evaluates the relationship between the regional policy toward the RFE pursued by the central government and the regional differentiation processes. The research is based on official statistics of Goskomstat, although these were insufficient. The process of differentiation is carried out here using two parameters: average per capita personal income and per capita gross regional product. In theory, both are closely connected to each other and have basically identical dynamics. However, analysis shows that for the Russian economy, with a significant share in the shadow sector and dubious statistics, these parameters are weakly correlated: in other words, the regions with higher levels of income do not necessarily have higher per capita production. Goskomstat has been carrying out estimations of gross regional product in the subjects of the Russian Federation in current prices since 1994. Considering that data in constant prices is required for interregional comparisons, GRP parameters for 1990–99 were estimated by means of a technique used by the World Bank for the countries of the Newly Independent States. The estimation of real personal incomes was carried out on the basis of official data on money incomes of the population and consumer price indices.

DIFFERENTIATION IN PRODUCTION

Nominal macroeconomic indices for the Far Eastern regions, calculated at current prices, are among the highest in Russia. The region ranks next to Western Siberia in average per capita GRP and occupies one of the country's top places in nominal average per capita income indicators. Nevertheless, the regional share in the all-

Table 4.1 Per Capita GRP in the Far East

	Per capita GRP (thousand rubles)				Compared to Russian average (percent)			
	1994	1995	1996	1997	1994	1995	1996	1997
Russia	3583.7	9562.2	13349.4	15794.1	100	100	100	100
Far East	4636.3	10829.7	15926.5	18859.9	129.4	113.3	119.7	119.4
Republic of Sakha	8079.6	19756	26682.6	29678.1	225.5	206.6	201.7	187.9
Jewish AO	2818.4	5637.1	7096.8	6302.2	78.6	59	53.6	39.9
Chukotski AO	5063.9	14138.7	26556.4	28745.4	141.3	147.9	200.7	182
Primorskii krai	3270.4	8519.3	11123.4	13720.9	91.2	89.1	84.1	86.9
Khabarovskii krai	3838.8	9543	15285.9	20227.3	107.1	99.8	115.4	128.1
Amurskaia oblast	4073.6	8011.4	12108.8	15248.4	113.7	83.8	91.5	96.5
Kamchatskaia oblast	5633.4	12973.7	19246.4	20360.8	157.2	135.7	145.5	128.9
Magadanskaia oblast	7552.1	12555.7	21469.7	25774.5	210.7	131.3	162.2	163.1
Sakhalinskaia oblast	4708.6	10490.5	14983.7	21335.5	131.4	109.7	113.2	135.1

Source: Goskomstat Rossii, *Natsional'nye scheta v Rossii v 1991–1998 godakh* (Moskva: Goskomstat Rossii, 1999).

Russian indicators is persistently decreasing. With less than 5 percent of Russia's population, the region's share in the country's GDP was 6.7 percent in 1994, 5.8 percent in 1995, and 6.0 percent in 1996–98.[1]

The Far East's per capita GRP at current prices has always exceeded Russia's average, although the difference between the Far Eastern and Russian averages has decreased since 1994 (see Table 4.1). In the northern territories—the Republic of Sakha (Yakutia), Magadan oblast, Chukotskii autonomous okrug—and in Kamchatka and Sakhalin oblasts, the nominal indicators of average per capita GRP remain higher than Russia's average. In the Republic of Sakha, the average per capita GRP is twice as high as the Russian average.

Until 1997 a steady decrease in the difference between the regional and the country indicators was only indicative of the Republic of Sakha and the Jewish autonomous oblast: in the remainder of the federation subjects, the relationship has fluctuated. In Primorskii krai, Amurskaia oblast, and the Jewish autonomous oblast, the GRP indicators are lower than the Russian average, while in the remainder of the territories the average per capita GRP in nominal terms exceeds the country average. The situation may be explained by inflation in the region being greater than in the country as a whole. That is why, despite the strained economic circumstances in the Russian Far East and a more intensive decline in production, the average per capita GRP is still higher than the country's average.

There has also been a change in the contributions made by individual territories to the establishment of the region-wide proportions (see Table 4.2). According to data on GRP at current prices, the contribution of the Republic of Sakha has become equal to and in some years greater than the contributions of Khabarovskii or Primorskii krais. In the period under review, a concentration of production facilities continued in these three major territories, which accounted for 62.5 percent of the Far Eastern GRP in 1994 and for 64.6 percent in 1999. These basic parameters are subject to significant variations should a price factor be eliminated.

According to official statistics, in 2000 industrial production in the RFE was 44.8 percent of what it was in 1990, and in Russia as a whole, 54.4 percent.[2] Although the decline in industrial production in the Far East proved greater than the country-wide average, as late as 1995 industrial decline in the RFE had been slower than in Russia as a whole.

A difference in the dynamics of the Far East and the country's average industrial production indices in 1992–94, when the region was in a relatively more favorable situation, was due to the difference in the extent of the decline in 1991, when all-Russia industrial production was 92 percent and the RFE's industrial output was 97 percent of the previous year. In 1992–93, the rates of industrial decline in the region were almost equal to the country's average, and by 1995 the regional production decline exceeded the country's average.

Table 4.2 Territorial Structure of Gross Regional Product
(as percent of total Far East GRP, in current prices)

	1994	1995	1996	1997
Republic of Sakha (Yakutia)	24.0	25.0	23.6	21.5
Jewish autonomous oblast	1.7	1.5	1.3	0.9
Chukotskii autonomous okrug	1.5	1.7	2.0	1.7
Primorskii krai	21.1	23.7	21.7	22.0
Khabarovskii krai	17.4	18.5	20.7	22.6
Amurskaia oblast	12.1	10.2	10.9	11.3
Kamchatskaia oblast	6.9	6.7	6.8	5.9
Magadanskaia oblast	6.3	4.2	4.7	4.6
Sakhalinskaia oblast	9.1	8.5	8.3	9.6

Source: Goskomstat Rossii, *Natsional'nye scheta v Rossii v 1991–1998 godakh* (Moskva: Goskomstat Rossii, 1999).

The main factors in the decline in industrial production in the Far East were the sharp drop in demand for military output and the relatively weak competitiveness of local consumer goods when the ruble was overvalued. But the dynamics of industrial production vary significantly throughout the Far East (see Figure 4.1). In the northern areas, where industry is based on mining valuable mineral resources, the drop in industrial production was less than in the southern areas, which are more process-industry oriented.

To judge from industrial production indices, the economic situation in the north of the Far East is better than throughout the region and Russia as a whole. It is worth mentioning that the Republic of Sakha was the first to show signs of industrial revival in 1998–99.

In those areas where the fishing industry, oriented to consumer demand, holds the lead in the industrial production structure, the decline in industrial production was also less than in the RFE as a whole. According to data for 2000, the signs in those areas of an increase in industrial production are more explicit. This is true of Primorskii krai and Sakhalin and Kamchatka oblasts.

Figure 4.1 Indices of Industrial Output in the Russian Far East
(2000 compared to 1990)

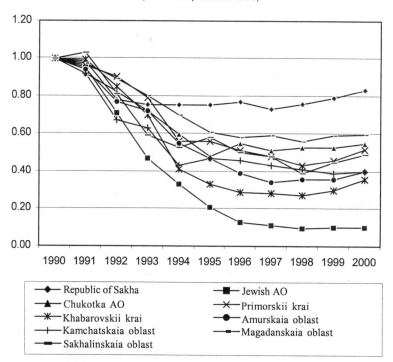

◆ Republic of Sakha	■ Jewish AO
▲ Chukotka AO	✕ Primorskii krai
✳ Khabarovskii krai	● Amurskaia oblast
+ Kamchatskaia oblast	▬ Magadanskaia oblast
▬ Sakhalinskaia oblast	

Source: Goskomstat Rossii, *Rossiiskii statisticheskii ezhegodnik* (Moskva: Goskomstat Rossii, 2000), 304; and Goskomstat Rossii, *Indeksy fizicheskogo ob'ema proizvodstva promyshlennoi produktsii,* 2000 (Moskva: www.gks.ru).

The industry of the southern areas—Khabarovskii krai, Amurskaia oblast, and Jewish autonomous oblast—is in the most strained economic situation. The industrial potential of the Jewish autonomous oblast is rather small, therefore the termination of machine-building and light-industry operation, which was the oblast's industrial basis, resulted in industrial output in 2000 that was about 12 percent of that in 1990.

Industrial production in Khabarovskii krai in 2000 was only 34 percent of that in 1990. There are at least two factors explaining the sharp drop in production in the krai as compared with other territories of the Russian Far East. First, the krai's industrial production was oriented toward markets in other regions of Russia and the former USSR, and the majority of these were lost with the onset of reforms. Second, it historically has an industrial structure primarily oriented toward military production. A sharp decrease in defense orders resulted in an 85 percent cut in machine-building output in the krai from 1990 to 2000.

Gross regional product indicators show results that differ significantly from the above. In addition to industrial production, the estimated GRP indicators at current prices account for the development of agriculture, transportation, construction, commerce, and other industries rendering services of a market and nonmarket nature.

According to our own estimate of the gross regional product, the decline in economic activity in the region was greater than the country's average as early as 1993. In subsequent years, the GRP-decline curve almost follows the shape of Russia's average-value curve, but the difference becomes greater over time. Thus, GRP in the Russian Far East in 1999 was 42 percent of that in 1990 (see Figure 4.2), while the GDP in Russia as a whole in 1999 was 59.4 percent of that in 1990.

It is in the northern areas that the decline in economic activity was the greatest. Production in Chukotskii autonomous okrug in 1999 was 25 percent of that in 1990; in Magadanskaia oblast—19 percent. It is only in the Republic of Sakha (Yakutia) that the decline in gross regional product was in rough correspondence with the decline in industrial production. In addition, the drop in economic activity on Kamchatka and Sakhalin when measured in GRP dynamics is greater than when viewed in terms of industrial production dynamics alone.

The situation is the opposite in the southern areas, including Khabarovskii krai and Amurskaia oblast, where the decline in GRP proves less than the decline in industrial production. In Primorskii krai, the estimate of production decline when measured in terms of both indicators turns out to be approximately the same.

The difference in GRP and industrial production dynamics is due to the variations in the production structure in the northern, island,[3] and southern areas of the Russian Far East. The basis of the economic system in the north is local industrial development using the most valuable and deficient natural resources. The economic systems of Kamchatka and Sakhalin are also of a very specific nature. Their economies are based on industrial production; the remaining branches of the economy are aimed at servicing the specialized industries. In those areas, the decline in nonindustrial sectors oriented to rendering services to the local industry has turned out to be greater than in industry. The outflow of population from the northern and island territories, which significantly exceeds the migration from the southern areas, has also made an important contribution to the process. The significant reduction in the population has brought about the curtailment of retail turnover, scope of services rendered, and construction. As a result, the economy of these regions is only maintained at the expense of other sectors. The reduction in agricultural output, construction activity, and service branches in the northern and island territories was greater than the general decline in GRP.

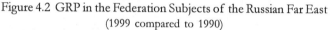

Figure 4.2 GRP in the Federation Subjects of the Russian Far East
(1999 compared to 1990)

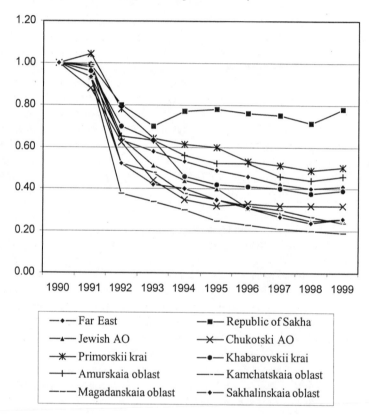

Source: Author's calculations.

In contrast to the northern areas, the southern krais and oblasts of the Russian Far East have always had a diversified production structure. The southern areas are responsible for the overwhelming majority of agricultural production in the region. Transport and transit functions performed by Amurskaia oblast, Jewish autonomous oblast, and Khabarovskii and Primorskii krais for both the northern areas and the country as a whole play an important role in their development. Development of domestic and foreign trade, which is primarily concentrated in the southern areas of the Russian Far East, has also turned out to be a stabilizing factor. Finally, a significant decline in industrial production observed in Khabarovskii krai, Amurskaia oblast, and Jewish autonomous oblast was counterbalanced by a more stable situation in other sectors of the economy.

Owing to the more intensive economic development of the southern portion of the Far East, the southern areas are increasingly perceived as more economically developed and more favorable for vital activity. In the post-Soviet period, tentative changes in the intraregional proportions of the Russian Far East economy have occurred. A manifest trend has been for the Republic of Sakha to make a greater contribution to regional production (from 16.5 percent in 1990 to 29.9 percent in 1999). During that same period, an increase in shares contributed by Primorskii krai (from 17.5 percent to 19.8 percent) and Amurskaia oblast (from 10.8 percent to 11.9 percent) has also occurred. A decrease in shares contributed to GRP was typical of other territories of the Far East (e.g., Magadanskaia oblast's share dropped by 5.6 percent and Sakhalin's by 4.8 percent).

A tendency also is observed toward an increase in the contributions made by northern and southern areas to the Far Eastern GRP structure at the expense of a decrease in the island oblast contributions. In 1990, the southern areas accounted for 48.7 percent of GRP, the northern areas for 29.1 percent, and the island oblasts for 22.2 percent. In 1999, the southern areas accounted for 50.1 percent of regional GRP, the northern areas for 36.3 percent, and the island oblasts for 13.5 percent.

The above data might lead to the misconception that regional economic activity is shifting to the northern territories. However, close scrutiny of changes in the distribution of production capacities over the territory of the Russian Far East reveals an evident concentration of production in the southern and western portions of the region. Indeed, the production is concentrated in Primorskii and Khabarovskii krais, Amurskaia oblast, and the Republic of Sakha. In 1990, these four territories were responsible for 63.2 percent of the gross regional product, while in 1999, already as much as 78.9 percent.

In the Republic of Sakha, the principal economic centers are located in the central and southern parts of the republic that are territorially adjacent to the southern regions of the Russian Far East. Thus, territorial shifts in GRP distribution in the

Table 4.3 Ratio of Per Capita GRP of Federation Subjects in the RFE to the All-Russian Average
(in constant prices of 1994)

	1990	1991	1992	1993	1994	1995	1996	1997	1998
Far East	1.23	1.25	0.99	0.97	1.02	1.04	1.01	0.96	0.94
Republic of Sakha	1.48	1.49	1.47	1.44	1.83	1.97	1.99	1.95	1.94
Jewish AO	0.87	0.84	0.7	0.6	0.6	0.56	0.48	0.44	0.39
Chukotski AO	1.54	1.44	1.3	1.22	1.19	1.26	1.45	1.47	1.62
Primorskii krai	0.76	0.85	0.71	0.68	0.73	0.75	0.66	0.64	0.63
Khabarovskii krai	1.12	1.15	0.98	0.97	0.83	0.78	0.8	0.79	0.75
Amurskaia oblast	1	0.97	0.8	0.88	0.89	0.89	0.91	0.8	0.81
Kamchatskaia oblast	2.18	2.27	1.41	1.47	1.35	1.43	1.44	1.33	1.3
Magadanskaia oblast	2.64	2.45	1.29	1.44	1.65	1.64	1.68	1.57	1.41
Sakhalinskaia oblast	1.64	1.56	1.08	0.93	1.04	1.04	0.92	0.84	0.77

Source: Based on author's estimations.

Far East resulted in the concentration of production in the more developed and populated portion and a decline in economic activity in the most remote territories.

As noted, the ratio of the average per capita GRP at current prices in the territories of the Russian Far East to that in Russia has varied. When the aggregate indicator of gross regional product is compared to the per capita GRP measured at current prices, then for all regions, excluding the northern, the ratio of the regional indicator to the country's average decreases (see Table 4.3).

The total production decrease is determined by the decline in employment and in productivity per capita.[4] During the reform period, the impact of both factors in the Far Eastern regions was stronger than in Russia as a whole. From 1990–98, employment in Russia decreased by 16.5 percent and productivity per capita decreased by 31.7 percent, while the decrease in employment and in productivity per capita in the Far East was 22 percent and 48.1 percent, respectively.

No data were available on the number of employed in all the federation subjects of the Russian Far East in 1990, so the share of production decrease due to the decline of population and decrease in per capita GRP were used in calculations. We found a substantial difference between the influence of the two factors in the southern and northern regions. Per capita GRP throughout the Far East decreased from 1990–98 by 14 percent due to population decline and by 86 percent due to a decline in productivity per capita. The same numbers for Magadanskaia oblast are 44.8 percent and 55.2 percent, respectively; for Chukotskii autonomous okrug—70 percent and 30 percent; for Kamchatskaia—22 percent and 78 percent; and for the Republic of Sakha—28.5 percent and 71.5 percent. Thus, population outflow was an important factor in declining production in the northern regions. In the southern regions, we found a significant role was played by productivity decline per capita, which caused 94.6 percent of the regional GRP decline in Khabarovskii krai, 92.5 percent in Primorskii krai, and 92.8 percent in Amurskaia oblast.

For the Russian Far East as a whole, the advantage of greater average per capita GRP compared to the country's average was lost immediately upon the onset of reforms. In 1998, average regional per capita GRP at constant prices was 94 percent of the country's average. These facts point to the further deterioration of the relative conditions for production in the Russian Far East and its declining relative competitiveness. These interregional and intraregional differentiation processes may be estimated by means of a standard deviation of regional indicators from the country's average and that of the Russian Far East as a whole (see Figure 4.3).

In the Soviet period, there was a significant gap between the average per capita GRP in the Far Eastern regions and the country's average, while the difference among the federation subjects in the Far East was less significant. In 1992–98, the indicators of interregional and intraregional differentiation grew to be almost equal.

This was due to the fact that the difference between the Far Eastern indicators and the country's average indicators decreased, while the intraregional differentiation became more intensive. This fact is of great significance in terms of formulation of economic policy toward the territories of the Russian Far East. The intensification of the intraregional differentiation means that the policy pursued should be not only specific with respect to the Russian Far East as a whole, but also differentiated with respect to its separate parts.

Figure 4.3 Standard Deviation of Per Capita GRP from the Country's Average
and from that of the Far East as a Whole
(constant prices)

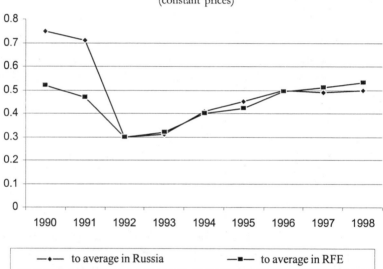

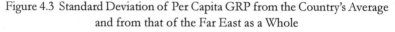

Note: Standard deviation calculated as $\sigma = [(1/n)\Sigma(a_r - a_0)^2]^{1/2}/a_0$, where a_r is per capita GRP production in region r, a_0 is country's average GRP production, and n is total number of regions.

Source: Based on author's estimations.

The estimates are built on developments in particular sectors of the regional economy generalized in terms of a gross regional product indicator. In our opinion, the estimates reflect basic tendencies in the development of the Far Eastern regions and provide a more complete representation of the results of regional development during reforms. On the other hand, these estimates may differ from the official data, which, unfortunately, were not at our disposal.

Our estimates show that the social and economic situation in the Russian Far East is worsening and the difference between the regional indicators and the country's average is increasing. The intraregional differentiation between individual krais and oblasts is becoming ever deeper.

INCOME AND LIVING STANDARDS

In the Russian Far East, high monetary payments have been meant to compensate for the severe natural and climatic conditions, remoteness, and shortage of infrastructure. The previous system of individual earnings, based on privileges and regional coefficients, has been partially retained to present. This was one of the reasons for the higher money income and average wage increases in the Russian Far East in general and individual regions in particular as compared to the country's average in 1992–93. But higher nominal ruble income did not result in a higher real standard of living, since nominal costs were also higher than elsewhere in Russia.

In 1994–99, the situation changed—the per capita personal income growth rates in the Far East were lower than Russia's average and, in fact, the average per capita personal income growth rate that some regions characterized by severe natural and climatic conditions (Kamchatka and Sakhalin) started to lag behind the country's average as early as 1992.

Within the entire period of reforms, the average per capita money income of the population in the Russian Far East has remained higher than the country's average, though the Far East's advantage in this regard is gradually disappearing. While in 1990 the level of money income of the population in the Russian Far East was 35 percent higher than Russia's average, in 1999 the average per capita income in the region was just 6.7 percent higher than the country's average, with the excess due mainly to the higher earnings of the population in the northern territories.

By 1999, the southern areas of the RFE (Jewish autonomous oblast, Amurskaia oblast, Primorskii krai) had lost the advantage of the highest money income even in nominal terms. The money income of the population in Khabarovskii krai, with the major portion of its territory located in the north, is about the same as the country's average.

As mentioned, the Far East is one of the most expensive regions in Russia. The rise in consumer prices was substantially higher than the country's average during both the pre-reform and the reform periods. From 1991–99, the aggregate growth in consumer prices in the Russian Far East was 7,404.8 percent (in Russia—6,144.8 percent). It was only in the Republic of Sakha that the aggregate consumer price index was lower than the country's average at 4,388.1 percent. Thus, from 1991 to 1999, the consumer price index in Magadanskaia oblast rose 9,375.5 percent; in

Sakhalinskaia oblast—17,165 percent. Moreover, the aggregate consumer price index in Kamchatskaia oblast rocketed as high as 21,254 percent to become more than three times the Russian average![5]

The price increases have been responsible for the greater decline in people's real earnings in the RFE. Again, the only region among the federation subjects in the Far East where the growth of real earnings was observed was the Republic of Sakha. According to our calculations, if a price index factor is taken into consideration, the relationship between earnings in the RFE and in Russia on average is essentially changed. It is only in the Republic of Sakha that real earnings exceed the country's average; we do not have any data on price indices in Chukotskii autonomous okrug; in Magadanskaia oblast they are close to Russia's average; and in Jewish autonomous oblast and Sakhalinskaia oblast they do not reach one-half of the country's average.

With regard to consumer prices, Kamchatskaia and Sakhalinskaia oblasts are in the most critical situation, with the level of real personal income being lower than in the southern areas of the region but with nominal earnings (average per capita monetary incomes) that are markedly higher than in the south.

The data on real personal income have been published in official statistics since 1994. On the assumption that 1993 is a basic year, which makes sense inasmuch as in terms of real money income the 1993 situation in the regions is more comparable than the 1990 situation, when a rationing system was actually functioning, the following points come to the fore. First, in spite of differentiation in the decrease in real personal incomes in the federation subjects in the Far East in 1993–99, real earnings in the majority of the territories in 1999 were about 50 percent of those in 1993, which approximately corresponds with the country's average. The situation is noticeably better in the Republic of Sakha and much worse in Jewish autonomous and Sakhalinskaia oblasts. Also, indicators of interregional per capita income differentiation testify that the Russian Far East has lost its position as a region with higher earnings.

The difference in per capita earnings in the territories of the Far East and the country's average follow the same tendency as the dynamics of average per capita income differentiation in Russia as a whole.[6] The differentiation, which was significant in the 1970s but had started to gradually smooth out by the onset of reforms, became more pronounced by 1992–93. From 1994, the RFE started to lose its advantageous position in nominal earnings quickly when the decline in the regional production became equal to that of Russia, and state support to the region weakened.

By 1999, real earnings in the federation subject with the highest earnings (Republic of Sakha) exceeded those in the region with the lowest level (Jewish autonomous oblast) fivefold. Actually, a pronounced difference in the level of earnings in different regions already existed in the Soviet period due to distinctions in the natural and climatic conditions, availability of resources, and level of economic development. This was especially true of the difference between the northern and southern territories of the Russian Far East. However, if previously the distribution of income corresponded to the administrative control over earnings, in the reform period signs of market regulation of earnings appeared. The highest income level has been found in territories that have the most intensive economic activity. At the same time, the regions that received an administrative surplus to wages and other types of income lost their leading position in the income distribution. First and foremost, these were Kamchatskaia, Sakhalinskaia, and Magadanskaia oblasts.

Only a portion of the people's earnings is registered by official statistics, with the share of unreported earnings in the federation subjects also varying. We have two sets of estimates of the share of unreported earnings in the territories of the RFE (see Table 4.4).[7] With regard to the "shadow" earnings, the former excess of the region's level of personal money income over that in the country as a whole was lost in the reform years, and earnings in the region move ever closer to the country's average.

As estimated in *Russian Economic Trends*,[8] the share of unreported income in all the territories of the Russian Far East, except for the Jewish autonomous oblast, is lower than Russia's average. In this case, a comparison of the money income level in the Far East with the average level in Russia yields an even more pessimistic evaluation of the people's earnings situation than the official statistics. In 1993, the average per capita money income was higher than the country's average by 38 percent, while in 1998 it was higher by only about 3 percent.

According to estimates compiled by Web Atlas,[9] the share of shadow income to total income in the RFE is higher than the Russian average, the larger value being due to the southern federation subjects, where the shadow income share is assumed to be the highest. The shadow income share in the northern regions is assumed to be lower than Russia's average. However, in this case the ratio of individual income in the Russian Far East proves to be close to the official data provided by Goskomstat. In 1995, per capita earnings in the region, taking into consideration the shadow portion, were 27 percent higher than the country's average (24 percent according to the official data). Should the portion of shadow income remain the same, then by 1998 the per capita income level in the RFE would have been higher by about 15 percent (12 percent according to the official statistics).

If shadow income is taken into account, then the ratio of income levels in the individual federation subjects changes compared to the official data (see Table 4.4),

Table 4.4 Estimates of the Unregistered Income Share in the Russian Far East
(percent)

	Russian Economic Trends (RET)	Web Atlas	Region's Rating		
			Goskomstat	RET	Web Atlas
Russia	31.5	59.0	-	-	-
Far East	14.5	62.7	-	-	-
Republic of Sakha	15.4	62.1	3	4	2
Jewish AO	35.1	68.2	9	9	9
Chukotski AO	10.4	54.8	1	3	1
Primorskii krai	25.1	68.7	6	6	6
Khabarovskii krai	18.3	69.0	7	8	7
Amurskaia oblast	28.2	65.8	8	7	8
Kamchatskaia oblast	25.9	48.9	4	2	4
Magadanskaia oblast	25.4	47.8	2	1	3
Sakhalinskaia oblast	18.4	56.3	5	5	5

Source: Based on author's estimations.

but these changes are not fundamental—the income ratings in the territories are mainly changed in the northern areas, while the ratio of income levels in the southern areas remains roughly the same.

Conclusions about the worsening social and economic conditions in the Russian Far East drawn from the analysis of real income are supported by a number of indicators depicting the standard of living. For example, the ratio of money income to the subsistence minimum in all the RFE federation subjects proves to be lower, and decreasing faster, than the national average. By 1999 the money income in Chukotskii autonomous okrug was only 88 percent of the subsistence minimum. In Primorskii krai, the Far Eastern region with the highest ratio, the money income exceeded the subsistence minimum by a factor of only 1.65 (Russia's average: 1.77).

According to 1999 data, the share of the population with income lower than the subsistence minimum varies from 28.2 percent in Khabarovskii krai to 70.9 percent in Chukotskii autonomous okrug, with the country's average being 29.9 percent. In 1999 the share of the population with income lower than the subsistence minimum exceeded the country's average in all territories of the RFE except Khabarovskii krai (see Table 4.5).

Although official income statistics are not reliable, the faster growth of the poor as a share of the population in the Russian Far East is confirmed by a number of indicators. For instance, the consumption structure in Russia changed during the reform period as the population had to spend a greater share of disposable income on food. On the other hand, because the average price level of nonfood consumer goods and services is relatively higher in the Far East, the shifts in consumption structure have had a greater impact on the standard of living here. According to a household expenditure survey, in 1998 the share of expenditures on foodstuffs in Russia made up 53.3 percent, in the Republic of Sakha—49.9 percent, in Primorskii krai—56.9 percent, in Amurskaia oblast—55.2 percent, in Magadanskaia oblast—59.2 percent, and in Sakhalinskaia oblast—54.4 percent.[10] Although the percentages for the RFE do not seem considerably greater than the Russian average of 53.3 percent, they are considerably higher than before the transition era. Previously the expenditures on foodstuffs in the Far East were substantially lower than average throughout the country, since the prices were considerably higher for clothes, housing and communal utilities payments, and transportation costs. The increase in the share of expenditures on foodstuffs shows that the population has had to give up purchasing other goods and services, in particular reducing the expenditures on durable goods, travel, and recreation.

Because of changes in consumption structure, the population of the Far East had to give up a number of goods and services that are still accessible to most

Table 4.5 Ratio of Monetary Incomes to Subsistence Minimum
and Share of Population with Incomes Lower than Subsistence Minimum
(percent)

	Ratio of monetary incomes to subsistence minimum					Share of population with incomes lower than subsistence minimum				
	1994	1995	1996	1997	1998	1994	1995	1996	1997	1998
Russia	238	195	206	226	197	22.4	24.7	22.1	20.8	23.8
Republic of Sakha	200	163	169	187	163	22.7	29.2	30.4	28.3	32
Jewish AO	152	121	137	141	120	—	—	—	—	—
Chukotski AO	—	156	141	140	95	—	—	—	—	—
Primorskii krai	176	149	156	168	147	18.2	31.8	30.4	28.6	34.5
Khabarovskii krai	183	140	157	179	176	21.8	29.4	27.4	24.1	24.8
Amurskaia oblast	145	159	168	183	148	47.1	37.9	29.8	27.9	33.5
Kamchatskaia oblast	218	181	174	190	161	16.7	22.7	28.7	25.9	32.9
Magadanskaia oblast	200	169	169	175	148	21.4	24.6	28.2	25.9	33.7
Sakhalinskaia oblast	153	137	150	151	136	23.3	24.6	33.2	32.8	38.5

Source: Goskomstat Rossii, *Rossiiskii statisticheskii ezhegodnik* (Moskva: Goskomstat Rossii, 1999).

populations in other regions, for example, travelling to western regions of the country or getting an education there. Growing poverty is also indicated by an increase in purchases of the cheapest products in the share of consumption. Consumption of the cheapest products such as bread and potatoes in the Far East is higher than in the rest of the country, while consumption of expensive products such as meat, milk, fruit, and vegetables is lower.

Although the life expectancy in the Far East has always been shorter than the Russian average, the gap has increased during the reform period. In 1989–90, life expectancy in Russia was 69.86 years, in the Far East—67.63; in 1998 the numbers were 68.12 years in Russia, 65.19 in the Far East, 64.2 in Sakhalinskaia oblast, and 64.68 in Kamchatskaia oblast.[11]

The increasing gap between the standard of living in the Far East and the average Russian standard is also indicated by a number of negative social phenomena that make Far Eastern regions even less attractive to live in. These regions, except the Republic of Sakha and Chukotskii autonomous okrug, are characterized by higher crime levels and are, unfortunately, leaders in the number of registered per capita crimes: in 1998, Magadanskaia oblast ranked second in Russia, the Jewish autonomous oblast was third, Sakhalinskaia oblast fourth, Khabarovskii krai took sixth place, and Primorskii krai seventeenth.[12]

The ever-growing negative trends in the social sphere are embodied in demographic statistics. All federation subjects in the Far East have a negative migration balance, which is caused by an absolute population decrease. Outmigration is most intensive from the northern territories. From 1990 to 2000, the population in Chukotskii autonomous okrug was halved, in Magadanskaia oblast it was reduced by 39 percent, in Kamchatskaia by 18 percent, and in Sakhalinskaia by 16 percent.

REGIONAL POLICY IN THE RUSSIAN FAR EAST

Throughout the reform period, economic policy toward the Russian Far East has varied with the changes in the national objectives of regional policy that have been based on modulating ideas of macroeconomic control.[13] In 1992–96, the Far East was under conditions governed by the economic standards and procedures inherent in the regional policy of the federal center. These were implicitly differentiated for individual federation subjects. The previous single economic policy pursued by the state with respect to the Far East, which was disaggregated on an administrative- and territorial-unit level, was replaced with a set of economic policies applied to individual territories. The agents of such economic policy were both the federation subjects themselves and Moscow.

In 1996 efforts began on a federal level to impart an institutional character to regional economic policy. These ideas were realized basically in terms of elaboration of state programs of regional development that were typical of a planned economy. For the Russian Far East, this stage meant revival of a single economic policy to be pursued by the state as regards the entire region as a single unit and to be complemented with consistent policies pursued by the federation subjects. Such an approach to RFE development was integrated into the State Program of Economic Development of the Far East and Trans-Baikal for 1996–2005. However, this program has not yet been implemented due to continued budget deficits. In fact, however, there is nothing like a single economic policy pursued toward the Russian Far East as an integral territorial unit.

During the reform era, in spite of the different goals declared at various stages of reform, the basic tool used to realize an economic policy with respect to all the country's regions was budget and tax policy. A budget and tax model of territorial development management is widely and efficiently used worldwide. The model implies that the government or special governmental bodies accumulate financial resources through a tax system and then appropriate funds to support efficient functioning of the economic system in the regions. In Russia, under conditions of ever-decreasing budget funds, the interregional redistribution of funds implemented through budgetary mechanisms is mainly aimed at elimination of the most urgent social and economic problems.

For a number of reasons associated with the difficult economic situation in the Russian Far East and the existing problems in establishing interbudgetary relations, all federation subjects in the Far East, along with the majority of other Russian regions, have budget deficits (see Table 4.6). The aggregate budget deficit in the Russian Far East comprises about 2 to 4 percent of GRP in the region. In some territories, the deficit is about 8 percent of GRP.

A formal mechanism to redistribute budgetary funds is interbudgetary transfers aimed at equalization of budgetary support to the regions. The results of the interbudgetary equalization policy are reflected in the situation in the budgetary sphere of the Russian Far East. Available data show that from 1992–97 a significant gap in the average budget revenues per capita among the Far Eastern federation subjects remained stable: in 1992, the ratio between the territories with the maximum and minimum per capita revenues (Republic of Sakha and Amurskaia oblast) was 6.15; in 1997, this ratio was 7.65 (between Chukotskii autonomous okrug and Jewish autonomous oblast).

For individual territories, a relationship between regional and national levels of budget revenue per capita by year fluctuates (recall that the relationship serves as a criterion to identify regions in need of support), although cases in which it fluctuates more than a factor of one, to one side or the other, are very rare. For the Far East as a whole, we may rather speak of a decrease (or, at least, of a non-increase) in the relationship between the average budget revenues in a particular territory and the country as a whole. Since the budgets of the federation subjects in the Far East are deficit-based, the decrease in the difference between the regional and all-Russian revenue levels, with per capita expenditures being higher, means further growth of the region's budgetary dependence on the center.

Table 4.6 Ratio of Budget Deficit (Surplus) to GRP
of Individual Krais and Oblasts in the Russian Far East
(percent)

	1994	1995	1996	1997
Far East	-7.7	-3.2	-3.6	-4.4
Republic of Sakha (Yakutia)	-0.8	-8.5	-11.0	-8.4
Jewish autonomous oblast	-7.4	0.2	-3.0	-10.7
Chukotskii autonomous okrug	-55.3	-29.9	12.6	-20.2
Primorskii krai	-7.2	-1.5	-1.4	-2.4
Khabarovskii krai	-8.1	0.1	-0.2	-1.3
Amurskaia oblast	-5.3	-0.3	-1.3	-1.9
Kamchatskaia oblast	-22.0	-0.2	-8.2	-11.2
Magadanskaia oblast	-14.6	-4.1	-1.3	-4.6
Sakhalinskaia oblast	-6.5	0.1	-1.0	-2.0

Source: Based on Goskomstat Rossii, *Regiony Rossii 1999*, vol. 2 (Moskva: Goskomstat Rossii, 1999); Goskomstat Rossii, *Natsional'nye scheta v Rossii v 1991–1998 godakh*, (Moskva: Goskomstat Rossii, 1999).

The northern areas, especially the newly established ethnic administrative units, where the share of their own revenues comprises less than half of total budget revenues, are most dependent on the federal budget. In virtually all the territories in the Far East, the extent of budget independence measured by a ratio of the amount of transfers to total revenues is lower than the country's average. According to 1996 data, the ratio of transfers to territorial budget revenues in these ethnic administrative units (Chukotskii autonomous okrug, Jewish autonomous oblast, and Koriakskii autonomous okrug) exceeded the country's average by 1.2–2.8 times. Transfers made up 27.7 percent of budget revenues in Chukotka, 47.7 percent in Jewish autonomous oblast, and 39.5 percent in Koriakskii autonomous okrug.[14]

Another important tool for the realization of economic policy by the federal and regional governments is budgetary investments in the regional economies. In the course of reforms, public capital investments were drastically decreased. Though the share of public investments in the Russian Far East is one of the country's largest, the funds of enterprises and credit facilities have failed to compensate for the gradually diminishing contribution by the state. In 1998, the amount of capital investment in the region at comparable prices did not exceed 15 percent of the 1990 level.

With a relative reduction in the amount of funds accumulated in the regional budgets, an ever-increasing share is spent on current social and cultural events and support to the vital branches of the regional economy. In all territories in the Far East, the share of investment from the federal budget markedly exceeds that from the regional budgets (see Table 4.7).

Under conditions of a shortage of investment resources, regional authorities try to attract foreign investment using various sorts of regional privileges and guarantees to the investors. The privileges provided for in the taxation and investment laws of the Far Eastern territories are diverse. In comparison with other regions in Russia, the Far East was somewhat late with the legislative support for both domestic and foreign investment. However, any close correlation between regional privileges provided and the investments attracted to the region has not been revealed.[15] The legislative initiatives are a necessary but not sufficient condition to attract investment.

The federation subjects of the Far East have a poor record of attracting both domestic and foreign investors. In the early 1990s, due to a number of investment-friendly projects that were related to the exploitation of natural resources, a fairly large volume of investment was attracted to the region. In 1995–99, the absolute amount of foreign investment to the RFE as a whole was steadily increasing, but in spite of this, the share of the region's investment in the country's total was decreasing, from 5.3 percent in 1995 to 3.5 percent in 1999.[16] Only in Sakhalinskaia oblast did a persistent growth of foreign investment take place. In general, foreign investment in the Russian Far East, like in many other federation subjects, has not yet become a significant factor in regional development.

Table 4.7 Share of Investment from Different Budgets in Total Volume of Investment in the Russian Far East (percent)

	1994		1995		1996		1997		1998	
	federal budget	regional & municipal budgets	federal budget	regional & municipal budgets	federal budget	regional & municipal budgets	federal budget	regional & municipal budgets	federal budget	regional & municipal budgets
Russia	13.4	10.6	10.1	10.3	9.9	10.2	10.2	10.5	6.6	12.7
Far East	17.2	15.9	10.2	12.7	15.2	8.9	14.3	8.9	13.0	9.5
Republic of Sakha	8.0	32.5	2.4	28.5	5.0	16.5	3.9	14.4	5.9	20.3
Jewish AO	34.1	9.3	11.5	4.6	10.2	4.8	43.1	4.0	76.1	7.5
Chukotski AO	44.6	13.2	50.9	25.4	58.6	10.0	47.6	27.4	57.2	12.3
Primorskii krai	20.8	10.9	16.8	7.8	14.2	4.0	10.6	4.3	13.1	11.0
Khabarovskii krai	25.7	6.7	14.0	5.1	20.6	8.2	17.1	9.4	18.9	10.1
Amurskaia oblast	24.9	9.8	4.7	6.3	29.4	6.4	24.0	9.0	27.4	6.5
Kamchatskaia oblast	10.4	12.1	13.4	14.1	26.5	10.8	21.0	9.5	21.6	4.1
Magadanskaia oblast	5.0	3.4	3.1	1.5	9.9	0.7	5.4	3.1	10.9	2.4
Sakhalinskaia oblast	22.6	7.5	17.1	2.7	16.6	4.2	25.5	4.3	4.6	3.6

Source: Goskomstat Rossii, *Regiony Rossii 1999*, vol. 2 (Moskva: Goskomstat Rossii, 1999).

With economic conditions in the Far East worse than in other areas of Russia, and the policy of interregional equalization of average per capita budget revenues failing to hit the target, one might conclude that economic policy toward the Russian Far East has not been successful. However, it is rather difficult to make a quantitative evaluation of the results of economic policy pursued with respect to a region, since the results cannot be isolated from the effect of other factors on regional development. Nevertheless, we have attempted to estimate the extent of the effect that policy tools used to manage economic development may produce on the economies of the territories in the Far East.

We have taken the rate of decline in production and the rate of decrease in real earnings observed in 1992–98 as the final indicators of regional development. The decline in production observed in the RFE between 1992 and 1998 is a phenomenon known to accompany economic reforms in all post-communist countries and is called the transformation recession. The mechanisms of the effect produced by particular causes on the recession dynamics have been investigated, and we base our analysis of the decline in production in the Far East on this literature.[17]

We have assumed that the difference in the rates of decline in production in the regions is due to the original conditions in the regions prior to reform as well as to the changes occurring in the course of reforms. A set of factors considered in the literature as the reasons for the interregional differentiation in the rates of decline in production is comprehensive and comprises economic, social, and political factors. The choice of factors incorporated into the present research has been limited to available statistical data.

We have used the following indicators as the variable original conditions in the regions: a ratio of average per capita gross regional product at constant prices to the Russian Far East's average; specific features of the regional economic structure pertaining mainly to the industrial or agricultural nature of the region's development; transport and transit functions; and development of service sectors. To evaluate the effect of the structural factors, we have used contributions made by the branches of the economy to the GRP. Contributions made by process industries (machine-building, light industry) and primary industries (nonferrous metallurgy, forestry, woodworking, and food industries) have been assumed to be important factors governing regional production dynamics, since the decline in production has varied according a territory's orientation toward primary or process industries.

Export orientation also has been viewed as a factor influencing regional production dynamics. A large export share means that a stable market for regional products is available. In addition, regional exports are a source of real money; therefore this factor, being an analog of trading conditions, has been included in regression equations.

Government influence on regional dynamics is exerted through a set of parameters reflecting the regional policy pursued by the state. Among them are all types of government expenditures in the region realized through various channels: social transfers to the region's population, interbudgetary transfers, investments from federal and local budgets, and a regional support fund. The regional statistics provide limited means to measure these factors, therefore we have used the readily available data indicative of the economic policy pursued by the central government with respect to the region. We have considered per capita regional budget expenditures as well as federal and local budget investment shares in the total investment volume as the data most suitable.

Table 4.8 Factors in the Regression Equation
of Annual Rates of GRP Reduction

	Far East		Northern zone		Southern zone	
	b (se)	P>|t|	b (se)	P>|t|	b (se)	P>|t|
Constant	0.899 (0.171)	0	1.591 (0.146)	0	0.506 (0.140)	0.001
Share of transport in GRP	1.278 (0.516)	0.017			2.293 (0.667)	0.002
Share of service in GRP	0.540 (0.211)	0.014			0.527 (0.178)	0.006
Share of agriculture in GRP	-2.166 (0.633)	0.001	-2.856 (0.698)	0.001		
Share of manufacturing sectors			-0.037 (0.014)	0.012		
Share of extracting sectors	-0.005 (0.001)	0	-0.006 (0.002)	0.007	-0.003 (0.001)	0.015
R2 (overall)		0.11		0.288		0.656
R2 (within)		0.474		0.592		0.623
R2 (between)		0.008		0.487		0.977

Source: Author's calculations.

Table 4.8 shows estimates of regression equations for GRP production rates in 1992–98 for the Russian Far East as a whole, the northern zone (Republic of Sakha, Magadanskaia oblast, Chukotskii autonomous okrug, Kamchatskaia oblast) and the southern zone, in which Sakhalin in this particular case was included along with Primorskii krai, Khabarovskii krai, Amurskaia oblast, and Jewish autonomous oblast.[18] Since the rates of change are rates of decline, then the positive coefficients in regression equations mean lower rates of decline. According to the estimates obtained, the difference in the rates of decline in production in the territories of the Far East has been mainly due to the structural peculiarities of production.

When the northern and southern groups of regions are considered rather than the Russian Far East as a whole, the statistical quality of the estimates turns out to be higher. For the southern regions, a positive effect on the decline value was produced by the transport and transit functions (transport share in GRP) performed by the regions and development of service sectors (comprising market and nonmarket services and commerce). A primary-industries factor was considered among the statistically significant with a negative value, though its elasticity is small. For the regions of the northern zone, the factors that produced a negative effect on the GRP were classified as statistically significant. Agriculture was among them—the higher the share of agriculture, the greater the decline in GRP. The same is true of the sectoral structure of industry, though the elasticity of primary and process industry share factors is small.

For the Russian Far East as a whole, the factors producing a positive effect on the annual average GRP turned out to be the share of transport service branches in GRP. Those acting to decrease the rate were the share of agriculture and primary branches of industry in GRP, although the elasticity of the latter factor is very small.

Factors associated with the realization of regional policy that are used in our analysis have not proven to be among the regressors statistically significant to affect the rates of GRP. Though a positive correlation between GRP and the indicators of regional policy exists, the correlation coefficient is 0.33–0.38 for the federal budget investment share and 0.43–0.46 for the local budget investment share. The correlation proves most weak for the factor of per capita budget expenditures.

A similar analysis was made to estimate the influence of the regional policy on the rate of decrease in real earnings. Just as with the GRP rates analysis, both specific features of particular regions and factors determined by regional policy govern the decrease in regional earnings. We have assumed that there is a positive relationship between the rates of decrease in the real earnings and GRP decline in the regions. The decrease in real earnings depends inversely on the original earnings level: the higher the earnings were at the initial period, the less the rate decrease. The following have been taken as regional factors: export orientation (it has been assumed that real earnings are to be higher in the regions with higher per capita export rates) and the share of population that is unemployed (this has been assumed to produce a negative effect on the real earnings rate).

Factors characterizing the influence of the regional policy were also used to analyze the real earnings of the population. Greater investm᷈ ᷈ from federal and regional budgets should also positively influence real earnings rates, since they are aimed at creation of jobs and, consequently, an increase in real earnings. It is more difficult to propose a hypothesis about the nature of the relationship between real earnings of the population and average per capita budget expenditures. In general, higher per capita expenditures should produce a positive effect on real earnings, since they make it possible to increase social allowance payment. On the other hand, according to the current scheme of budgetary management, budget expenditures are highest in the poorest regions. Therefore, in the budget-deficit regions (the Far East territories, for example), the highest average per capita budget expenditures are observed in the poorest regions. The estimated correlation between the rates of change in real earnings and average per capita budget expenditures is negative.

The results of a regression analysis for the relationship between the rates of change in real earnings among the territories in the Far East in 1992–98 are shown in Table 4.9. As distinct from the analysis of the GRP rate, where the differentiation is mainly due to previously existing conditions in the territories, a significant effect on the real earnings dynamic is produced by factors associated with the federal government's regional policy. For the Russian Far East as a whole, 56 percent of intraregional differences in the rates of change in real earnings may be explained by the differences in the regional policy parameters. Fairly good statistical estimates have been obtained for the southern territories of the Russian Far East. In addition to regional policy factors, an export orientation is included into the statistically significant factors applied in this category. The higher the rate of average per capita exports in a region, the higher the real earnings will be.

It is of interest that the factors associated with the production dynamics in the region have not been considered statistically significant to be incorporated into the equations for the rates of change in real earnings (i.e., a statistical relationship between the rates of decline in production and real earnings dynamics is not essential). However, the correlation efficient between these parameters is a positive 0.48.

Average per capita budgetary expenditures have been incorporated into the regression equations with a negative effect. In other words, under conditions in the Russian Far East, it turns out that the interbudgetary equalization has had the effect of the high budget expenses being used to maintain vital functions in the most unfavorable regions rather than to increase the real earnings of the population.

Table 4.9 Factors in the Regression Equation
of Annual Rates of Real Income Reduction

	Far East		Northern zone		Southern zone	
	b (se)	P>|t|	b (se)	P>|t|	b (se)	P>|t|
Constant	0.637 (0.098)	0	0.515 (0.095)	0	0.246 (0.157)	0.117
Budget expenditures	-0.206 (0.081)	0.013			-0.627 (0.284)	0.027
Investment from federal budget	2.075 (0.396)	0				
Investment from regional and municipal budgets	2.599 (0.632)	0	3.024 (0.654)	0	10.202 (0.845)	0
Per capita export revenues					0.228 (0.079)	0.004
Unemployment share					0.032 (0.007)	0
R2 (overall)		0.559		0.451		0.862
R2 (within)		0.641		0.458		0.863

One of the statistically significant factors in the regression equation for the southern regions is the unemployment rate. The fact that it is positive contradicts the hypothesis according to which a higher unemployment rate leads to a decline in population incomes. We suppose that this contradiction arose due to unreliable unemployment data. We used the official unemployment statistics, which do not reflect hidden unemployment, a factor that varies significantly from region to region. As elasticity of unemployment in the regression equation is not high, its quantitative impact on the resulting indicator is insignificant.

The analysis shows that the effect of the regional policy parameters varies among federation subjects: the regression equation estimates prove different for the northern and southern regions. This also supports the assumption we have made above on the lack of a single economic policy with respect to the Russian Far East as a whole.

In the RFE, the effect produced by the federal government's regional policy on social and economic development is manifest mainly in the field of personal income rather than in the field of production. These results are consistent with the notion of a regional policy being aimed primarily at the solution of the most urgent social and economic problems rather than at the creation of conditions for economic growth. The regional policy pursued with respect to the Russian Far East also has been focused on elimination of abnormal interregional discrepancies— this allows for a smoothing-out of the most thorny regional problems, but is in no way stimulating development.

In conclusion, we would like to mention that in view of the specificity of the regional development and tasks facing the Far East of Russia, the federal government needs to pursue a stimulating rather than leveling regional policy that would provide the region with a chance to create an efficient economic system.[19] In essence, the Far East of Russia needs a policy aimed at equalization of the regional economic conditions with, or at least drawing near to, the country's average economic conditions, and provision for opportunities to realize the relative advantages of the regional economy.

METHODOLOGICAL APPENDIX: ESTIMATION OF GRP INDICATORS IN THE FAR-EASTERN REGIONS

Goskomstat has published gross regional product statistics compiled according to SNA-1993 methodology for 1994–98 only, and at current prices.

Estimations of GDP at comparable prices have not yet been performed, even on the national level. However, a number of methods allow one to estimate the indicators at comparable prices. The methods to compile GRP indicators at constant prices have been offered by Goskomstat.[20] A similar approach has been used by the World Bank to examine the results of GDP compilations by individual countries and in a number of papers aimed at estimating the dynamics of macroeconomic parameters.[21] Therefore, to estimate the differentiation in the field of production, we have calculated the gross regional product at constant prices on the basis of officially published data on the dynamics of particular physical indicators.

The core of the compilation consists of the following: On the assumption that there are independently estimated indices of the dynamics of production for certain sectors $g_i(t)$, an aggregate index characterizing the dynamics of GRP may be computed by using them as a basis.

Assuming that $Y_i(t)$ is a gross regional product (or national income) produced in sector i of year t, and $g_i(t)$ is a production increment rate in sector i estimated on the basis of a corresponding physical index, then:

$$Y_i(t+1) = (g_i(t)+1)Y_i(t), t = 0,\ldots,T.$$

The gross regional product of year t is defined as $Y(t)$: $Y(t) = \Sigma_i Y_i(t)$, and, accordingly, a rate of increment of the general index is

$$G(t) = \Sigma(Y_i(t) - Y_i(t-1))/\Sigma Y_i(t), t = 1,\ldots, T.$$

The gross regional product dynamics were compiled on the basis of the following factors reflecting the dynamics of physical production volume: for industrial production—physical indices of production in the particular industry; for agriculture—rates of agricultural production at comparable prices; for the construction industry—dynamics of completed dwellings (m^2); for transport and communication—dynamics of freight turnover; for the marketing sector—dynamics of retail turnover at comparable prices; for the services sector—dynamics of the number of employees in the sector. Other sectors of material production have not been taken into account.

Regional data on production accounts (sectoral profile of the gross regional product) are available as of 1994, therefore that year has been chosen as the base year, wherefrom computations by physical indicator indices have been performed from 1994 back to 1990 and from 1994 up to 1998. The estimates obtained reflect the GRP dynamics at 1994 prices.

NOTES

1. Goskomstat Rossii, *Rossiiskii statisticheskii ezhegodnik* (Moskva: Goskomstat Rossii, 2000).

2. Goskomstat Rossii, *Rossiiskii statisticheskii ezhegodnik* (Moskva: Goskomstat Rossii, 2000); and Goskomstat Rossii, *Indeksy fizicheskogo ob'ema proizvodstva promyshlennoi produktsii*, 2000, <www.gks.ru>.

3. Kamchatka, as is well known, is a peninsula, the Russian term for which is *poluostrov*, or "half island." Therefore, it is considered an "island oblast" here.

4. The shares of factors were defined as follows. When G was GRP, p was GRP per capita, and H was population, the production decrease due to decline of population was defined as $[(H_{98} - H_{90}) * p_{90}]/(G_{98} - G_{90})$, due to decline of production per capita as $[(p_{98} - p_{90}) * H_{98}]/(G_{98} - G_{90})$.

5. Goskomstat Rossii, *Rossiiskii statisticheskii ezhegodnik*.

6. N. Mikheeva, "Differentiation of Social and Economic Situation in the Russian Regions and Problems of Regional Policy," EERC Working Paper Series, no. 99/09 (1999).

7. S. Nikolaenko, Y. Lissovolik, and R. MacFarquar, "Special Report: The Shadow Economy in Russia's Regions," *Russian Economic Trends*, no 4 (1997); A.S. Martynov, V.V. Artjukhov, V.G. Vinigradov, "Rossiia kak sistema," Web Atlas <www.sci.aha.ru>.

8. S. Nikolaenko, Y. Lissovolik, and R. MacFarquar, "Special Report: The Shadow Economy in Russia's Regions," *Russian Economic Trends*, no 4 (1997).

9. A.S. Martynov, V.V. Artjukhov, V.G. Vinigradov, "Rossiia kak sistema."

10. Goskomstat Rossii, *Regiony Rossii 1999,* vol. 2 (Moskva: Goskomstat Rossii, 1999), 120–21.

11. Ibid., 60–61.

12. Ibid., 257.

13. *Economika Dal'nego Vostoka: Pyat' let reform* (Khabarovsk: DVO RAN, 1998); V. I. Ishaev and P. A. Minakir, eds., *Dal'nii Vostok Rossii: Real'nosti i vozmozhnosti ekonomicheskogo razvitiia* (Khabarovsk: DVO RAN, 1998); *Economicheskaia politika na Dal'nem Vostoke Rossii: Konseptsiia i programma* (Khabarovsk: DVO RAN, 2000).

14. *Economicheskaia politika na Dal'nem Vostoke Rossii.*

15. S. V. Badiina, "Rol' l'gotnogo nalogooblozheniia v privlechenii investitsii v sub'ektakh DVR," in *Economicheskaia politika na Rossiiskom Dal'nem Vostoke: Materialy nauchno-prakticheskoi konferentsii* (Khabarovsk: DVO RAN, 1999).

16. *Rossiiskii statisticheskii ezhegodnik.*

17. M. Ellman, "Transformation, Depression, and Economics: Some Lessons," *Journal of Comparative Economics* 19 (1994); J. Kornai, "Transformational Recession: The Main Causes," *Journal of Comparative Economics* 19 (1994); N. N. Mikheeva, "Analiz differentsiatsii sotsial'no-economicheskogo polozheniia rossiiskikh regionov," *Problemy prognozirovaniia* 5 (1999): 91–102; L. Taylor, "The Market Met Its Match: Lessons for the Future from the Transition's Initial Years," *Journal of Comparative Economics* 19 (1994); V. Popov, "Reform Strategies and Economic Performance: The Far East Compared to Russia's Other Regions," paper presented at the conference "Security Implications of Economic and Political Development in the Russian Far East," The National Bureau of Asian Research, Washington, D.C., May 2000; V. Matvienko, E. Vostroknutova, and M. Buev, "Transformatsionnyi spad i predposylki rosta v Rossii," EERC Working Papers, no. 98/03 (1998); and V. Polterovich, "Transformatsionnyi spad v Rossii," *Economika i matematicheskie metody* 32, no. 1 (1996):54–69.

18. We used a panel data set. The regression equation with fixed effects was constructed according to statistical criteria.

19. Ideas for creating development stimuli have been proposed. See, for example, *Economicheskaia politika na Dal'nem Vostoke Rossii.*

20. *Metodologicheskie polozheniia po statistike,* no. 1 (Moskva: Logos, 1996).

21. See, for example, M. Kuboniwa, "National Income in Post-War Central Asia," Institute of Economic Research of Hitotsubashi University Discussion Paper, no. D96-6 (June 1996).

5

The Russian Far East's Competitive Position in Northeast Asian Markets

Alexander S. Sheingauz, Victor D. Kalashnikov, Natalia V. Lomakina, and Grigoriy I. Sukhomirov

The development of the regional economy of the Russian Far East was neither even nor balanced. During the Soviet period, production competitiveness on the domestic market did not exist in practice, and on the external market the problem was resolved through compulsory regulation of the domestic prices of inputs. Therefore, the question of real profitability was not primary, and activity on the external market was determined by the so-called hard currency effectiveness, which was dependent on the huge gap between the internal prescribed and external free market prices.

Since the late 1980s, RFE firms have acquired an opportunity for independent trade on the external market. However, they have lost the guaranteed support of the state and, more importantly, a market for those industries that had been created and developed almost exclusively for the demand generated by state planning. Foreign trade has not been able to make up for the loss of the guaranteed state market, which absorbed up to 80 percent of the gross regional product. After the shift to free pricing, competitiveness of industries became one of the main problems on the domestic regional, interregional, and external markets.

In this chapter, the problem of competitiveness in the Russian Far East is considered on the basis of the natural resource industries that have the longest involvement on all the aforementioned markets in the pre-reform and post-reform periods.

GENERAL CONDITIONS OF COMPETITIVENESS OF INDUSTRY IN THE RUSSIAN FAR EAST

In the Soviet Union, production costs in the RFE often considerably exceeded the average all-Union values. In particular, the production costs of coal and commercial timber exceeded the analogous indicators in the country's western regions by 25 and 75–100 percent, respectively. That is why a number of industries turned out to be relatively inefficient when oriented toward internal markets.[1] The entrance to foreign markets on the basis of advantages of the region's economic or geographic position was restricted by foreign economic policy, which was based on the leadership's lack of desire to integrate the Soviet economy with world markets. In those conditions, trade relations between the RFE and foreign markets only supplemented domestic interregional exchange, although the necessity of greater participation of the Russian Far East in the international economy, and above all with countries of the Asia Pacific region for the purpose of development in the RFE, was recognized.[2]

Export specialization of the RFE began to form in the mid-1950s, and it was based on the development of natural resource sectors. However, the extensive use of natural resources increased costs and lowered the quality of production—especially production of biological resources. It exacerbated ecological problems as well—a situation that continues to this day.

During the reform period, the raw-materials orientation of the RFE economy has been intensified; the share of the primary sector in gross regional product rose from 35 to 43 percent. At the same time, the nominal output in all industries of the sector has declined. Comparative production costs in the RFE have proved the largest among Russian regions.[3] An additional problem is that despite a high endowment of various natural resources, a large portion is no better in quality than the natural resources of other Pacific-Rim countries.

The internal market of the RFE has always been rather small, and during the post-Soviet economic crisis, it shrank considerably. This was exacerbated by increasing transportation and energy tariffs, which have almost cut off the RFE from the rest of the Russian economy. The possibility of competing with producers in other regions is negligible without a large-scale modernization of production technology and organization. The financial crisis of August 1998 aggravated the problems of the RFE economy, which on the eve of the twenty-first century appeared to be more connected with Pacific-Rim markets than with the domestic market. The region faces a difficult choice: either to focus on realization of its comparative advantages and active economic cooperation with Asia Pacific countries, or to concentrate on rather modest internal sources of development and attempt to market products domestically.

Competitiveness on the external markets depends on a variety of factors.[4] The main ones are labor productivity, wage levels, technology, transportation tariffs, and the currency exchange rate. The set of factors that influence competitiveness is different for each industry. Therefore each sector is analyzed separately below, with the attainment of competitive advantages considered as a dynamic system and not as a set of basic components.[5]

CONDITIONS OF INDUSTRIAL COMPETITIVENESS
IN THE NATURAL RESOURCE SECTOR

Agricultural Products and Markets[6]

Agricultural markets in the northern RFE territories are inevitably deficient because of the impossibility, due to natural factors, of developing full-scale agriculture there. Markets in the southern territories are also deficient, largely due to inadequate organization of production. Thus, a longstanding practice has been to import potatoes into the RFE from Siberia and, to a lesser extent, from China. Now, however, locally produced potatoes in the southern territories meet local demand, and 86 percent of this crop is produced not at large enterprises, but on individual farms. At the same time, conditions in the Russian Far East are favorable for soybean production. There is practically an unlimited market in other Russian regions, first of all in Siberia, for Far Eastern soybeans. Exports of soybeans to northeast China also recently began. Soybeans, therefore, appear to be competitive even under conditions of relatively low crop yield (0.6–0.7 tons per hectare).

At the turn of the century, the leading agricultural markets in Northeast Asia are either self-sufficient (Japan) or partially overabundant (the Republic of Korea, northeast China) in virtually all products. Potentially, the situation could change because of a reduction of land under cultivation in those countries and because of continued population growth.

According to one projection, by 2015–20, China could turn from a net exporter to a net importer of foodstuffs.[7] The land of the Russian Far East could then become a major reserve for the expansion of Northeast Asia's food base. The implementation of advanced agricultural techniques would make it possible to raise productivity on the developed lands of the RFE, in some instances at least doubling it. There is also the potential for an almost twofold expansion, by 2–2.5 million hectares, of arable land in the southern RFE.

Timber Products and Markets

The northern part of the Russian Far East has always depended on imports from the southern, timber-abundant territories of the region. The latter also exported timber products abroad and to other regions of the USSR. Current transportation tariffs have created a powerful barrier for the transport of timber westward and turned the flow of timber from the RFE toward the Asia Pacific region, where the timber market is the largest in the world. The total annual demand in China, Japan, and South Korea exceeds 260 million cubic meters, of which 65 percent is imported. The amount of imports into these three countries is five times greater than the peak RFE timber production (reached in 1986) and exceeds by almost twenty times the former maximum timber exports from the region.

With an annual capacity of 95.3 million cubic meters, the Russian Far East is the closest supplier of timber to these countries, but the region does not come close to reaching its maximum capacity (see Table 5.1). Timber exports reached 8.6 million cubic meters in 1987, and 7.7 million cubic meters of timber were exported in 1998.

Table 5.1 Output of the RFE Forest Sector

Product	1985	1990	1995	1998
Total wood cutting, million m³	34.5	29.6	10.5	6.3
Commercial timber, million m³	26.1	23.5	7.4	4.9
Lumber, thousand m³	6179.0	5414.0	973.0	476.0
Plywood, thousand m³	35.9	25.3	1.0	–
Particle board, thousand m³	117.1	189.4	22.1	5.1
Fiber board, million m²	23.0	23.8	5.6	2.6
Cellulose, thousand tons	418.3	539.9	60.0	2.2
Paper, thousand tons	228.3	215.5	14.1	0.2
Cardboard, thousand tons	192.0	240.6	13.1	6.1

Source: Database of Economic Research Institute, Far Eastern Branch of the Russian Academy of Sciences, 1999

In the Soviet period, timber from the RFE was exported to fifteen countries,[8] which decreased their dependence on the Japanese market. There now remain only four major importers of timber from the RFE: Japan, China, South Korea, and

Taiwan. The region's dependence on the Japanese market has grown, and competition is increasingly strong. The former monopoly of the three Russian exporters has been replaced by the activity of several hundred export firms. This has led to unfair competition, to supplying materials inadequate to the demands of the market and the terms of contracts, and, as a result, to undermining the reputation of Russian timber and to a drop in prices. Since 1996, among importers of timber into Japan, Russia has shifted from third to fourth place.[9]

The structure of Japanese demand for imported timber was stable for a long time, but is changing toward increases in the share of lumber, wood chips, wood panels, and plywood. The demand for sawn wood imports in Japan has grown threefold over the last ten years.[10] However, wood processing facilities in the Russian Far East cannot provide sawn wood to meet the quality requirements of the Japanese market.

Softwoods have predominated in RFE timber exports, but in recent years the demand, primarily from China, has grown for ash and oak. Hardwoods amounted to 15 percent of total timber exports from the RFE in 1999. In China in 1996, the price for ash exceeded the price for cedar by 1.5 times, the price for spruce by 2.0 times, and the price for larch by 2.6 times.

Owing to proximity to the markets, the competitiveness of RFE timber exports has always been higher than exports from other Russian regions. However, competitiveness has been declining due to growing production and transportation costs. Siberian timber, produced with relatively cheap energy, has been successfully replacing Far Eastern timber. Currently, Siberian timber constitutes 30–40 percent of all timber exported from RFE territory.

The prices for Russian timber on the Japanese market are 2.5–3.0 times lower than for American and Canadian timber, and 1.1–1.4 times lower than for Finnish timber. Recently, the profitability of RFE exports has dropped and in the summer of 1998 was close to zero. After the crisis in August 1998, it rose to an average of 25–30 percent, but even following the crisis, logs of third-grade quality (the lowest quality commercial timber) remained unprofitable.

The shortage of timber products forecast for the Asia Pacific region will be worse than in any other region of the world and will require the rapid growth of imports.[11] According to the United Nation's Food and Agriculture Organization (FAO) calculations, average annual Russian exports of commercial timber to the Asia Pacific region will grow 1.4 percent, wood panels exports will grow 3.6 percent, and paper and cardboard products—2.0 percent. Export of raw fiber material will begin and by 2010 will amount to one million tons.[12]

Despite significant competition, Far Eastern timber can play an important role in the Pacific Rim, and especially Northeast Asian, markets. Wood from the region has high density and is suitable for construction. Finished products (hardwood parquet, veneer, furniture parts, etc.) can be sold on more remote markets in the United States, Canada, the Baltic countries, Poland, Germany, European Russia, Ukraine, and so on.

The stability and state of the Russian timber trade in the Asia Pacific region will be determined by the following factors:

(1) The degree of adaptation to market conditions in each country, including conformity of products with each country's specifications and technical conditions, and delivery of products that are in greatest demand in these countries;

(2) Rational distribution of export resources, taking into account the demands of quality and pricing conditions in each country;

(3) Reliability of Russian suppliers to fulfill obligations and guarantee all contract conditions; and

(4) Coordinated action by the leading Russian timber exporters on the Japanese and other timber markets in matters of general conditions of deliveries and pricing policy.

Seafood and Seafood Markets[13]

Russia's exclusive economic zone in the Far East includes the most productive fishing grounds in the North Pacific. The cod, flounder, herring, and sardine resources remain undeveloped.[14] Fish products from the Russian Far East have always been competitive throughout the territory of the former USSR. In 1997, average prices in the RFE for fish products were 1.3–1.4 times lower than average prices in Russia. Because the domestic market is not saturated with fish products, prices for fish products in 1992–97 on the internal RFE market grew 1.3 times quicker than for foodstuffs as a whole.[15]

Labor productivity in the Far Eastern fishing industry considerably exceeds average Russian productivity and creates a basis for the competitiveness of the regional fishing industry on the domestic market. In 1995–99, fishing industry profits increased slightly. However, the increase in tariffs for harbor services and for transportation increased prices for Far Eastern fish in European Russia by two to three times, so now fish from the Far East often proves uncompetitive there. In 1990, fish products from the RFE were delivered to 170 provinces of the USSR. Today, approximately 50 Russian provinces receive fish from the Far East. At the same time, in the 1990s the volume of Far Eastern fish production that was exported abroad expanded because many countries in the Asia Pacific region cannot satisfy their demand for seafood with resources from their own waters.[16] The traditional consumption of seafood products by Pacific Rim countries, their developed economies, and proximity to Russian fishing zones promote the export of seafood products, which increased 3.1 times in weight and 1.9 times in gross receipts from 1993 to 1997 (see Table 5.2).

Table 5.2 Fish Exports of the Russian Far East
(million US dollars)

Province	1992	1993	1994	1995	1997
Primorskii krai	234.1	212.2	388.7	565.8	549.1
Khabarovskii krai	41.8	14.1	8.7	16.3	39.4
Kamchatskaia oblast	131.9	168.2	153.0	164.6	261.1
Magadanskaia oblast	52.4	7.4	7.7	2.3	25.9
Sakhalinskaia oblast	162.5	138.6	70.9	66.1	153.6
Total RFE	622.7	540.5	629.0	815.1	1029.1

Source: Data of joint-stock company Dalryba, 1998.

In 1997, seafood products were exported from the RFE to twenty-four countries. The largest share of exports went to the United States (24 percent of export volume), the Republic of Korea (19 percent), Japan (16 percent), Germany (7 percent), and Hong Kong (6 percent). Japan, China, and South Korea import from the RFE fresh and frozen fish, caviar, liver, milt, crab, shrimp, mollusks, and algae. Frozen fish and filleted fish have been bought at various times by Germany, Poland, Great Britain, and other European countries. Cheap raw fish and semi-processed products—and unprocessed products—also constitute a large share of exports.

Abolition of the state monopoly on the export of seafood products, the emergence of a new type of exporter, and unfair competition resulted in excessive supply, price imbalances, and sinking prices, especially on Japanese markets. They also resulted in a sharp decrease in the amount and assortment of fish on the domestic market, and in an absolute reduction of currency receipts. According to FAO data, the average price for Russian fish products is less than half of the world level.

On the whole, the RFE raw material base will make it possible in the next decade to increase the total volume of production to 4.2–4.3 million tons of seafood products—from 3.3–3.8 million tons of fish and 0.5–0.9 million tons of marine products (scallop, sea cucumber, laminaria, etc.). At that, the bulk of the catch (up to 90–95 percent) will be harvested in the Russian economic zone.[17]

It is forecast that the global trend toward depletion of marine resources will continue, catches of marketable fish will decrease, and difficulties with supplying the growing populations of the Asia Pacific with proteins will be exacerbated. The volume of fish from the Far East consumed on the domestic market will grow if the purchasing capacity of the Russian population increases. Prices for fish products probably will rise gradually both on the foreign and domestic markets.[18]

The fishing industry has substantial reserves to further increase its competitiveness, including:

(1) Substitution of production of finished fish products for raw fish for the domestic and export markets;

(2) Increase in labor productivity;

(3) Modernization of the fleet;

(4) Regulation of customs duties;

(5) Restoration of inspector supervision over production technology; and

(6) Creation of an independent system of fish product certification.

If these conditions are met, the export of Russian seafood products at least to Japan and South Korea would grow by 10–15 percent, which would amount to US$150–200 million.

Fuel and Energy Products and Markets[19]

The RFE's comparative advantages in the energy sector are ambiguous. In the last fifteen years, the region's balance of trade in all kinds of primary energy resources in interregional exchange has been sharply negative. The share of imports from other Russian regions in total energy consumption is rather high—46 percent in 1990 and 36 percent in 1996. At the same time, for many years the Russian Far East has exported primary energy resources, as well as some electricity, which provides today about 15 percent of the region's export income.

The geographic position of the region and its fairly developed infrastructure in the south favor the evolution of energy exports to neighboring countries of Northeast Asia. Except for North Korea, Mongolia, and the RFE, economic development of other countries in Northeast Asia in the last fifteen years has been accompanied by a steady growth of total energy consumption and of their share in world energy consumption. In 1996, Northeast Asian countries consumed almost one-fifth of the world total.

Natural and economic conditions (mountains, large rivers, dispersed industrial enterprises, etc.) impede the creation of an integrated fuel and energy system in the

RFE similar to those in Siberia and Europe. During the transition period, the region's consumers have enhanced their quality expectations for primary energy resources, but the region's level of quality still remains incomparable with the world standards. The low concentration of energy consumers (especially in the vast northern and northeastern areas) has led to a situation in which the energy supply of industrial units comes from rather small (with rare exceptions) providers. It is impossible to count on the creation of powerful suppliers of fuel and energy on the basis of large deposits in the region, even if one were to proceed from the most optimistic assessment of internal energy consumption. However, projects to develop the region's energy resources are commercially well-grounded.

For suppliers of primary energy resources, the markets of the Asia Pacific region are very competitive. The RFE competes on this market not only with foreign suppliers, but also with firms from East and West Siberia, where powerful, economical energy producers are located. The ratio of consumption and production in Japan, China, and South Korea, which together account for 96 percent of energy consumption in Northeast Asia, shows their high dependence on imports of oil, gas, and coal. Further increases in total demand for energy in these countries are predicted, as is an increase in imports of primary energy resources and a shift toward natural gas and, possibly, electricity.[20] So far, the participation of RFE suppliers in the energy markets of these countries remains symbolic.

Competitive positions of the RFE in the power industry can be improved through the following major projects that are at different stages of technical and economic feasibility:

(1) Further progress at Sakhalin 1, 2, and 3 oil and gas projects, and the expeditious approval of production-sharing agreements for, potentially, up to seven additional projects;

(2) Construction of several interstate electricity transmission lines across the border into northeast China:

(3) Development of the Solntsevskoe coal deposit on Sakhalin;

(4) Construction of two large electric power plants on Sakhalin Island that would use natural gas from the Sakhalin shelf and coal from the Solntsevskoe deposit, with electricity transfer from these plants through transmission lines to Hokkaido and Honshu;

(5) Construction of the large Elginskii open-cast mine, which contains high-quality coals (confirmed reserves of the deposit are over 2 billion metric tons);

(6) Development of oil and gas resources of the central and west regions of the Republic of Sakha, with orientation towards pipeline export of natural gas to Northeast Asia;

(7) Construction of hydroelectric power plants on tributaries of the Aldan River with aggregate capacity of about 5 million kilowatts, with a view to develop a Russia-Japan energy bridge; and

(8) Geological survey and development of hydrocarbon resources of the East Siberian Sea, Chukchi Sea, Bering Sea, and the Sea of Okhotsk.

Mineral Products and Markets

As in previous years, data on these industries remain least accessible, although some information is available (see Table 5.3). The transition period in Russia coincided with a difficult period on the world market for nonferrous metals in which prices fell for almost all basic metals. For example, the price of gold in January 1999 dropped to its lowest level in over twenty years to $286 an ounce.[21]

Table 5.3 Excavation of Nonferrous Metals in the Russian Far East

Metal	1991	1992	1993	1994	1995	1996	1997
Gold, tons	96.6	92.3	94.7	91.5	83.1	74.0	73.2
Silver, tons	–	–	202.6	54.2	97.2	–	–
Platinum, tons	–	–	3.7	4.7	5.6	–	–
Tin, thousand tons[a]	11.8	10.8	7.3	6.3	6.2	–	–
Lead, thousand tons	26.8	26.3	23.5	18.6	17.8	16.5	18.1
Zinc, thousand tons	36.9	98.9	33.4	25.6	23.9	23.6	24.7
Wolfram, thousand tons	5.7	4.9	2.8	1.9	3.1	1.0	1.4

[a]without Sakha republic

Sources: *Main Problems of Exploration and Excavation of Mineral Raw Materials in the Far Eastern Economic Region* (Khabarovsk, 1999); Database of Economic Research Institute, Far Eastern Branch of the Russian Academy of Sciences, 1999.

The orientation of producers toward world market prices and entrance to the external market in 1992–93 helped many producers of nonferrous metals in the RFE survive. But by 1994, domestic prices exceeded world market prices by 13–20 percent.[22] Between 1994 and 1996, the profitability of nonferrous metallurgy production in the RFE declined from 56.7 to 32.2 percent of production costs. The narrow domestic market could not support the increase in production costs, and profitability declined. The Russian Far East has a 20 percent share in the world production of unprocessed diamonds.[23] In 1985 and 1990, profitability at the firm Yakutalmaz (Yakutia Diamonds) constituted 52.8 and 46.8 percent of the sales at the firm, respectively. In 1995, the share of net profit in total revenue of the company Alros (successor of Yakutalmaz) was 10.5 percent.[24] Explored reserves of diamonds in Yakutia are substantial, but two-thirds of active reserves require additional capital construction.[25] Maintaining and increasing the level of diamond extraction over the next 10–15 years will only be possible if untapped but already discovered deposits are put into operation and new deposits are discovered.[26]

In Russia, deposits have been worked with a diamond content of not lower than 2.5 carats per ton of ore, while the richest deposits of the world have diamond content of about 1 carat per ton of ore. Total income will decline approximately threefold if the diamond concentration is cut in half. Such is the case with the diatreme Yubileinaia, which was commissioned at the end of 1996. The average content of diamonds here is about 1 carat per ton, and the size of crystals (and, therefore, their value) is somewhat smaller than at the Udachnaia diatreme.[27]

The prospects for marketimg platinum and related metals are favorable. In recent years, demand has grown for these metals due to the development of new applications and the growth in the popularity of platinum as an alternative to gold and silver in jewelry production.[28]

In spite of a favorable mid-term forecast for some metals, the general assessment of the situation on the mineral resource markets does not seem optimistic for the RFE and gives no reason to hope that the region can attain internal and external competitiveness without special measures. Under present circumstances, 30–60 percent of reserves cannot be considered profitable for development. The state of the world market and the extremely rigid Russian system of taxation have led to the unprofitability of about 50 percent of the gold mines.[29] Given the existing extraction in the RFE, it is economically inefficient to develop 30–70 percent of nonferrous metal ore deposits.[30] At present, the inefficiency of applied technologies is one of the major problems in nonferrous metallurgy and the reason for its low profitability.

IMPROVING THE COMPETITIVENESS
OF THE RUSSIAN FAR EAST ECONOMY

An analysis of competitiveness of RFE industries shows that practically all standard elements and procedures characteristic of market competition exist in the

region. Some of these still act as permanently negative factors: relatively high production costs; inferior product quality compared to world standards; and low
profitability. Other factors exert positive influence on competitiveness in the Russian Far East, including: relatively low wage levels; proximity to unsaturated raw-
materials markets of Northeast Asia; and the unique character of some resources.
Additionally, some factors have multiple influences on competitiveness. These
include the quality of specific natural resources; traditional trade relations; consumption habits; and state monopoly regulation on use of such resources as
precious metals and diamonds. There is, therefore, considerable potential to increase competitiveness.

The natural resource sector is the most important sector of the RFE economy.
As mentioned above, at present its share of the gross regional product is 43
percent. In 1998, 51 percent of the regional industrial employees worked in the
sector. In Kamchatskaia and Magadanskaia oblasts, this share increases to 64–66
percent; and in Sakhalinskaia oblast—to 83 percent (see Table 5.4).

The question arises about labor resources for the expansion of production if
competitiveness were to improve. With current unemployment at 13.7 percent,
even if all of these labor reserves were involved in the natural resource sector
completely (which is unlikely), this sector would not provide a great expansion in
employment. The Soviet way to recruit labor force from other Russian regions is no
longer realistic because the average income per capita in the RFE was just 93.4
percent of the Russian average income in 1997, and since then the disparity has
grown worse.[31] Thus, the main means to expand production is to increase labor
productivity. Increased labor productivity would also be the main factor in the
decrease of production costs.

Labor productivity in most of the natural resource sectors seriously lags behind
the analogous indicators in developed countries. For example, labor productivity in
agriculture in the Russian Far East is five to seven times lower than in Japan, the
United States, and Canada. In the region's timber industry, at the peak of development in the mid-1980s, it was ten, and now twenty, times lower than in western
Canada and the United States. Unfortunately, examples are numerous. Low labor
productivity is a basic factor that does not permit the realization of the effect of
comparatively low wage levels.

The current average salary in the Russian Far East is about ten times less that in
Japan, the United States, and Canada and about the average wage in the northeastern provinces of China (see Table 5.5). Such low compensation levels do not
correspond to the relatively high professional skill of the labor force, which cannot
be revealed completely under conditions of bad production organization and cannot provide a decrease in the cost of production materials.

Table 5.4 The Share of Industrial Employees that Work in the Natural Resource Sector, 1997
(percent)

	Oil and Gas	Nonferrous Metallurgy	Forestry	Construction Material Manufacturing	Fisheries	Natural Resource Sector, total
Sakha Republic	11.7	37.7	7.4	0.0	0.0	56.8
Jewish autonomous oblast	0.0	7.1	4.4	13.3	0.0	24.8
Primorskii krai	7.7	3.5	7.4	4.7	18.7	42.0
Khabarovskii krai	3.5	6.7	17.4	3.8	11.6	43.1
Amurskaia oblast	7.4	18.6	11.7	7.8	0.0	45.5
Kamchatskaia oblast	0.0	1.2	3.4	1.9	57.0	63.6
Magadanskaia oblast	5.0	44.5	1.3	2.1	13.4	66.4
Sakhalinskaia oblast	23.1	0.0	19.5	1.6	38.4	82.7
RFE[a]	8.0	11.5	10.9	3.7	16.9	51.0

[a]without Chukotskii or Koriakskii autonomous okrugs
Source: Calculated on the basis of O. M. Prokapalo, *Socioeconomic Potential of the Federation Subjects of the Russian Far East* (Khabarovsk: Kabarovsk State Technical University, 1999), 143.

Table 5.5 Average Monthly Wage, 1997
(U.S. dollars)

	Oil & Gas	Nonferrous Metallurgy	Forestry	Silviculture	Fisheries	Total industry, average	Agriculture	Total economy average
Sakha Republic	610	548	n/a	206	208	553	211	392
Jewish autonomous oblast	106	117	n/a	n/a	–	151	79	154
Primorskii krai	367	177	170	153	332	246	124	204
Khabarovskii krai	n/a	296	225	142	214	260	147	226
Amurskaia oblast	405	159	n/a	146	209	246	87	196
Kamchatskaia oblast	492	1337	263	206	495	472	292	374
Magadanskaia oblast	544	549	–	256	468	379	268	349
Sakhalinskaia oblast	408	–	n/a	165	267	303	266	289

Note: The average exchange rate in 1997 was 5,780 rubles per U.S. dollar.
Sources: Calculated on the basis of provincial statistical yearbooks.

The other cause of large production costs is high energy consumption in production, which is a general feature of the Russian economy. In the RFE, this factor is intensified by the application of high tariffs for electric and thermal energy. In 1999 the average price of electricity in the RFE was 2–3 times higher than the all-Russian average. This has resulted in a large increase in share of energy costs in the structure of product prices. For example, in Khabarovskii krai in the first half of the 1990s, the share of fuel and energy in the product price increased from 5.8 to 15.0 percent.

The problem should be resolved with a two-pronged approach for the natural resource industries of the region: by a reasonable reduction of tariffs and by use of regional energy sources. The latter can be created within these industries (burning of wood wastes in the forest sector, generation of biogas in agriculture, and so on).

Needlessly high transportation tariffs, especially for rail transport, greatly impact the competitiveness of products in the natural resource industries, which often ship large volumes. A reasonable mutually beneficial compromise should be found between the cargo carrier and the sender.

High resource consumption is connected with wasteful and poorly managed use of primary resources. For instance, 15 to 65 percent of timber that is permitted to be cut is not extracted from the cutting sites. Moreover, of every four extracted cubic meters, one is lost in further primary treatment and transportation. The waste of wood in the next stages of production of finished or semi-finished products is, on average, 40 percent of the raw material.[32] Therefore, the total waste before product manufacturing averages about two-thirds of the initial raw material.

There are a number of such examples. It should be noted that the problem is often connected not only with poor organization of production but also with obsolete technologies that are involved in the production process.

The above-mentioned waste causes low profitability or outright unprofitability for producers (see Table 5.6). The solution lies in modernization of manufacturing processes and substitution of obsolete equipment with new technology and machinery, which demands significant investments. Several projects in Khabarovskii krai, for example, demand considerable investment to bring the quality of products up to world standards. The renovation of the Komsomolsk-na-Amure fishing and industrial complex, with annual output of 2,380 tons, would cost $8.6 million. The construction of an open pit at the Lian brown coal deposit, with expected annual output of 300 thousand tons, would demand $6.3 million. The construction of an open pit with annual output of 3 million tons at the Urgal coal deposit would cost $146 million. Construction of a modern cellulose-paper plant in Amursk is estimated at $500 million. Recouping capital investments for these projects is expected to take three to ten years.[33]

Table 5.6 Profitability of Production, 1997
(percent)

Industry, Province	1997
Fuel Mining, Primorskii krai	15
Nonferrous Metallurgy, Primorskii krai	-15
Forest Industry:	
Primorskii krai	17
Khabarovskii krai	-17
Amurskaia oblast	-12
Kamchatskaia oblast	-20
Agriculture:	
Primorskii krai	-42
Amurskaia oblast	-34
Magadanskaia oblast	-33

Source: Social-Economic Status of Primorskiy Krai in Comparison with Regions in 1997 (Vladivostok: 1998).

CONCLUSION

In the past several years, the decline of prices for the majority of raw materials has been evoked by great structural changes in the economies of advanced industrial countries as well as by substantial technological changes. The total reorientation of companies to energy-saving technologies, utilization of waste products, and multiple processing of natural resources has become an additional factor. The price decline for raw materials began before the financial crisis in Asia, and the latter only aggravated this process. Lower prices will be preserved in almost all segments of the world markets for raw materials, at least in the short term. The consequences for a region producing raw materials can be grave if purposeful measures for restructuring and modernization of the natural resource sectors of the regional economy are not implemented.

The actual and long-term increase of competitiveness of RFE industries can be achieved only through a combination of stability in the external market with indispensable development of the internal market. From this point of view, it is necessary to consider the competitiveness of RFE products more extensively and in the context of the optimal combination of the regional, national, and international markets, as well as the optimal combination of national and foreign capital.

Creation of a mechanism that stimulates the formation of optimal proportions between internal and external economic cooperation for the Russian Far East is increasingly becoming the aim of regional development authorities. It will be extremely important to create a system of actions, incentives, and protective mechanisms for raising competitiveness.

Although some of these problems can and must be solved on the regional level, a significant portion (transportation tariffs, rate of exchange, etc.) depends on federal policies to create a favorable climate for investment and entrepreneurship in Russia.

NOTES

1. P.A. Minakir and N.B. Pisarenko, "Vzaimosviaz mezhraionnykh sviazei i transportnogo proizvodstva v otrasliakh spetsializatsii," in *Sovershenstvovanie mezhraionnykh ekonomicheskikh sviazei na Dal'nem Vostoke* (Vladivostok: Dal'nevostochnii Nauchnii Tsentr AN SSSR, 1978).

2. V. S. Nemchinov, *Izbrannie proizvedeniia,* Tom 4, *Razmeshchenie proizvoditel'nykh sil* (Moskva: Nauka, 1967), 46–47.

3. P. A. Minakir and N. N. Mikheeva, eds., *Dal'nii Vostok Rossii: Ekonomicheskii potentsial* (Vladivosotok: Dal'nauka, 1999), 594.

4. P. F. Krugman and M. Obsfeld, *Mezhdunarodnaia ekonomika: Teoriia i politika,* in Russian, translated from English (Moskva: Ekonomicheskii fakul'tet MGU, 1997), 799.

5. M. Porter, *Mezhdunarodnaia konkurentsiia,* in Russian, translated from English (Moskva: Mezhdunarodnie Otnosheniia, 1993), 61.

6. For a detailed case study of the RFE's agricultural sector, see Jennifer Duncan and Michelle Ruetschle, "Agrarian Reform and Agricultural Productivity in the Russian Far East," chapter 8 in this volume.

7. Lester R. Brown, *Who Will Feed China? Wake-up Call for a Small Planet* (New York: W. W. Norton & Co., 1995), 163.

8. N. L. Shlyk, "Dal'nevostochnii ekonomicheskii raion v razvitii sovetsko-iaponskikh ekonomicheskikh sviazei," in *Sovetsko-iaponskie otnosheniia v Tikhookeanskuiu eru* (Khabarovsk: IEI DVO AN SSSR, 1989), 213–32.

9. "Obzor lesnogo rynka v stranakh ATR za 1996 god" (Khabarovsk: Investitsionnii departament AO "Dal'les," 1997), 36.

10. Ibid.

11. United Nations Food and Agriculture Organization, "FAO Provisional Outlook for Global Forest Products Consumption, Production and Trade," Rome, 1997 <www.fao.org/waicent/faoinfo/forestry>.

12. Ibid.

13. For a detailed case study of the RFE fishing industry, see Tony Allison, "The Crisis of the Region's Fishing Industry: Sources, Prospects, and the Role of Foreign Interests," chapter 6 in this volume.

14. V. P., Shuntov, "Sostoianie pelagicheskikh nektonnykh soobshchestv dal'nevostochnykh morei," *Rybnoe khoziaistvo,* no. 1 (1996):35–37.

15. Primorskii komitet gosstatistiki, *Rybnaia promyshlennost' Primoriia* (Vladivostok: Primorskii komitet gosstatistiki, 1998).

16. E. A. Piliasova, *Formirovanie rynka ryby i moreproduktov v Dal'nevostochnom ekonomicheskom regione: Nauchno-statisticheskii sbornik* (Magadan: SVKNII DVO RAN, Magadanskii oblastnoi komitet gosstatistiki, 1995).

17. Ibid.

18. "Polozhenie na rynke promyslovoi ryby," *BIKI, OF,* no. 26 (July 1997).

19. For a detailed case study of energy production on Sakhalin Island, see Judith Thornton, "Sakhalin Energy: Problems and Prospects," chapter 7 in this volume.

20. *Regional Economic Cooperation in Northeast Asia: Proceedings of the Seventh Meeting of the Northeast Asia Economic Forum,* August 19–21, 1997, Ulaanbaatar, Mongolia; "Energy and Security in Northeast Asia: Supply and Demand; Conflict and Cooperation," IGCC Policy Paper, no. 36 (February 1998); and "Vostochnaia energeticheskaia politika Rossii i problemy integratsii v energeticheskoe prostranstvo Aziatsko-Tikhookeanskogo regiona," *Trudy mezhdunarodnoi konferentsii* (Irkutsk, ISEM SO RAN, 1998).

21. "Sostoianie i perspektivy mirovogo rynok zolota," *BIKI,* no. 4 (February 1999):15.

22. V. Kapitonenko, "Modelirovanie protsessov sblizheniia vnutrennykh tsen s mirovymi," *Rossiiskii ekonomicheskii zhurnal,* no. 2 (1997), 55–62.

23. "O proizvodstve i prodazhakh rossiiskikh almazov," *BIKI,* no. 16 (February 1999):15.

24. V. V. Teslenko, *Organizatsiia torgovli dragotsennymi kamniami* (Moskva, INFRA-M, 1997), 240.

25. V. I. Vaganov and V. A. Varlamov, "Diamonds of Russia: Raw Material Base, Problems, Perspectives," *Mineral Resources of Russia: Economy and Management,* no. 1 (1995) (in Russian).

26. V. I. Vaganov and Iu. K. Golubev, "Almazy Rossii: mineral'no-syrievaia baza, problemy, perspektivy," in *Mineral'nie resursy Rossii: Ekonomika i upravlenie,* no. 1 (1995):6–10.

27. Ibid.

28. "Perspektivy rynka metallov platinovoi gruppy," *BIKI,* no. 17 (April 1999):15.

29. V. P. Orlov, "Mineral'no-syrievoi sector stran SNG: Osnova ekonomicheskogo razvitiia," *Mineral'nie resursy Rossii: Ekonomika i upravlenie,* no. 1 (1999):2–6.

30. M. Mkrtchyan, R. Sarkisyan, and A. Spector, "Neobkhodimost' i factory perekhoda

k resursoekonomicheskomu razvitiiu," *Rossiiskii ekonomicheskii zhurnal*, no. 11/12 (1997): 43–52.

31. Pavel A. Minakir, ed., *Ekonomicheskaia politika na Dal'nem Vostoke Rossii (kontseptsiia i programma)* (Khabarobvsk: Izd. Khabarovskogo gosudarstvennogo tekhnicheskogo universiteta, 2000), 92.

32. Alexander S. Sheingauz, ed., *Prirodopol'zovanie rossiiskogo Dal'nego Vostoka v Severo-Vostochnaia Aziia* (Khabarovsk: RIOTIP, 1997), 224.

33. "Investments," *International Business Magazine*, no. 8 (1997).

SECTORAL CASE STUDIES:
FISHERIES, ENERGY, AND AGRICULTURE

6

The Crisis of the Region's Fishing Industry: Sources, Prospects, and the Role of Foreign Interests

Tony Allison

The fishing regions of the Far East are threatened with an ecological disaster that has no analogies in terms of consequences, of economic and social destruction in the eastern borderlands of the country. Therefore we strongly demand the expulsion of the foreign fleet (including the foreign fleet under Russian flag¹) from the Exclusive Economic Zone of Russia in order to prevent a catastrophe in one of the most important fishing areas (along with the Sea of Okhotsk) of the North Pacific—the Bering Sea.

—Excerpt from a letter of top RFE fishing executives to President Putin, September 2000.

According to many long-time participants, the fishing industry of the Russian Far East is experiencing a severe and enduring crisis. Given the critical importance of the fishing industry to the RFE and to its neighbors, this crisis bears directly on the economic and political stability of the region.

During the Soviet era, the Russian Far East, because of its vast resources and shorelines, received the greatest share of investment in vessels and related infrastructure, and produced well over one-half of all seafood harvested by the USSR by the late 1980s.[2] In the post-Soviet era, fishing, including fish processing, storage, transport, and related activities, is the region's largest industrial sector, and in many localities it represents the only significant form of economic activity.[3] Taking into account estimated unrecorded high seas shipments, products of the fishing industry constitute roughly one-half of all export revenues for the region.[4] Because of the fishing industry's pervasive economic influence and its connection to foreign currency earnings, regional politics are closely tied to the industry's development, and, in the past decade of decentralization, regional governors have not hesitated to lobby publicly and strenuously for their territory's fishing interests—whether against the influence of other regions or against Moscow's policies.

Fishing is also crucial to the region's international dimension. Foreign companies and governments, especially those of Japan, South Korea, China, and the United States, have been more active in the fishing industry than in any other sector of the Russian Far East economy.[5] The forms of this activity have ranged from bilateral and multilateral conventions on preservation of stocks, to fishing by foreign fleets in Russian waters, to joint ventures, seafood trading, fleet modernization, and supply of provisions for vessel operations. Japan's seafood market, the largest in the world, has been dependant on output from Russia's Far East for several decades. China and Korea both serve as centers for the transit and reprocessing of Russian seafood, as well as end markets in their own right. Crab, salmon, pollock, scallops, and bottomfish from the RFE are familiar to seafood importers throughout Asia, North America, and Europe.

Through these multifaceted connections, foreign interests have played a key role in transforming the RFE fishing industry. Enormous modern trawling fleets, built in Norway, Spain, and Germany and financed through long-term bareboat charters, have appeared in RFE waters. Russians have bought large, state-of-the-art crab catcher-processors from the United States, where crab stocks have declined sharply. Dozens of Russian-built vessels have been refitted in Korea, China, and the United States for crabbing, shrimping, and longlining operations.

The Russian fleet also has come to rely on foreign ports for repairs, crew changes, and even transshipment of products, leaving Russian port facilities inactive and decaying. The numerous shoreside plants that functioned throughout the Russian Far East in Soviet times have deteriorated, and many have ceased operations. Large state-owned fishing companies have disappeared or have become privatized holding companies for smaller entities, and most are struggling under imposing debt loads and tax arrears. Russian sources of financing for the industry have been almost nonexistent, resulting in widespread reliance on foreign credits.

Fisheries management problems have also plagued the RFE seafood industry since the collapse of the USSR, placing increasing stress on dwindling resources. Throughout the Soviet era most fisheries stocks of the RFE and in accessible foreign waters generally underutilized, and therefore sufficiently available for those with harvest capacity. Moreover, the entrenched, centralized Soviet allocation system was relatively resistant to influence by regional leaders and by enterprises, and was largely capable of enforcing harvest limits. Anecdotal evidence suggests that corruption in the form of personal gain by regulatory officials played almost no role in the system of establishing and allocating quotas, and only a marginal role in the activities of enforcement agencies. Disputes between regions and the center over the allocation process were not allowed to develop; complaints between or from the regions were resolved through Moscow's all-encompassing administrative power. In stark contrast, in the post-Soviet era Moscow has struggled with the federation subjects (and they with each other) for control of the resource, while the most important commercial stocks, king crab and pollock, have been sharply reduced in many areas due to overfishing and ineffective management. Falling quotas have recently been accompanied by unprecedented hostility between the krais and oblasts over rights to a shrinking resource, and by aggressive statements—backed by policy changes—from Moscow and the region vilifying foreign participation in the fishing industry.

In this situation investors from neighboring countries are pulling back from the RFE fishing industry, frightened by the decline in some stocks, the unpredictability of the resource allocation system, and the larger uncertainties of the business environment. Recent rapid changes in the Russian government and the collapse of the banking system have added to the confusion. But because the fishing industry is export-oriented and involves an easily extracted and valuable resource, foreign involvement is nonetheless likely to remain an important factor in the future.

The crisis in the Russian Far East's most important traditional industry raises several questions of interest to Russian and foreign policymakers: What are the main characteristics of this crisis? What are its sources? What are the ramifications for the region and for individual oblasts and krais? Have foreign interests helped to create this crisis, and what should the role of foreign interests be? Finally, what are the prospects for success of the solutions currently being implemented by Russian policymakers? What alternatives should be considered?

THE CHANGING ROLE OF GOVERNMENT

The end of the USSR's command economy caused an abrupt decline of powerful state industrial structures such as the Ministry of Fisheries. In the late 1980s the Ministry began to shed its traditional industry-leading role, and its authority was increasingly restricted to management, instead of exploitation, of fisheries stocks. In 1991 the Ministry of Fisheries became the Russian Committee of Fisheries, which was reduced to a constituent department of the Ministry of Agriculture.[6] In 1992, it was elevated to the status of an independent state committee, although with its staff reduced by one-third.[7] It was downgraded again to a department in

the Ministry of Agriculture in 1997, but was once more restored to its state committee status soon thereafter (it will be referred to here as the Committee). These
periodic re-designations, along with reductions in staff and authority, have been
accompanied by frequent changes in the top position of chairman: seven different
individuals have held the job since 1991.

Although many powers were ceded to regional entities, the all-important function of setting and allocating overall harvest levels has remained in Moscow, and
chiefly with the Committee (as has the licensing of vessels and fishing companies). However, the authority of the Committee in this most crucial of areas has
increasingly been impinged upon, and by the late 1990s the Committee was forced
to share the establishment and approval of quotas with other government bodies. In 2001 the Ministry of Economic Development was charged with establishing and administering a system of auctions for the most valuable species, thus
introducing both a new entity and a radically new approach into the allocation
process. Important results of such changes have been serious delays and uncertainty around the issuance of quotas, which have in turn caused lost fishing time
and missed revenues for the fleet.

The reasons cited by industry participants and observers for inserting additional
controls, in the form of approving agencies, into the quota allocation system are
various. Many in the industry have pointed to the extremely negative public image
of the fishing industry in the Russian press, where it has been described as a
"criminal industry," "mafia-controlled," with hundreds of millions, if not billions, of dollars disappearing every year through bribes to officials, illegal fishing,
and unrecorded exports. Another view has been that the Committee, as a former
ministry filled with pro-industry apparatchiks, is ill-equipped to regulate fishing in
the long-term public interest. Yet another element mentioned is the eagerness of
other bureaucratic agencies to enjoy the fruits of control over an industry with
substantial hard currency earnings, and whose participants are more than willing to
pay off obstructive officials to achieve their goals.[8]

By the late 1990s, the Soviet fisheries management and quota allocation system
had evolved into a complex and somewhat confusing structure (see Figure 6.1). At
the base of the structure, the local scientific work is done by oblast/krai scientific
institutes.[9] The oblast/krai fisheries science centers have gained increased independence from Vladivostok and Moscow. The head of one oblast scientific institute
estimates that only 30–40 percent of his funding comes from the government, and
the rest must be obtained through contracts for research with fishing companies.
This has caused great concern that the very data on which quota decisions must
ultimately be based is inadequate or suspect. According to one long-term industry
insider and former fisheries researcher, data gathering and analysis in Russian Far

Figure 6.1 Structure of the Fishing Industry in the RFE

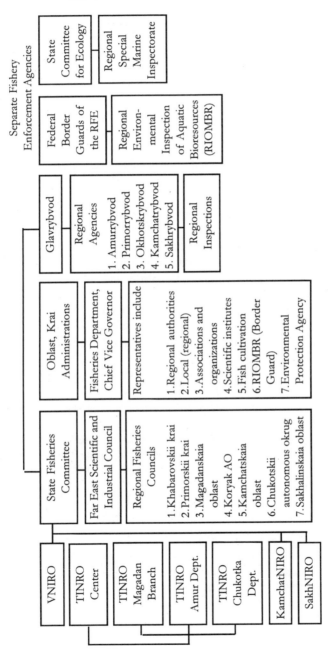

Source: Russian industry representatives.

East waters has dropped dramatically in the last ten years, and whereas well over one hundred different species were previously studied, "today almost all of the effort is devoted only to crab and pollock." The same source notes the suspect quality of much of the data gathered today, since it comes mainly from commercial fishing boats that allow scientists on board in exchange for utilizing valuable special "scientific" and "control" quotas.

Formally, the main steps in determining quota allocations are much the same as in the Soviet period: Tinro-Center in Vladivostok collects the data and makes recommendations to its parent, Moscow-based Vniro. Next, in an increasingly politicized process, the Committee divides the recommended allocations by fishing area and species between oblasts and krais. Now, however, instead of having the final word, the Committee sends its recommendations for review to a government commission of "experts"—mainly ichthyologists from various institutes appointed by the State Committee for Ecology—and then to the State Committee for Ecology itself. Once any questions or objections are resolved, this entire set of harvest recommendations, by fishing area and by species, with rights of harvest divided between oblasts/krais, is forwarded to the Russian prime minister for signature.

After the highest government official approves the harvest limits, they are passed to oblast/krai administrations for distribution among companies, sometimes through an intermediary industry association group. This distribution of long-awaited quotas, with subsequent issuance to specific vessels by the local fisheries enforcement agency, *rybvod*, of a fishing "ticket," is based on the types of vessels owned (or operated through charter) by each company and their historical catch levels. Additional criteria explicitly considered by territorial governments are the vessel operator's record in tax and wage payments, its importance as an employer and social service provider for the territory, and any record of fisheries violations. Less formal criteria, according to industry observers, range from family ties to political leanings to outright bribery. Instances also occur of "special" quotas of considerable value being awarded directly from Moscow to individual firms, including even to firms without vessels to harvest the quota received.[10]

The quota allocation system is complicated additionally by the existence of different types of quotas. There are four basic types for domestic users:

- *industrial quotas,* which constitute the great majority of all quotas, and have been usually free of charge (a part of these quotas, and indeed a very large percentage of industrial quotas for valuable species such as crab, are being handled through auctions beginning in 2001);
- *control catch quotas,* which are typically in biologically sensitive areas not generally open for operations and require fishing with a scientist on board who monitors and analyzes the catch;

- *scientific quota,* which requires fishing according to a program devised by scientists for an area and species about which information is insufficient to establish an industrial quota; and
- *paid, or commercial, quotas,* which have been sold through designated agencies (usually in Moscow) for fees that are ostensibly used to support fisheries science, enforcement, search and rescue, and other functions needed by the industry. These quotas seem to have been largely eclipsed by the auction system in 2001, although it is unclear if this is a permanent development.

In addition, there are separate quotas set aside for bilateral fisheries agreements that allow foreign vessels to fish in Russian waters. These quotas are provided to foreign governments in exchange for payment in cash or in kind (for instance, construction of salmon hatcheries or delivery of scientific vessels or, less frequently in recent years, in exchange for reciprocal fishing rights. The scope of these quotas has been reduced as pressure on Russian stocks from Russia's own fleet has grown.

The possibility of moving allocations between categories or even of creating new "special" quotas, and of treating the criteria and rules for each category subjectively, has created a high potential for corruption. In this context, it is not surprising that the top executives of fishing enterprises and the heads of oblast and krai fishing departments spend several months of every year in Moscow trying to protect and enhance their interests. There are additional obvious moral hazards that arise on the local level when territorial administrations divide quotas between companies based on the changing mix of objective and subjective criteria described above.

A third level of vulnerability in the fisheries management system is monitoring and enforcement. Underpaid (or unpaid) scientists and enforcement officers are often offered cash, alcohol, or valuable seafood products in return for falsifying records, easing the rigor of scientific fishing programs, or simply overlooking violations. Although such hazards may be encountered in every country, in Russia the sense of abandonment often felt by scientists and enforcement officers, and the widespread view held by Russian fishermen and their employers that success can only be achieved by violating the formal rules, makes this a particularly serious problem.

As with the Committee in Moscow, during the 1990s the traditional en-forcement agency, Glavrybvod and its local rybvod branches, has faced growing criticism for unregulated exports and unpunished fishing violations. In the 1990s another organization, the Special Marine Inspectorate (*Spetsmorinspektsiia*), a division of the State Committee for Ecology, was empowered to patrol and pursue violators alongside the rybvods. Capture of violators became the sub-ject of competition, and sometimes of conflict, between the two organizations, leading to confusion and often to needlessly interrupted legitimate fishing operations. Finally, in 1998 the enforcement functions of the rybvods were rred to the Federal Border Guard, a further impingement on the power of the Fisheries Committee, and another case of an outside entity receiving decisive authority over an activity with which it was only generally familiar. It appears that this inexperience was recognized, and many rybvod personnel have been integrated into the border guard units involved in fisheries enforcement. However, anecdotal evidence indicates that problems of corruption have not eased significantly. Indeed, some industry participants have portrayed the take-over as an effort to find a source of unofficial revenue in the form of bribes to appease the border guard, whose troops are usually asked to serve in diffi-cult and remote areas of the Russian borderlands with little recompense.

Quotas, the status of the resource, and enforcement of fishing rules are all central topics at sessions of the RFE Scientific-Industrial Council, which meets either in Moscow or at a RFE location at least two times per year. The Council is made up of government and industry representatives from each Far Eastern oblast and krai, Tinro, and rybvod, and its meetings are also attended by top representatives of the Committee. The Council has served as a forum to dis-cuss regional resource issues, to negotiate trade-offs on quotas between federa-tion subjects, and to generate proposals or demands to the Committee and to other fisheries-related entities. In the past, Council meetings were often marked by common positions and actions by RFE territories in support of the indus-try and the region; more recently, however, conflicts among oblasts and krais over fishing rights have diminished the Council's role and reduced its effectiveness.

In some respects the Council has replaced Dalryba, the traditional umbrella unit of the regional fisheries branches, as the voice of the RFE fishing indus-try. A key difference, however, is that the Council does not, as Dalryba did in the Soviet era, speak with one authoritative voice; another is that it does not attempt to involve itself directly in the economic activities of the fishing com-panies that are its constituents. These constituents now aggressively compete with each other for markets, financing, vessels, and, above all, quotas. Indeed, the time of unanimous resolutions and unquestioned fisheries policies ema-nating from Vladivostok or Moscow has long passed. A new era, dominated by the actions of a dynamic, export-oriented, and fragmented private industry, has taken its place.

THE EMERGENCE AND THE STRUGGLES OF PRIVATE INDUSTRY

In 1990 in the waters of the Far East we caught 4.2 million tons of fish with a (vessel) tonnage of 460,000. In 1997 we caught 3.2 million tons there with a vessel tonnage of 670,000. It follows that on the fishing grounds we have 1.5–2.0 times the (vessel) capacity needed. This negatively affects the stocks.... Failure to observe a balance in the pollock fishery will lead to the complete undermining of those stocks.

—B. N. Kotenov, Director, VNIRO (the National Fisheries Scientific Research Organization), at a government hearing on the Russian fishing industry, December 1999.

While the Russian State Committee for Fisheries managed to retain quota and licensing powers after it lost control of production, the huge regional branch (*bassein*) and oblast/krai Soviet fishery entities lost almost everything and either disappeared or began a new life. Dalryba shrank from an enormous production-oriented bureaucracy to a modest association in the early 1990s after its constituent firms had almost all established themselves as independent business entities. The powerful oblast and krai umbrella companies, called *rybproms*, sometimes managed, as did Dalryba, to acquire their own small fleet of fishing vessels through a combination of appropriated state assets and foreign credits, and reappeared, usually under the previous management, as colleagues and competitors of their former subordinates.

The number of independent firms in the fishing industry exploded in the 1990s. Not only did the former state enterprises and the fishing kolkhozes break free from their umbrella associations, but a myriad of entirely new ventures appeared. One source, writing in 1996, cites an "incomplete assessment" that found over one thousand firms active in the RFE fishing industry.[11] Recent data indicate that in Sakhalin oblast alone some 598 enterprises are active in the fishing industry, a ten-fold increase since 1990.[12] Although every region has seen a proliferation of small firms, in Primorye and Kamchatka, large former state enterprises, along with fishing kolkhozes, have continued to dominate the scene, while on Sakhalin newly formed companies, often with foreign participation, emerged at an early stage alongside the kolkhozes as industry leaders. Given the upheaval and change that have pervaded the industry, it is additionally noteworthy that the CEO's of the largest companies in Primorye and Kamchatka—the leading localities in the RFE for seafood production—were almost all the same at the close of the decade as at the beginning.[13]

However, these examples of continuity belie the deep sense of chaotic change and growing crisis that has prevailed throughout the RFE during this period. The RFE catch plummeted from 4.6 million tons in 1990 to a nadir of 2.3 million tons in 1994. After recovering to about 3 million tons annually during the next four years with the help of chartered ships built in Europe and modernized Russian vessels, the catch dropped by some 350,000 tons in 1999. The total quota for 2000 was substantially below that for 1999, and catches during the year were below the 1999 level.[14] The quotas for most species in 2001 were again reduced compared to the previous year. While the initial reduction in catch in the early 1990s was connected to national political-economic collapse and industry restructuring, the latest trend reflects primarily a resource constraint. Of particular concern is the most abundant commercial species, pollock, which despite its decline still represents well over half of the RFE harvest. Meanwhile the annual harvest of the other most important commercial species, king crab, probably peaked in 1996. A moratorium on additional boats in the crab fishery was introduced several years ago, but the king crab resource shows increasing signs of stress every year due in large part to illegal fishing (see Figure 6.2).

With the exception of imported or refit pollock and crab vessels, most of the fleet has continued to deteriorate. The technical norms for the industry imply that by the year 2010, over 90 percent of the total existing Primorye fishing fleet will need to be scrapped.[15] The situation is similar in other RFE areas.

A sharply reduced and declining overall catch, overfished pollock and crab stocks, and an aging and decrepit fleet are only the most blatant signs of an industry in crisis. Production by shoreside plants declined even more precipitously than that by the fleet—by almost 60 percent between 1990 and 1994.[16] Unlike in the case of the fleet, however, there have been almost no significant investments in modern shoreside technology, and almost no exceptions to the rule of deterioration and steep decline.[17] According to the State Committee, shoreplants and ship repair facilities are utilizing only 20–30 percent of their capacities. Turnover at fishing ports, formerly bustling centers of repair, resupply, and transshipment, has been curtailed by a factor of three.[18]

As a result of these developments, the fishing industry throughout the RFE has reportedly lost roughly 30 percent of its workforce in the 1990s, a striking figure for the region's leading industrial employer.[19] Of course, this drop should be seen against the background of a region-wide population decline, including a 20 percent drop in the working-age population through outmigration since 1991.[20] Indeed, because of these overall regional trends, the fishing industry appears to have *increased* its importance as an employer relative to other industries in the RFE: in Primorye as of 1999 some 17 percent of all employed industrial workers were in the fishing industry, in Sakhalin 25 percent, and in Kamchatka 50 percent—all slightly above figures of the early 1990s.[21] Therefore, further industry decline will likely have increasingly powerful socioeconomic effects on the region unless alternative sources of employment are developed.

Reliable data on the profitability of companies in the fishing industry is virtually impossible to obtain, given the ubiquitous practice of underreporting catches, revenues, and profits. However, the fragile state of the industry's financial condition is attested to by frequent and well-publicized cases of tax arrears, vessel arrests

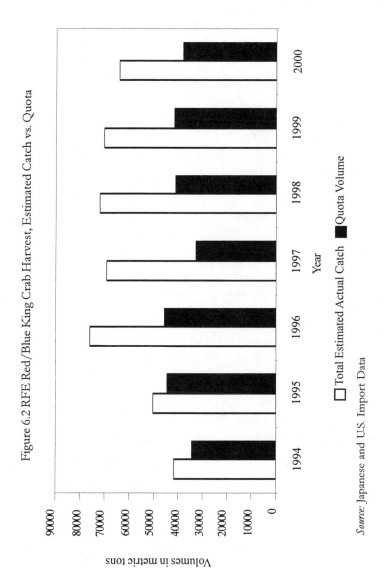

Figure 6.2 RFE Red/Blue King Crab Harvest, Estimated Catch vs. Quota

□ Total Estimated Actual Catch ■ Quota Volume

Source: Japanese and U.S. Import Data

by unpaid creditors, and bankruptcies. Most importantly, the lack of capital investment has contributed to the downward spiral of undercapitalization, underperforming
assets, increased reliance on foreign financing, and additional scrutiny and bureaucratic interference in attempts to stem capital flight.

A conference of the Primorye fishing industry in May 1998 provided a summary
list of factors contributing to the industry's state of crisis:[22]

- the end of government financial support and the implementation of harsh
  tax and credit policies;
- the absence of an effective legislative system that could protect domestic
  producers;
- a chronic deficit of operating funds experienced by companies, which is intensified by the high costs of maintaining the fleet and shoreside assets and
  of conducting fishing operations—costs which exceed the sales price of
  seafood products;
- a constant lack of quotas for harvesting seafood up to full production
  capacities; and
- the inadequate level of technology in fish processing, which does not provide
  competitive seafood products for the export market.

Putting aside questions of the efficacy of Soviet-era subsidies and the dangers
of protectionism, this list reflects fundamental industry problems that have persisted throughout the 1990s: lack of domestic capital; a confiscatory tax system;
outdated technology (especially in shoreplants); and, by the late 1990s, lack of
adequate quotas for some species, especially pollock and crab. Most commentators would add to this list the underfunding of fisheries science and the confusing, inefficient, and corrupt system of quota allocations and fisheries enforcement
discussed earlier.

Another issue that has received increasingly negative attention in recent years is
the role of foreign interests. This role has several dimensions, and it is one of
the most controversial elements of the current debate over the crisis in the RFE
fishing industry.

THE ROLE OF FOREIGN INTERESTS

*The experience of recent years has shown that foreign investors enter the Russian
fishing industry with one goal: to get access to Russia's marine biological resources
and supply seafood products to the international market. In doing this foreigners
are not in the least interested in the preservation of our resources, or in the life
of our villages, and less so in Russia's food security. And although we continue to*

*work with foreign investors, trying to find mutually profitable alternatives, basi-
cally we rely on our own capabilities.*

—Yevgenii Nazdratenko, Governor of Primorskii krai, December 1999
(in February 2001 Nazdratenko was appointed Chairman of the State
Committee for Fisheries).

The proliferation of new firms in the fishing industry in the early 1990s was
accompanied by a radical three-fold reorientation of business strategy: toward
foreign markets, foreign financing, and foreign technology. The shift was caused
by factors common to other industrial sectors in post-Soviet Russia, especially
lack of domestic capital and the need to upgrade assets to competitive international levels. But this movement into the international marketplace was particularly abrupt and widespread in the RFE fishing industry because of several
factors peculiar to it:

- a history of close international contacts, including joint fishing operations
  with foreigners (especially with Japan and the United States);
- the relative insulation of the fishing industry, and especially its export activities, from the imposing barriers of Russia's physical, legal, and regulatory
  infrastructure that inhibited foreign involvement in other industries;
- the established value of many RFE seafood products in international markets,
  along with the relative ease with which these products could, with limited
  infusions of technology and management expertise, be increased in value; and
- the decline of fisheries, and of access to fisheries, throughout much of the
  world, which affected the major potential foreign partners of the RFE fishing industry. This decline made foreign shipbuilders particularly eager for
  new buyers, made foreign vessel owners enthusiastic about sending their
  vessels to Russian waters in search of better catches, and made international
  seafood marketers hungry for new sources of product.

Foreign-built vessels have attracted perhaps the most attention of all aspects of foreign involvement in RFE fisheries. In the first half of the 1990s,
some fifty large new pollock "supertrawlers" were delivered under bareboat
charter from the shipyards of Norway, Spain, and Germany in the largest infu-
sion of foreign capital the industry has ever seen. A fleet of twelve new longline
vessels arrived from Norway under similar conditions during the same period.
Approximately fifteen large existing crabber-processors and at least one newly
built one, with capacities roughly three times greater than Russian crab vessels,
entered RFE fisheries between 1990 and 1996 from the United States, where

crab stocks had declined sharply. In addition, a large number of smaller used vessels of various types have been sold or chartered to RFE fishing companies from Japan and Korea.

These foreign vessels were typically placed under Russian flag, and the effective charterers/operators have been Russian companies based in the RFE. Arrangements have commonly included operational management and product marketing by a foreign company, foreign specialists in key positions on the vessel, and financial control through chartering or mortgage obligations to foreign entities. Operational control has tended to revert to the Russian side as financial obligations are satisfied and as the Russian fishermen gain experience with the new vessels and their technology.

The supertrawlers from Europe have received by far the most publicity of these transactions, mainly because of their high cost, their failure to fulfill financial obligations, their complex offshore chartering arrangements, and government guarantees supplied originally by the Russian side, which were said to amount to $1.5 billion in the year 2000.[23] This publicity has become increasingly hostile as reduced pollock stocks have caused these vessels, with their enormous capacities, to compete for raw material among themselves and against less efficient traditional Russian vessels. Recently, the abrupt transfer by the State Fisheries Committee of eleven of the largest of these supertrawlers from one RFE operator to another has sparked a rash of legal actions in Russia and abroad.

Besides providing new and used foreign vessels to Russian companies, international business dealings have served as a channel for Russian shipowners to upgrade their existing vessels. These upgrades, often including a complete revamping of the fishing and processing systems, have taken place mostly in the ports of Pusan, South Korea, and Seattle. The number and value of such projects is difficult to estimate because shipowners are careful to avoid declarations that could trigger large customs or tax payments. However one U.S. company estimates that between 1990 and 1996 it conducted major refits of over twenty Russian vessels in Seattle, with the value per project ranging from about $500,000 to $1.8 million. Most large RFE fishing companies have contracted for multiple refit projects in Seattle and in Pusan. Much of this work has involved converting vessels for crab operations, but bottomfish longlining, salmon processing, and netting operations for bottomfish and salmon have also been targeted.

Impressive as this refit business has been, it is probably dwarfed by the volume and value of repair work on Russian vessels conducted in Pusan and Seattle, and also in other foreign locations such as Dalian, China, and Victoria, Canada. The large-scale acquisition of foreign-built vessels and shipboard systems has enhanced dependence on foreign shipyards because of the subsequent need for foreign vendor-supplied parts and technical expertise. The outdated technology and general deterioration of RFE shipyards, together with prohibitive duties and burdensome regulatory processes, have helped to drive much of the fleet overseas for repairs.

All of these factors, but especially high taxes and duties, have caused many Russian operators to keep their foreign-built vessels out of RFE ports: even crew changes often are done at sea or in foreign locations. Russian-built vessels are more likely to call in Russian ports between voyages, but almost uniformly ship or carry their exports directly from the high seas to international markets. Russian-flagged vessels, or those delivering their product, then stock up with provisions from these ports to be delivered directly to the Russian fleet at sea. During the 1990s, Pusan, because of its nearby location and its marine service capabilities, came to resemble an offshore Russian port city: drydocks full of Russian vessels, business hotels hosting Russian fishing industry entrepreneurs, and one entire area of town, around "Texas Street" (*ulitsa Texas*), catering to Russian fishermen and shuttle traders and resembling a Korean version of Brighton Beach's commercial strip.

The financing by foreign interests of vessel acquisition, refits, repairs, and provisioning has been closely connected with obtaining marketing rights to product. These rights provide some ability to control cash flows, and therefore give increased security to the financing entity in an environment where mortgages and other legal instruments lack sufficient power. The foreign side inevitably requires export of the product to foreign markets where, often, existing marketing channels allow the rapid conversion of the product to hard currency which is, in turn, used to satisfy the financial obligations of the vessel operator.

An additional factor closely connected to the end of the USSR and its command economy underlays the industry's reorientation to hard currency exports: in effect, Russian producers had no alternative. A recent survey describes the problems of Russian seafood producers supplying the formerly huge Soviet domestic market in an era of terminated or unpaid industry subsidies: Increased costs of production, inflation, and the reduced purchasing power of the general population led to a drop in demand for fish products on the internal market (between 1990–96 per capita consumption of seafood products fell by more than 10 kg per person).[24]

The fall in the purchasing power of Russian consumers was accompanied by a breakdown of Soviet marketing channels, a lack of financing for producers to offer the extended terms of sale required by most Russian buyers, and a business environment that made collection of sales proceeds problematic. Additionally, rail tariffs on the Trans-Siberian delivery route from the RFE to population centers in European Russia skyrocketed, and reliability of the service declined. In sum, the domestic market quickly became nonviable for most seafood producers in the Russian Far East.

Because of the extent of unrecorded and underreported export shipments, it is difficult to measure the true quantity of seafood exports from the RFE in the 1990s. Yet official figures make the trend plain: revenues from export shipments roughly doubled from the late 1980s to 1992, and then doubled again by 1996.[25] This jump is particularly striking in the context of a fall in harvests of approximately 40 percent over the first period and another 10 percent over the second. The sharp rise in export revenues in the face of large declines in harvest were achieved through improved technology and a reorientation to export markets, but also by terminating or decreasing fishing for species—especially saury, sardines, and herring—that made up a significant portion of the catch in the Soviet period but have a relatively low value on international markets.

While the catch by Russian vessels of pollock, the most abundant species in RFE waters, has also fallen steeply (by some 50 percent since 1988), this drop has been offset to some degree by an increase in product value. The arrival of the European supertrawlers, whose predominant finished product is frozen fillet block, along with the refitting of several large Russian trawlers for producing the same products, has caused Russia to become a major supplier of relatively high-value pollock fillet blocks to international markets. These fillet blocks are sent overseas, usually to large, relatively stable markets in the United States and Europe.

A different and extremely controversial form of pollock exports is the sale of quotas to foreign entities, which harvest these quotas with foreign-flagged vessels. While the total tonnage taken in this manner has declined, there is a great deal of speculation in the industry, sometimes voiced by political leaders, about systematic and gross underreporting of catches by foreigners.[26] The prominence of these issues should recede somewhat due to declarations by the State Fisheries Committee that all foreign fishing for pollock in the Sea of Okhotsk will be terminated.[27]

Skeptics on the issue of foreign fishing abound, however. Many industry participants believe that the sale of quotas to foreigners provides funds for the political and personal purposes of government officials, and that gross underreporting of foreign catches is agreed to in advance and simply increases the amount that foreigners are willing to pay for the right to fish. Also, large-scale harvests of pollock by vessels of several foreign countries inside the "peanut hole," a central area of the Okhotsk Sea just beyond Russia's EEZ, had reportedly reached some 700,000 tons annually in the early 1990s. These harvests were ended by a 1995 agreement to provide pollock quotas to those countries within Russian waters so their fishing activities could be properly monitored. Termination of these quotas raises the question of how these countries will behave in the future toward the "peanut hole" area, and this question is critical both to the health of pollock stocks and to international relations on fishing issues in the region. Most recently, the participation by foreigners in quota auctions for pollock and other species has stirred new controversy.

The other major RFE seafood product contributing to export sales, and the one most associated with problems of unrecorded shipments, illegal fishing, and underreported foreign-source revenues, is king crab. Prior to 1990, only a few RFE companies fished for king crab, and they used small Japanese-style conical pots. Most of the catch was canned for deliveries to Europe. With the arrival of U.S.-style crabbers and large rectangular pots, and with the deterioration of Russian monitoring and enforcement capabilities, both the legal and illegal catch expanded quickly. The catch rose from approximately 15,000 metric tons per year in the late 1980s to over 70,000 tons by the late 1990s (see Figure 6.2, above). Because harvesting king crab and delivering it in live, chilled, or frozen form is possible and potentially very lucrative with a relatively small boat, incentives for illegal fishing and unrecorded exports are very high.

As a result, reasonable estimates of Russian king crab harvest levels come not from official Russian catch and export data, but by extrapolating from import data of the two major importing countries, Japan and the United States. By this method, it appears that from 1994 through 1999 catches of the two predominant forms of king crab—red and blue—exceeded the total quota in the RFE by about 139,000 metric tons, which represents an average overharvest of 58 percent. Moreover, the problem has been worst in recent years: implied overharvests average 78 percent from 1996 through 1999. Put another way, about 44 percent of the catch of the predominant and most lucrative crab species caught in the RFE between 1996 and 1999 represents overharvest and illegal fishing. Based on these estimates, the average annual value of illegal shipments of red and blue king crab in 1996–99 would be approximately $188 million. Statistics indicate that the rate of illegal harvest showed no signs of decreasing in 2000.

These figures relate only to the problem of overharvest. They do not count underreporting of revenue through transfer pricing, misidentification of species, or other techniques used for avoiding income reporting or quota limitations. Furthermore, the above analysis relates only to red and blue king crab. A similar situation exists with other crab species, although on a smaller scale. Still, the above estimate for red and blue king crab covers what appears to be the most significant single aspect of illegal seafood exports from the RFE.

Some Russian industry officials have suggested that Japanese sources are overstating deliveries of illegal live crab in import data as a tactic for justifying lower prices on all crab purchases. Unfortunately, based on Japanese inventories and on reports by observers of offloads of live crab, this is probably wishful thinking. Other officials have expressed frustration at Japan's unwillingness to help stop these deliveries.[28] Indeed, Japan's northern ports, processing plants, and entrepreneurs have benefited greatly in the short term from illegal live crab exports from Russia. But it is clear that such rates of overharvest, or rates even close to those indicated here, represent a serious danger to one of the RFE's most valuable resources, and to all who rely on it for economic sustenance. Given the dependence of foreign markets on this resource, as well as the substantial income represented by the various services provided by foreign businesses in support of the Russian crab fleet, it appears to be in the self-interest of Russia's neighbors to assist in establishing an orderly export regime for king crab and other products.

Developments in king crab and pollock fisheries reflect the complex and sometimes paradoxical role of foreign interests in RFE fisheries. New fishing and processing technology, financed by foreigners, has sharply raised harvest efficiency and has greatly improved the quality of products. This harvest efficiency, combined with ineffective control and monitoring of fisheries, has pushed pollock and crab stocks into decline, with further depletion sure to follow if current trends continue.

As industry observers have often pointed out, financial obligations attached to deliveries of technology have led to many cases of substantial foreign control of RFE fishing operations, and especially of marketing channels (though these channels relate to processed products, and have nothing to do with the largest problem, that of live crab shipments). At the same time, international transactions, including unreported deliveries of product to foreign ports, have allowed Russian entrepreneurs to hide income, accumulate personal and corporate wealth abroad, and reduce Russian government rents from use of this valuable public resource.

However, undoubtedly far greater rents, both public and private, have been lost to Russia through the wholesale shift of industry support activities—shipbuilding, repair, provisioning, transshipment, crew rest and recreation—to foreign ports. This shift, as opposed to the shift to export markets, is not stimulated by the logic of geography and markets. It is instead largely the result of Russian tax and customs regimes, regulatory practices, and the deterioration of port facilities throughout the RFE. This result has greatly benefited foreign shipyards, foreign ports, and foreign vendors of marine equipment and supplies.

In this situation it is no surprise that proposals for improving the performance and prospects of the RFE fishing industry often involve recasting the role of foreign interests, as well as reforming Russian management of the country's fisheries resources.

PROPOSALS FOR SOLVING THE CRISIS

Lessons from the experience of the RFE's neighbors are important to consider as Russia formulates proposals to deal with the crisis in RFE fisheries. In the recent past, other Pacific maritime states have, like Russia, faced major declines in their national harvest volumes and threats to their most important stocks, as well as bitter conflicts between resource users and arguments over the role of foreign interests in the fishing industry. However, none of Russia's neighbors has faced these problems while simultaneously confronting dramatic national political and economic change on the scale of that experienced in Russia.

The key economic issue for RFE fisheries is how to maintain the stocks of these valuable resources in order to assure long-term sustainability of harvest. Pollock and king crab, taken together and considering estimates for illegal fishing and unrecorded exports, probably account for well over two-thirds of all revenues earned from RFE fisheries in the past decade. The status of these stocks is likely to determine, in large part, the health and viability of the RFE fishing industry in the coming years.

In the U.S. Pacific area, where pollock and king crab stocks have had a similar economic importance, stocks have also seen startling vicissitudes in abundance, and have been the subject of ferocious debate over the reasons for these vicissitudes. Political battles continue both regionally and in Washington, D.C., over the allocation of quotas to users of these species. The United States has had significant success in recent years in resuscitating its pollock stocks and increasing the value of pollock products produced at sea through management measures such as limited entry and individual transferable quotas. Meanwhile, Russia's pollock stocks have continued to decline, with Chairman Nazdratenko, among others calling for further radical reductions on fishing for pollock in the Okhotsk Sea.[29] Exchange of management experience and scientific data with the United States may be useful in exploring management alternatives for Russian stocks, but will have no lasting impact until uncontrolled fishing in RFE waters, by Russia's own fleet and by foreigners, is sharply reduced or eliminated.

Regarding king crab, the enormous Alaskan stocks declined precipitously in the early 1980s, and at present the fishery is a fraction of former levels. It is still a matter of argument in the United States as to the role that overfishing, environmental change, and other factors have played in this dramatic and enduring downturn. Negative lessons may be the key here: once a king crab stock is driven below a certain level, its recovery may be problematic even if the fishing effort is tightly controlled, as it has been in Alaska. The Russian catch appears to have peaked in 1996, then declined slightly in annual tonnage through 2000, but with a substantial drop in average size of crabs caught according to fishing and market data. Quotas for king crab were slashed by over 40 percent in 2001.

Although stock assessment and fisheries management are inexact sciences in any country, most experts believe that environmental change and fishing pressure interact, so that a stock under fishing stress is more susceptible to climate change, and climate change can accentuate the effects of overfishing. This is one reason why the problems of unreported catches and ineffective monitoring and enforcement are so troubling for the future of Russia's pollock and king crab stocks. It is not just overfishing that is worrisome; it is the perceived inability to accurately monitor stocks and to set and enforce rational rules at all.

The Putin government came to power in Russia with the expressed purpose of establishing the rule of law and attacking illegal activities, especially those that directly harm Russia's national interest. The fishing industry appears to be a good place to start. The main danger in such efforts would be to make more burdensome an already harsh and complex regulatory regime in the name of law and order, without actually reducing illegal fishing and corruption. Another mistake would be to further damage national interests by seeking scapegoats in the form of foreign involvement.

Since taking power, the Putin administration has, chiefly through top officials in the State Committee for Fisheries, consistently advocated certain planks of federal fisheries policy, which may be summarized as follows:

- The current shortage of resources for the fleet in RFE waters must be offset by increased fishing in the open ocean and in the fishing zones of other countries;
- More emphasis must be placed on development of inshore, small-boat fisheries, which deliver to shoreside facilities, thus increasing employment and other benefits to the local economy;
- Tax and customs regulations must be altered to attract the Russian fleet back to Russian ports for repairs and other services. Other regulations must also be streamlined to avoid costly delays of vessels in RFE ports;
- Shipbuilding in Russia, as opposed to abroad, should be stimulated by offering guaranteed quotas to those companies that have fishing vessels built in Russian shipyards;
- The quota allocation system should be reformed to provide greater "transparency," should tie each allocation to a specific vessel capable of fishing for it, and should reward those companies that have no tax arrears and that "integrate" their business activities with the Russian economy (through delivery of product to the Russian market as well as through ordering vessels from Russian shipyards). In fact, certain quotas may be available only to those shipowners who agree to deliver the resulting product to the Russian market.

The goal of "transparency" has been pursued, beginning in 2001, through open auctions of many valuable quotas (e.g., most king crab), where the buyers has no obligation other than to pay for the quotas in full in advance of fishing for them; and

• There must be a crackdown on illegal fishing and illegal exports. A continuous monitoring system, based in Petropavlovsk-Kamchatskii and Murmansk, whereby vessels are required to install and operate approved electronic transmitting systems, has been introduced to track catches and ship locations. Mandatory port clearance calls may be introduced for all vessels carrying product for export, especially crab.

These policies have not all been implemented (and indeed could not be) and thus far have brought little or no improvement to the problems they were designed to address. The reason for such ineffectiveness is a combination of the unrealistic, ill-informed character of some of these policies and the deep, recalcitrant nature of many of the political and economic problems affecting the industry and its environment.

To review these proposed policies in turn:

First, although some Moscow and regional officials, including Chairman Nazdratenko, continue to advocate a return to fishing in open ocean areas and in foreign zones as was done in Soviet times, experienced industry participants point out that such operations would have been extremely unprofitable to shipowners without subsidies and would be disastrously so at present given the cost of inputs such as fuel. These same industry participants also note that in any case the entire access regime in foreign zones has changed completely and would no longer be open to the Russian fleet on an acceptable basis.[30] Advocacy of this policy appears to be based more on nostalgia for the Soviet worldwide fishing presence, and desperation regarding the state of the RFE's own stocks, than on sober and realistic strategy.

Second, widespread development of inshore fisheries and related shoreside plants will remain extremely unlikely since the existing large fishing fleet, which processes its products on board, lacks sufficient quota and has already depleted many key RFE species. In addition, any shoreside-based operation will encounter all of the regulatory and infrastructure problems that the offshore fleet has attempted, with some success, to avoid by basing many of its operations overseas. For these reasons, most attempts to attract investment, either foreign or domestic, in shoreside development projects in the RFE have failed completely in recent years.

As for reforming regulations in order to attract the fleet back to Russian ports, Chairman Nazdratenko recently complained publicly that some 17 separate agencies harass fishermen in their attempts to earn a livelihood, and that to receive the proper licenses and permits for fishing operations requires 102 separate signatures.[31] Putin's efforts at strengthening government controls in all sectors may run counter to the goal of reducing and simplifying port procedures. In any case, there appears to be little meaningful progress in this area, which is so crucial to the future of RFE fishing ports, and Pusan today remains a center of offshore Russian fleet activity.

Any attempt to stimulate shipbuilding in Russian yards through quota allocations is wrongheaded and doomed to failure as long as those yards cannot turn out vessels of acceptable quality under competitive terms. At the present time Russian shipyards produce an inferior and inconsistent product at a high price. While far fewer vessels are entering the RFE fisheries today than previously, those vessels that are entering are typically older, foreign-built hulls with lower fixed and operating costs, and higher productivity, than new Russian-built ships. For the federal government to force Russian operators nonetheless to purchase Russian-built ships in order to procure quotas would undermine the industry's chances of achieving economic viability.

The most controversial and visible change enacted by the Putin administration is the introduction in 2001 of auctions for the most valuable quotas, especially crab. It is too early to identify clearly the many effects of these auctions, much less to measure their overall impact on the industry and the stocks. The auctions do seem to be achieving one of their purposes: they are open and relatively transparent compared to the almost totally opaque traditional quota allocation system described earlier. However, purchase of auctioned quotas depends strictly on financial wherewithal (whether from foreign credits, "mafia" money, or other sources) and possession of requisite vessels. Social and historical criteria, and other economic factors, are not considered. This system is likely to propetuate upheaval in the industry and the communities dependent on it if quotas are bid up for monopolistic and other anti-competitive reasons, and thus lost to companies and regions. On the schedule used thus far, auctions also make planning and financing efficient fleet maintenance and fishing operations almost impossible, since until the auctions are held no company can be certain what its fishing quotas will be. Perhaps more challenging still, most industry observers are convinced that many companies have bought small amounts of quotas at high prices only with the intention to abuse their access to licenses through illegal fishing of volumes far above those purchased. Finally, the financial impact for the government budget is questioned by top officials: Chairman Nazdratenko has recently stated that the auctions have not brought more money to the Russian treasury, but in fact have "brought Russia only losses," which he assesses at $33 million (the auctions have contributed some $190 million in total to the Russian budget in 2001).[32] The Fisheries Committee, under Nazdratenko's direction, is currently drafting an evaluation of the auctions for review by the Putin government.

Finally, in regard to the central problem of enforcement, despite several highly publicized arrests of both foreign and Russian vessels for violating fishery rules, the picture remains bleak. The total amount of illegally caught live red and blue king crab shipped to Japan was virtually the same in 2000 as in 1999. Since the total volume of this crab caught in the RFE was lower due to resource depletion, illegal crab actually made up a larger percentage of the catch in 2000 than in 1999. The data for 2001 is far from complete but is not encouraging, and informed speculation about the role of auctions in stimulating illegal fishing continues. Meanwhile, as in the case of zealous regulators in Russian ports, enforcement agencies, as they try to fulfill their mandate to end illegal fishing, take little note of increasingly costly disruptions they cause to legitimate operators. In the end, successful and cost-effective enforcement depends not only on public campaigns and on more and better equipped (and better paid) officers, but also on creating a management regime that provides sufficient stability, predictability, and opportunity for operators to make a profit without resorting to illegal actions.

In summary, it is possible that current policies, particularly nationalistic ones, ostensibly aimed at correcting the industry's problems could make the situation worse rather than better. The RFE would bear high costs if government policy ignored the advantages of international trade and insisted that seafood products be delivered to the Russian market or to Russian shoreplants even if these products have a far higher value abroad. The importation of supertrawlers and other sophisticated fishing vessels in the 1990s gave the industry access to expensive foreign technology and expertise, and the potential, under the proper management regime, to conduct profitable operations. Policies that force operators to make uneconomic trade and investment decisions will ultimately lower, not increase, the industry's potential contribution to the regional and national economies.

An expansion of domestic activity in Russia will require fundamental reform of tax, duties, and regulatory procedures to attract the fleet back to Russian ports. Predictability and equity, as well as transparency, is needed in the quota allocation process. Success will also undoubtedly require a determined, focused government effort aimed at prevention and interdiction of illegal fishing, along with the opportunity for legitimate operators to earn a healthy return without resorting to illegal actions. It remains for Russia's neighbors, particularly Japan, to assist these efforts through tighter controls and exchange of information regarding imports of RFE-origin seafood, especially live crab

A paradox of the RFE fishing industry is that it alone among the region's economic sectors has succeeded in attracting large amounts of foreign and domestic capital, albeit almost exclusively in the form of vessels rather than shoreside assets—but it has succeeded so well that fishing power has outstripped the resource base upon which it is dependent. The implications for individual fishermen and their families, for shoreside communities, and for the region's tax base and overall economic well-being are deeply troubling. Given the recent vociferous clashes between federation subjects over fishing rights and Russia's fundamental weaknesses in fisheries management and enforcement, it is difficult to envision how a rational division of a shrinking resource "pie" and a downsizing of fishing capacity can take place. Discussions of a vessel buy-back program, as practiced in the United States and other countries, and other capacity-reducing measures, must begin. The alternative may well be the destruction of the RFE's most important traditional industry.

Russia's Pacific neighbors, especially the United States and Japan, have had their own struggles in managing dwindling fisheries resources and allocating access to them, as well as balancing national political interests against the benefits of international commerce. Their experiences should be drawn on broadly in devising alternatives for Russia's policymakers. Moreover, the fishing industries of Korea and China, as well as those of Japan and the United States, have interacted closely and profitably with the RFE fishing industry over the past decade. This interaction has usually focused on quick returns and has reflected the short-term perspective of Russian entrepreneurs—often unfortunately bolstered by government officials—which places a premium on immediate cash flow because of the perceived uncertainty of the future.

A more stable and sustainable system of resource management is thus a prerequisite for the long-term health of the RFE fishing industry and for the well-being of the communities that depend upon it.

NOTES

1. The "foreign fleet under Russian flag" refers to foreign-built vessels chartered to Russian companies.

2. Food and Agriculture Organization (FAO) of the United Nations, country and area catch data for the USSR and Russia 1950–97, FAOSTAT Database <www.apps.fao.org>.

3. This statement is based on data for industrial output and employment by sector from oblast/krai Goskomstat data for selected recent years. Also see P. A. Minakir and N. N. Mikheeva, eds., *Dalnii Vostok: Ekonomicheskii Potentsial* (Vladivostok: Dalnauka, 1999), 87, which provides data showing that in 1995 the food industry, which is heavily dominated by seafood, represented over 25 percent of the region's industrial output, with nonferrous metallurgy and energy each around 20 percent. Since then the fishing industry has generally retained its production levels, while the RFE economy as a whole has continued to shrink. Also, the fact that a very large part of the fishing industry's production and income is unreported means that the industry's role tends to be heavily understated in official statistics. Visits to remote coastal areas of the RFE, and discussions with resi-

dents and officials, are sufficient to convince any observer of the utter dependence of these areas on fishing activities.

4. "The Russian Far East: A Survey," *The Economist,* September 1999, 6–8, contains official data and an estimate of $1 billion per year of unrecorded seafood exports. Also see Minakir and Mikheeva, *Dalnii Vostok: Ekonomicheskii Potentsial,* 213, for RFE export data by sector 1991–96.

5. While foreign activity is a difficult measurement to quantify—especially since the activity is often not only unrecorded but also very diverse: bilateral and multilateral treaties, direct fishing, commercial and government credits, scientific exchanges, chartered vessels, and vessel management support are all part of the picture—it is doubtful that this statement would be disputed by anyone who has tried to compare this situation with other Russian Far East industries. However, from the standpoint of foreign financial investment and employment, it is likely that the oil and gas sector on Sakhalin will soon surpass the fishing industry, if it has not already done so.

6. The fact that during Soviet times regulation of the fisheries was elevated to ministry-level status indicates the importance of the industry in comparison to that in most other maritime countries, including the United States and Japan, where fisheries have traditionally formed a subunit of other ministries in federal bureaucracies.

7. Milan Kravanja and Ellen Shapiro, *World Fishing Fleets: An Analysis of Distant-Water Fleet Operations, Past-Present-Future,* vol. 5, *The Baltic States, The Commonwealth of Independent States, Eastern Europe* (prepared by the Office of International Affairs, National Marine Fisheries Service, U.S. Department of commerce, 1993), 108.

8. Such views are voiced frequently in the RFE press. For a good summary article from the national press on views of the fishing industry and its bureaucracy, see Viacheslav Zilanov, "Morskoi uzel" ("Marine Knot"), *Nezavisimaia Gazeta,* October 10, 1999. Zilanov is a former deputy minister of fisheries of the USSR.

9. During the Soviet-era, Vladivostok was the headquarters of Tinro, the entity responsible for fisheries science in the Russian Far East, and of Turniff, which operated the vessels on which most of Tinro's scientific research was conducted.

10. A well-known instance of this was a large crab quota awarded to the Kamchatka company Ekofim in 1999. For an industry view of the quota allocation system, with reference to the above case, see "The Misfortune Is That There Is No Unity," interview with Valery Vorobiev, general director of ZAO Akros, one of the largest RFE fishing companies, in *Rybak Kamchatki,* April 20, 2000.

11. Pavel A. Minakir, ed., *The Russian Far East: An Economic Survey,* trans. Gregory L. Freeze (Khabarovsk: RIOTIP, 1996), 112.

12. Goskomstat fisheries data for Sakhalin, 1999.

13. On Kamchatka the largest companies and their directors, who have not changed since the early 1990s, are: Okeanrybflot—V. Topchii; UTRF—A. Abramov; Akros—V. Vorobiev; Kamchatrybprom—V. Potapenko; and Lenin Kolkhoz—V. Drachev (Drachev was briefly replaced in the mid-1990s).

In Primorye, apart from the demise and split-up of the huge VBTRF enterprise, the two largest fishing companies have also retained their CEOs: Dalmoreprodukt—Y. Didenko; and BAMR (Nakhodka)—A. Kolisnechenko.

14. Goskomstat and State Committee for Fisheries data for selected years, and quotas and data for 2000 announced by the State Committee and by the RFE Scientific-Industrial Council, report of meeting, July 25–27, 2000.

15. A. P. Latkin, *Na Rubezhe Vekhov (The Fishing Industry of Primore Between Two Eras)* (Moscow: More, 1999), 46–47.

16. Minakir, ed., *The Russian Far East: An Economic Survey,* 112–13.

17. Notable exceptions include the Tunaicha salmon plant on Sakhalin and the Kholkam bottomfish plant on Kamchatka. Several smaller operations also have installed modern equipment, but this does not change the general picture of deterioration and neglect.

18. State Committee for Fisheries, materials prepared for an industry conference on Sakhalin, July 1–2, 1999.

19. Minakir and Mikheeva, eds., *Dalnii Vostok: Ekonomicheskii Potentsial,* 123.

20. Ibid., 36–37 and 323.

21. Goskomstat data for fisheries in Primore (also contains data on other oblasts and krais), 1999.

22. Latkin, *Na Rubezhe Vekhov (The Fishing Industry of Primorye Between Two Eras),* 32.

23. Figures and strong views on these issues can be found in a recent and widely discussed interview with the Chairman of the State Committee for Fisheries, Yuri Sinelnik, "My vozmem Primorye pod osobyi kontrol" ("We Will Put Primorye under Special Control"), *Zolotoi Rog,* March 14, 2000.

24. Minakir and Mikheeva, eds., *Dalnii Vostok: Ekonomicheskii Potentsial,* 125.

25. Ibid., 126; and Goskomstat, various years.

26. See, for example, the speech by then-Governor Nazdratenko of Primorskii krai at a government hearing regarding the fishing industry on December 9, 2000, as reported in the *Digest of Fishermen's News and Regional Press,* December 10, 2000. Nazdratenko claimed that an analysis by the Primorye administration concluded that foreign vessels, on average, catch five times more than the volumes they are allocated and that these volumes show in catch records.

27. Interfax News Agency, "The Sea of Okhotsk Is Being Closed to Foreign Fishermen," March 30, 2000.

28. Ibid.

29. "Headquarters Takes Responsibility," an interview with Chairman Nazdratenko published in *Tikhookeanskyi Vestnik* 41, no. 16 (August 9, 2001).

30. "We Don't Need the Shores of Chile," an interview with Anatoly Kolisnechenko, General Director of NBAMR, published in *Tikhookeanskyi Vestnik* 41, no. 16 (August 9, 2001).

31. "Headquarters Takes Responsibility," *Tikhookeanskyi Vestnik.*

32. "At the Collegium of the State Committee for Fisheries of the R.F.," *Tikhookeanskyi Vestnik* 41, no. 16 (August 9, 2001).

7

Sakhalin Energy: Problems and Prospects

Judith Thornton

For decades, energy experts have promoted energy prospects in Northeast Asia. Here, they noted, is a rapidly growing region with an energy deficit and high energy prices adjacent to Pacific Russia, a major potential supplier of oil, gas, and electricity. Here is a region where capital-rich lenders could unlock the wealth of resource-rich producers. Yet, while the Asian economy boomed, nothing happened.

Authors from the National Pipeline Research Society of Japan, the Hyundai Research Center, the Royal Institute of International Affairs, and the East-West Institute produced elaborate programs—the Asia Pacific Energy Community, the Vostok Plan, the Energy Silk Route Project, the Kovyktinsk Gas Project, and the Trans-Asian Gas Pipeline Network.[1] The L. A. Melentev Energy Systems Institute in Irkutsk estimated multilevel, multisectoral models of each program for four regions, eighteen sectors, and twenty-five years.[2] Yet, few of these paper plans were realized.

In the Cold War era, political differences complicated agreement on long-term economic projects. With the onset of economic reform, competition for owner-ship of Russia's resources, the country's weak rule of law, and capital flight led to higher, not lower, levels of political and economic risk. In 1992, with the opening of the Russian market, Western oil and gas producers and equipment suppliers began to seek links to Russia's newly privatizing oil giants. Companies which initiated projects found a chaotic environment with fuzzy property rights and rapidly changing regulations and taxes, so many withdrew after a few unprofitable ventures, convinced that Russian policymakers saw little role for foreign producers in their domestic energy sector.

In the decade following economic reform, the Russian economy received a trickle of foreign direct investment. In 2000, gross flows of financial capital to Russia amounted to $11 billion, but, of this, foreign direct investment totaled only $4.4 billion. Of that modest amount, about 10 percent went to the energy sectors—oil, gas, and electric power.[3]

Investment in offshore oil and gas development on Sakhalin Island's shelf is a crucial exception. By the beginning of 2001, two major Western consortia, called Sakhalin-1 and Sakhalin-2, had committed approximately $1.6 billion to exploration and development of Sakhalin's energy, making direct payments of $67 million into the local Sakhalin Development Fund.

In July 1999, Sakhalin-2 celebrated production of first oil. In 2000, total oil production reached 1.7 million tons. The total cost of the first phase of development of the Piltun-Astokhskii field is estimated to be $733 million, $348 million of which is funded by loans from the European Bank for Reconstruction and Development (EBRD), the U.S. government–funded Overseas Private Investment Corporation (OPIC), and the former Export-Import Bank of Japan, which, in late 1999, merged with several other banks to form the Japan Bank for International Cooperation. Both consortia are seeking commitments from potential consumers of natural gas in Asia, while the Russian government itself has allocated a modest first installment of investment to an extension of the local pipeline network between Sakhalin Island and adjoining Khabarovsk territory to deliver energy to consumers in the Russian Far East.[4]

Although promising, the success of energy development on the Sakhalin shelf is by no means assured, for there are barriers on both the supply and demand sides of the market. Russian policymakers are badly divided on whether to develop their energy sector as part of the international market. In the late 1990s, with world oil selling at $10 a barrel, it seemed that only foreign multinationals could bring in the investment to reverse declining production. However, in 2000–01, with the price of oil at more than $25 a barrel, there are strong pressures from domestic producers to enforce domestic control of energy against foreign participation. At the same time, domestic consumers, whose value-subtracting enterprises depend on hidden subsidies of cheap energy, seek to block export of energy to world markets. Thus, Russia's energy wealth could be a catalyst for regional growth; but, as in other countries, there are also strong protectionist interests that would benefit if high levels of political and economic risk insulate them from foreign competition and preserve their monopoly role in the domestic economy. In September 2000 President Putin visited Sakhalin, promising to speed production-sharing legislation to attract foreign investment and technology into the Russian energy sector. However, in early 2001, the legal framework for resources remained uncertain. Only 3 of the 28 projects approved for production sharing by the Russian Duma were actually underway.

In this chapter, I examine foreign involvement in the energy sector of Sakhalin's shelf, asking several questions: How has the small energy sector of Sakhalin managed to attract major international investment at a time when other Western investors were fleeing from Russia? What strategies do the operating partners use to protect investment from expropriation? How are the benefits and costs of development divided between foreign investors, the Russian Federation government, and local communities?

Then, looking ahead, I inquire: What domestic and foreign developments will determine the directions and prospects of these projects? Can Sakhalin's energy sector play a decisive role in reversing the fortunes of what will otherwise be Russia's declining periphery? More broadly, could a network of pipelines and ports linking energy producers in Russia with consumers in Japan, Korea, and China create links among the economically and politically disparate states of Northeast Asia?

THE RISK OF EXPROPRIATION

Investment on Sakhalin has gone ahead in the face of significant risk. Investors point to high levels of political and economic risk, corruption and illegal activity, fuzzy property rights, weak rule of law, weak corporate governance, and unequal competitive conditions as some of the major impediments to investment. In the case of natural resources, where rights of access are defined and controlled by the federal government, foreign investors lament the lack of a "level playing field," claiming that insider elites with close relationships to government officials gain control of resource rights and the resulting incomes. In the absence of a clear, enforceable framework defining ownership, taxation, and regulation, foreign investors face a high risk of expropriation, either by administrative intervention or by "creeping expropriation" through unpredictable changes in laws, regulations, and taxes.

Businesses, recognizing that they may be subject to "hold up" once their capital is sunk in a host country, undertake many strategies to reduce the costs and risks of expropriation. When a weak legal framework makes third-party enforcement of agreements difficult, parties seek to set up implicit, self-enforcing agreements to provide a framework for cooperation. Agreement is possible when the benefits of continued agreement for both partners are greater than the potential gains to either from deviation, but one of the difficulties of self-enforcing agreements is that each party must have the means to punish a partner who deviates from the contract.

It is in the interest of the host country to alter its own payoffs so that a promise to charge low taxes would clearly be in its own interest. For example, it might post a bond, which would go to the firm if it raised taxes. A country's reputation—reflected in international investment ratings of political and financial risk—provides additional powerful incentives. Reputation is a powerful mechanism for enforcing contracts, because a host country that lives up to agreements and provides a transparent framework of business law gains access to international capital markets on favorable terms. Multinational corporations attempt to spread risk by involving a group of complementary firms and international banks in each project. A consortium can share both risk and information about the reliability of a partner.

Although limited at present, production-sharing legislation in Russia is a potential means for reducing certain sources of risk, such as the risk of arbitrary changes in taxation. Production sharing allows the operating company and the host government to share the price risk of changing costs and prices on the world market. Other mechanisms involve "posting a bond" or holding each other's assets hostage in order to guarantee good performance. For example, revenues from energy sales may be held in escrow, or a domestic firm may accumulate its earnings as equity in a foreign firm in order to balance control of the foreign firm's assets in the home market. Additionally, investors may commit resources gradually so that a host country's short-term incentive to expropriate will be offset by the long-term incentives to gain access to future financing, technology, and know-how.

For a self-enforcing arrangement to work, each party to the agreement at every point in time needs to be better off abiding by the mutual commitment than deviating from it. In an uncertain world where costs and benefits are impacted by unanticipated shocks, it is difficult to negotiate arrangements that will survive every contingency. In the case of Sakhalin, issues of fiscal federalism further complicate formal agreement, because territories that earn increased direct budget revenues are penalized by losing an offsetting amount of federal transfers. Moreover, as the legal owner of the shelf's resources, the federal government may choose to trade the revenue benefits of a current project against the interests of the domestic oil and gas industry—expressed in their lobbying and political support—which may want to hold an option to invest in the future.

Large capital-intensive projects are particularly risky because capital must be sunk before production begins to provide a flow of earnings. Natural gas projects, which extend across national borders and over many years, are exceptionally difficult, because both producers and consumers must commit to long-term guarantees even when they face great uncertainty as to future costs, prices, and technologies.[5] So, even when energy projects offer great potential benefits, there are significant obstacles to their realization.

SAKHALIN'S ENERGY SECTOR

In the Soviet era, Sakhalin Island was a heavily subsidized military outpost, but in the reform period few workers could support themselves in the region's fishing, farming, and forestry industries. Civilian employment fell from 395,000 to 254,000. Population fled to more prosperous regions, and local officials had enormous incentives to stem the decline (see Figure 7.1).

Figure 7.1 Sakhalin Population and Employment

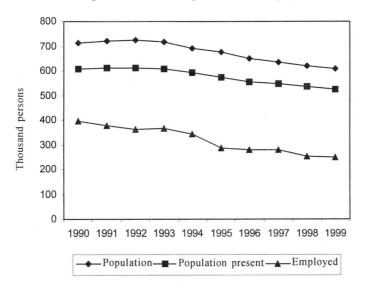

Development of oil and gas promised to serve as a catalyst, generating know-how and employment, and reducing energy costs for the whole region. A case study of development of the Sakhalin shelf provides a test of attempts to build a framework for investment when the domestic setting for contract enforcement is weak.[6]

The oil and gas industry is Sakhalin's oldest. When native people told of a "black lake of death," Russian surveyors in the 1890s found surface deposits of oil on northern Sakhalin. The first well was drilled in 1911. The first oil field with twenty derricks was established in 1928 at Okha, which was soon connected to the coast by railroad and pipeline. From 1965 until the late 1980s, Sakhalin produced about 2.4 million tons of oil per year. Nineteen of these onshore fields are still in operation, although most are nearing the end of their commercial life.

After the oil shock of the early 1970s, the Soviet Union agreed with an international consortium to undertake exploration of offshore sites. Exploratory work began in 1976 with a Japanese consortium, Sodeco. Under terms of the agreement, Japan advanced credits of $176 million, to be repaid only if sufficient fuel was found and the Russian side deemed the fuel profitable. Japan was to receive half of the output. From 1976 to 1982, the project, Sakhalin-1, discovered two fields, Chaivo and Odoptu, but neither field was deemed profitable at the lower fuel prices prevailing in the 1980s.

Subsequently, several additional offshore fields were discovered, including Piltun-Astokhskii, Lunskii, and Arkutun-Dagi. In 1988, the Russian government authorized the Ministry of Oil and Gas to develop the first two of these, but the domestic industry's lack of experience in an arctic offshore environment meant that foreign participation would be required.

In May 1991, Russia invited competitive international bidding for a feasibility study of two large deposits off northeastern Sakhalin—Lunskii and Piltun-Astokhskii. After intense competition between six consortia, a group that included Marathon Oil, McDermott, and Mitsui was chosen to undertake exploration, and a holding company, Sakhalin Energy Investment Company (SEIC) was established. Later, Royal Dutch/Shell and Mitsubishi joined the group and, subsequently, McDermott withdrew. In 2000, Royal Dutch/Shell bought out Marathon, in an exchange of assets, taking over 62.5 percent of SEIC.

The resource stocks that have attracted such intense interest are large, but not giant, and Sakhalin's offshore environment presents sub-arctic conditions, violent storms, and risk of earthquakes. A recent publication by the Sakhalin government estimates total recoverable reserves of oil, gas, and condensate at 99.6 million tons of oil equivalent onshore and 791 million tons on the Sakhalin shelf.[7] This is more than half the size of reserves in Alaska's Prudhoe Bay. However, it appears that three-quarters or more of the reserves of Sakhalin-1 and -2 are natural gas, the consumption of which will require either an expensive pipeline network or facilities to process and transport liquefied natural gas (LNG). Table 7.1 provides a conservative itemization of reserves by individual field, which shows that Pilton-Astokhskii and Odoptu represent the primary stocks of oil and condensate (104 and 70 million tons respectively), while Chaivo and Lunskii are primarily gas fields (147.5 and 350 billion cubic meters). With much of the region still unexplored, recoverable reserves may prove considerably larger.

The four large fields currently under development are:

(1) Odoptu, 15–20 kilometers offshore, in waters 22–40 meters deep;
(2) Chaivo, 12–15 kilometers offshore, in waters 18–32 meters deep;

(3) Lunskii, 112–115 kilometers offshore, in waters 40–50 meters deep. Primarily gas; and

(4) Piltun-Astokhskii, 12–15 kilometers offshore, in waters 26–33 meters deep. Oil and associated gas.

Other fields listed in Table 7.1 are nearing development or awaiting approval of production-sharing legislation.

THE RUSSIAN PARTNERS

The main Russian partners in all prospective projects are Rosneft and Sakhalinmorneftegaz (SMNG). SMNG-shelf, a branch of SMNG, participates separately as a partner in Sakhalin-1. Although most of the Russian oil industry has been privatized into about eight vertically integrated, closed joint-stock companies, Rosneft and SMNG operate as separate, mainly state-owned corporations.

Rosneft is a state oil holding company that controls a miscellaneous assortment of assets that were not integrated into the original twelve vertically integrated, closed joint-stock companies formed after the breakup of the former Soviet Union. Rosneft serves as the exclusive exporter of the federal government's share in all oil production-sharing contracts and runs a vast sales network for refined products. It controls the Komsomolsk-na-Amure oil refinery in Khabarovskii krai, which receives Sakhalin crude oil by pipeline, processes it, and exports half of the products to the Pacific market. Officials of the federal government have announced conflicting plans either to sell the state share of Rosneft or to establish a national oil company in the future. In 1998, low oil prices made Rosneft unprofitable, so it was unable to contribute to development costs of Sakhalin-1, but its financial balance improved as the price of oil rose in 2000, and it is beginning to undertake new investment.

Sakhalinmorneftegaz is a medium-sized oil producer, formed on the basis of a former government production association. It currently produces about 1.49 million tons of oil and 1.78 billion cubic meters of gas annually. SMNG delivers to the Russian market by two pipelines, but two-thirds of its oil production is exported to the world market. It was partially privatized in 1994, when an 18.36-percent stake was sold at a voucher auction and another 0.31 percent of the company's charter capital was sold at a cash auction. In 1995, under a presidential decree, it was amalgamated with Rosneft, which now holds a 51-percent stake in it. In early 1997, SMNG, Rosneft, and ABN-AMRO bank signed an agreement under which the bank would provide $8 billion of a total of $13 billion in capital costs over the lifetime of Sakhalin-1.[8] The Russian partners have also received credits from OPIC, Japan's former Export-Import Bank, and the EBRD.

Table 7.1 Sakhalin Shelf Projects

Project	Fields	Reserves oil (million tons)	Reserves gas (billion meters³)	Operating Company	PSA	Duma list	Members	Investment ($ billion)
Sakhalin-1	Chaivo Odoptu Arkutun-Dagi	310	335	Exxon Neftegas	1995	yes	Exxon, Sodeco, SMNG, Shelf, Rosneft	12
Sakhalin-2	Piltun-Astokhskii Lunskii			Sakhalin Energy (Shell)	1994	yes	Shell, Mitsui, Mitsubishi	10
Sakhalin 3a	Kirinskii Mynginskaia	450	970	Pegastar	yes	yes	ExxonMobil, Rosneft, Texaco	15
Sakhalin 3b	Ayashskii East Odoptinskii	114	513	Exxon Neftegas	no	no	ExxonMobil, Rosneft, Rosneft-SMNG	13.5
Sakhalin-4	Astrakhanovskii Shmidtovskii	115	440	Rosneft, SMNG	yes	yes	Rosneft, SMNG	
Sakhalin-5	East Shmidtovskii	115 30ª	450	BP Amoco	no	no	BP Amoco, Rosneft will tender	
Sakhalin-6	Pogranichnyi	150	200	Pegastar			ExxonMobil, Rosneft, Texaco will tender	

ªMillion tons condensate.

Source: Sakhalin Government, *Neft i gaz Sakhalina,* 1998, Pacific Russia, Oil and Gas Report (Spring 2001).

Recently, new state-owned corporations appeared as Russian bureaucracies vied for control and cash flow rights to oil projects. The Sakhalin regional government set up Sakhalin Oil Company (SOC), which, it argued, should receive a percentage share of ownership in each project without cost. In 1999, Rosneft-SMNG did, in fact, sign over a 10-percent stake in the Kirinskii block to a joint venture with SOC, named Vostok-Shelf.

In spring 2000, a new subsidiary of Rosneft was created, AO Dalneftegas, to represent Russian regional interests in gas development. Fifty-one percent of its shares went to Rosneft and SMNG. The other 49 percent were divided between Rosgasifikatsiia (the gas pipeline contractor) and the regional governments of Khabarovsk, Primorye, and Sakhalin, the primary domestic consumers of natural gas. The agreement stipulates that the Rosneft and SMNG shares of gas production must be delivered to the domestic market—on what terms is not clear. The three regional governments also organized a state pipeline company, Daltrans, to construct pipeline capacity between Sakhalin and the mainland, funding it initially with a federal allocation of 97.5 million rubles ($3.4 million). Then, in 2000, the territorial government established a local gas company, Sakhalingazprom, to develop the onshore Anivskoye gas deposit with the help of a subsidiary of Gazprom.

CURRENT AND FUTURE PROJECTS

Western participants in the first three offshore projects are major international oil companies and a Japanese consortium, Sodeco. Sakhalin-1 brings together Exxon Neftegas (30 percent), Sodeco (30 percent), Rosneft-SMNG (17 percent), and SMNG-shelf (23 percent) in a project to develop Chaivo, Odoptu, and Arkutun-Dagi fields (see Table 7.1).[9] A production-sharing agreement (PSA) was signed in 1995, and work has been underway since 1996. However, the project is still in the exploration phase, meaning that the partners have yet to determine commercial feasibility. After completing 3D seismic surveys and appraisal drilling, Exxon found potential commercial reserves of gas, but development of natural gas would require long-term agreements with consumers before a project could be funded. Exxon has contracted with the Japan Sakhalin Pipeline Study Consortium, which includes Japex, Marubeni, and Itochu, for a pipeline feasibility study. This group is to investigate both a land pipeline route to Northeast China and an underwater pipeline to Hokkaido.

Exxon cancelled exploration drilling during summer 1999 when it failed to reach agreement with the Russian environmental agency, Goskomekologiia, about the treatment of drilling mud and cuttings, but, after the issue was resolved in

2000, drilling at Chaivo-6 showed a "sizeable" oil rim with a potential production rate of 6,000 barrels per day.[10]

The Sakhalin-2 consortium was more fortunate in finding commercial quantities of oil. In July 1999, they began production of early oil under a production-sharing agreement. The operating company, Sakhalin Energy Investment Company, originally brought together Marathon (37.5 percent), Mitsui (25 percent), Mitsubishi (12.5 percent), and Royal Dutch/Shell (25 percent) in developing the Piltun-Astokhskii and Lunskii fields. In 2000, Royal Dutch/Shell bought out Marathon, reselling a portion to Mitsubishi, giving the company 55-percent ownership and increasing Mitsubishi's share to 20 percent. SEIC proposed a phased development of the Piltun-Astokhskii field starting with Astokhskii.[11] In 1999, production started at SEIC's Vityaz complex, which consists of the Molikpaq offshore drilling rig and an adjoining offshore oil storage tanker from which oil tankers offload product for transport to the market. Production began in 1999, and in 2000, output reached 11 million barrels, or 1.4 million metric tons, earning about $300 million and doubling the region's total production.

SEIC has begun development of an onshore natural gas pipeline and an LNG plant with an eventual capacity of 9.6 million metric tons per year. In autumn 2000, it awarded a $10 million contract for technical specifications to the Scientific Research Institute of Gas Processing (Russia), Chiyoda (Japan), and Fluor Daniel (United States). Another $100 million in major contracts were awarded for design of offshore and onshore pipelines, pump and compressor stations, offshore platforms, and an export terminal. In 2001, a $250 million contract for construction of a water-flood module was awarded to Amur Shipbuilding, Khabarovsk.

The new LNG plant will be the first to apply cutting-edge refrigeration from Shell, but demands by the Russian Energy Ministry that technical design parameters include domestic equipment are a serious constraint. An LNG plant on Sakhalin will be able to serve Japan, South Korea, Taiwan, and/or coastal China once the considerable infrastructure for regasification is put in place on the consuming side.

As a primary producer and distributor of LNG in the Pacific, Shell is in a good position to negotiate the long-term purchase commitments that would be required to provide security for investment. Development of natural gas infrastructure intensifies the need to secure commitment against creeping expropriation from all parties, and it raises significant demand-side constraints.

TAXATION AND THE LEGAL FRAMEWORK
FOR USE OF NATURAL RESOURCES

Western interest in the Russian energy sector was delayed by the need to put in place the legal structure for production-sharing agreements similar to those used in most other countries. Production-sharing legislation was intended to simplify the complex and changing tax structure that businesses faced and to divide project risk between the operating companies and the Russian government. In the absence of a production-sharing agreement, projects would face an overwhelming tax burden. They would pay royalties (6–16 percent), geology fund payments (10 percent), VAT (20 percent), and excises (approximately 14 percent) on production or sales; profit tax (38 percent); payments to pension fund (28 percent), state employment fund (2 percent), social insurance (5.4 percent), medical insurance (3.6 percent), education fund (1 percent), militia fund (2 percent), and transport fund (1 percent), plus excess wage tax (38 percent less deduction) on wages bill. On imports there would be customs duty, excise, VAT, and customs clearance. Then there would be property tax (2 percent of assets), land use payments, and, in the case of oil, payments for loss of fish.[12]

Production-sharing agreements simplify the legal framework. The original Russian Federation Law on Production-Sharing Agreements, signed in 1995, allowed the federal government to enter into an agreement with an investor granting the investor exclusive rights to prospect for and extract mineral raw materials from a designated site.[13] A license is to be issued jointly by the Federal Agency for State Mineral Resource Management and the territorial administration. However, international contracts are subject to parliamentary approval, and there are strict domestic content conditions. Moreover, the Russian side reserves the right to make unilateral alterations in arrangements in response to changes in world markets. There are few safeguards for the foreign investor in the event of a dispute. The production-sharing law explicitly exempts the investors, their contractors, and subcontractors from taxes, fees, excises, and other obligatory payments except for profits tax, royalty payments, bonuses, exploration payments (levied on the user of subsoil resources), land use payments, and insurance coverage of Russian employees.

A number of enabling laws and regulations followed, which eliminated many inconsistencies between PSA and preexisting legislation.[14] The Duma placed a cap of 30 percent on the share of sites that could be developed under a PSA in any individual region. For "strategic resources" (such as the Sakhalin shelf), the ceiling was 10 percent. They ruled that 80 percent of employees and 70 percent of inputs should be Russian. In addition, the federal Duma passed a law requiring Duma approval for PSAs and limiting the number of projects that would be eligible. Passage of part I of a new tax code in January 1999 and part II in summer 2000 simplified the tax burden, but part II specifically precludes payment of tax revenue in the form of natural resources.

Russian economic development plans published in 2000 promised an improvement in the tax and regulatory framework, but implementation still lags. Minister of Economic Development German Gref's "Strategy of Russia's Development until 2010" promised changes to protect property rights, provide rule of law, improve state capacity, reform taxes and regulation, and, gradually, provide market-supporting infrastructure. President Putin announced that improvement of production-sharing legislation would be a cornerstone of his proposed measures to attract investment and technology, and instructed a working group headed by Gref to identify legislative barriers to the implementation of PSAs. This working group, which includes top officials of the ministries of energy, natural resources, taxation, justice, and the customs committee, has prepared a list of amendments to PSA legislation, addressing issues including VAT, marine drilling, and customs barriers to export of production. Changes in the leadership of the energy ministry and appointment of a governmental commission headed by Deputy Prime Minister Viktor Khristenko are intended to provide greater executive control over the proposed revisions in policy. Yet, the promised Normative Acts still have not emerged and no new PSA projects have been signed.

Russian tendering of resource stocks is based on a set of model PSAs. Tenders for offshore fields are conducted by the Committee on Geology and Sub-Soil Resources of the Russian Federation (Goskomnedra) and by the Sakhalin administration after authorization by federal decree. For each project, a tender committee of federal and territorial officials considers the bids. Interested firms receive a copy of a model PSA and submit sealed bids by a specified deadline. Submitted bids must include a minimum guaranteed commitment of exploration activity for each of the first five years as well as any proposed changes to the PSA.

The PSA for Sakhalin-4 is an example. It includes a royalty of 8 percent on production and profit tax of 35 percent.[15] There is a cost recovery limit of 80 percent.[16] The share of production depends on a company's accounting of its internal rate of return after payment of profit taxes. At a rate of return lower than 22 percent, the split is 70 percent to the company and 30 percent to the Russian Federation. For rates of return of 22–26 percent, there is a 60–40 split. Above that point, the production split changes by 10 percent for every 2-percent increase in rate of return. Based on long-term projections of production and cost, the model PSA provides a company–Russian Federation division of 55–45.

The Sakhalin-1, -2, and -3 contracts also provide bonus payments to the federal government upon reaching certain milestones, such as initial signing and the start of production. Under the PSAs, each consortium contributes to the Sakhalin Development Fund after a commercial discovery is announced and annually for five years after that. In the case of Sakhalin-2, these early payments were a $15 million signing bonus, $15 million commercial development payment, $16 million reimbursement of Russian exploration costs, and a total of $100 million in payments into the Sakhalin Development Fund over five years. Royalty payments are 6 percent for Sakhalin-2, 8 percent for Sakhalin-1, and 10 percent for Sakhalin-3.[17]

Negotiations between federal authorities and the territorial government determine the division of payments between the federation and territorial governments. The Federation Treaty and Federation Law on Sub-Soil Resources specify a division of royalties that gives the federal government 40 percent, the territory 30 percent, and the local government 30 percent of total payments. Table 7.2 shows Sakhalin's income shares under an agreement negotiated between the Sakhalin administration and the federal government.

The SEIC Development Plan for the Piltun-Astokhskii Field provides the following estimates of Russian government revenues for phase I of the project (prior to development of natural gas reserves—see Table 7.3).

The financial projections of Pegastar for the South Kirinskii portion of Sakhalin-3 are similarly optimistic.[18] If South Kirinskii contains a recoverable reserve of 450 million tons of oil plus 720 billion cubic meters (bcm) of gas, then during peak production the Russian government would receive about $1 billion per year from royalties, taxes, and the sale of profit oil. This would total $20 billion over the life of the project (without discounting).

Although in theory introduction of PSAs should represent a breakthrough, in practice their implementation remains chaotic. Until German Gref's working group succeeds in removing inconsistencies between PSA and other legislation, major barriers will remain.

SAKHALIN ISLAND: A TEST CASE

How did the small energy sector of Sakhalin manage in 1999 to become the second largest recipient of foreign investment in Russia after Moscow? In a number of respects, Sakhalin differs from other resource-rich regions. Its location on Russia's periphery, only 60 kilometers from Japan, gives it strategic importance to Moscow. Moreover, the rapid fall of population from 714,000 to 594,000 between 1990 and 2000 signaled the consequences of Moscow's inability to provide its previous rate of subsidy. Policymakers are therefore concerned with the economic health of Russia's Pacific gateway, recognizing that farming, logging, and fishing could support no more than a small share of the existing population.

Table 7.2 Sakhalin's Percentage of Total Consortium
Payments to Federal, Territorial, and Local Governments

Regional share	Percentage
Sakhalin Development Fund	100
Royalties	50
Bonuses	60
Profit oil	50

Source: Interview with Galina Nikolaevna Pavlova, head of the
Department on Development of Mineral Resources of Sakhalin
Shelf, September 15, 1999.

Table 7.3 SEIC Estimates of Russian Government Revenues from Sakhalin-2
and Portion Paid to the Sakhalin Oblast Government

Estimated Russian income (without discounting)	Total (million U.S. dollars)	Region (million U.S. dollars)
Royalties	417.0	208.5
Profit shares	1,137.5	568.8
Sakhalin Development Fund	100.0	100.0
Exploration reimbursement	160.0	–
Bonuses	30.0	18.0
Profit tax[a]	854.9	581.3
Total Russian income[b]	2,699.3	1,476.6

Notes: [a]Of the 32-percent profits tax on investor income, Sakhalin receives 22 percent.
[b]Of the projected Russian government income of $2.7 billion dollars, $470 million
would be received by 2005. Galina Pavlova, head of the Department on Development
of Mineral Resources of the Sakhalin Shelf, said that she expects the Sakhalin-2
project to generate government revenue of about $500 million by 2005.
Source: Data provided by Sakhalin Energy Investment Company (SEIC).

Moreover, in the past, Sakhalin's remoteness from Moscow weakened the interest of domestic oil and gas interests in blocking foreign involvement in development. Before the rise in oil prices in 2000, the domestic oil industry faced severe capital constraints. Investment in the sector was inadequate even to maintain existing wells and pipelines, so oil production was falling. Gazprom, too, has done little investing in the domestic industry. The natural gas resources of the Sakhalin shelf were separate and distant from Gazprom's network of pipelines linking West Siberia to Europe, and the company's priorities lie elsewhere.

There were technological reasons as well favoring Western companies with experience in offshore development in difficult environments such as Alaska and the North Sea. Russian domestic firms had little such experience. An empirical comparison of Russian and Western oil extraction shows that the Russian industry experienced rapidly declining yields and short reservoir life compared with similar reservoirs in the West. James Smith estimates that Russian producers lost approximately 40 percent of the total economic value of resource stocks compared with similar fields in the West.[19] Policymakers could, therefore, expect foreign development to provide a substantially larger flow of rents to the government budget, and they expected, through strict domestic content rules, to generate a substantial upgrading of the technology of domestic oil equipment and production as well. The local producing firms expected to gain new skills and further employment with Western firms as the local onshore fields were depleted.

Environmental concerns also favored Western involvement. In the past, Russia's oil industry demonstrated a weak environmental record. In an interview conducted by editors of *Petroleum Economist* in 1996, senior executives of Rosneftegazstroi, Russia's premier oil and gas contractor, explained:

> The majority of the pipeline construction projects, except for the trunk ones, did not comply with, or meet, world standards.... No provision was made in the projects for monitoring pipeline conditions during operations.... The inappropriate use of corrosion inhibitors and electrochemical protection units has resulted in high corrosion rates in pipelines.... The lack of on-line pipeline diagnostics has meant it has been difficult to detect damage and so prevent leakage of gas, oil and oil products. As a result, the number of registered accidents at pipelines runs to thousands a year. The number of "insignificant" leaks exceeded 40,000 per year. Instead of the design service life of 15 to 20 years, many in-field pipelines become unserviceable, due to internal corrosion and erosion, within as little as two to five years.[20]

The Russian fisheries industry is concerned with the risk to its important fishery in the Sea of Okhotsk. Local policymakers and scientists reversed their traditional opposition to energy development only after onsite visits to Alaskan offshore fields, such as Cook Inlet, where strict environmental monitoring allows offshore production to coexist with a rich fisheries resource. They were willing to support offshore energy only if similarly strict safeguards were maintained.

THE INTEREST OF WESTERN FIRMS

Large multinational energy companies assume that they must maintain a presence in any country that is both a major producer and a major market for energy, as Russia is. Nevertheless, energy executives found the Russian environment uniquely difficult. In industrialized countries the oil producer finds strong physical and institutional infrastructure, a strong network of suppliers and services, developed financial markets, and an effective legal framework. But there are also many competitors in such markets.

In developing countries, there is little local infrastructure or industrial support, a weak capital market, and an incomplete legal framework. But in these markets, policymakers are open to modernization and are willing to construct physical and institutional infrastructure to foster development. In these countries, the formation of strong relationships can create a relatively stable business environment for a firm and provide some barriers to competition.

The Russian environment, in which there is a large and politically powerful domestic oil and gas industry that has incentives to block foreign competition, represents a third case. Russia also has a large body of administrative regulation and practice, most of which is unproductive in a modern, competitive business environment. New legislation that reflects world practice contradicts past administrative law. When the two legal frameworks conflict, administrators usually follow past administrative practice.

In spite of these difficulties, Western firms were attracted to Sakhalin because they could have direct access to the Pacific market without facing potential hold-up by Transneft, the Russian government pipeline monopoly. They expected production-sharing legislation to establish a secure framework of taxation, eliminating some of the opportunities for creeping expropriation of potential rents. On this score, they have been disappointed.

Western firms have the ability to impose some potential penalties (or to withhold some benefits) in the face of expropriation. They can easily transfer their centralized technologies, skilled personnel, and support services to numerous other projects around the world. The potential loss of Russian employment would be concentrated on skilled industrial workers and manufacturing capacities, which bore the sharpest drop in demand after the collapse of the Soviet Union. Moreover, offshore production facilities have some physical mobility: if production were terminated, Sakhalin Energy Investment Company could physically remove its oil storage facility, the tanker Okha, and even its oil-drilling platform, the Molikpaq, which was towed to the Pacific from Newfoundland.

Investment in natural gas production and transmission facilities, on the other hand, would be sunk costs. Still, the presence of Exxon and Shell on both sides of the market will lower transaction costs and provide some leverage.

IMPLEMENTATION ISSUES

Interviews with oil company executives, subcontractors, and government officials in September 1999 revealed frequent examples of what might be called "hold-up" problems. However, companies anticipated many of these problems and were prepared to deal with them—albeit at a considerable cost. In some ways, they said, the Sakhalin environment is like a "tragedy of the commons," with each regulatory agency trying to hold up the project for a piece of the rent. One executive of a company drilling an exploratory well listed 32 permits and licenses that were required before drilling could start. "None of these permits is trivial," he said. "Each requires reports, fees, and negotiations. Each agency can shut down everything." Often the problem has been competition between agencies with overlapping jurisdictions, which had conflicting requirements. On environmental issues, the environmental agency Goskomekologiia, the Committee for Sanitary-Epidemiological Oversight, and the Oblast Shelf Department often have three conflicting views. There are cases in which federal authorities at the center overrule both the territorial branch of the same federal agency and Sakhalin's own regulatory agency. For example, both the local branch of the Ministry for Emergency Situations and the Coast Guard Agency of the Ministry of Transport have been developing a system for oil spill response, so they objected when federal authorities insisted on a totally new, centrally directed program.

Clearly, there is a necessary role for environmental, health, and safety regulation: however, on Sakhalin, more than 40 percent of the civilian-employed population is in government service. The Director of Environmental Programs for one project estimated the annual extra costs of getting approvals and permits at nearly $500,000. Still, this is a relatively minor impediment compared with other sources of uncertainty. The oil companies accept that a large part of the potential rents will be eaten up by regulation, so they make some effort to direct these overhead expenditures toward activities that will benefit the community, such as enhancement of fisheries stocks or social welfare programs. Yet, one company executive estimated that 95 percent of the regulatory delays were due not to local, but to federal, authorities.

Some of the rulings by federal agencies have threatened the foundations of the production-sharing legislation. Although the 1995 production-sharing law specifically exempts project equipment from the Russian VAT, the Customs Authority levied VAT on all equipment imports. By mid-1999, more than $70 million in illegal VAT had been collected. The Tax Authority promised that investors would be allowed to add VAT to the capital cost of the project before calculating profits, but this capture of taxes up-front before the projects produced any income sabotaged the timing of bonuses and payments to the Sakhalin government. (In 2000, the federal government began repaying VAT collected illegally after project managers postponed distribution of royalty payments pending return of VAT.)

In addition, collapse of the Russian banking system in August 1998 disrupted project accounts. Many foreign companies lost the balances in their local hard currency accounts. One company, which had just transferred $10 million in payments into a Russian bank, lost the full amount when the bank went bankrupt.

On September 21, 1999, the tanker Seamaster loaded the first 81,000 tons of Sakhalin oil to transport to Korea. However, before it could set out, the Far Eastern Directorate of the Customs Authority issued a ruling that since SEIC was not a joint venture, it did not have the authority to export oil. In this case, too, the Customs ruling was directly contradicted by production-sharing legislation, which guarantees the right to export product. SEIC ultimately was able to export its oil, but the possibility that export rights could be blocked in contradiction to PSA legislation remains a concern.

SEIC's strategy is to try to ensure that the government, and especially the territorial government, derives a substantial, predictable income from the project in every period beginning well before the project itself generates a flow of income. Yet the implicit possibility of withdrawal comes up each time a serious problem arises.

OWNERSHIP ISSUES

Resource projects are considerably more complicated when there is joint foreign-Russian ownership. Rosneft and SMNG, which are obligatory partners in most projects, were initially unable to contribute to project costs. Difficulties sometimes arise when SMNG or its subsidiaries want to function as project subcontractor, receiving payment from Exxon. Such a dual role makes it difficult to enforce cost and quality constraints on work. A recent ownership issue is the founding of Sakhalin Oil Company, owned by the Sakhalin oblast administration and administered by the Shelf Department of the administration. If the oblast administration receives its royalty oil and gas in kind, SOC plans to be marketing agent as well. It also intends to construct a local refinery.[21]

THE MARKET FOR SAKHALIN ENERGY

Sakhalin's oil and gas condensate can find a ready market in the Pacific without influencing world prices. At 2–3 million tons per year, RFE total annual production is less than one percent of Japanese total consumption of 255 million tons. The main barriers to oil export are domestic taxes and regulations. Russian export taxes have changed frequently. In 2001, they were set at 34 euros per ton (about $4.50 per barrel of oil). Export regulations (currently quotas) restrict the share of refined products that may be exported, requiring refiners to sell most of their output on the domestic market at low internal prices.

At 929 million tons, total Asian consumption of oil products in 1999 accounted for about one-fourth of world demand (roughly equal to U.S. total consumption). Production of oil and condensate on Sakhalin is projected to rise from 2 million to 8.5 million tons in 2005, and to 16.2 million tons in 2010, bringing total RFE production (including Sakha) to about 18 million tons in 2010, still less than 2 percent of total Asian consumption.

In contrast to oil, designing successful natural gas projects will be much more difficult. Small and large LNG projects have roughly similar average costs, but the average costs of supplying pipeline gas fall sharply as the size of the project increases. The largest single element in cost is the pipeline itself. So the average cost of pipeline gas falls rapidly until production rates equal about 20.5 bcm per year. In order to gain potential economies of scale, a natural gas pipeline from Sakhalin would need to be more than ten times larger than the current pipeline delivering natural gas to Khabarovsk, which was built in 1942. Moreover, to supply this rate of output for twenty-five years, a natural gas reservoir would need to have about 800 bcm of gas. The willingness of SEIC and Exxon to move forward with separate gas programs indicates they believe that reserves are large enough to support two separate projects and that currently published reserve estimates understate potential stocks.

There are also significant constraints on the demand side. Most natural gas consumption in Asia is in the form of LNG. In 1998 the largest Asian importers of LNG were Japan (69.5 bcm) and South Korea (15.6 bcm). China supplied most of its natural gas consumption of 19.3 bcm. Before investing in natural gas projects, capital markets require firm, long-term contracts and a strong legal framework.

Where are the markets for Sakhalin's natural gas? Its closest neighbor, Japan, pays the highest energy prices of any industrialized country, although with current low rates of growth, Japan has weak short-run incentives to seek new energy sources. Nevertheless, Japan is rich in capital, and access to pipeline gas would give Japan substantial savings on energy costs.

In contrast, China's economic growth has exceeded 9 percent per year for the past decade. It pays heavy environmental costs for the high share of coal in its current energy balance. With natural gas accounting for less than 2 percent of total energy consumption, China has strong economic and environmental reasons to increase the share of gas in its expanding consumption, but domestic price controls and regulations make investment unprofitable. South Korea, too, seems to be returning to rapid growth after the Asian financial crisis. Its focus on production of heavy industrial products means that several of its industries are energy-intensive. In the past, Korea has tried to foster growth by providing industry with access to low-cost energy, but its domestic gas market is still too small to support a pipeline alone.

The Russian Far East economy itself is a potential market for energy. In the Soviet era, when the relative prices of energy products were one-tenth or less of world prices, the region was a heavy consumer of energy for metallurgy, military machine building, fishing, and timber. Producers faced high fixed costs for district heating in a severe climate. Today, the region's industries seek access to energy on heavily subsidized terms, but they are unable or unwilling to cover its costs. Their presence increases the likelihood that Russia would have incentives to expropriate all or part of the production after the fixed capital is in place, contributing to the risk that investors foresee.

If prospects for RFE natural gas extraction depend on firm long-term international contracts, then prospective domestic demand complicates, rather than resolves, future market conditions. Currently, SMNG delivers natural gas to power stations and municipal, industrial, and government installations at prices that are well below its costs. In July 1999, net price equaled approximately $7–$8 per thousand cubic meters (equivalent to less than $.20 per million cubic feet, or less than half of cost), with the net of VAT and excise taxes collected at the rate of 24 rubles per dollar of revenue.[22] Mikhail Korchemkin estimates that about two-thirds of natural gas consumers pay for their gas, and the remaining one-third accumulates arrears, which after the fact turn out to be an in-kind subsidy.[23] (In the case of oil, Rosneft compensates SMNG for nonpayments in Khabarovsk by giving it the right to export one million tons of West Siberian oil, acquired under mandatory sales to the federal government, to western Europe.) Under Russian law, it is illegal for energy suppliers to halt supply to government and strategic consumers.

Sakhalin's natural gas could flow to one or more of these potential demanders, but there are barriers to be overcome in each case. Japan is the region's largest gas market, accounting for more than a third of all gas sales in the Pacific and more than three-quarters of regional LNG demand.[24] However, Hikaru Yamada and Arlon Tussing argue that the most serious obstacle to the introduction of piped gas (or even expanded use of LNG) is Japan's lack of an internal gas transmission and distribution network together with the high level of stranded costs that existing energy utilities would bear if lower cost energy suppliers were to emerge.[25] Currently, they claim, Japan is at a serious competitive handicap, with LNG imported at twenty widely dispersed and unconnected terminals. A network of open-access gas pipelines could link LNG import terminals with one another and with industrial and population centers. Without such links, Japan lacks the flexibility to shift supply from high-value district heating to interruptible industrial uses. Still, if Japan could open its energy market to competitive sources of supply, it might lower its energy costs to half of present levels.

Between 1989 and 1997, the Mitsubishi Research Institute organized the National Pipeline Research Society of Japan to study the feasibility of a pipeline system. The society, whose corporate members included Japan's main gas and electric companies and energy equipment manufacturers, drafted the design of a major gas trunk line system for Japan. This plan could serve as a blueprint for the improvement of Japan's gas transmission system. The feasibility study, initiated by Exxon and prepared by the Japan Sakhalin Pipeline Company for an undersea pipeline route to Hokkaido, increases the probability that pipeline gas would be directed first to Japan.

Accessing the Chinese market presents slightly different problems. China's energy balance is still heavily influenced by central planning, price controls, and the policies of China's energy monopolies, China National Petroleum Corporation (CNPC), China Petroleum Corporation (Sinopec), China National Offshore Oil Corporation, and (recently) China National Star Petroleum Corporation. Currently, China's Prime Minister Zhu Rongji is promoting a program to import LNG into southern China. Construction has started on a 3-million-ton-per-year import terminal in Guangdong that will link the cities of Shenzen, Dougguan, and Guangzhou by a 400-km pipeline. Royal Dutch/Shell, a partner in Sakhalin-2, is expected to play a lead role in finding markets for Sakhalin's LNG. Yet, questions remain as to who will fund the costs of building municipal infrastructure to provide gas supply.

Meanwhile, Sakhalin-1 is focusing on the potential of pipeline gas, exploring the options of a pipeline from southern Sakhalin to Hokkaido or a line to the Russian mainland and, from there, to Northeast China or South Korea. For all of the major customers in Asia—Japan, China, and South Korea—Sakhalin's natural gas could be supplied sooner and at lower cost than alternative sources from Irkutsk (including Kovyktinsk), the Viliusk Basin of Sakha, or the Sobinsk field in Krasnoyarsk.

If strong institutional infrastructure were in place to support long-term international energy contracts, then Russian producers and Asian consumers could enjoy major benefits from access to low-cost energy. Northeast Asia could enjoy something of an energy boom. However, until the legal framework is strengthened, these projects may remain pipe dreams.

On economic, technological, and environmental grounds, there is a strong case for a rising share of natural gas in the energy mix in Northeast Asia. Elsewhere, the natural gas share of world energy supply has increased from one-fifth to one-fourth over the past decade. Japan, South Korea, and China account for almost one-quarter of the world's population but only four percent of world consumption of natural gas.[26] Between 1986 and 1997, Northeast Asia's total energy consumption grew at five percent per year. Extrapolations based on this past rate seem unrealistic in the wake of the Asian financial crisis, yet even at lower rates of increase, total energy demand in these three countries is likely to exceed either U.S. or European Union energy consumption by 2010, accounting for more than a quarter of global consumption.

ISSUES AND POLICIES FOR FOREIGN PARTNERS

Development of Sakhalin's offshore energy has moved ahead with Western involvement because the Russian domestic industry had relatively little experience in an arctic offshore environment, because the Russian Federation government hoped to stem the exodus of population from its gateway to the Pacific, and because the region's fishing and maritime industries feared that Russia's domestic oil and gas producers would damage the valuable Pacific fishery if they undertook development alone.

Both parties to Sakhalin-1 and Sakhalin-2 have adopted strategies to make agreement possible and to protect themselves against "hold up." The Russian government tendered the offshore fields in separate agreements. It tried to ensure that each project would have both an oil and a gas resource, which could be developed in sequence.

The Western partners designed production-sharing agreements to provide a steady flow of benefits to the local government in each period. As cost escalation has threatened this goal, Western advisors and the Sakhalin government are designing a development bank which would allow the territory to borrow money to fund infrastructure projects, with repayment guaranteed by future oil and gas revenues.

Investment is phased in over time, so that the government must trade off the short-run gain from expropriation against the long-term loss of future investment. With current high world oil prices, concerns about capital have lessened. However, institutional barriers, which have been overcome in the case of oil extraction, will be more difficult in the case of a large-scale natural gas pipeline. Both Japanese and South Korean energy companies express interest in a multilateral governmental agreement providing investment guarantees. (China, on the other hand, appears to want to negotiate bilaterally with Russia.)

Although there are clear revenue-sharing rules for the division of royalties, profits, and profit-oil between the companies and the federal and territorial governments, in practice the federal government uses its regulatory powers to impose in-kind taxes on energy producers and to give certain energy users in-kind subsidies. The prohibition against export forces producers to sell at low domestic prices, and the obligatory delivery of natural gas to nonpaying users creates enormous in-kind taxes and subsidies. Thus, the main risk to energy projects is not outright, but hidden, expropriation.

A survey of problems arising during implementation suggests that even relatively minor issues, such as the procedure for disposal of drilling mud, can threaten a whole project. However, the main barrier that needs to be overcome, at least in the case of natural gas, is the willingness of foreign partners to view Russia as a reliable long-term supplier. Until Russia overcomes these perceptions of high political and economic risk, potential foreign partners will be reluctant to invest in the infrastructure to consume Russian gas, and international capital markets will be reluctant to finance the pipelines to deliver gas.

In the long run, the Western policy agenda should include the possible establishment of a multilateral mechanism providing investment guarantees for large multilateral projects. All of Northeast Asia would benefit from a network of pipelines and ports linking energy producers in Russia and elsewhere with consumers in Japan, Korea, and China. Sakhalin is poised to play a catalytic role in initiating cooperation, particularly in the large Japanese market, but, as always, the devil is in the details.

APPENDIX: ENERGY PRODUCTION

Appendix 7A: RFE Oil Production
(million barrels)

	Far East total	Sakhalin	Republic of Sakha	East Siberia
1985	2,632.0	2,597.0	35.0	0.0
1986	2,492.7	2,451.8	40.9	0.0
1987	2,477.0	2,408.2	68.8	0.0
1988	2,165.1	2,084.9	80.2	0.0
1989	2,208.0	2,119.5	88.5	2.3
1990	2,026.0	1,918.0	108.0	4.6
1991	1,890.1	1,771.1	119.0	49.1
1992	1,809.4	1,677.4	132.0	3.0
1993	1,696.0	1,561.0	135.0	1.0
1994	1,769.6	1,626.6	143.0	78.0
1995	1,908.7	1,723.7	185.0	108.0
1996	1,873.3	1,662.3	211.0	100.0
1997	1,950.0	1,720.3	230.0	100.0
1998	1,935.0	1,695.9	239.0	–

Source: Goskomstat, Promyshlennost, Neftedobyvaiushchaya promyshlennost

Appendix 7B: RFE Natural Gas Production (Including Gas Condensate)
(million cubic meters)

	Far East	Sakhalin	Republic of Sakha
1985	1,826.0	809.0	1,017.0
1986	1,955.3	807.3	1,148.0
1987	2,269.8	945.1	1,324.7
1988	2,909.5	1,581.8	1,327.7
1989	3,375.2	2,016.2	1,359.0
1990	3,234.3	1,832.3	1,402.0
1991	3,416.2	1,888.2	1,528.0
1992	3,268.0	1,730.0	1,538.0
1993	3,204.7	1,618.7	1,586.0
1994	3,115.1	1,481.1	1,634.0
1995	3,303.5	1,636.5	1,667.0
1996	3,414.0	1,790.0	1,624.0
1997	3,420.7	1,843.7	1,577.0
1998	3,366.7	1,862.7	1,552.0
1999	–	1,763.6	–

Source: Goskomstat, Regiony Rossii 1999.

NOTES

1. Keun Wook Paik, *Gas and Oil in Northeast Asia: Policies, Projects and Prospects* (The Royal Institute of International Affairs, Energy and Environmental Programme, 1995); Kengo Asakura, "Concept for a Natural Gas Pipeline That Will Support Asia's Symbiosis," *Energy* (November 1998).

2. Iu. D. Kononov, E. V. Gal'perova, O. V. Mazurova, V. V. Posekalin, *Energoemkost' ekonomiki i tseny na energonositeli: Global'nye tendentsii* (Irkutsk: Institut Sistem Ekergetiki im. L. A. Melent'eva SO RAN, 1999).

3. Juhani Laurila, "FDI and the Russian Energy Sector: An Ill-Managed Partnership?" Bank of Finland, *Russian Economy: The Month in Review*, April 6, 2001.

4. Goskomstat Rossii, *Regiony Rossii: Informatsionno-statisticheskii sbornik*, vol. 1 (Moscow: Goskomstat Rossii, 1997), 180.

5. Moreover, the structure of a natural gas agreement is a bilateral monopoly, creating strong incentives to seek some form of vertical integration.

6. In September 1999, I visited Sakhalin to interview executives of Western energy firms, subcontractors, local government officials, and academic specialists. I asked what strategies the firms and policymakers used to establish agreements, resolve disputes, and minimize the risk of outright or creeping expropriation, and what benefits each party expected to receive from the projects. In the ensuing year and a half, it has been possible to see how both sides to these agreements attempted to resolve disputes.

7. Goskomstat Rossii, *Regiony Rossii*, 123.

8. Sakhalinmorneftegas, *Company Report* (ISI Emerging Markets: April 1997).

9. Former Rosneft executives also hold part of Rosneft's shares in Sakhalin-1, although they are under pressure to contribute to project funding or relinquish their shares.

10. See discussion in *Gubernskie Vedomosti*, March 24, 2000 and April 19, 2000 (excerpted by *Sakhalin Oil and Gas News Service*, Pacific Russia Information Group LLC, 2415 La Honda Drive, Anchorage, AK 999517).

11. "Sakhalin Energy Investment Company Ltd. Development Plan for Phased Development of Piltun-Astokhskoye Field" (processed draft).

12. Tax estimates provided by Sakhalin government authorities, September 1999.

13. Russian Federation Law No. 224-FL on Production-Sharing Agreements, December 30, 1995, cited in *Rossiiskaia gazeta*, January 11, 1996, 3–4.

14. The President's Decree on Measures for Enforcement of the Federal Law on Production-Sharing Agreements, issued in 1997, allowed the Ministry of Finance and the State Tax Committee to establish taxes. The Federal Law on Amendments and Additions to the Russian Federation Legislative Acts, passed in February 1999, amended twelve federal laws to remove inconsistencies with PSA legislation.

15. The tax data provided by Jack Holton, "Sakhalin: Giant Reserves and Hungry Markets," *Gas in the Former Soviet Union* (Petroleum Economist, 1993).

16. Cost recovery refers to the share of initial investment and development costs incurred by the Western firm that will be reimbursed from product sales prior to the division of net revenues between taxes and net profit shares.

17. Data from a discussion with Michael Allen, Director, American Business Center, Sakhalin. August 15, 2000, at the Foundation for Russian American Economic Cooperation, Seattle, Wash.

18. Sakhalin Government, *Neft i gaz Sakhalina* (Sakhalin government: 1998), 172–73.

19. James Smith, "Cost of Lost Production in Russian Oil Fields," *Energy Journal* 16, no. 2:25–33.

20. Interviewed in a sponsored supplement, "Seeking Western Involvement for Rebuilding and New Developments," *Petroleum Economist* (January 1996): 10–14. In September 1999, I talked with the head of an environmental remediation firm who reported that in Komi, en route to inspect a major oil spill, he counted sixteen other pipeline leaks in the space of thirty kilometers. Author's interview on Sakhalin Island, September 1999.

21. Interview with Galina N. Pavlova, head of the Department on Development of Mineral Resources of the Sakhalin Shelf, Sakhalin administration, September 15, 1999.

22. Mikhail Korchemkin, "Local Gas Pricing Hurts Sakhalin Gas Export," *Oil and Gas Journal* 19 (July 1999):61.

23. Although Khabarovsk consumers were making partial payments, one Sakhalin source estimated that Khabarovsk had accumulated more than one year of arrears in nonpayments for oil as well as gas.

24. Alan Troner, "Russian Far East Natural Gas Searches for a Home," *Oil and Gas Journal*, March 5, 2001, 68–72.

25. Hikaru Yamada and Arlon Tussing, "Japanese Gas Pipeline Grid Mapped Out: Seeking U.S. Help," *Natural Gas Journal* (May 1998).

26. British Petroleum, *World Energy Statistics*, 1999.

8

Agrarian Reform and Agricultural Productivity in the Russian Far East

Jennifer Duncan and Michelle Ruetschle

The agricultural sector in the Russian Far East employs eight percent of the regional labor force. Primary crops are soybeans, oats, wheat, barley, potatoes, tomatoes, cucumbers, cabbage, and livestock fodder. Meat, milk, eggs, and honey are also produced in the RFE.[1] Agriculture in the RFE accounts for 1 percent of the total grain production in the Russian Federation, 5 percent of the potato and vegetable production, 50 percent of the honey production, and 74 percent of the soybean production.[2]

Soviet policies from the 1960s through the 1980s propelled the expansion of agricultural production in the region through the creation of very large collective and state farms. The total amount of plowed land in the RFE peaked at 2,756,000 hectares in 1988, bolstered by heavy subsidies from Moscow that propped up agriculture.[3] Even while highly subsidized, however, the collective and state farms were unable to produce at the level realized in countries with private land ownership and market economies.[4] Natural limitations, including mountains, forests, and a severe climate, restrict agricultural production in the RFE to narrow bands of land in the south, mostly in Amurskaia oblast, Primorskii krai, Khabarovskii krai, and the Jewish autonomous oblast. Amur accounts for nearly 60 percent of the arable land in the RFE, and one-half of the region's agricultural production.[5] The area of land under agricultural production in the RFE has substantially decreased since the reduction of state subsidies in the early 1990s. Out of 1,760,000 hectares of arable land in

Amurskaia oblast, for example, only 600,000 hectares were in production in 1999 (a decrease of 200,000 hectares since 1997).[6]

Though it is doubtful, given difficult climatic conditions, that the RFE will ever be able to fully support its population with agricultural production, several factors indicate that the Russian Far East has not, at least since collectivization, produced at even a fraction of its potential. Although many areas of the RFE may be unsuitable for crop production, the Amur River valley contains some of the most fertile soil in Russia. Some agricultural land in Amurskaia oblast, for example, is considered equally as valuable for agricultural production as the "black earth" areas of western Russia.[7] It seems quite possible, then, that this area could produce a wheat yield on par with that realized in countries with similar growing conditions, like Canada or Finland (roughly between 2.2 and 2.7 tons per hectare). Historian John Stephan has attributed the failure of the RFE to achieve self-sufficiency in foodstuffs during the Soviet era to human error, such as the misuse of machinery and repeated failures to deliver produce on time. This resulted in a widespread, progressive failure of agriculture in Amur, which he described in these terms: "Once the bread-basket of the Far East, the Amur District in the early 1980s had one of the worst production rates in the USSR."[8]

One final curious note pointing to the potential for higher yields in the RFE is that in 1913, peasant farmers in Amurskaia oblast produced 0.9 tons of grains per hectare and 7.4 tons of potatoes, using completely manual labor. These grain yields were only 0.1 tons per hectare less than yields produced in the oblast from 1986 to 1990; potato yields were only 3.5 tons less per hectare than those produced from 1986 to 1990.[9]

The RFE relies heavily on imports of agricultural products, leaving it vulnerable to fluctuations in the exchange rate and protectionist measures taken by agricultural regions in western Russia.[10] Both the Russian government and the international press have reported potential food shortages and hunger in the Russian Far East as recently as 1999, which has become one of the central rationales put forward by Russia and donor governments for emergency food aid to Russia.[11]

SUMMARY OF THE AGRARIAN REFORM PROCESS IN THE RFE

A series of laws and decrees issued in 1991 ushered in the privatization process in the agricultural sector in Russia.[12] As a result of the reforms, the majority of land held by collectives and state farms should have been transformed into land shares privately owned by farm members.[13] Some of this land was later withdrawn by shareowners to start peasant (farm) enterprises (PFEs). A portion of land from each collective also went to the raion land redistribution fund, to be reallocated by the raion governments to PFEs. Finally, the reforms left house-hold plots under the control of individual families, and provided for full own-ership rights to these plots.

Agrarian reform legislation also called for privatization of non-land assets of collective and state farms.[14] This legislation directs state and collective farms to determine the value of their total non-land assets (known as property shares) by deducting net liabilities from net assets, then dividing this total net value into shares among several categories of people, including farm workers, workers tem-porarily absent from the farm, and pensioners. Shares to eligible individuals were to be determined by their former contribution to the fund (e.g., by the relative amount of hours they had worked). Persons withdrawing from a collective or state farm have the right to withdraw their property share in kind. While most farms originally completed the process of dividing up non-land property and assigning monetary value to individual shares, they have often prohibited indi-viduals from withdrawing a reasonable property share in kind.

Following privatization, three types of agricultural producers emerged in the private agricultural sector: large agricultural enterprises; peasant farm enterprises; and household auxiliary plot owners.

Large Agricultural Enterprises

Agricultural enterprises are former collective farms now registered as agricultural production cooperatives, joint stock companies, limited liability companies, or, in some cases, even (mistakenly) PFEs.[15] Most of these farms have barely changed in structure or productivity, with only a cosmetic name change and the distribution of shares (on paper) to reflect any movement toward privatization. One former collec-tive we visited had managed to make more significant changes through a radical change in leadership, transforming from a failing business in 1995 to a fairly suc-cessful enterprise. Such instances are rare, however, indicated by the wry observa-tion of an oblast official in Amur that "finding failing former collectives would not be difficult." In 1998, Khabarovskii krai had 58 agricultural enterprises (down from 76 in 1993), and Amurskaia oblast had 54 such enterprises.[16]

One typical former collective we visited in Khabarovskii krai consisted of 11,000 hectares, all of which were under production in 1999. It was negotiating to acquire more of the neighboring land: however, this was difficult because that land was divided into shares and required the consent of numerous shareowners. The enter-prise had undergone some reorganization in 1991, when the collective's land was converted into shares. In 1999, the enterprise rented shares from 500 people, while only 280 people worked on the farm. The enterprise has three-year rental contracts with the shareholders, many of whom are pensioners. Rental compensation was in kind, in the form of one ton of grain per year, as well as in various services, such as transportation and plowing of household plots. Workers were paid additional monthly wages, including advance and post-harvest payments, and received favorable purchase rates for farm produce.

This enterprise, like many throughout Russia, is slowly failing.[17] Workers are not paid on time, and may only be paid in-kind after harvest. Many enterprises have had their bank accounts frozen for failure to make timely payments to government budgets, which has forced those enterprises to operate almost completely through barter arrangements. In 1997, one Khabarovskii krai official estimated that perhaps 50 percent of all agricultural enterprises in the krai had their bank accounts frozen pursuant to a 1996 Presidential Decree.[18]

While large agricultural enterprises use the majority of the RFE's agricultural land, these enterprises generally do not own the land. Rather, it is owned in common by individual shareowners, who are permitted to dispose of their shares by permanently contributing them to the enterprise charter capital; temporarily contributing them (for use) to the enterprise; leasing them to the enterprise or to a peasant farm; or withdrawing them to create a peasant farm, add to an existing peasant farm, or to augment an existing small plot. Some 108 million hectares, or 49 percent of Russia's 222 million hectares of agricultural land, were transferred into private ownership through land shares in the early to mid-1990s.[19]

The majority of land share owners in the Russian Far East have been unable to formally dispose of their shares, and enterprise management continues to use them with no written agreement with the shareowner.[20] For example, one female pensioner interviewed in the village of Korsakovo near Khabarovsk suspected that her land was being used but did not dare to request compensation from the boss of her former collective farm. This same woman was also unable to afford the cost to ascertain the location of her land by a surveyor. Based on this and other fieldwork findings, the absence of a written agreement often signifies that lessors/land share owners are in fact receiving little if any compensation for use of their land by the enterprise.

Peasant Farm Enterprises

Peasant farms occupy about six percent of Russia's agricultural land, and represent roughly six percent of all agricultural households. The relative size of the peasant farm sector in the RFE roughly mirrors that of Russia as a whole, although the average size of PFEs appears greater in the Russian Far East. In Amurskaia oblast, for example, the average size of a PFE was 148 hectares in 1999, according to official statistics. This average could be inflated and misleading, however, due to the registration of some large former collectives as PFEs. Most PFE members interviewed were formerly collective farm members who had withdrawn their shares from the collective, often also leasing or purchasing additional land.

A consolidation trend has emerged within the peasant farm sector in the Russian Far East, as in the rest of Russia, where the amount of land owned and leased by peasant farms has increased while the number of peasant farms has decreased slightly.[21] This consolidation trend has been especially prominent in Amur, where the number of PFEs decreased from 2,783 in 1993 to 1,926 in 1999 (a 31-percent decrease). Peasant farm enterprises possessed an aggregate of 333,497 hectares of arable land (not all of which was in production) in the oblast in 1993, compared with 284,534 hectares in 1999 (a decrease of only 15 percent). The result is an increase in average farm size from 120 hectares in 1993 to 148 hectares in 1999.[22]

In Khabarovskii krai, however, PFE land holdings have not consolidated as they have elsewhere in Russia. The number of PFEs in the krai decreased from 1,850 in 1993 to 886 in 1999 (a 52-percent decrease). Aggregate land holdings by PFEs fell from 45,451 hectares of arable land in 1993 to 18,059 hectares in 1999 (a decrease of 60 percent), signaling a *slight* decrease in average peasant farm size. One reason for this deviation from the national trend may be the high concentration of PFEs producing livestock rather than crops. Since livestock production requires less arable land mass than crop production, a consolidation of resources among fewer farms may not necessarily be reflected in consolidation of land.

On one PFE that we visited in Khabarovskii krai, the farmer had to travel some distance to his farm of 98 hectares. He began his PFE in 1992 by purchasing virgin land from the rural administration. He purchased land in parts, beginning with 30 hectares of land and gradually expanding with additional applications to the rural administration for more land. With his first 1,000 rubles of profit, the farmer purchased some machinery. The farmer was deeply discouraged by fuel prices, and feared that his farm would fail as a result. Competition with middlemen purchasing cheaper potatoes from Amur made it impossible to maintain a competitive price and still account for the additional fuel costs. The farmer raised pigs and grew potatoes and soy; however, he was unable to slaughter the 20 pigs he had prepared for sale because he could not afford the fuel to transport them to the market. He was also unable to afford the fuel necessary to harvest and transport his soy crop.

Reasons for reductions in numbers of peasant farms and the amount of land they control may include limited access to machinery by the smaller farms, receipt of poor quality land from the land redistribution fund (rendering small-scale, intensive farming more difficult), and a formal deregistration of many PFEs, whose owners now continue their farming activities in the informal sector. Peasant farms in the RFE that have grown in size have generally done so by leasing land from either shareowners on agricultural enterprises or from the land fund.

Small Plots

Household auxiliary plots (or "small plots," which include garden plots, household vegetable plots attached to houses in former collective villages, and household vegetable plots located in a field some distance away from the family house) constitute the most efficiently used agricultural land in the Russian Far East. Almost all interviewees obtained a significant portion of their daily subsistence food from their household plots.

The only sector in which a nearly functional land market is emerging in the RFE, and in Russia as a whole, is that of small plots, which have been "owned" in the full sense for almost seven years. The minimal capital requirements for small plot cultivation contribute to higher market demand for small plot land. The ability to transact small plots has allowed their allocation to efficient users, and has probably facilitated sustained high levels in production on these plots over the past decade. More importantly, tenure security has encouraged more hard work and investment on the land.

Household plots are larger in the RFE than in Russia as a whole, reflecting the high ratio of arable land per RFE resident. In Khabarovsk, for example, garden plots are 1,200 square meters on average, compared with 600 square meters in Moscow oblast. In Khabarovsk and in Amur, as in the rest of Russia, household plots produce a great quantity of high-value crops, such as vegetables and potatoes. In Russia, small plots represent only about 3 percent of all agricultural land, but account for significant percentages of total agricultural output for many crops, including potatoes (90 percent); vegetables (77 percent); meat (52 percent); milk (45 percent); and eggs (31 percent).[23] In Khabarovskii krai, the estimated contribution from small plots (which occupy 10,000 hectares, or only 10 percent of the cultivable land) range from 50 to 80 percent of the total production of these crops. Small plot production is also important in Amurskaia oblast, where the land committee reported that more people each year were relying on household plots for survival as production on the former collectives continued to fall and unemployment continued to rise.

Families generally use produce from small plots for household consumption, and occasionally sell surpluses at local markets. Many vendors we interviewed at the Khabarovsk central market, for example, had come to sell pork from their family pig or milk products from their family cow. Small plot vegetable growers sell potatoes, beets, carrots, and other products along the roadside not far from the central market, as the central market stalls for fruits and vegetables are taken by middlemen selling mostly imported products.

Many families located in villages on former collective farms receive some degree of subsidy for their small plots from the collective farm management. This often takes the form of free plowing and sometimes of reduced-cost inputs for planting. In some cases, collectives offer to plow their members' household plots as a lease payment for the use of the members' land shares. Resource transfers (both explicit and implicit) from collectives to farm members for their household plots, although of immediate benefit to small plot owners, could discourage members from withdrawing their land shares for private farming, as this would terminate the flow of resources from the collective.

ISSUES RELATED TO LAND PRIVATIZATION AND FARM RESTRUCTURING

Despite the current surplus of agricultural land in the RFE, allocation of this land continues to be an important factor in increasing productivity. This is true for three reasons. First, while much land currently goes unused, the supply of readily cultivable land that does not require a large initial investment (in leveling or clearing, for example) is more scarce. Second, land in desirable locations is also more scarce. Most potential buyers or lessees are interested only in land that adjoins parcels currently in their possession. When this land is owned by private shareowners or PFEs rather than by the land redistribution fund, the potential buyers rely on functioning lease and/or sales markets to obtain the land. Land near urban centers such as Khabarovsk and Blagoveshchensk is also highly desirable and in shorter supply than land further out. Third, and perhaps most importantly, any increases in production brought about through a future increase in the availability of credit and capital will be limited if land cannot transfer via the market to successful enterprises, and away from those unlikely to succeed even with greater access to capital.

Privatization and Farm Restructuring

Where collectives have been "privatized" into land shares, shareowners are often unable to exercise the rights to their shares in any meaningful way. Most collective farms have undergone superficial restructuring at best, and continue to operate as collectives with over 5,000 hectares. Few operate efficiently, nor would they be able to operate efficiently even with more capital. Most have retained their exact past dimensions and characteristics, including size (some remain as large as 10,000–12,000 hectares), a large number of employees, methods of production, and decision-making. In most cases, the only difference has been a marked drop in production resulting from the ending of state subsidies. While most managers we interviewed acknowledged that workers and pensioners now own the land of the collective in the form of land shares, they rarely compensated these land share owners in any way for the continued use of their shares by the collective.

In addition, some collective farms in Khabarovskii krai have not yet restructured and have not been divided into land shares as directed by agrarian reform legislation.[24] According to the Khabarovsk land committee, 23 out of 53 former collective farms in the krai (representing 29,700 hectares, or about 14 percent of the total agricultural land in the krai) have been "reorganized," but without privatizing the land and property that are supposed to be owned by the members. These 23 enterprises are distinct from those enterprises exempted from privatization for purposes of specialized state production. Officials explained how this reorganization without privatization might have occurred by telling us that each of these collective/state enterprises may have adopted a provision in its new enterprise charter that all land shares held by individual members would automatically be contributed to the new enterprise. This explanation is not sufficient, however, as these shares should then have been included among the official tallies of "permanently contributed shares." Instead, it appears that land shares were never even calculated on the 23 farms, depriving farm members of all rights to the land to which they were entitled.

One of the defining characteristics of agrarian reform in the RFE relative to anywhere else in Russia is the great amount of land that regional governments have retained in the land redistribution funds. In fact, the majority of agricultural land in the RFE remains unprivatized in the raion land redistribution funds. In 1999, Khabarovskii krai held 93,900 hectares of arable land in its fund, while Amurskaia oblast held over 900,000 hectares of arable land. In 1999, the Amur land committee leased out 251,176 hectares from the fund to agricultural enterprises and only 700 hectares to peasant farmers.[25] The amount of land held in the land fund in both regions has increased since 1997 (in Amur by 13 percent and in Khabarovsk by 45 percent).[26]

It is unclear exactly how the land funds in Khabarovskii krai and Amurskaia oblast became so large. In Amur, the size of the fund may be related to the oblast land committee's aggressive policy of land monitoring and penalties pursued in the years following reforms.[27] It may also be related to an oblast-wide policy limiting land shares to ten hectares each, which probably resulted in large amounts of land on some farms being unallocated "residual" land slated for the land fund; or to a depressed demand for agricultural land, which in turn is related to the economic inefficiencies of farming in the Far East given current input/output price ratios and, above all, an intense and increasing scarcity of capital.

The notably high level of land held in state control through the land funds in the RFE has important implications for the agrarian reform process. It indicates that the oblast and raion-level officials in the RFE have only partially implemented federal privatization and agrarian reform policies.[28] The purpose behind the funds was to redistribute land to peasant farmers, not to hold it en masse at the local or regional level. Reform-oriented legislators certainly did not anticipate that over 50 percent of the arable land would be withheld from privatization in the land funds.

Rather than allocate ownership of this land to agricultural enterprises or PFEs, regional governments have chosen to lease some of it out on five-year terms (for free or, at most, nominal rates), retaining the option to terminate the lease at the end of the term in the event of misuse or nonuse. The Amur land committee has shifted its policies over the last two years to encourage more land to be in production, partly by allocating land in lease (or use) to almost anyone who applies for it.[29] In some cases the land committee has allowed immigrant farmers from China, Korea, Holland, and the United States to lease land in the fund for farming.

The strategy of Amurskaia oblast appears to be to maximize agricultural production by retaining ownership of most arable land and allocating it to supposedly efficient private users for short terms. This policy, coupled with strict management policies of land held in private ownership, appears to have comprised a regional strategy to reduce inefficient land use by private owners. This strategy leans heavily on the supremacy of central state planning in organizing efficient production.

The policy of retaining most arable land in state control is a dangerous one for several reasons. First, it assumes the state is a better regulator than the market for moving land into efficient use. However, data shows that a well-functioning market is the best way to ensure allocation of land into efficient use.[30] Second, the more resources retained by the raion and oblast-level governments, the more opportunity for corruption and nepotism in distributing them. Third, the government accrues administrative costs for monitoring the land, making and reviewing lease contracts, and executing penalties. (These costs could, of course, be considered advantageous from the perspective of the oblast and raion-level officials whose employment currently depends on them.) Fourth, short-term leases fail to provide the type of security of rights required by farmers to make long-term investments to boost productivity. Any government policy of strict monitoring and intervention into the nonuse of privately held land is also likely to decrease farmers' incentives to make these longer-term investments.

Finally, holding large quantities of land in state ownership, available for lease at nominal rates (quoted as anywhere between zero and five rubles per hectare per year) may ensure the availability of inexpensive land to many of those desiring to use it, but at the cost of developing a market in private transactions.[31] As long as large quantities of land are available at no cost, or practically no cost, land will continue to have very little, if any, commercial value. This point brings us back to the initial reasons for developing a land market, which include the creation of wealth in rural areas.[32] Attaching commercial value to land allows shareowners to exit the farming sector. This may be especially important for pensioners and for people wishing to migrate to urban settings. Without real land privatization and the development of a functioning land market to facilitate the movement of agricultural land from inefficient to efficient users, obsolete farms will continue to sit on large tracts of land and production will continue to stagnate. Furthermore, banks cannot accept land for collateral in the absence of a land market, impeding farmers from leveraging credit for major infrastructure improvements. Clearly, the best way to hasten the development of a functional agricultural land market in the Russian Far East would be to privatize the great majority of land that is currently contained in raion land redistribution funds.[33]

Another problem with the process of privatization is that PFEs established on land-fund land in the early period of the reforms often received poor quality land. This meant that many of the "pioneer" peasant farmers, even if they may have received subsidized credit for machinery purchase (a significant advantage relative to PFEs established later in the reform period), faced an additional obstacle to survival in the ensuing years. One official in Khabarovskii krai estimated that only 70 out of 307 PFEs in one raion produce efficiently due to the poor soil quality possessed by most. Several interviewees remarked that the land they now lease is of better quality than the land received in early land-fund distributions.

In privatizing land-fund land, PFEs should be given priority through (1) offering PFEs the first rights to land currently leased out to them from the land fund, and (2) assigning a preference to PFEs in auctioning the remainder of "unleased" land-fund land.

A final problem with privatization and restructuring in the RFE, as in the rest of Russia, is the inclination of large farm enterprises to impede people from withdrawing property shares in kind upon leaving to start a peasant farm. Property shares are still a largely untapped source for machinery and equipment for peasant farms, and the laws regarding property share valuation and withdrawal are largely ignored. Presently, individuals who leave agricultural enterprises continue to have great difficulty exercising their right to withdraw property in kind or receive the cash value of their property shares. Many agricultural enterprises may have a shortage of working machinery since the enterprises have not had funds to make repairs, and enterprise workers have little incentive to care for the machinery. Whether for this reason or others, the enterprises are reluctant to give property shareowners any functioning machinery or other capital assets. Nor do the enterprises have sufficient funds to redeem the property shares for cash. Moreover, property shares on the great majority of farms have not been adjusted for inflation for several years, so the denominated value of property shares is ridiculously low, sometimes being undervalued by a factor of several thousand.

Government Regulation of Privately Held Land

The land committees in both Khabarovskii krai and Amurskaia oblast continue to monitor privately held land used by PFEs for irrational use or nonuse, whether this land is leased from the land fund or owned. Punishment for irrational use or nonuse by a lessee is refusal to renew the lease contract upon its expiration; punishment for irrational use or nonuse by a private owner ranges from warnings to fines to outright confiscation. Although land committee personnel in both Khabarovsk and Amur strongly believe they have the legal right to enforce land use regulations on farmers who hold land in ownership,[34] they have become increasingly reluctant to do so since the amount of land not being cultivated has increased. One official from the Khabarovskii krai department of agriculture, however, thought that stricter monitoring policies would increase productivity.

In our fieldwork in the fall of 1999, farmers did not appear to be concerned that the land committee might fine them or confiscate land for failure to use it properly. However, it is important to note farmers' concerns in interviews in 1997 that the land committee could fine them or withdraw their land if they did not use it in a manner that satisfied the land inspector. The threat of withdrawal affected the manner in which peasant farmers chose to expand their operations. The difference between 1997 and 1999 in perceived threat of land committee interference appears to be due to oblast/krai decisions to relax strict monitoring and penalties on private land.[35]

Land Transactions

As noted, working land markets function as a powerful tool for encouraging productivity and investment among land users.

Lease

A land share lease market is developing in the RFE, defined by a number of different participants and variations. The most common type of lease agreement between private actors takes place when a land share owner leases out his or her share to the agricultural enterprise (former collective farm) that occupies it. Sometimes an agricultural enterprise leases land from shareowners on a neighboring enterprise. In a few instances, peasant farmers also lease land from shareowners, usually at a higher rate than the average paid by agricultural enterprises.

Lease agreements between land share owners and large enterprises vary greatly in their terms and level of payment. In most instances, terms are for three to five years, with an option to renew at the end of the term. Terms offered by at least one former collective we encountered were much longer, however, ranging from 10 to 49 years. Payment ranged from zero to 10 percent[36] of the gross production and was usually in kind, offered in a combination of grain, soy, and discounts on items such as hay and coal (bought in bulk by the enterprise). Payment sometimes also included plowing the lessor's household auxiliary plot. Some farm managers also cited payment of land tax as part of their lease payment to the land share owner.

Many lease transactions also take place between the land fund (making the raion government the lessor) and private farms as lessees, including both former collectives and PFEs. In a few instances, peasant farmers work out informal "sublease" arrangements where one larger, wealthier farmer leases land from the land fund, and smaller neighboring farmers use part of this land for a very nominal fee paid to the primary lessee.

Where former collectives produce on only a portion of the land they possess, they generally provide lease payments for only those shareowners whose shares are located in the fields under production (if they provide lease payments at all). This is true even though a land share represents a right to common ownership of the enterprise land: if one hectare of land is cultivated, that hectare represents a minute part of everyone's land share. At a former collective in Amurskaia oblast, for example, one pensioner told us she had approached the farm management about lease payments on her land share, which the farm was currently using. The manager, who was also the chairman of the former collective, responded that if she demanded payments, he would simply stop cultivating her land and shift production to another field where shareowners did not make such demands. This response underscores the imbalance of power between the management of agricultural enterprises and former collective farm members who are now land share owners, and indicates a low level of organization among former members/ shareowners. Most importantly, this response exposes illegal activity by the enterprise management.

Further reports by land share owners at the same farm in the RFE reinforced the level of coercion employed by management in avoiding payments for use of land shares. One pensioner couple reported that their shares were located in a field the farm management was not currently cultivating. The couple approached the farm manager, asking him to lease in their shares. Management responded with an offer for a ten-year lease at 1,000 rubles ($40.00) per year. This, said the couple, was "crazy!" The manager went on to say that he would only lease the land on these terms if and when the couple convinced the additional ten people who owned land shares in their field to lease out on the same terms.

A final problem relating to the lease market is that even when farm managers do make lease agreements, they often breach them without suffering consequences. In several cases we encountered, farm managers (of agricultural enterprises and, in one case, a peasant farm) claimed they were "unable" to pay the in-kind lease payments they had contracted to, and so did not plan on making any payments in that year. In another case, the manager of a former collective in Amurskaia oblast planned on "renegotiating" the terms of his five-year leases with shareowners after only three years. The first shareowners selected for termination of the lease agreement or reduced payment would be those who were no longer employees of the farm, and the last shareowners selected would be pensioners, he said.

Inheritance

Inheritance transactions are, and will continue to be, an essential component in transferring the lasting benefits of agrarian reforms to rural households. Of the roughly 108 million hectares (49 percent) of Russia's 222 million hectares of agricultural land that were transferred into private ownership through land shares in the early to mid-1990s, about 40 percent of these shares went to pensioners. By 2010, it is likely that rights to roughly three-quarters of these pensioner-owned land shares, representing about 32 million hectares, will have passed by inheritance to their children.

Despite the importance of inheritance as a means of transferring land rights within rural households, apparently only 158,512 "successions" (inheritances), with an average size of less than one-third hectare each, were formally registered in all of Russia in 1997.[37] Virtually no inheritances of land shares, which are likely the principal source of land for new and expanded family farms, are being formally documented and registered. Many collective farm managers currently attempt to restrict the inheritance of land shares, leading to additional delay, expense, and discouragement for the heir attempting to claim his or her rights to the land share or to sell or lease out those rights.

In the RFE, however, many heirs simply do not claim inherited land shares or plots. This may be because they cannot afford to pay land tax on it and, in the presence of an insecure legal framework about their rights to dispose of the land through sale or lease, they may view assuming rights to the land as a net liability. This scenario is especially likely for heirs living in urban areas who are unable to benefit from farming the land themselves.

Purchase and Sale

As in the rest of Russia, a market in agricultural land purchase-sale has been slow to develop in the Russian Far East.[38] A number of factors impede the development of a market in the purchase and sale of agricultural land in the RFE. First, farmers and officials are unclear about legal rights to purchase and sell land. Current legislation does not provide a solid framework for buying and selling agricultural land and land shares. On the one hand, Article 36 of the Constitution of the

Russian Federation establishes a right to dispose of land, and presidential decrees clearly provide for private purchase-sale transactions in agricultural land. However, the federal legislature has not adopted a law confirming these rights; this absence of parliamentary confirmation has led many rural residents to believe these rights are not secure. The unclear legality of purchase-sale transactions depresses demand for land in two ways: people do not want to buy land for fear the transactions could be revoked at a later time; and people do not want to own land because they are not certain they would be able to sell it in the future. Perceptions that it is illegal for PFEs to lease out their land also reduce the demand for land purchases and ownership.

Second, at least some shareowners believe they must go through a potentially time-consuming and difficult process to obtain approval from farm management and/or the farm's general meeting to sell their shares. A third factor impeding the development of a land market is the high availability of land at low lease rates, which undermines a market in sales. As long as people are able to lease land from the land fund at nominal rates, the demand to purchase land from private shareowners will remain low. Finally, a lack of information about buyers and sellers increases transaction costs and further impedes purchase and sale.

Mortgage

The federal law "On Mortgage" explicitly prohibits the mortgage of agricultural land.[39] Even if mortgage becomes legal, until a stronger agricultural land market develops in the RFE, it is unlikely that banks will engage in mortgage transactions. Meanwhile, farmers are unable to secure credit for machinery and inputs, which would foster higher productivity and thus contribute to increased land values. The majority of peasant farmers in Khabarovsk and Amur were familiar with the concept of using land for collateral, and many expressed an interest in mortgaging their land if federal law allowed. Most farmers would use credit secured through mortgage for the purchase of much-needed machinery or processing equipment.

Registration

The registration and mapping processes in Russia give rise to several issues that affect sale transactions, including delays in and costs of demarcation and registration of land plots, and broader institutional shortcomings related to the establishment of a new registration apparatus under the Ministry of Justice. The 1997 law "On Land Registration" and accompanying regulations transferred land registration functions from the land committee to the Ministry of Justice.[40] The ministry has been working to set up registration offices (known as "chambers") in every raion in Russia. The Amurskaia oblast government, according to officials in the land committee and Ministry of Agriculture, has yet to implement the new chambers, with the result that the land committee continues to perform registration functions, as well as to manage and allocate state and privately held land. Maintaining both functions allows a consolidation of a large amount of authority within one branch of government, an outcome the new system avoids.

In Amurskaia oblast and Khabarovskii krai, procedural requirements related to demarcation and registration may deter some land share owners from selling their plots, according to reports by pensioners and other shareowners. Anyone wishing to sell his or her land must first confirm the boundaries with the oblast/krai land committee, then register it with the land committee (or in the case of Khabarovsk, with the Ministry of Justice). The registration process costs 200 rubles ($8) and takes two to three days, according to krai officials. Perceptions of the demarcation/registration process by land share owners vary from straightforward and fairly efficient to extremely onerous, expensive, and time-consuming.

Bankruptcy

It may be possible to use bankruptcy as a tool for transferring land and other resources from broken, inefficient agricultural enterprises to productive new or existing enterprises.[41] Officials in Amur have, in fact, exercised bankruptcy on roughly 20 farms. In some cases, outside buyers have purchased farm resources (often one or two of the "productive sections" of the former collective) from the state after it has carried out bankruptcy proceedings.

An important question relates to the outcome of individuals' rights to land and property shares in the event that the state declares bankruptcy on an agricultural enterprise. According to federal legislation, land shares that have not been formally contributed to the charter capital of the agricultural enterprise belong to the individual land share owners (not the enterprise), and can be withdrawn or transferred at any point through the liquidation process in accordance with Presidential Decree No. 337. Land shares that have been contributed to an enterprise may still be withdrawn if allowed by the enterprise's charter. In that case, however, the land to be allocated in kind may be subject to some debt, since the land was "owned" by the enterprise (subject to withdrawal rights). What has actually happened with shareowners' rights in the 20 cases of bankruptcy in Amurskaia oblast is not clear.

ECONOMIC AND INSTITUTIONAL FACTORS AFFECTING IMPLEMENTATION OF AGRARIAN REFORMS

In addition to land privatization and farm reorganization, a complex set of issues related to physical capital, credit, marketing, taxes, and labor affect agrarian reform in the Russian Far East. These additional factors provide an important backdrop for understanding the climate in which agrarian reforms take place in the region.

Physical Capital

One of the primary constraints on agricultural productivity (and hence demand for agricultural land) in the RFE is inadequate physical capital, including machinery, storage, seasonal production inputs, processing facilities, and public infrastructure.

Machinery

One of the greatest cited impediments to effective land use by farmers and officials alike is a lack of adequate machinery. Particularly in the Far East, where land is in abundant supply and farms tend to be larger, the aging arsenal of farm machinery has significantly constrained growth and production. Statistics show a steady decline in agricultural machinery throughout the Russian Far East. Throughout the region, tractor supplies have decreased 47 percent and grain harvesting combines 44 percent between 1991 and 1997. Taking into account the deteriorating condition of the remaining supply, this sharp decline in machinery reduces the plowing and harvesting potential of the region by almost half. [42]

With the passage of time, the situation has only grown worse. The price of farm machinery and equipment across Russia rose exponentially between 1990 and 1997. [43] Some farmers predicted that they would only continue to farm for a short time before the inevitable breakdown of their machinery. Without access to new machinery in the near future, those farmers still able to farm at all will be forced to work smaller and smaller plots of land with fewer and fewer modern agricultural aids. In Amurskaia oblast, lack of machinery was cited as the main cause for the removal of 200,000 hectares from production between 1997 and 1999.

Most farmers have not purchased new machinery since the beginning of land reform in 1991–92, when subsidized credit was widely available. Others had received their machines as property shares from their former collectives. This option is also largely obsolete today, as many of the most valuable machines have already been distributed among the earliest shareowners to withdraw from collective farms. What machinery remains is often decrepit and unsuited to the smaller parcels farmed by peasant (farm) enterprises. In fact, unusually large numbers of farmers stated that they had sufficient machinery, but that it was of poor quality or unsuitable for their needs. Moreover, due to the scarcity of machinery, many agricultural enterprises, including small farmers, used tractors and combines well in excess of their recommended capacity—in some cases more than double the standard amount.

Lack of access to long-term credit prevents farmers from purchasing machinery. In 1999, rates of credit from banks could be obtained with interest rates as high as 180–200 percent, for the maximum period of one year. The fragile state of Russia's undercapitalized and institutionally unstable banks has contributed to unpredictable and often very high interest rates.[44] Moreover, agriculture is seen as a risky investment due to the low profitability of farms. The credit histories of small farmers further discourage loans, and mountains of paperwork hamper even the initial application process. As noted, land cannot be used as collateral under the existing moratorium on mortgages, and the practice of using the new machinery itself as collateral for loans is still uncommon and unreliable in a volatile market riddled with high inflation.

One consequence of the machinery shortage in Amurskaia oblast is increasingly intensive production of such profitable crops as soy in order to maximize use of machinery.[45] To grow soy over an extended period of time, it must be rotated annually with other crops. Without fertilizers, soy can be grown on only two-fifths of the land each year. Even under ideal circumstances with fertilizers, it can be grown on only one-half of a farmer's arable land. Currently, farmers violate crop rotation norms by increasing the relative amount of land grown in soy. Overuse endangers the already fragile quality of the soil and the sustainability of production.

Storage

Inadequate storage further reduces farmers' profitability. Where storage is available, farmers are able to maximize profits by storing their produce until spring, when prices are higher. Where storage is not available, however, farmers attempt to sell all their produce (at lower prices) in the autumn, leaving any surplus to spoil. In some cases, vegetable farmers without access to storage have lost up to 45 percent of their production to rot. Meat-producers also have difficulty finding storage for their fodder hay through the winter season.

Farmers living near former collectives sometimes have the option of leasing storage space from the collectives. The cost of leasing was often deemed excessive, however. The possibility of cooperation in building and sharing storage facilities, while attractive, is unrealistic for many farmers living too far apart.

Competition from Chinese farmers with adequate storage across the border further exacerbates the problem. According to reports from farmers and officials in the RFE, Chinese farmers purchased vegetables at low prices from the Russians in the autumn and sold their own produce on the Russian market at higher prices in the spring. One farmer complained that even though he managed to save his produce for the spring, the early sale of large quantities of Chinese products that spring drove down prices, reducing his profit.

Seasonal Production Inputs

A rising disparity between the high costs of inputs and the low prices of agricultural products impedes farmers' ability to make a profit. Fuel prices, for example, quadrupled between 1998 and 1999 while the prices of produce only doubled or tripled. With profits already slim, these differential increases between expenses and returns have been sufficient to seriously harm farmers. Some were unable to use their machines or harvest their entire crops because they could not afford fuel. Other farmers located far from urban areas and markets were still more hard-pressed because of the high cost of transporting their produce.

In addition to high fuel costs, high costs of fertilizers and herbicides raise farmers' production expenses. Prohibitively high prices force many farmers to abandon using these inputs altogether. Because fertilizer is both difficult to obtain and expensive, farmers often sow the soil with hay or use crop rotation to maximize production. One cause of the expense and scarcity of herbicides is that they are imported from Japan, Germany, and the United States.

Cooperation among farmers may help to reduce the cost of inputs. In Romnetskii raion in Amur, for example, the Organization of Peasant Farms and Cooperatives of Russia (AKKOR) helped to reduce the cost of inputs to PFEs by purchasing large quantities of fuel from wholesale suppliers and reselling them at no profit to those enterprises. Again, one of the underlying problems is lack of available short-term credit at reasonable rates to purchase inputs. Many farmers are forced to rely on contracts with state organizations or processors at disadvantageous rates of exchange to receive the necessary inputs.

Processing Facilities

As in any economy, processing greatly increases the value and profitability of agricultural products in the Russian Far East. Without adequate capital or access to credit, however, the agricultural processing industry has grown slowly. The processing facilities that do exist appear to monopolize the sector, forwarding farmers' fuel and other inputs in exchange for a promise from the farmers to deliver produce after fall harvest at prices substantially below market levels. Most farmers we interviewed complained bitterly about these future contracts with processors, saying they paid dearly in the fall for advances of fuel and fertilizer the previous spring. Many, however, said they had no other option either for obtaining seasonal credit for planting or for selling their products.

In Amurskaia oblast, for example, soy processing is dominated by several processing plants in Irkutsk, Khabarovsk, and Ussuriisk. (It is an example of lingering Soviet-era inefficiency that while the oblast produces by far the most soy in the country, it has virtually no soy processing facilities.) We found one exception in Romnetskii raion, where several farmers purchased their own small-scale soy processing equipment. The AKKOR helped these farmers obtain loans to purchase processing equipment from an agricultural bank at an interest rate of just 18 percent, with the AKKOR serving as the guarantor. After ensuring capacity to process their own raw soy, the equipment owners give priority to other farmers in the raion, and then to farmers from neighboring raions.

Access to foreign direct investment may be necessary for the development of the food processing sector of the RFE. This may leave processors (and indirectly farmers) vulnerable to fluctuations in the exchange rate, however. When the ruble collapsed in August 1998, some processors in the RFE realized net losses due to an increased loan repayment burden to foreign investors during a period when they could have benefited from the increased demand for domestic production created by the rapidly declining value of the ruble.[46]

Public Infrastructure

Several farmers located in more remote areas complained of lack of road access to fields. Roads once actively used by collectives are now falling into disrepair as more and more land falls out of production. Electricity supply lines often do not reach remote "homestead" farms, and many farmers operate without reliable electricity or are forced to invest in their own power sources. One enterprising farmer had installed his own wind propeller to produce an increased amount of electricity to his remote farm.

Credit

Commercial bank credit is a rare form of credit financing under current circumstances. Most farmers absolutely ruled out the option of obtaining bank loans because of interest rates ranging from 60 to 220 percent, even taking into account current rates of inflation. Banks, in turn, are reluctant to invest in farm enterprises. Agricultural profitability is down and collateral is of questionable value. Under any circumstances, banks take relatively high risks investing in agriculture because of the unpredictability of weather and harvesting factors.

A more common form of credit is the "budget loan," a state-subsidized loan from a commercial bank at a fixed low interest rate of approximately 18 percent. These can enable significant capital purchases and investments to those who qualify, although qualification (requiring solid credit history, a lengthy application procedure, and proof of sufficient collateral) may elude many farmers. Cooperative loan efforts with AKKOR-type assistance may be an effective means to overcome the stringent requirements needed to receive state subsidized bank loans.

Another type of credit involves contracts with state organizations. In Khabarovsk, for example, the krai administration helps farmers with spring planting in return for delivery contracts with state organizations. Farmers who agree to deliver a fixed amount of their production to a state institution such as a military barracks, hospital, or public school may be eligible for these contracts. The state agrees to pay for the delivery in two parts: an initial payment for operating expenses (fuel, fertilizer, herbicide) in the spring and a second payment in cash upon delivery in the fall. The agreement resembles a commercial forward contract; the advantage to farmers is low interest rates for the value of the forwarded inputs.

In practice these contracts have been problematic. Most noticeably, the state repays contracts late, often one to three years after delivery. With high inflation rates, these delays make payments virtually worthless. Furthermore, state payments generally consist of in-kind deliveries of fuel or other inputs or repayment of old loans. Thus, if farmers need cash for other needs, state delivery contracts are not an option.

An alternative form of credit available mainly to soy producers is future contracts with processing enterprises, as discussed above. Under these contracts, processors lend farmers in-kind operating expenses (such as fuel and fertilizers) for the spring planting season and charge high interest rates that must be paid by the farmers upon delivery of their goods. Farmers who participate in these contracts (only some of which are written) receive inputs in the spring for no cash up front but, by promising to deliver a fixed amount of product to the processor/lender at a submarket price, give up the potentially higher prices for soy they could receive in the open market.

The formation of credit cooperatives may offer an alternative means for farmers in the RFE to secure credit. Although these are not common among farmers in the Far East, we did encounter one example of a successful credit cooperative in Amurskaia oblast. Membership in the cooperative consisted of 12 PFEs, one former collective, and AKKOR. Members contributed machines and cash as charter capital and collateral.

While this innovative method of credit access appears promising, it still faces considerable hurdles. The law of the Russian Federation "On Cooperatives"[47] is tailored to production cooperatives rather than "secondary" cooperatives (such as credit, marketing, or service cooperatives) and so applies clumsily to credit cooperatives. The paperwork is complicated, and a cooperative's income may be subject to double taxation (as income to the cooperative enterprise and to the individual members). In a period where taxes are not always collected, the threat of double-taxation may not be a significant detriment to the individual cooperative, but it will most certainly discourage the proliferation of such organizations in the future. In an attempt to address some of these gaps, a federal law on credit cooperatives that defines its legal status, goals, specific features, and basic principles of operation was finally approved by the Russian government in January 2001, and was introduced in April of the same year.

Marketing

Farmers in the Russian Far East market their products through a variety of channels, including foreign importers, domestic processors, stalls at central or local markets, and roadside trucks. Sale of agricultural production directly to consumers is a prime means of cash for farmers. Many farmers reported, however, that they could not afford the time or transport costs of selling at consumer markets. These farmers had instead reluctantly chosen to sell their goods to middlemen at lower prices. Other farmers found an abundance of demand, selling their goods at the roadside or to an established round of customers.

The middleman sector in the RFE has grown over the past decade. By purchasing goods in bulk directly from farmers at lower-than-retail market prices, middlemen are able to profit even after deducting transport and marketing costs. Although farmers prefer to receive retail market prices for their goods, selling to a middleman saves transportation, transaction, and market costs and so presents an important alternative. Despite additional marketing choices presented by an evolving middleman sector, many farmers view middlemen as corrupt, usurious, or monopolistic. Middlemen often gain access to premium stalls in local markets that are inaccessible to farmers, and some farmers suspect collusion between market operators and middlemen. Some middlemen also import goods at lower rates from other areas, thereby creating competition for local farmers.

A dearth of processing equipment further restricts the marketing potential for farmers in the Far East, as it does throughout Russia. Farmers bear the brunt of the extra costs required to deliver soy (for example) to processors in distant regions, and lack the bargaining power to demand higher prices for their deliveries. Instead of benefiting from the apparently strong demand for soy products, farmers make unfavorable deals with middlemen who represent these processors in the spring when the farmers are cash vulnerable and in great need of inputs for planting.

The demand for soy products appears high. Soy farmers seemed to have no trouble selling everything they produced. Much of the demand for processed soy comes from markets overseas. Seventy percent of soy oil exports from the Russian Far East have gone to China over the past four or five years. Soy meal is largely exported to Japan. Other countries such as Holland and Israel have also imported soy from the Russian Far East.

The market for grains seems somewhat less dependable, and even the largest collectives appear to have no stable buyers, while the market for local grains is also suffering from competitively priced imports. Although some local producers briefly profited from the fall of the ruble in August 1998, importers were quick to adjust prices to remain competitive. For example, one dairy farmer in Amurskaia oblast capable of producing 80 tons of milk per day produces only 5 tons per day because of competition from high-quality, inexpensive Swedish dairy products. Similarly, competition from U.S. chicken drumsticks had virtually wiped out profits of local poultry producers until the fall of the ruble in August 1998. For a brief period after August 1998, Russians could not afford the U.S. chicken, and Russian poultry factories began to work in full swing again. Later, drumstick prices from the European Union dropped dramatically to compete with local prices. Officials in Amurskaia oblast thought that highly subsidized farms in EU countries could afford these competitive actions to ensure long-term demand for their products. Because Russian farmers lack long-term credit, technology, storage, and subsidization, they are being driven out of the market by their more robust foreign counterparts.

Taxation

Many farmers cite agricultural taxes, which they claim absorb from 68 to 90 percent of gross receipts, as a major burden on their resources. Land share owners who were considering withdrawing their land to start a PFE feared taxes, as much for their complexity as for their actual financial burden. Support for a uniform tax appeared widespread. While former collective farms have been able to maintain accountants, smaller PFEs often negotiate the maze of financial requirements alone or with limited assistance.

The Russian tax structure is extremely complex and includes profit taxes, value-added taxes, road fund taxes, income taxes, property taxes, and land taxes.[48] The most significant payments required of agricultural enterprises are the compulsory deductions for extra-budgetary funds such as the pension, social security, medical insurance, and public employment funds, amounting to a total of 31.1 percent.

As a final note, tax enforcement appears inconsistent. While most farmers deemed the tax burden onerous, we interviewed several peasant farmers and managers on former collectives who had not paid their taxes for several years, raising questions of the efficiency of enforcement.

Labor

An ineffective labor force may also impede agricultural production in the new market system in the Russian Far East. Several enterprising farmers complained that they had difficulty finding workers willing to labor more than eight hours per day in order to make a profit. Some PFEs in the Russian Far East hire Chinese laborers to supplement their work force. These seasonal workers usually work in exchange for a percentage of the crop, which they then take with them to sell in China upon their return. The Chinese workers, according to officials and farmers, are hardworking and willing to work for lower wages than Russians. They often bring with them useful techniques to maximize production. Particularly in the areas of soy and melon production, Chinese and Korean immigrant laborers have brought valuable expertise to Russian farmers. The official numbers of such immigrants are relatively few, however. In Khabarovskii krai, for example, officials reported that only 200–300 Chinese agricultural workers participated in farming in 1998.[49] Aside from immigration restrictions, cultural attitudes and suspicion of Chinese intentions may contribute to the relatively rare usage of this valuable labor resource.[50]

Immigrant laborers do not, for the most part, have the benefits of land tenure security available to Russian farmers through ownership or long-term leases. Russian law does not provide for foreign ownership of land. Furthermore, at least some of the foreign laborers lack valid immigration documents, increasing their vulnerability to poor wages and reducing their security in crop-sharing arrangements. Pursuing a policy of leasing out land-fund land to foreigners who have the means to effectively cultivate it would be one way to increase the contribution of immigrant laborers to agricultural production in the RFE.

RELATIONSHIP OF AGRARIAN REFORM TO REGIONAL SECURITY

Eight percent of the labor force of the Russian Far East currently works in agriculture, indicating an even greater percentage of people who depend on a family member's income from agricultural employment. In addition, the vast majority of households in the RFE cultivate small plots that provide a major source of food supply. Many of the people who depend on agriculture to earn their living or feed their families are living in poverty, or are struggling day to day to avoid descending into poverty. Reform of the agricultural sector to enable these people to make choices for themselves that will increase their production, and by corollary their household incomes, should result in a more stable population and thus a more stable region. Production increases should also benefit the RFE population living in the cities, who will have access to a larger, less expensive, and more stable supply of food.

Policymakers in the Russian Far East have the power to make key changes to the legal and policy structure that would increase agricultural production—and thereby improve food security and standards of living throughout the region. The basic steps they could take might include:

- privatizing the large stores of land currently held (mostly out of production) by the raion land funds;

- helping owners of land shares currently being used by large agricultural enterprises to understand their land rights, and then to exercise their land rights to increase their incomes. Such exercise could be through leasing, selling, or using the land themselves in private farms. Enforcement of rights is also crucial; and
- adopting policies encouraging foreign workers with farming expertise and access to capital to lease unused, nonprivatized land from the raion land funds.

At the federal level, lawmakers need to:

- ensure that rights to purchase, sell, lease, and inherit agricultural land are clear, widely understood, and enforced; and
- amend the Law on Mortgage to allow for mortgage of agricultural land.

The above changes would be greatly facilitated by private capital investment, especially in machinery. Creating the proper policy environment for such investments is therefore also crucial.

Finally, when viewing the Amur River Valley, it is clear that national boundaries impose constraints on production. While the Russian side of the valley has a surplus of land and a scarcity of labor and capital, the Chinese side has a scarcity of land, a surplus of labor, and greater access to capital. While recognizing the obvious political issues, it is nevertheless possible to imagine a transformation of agricultural production in the RFE brought about by a fluid exchange of labor and capital across the Russian-Chinese border. Production could be increased, and the benefits could be shared by all concerned.

NOTES

1. *Bulletin: Development of Economic Reforms in Primorskii Krai from January to June 1997* (Primorskii krai Committee on Statistics), 20; *Amur Region: Guidebook for Businessmen* (VOSTOKINCENTER, 1994); *The Russian Far East: A Business Reference Guide*, 3d ed. (1997–98), as cited in Bradley J. Rorem and Renee Giovarelli, *Agrarian Reform in the Russian Far East*, RDI Report, no. 95, The Rural Development Institute, Seattle (October 1997), 7.

2. Discussions with officials in Khabarovskii krai and Amur oblast land committees (October 1999).

3. From 1986 to 1990, for example, the Soviet government spent 3.5 billion rubles (officially equivalent to $3.5 billion because at this time the exchange rate was pegged at one ruble to one U.S. dollar) on the development of the agro-industrial complex of the Russian Far East. Pavel A. Minakir, ed., *The Russian Far East: An Economic Survey*, trans. Gregory L. Freeze (Khabarovsk: RIOTIP, 1996), 97.

4. Even when agriculture was more heavily subsidized by the Soviet Union, it did not

achieve yields at levels experienced by noncollectivized agriculture in countries with agro-climatic conditions similar to Russia.

5. FT Asia Intelligence Wire, *International Market Insight Reports,* October 21, 1998, 6.

6. Interview by author with Anatoly Bonetskii, head of the State Committee on Land Resources and Land Tenure for Amur oblast (October 1999).

7. International Industrial Information, Ltd., *Russia Express-Perestroika, Executive Briefing,* April 8, 1996 (available on Westlaw).

8. John J. Stephan, *The Russian Far East: A History* (Stanford, Calif.: Stanford University Press, 1994), 269.

9. Minakir, *The Russian Far East: An Economic Survey,* 438–39.

10. For example, several of the primary agriculture-producing federation subjects of western Russia erected regional trade barriers in the wake of the crash of the ruble in August 1998. Objectives included protecting local consumers from rapidly rising demand for domestic agricultural products from Moscow, and in some cases protecting local producers from rising competition from other regions. See Yevgenia Serova, "Influence of Interregional Trade Barriers on the Development of Agro-food Markets in Russia," unpublished paper presented for a conference on "Interregional Trade Barriers," Moscow, March 13, 2000.

11. See Dmitrii Kirsanov, *Russia to Start Receiving Food Aid on January 1, 1999,* ITAR-TASS, December 15, 1998; Dan Glickman, U.S. Secretary of Agriculture, Prepared Statement before the House Agricultural Committee (as reported by Federal News Services, October 6, 1999).

12. See, for example, the law of the Russian Soviet Federated Socialist Republic, "On the Peasant (Farm) Enterprise," as amended January 5, 1991; Presidential Decree No. 323, "On Urgent Measures for Implementation of Land Reform in the RSFSR," December 27, 1991, Article 6; Government Resolution No. 86, "On the Procedure for Reorganization of Collective and State Farms," December 29, 1991; and Roy L. Prosterman, Robert G. Mitchell, and Bradley J. Rorem, "Prospects for Family Farming in Russia," *Europe-Asia Studies* 49, no. 8 (December 1997): 1384–85.

13. Each land share on a particular enterprise is of equal size and represents its holder's ownership, in common with the other land share owners, of the land being used by the enterprise.

14. See the laws and decrees cited in note 12. Of particular relevance for the remainder of this paragraph are articles 13–17 of the regulation, "On Reorganization of Collective and State Farms and Privatization of State Agricultural Enterprises" (approved by Resolution No. 708 of the Government of the Russian Federation, September 4, 1992).

15. See Rorem and Giovarelli, *Agrarian Reform in the Russian Far East,* for further discussion.

16. For Khabarovsk, see *International Market Insight Reports,* information provided by an official from the Khabarovskii krai Ministry of Agriculture. For Amurskaia oblast, see Bonetskii, interview by authors.

17. The Economic Research Service of the USDA estimated in 1997 that 75 percent of former state and collective farms in Russia were unprofitable in 1995, even if all subsi-

dies were included in revenue. "International Agriculture and Trade: Newly Independent States and the Baltics" (Washington, D.C., USDA Economic Research Service, May 1997), as cited in Rorem and Giovarelli, *Agrarian Reform in the Russian Far East,* 32.

18. Presidential Decree No. 1212, "On Measures to Improve the Collection of Taxes and other Mandatory Payments and Streamlining Cash and Noncash Money Turnover," August 18, 1996.

19. Data from Russian Federation State Land Committee, 1996.

20. Data from Primorskii krai (the second largest agricultural region in the RFE) gathered in 1997 shows that nearly 45 percent of all shares in this region (37,765 out of 86,021 shares) are used without consideration by agricultural enterprises. Of even greater notice, as of 1997 Primorskii krai had issued only approximately 45 percent of shares to entitled owners in the region. Rorem and Giovarelli, *Agrarian Reform in the Russian Far East,* 16, Table 5.

21. As discussed on p. 198 under the section "Small Plots," some of the recorded decrease in the number of peasant farms may be attributed to deregistration of smaller farms to operate as household plots rather than as PFEs. (Reasons to deregister include tax advantages and less bureaucracy.) See, for example, V. Ia. Usun, "Privatization of Land and Farm Restructuring: Ideas, Mechanisms, Results, Problems," August 23, 1999, 6.

22. Data from Amurskaia oblast, State Committee on Land Resources and Land Tenure, 1999. Note that nationwide the amount of land in production by PFEs has increased.

23. Russian Federation State Land Committee, *Russia in Figures, 1997.* See also Aleksey Filatov, *Private Plots Supply Over 50 Percent of Food in Russia,* ITAR-TASS, April 3, 2000. (Small plots account for 50 percent of the food consumed in Russia.)

24. See especially, "On Reorganization of Collective and State Agricultural Enterprises," approved by Resolution No. 708 of the Government of the Russian Federation on September 4, 1992.

25. Data from Amurskaia oblast State Committee on Land Resources and Land Tenure, October 1999.

26. In 1997 Khabarovsk had 65,000 hectares and Amur had 779,000 hectares of arable land in their respective land funds. Ibid.

27. Rorem and Giovarelli, *Agrarian Reform in the Russian Far East,* 22–30.

28. For a full discussion of laws and regulations directing land fund creation and sources, see Ibid., 19–21.

29. One official from the Amurskaia oblast land committee was aware of only three cases in the past two years in which the oblast denied applications. In each case, officials deemed that the applicant had insufficient machinery to productively farm the land.

30. Rorem and Giovarelli, *Agrarian Reform in the Russian Far East.*

31. For further discussion, see Ibid., 19–20.

32. Experience in other countries underlines the potential for creating wealth through rural land market development. The average price of agricultural land in the eastern region of Germany has recently been estimated at $4,000–$5,000 per hectare. Roy

Prosterman and Leonard Rolfes, Jr., *Review of the Legal Basis for Agricultural Land Markets in Lithuania, Poland and Romania, and Implications for Accession to the EU,* report presented at the Second World Bank EU Accession Workshop, "Structural Change in the Farming Sectors of Central and Eastern Europe: Lessons and Implications for EU Accession," June 26–29, 1999, Warsaw, Poland. In the United States, nonirrigated wheat cropland is worth between $300 and $1,200. Information from Dr. Steven Tass, University of Minnesota; and "Agricultural Land Values," United States Department of Agriculture, March 20, 2000.

33. It is possible that some of the agricultural land in the RFE that is not currently in production has, at best, marginal productive capacity. Oblast governments should decide whether to remove some or all of this land from agricultural production, allowing it to return to its natural state.

34. In fact, legal authority for some land-monitoring activities is lacking. Federal legislation includes irrational use, but not nonuse, as a violation. In fact, under the rules for fining owners, it would be irrational to include nonuse, which is equivalent to allowing the land to lay fallow for a longer period of time and generally improves the fertility of the agricultural land. See Rorem and Giovarelli, *Agrarian Reform in the Russian Far East,* 23–30, for a detailed discussion of legislative authority for land monitoring.

35. Ibid.

36. Even a lease rate equal to 10 percent of the gross production is low relative to that in developed market economies, where lease payments for agricultural land constitute on average 25 percent of gross production.

37. Yevgenia Serova, "The Impact of Privatization and Farm Restructuring in Russian Agriculture," September 1999, 21, Table 11.

38. The only sector in which a market in land turnovers is functioning well in the RFE is the small plots (household auxiliary plots, *dacha* plots, garden plots). A law adopted by the Russian parliament in late 1992, complemented by a regulation issued in May 1993on how to actually carry out such sales, has given potential buyers and sellers high confidence in the legality of such transactions. As mentioned above, the ability to freely transact small plots has probably contributed to their high productivity.

39. Law of the Russian Federation, "On Mortgage," June 24, 1997.

40. Law of the Russian Federation, "On the State Registration of Rights to Immovables and Real Estate Transactions," June 17, 1997; Resolution No. 1378 of the Government of the Russian Federation, "On Measures to Realize the Federal Law on State Registration of Rights to Immovable Property and Transactions With It," November 1, 1998.

41. See, for example, V. Ia. Usun, "Privatization of Land and Farm Restructuring," 5.

42. Figures from V. A. Uvarov, *Agriculture of the Russian Far East: Choosing the Form of Production* (Rosseskogo Dalnego Vostoka: Khabarovsk, 1998), 315.

43. The deputy general director of Rosagrosnab, a company administering a government fund for the lease of machinery, was quoted as saying that the cost of equipment rose as much as 20,000 times during that period. FT Asia Intelligence Wire, "Russia Farming Equipment Lease Deal Signed," *International Market Insight Reports,* August 14, 1997.

44. Ro bert L. Walker, *Russian Agriculture from an American Perspective* <www. riaea.hypermart.net/book98/e02.htm>. For analysis of the banking system, see Pavel Minakir, "Influence of the 1998 Financial Crisis on the Russian Far East Economy," chapter 3 in this volume.

45. The Amur region produces 90 percent of Russia's soy.

46. FT Asia Intelligence Wire, *International Market Insight Reports*, October 21, 1998, 6.

47. Law of the Russian Federation, "On the Consumer Cooperative System in the Russian Federation," July 1992.

48. For example, one major tax for some agricultural producers is the profit tax, which amounts to 35 percent of an enterprise's gross profit less expenditures. See the Law of the Russian Federation, "On Tax on Profit of Enterprises and Organizations," December 27, 1991, with amendments made on July 16, and December 22, 1992; on August 27, 1993; on October 27, November 11, and December 3, 1994; and on April 25, 1995.

49. Interview with Sergei Egorov, Chief Specialist on Peasant (Farm) Enterprises, Khabarovskii krai Agro-Industrial Committee, October 18, 1999.

50. For an evaluation of the perceived Chinese threat, see Mikhail Alexseev, "Chinese Migration in the Russian Far East: Security Threats and Incentives for Cooperation in Primorskii Krai," chapter 13 in this volume.

THE MILITARY, THE PACIFIC FLEET, AND DEFENSE CONVERSION

9

Russian Reforms: Implications for
Regional Security Policy and the Military

Sergey Sevastyanov

CRISIS OF COMPREHENSIVE REFORMS

Currently, Russia finds itself in a unique moment in its history: the country does not face any immediate external threat, and it, in turn, is not a threat to anyone. Nevertheless, Russians can only dream about a "comprehensive security" environment. This term refers to a broad definition of security that characterizes threats that are mostly unrelated to traditional military power but which directly affect the basic political, economic, and social fabric of the nation. Security, in this case, is defined as a protection against loss.

During the last eight years, Russia has suffered many losses, including: (1) loss of half of its gross domestic product; (2) devaluation of the ruble against the U.S. dollar by two-thirds in a single day, August 17, 1998; (3) decrease of political influence and international standing; and (4) social degradation, among others. Today Russia's security concerns are largely *internal*. However, the scope and magnitude of these concerns are so tremendous that their culmulative effect has resulted in a "comprehensive insecurity syndrome."[1] This syndrome is comprehensive in the sense that all conceivable types of threat are present in Russia: endemic corruption; drug trafficking; environmental pollution; technological breakdowns; energy and food supply shortages; and violent outbreaks of terrorism and separatism.

In the early 1990s, the reform tasks seemed obvious: (1) change the pattern of the relationship between politics and economics by placing emphasis on the development of the market; and (2) demilitarize the state and civilian life to promote the growth of civil society and personal consciousness and freedoms.

Former President Boris Yeltsin tried to forcefully impose a market economy on post-communist Russia in a short period of time. However, it is well known that while formal institutions, such as constitutions and laws, may be established relatively quickly, informal institutions, such as customs, taboos, traditions, and codes of conduct, are culture-specific and slow to change. Yeltsin's reforms were extremely difficult to implement in Russia, where communism was a natural product of the country's historical development, rather than a form of government that was imported from abroad, as was the case in East European countries.

For this reason, fighting communism in Russia is to undermine the integrity of society. Not surprisingly, Russia's old informal institutions rejected the proposed reforms, and in 1998 Russia entered into a major crisis. Owing to a combination of domestic and external factors—including a high budget deficit, declining oil prices, and economic fallout from the Asian crisis—the Russian financial system collapsed.

The Russian Far East was not immune to these problems. In fact, the region was extremely hard hit by ten years of wild market reforms. As elsewhere in Russia, the crisis in the Russian Far East manifested itself through negative consequences in all spheres of public life, including economics, security, and social standards. As a result, consensus about the need to "reform the reforms" was the theme of the 1999–2000 electoral season. In response to the comprehensive insecurity syndrome, Vladimir Putin and his campaign staff effectively used forceful actions in Chechnya to boost his ratings as the March 2000 presidential elections approached. Furthermore, so as not to decrease the number of his supporters, Putin did not declare a clear economic program while campaigning, and this strategy also worked very well. In Russia people still vote for personalities, not for sophisticated economic programs. The RFE was no exception, and most of the region's population supported Putin.

This chapter examines two basic factors in order to address the impact of Russia's political reforms on RFE security. First, the influence of the Yeltsin reforms on security is analyzed using regional trends in three critical areas: Russian foreign policy in Asia, the military-industrial complex (MIC), and the status of the military. Second, the first initiatives proposed in the field of RFE security and economics by President Putin are explored in order to grasp their possible effect on the future security of the RFE.

DEVELOPMENT TRENDS IN THE RUSSIAN FAR EAST'S MILITARY-INDUSTRIAL COMPLEX

From the 1930s to the 1990s, a main purpose of the centrally planned socialist economy was to build up and support a military power in the Pacific. To achieve that goal, great economic and financial resources were constantly poured into the region, while about 50 percent of the region's gross industrial output was of military character.

The peaceful initiatives of the Gorbachev era first hit the local engineering industry, which began to suffer a reduction of military orders after 1989. In 1992 these reductions, averaging about 50 percent, affected almost all sectors. At the same time, the Yeltsin government stopped all subsidies to the RFE (transport, energy, wages, etc.). These circumstances coincided with the region's loss of the Russian domestic market due to a decrease in overall demand.

The first years of the reforms (1991–94) were the most painful for the regional military-industrial complex. Military orders were stopped, advertising to potential foreign customers was not yet in place, and the only clear signal coming from Moscow was to begin conversion to civilian production. Although it was easy to propose conversion, it was very difficult to implement it. Most of the RFE, and especially enterprises in Primorskii krai, had strong connections with the Pacific Fleet. A number of huge shipyards, such as Dalzavod and Zvezda, dealt with surface ships and submarine repairs, and the Pacific Fleet continued to send ships and submarines for repairs without having the money from Moscow to pay for them. For many years the main task for Zvezda was to repair Pacific Fleet submarines, so it was very difficult to convert its production lines. Moreover, civilian submarines still do not have a market niche. In addition, the RFE civilian ship-owners ignored Dalzavod, sending their vessels to foreign shipyards in Korea, Taiwan, and China, where repair quality was guaranteed and the cost-benefit ratio was more acceptable.

Other Vladivostok MIC enterprises in the communications and electronics businesses also met a number of obstacles as they tried to convert their production. After 1992, due to a general liberalization of foreign trade in Russia, it became possible to partially reorient the RFE's financial and commercial transactions toward the Asia Pacific market. The increase in international trade played a very positive role in meeting the demands of the local population by compensating for the reduction in domestic production. However, this situation created a nightmare for local MIC enterprises, because, after a few months, the RFE (as well as Russia as a whole) was adequately supplied with high-quality and affordable electronics, refrigerators, and other such goods produced in South Korea or Southeast Asia.

After 1991, Russian military production declined dramatically as state orders for weapons and military equipment were reduced by more than 90 percent until 1995.[2] This situation resulted in partial layoffs for workers in MIC enterprises. From 1991 to 1995, industrial output in all sectors of the RFE economy declined by about 58 percent because the regional domestic market was too small to support output.

During the Soviet era, the RFE received huge subsidies from the central budget. (The region's contribution to the national income was far less than what the RFE received in subsidies.) With an end to subsidies, the situation changed radically. Unfortunately, during the initial years of the reforms, Moscow considered Russia as a single economy. It was not until 1995 that the central government began to search for new policies to be implemented in different regions that took into account their specific economic profiles, geography, and specialization.

In 1996, a new federal program was proposed for the economic and social development of the RFE and Trans-Baikal for 1996–2005. The main idea of the program was to integrate the RFE with the Northeast Asian market, and at the same time to place the RFE within a framework of Russia's domestic division of labor. The latter issue was of primary importance because a type of geopolitical paradox was incorporated into it: more than 4,000 miles from Moscow, the geographic distance between the RFE and production facilities in western Russia threatens to isolate the region and force it to seek assistance—economic or otherwise—in Northeast Asia.

Although the central government agreed that it was a national priority to prevent the separation of the Far East from the central part of Russia, very few practical steps were taken to help the region. Furthermore, neither the president's program nor federal economic policy included any real incentives for the RFE to promote its international economic activities.

In recent years, however, MIC enterprises in the Russian Far East have received much more optimistic signals from Moscow about the possibility of their survival in the market economy. The Russian government changed its attitude toward the military-industrial complex and promised to allocate credits for new military orders and dual-purpose (both military and civilian) production. As a result of this change in government policy, most MIC enterprises in the region remain oriented toward military production. Only some have been able to develop dual-technology products and to find their niche in foreign or domestic markets. At the same time, 1998 was a stabilizing year for some MIC enterprises due to effective production diversification efforts, strong local government support, improvements in advertising campaigns, and the drastic change in the ruble to dollar ratio after August 1998.

Progress, one of the largest MIC enterprises in Primorye, achieved some stability between 1998 and 2000. Its internationally competitive helicopters, the Ka-50 Black Shark and the Ka-52 Alligator, were included in international tenders declared by Turkey and South Korea. However, in order to push its own helicopters, the United States exerted strong political pressure on both countries not to purchase Russian equipment. Production diversification efforts at Progress also brought positive results: contracts have been signed to sell 5 Yak-55 civilian aircraft to the United States, 6 civilian helicopters to domestic customers, and 700 cargo containers to Japan.

Zvezda has been able to exploit its position as one of the best submarine repair facilities in Northeast Asia and has secured an order to repair two Chinese submarines. In addition, Zvezda, Dalzavod, and Eastern Shipyard became participants in the Primorskii krai administration's very ambitious program to build several hundred small- and medium-sized fishing boats using MIC facilities. This program would serve the dual purposes of helping these shipyards overcome the current crisis and renovating the obsolete fishing fleet. The Primorskii krai administration is already granting credits and tax privileges to program participants and is ready to allocate guarantees to foreigners who would like to invest in the project.[3]

In another military conversion program supported by the Primorye administration, the leadership of the enterprise Askold decided to partially switch from swords to ploughshares. In addition to producing auxiliary military equipment, they began to construct 17 types of agricultural machinery. Because its clients did not have enough money to buy its products, Askold did not earn a profit in 1999. In 2000, however, the situation improved when the Primorye government allocated credits to the best agricultural farms to buy Askold machinery.

In Soviet times, Vladivostok-based MIC enterprises Izumrud and Radiopribor produced communications and electronic equipment to support military orders. Fortunately, an efficient diversification effort was possible in this field. Both plants were able to secure profitable foreign military contracts and to diversify production. In an interview, the Radiopribor director said that the plant is ready to start manufacturing any product that could bring profit.[4] This statement indicated a sea change in the director's mentality. Radiopribor's development program through 2001 is based on increasing production in the civilian sector.

The current situation is much less favorable at the oldest and most famous Vladivostok shipyard, Dalzavod. Due to its very substantial ship-repairing obligations to the Pacific Fleet, Dalzavod found it difficult to implement any sound conversion program. Dalzavod leadership now has the more realistic hope that it will continue to service the Pacific Fleet on a long-term basis. It is expected that Dalzavod will be included in the "National Shipbuilding Program until the Year 2010," which is currently under discussion in the Russian government.

To support the military-industrial complex, the parliament approved a law in December 1999 that made bankruptcy of MIC enterprises very difficult. According to that law, the bankruptcy process could be initiated only if the MIC enterprise's liabilities were larger than its assets, and an enterprise now has twice as much time to overcome its debt crisis.[5] The MICs are also supported on the provincial level. In

January 2000, twelve Primorskii krai MIC enterprise directors formed a new council to coordinate cooperation. The Primorye government's MIC Committee Chairman Alexander Polusmak became chairman of that council.

Center-regional relations have changed drastically during the reform period. In the Soviet era, the role of the governor (at that time, the first secretary of the regional committee of the Communist Party of the Soviet Union) was mostly to control the socioeconomic situation in the region. Now the RFE governors and their deputies have become vigorous lobbyists for the interests of their territories in the central government, especially for the MIC. This change is quite understandable, because before the reforms about 50 percent of the regional industrial output was devoted to military purposes, and in 1997 the overall RFE output in the military and civilian sectors combined was estimated at 24 percent of the 1990 level.

Since 1993 one of the most visible political figures in the RFE was former governor of Primorskii krai, Yevgenii Nazdratenko. His long-term socioeconomic agenda was to level the playing field for RFE enterprises by introducing tariffs equal to those in the rest of the Russian Federation, including tariffs for railway transportation and electricity. Nazdratenko was also a great help to the MIC enterprises in Primorye. He proved capable of winning state orders and of securing state budget funds to help in fulfilling the orders.

For the MIC enterprises, obtaining well-paid state orders to produce armaments for foreign countries is the best and easiest way to survive in Russia's new economic environment. However, arms exports in 1997 and 1998 dropped to $2.5 billion and $2.0 billion respectively, the country's worst performance since 1993. One possible explanation for the decrease is the fact that all military sales to Southeast Asia were suspended due to the Asian economic crisis.

In these circumstances, the role of Rosvooruzhenie, the state arms-exporting corporation, became critically important for both the central and regional governments. To improve its ties with regional MIC enterprises, Rosvooruzhenie has established fourteen offices throughout the country. These offices are also intended to serve as a channel for the regions to influence Moscow and to be an effective means by which the center might coordinate the work of the regional administrations, armed forces, and MIC leadership in order to support MIC interests at both the state and provincial levels and to increase foreign arms sales.[6] As a result of these efforts, in 1999 Russian arms exports increased to about $2.8 billion (other Russian experts estimate that the figure was about $3.4 billion). During 2000 that positive trend continued, and, according to preliminary data, total Russian arms exports reached $4.0 billion in 2000.

To further strengthen its position in the world armaments market, in November 2000 the Russian system of military technical cooperation with foreign countries was again reorganized. According to presidential decree, Rosvooruzhenie and another state arms exporting corporation, Promexport, were combined into one federal state enterprise, Rosoboronexport. Some experts predict that the effects of the centralization effort of those arms sales, as well as continuing strong global demand for new and secondhand Russian armaments, could soon increase Russia's annual military exports to $5–6 billion.[7]

In March 2000, two Russian newspapers published information on total military armament production for an eight-year period (1992–99) and its distribution between the armed forces of the Russian Federation and foreign countries. Although there have been reports that these numbers are not absolutely accurate, the information gives a clear picture that for years the Russian armed forces were unloved stepchildren of their own government (see Table 9.1).[8]

Table 9.1 Distribution of Russian Military Production (1992–99)

	Domestic Sales	Foreign Sales			
		China	India	Other countries	Total
Aircraft	7	101	85	92	278
Helicopters	8	6	16	76	98
Tanks	31	140	175	120	435
Submarines	2	4	6	–	10
Surface ships	2	4	3	4	11
Armored troop-carriers	17	60	36	121	217
Anti-air missile systems	1	8	10	4	22

Source: "Nesokrushimaia i legendarnaia," *Komsomol'skaia Pravda,* March 31, 2000.

It is clear that the Chinese and Indian armed forces are currently equipped with Russian armaments, while Russia's own armed forces can only dream about access to domestically produced weapons. All the same, the idea to increase Russian arms sales to Asia is still one of the main tenants of Moscow's foreign policy.

REGIONAL SECURITY PROSPECTS

Security policy cannot be considered in isolation from economics. As a country in economic turmoil, Russia does not have much room for effective maneuvering in the Asia Pacific. However, due to its location, nuclear capabilities, and abundant natural resources, its strategic and economic interests remain important.

Some political experts in Russia argue that in the foreseeable future Russian foreign policy should be based on the concept of "limited globalism."[9] This theory assumes that, although it is a global power, Russia should pursue a pragmatic policy and selectively seek to engage in world and regional affairs. In this scenario, Russia's vital interests are primarily located in the regions adjacent to its borders. In view of this, it is quite natural for Russia to focus its foreign policy on its neighbors to the west, south, and east (paying special attention to the core regional triangle— China, Japan, and the Korean Peninsula).

The main regional security threats to Russia are perceived to be:

- potential armed (or even nuclear) conflict on the Korean Peninsula;
- the military growth of China and its potential conflict with Taiwan and neighboring states;
- tension with Japan over unresolved territorial disputes;
- proliferation of weapons of mass destruction and illegal arms trade;
- development of the U.S. theater missile defense (TMD) and national missile defense (NMD) systems;
- nontraditional security threats such as illegal immigration and poaching in Russian waters; and
- isolation of the RFE from the Asia Pacific region.

Notwithstanding its internal problems, the eastward dimension of Russia's policy is becoming an increasingly important priority. Since 1998 Russia has substantially increased its political activities in Northeast Asia. In 1998 Russia was officially admitted to the Asia Pacific Economic Cooperation (APEC) Forum, and, in recent years, numerous high-level meetings have taken place between the Russian leadership and that of its regional neighbors.

China

China has continued to be the main focus of Russian policy in the Asia Pacific. The latest important visit to Moscow of a Chinese high-ranking military official was that of General Zhang Wannian, deputy chairman of the Chinese Central Military Council, in June 1999. An important agreement for further increasing the level of military and technical cooperation was reached during his meeting with then Russian Minister of Defense Igor Sergeyev.

General Zhang's visit took place during the political crisis that followed the bombing of the Chinese embassy in Kosovo, when the need for greater coordination between Russian and Chinese foreign policies became imminent. In fact, Russia and China share the view that all post–World War II security arrangements were damaged by the United States in 1999. Moscow and Beijing assert that the most devastating blows to that system were the U.S. bombing of Kosovo without UN approval, the disagreement in the U.S. Senate over ratification of the Comprehensive Test Ban Treaty (CTBT), and the Clinton administration's attempts to abrogate the Anti-Ballistic Missile (ABM) treaty.

According to the Stockholm International Institute of Peace, between 1991 and 1997 Russia sold China armaments worth more than $6 billion, and in 2000–05, the overall value of Russian arms exports to China is projected to be $5–6 billion. As a result, military sales to China have become critically important for the survival of Russia's MIC, and the RFE military-industrial enterprises in particular. Su-27 fighters and Moskit antiship missiles are produced in the RFE, and Zvezda has an order to repair Chinese kilo-class submarines. Consequently, this arms sales dependence is becoming mutual: China depends on Russian military technology to boost its military capabilities, while the Russian Federation depends on Chinese purchases of arms to sustain its MIC, at least for the next four to five years.

On his way back to Beijing, General Zhang met with both the Pacific Fleet Commander in Vladivostok and the Far Eastern Military District Commander in Khabarovsk, where he visited a number of MIC enterprises. In Vladivostok, Zhang declared that Russia's Pacific Fleet had great prospects for military-technical cooperation with the Chinese navy, and that the RFE had many MIC enterprises that could fulfill Chinese orders. General Zhang's words were confirmed in October 1999, when, to mark the fiftieth anniversary of the People's Republic of China, two Russian ships came to Shanghai for the first naval exercises with China. During that visit, China's leadership praised the warming ties between the two countries and expressed hope that a strategic partnership would develop further.

In December 1999, a contract worth about $1 billion was signed for Russia to sell to China a large group of advanced fighters. In that same month, a newly built Sovremenny-class destroyer was officially transferred to the Chinese navy at the Northern Shipyard in Saint Petersburg. In May 2000, 24 Moskit antiship missiles were sent to China from the enterprise Progress to arm the new ship. A second Sovremenny-class destroyer and 24 more antiship missiles were to be sent to China by year-end 2000.[10]

During President Yeltsin's December 1999 meeting with Chinese President Jiang Zemin in Beijing, both presidents expressed their dissatisfaction with the U.S. position on the ABM and CTBT treaties and criticized Taiwanese and Chechen separatism. They signed protocols on border demarcation and defined priority areas for future economic cooperation as follows: joint extraction and transportation of oil and gas, new technology exchanges, and further development of direct economic links between adjacent border provinces. The meeting indicated that for the foreseeable future, Russia can be expected to maintain close ties with China. However, if Russia cannot overcome its extended economic crisis, the geopolitical tendencies in this bilateral relationship may work against Russia in the long run.

Japan

The Russian-Japanese relationship has been characterized by contradictions. On the one hand, the geopolitical interests of both countries depend on the radical improvement of bilateral relations. Yet, while work on a bilateral peace treaty continues, Russia emphasizes the idea of joint economic exploitation of the Northern Territories/Kurile Islands—without the transfer of sovereignty—and economic exchanges between Russia and Japan remain fairly insignificant.

Japan's desire to support reforms in Russia was reaffirmed during then Prime Minister Keizo Obuchi's visit to Moscow in November 1998 (the first official visit at that level in twenty-five years). Furthermore, Moscow appreciates Tokyo's limited input into the TMD program and hopes that Japan will not go further than the research phase. Recent positive changes in Tokyo's policies toward Russia may be explained not only by Japan's desire to solve the territorial dispute but also by the recent improvement in Sino-Russian relations. The warming in the Sino-Russian relationship induced Tokyo to implement a policy change to increase Japan's own diplomatic maneuverability.

One way to show a change in foreign policy is to increase the level of state visits, which has already begun. The next step in improving ties is to change the paradigm of bilateral military cooperation. In 1996 a Japanese Maritime Self-Defense Force (MSDF) ship paid a visit to Vladivostok. It was the first visit to Russia by an MSDF ship since the end of the Cold War (Canada, the United States, China, and South Korea had sent official naval delegations to Vladivostok in the early 1990s). In 1997 Russia reciprocated with an official naval visit to Tokyo—104 years after the last port visit of this kind. In 1998, the first joint Russo-Japanese search-and-rescue naval exercises were held in the Vladivostok area.

In August 1999, then Japanese Minister of Defense Hosei Norota paid an official visit to the Russian defense minister and met with the Pacific Fleet commander in Vladivostok. In Moscow, Norota signed an important memorandum on bilateral understanding and military cooperation. In Vladivostok, he approved a plan for a hotline between the Japan MSDF and the Russian Pacific Fleet and proposed annual bilateral search-and-rescue exercises.

The level and agenda of Norota's meetings in Russia very much resembled General Zhang Wannian's visit to Russia earlier that year. This resemblance was not a coincidence, but a manifestation of the Japanese leadership's desire to demonstrate to the world that they enjoy the same level of military contacts with

Russia that China does (the difference is that Russian-Chinese military cooperation has a strong economic component).

In September 1999 another Pacific Fleet ship made a visit to Japan, and in February 2000 Japan MSDF Chief of Staff Admiral Kosei Fujita visited Moscow and Vladivostok. In the capital of Primorskii krai, he was permitted to board the Variag missile cruiser and declared that Japanese-Russian naval cooperation would be strengthened further. His words were confirmed in September 2000 when MSDF ships visited Kamchatka.

In February 2000 Russian Minister of Foreign Affairs Igor Ivanov made the first official trip to three Asian countries (Japan, North Korea, and Vietnam) since Putin became president. During his meeting with Prime Minister Obuchi, Ivanov declared that Russia was not ready to define an exact date for the signing of a bilateral peace treaty and that Moscow would solve the territorial dispute without jeopardizing its national interests.

Korean Peninsula

During the February 2000 trip, Ivanov also made an official visit to Pyongyang (the first by a Russian minister of foreign affairs in ten years). During the 1990s, Moscow lost almost any leverage it had over North Korea, and now all Russian politicians agree that a strategic mistake was made in the early 1990s, when official relations were fully switched from North to South Korea. Ivanov's visit was a first step toward improving the bilateral relationship with North Korea. During the visit, a new bilateral treaty on cooperation and friendship was signed. (The treaty was not aimed against third countries and was free of any ideological bias.)

The historic meeting between the leaders of North and South Korea in June 2000 received very positive coverage in the Russian media. Moscow's official position is that Russia will try to secure full-scale participation in dealing with problems on the Korean Peninsula and will maintain balanced relationships with both Koreas.[11]

Southeast Asia

The Asian economic crisis destroyed Russian hopes of expanding arms sales to most countries in Southeast Asia, especially Indonesia. However, the effort to reestablish friendship with Vietnam was successful. Moscow plans to sell its former ally 24 Su-27 fighters and several naval vessels. Despite severe financial problems, Russia extended its lease to maintain the Cam Rahn Bay supply facility beyond the year 2000 (that small facility in Vietnam has become one of the few remaining assets symbolizing Russia's previous status as a superpower in the Asia Pacific).

The United States

The political relationship and military cooperation between the Russian Federation and the United States in the Asia Pacific for the last five or six years are very curious issues. Since 1993, NATO's imminent eastward expansion has become a problem in Russia's relations with the United States. Moreover, disagreement over Russian proposals to lift the trade embargo against Iraq has been exacerbated by Moscow's irritation over the Kosovo bombing.

However, U.S. politics in Asia do not seem to contradict any critical Russian interests in the region. In fact, on a number of diplomatic issues, they have effectively coincided. Moscow appreciates U.S. financial help in dealing with Russia's nuclear submarine waste and Washington's rejection of a Japanese proposal to remove part of the U.S. military bases and personnel from Okinawa to Hokkaido. In addition, Russia has not called for the dismantling of America's Cold War–era treaties with Japan and South Korea; and during his May 1997 visit to Japan, then Russian Defense Minister General Igor Rodionov even called the U.S.–Japan Security Treaty a stabilizing factor in Northeast Asia. The only visible problem in this bilateral relationship in Asia now is a U.S.-Japanese effort to install TMD against North Korea. From the Russian standpoint, the North Korean threat is exaggerated in order to justify these plans. The realization of this program would involve colossal military expenditures and may bring instability in the regional balance of power.

From 1994 to 1998, Russian-American military contacts in the Asia Pacific were very positive, including a series of search-and-rescue exercises, the *Cooperation from the Sea* series of amphibious disaster relief exercises, U.S. Pacific Command and Russian Far East (0–6) Working Group meetings,[12] and others. The centerpiece of those annual events was the *Cooperation from the Sea* exercise series. So far, it is the only series of bilateral naval exercises between Russia and the United States in the post–Cold War era. However, in the spring of 1999, the post-Kosovo effect put bilateral political and military cooperation in Asia on hold indefinitely.

Since the end of the Cold War, Moscow has emphasized diplomacy, not raw power, in its relationship with countries of the region. In 1996 Russia became a full participant in the ASEAN Regional Forum and in 1998 a member of APEC. Being a member of practically all Track I (governmental) and Track II (nongovernmental) regional security and economic cooperation organizations, Russia will definitely try to gain more influence by working through these channels. But what Russia may now face is a credibility problem. Some may wonder how Moscow will support Russia's international obligations (whatever they may be) with limited resources to pursue a consistent regional policy.

PACIFIC FLEET STATUS

One of Russia's most valuable assets in implementing its regional security obligations is the Pacific Fleet. As then Pacific Fleet Commander (now Commander-in-
Chief of the Russian Navy) Admiral Vladimir Kuroyedov declared in November
1996, the Pacific Fleet's main operational tasks are:

- to maintain nuclear deterrence;
- to defend Russian territory;
- to secure the Russian Federation's economic zone;
- to protect the sea lines of communication; and
- to conduct "show-the-flag" missions in the ocean areas of strategic importance (including port visits, joint exercises, and peacekeeping missions).[13]

To accomplish these tasks, the Pacific Fleet has different types of submarines, surface combatants, auxiliary vessels, sea aviation, a marine corps, shore
missiles, and artillery units. Unfortunately, for several years the Pacific Fleet received no new surface ships or aircraft, and meeting the same commitments
with considerably fewer resources is becoming a very difficult task. The smart
advice—to do more with less and apply limited resources where they achieve
the greatest effect—is easy to give, but hard to implement.

At the height of the Cold War, the Russian navy had a popular saying that its
two most dangerous enemies were the U.S. Navy's Submerged Ocean Surveil-
lance Underwater System (SOSUS), used to detect Russian submarines, and the
Airborne Warning and Control System (AWACS), used by the U.S. Air Force to
detect Russian aircraft. For the last ten years, Russia's navy has had only one
enemy, but it is a more formidable one—the lack of adequate finances.

In the reform era, the government budget has not been able to meet defense requirements. Military spending in Russia has been reduced annually, and
now constitutes less than 3 percent of the nation's GDP. From 1992 to 1997,
the total reduction in spending amounted to 60 percent, with a further 40
percent cut in 1998 alone. As a result, in comparison with 1992 levels, in 1998
Russia was spending only 27 percent on operation and maintenance of the
armed forces, 10 percent of which went toward research and development and
a mere 7 percent to procurement.[14]

A considerable portion of the Russian Federation's financial burden for supporting the armed forces has been transferred to the Primorskii krai budget. Since
the early 1990s, the regional budget has provided the Pacific Fleet, Far Eastern
Military District, border guards, and other federal service units with electricity,
fuel, water, and food. The federal government paid for only part of those needs.

Its current debt to Primorskii krai is about 3 billion rubles (including a 500-million ruble debt to MIC enterprises for armaments produced to fulfill state military orders). Not receiving this money, MIC plants and shipyards have not been able to pay taxes to the provincial budget.[15]

Fortunately, this problem did not provoke confrontation between Nazdratenko and the leaders of federal agencies in the region. Quite the contrary, they have made joint efforts to attract the attention of the president and prime minister to the arrears. The point that the central government must more adequately share the military burden with the region was raised during then Prime Minister Putin's visit to Vladivostok in October 1999. In a February 2000 interview, Admiral Kuroyedov acknowledged that for the last ten years the Russian navy decreased by about 1,000 ships and patrol boats. He predicted that if the trend continues, by 2010 or 2015 the navy would encounter a real shortage of surface vessels.[16] Regarding the Pacific Fleet, in 1992 it had 345 ships and patrol boats, in 1996 it had 140, and the decline is still continuing.[17]

A critical part of the national strategic balance of power, Pacific Fleet nuclear submarines with ballistic missiles (as well as multipurpose nuclear submarines) receive priority in all kinds of material and financial support. Nevertheless, for the last several years the number of their sea deployments has decreased, and some of the submarines are becoming outdated. Two newly built multipurpose nuclear submarines, Tomsk and Cheetah (Hepard), which came to the Pacific Fleet in 2000, were the only exceptions to that negative trend.[18]

In the late 1990s, due to the lack of adequate base and repair infrastructure as well as to financial shortages, the Pacific Fleet lost a number of unique oceangoing ships (the space control ship Marshal Nedelin,[19] the command and control ship Ural, and several cruisers and destroyers). In addition, some years earlier two helicopter carriers were sold abroad.[20]

For the last several years, severe shortages of fuel and money have been constant impediments to the Pacific Fleet's exercises at sea and implementation of foreign visits. Despite several widely publicized naval exercises, average training levels have remained low. Due to lack of fuel, in July 2000 the Naval Day's sea parade of Pacific Fleet ships was cancelled for the first time in many years.

For the last ten years the Pacific Fleet has been a valuable asset to Russian diplomacy in the Asia Pacific. Since 1990 a great number of foreign naval vessels have visited Vladivostok. Pacific Fleet ships have also visited the United States, China, South Korea, Japan, Thailand, Malaysia, India, and Vietnam. The first visits paid to each of these countries, especially to the United States (1990), China (1993), South Korea (1993), and Japan (1997), were real breakthroughs in reestablishing bilateral relationships after many years of confrontation and distrust. Those visits were supplemented by bilateral communications, joint maneuvering, and search-and-rescue exercises, thus contributing to increased trust and interoperability between the navies.

However, for the last three or four years the Pacific Fleet has had difficulty reciprocating annual visits to its foreign partners. Since 1995, all *Cooperation from the Sea* exercises were either implemented in the Vladivostok area or cancelled. In October 1998, due to financial constraints, Russia's Pacific Fleet could not send a ship to Pusan (one of the closest foreign naval bases to Vladivostok) to participate in the international parade of ships held in conjunction with the Republic of Korea's fiftieth anniversary. The situation improved in 1999 when the Pacific Fleet reciprocated with visits to Japan and China.

The Pacific Fleet has gained valuable interoperability experience with foreign navies. In the annual *Cooperation from the Sea* exercises, the Pacific Fleet commanding officers and crews have demonstrated excellent seamanship and amphibious landing capabilities. If a multinational search-and-rescue or a UN-led naval operation were necessary in the Asia Pacific, the Pacific Fleet (if the operation coincided with Russia's national interests) could allocate ships.

Problems of Decommissioned Nuclear Submarines

The difficulties associated with decommissioning the Pacific Fleet's nuclear submarines and processing nuclear waste are extremely important. A number of decommissioned submarines currently wait for full dismantlement and deactivation of their nuclear reactors. Substantial nuclear waste stocks at Bolshoi Kamen also need to be processed. The United States and Japan, both very concerned with nuclear safety issues, have already allocated money for the problem. In October 1999 the Zvezda management signed two documents to cooperate with Japan and the United States on safe nuclear waste disposal. The first certified that the Japanese-funded floating filtration plant, Landysh, was in adequate technical condition and run by highly qualified personnel. Since autumn 1999 that floating plant has been undergoing active water tests, and in the autumn of 2000 Landysh became operational.

The second agreement was a contract signed with the U.S. Department of Defense to build a technical shore base at Zvezda. Russian specialists designed the project to support the full technological cycle of nuclear submarine dismantlement. Its implementation would lead to several positive outcomes. First, it will help to improve the ecological situation in the area. The unloading of nuclear reactors and the processing of liquid and solid waste would be implemented at this shore base by highly qualified personnel using the newest Russian and foreign technologies. Second, it has a profound socioeconomic dimension. It will create new jobs and bring money to the city of Bolshoi Kamen, where Zvezda is the largest industrial enterprise.[21]

For many years the politically sensitive problems of nuclear waste disposal and nuclear security were highly classified. They came into the spotlight around 1998 when Pacific Fleet journalist Captain Second Rank Grigorii Pasko was arrested for allegedly passing secrets on nuclear waste disposal areas and transportation routes to the Japan Broadcasting Corporation NHK press bureau chief in Vladivostok.

It turned out that Pacific Fleet Federal Security Service (FSB) Department Chief Admiral Nikolai Sotskov got all the heat in Pasko's controversial trial. In several interviews, he confirmed that the Pacific Fleet commander and the FSB, as well as Moscow research institutes and Far Eastern Academy of Science scholars, were doing their best to solve the Pacific Fleet's nuclear safety problems. However, due to the Fleet's acute financial problems and lack of adequate technical facilities, the problems would not be completely solved in the immediate future.[22] Russia is ready to accept foreign advice and financial help in solving these problems, but it will never agree to foreign control of the nuclear arsenals, which it would consider a breach of sovereignty.

Lacking sufficient finances to make adequate technical decisions, the FSB and the Ministry of the Interior implemented a series of joint preventive actions to support nuclear security and to stop economic crimes and the illegal sale of armaments. In 1999–2000 they were able to confiscate grenades, artillery shells, 9 small arms, an anti-aircraft missile launcher, and about 18,000 cartridges that had been stolen from Pacific Fleet arsenals.[23]

An unfortunate incident happened on October 20, 1999, when three warrant officers and two seamen illegally entered a decommissioned nuclear submarine module (without a nuclear reactor) that was waiting to be dismantled in Chazhma Bay. The thieves planned to steal nonferrous metals and sell them at the local metal collection point. Unfortunately for the thieves, there was not enough oxygen inside the module, and all five of them died.

To present a clear picture, several negative incidents and serious problems involving decommissioned submarines and nuclear waste disposal have been mentioned here. However, it is important to clarify that, for many years, no serious incidents involving the Pacific Fleet's combat-ready nuclear submarines have occurred, although incidents with decommissioned nuclear submarines occasionally have taken place.

Recently the morale of Pacific Fleet personnel has shown signs of improving. Several years ago, officers and seamen received their small salaries up to five months late. Since 1999, salaries have increased and are now paid on time. In 1997–98, many officers left the navy voluntarily. Not all of them found good civilian jobs, and as a result, this process has practically stopped. Though lack of adequate finances could be considered a threat to the safety of the nuclear complexes, the Pacific Fleet

Command has the situation under control. For that reason, characterizations of the Pacific Fleet status as having salary arrears or allowing possible sale of decommissioned submarines or the theft of nuclear weapons are clearly exaggerations.

PRESIDENT PUTIN'S REFORMS

After ten years of the Yeltsin presidency, it was imperative for the new Russian president to implement new policies toward the economic and regional security concerns of the Russian Far East. In July 2000 President Putin expressed his strong dissatisfaction with the present situation in the RFE and demonstrated his political willingness to improve it.

Reviving the military became one of the policies that gave Putin a commanding lead in the elections. To give everybody, including himself, the proud feeling that he was the leader of a strong military power, he flew on a modern fighter (Su-27) and attack aircraft (Su-25) in autumn 1999 and spring 2000, respectively. Putin also made short visits on board the Pacific Fleet's missile cruiser Variag and on the Northern Fleet's strategic nuclear submarine Karelia.

Putin used his Variag visit in October 1999 as a chance to declare his presidential campaign priorities. As far as security issues were concerned, the most important among them were:[24]

- to champion Russia's national interests in the world, the country must have strong armed forces and MIC;
- the MIC is the only sphere in which Russia is still competitive on the international industrial market, and, therefore, it is the only engine capable of getting Russia out of its economic crisis (this view is a 180-degree turn from the previous economic course);
- the 2000 Russian military budget was to be increased from 93 billion rubles to 146 billion rubles, and more than 26 billion rubles of that money was to be assigned to arms procurement; and
- naval development is to become a priority in the Russian Federation military doctrine.

Offering practical interpretations of these policies, Russian officials proposed their own ideas for security policy. Deputy Prime Minister Ilia Klebanov expressed his satisfaction with the fact that the 2000 state military order was increased by 50 percent, in addition to an 80-percent increase in research and development and arms procurement. Admiral Kuroyedov reported that Russia's main naval staff was working hard to prepare the "Russian Federation Naval Doctrine until the Year 2020." He declared that Russia would need to allocate about 50 billion rubles to sustain the naval component of its nuclear deterrence until 2010. He added that overall financing of the naval component in the Russian annual military budget should increase from the current lower level to 20 percent.[25]

Addressing an audience at the Financial Academy in Moscow in March 2000, Andrei Kazmin, chairman of Sberbank, the largest Russian bank, said that the bank's priority would be to allocate credits to the industrial sectors of the Russian economy, laying special emphasis on export-oriented MIC enterprises. Sberbank's reasons for giving priority to MIC export orders may be twofold: sound expectations to receive financial profit and striving to block foreign investment in this strategic sector of the Russian economy.

Winning the presidential election in the first round, Vladimir Putin received a solid endorsement not only from the Russian population but also from the Duma (the lower chamber of the Russian parliament). His first actions as president demonstrated that he was ready to apply new approaches to solving old problems. In one month's time, Putin was able to persuade the Duma to ratify the Strategic Arms Reduction Treaty-II (START-II), which Yeltsin could not do in seven years, and the CTBT, which was turned down by the U.S. Senate in October 1999. Both ratifications became a part of the political bargain proposed by Putin to persuade the United States not to abrogate the ABM Treaty.

The ABM Treaty was discussed during President Clinton's visit to Russia in June 2000, but the two presidents could not reach a compromise. Nevertheless, a few days later in Italy, Putin made an innovative proposal to build a European ABM nonstrategic system. European leaders commented very cautiously on his proposal, but most of them demonstrated either a negative or vague attitude toward the U.S. plan to build a national missile defense system.

In July 2000 Putin effectively used his Asia trip to declare new approaches to Asia policy and also to express his strong dissatisfaction with the present economic and social situation in the RFE. On the eve of that trip, Putin declared that Russia was both a European and an Asian state, and therefore Russian foreign policy would be balanced.[26]

During the Russian president's visit to China (July 18–19, 2000), both countries confirmed their course for strategic partnership. Presidents Putin and Jiang Zemin agreed to further develop cooperation in a number of joint economic projects, to increase Russian arms sales to China, and to deepen border trade. In a joint statement, both leaders expressed their strong disagreement with U.S. plans to build an NMD system and to include Taiwan in a TMD system. That visit's success was well predicted, and it demonstrated once again the coincidence of the Russian and Chinese approaches toward "the most critical issues of world politics."[27]

Putin's visit to the Democratic People's Republic of Korea (DPRK) was a real breakthrough in the bilateral relationship. Putin and Kim Jong Il discussed economic cooperation, bilateral trade, and other issues, but the most sensitive topic was North Korea's long-range missile program. President Kim expressed the possibility that if developed countries help Pyongyang launch communications satellites, DPRK might abandon the missile program.

After his visit to Pyongyang, President Putin made his next stop in Blagoveshchensk (the capital city of Amurskaia oblast—across the Amur River from China) for a meeting with the RFE leadership. On the eve of that event, Viktor Ishaev, chairman of the Far East and Trans-Baikal interregional economic cooperation association and Khabarovskii krai governor, disclosed that the RFE governors would like to discuss three critical issues with President Putin: (1) the failure of the Russian government to execute federal programs for the economic and social development of the RFE and Trans-Baikal for the years 1996–2005; (2) the ongoing energy crisis; and (3) demographic problems.[28]

At that meeting, Putin asserted that during the last several years the RFE and Trans-Baikal were developing at an extremely slow pace. He declared that Russia must fundamentally change its policy toward the RFE to convert this region, which possesses abundant natural resources and high industrial potential, into a prosperous part of the country. To start moving towards that ambitious aim, he set two principal tasks: (1) to develop a concept that defines several principal spheres for concentrated allocation of federal money in order to change the operational mode of the entire RFE economy; and (2) to strengthen the federal powers of the presidential representative in the RFE. Putin declared that the presidential representative must play first fiddle in the more efficient inclusion of the RFE into Russia's federal system and in strengthening its ties with the other parts of Russia.[29]

The Blagoveshchensk meeting produced a number of critical outcomes. Most important, it clarified the role that the presidential representative would play in the region. In a few months, it changed from exercising control over the governors' policies and actions to assuming full responsibility for the RFE. A few days after the meeting, the presidential envoy, Konstantin Pulikovskii, declared that for effective realization of federal decisions, he would form the RFE Federal District Council. RFE governors, provincial Duma chairpersons, and leaders of federal structures— Ministry of Defense, Ministry of Interior, etc.—would be its members. According to a statement by Pulikovsky, the Council would become a regional-level branch of the executive power with its decisions binding for all RFE provinces.[30]

However, due to very serious opposition from the governors and from the presidential administration, such a plan has not materialized. In a September 2000 interview, Pulikovsky said that the RFE Federal District Council would help the Far East

and Trans-Baikal interregional economic cooperation association to implement regional development plans and that the RFE Federal District Council would not
play the role of an executive power.[31]

However, Pulikovsky is still a very influental figure in the RFE political scene.
In February 2001 he initiated the "voluntary," preterm retirement of the Primorskii
krai governor and "strong man" Yevgenii Nazdratenko.[32]

At an Irkutsk meeting of the Baikal Economic Forum that took place following
the Blagoveshchensk meeting, a joint concept for the development of the Russian
Far East and Siberia was elaborated. *Russian Asia-Pacific Strategy for the Twenty-First
Century* proposed complex measures to support a favorable investment climate,
preferential customs duties, the formation of the Russian Asian Bank, and the realization of a number of infrastructure development projects (international energy
transmission system, gas pipelines, highways, etc.).[33] Currently, the federal government is considering what first practical measures should be implemented in the
framework of this concept.

CONCLUSION

In an address to the Federal Assembly in July 2000, President Putin outlined a plan
for strategic, economic, and social development programs and federal control priorities. In that address, Putin proposed a number of measures to strengthen executive power and to implement liberal economic reforms in Russia. The essence of the
address was that strengthening the federal component of executive power was the
only practical way to implement any reforms in a country as large as Russia.[34]

One of the clear priorities declared by the president was to maintain a strong
armed forces to champion Russian national interests in the world. Another of
the president's ideas was that the military-industrial complex would be able to
serve as a locomotive to haul all civilian sectors of the Russian economy. Putin's
declarations indicate that, for the immediate future, the RFE's military-industrial
complex will receive more financial support from the federal government, particularly for export-oriented weapons production. However, over the long term,
the RFE must convert most of its economy to civilian purposes, which would be
harmonious with the neighboring economies in the region. The RFE cannot
survive long on the basis of the MIC only. The best MIC enterprises like Progress,
Askold, Radiopribor, and others are already moving toward civilian production.

As far as Russia's Pacific Fleet is concerned, the commanding officers and crews
are doing their best to maintain the combat readiness of their submarines and ships.
In this context, it is worth mentioning two recent events that became very positive
highlights for the military people of the Russian Far East. First, on October 17,

2000, two pairs of Russian Air Force fighters freely flew over the flight deck of the U.S. aircraft carrier "Kitty Hawk" (such actions had not been performed by Russia's Air Force in the region for many years).[35] In training terms, it meant that the aircraft carrier would have been successfully attacked and sunk. Secondly, from January to March 2001, a Pacific Fleet naval detachment consisting of two large antisubmarine ships and a tanker made a successful foreign visit to India and Vietnam (the first oceangoing deployment for the Pacific Fleet surface combatants in five years).

Those events were symbolic of the fact that new Russian leadership agreed with a simple argument that in order to sustain combat readiness, naval ships must go to high seas, and military pilots should have more real flight hours. In addition, it means that in the future Russia would do its best to sustain its status as a sea power. While that may be a good omen for the military people, to radically improve the situation, significant financial allocations are needed to purchase new equipment and repair old ships, to improve the infrastructure of the Fleet bases, and to support adequate combat training at sea.

For the last several years, the Russian military budget did not permit the armed forces to sustain their basic needs. President Putin recently declared that Russia should increase its extremely small military budget, which in 2000 was equal to one percent of its U.S. counterpart.[36] The Russian government initially planned to increase the 2001 military budget by about 30 billion rubles to roughly 176 billion rubles ($6.3 billion).[37] However, following the tragic events surrounding the Northern Fleet's nuclear attack submarine Kursk in August 2000, the 2001 military budget was finally approved by Russian Parliament in the sum of 214.7 billion rubles (roughly $7.6 billion), which equals 2.8 percent of the Russian GDP planned for the year 2001.[38]

In the foreign policy sphere, President Putin has already demonstrated new innovative approaches toward solving some sensitive security issues that are of critical importance to Russia. Pragmatic economic interests are the most effective stimuli for Russia to strengthen its ties with China as its key Asian partner and to strengthen the bilateral relationship with both Korean states. This might also be an appropriate time for Russia to propose new initiatives to solve the Northern Territories issue, since Moscow definitely needs Tokyo's assistance for the effective implementation of its *Russian Asia-Pacific Strategy for the Twenty-First Century*. During his September 2000 visit to Japan, Putin proposed two grand economic development plans: one to extend the Trans-Siberian railway to Japan and the second to build an energy bridge between the two countries.

In the short run, the Sino-Russian strategic partnership is secured by common reform tasks, strong interdependence in military technical cooperation, new opportunities for large-scale export-oriented projects, and sharp contradictions with the

West, particularly with the United States. Whether this strategic partnership with China will become a strategic alliance is unclear. It will depend heavily on the kind of foreign policy (engagement or containment) Washington will pursue with regard to Moscow.

It is worth noting that a possible negative turn in Russian-American relations may result from the "new bipolar world theory" that is gaining strength in Russia.[39] According to this theory, the post–Cold War world is moving to a new bipolarity— this time between the developed and prosperous West and the underdeveloped East and South, which is struggling for survival. The authors of this theory believe that if the West tries to forcefully impose its political and economic models on the rest of the world, then U.S. or NATO policies might drive Russia, China, India, and other countries to an even more antiwestern posture and political confrontation in the twenty-first century. Recent use of military force by NATO in Yugoslavia as well as U.S. plans to build an NMD system that would abrogate the ABM Treaty may be regarded as an impetus for the underdeveloped countries to unite.

Realistically, however, the possibility of a Russian-Chinese-Indian alliance is not very high, given Sino-Indian hostilities. During some periods of the Cold War, the so-called quasi-alliance model—the relationship between two states that are not allied but share a third great-power patron as a common ally due to the common patron's security commitments—could explain the status of the Russian–Chinese–Indian relationship. (The current U.S.–Japan–Republic of Korea relationship is a good example of such a quasi-alliance.) Nevertheless, Russia is definitely not now in a position to play such a role in supporting the security of India and China.[40]

In the future, Moscow will do its best to develop a better bilateral relationship with Northeast Asian regional powers and both Korean states. Modest progress achieved by Russia in any of these relationships might well stimulate movement in other relationships. We have already seen how Japan and China were competing to engage the RFE in their military-political spheres of influence. Such a trend may be used by the RFE to establish more advantageous economic ties with its neighbors.

Considering Russian long-term state interests in the Asia Pacific, one may assume that the best alternative for Moscow would be to develop balanced partnerships with China and the U.S.-Japan alliance. Such a "balanced" system complemented by active Russian work in multilateral regional channels of cooperation may constitute a reliable basis for the effective implementation of the *Russian Asia-Pacific Strategy for the Twenty-First Century.*

NOTES

1. This term was developed during the author's cooperative research with Viktor Sumsky at the Institute of World Economics and International Relations (IMEMO) in Moscow in October 1999.

2. East-West Center, *Asia-Pacific Security Outlook* (Honolulu: East-West Center, 1997), 112–15.

3. "Predpriiatiia VPK Primoria stanut nemnogo morskimi," *Vladivostok,* August 8, 2000.

4. "Dividendi doveriia 'Radiopribora'," *Vladivostok,* March 21, 2000.

5. "Ob osobennostiakh nesostoiatelnosti VPK," *Vladivostok,* February 8, 2000.

6. "Mat rodna," *Izvestiia,* May 5, 2000.

7. Sergey Akshintsev, "Rossiya na mirovom rinoke vooruzheniya," *Rossiiskaia biznisgazeta,* March 20, 2001.

8. "Nesokrushimaya i legendarnaya," *Komsomolskaya Pravda,* March 31, 2000.

9. Evgeny V. Afanasiev, "Asia-Pacific Region: A Russian Perspective" (paper presented at the Pacific Symposium sponsored by National Defense University and U.S. Pacific Command, Honolulu, Hawaii, March 1–2, 1999).

10. "Mat rodna," May 5, 2000.

11. "2000 Russian Foreign Policy Concept," July 11, 2000.

12. Comprised of Russian and U.S. colonels and Navy captains (equivalent to 0-6 rank in the U.S. military system), that working group met each year to develop programs of military contacts involving all services and personnel of all ranks. For more information on the U.S.-Russian military-to-military contact programs in the Pacific, see Bill Smith, "A New Era of Partnership," *Asia-Pacific Defense FORUM Special Supplement* (Honolulu: USCINCPAC, Spring 1996).

13. Vladimir I. Kuroyedov, "Russian Security Politics and Its Role in Building Trust among Asia-Pacific Nations" (paper presented at the fifth Western Pacific Naval Symposium, November 25–27, 1996, Tokyo).

14. *Asia-Pacific Security Outlook,* 158.

15. "Prinimaiutsia meri po stabilizatsii ekonomiki," *Vladivostok,* November 5, 1999.

16. "Bez opyta proshlogo net budushchikh pobed," *Krasnaia Zvezda,* February 1, 2000.

17. Kuroyedov, "Russian Security Politics."

18. "Poteryaet li Rossiya status yadernoi derzhavi?" *Vladivostok,* February 4, 2000 and "Iz glubin mirovogo okeana mi ne uidem," *Krasnaya Zvezda,* March 18, 2000.

19. The Marshal Nedelin is a special ship that controls and tracks objects (such as strategic missiles and satellites) flying in space orbits.

20. "Flot potopili. Ostalis odni admirali," *Vladivostok,* February 11, 2000.

21. "Zvezdno-polosatii kontrakt 'Zvezdi'," *Vladivostok,* November 2, 1999.

22. Nikolai Sotskov, "U nas est pravo smotret' liudiam v glaza," *Vladivostok,* August 13, 1999.

23. "Tikhookeanskii Vikhr," *Vladivostok,* March 30, 2000.

24. "Voenno-morskoi kortik Vladimira Putina," *Vladivostok,* November 2, 1999.

25. "Bez opyta proshlogo net budushchikh pobed," February 4, 2000.

26. This declaration does not seem like a new direction from that of the Yeltsin administration. However, there is a difference in its implementation. During his first presidential year, Putin paid much more attention to Russian policy in Asia: he visited *all* the Northeast Asian countries (China, Japan, Mongolia, both Koreas) and Vietnam. In addition, he visited the Russian Far East several times and made a strong commitment to improve the socioeconomic situation there.

27. "2000 Russian Foreign Policy Concept," July 11, 2000.

28. "Vladimir Putin sobiraetsia na Dal'nii Vostok," *Vladivostok,* July 12, 2000.

29. "Rossiia obiazana meniat' politiku na Dal'nem Vostoke," *Rossiiskaia gazeta,* July 22, 2000.

30. "Ot sovetov k resheniiam," *Rossiiskaia gazeta,* August 3, 2000.

31. Interview by Konstantin Pulikovsky in *Vlast i biznis,* September 2000.

32. Nazdratenko was accused of ineffective leadership that caused an energy crisis in Primorye, and his retirement was accepted by Putin. Nonetheless, several weeks later, Nazdratenko was appointed to the post of chairman of the State Federal Fishery Committee in Moscow.

33. "Nuzhen vitse-premier po Dal'nemu Vostoku," *Vladivostok,* August 15, 2000; and "Cherez strategiiu uvidim Iaponiiu," *Vladivostok,* August 16, 2000.

34. Vladimir V. Putin, "Kakuiu Rossiiu mi stroim" (Address to the Federal Assembly), *Rossiiskaia gazeta,* July 11, 2000.

35. "Mi 'sdelali' Kitty Hawk!" *Vladivostok,* December 28, 2000.

36. "My ne pozvolim privatizirovat' gosudarstvennuiu vlast'," interview by Vladimir Putin to German newspaper *Velt am zontag,* published in *Rossiiskaia gazeta,* June 15, 2000.

37. "Oborona—delo obschee," *Rossiiskaia gazeta,* June 8, 2000. One might wonder whether such a modest Russian budget change of about $1 billion provoked an increase in the year 2001 U.S. military budget of more than $20 billion (see "Novosti," *Krasnaia Zvezda,* July 27, 2000).

38. "Rossiiskaya gazeta," December 29–30, 2000, statistics on Russian Federal budget 2001.

39. Evgeny V. Afanasiev, "Asia-Pacific Region: A Russian Perspective" (paper presented at the Pacific Symposium sponsored by National Defense University and U.S. Pacific Command, Honolulu, Hawaii, March 1–2, 1999).

40. Viktor D. Cha, "Abandonment, Entrapment, and Neoclassical Realism in Asia: The United States, Japan, and Korea," *International Studies Quarterly* 44, no. 2 (June 2000).

10

Russian Nuclear Regionalism: Emerging Local Influence over Far Eastern Facilities

James Clay Moltz

The simultaneous processes of political pluralization and economic decline that have characterized Russia since the late 1980s have weakened or ended central controls over a large range of economic, political, and defense enterprises for which Moscow was once responsible. As the old system of state ownership, communist party oversight, and central planning has collapsed, a confused mixture of private, semiprivate, and remaining state-owned enterprises has emerged. These actors face new and often conflicting federal, regional, and local political regulations and must also deal with the rise of local criminal organizations. For those still under the authority of the central ministries, Moscow's failure to deliver promised support to regional subunits means that the regions must find new sources of funding. This emerging environment affects both civilian and military enterprises, as well as active-duty units of the Russian military. In these conditions, it is not surprising that various forms of "regionalism" have taken root, often without Moscow's control or approval.

Within this complex picture, no area is of greater concern than the status of nuclear enterprises—both civilian and military—located in Russia's periphery. New evidence of regionalism raises a broader set of concerns related to the center's ability to conduct an effective foreign policy. As former Senator Sam Nunn and Adam Stulberg wrote in a *Foreign Affairs* article published in the spring of 2000, "Unchecked regionalism and the spontaneous privatization of the Russian military jeopardize control and other security arrangements, holding them hostage to the parochial concerns of local authorities."[1] Thus, regionalism is creating conditions where nuclear safety and even arms control arrangements may be seriously threatened. Former British diplomat Martin Nicholson characterizes the impact of these unique changes in center-periphery power relations in a nuclear weapons state by saying: "The central government cannot ... implement treaties governing the destruction of weapons of mass destruction (WMD) without regional cooperation."[2] This type of local influence over nuclear decision-making creates new and historically unprecedented problems. However, because no other nuclear weapons state has suffered from the kind of economic meltdown and extreme political transformation that has characterized Russia in the past decade, no systematic study exists, either positive or negative, on the possible net effects of the devolution of central authority over fissile material and nuclear-related technologies.

Conceptually speaking, certain types of regionalism might be expected to have a positive effect on nuclear controls (for example, local efforts to hold the center's feet to the fire in dealing more responsibly with nuclear waste). However, other forms of regional influence must be viewed more negatively, particularly when they imply losses of central control over nuclear weapons or fissile material. Although Alexander Lebed's 1998 comment that his government in Krasnoyarsk "controlled" hundreds of strategic missiles was meant mostly for political effect, it is worth questioning whether central control at both military and civilian facilities is still adequate to ensure the safety of nuclear-related technologies and nuclear materials outside of weapons. Unfortunately, as will be discussed in this study, evidence seems to be mounting that Russia faces new types of safety problems and continuing cases of attempted diversion, theft, and sale of nuclear materials from regional facilities.

Officially, responsibility for nuclear weapons, materials, technologies, and facilities in Russia's regions is divided mainly among the Ministry of Defense, the Russian Shipbuilding Agency (which took over responsibility for the nuclear shipyards in 1999),[3] and the Ministry for Atomic Energy (Minatom). However, increasing evidence suggests that the stability of central control may be weakening, or at least subject to mitigating factors. Primary among these influences are economic hardship, which has caused desperate individuals to carry out a number of dangerous acts involving the seizure and attempted sale of nuclear materials and, in one case, even the takeover of a nuclear-powered submarine. Similarly, criminal forces may be exerting additional pressures on the directors, engineers, and workers at regional nuclear facilities that may cause them to violate the security regimes at these facilities. Peter Kirkow has noted, for example, that "the decline of the Pacific Fleet has had a profound impact on the criminal underworld,"[4] increasing the chances that ports and other points of access to nuclear facilities may be compromised. In border areas like southern Primorskii krai, the threat of possible foreign infiltration at naval facilities and the diversion of nuclear materials and technologies abroad cannot be ruled out, particularly given the known presence of North Korean and Chinese agents in this region.[5]

The literature on Russian regionalism provides considerable discussion and analysis of the new forms of local governance and coalition-building that are emerging in Russia's hinterlands.[6] Only a few authors, however, have touched upon conditions at regional nuclear facilities, and most of these analysts have looked through the somewhat narrow prism of civil-military relations.[7] Dale Herspring's work, for example, describes the emergence of "alarming" incidents at regional facilities, including shootings and thefts. He also highlights the "increasingly close ties between the country's military officers and local political and economic authorities."[8] But while civil-military relations are certainly an important aspect of the nuclear problem, there are a number of other actors involved in handling nuclear materials, including civilians within the defense industry and workers at civilian enterprises that possess nuclear material, such as power plants, lighthouses, storage sites, and shipyards.

This chapter assesses the status of control at this broader range of facilities in the Russian Far East, and attempts to determine how regional factors may be influencing Russia's nuclear security across the full spectrum of possible vulnerabilities. In addition, it analyzes enterprises and military units with responsibility for nuclear weapons, materials, and technologies in the Far East and investigates how changing center-periphery relations in Russia have affected central control. It seeks to determine whether we need to fear the rise of "nuclear regionalism" in the Far East, even without the formal breakup of the Russian state.[9]

OVERVIEW OF NUCLEAR FACILITIES IN THE RUSSIAN FAR EAST

By any standard, the Far East represents an important test case of the possible implications of "nuclear regionalism" in Russia. The region lies at the end of the central supply chain, much farther from Moscow than the large nuclear complexes located on the Kola Peninsula, in the Ural Mountains, or in western Siberia. It is also subject to a variety of economic and political stresses, including significant mafia-related threats associated with its extensive network of ports. In addition, due to its location, the region is much more vulnerable to possible foreign influences.

Although perhaps less well-known to Western observers than the nuclear weapons facilities at such closed cities as Arzamas, Cheliabinsk, or Krasnoyarsk, the scattered nuclear-related enterprises in the Far East house a significant amount of nuclear material and technologies, including hundreds of strategic and tactical nuclear weapons, over 75 decommissioned nuclear submarines (many with operating reactors), more than a dozen active-duty nuclear submarines, a strategic bomber base, and a half-dozen storage facilities with either fresh or spent submarine fuel (which contain highly enriched uranium [HEU] and plutonium, respectively). The region also has a number of lighthouses powered by radioactive materials, one civilian nuclear power plant, and thousands of gallons of liquid radioactive waste from submarine reactors in various locations. The numerous facilities that house these materials are stretched across a vast region, making them difficult to protect.

Magadanskaia oblast is home to the region's only civilian nuclear power plant at Bilibino, whose four boiling-water reactors provide a 48-megawatt (MW) capacity to generate heat and electricity for this frozen region.[10] The reactors have been operating since the mid-1970s and are to be decommissioned between 2004 and 2006. Local officials are eager to replace them with a larger 96-MW plant. Given the lack of funds for new construction, however, the plant is still running its aging reactors, which it may try to extend beyond their recommended service lives, despite the safety hazards involved.[11]

In Kamchatskaia oblast, all of the remaining active-duty nuclear-powered ballistic missile submarines (SSBNs) in the Pacific Fleet are home-ported at the Rybachii Naval Base, south of Petropavlovsk. Officially, they comprise an impressive force of 9 Delta III nuclear submarines with a total of 143 long-range SS-N-18 missiles carrying 429 nuclear warheads, plus 1 older Delta I submarine with 12 SS-N-8 missiles each carrying 1 nuclear warhead.[12] However, due to problems of financing and maintenance, recent estimates suggest that only four of these vessels (all of them Delta IIIs) are fully manned and seaworthy. There are also twelve nuclear-powered attack submarines (SSNs) and nuclear-powered guided-missile submarines (SSGNs) capable of carrying nuclear-tipped cruise missiles and torpedoes, as well as more than two dozen decommissioned nuclear submarines (half with still operating reactors).[13] The base faces a number of problems due to the lack of equipment to dismantle the decommissioned boats and to safely dispose of the liquid waste and spent fuel. Some work is going on at the nearby Gorniak Shipyard to defuel several boats per year, but the fuel can only be removed during the summer months by a supply ship from the Chazhma Bay Shipyard in Primorskii krai. Conditions at the Gorniak Shipyard are poor due to significant wage arrears and the departure of many skilled personnel from Kamchatka since the breakup of the Soviet Union.[14] The facility has a radioactive waste storage area nearby, and concern over the buildup of spent fuel and other radioactive material has caused the Russian navy to request support from the U.S. government to refit the Gorniak Shipyard with equipment that will enable it to dismantle nuclear submarines.

Khabarovskii krai is home to two nuclear submarine facilities. At the Amurskii Zavod, two nuclear submarines have been under construction since before the

Soviet breakup—one vessel is now said to be 60 percent complete and the other 80 percent complete.[15] The latter submarine had its reactor started in dry dock two years ago, meaning that the factory has HEU submarine fuel on its premises. It is unclear when additional fuel will be brought to the facility for the completion of the second vessel's reactor. Two factors make this situation worrisome: (1) the federal government has repeatedly failed to provide funding for completion of the submarines; and (2) according to the factory's director, the necessary technical personnel required to finish installing the reactors and other systems have left the facility due to unpaid wages, meaning that the enterprise is not capable of completing the construction work even if funds could be found.[16] The second facility in the krai, the Zavety Ilycha Naval Base, houses a small number of decommissioned nuclear submarines with operating reactors. As at other sites, the fuel in these reactors poses both an environmental threat if not properly controlled and a proliferation risk if the fuel is removed from the reactor without adequate local storage facilities and physical protection measures. The long presence of these vessels at the Zavety Ilycha base stems from the lack of capacity at the fleet's major spent fuel storage site in Primorskii krai and the failure of the Russian government to provide adequate transportation of the fuel cores already at the Primorye storage facility to the central storage site at the Maiak facility in Cheliabinsk.

Nearby Amurskaia oblast houses a large, long-range, nuclear-capable bomber base at Ukrainka. The Ukrainka base has 27 Bear-H6 bombers and 21 Bear-H16 bombers,[17] each of which can carry long-range air-launched cruise missiles. Due to closures of air bases elsewhere, the number of bombers at Ukrainka has actually increased in the past few years. These aircraft are capable of delivering 498 nuclear weapons. Bombers from Ukrainka continue to conduct training missions, despite electrical outages and serious shortages of fuel and funding.

Finally, Primorskii krai has the greatest density of nuclear materials of any of the Far Eastern regions. The Shkotovo Peninsula is home to a major Russian submarine base at Pavlovsk Bay, which officially has more than a dozen nuclear attack submarines listed as active and 1 START I–countable Delta I SSBN with 12 nuclear weapons. However, recent sources suggest that—while all of their reactors remained fueled and are still operating—only one of the attack submarines is actually fully manned and is going to sea, while the Delta I SSBN has been decommissioned (although it has not yet been dismantled).[18] The Pacific Fleet's main storage sites for fresh submarine fuel (Chazhma Bay) and spent submarine fuel (Dunai) are located nearby. In addition, a large number of decommissioned nuclear submarines and separated reactor compartments are stored at Chazhma Bay and Pavlovsk Bay. Slightly further north is the most active nuclear facility in the Far East: the Zvezda Far Eastern Shipyard at Bolshoi Kamen. This enterprise is the official

START I–designated submarine dismantlement facility for the Pacific Fleet—responsible for cutting up SSBNs. The facility experienced serious difficulties during the 1990s—with labor unrest, a murder-for-hire, and attempts to smuggle nuclear materials, blueprints, and technologies. The Zvezda Shipyard has received considerable attention from the U.S. government, which has provided over $8 million in dismantlement technology[19] and more than $30 million in contracts for SSBN dismantlement.[20] Without these funds, it is doubtful that the shipyard would have survived the 1990s or that Russia would have dismantled even the small number of SSBNs that it has been able to complete to date. The facility recently received a contract from the Chinese government to conduct repair and maintenance work on a number of Kilo-class diesel submarines sold to the Chinese navy in the early 1990s.

Although they do not pose a serious proliferation threat, it is also worth noting that the Far East is home to dozens of lighthouses at various coastal sites operating on radioactive power sources. These radioisotope thermal generators, when operated safely, pose little threat to the environment or to local personnel. Unfortunately, there is considerable evidence that safety has not been a high priority, and that radioactive sources have not been well accounted for.

Many of the nuclear enterprises in the Russian Far East are civilian facilities, and thus each can be expected to face certain unique problems and pressures when compared to military enterprises and bases. However, in general terms, these facilities share similar circumstances in carrying out federation-level nuclear responsibilities under difficult conditions and far from the major funding sources in Moscow. Civilian facilities merit concern by international policymakers because they house a significant portion of Russia's fissile material, nuclear technology, and nuclear weapons—all highly sensitive from the perspective of safety and proliferation.

It is worth mentioning that factors that might seem manageable in normal periods could become harder to deal with during times of crisis, which may yet be in store for Russia's regions.

REGIONAL POLITICAL AND ECONOMIC FACTORS AFFECTING CONTROL AT FAR EASTERN FACILITIES

In order to categorize the types of influence that regional political and economic factors may have on central control of Far Eastern nuclear facilities, it is necessary first to consider the dynamics at work in the control over any nuclear materials or technologies.[21] Drawing on the literature and concepts already developed regarding command and control of nuclear weapons, it can be observed that regional political actors may attempt to exert either "positive" or "negative" control over nuclear materials and facilities, or nuclear facilities may be affected by "loss of control" events.[22] Extreme cases of positive control may involve regional efforts to commandeer fissile material, nuclear technology, or means of delivering nuclear weapons. In some cases, the groups or individuals involved might represent nonofficial elements: workers seizing control of equipment in order to bargain with enterprise managers to recoup lost wages, or members of an organized crime syndicate seeking to seize material for the purpose of smuggling. Alternatively, regional actors may seek to take possession over whole facilities—such as shipyards, waste disposal sites, or fresh fuel depots—in order to operate them for profit. Such administrative seizures may be less worrisome in the short term, but could be problematic over the longer term if varying regional standards emerge for nuclear safety and export control.

In a second category of cases, regional actors may seek to exert so-called negative control. In the weapons literature, this involves state efforts to establish mechanisms to prevent an unauthorized nuclear launch. As applied to regionalism, we can redefine negative control as encompassing local efforts to *block* the use or operation of nuclear facilities by central authorities. Examples of negative control might include preventing access to facilities through the use of local police, preventing the transit of nuclear materials via rail lines or roadways, or cutting off the supply of key inputs (water, heat, food, or electricity) to sites with nuclear materials. These actions could render central control ineffective and provide greater influence to regional officials. Examples might include organized groups of striking workers at a facility preventing a nuclear vessel from going to sea by refusing to operate the dry docks, environmentalists undertaking a sustained protest (perhaps in conjunction with occupation of part of a facility), or regional power companies cutting off the electricity supply to nuclear facilities due to unpaid debts (of which there are numerous actual cases). In such incidents of attempted negative control, the aims of the groups would not be to operate the facility or possess material (in contrast to positive control), but to stand between Moscow and its ability to undertake these activities and, thus, to implement its nuclear policy. In certain cases, such local efforts could have a beneficial effect, for example, if the center's plans for operating a facility (such as a nuclear waste dump) could cause environmental damage. In other cases, such actions could prevent work on weapons dismantlement, thereby blocking Russian arms control compliance.

Finally, a third possible influence exerted by regional factors at nuclear facilities might be characterized by the term "loss of control events." These cases might involve circumstances in which systemic failures at regional facilities, caused by budget cuts or staff reductions, might lead to general problems of oversight for which no group or individual is at fault. These might include a decision by the Ministry of Defense or Minatom to abandon a nuclear facility (such as a decommissioned nuclear submarine or a spent fuel storage site) due to a lack of funding for its maintenance. Such cases might occur especially in the area of nuclear waste management, where the government might decide to leave a storage facility unguarded or fail to conduct adequate searches for lost materials (due to inadequate funding). These incidents could lead to environmental disasters or to proliferation problems, particularly if they contributed to positive control by a group or individuals who might seek to exploit the situation for their own purposes.

EVIDENCE OF CONTROL PROBLEMS
AT FAR EASTERN NUCLEAR FACILITIES

These three general types of possible influences by regional actors on central control over nuclear sites can be used as a framework for examining the evidence of control problems at Far Eastern nuclear facilities to date, although some cases may not fit neatly within the three categories. The main point, however, is to gain a better understanding of the existing data and some perspective on general trends at regional facilities. Such information is a prerequisite to crafting effective policy measures aimed at reducing the negative implications of regional factors for nuclear safety and control.

Positive Control

In the category of positive control, fortunately, there is little available evidence of efforts by political leaders in the Russian Far East to seize or establish authority over nuclear weapons. There is also little data on efforts by other groups, such as the mafia, to seize nuclear weapons. The same cannot be said, however, about nuclear materials or nuclear facilities themselves. A few cases are worth discussing in detail.

One area of particular concern is the possibility that facilities with nuclear material and technologies might fall under the control of regional mafia groups. While this notion may seem far-fetched, in March 1999 law enforcement officials in Sakhalinskaia oblast apprehended two suspects apparently involved in a string of murders-for-hire since the early 1990s.[23] During their interrogation, the criminals confessed to the 1993 murder of Alexander Makarov, deputy director of the Zvezda Far Eastern Shipyard in Bolshoi Kamen. Even more troubling than the tragic murder, however, was the criminals' revelation that the mafia's real aim was to threaten Makarov into helping them seize control over the factory (in order to set up an extortion and profit-skimming operation). But Makarov refused to cooperate with the criminals and was killed. Had he succumbed to the pressure, this mafia clan would have gained control over dozens of decommissioned nuclear submarines and a variety of nuclear materials and technologies, opening the way for possible diversions to North Korea, Iraq, and other states of concern.

Unpaid civilian workers with access to nuclear reactors also make for a very dangerous mix. As one Zvezda plant mechanic threatened during a strike in July 1997, "I can see only one way out—to go to a nuclear submarine and do something." He added that it would not be difficult to cause a "tragedy worse than Chernobyl."[24] While some of these comments were clearly aimed at increasing the strikers' bargaining leverage with central authorities, such desperation and the ability to act upon it if provoked typifies the volatile situation that exists at many regional nuclear facilities. When workers face conditions in which they cannot feed their families, they are liable to behave in unpredictable and sometimes dangerous ways.

Within the military, problems associated with low or unpaid salaries, the breakdown of discipline, and even food shortages at many bases have been particularly acute.[25] A September 1998 incident at the Northern Fleet base at Gadzhievo on the Kola Peninsula underlines the type of disaster that could potentially occur in the Pacific Fleet as well. In this case, a lonely and frustrated sailor lashed out against conditions in the navy by seizing control of an Akula-class nuclear attack submarine, killing eight of his shipmates before barricading himself in the torpedo room.[26] He held the ship hostage for nearly 24 hours. When commandos finally stormed his stronghold, they found him dead from an explosion he had caused while trying to ignite the weapons stored there. Had his attempt to detonate the vessel's torpedoes succeeded, the ensuing fire might have ignited the propellant and spread the blaze to the reactor compartment, where it could have caused a serious accident— spreading a highly radioactive nuclear cloud that would have contaminated a large area of the Kola Peninsula, killing hundreds and causing perhaps thousands of long-term illnesses and related deaths.

Other cases of attempted positive control relate to efforts at theft or diversion of nuclear materials for profit. So serious is the ongoing criminal situation in the Kamchatka region that Rear Admiral Yuri Kirillov complained recently to the oblast governor that civilian smuggling of various metals and other materials from military facilities represented an actual "regional conflict," given its possible effects on readiness and the safety of weaponry and military vessels.[27] A serious case took place at Bolshoi Kamen in early 1999, when a former Zvezda Shipyard employee was caught trying to sell radioactive materials, allegedly taken from the factory, to undercover agents posing as brokers for North Korea.[28] When such information is put alongside well-known cases involving the smuggling of drugs and counterfeit money by North Korean agents into Primorskii krai, the reality of the proliferation threat becomes readily recognizable—these channels could easily be reversed to smuggle fissile material desperately desired by the North Korean military. It is certainly no coincidence that a former Chinese citizen was recently convicted in the United States of attempting to export specialized speedboats (capable of reaching over 100 mph) to North Korea.[29] Many Pacific Fleet nuclear bases and enterprises are located less than 100 miles by sea from North Korean shores.

Several other incidents of attempted foreign diversion have already come to light following arrests. In early 1996, for example, 17 North Korean workers attached to a Russian farm brigade were caught trying to infiltrate a nuclear submarine facility in Primorskii krai. In similar cases, North Korean agents have been arrested for trying to buy dismantlement schedules for nuclear submarines and cruising patterns for active-duty nuclear vessels.[30] These cases show that the North Korean threat is not an abstract one, and that Pyongyang is fully cognizant of the value of the materials to be had in poorly guarded and underfunded enterprises not far from its borders.

Still other cases involve attempted "insider" diversions. In at least two cases in 1994, Russian sailors were involved in the theft of HEU submarine fuel from storage facilities in the Northern Fleet. There is a similar reported case involving a diversion from the Far Eastern naval base at Zavety Ilycha.[31] In all of these cases, the motive was profit. Fortunately, in these instances at least, the perpetrators were caught and the material recovered.

Still other attempts at positive control involve nonnuclear materials or technologies crucial to the operation of a nuclear facility. For example, in one recent case, a sailor serving on a nuclear attack submarine on the Kola Peninsula cut out several lengths of special palladium-vanadium wire from his vessel and sold it to an officer from another submarine.[32] Although the sailor eventually was arrested, the wire he removed was part of an important control system for the submarine's nuclear reactors, and the submarine had to be withdrawn from service for several months for repairs. If the theft had not been discovered, the results potentially could have caused a Chernobyl-like accident.

Similar incidents have taken place in the Pacific Fleet. In January 2000 near the Rybachii base on Kamchatka, for example, two sailors bribed a security guard and boarded a decommissioned nuclear submarine (with an operating nuclear reactor) in search of material that could be sold for profit.[33] They broke open the hatch leading to the reactor control compartment and began to remove cables and anything that seemed to be of value. They stole several sheets of gold-colored metal that turned out to be radioactive calibrating plates, which they later stashed under their mattresses. They tried to operate the lever for the reactor control rods, but were unable to do so only because an engineer had welded down the handle just the day before. Had this not been the case, the two sailors could have caused the reactor to overheat and risked a dangerous nuclear explosion. While these two sailors were eventually caught, the vulnerabilities highlighted in this case are certainly grounds for concern.

Other attempts at positive control in the Far East have involved efforts by local authorities in energy-deficient cities to draw electricity from nuclear vessels stationed in their ports. The case of the nuclear cruiser Ural near Vladivostok is one such example. In November 1997 Primorskii krai Vice Governor Konstantin Tolstoshein discussed this issue in Moscow with the Russian National Security Council in an attempt to allow the krai to take power from the Ural in exchange for unpaid debts owed to the region by the Russian government.[34] However, his attempts were unsuccessful, and the Ural is now scheduled to be decommissioned.[35] Nevertheless, the closed city of Viliuchinsk near the Rybachii Naval Base on Kamchatka made a similar request and may temporarily have received electricity from three nuclear submarines.[36] Although these actions may seem benign, accidents could occur if cables, cooling systems, or other equipment associated with this work were to malfunction. There are good reasons to believe the chances for malfunctioning are considerably higher in a submarine than at a commercial nuclear power plant, since these military vessels were not designed to produce and transfer electricity to onshore sites.

Negative Control

There is also a considerable amount of evidence from nuclear facilities in the Far East of negative control. In the summer of 1997, for example, a referendum of the residents of Bolshoi Kamen temporarily postponed the delivery of a floating liquid waste filtration facility to the Zvezda Shipyard.[37] Residents opposed Moscow's plans to force their city to become a repository for the additional solid and liquid radioactive wastes that would be deposited as a result of the heightened rate of submarine dismantlement that would occur at the Zvezda plant. This effort provides one of the few positive examples of "nuclear regionalism," where the exercise of democracy by local citizens sought to raise federal awareness of an important environmental issue. However, federal and Zvezda plant authorities chose not to recognize the 94 percent of voters opposed to the new facility, because less than 50 percent of the electorate had participated in the referendum. Furthermore, local political opinion changed in September 1997 when new evidence of leakage from one of the shore-based tanks holding liquid radioactive waste at Bolshoi Kamen caused the residents to drop their protest. The city council then officially voided the referendum and allowed the facility to be delivered that October.[38]

Given the Far East's considerable nuclear legacy and current fissile material stock-pile, it is troubling (but not surprising) that the region has also witnessed numer-ous strikes by workers attempting to halt operations at nuclear facilities, including the Amurskii Zavod and the Zvezda Shipyard. Almost all of these incidents in-volved unpaid wages rather than more "lofty" goals, but they still represent distinct regional efforts to exert greater control over nuclear decision-making.

Prior to the referendum in 1997, for example, striking workers from the Zvezda plant blocked the Trans-Siberian railroad from shipping materials past Bolshoi Kamen to Nakhodka until officials in Moscow promised to pay at least part of their back wages. In June 1997 workers at the Amurskii Zavod staged a similar strike in response to over eight months of wage arrears. Numerous strikes have also halted work at other enterprises associated with the Far Eastern nuclear and defense complex. Even more incidents might have taken place in the region ex-cept for the fact that many of the nuclear facilities remain under military control, which prevents workers from organizing or striking.

A final negative control incident of possible relevance to the Far East took place in the Northern Fleet in 1995, when the crew of an Akula-class nuclear attack submarine refused to take their vessel to sea until their back wages had been paid.[39] One of the key reasons was the shortage of food at the base and the need for money to ensure their families' survival before the ship went to sea. Similar conditions have plagued active-duty bases in the Pacific Fleet.

Overall, incidents of negative control have been somewhat more benign in their impact on nuclear safety than most positive control events. They also high-light efforts by regional actors to encourage greater environmental and financial responsibility by Moscow in its nuclear activities. Nevertheless, they indicate a weakening of Moscow's ability to control its nuclear arsenal, which sets a possi-bly dangerous precedent that could encourage future positive control events.

Loss of Control

Given their implications, it is particularly disturbing that incidents of the third category of events—loss of control situations—are becoming ever more fre-quent. What is particularly worrisome about these incidents is that often neither national nor regional authorities are in a position to prevent them from occur-ring, due to losses of necessary staff. Similarly, the lack of financial means to clean up, safeguard, or recover radioactive materials means that the environmen-tal implications of these incidents are often left unaddressed, even when there is evidence of such problems.

In May 1997, for example, a decommissioned nuclear submarine docked near the Rybachii base in Kamchatka sank at its moorings.[40] While the submarine had reportedly already been defueled, the breaching of the hull may have contaminated coastal waters. Although the submarine was refloated some weeks later, whether it is still floating is not known, and there are dozens of submarines in similar condition or worse (those with fueled reactors).

Another loss of control incident occurred off Sakhalin Island in August 1997 when a helicopter carrying a radioisotope thermal generator (RTG) for a lighthouse mistakenly dropped the unit into the ocean off the coastline. This was not the first such incident involving an RTG. When a ship later returned to retrieve the radioactive source material, however, it was unable to locate it.[41] While the Strontium-90 in the generator cannot be used to make a nuclear weapon, it can cause serious medical problems to individuals who handle it (or get too close), as well as contaminate fish and other wildlife. The existence of such slipshod control over radioactive material lends at least some credence to the future possibility of more dangerous loss-of-control scenarios involving bomb-quality fissile materials.

What remains troubling about these loss of control events is that the lack of specific individual perpetrators makes it more likely that they will remain undetected and unaddressed for years, despite the clear hazards they pose. Thus, there may be sites with small amounts of nuclear waste or fissile material that have already caused damage to local populations or been the source of a proliferation-related diversion without officials or the media even knowing about them.

FUTURE POLICY OPTIONS

The instability in the current Russian political and economic scene makes predictions about the status of control at nuclear facilities very difficult. However, based on the evidence to date and a conservative assessment of the coming five years in Russia, it can be predicted that conditions at Far Eastern nuclear facilities are not going to improve dramatically in the near term. Instead, they may get worse before they get better, particularly if there is instability as a result of President Putin's efforts to rein in Russia's regions, unforeseen developments in Chechnya, or some new center-regional crisis. The best hope is for gradual reform under Putin and steady progress. Unfortunately, this means that threatening incidents are likely to continue at least over the near term. Moreover, any solution to these problems is going to require new funding. Thus, while it appears that President Putin is concerned about center-regional power relations, it is less clear that he has the resources necessary to address the roots of the problems.

In this complex environment, there are still several basic areas in which new policy initiatives by Russian leaders and providers of foreign assistance could make a difference in improving the situation at Russian Far East nuclear facilities.

The rest of this chapter will briefly discuss the integrated role of three possible policy lines: (1) defense conversion; (2) material consolidation; and (3) new non-proliferation and arms control initiatives.

Defense conversion is at once the most important and most difficult task in regards to existing nuclear facilities.[42] According to Russian sources, there have been no cases in the Far East to date of successful conversion at a nuclear enterprise.[43] New Russian initiatives and foreign assistance, however, could play a significant role in preventing control problems even short of immediate conversion. Work needs to be done first and foremost within the facilities themselves to help them get over the mindset and expectations set up during the Soviet period. There is still a tendency among Soviet-style managers to "hunker down" in the vain hope of renewed state orders. Recent interviews with officials in Vladivostok and Khabarovsk find a large number of officials who still believe that eventually the Russian navy will be rebuilt and there will be demand for the construction of more nuclear submarines.[44] They listened appreciatively in the fall of 1999 when then Prime Minister Putin pledged increased defense orders, but the new budget delivered in spring 2000 lacked funds for such orders. In this context, a positive approach by foreign assistance providers would be to offer programs for retraining workers at large defense enterprises. The provision of seed money for new businesses in the civilian sector would be another worthwhile direction. By undertaking these and similar efforts to reduce the number of workers active in the nuclear sector, foreign assistance programs would be taking effective measures toward reducing the present threat, as well as preventing future problems. The good news (if it can be called that) in the nuclear sector is that there does not appear to be a significant pool of new workers entering the field. Thus, many of these enterprises need only survive as long as it takes for the older generation of workers (most in their late 40s and 50s) to reach retirement age. Russian and foreign assistance programs could help bridge the gap for remaining workers toward a stable, phased shutdown of military work. In this regard, new efforts by foreign governments to begin cooperative programs to engage these facilities in weapons dismantlement or in new civilian joint ventures could help buy time until these workers retire.

But the Russian side must do its part, too. Much more needs to be done to increase transparency at facilities and to facilitate access to sensitive sites by foreign assistance providers, which has often not been the case in the past. Instead, many formerly secret cities in the defense industry are seeking to return to their old "closed" status in order to receive the small amount of guaranteed funds from the federal budget allotted to closed cities. However, such efforts make chances for attracting foreign investment and undergoing successful conversion much more difficult. Thus, Moscow needs to discourage these practices and instead provide incentives for these cities to remain open and to make themselves more attractive to both Russian and foreign investors through tax incentives and legal protections. Similarly, the central government's willingness to channel at least some new investment funds to the Far East to stimulate civilian industries and to facilitate greater foreign investment will also be a factor in the success of conversion efforts.

In addition to conversion, material and technology consolidation programs can reduce the number of facilities that are vulnerable to dangerous influences. It is easier to create effective physical protection systems at a handful of facilities than it is to protect dozens spread across a vast area. Eventually the goal must be to help Russia reduce its nuclear infrastructure to a point where the quantities of material, technology, and workers reach levels that will be manageable for the Russian government to handle on its own. In the Far East, this is likely to mean a situation—hopefully sometime near 2010—when the backlog of old material has been overcome and Russia is deploying only a handful of nuclear submarines and bombers in order to maintain a minimum defensive capability in the Pacific. In the meantime, new efforts need to be made to reduce the number of locations with sensitive material and technologies. Assistance programs run by the U.S. Department of Energy have facilitated consolidation of fresh submarine fuel stockpiles and improved physical protection at remaining sites. However, more work needs to be done to consolidate spent nuclear fuel and liquid wastes, which are dispersed among a dozen separate facilities. This will reduce the geography of the region's nuclear safety problem and make protection of these proliferation-sensitive and environmentally hazardous materials easier to accomplish.

The Amurskii Zavod in Komsomolsk-na-Amure is a case in point. It would make sense for foreign governments to initiate a new program to pay the facility to dismantle the two submarines that are now partially completed (before the Russian government finds funds to complete them) and to safely store the fuel. Such an effort, which might be accomplished for as little as $5 million, could provide at least two years of support to desperate workers at the facility. It would also make sense to undertake greater efforts, in cooperation with the regional government perhaps, to offer funds to shut down the nuclear production line at the site to ensure that no more nuclear vessels are produced in the Far East. Indeed, such an action was formally decreed by the Yeltsin government in 1992 as part of an effort to consolidate all nuclear construction to the Sevmash Shipyard in Severodvinsk (near Arkhangelsk), but the managers at the Amurskii Zavod continue to cling to hopes of renewed state orders. The United States and its allies in the Pacific (particularly Japan) could support conversion efforts by stimulating their respective companies doing business in the Far East—through tax incentives at home—to provide orders for civilian vessels and other equipment at the shipyard.

Even a very small number of orders for oil rigs, barges, and other craft could mean the difference between a satisfied worker who can feed his family and one who might be motivated to undertake a dangerous act of sabotage or theft involving nuclear materials.

A third area worth additional emphasis is the use of foreign assistance to engage facilities in new nonproliferation and weapons elimination work. Ironically, the one facility in the region that has begun to thrive since 1998 is the Zvezda Far Eastern Shipyard, due primarily to direct U.S. funding to the shipyard for SSBN submarine dismantlement. These payments do not go through Moscow, and the factory directors have used them to pay back wages owed to workers. Now, the facility has actually begun to hire new staff.[45]

An area where there is considerable new opportunity for such arms control and nonproliferation work is in possible dismantlement of nuclear attack submarines. Although there are over thirty such decommissioned vessels that still contain nuclear fuel and operating reactors (and are capable of carrying nuclear-tipped cruise missiles and torpedoes), no country has yet established a plan to assist Russia in their dismantlement. The good news is that Japan has recently pledged to contribute as much as $120 million to such an effort,[46] but has yet to develop any specific plans or timetable. Unfortunately, to date the United States has viewed these submarines as outside its mandate for weapons elimination because they do not carry strategic missiles. Clearly, the threat that these vessels pose in terms of possible accidents, sales to foreign countries, or recommissioning merits international attention, in cooperation with some Russian funding. Such a joint effort between Russia and a number of states, with the vessels to be dismantled apportioned among several shipyards over a five- to seven-year period, could make a significant contribution in helping to transition remaining workers while the regional economy seeks to rebuild and reorient itself. Nuclear shipyards involved in this effort (besides Zvezda) would require some modest amount of funding to provide the technical infrastructure to conduct dismantlement work. They could then receive a fixed sum for each attack submarine dismantled. Such a program has worked effectively in dismantling SSBNs at Zvezda under U.S. contracts. This model could be transferred to work on attack submarines as well, although the funders might be other foreign governments.

Of course, foreign assistance alone cannot solve the problems in the Russian Far East's nuclear sector. Moscow must work to clean up its own house economically while simultaneously encouraging regional governors to create a more favorable investment climate in their territories. A new division of responsibilities and stricter enforcement of nuclear safety regulations are also needed, along with greater public oversight. In the meantime, foreign assistance can help alleviate some of the negative manifestations of today's "nuclear regionalism," particularly in areas related to weapons technologies and proliferation of sensitive materials such as submarine fuel. Overall, future policy needs to consider how the various initiatives outlined above might complement each other substantively, and how a phased strategy of simultaneous conversion, material consolidation, and support for weapons dismantlement efforts could serve the long-term interests of both Russian workers and Western governments interested in nonproliferation goals.

CONCLUSION

The stability of central control over Far Eastern facilities is a subset of the general future of Russia's political and economic integrity as a country and as a united economic space. As shown here, nuclear facilities are particularly sensitive elements due to the possibly catastrophic implications of control problems related to center-regional conflicts or a worsening of the regional economic crisis. The Russian Far East has already experienced a number of dangerous incidents that raise serious questions about the integrity of control at these facilities. Given the technical and personnel requirements for protecting these sites, it is clear that the Russian system is currently incapable of performing these tasks. The large volume of nuclear material and related technologies (including nuclear vessels) that were created during the Soviet period has overwhelmed the new (and still emerging) system. In the coming decade, if the economy recovers and center-regional relations become more stable, Russia should become increasingly able to deal with a smaller, post–Cold War nuclear infrastructure. A healthier economic climate will also reduce workers' incentives to risk stealing materials and technologies from nuclear facilities. Until then, however, foreign governments need to help ensure that the security threats posed by "nuclear regionalism" in the Russian Far East are prevented through timely and appropriate assistance programs, in cooperation with both central officials and politicians and facility representatives on the ground.

NOTES

1. Sam Nunn and Adam Stulberg, "The Many Faces of Modern Russia," *Foreign Affairs* 79, no. 2 (March/April 2000):47.

2. Martin Nicholson, "Towards a Russia of the Regions," Adelphi Paper no. 330 (September 1999), 63.

3. Russian Government Decree No. 878, "Voprosy Rossiiskogo agentstva po sudostroeniiu," July 30, 1999, in *The Legislation in Russia* <law.optima.ru>.

4. Peter Kirkow, *Russia's Provinces: Authoritarian Transformation versus Local Autonomy?* (New York: St. Martin's Press, 1998), 11.

5. See James Clay Moltz and Tamara C. Robinson, "Dismantling Russia's Nuclear Subs: New Challenges to Non-Proliferation," *Arms Control Today* 29, no. 4 (June 1999):11.

6. See, for example, Kirkow, *Russia's Provinces*, 11; Daniel S. Treisman, *After the Deluge: Regional Crises and Political Consolidation in Russia* (Ann Arbor, Mich.: The University of Michigan Press, 1999); Mikhail A. Alekseev, ed., *Center-Periphery Conflict in Post-Soviet Russia: A Federation Imperiled* (New York: St. Martin's Press, 1999); and Kathryn Stoner-Weiss, *Local Heroes: The Political Economy of Russian Regional Governance* (Princeton, N.J.: Princeton University Press, 1997).

7. For example, Geir Honneland and Anne-Kristin Jorgensen, *Integration vs. Autonomy: Civil-Military Relations on the Kola Peninsula* (Aldershot, UK: Ashgate Publishing, 1999); and Eva Buzsa, "From Decline to Disintegration: The Russian Military Meets the Millennium," *Demokratizatsiya* 7, no. 4 (fall 1999).

8. Dale R. Herspring, "The Russian Military Faces 'Creeping Disintegration'," *Demokratizatsiya* 7, no. 4 (fall 1999):581.

9. Although there is less evidence of pro-independence sentiment today in the Russian Far East than in the early 1990s, some authors continue to worry that the Far East may yet break off, either willingly or unwillingly. See, for example, Anton Surikov, "Bezopasnost natsii: Sekvestrom po samii Altai," *Pravda*, May 23–30, 1997, 1. For one of the original articles arguing that a breakup of Russia is imminent and warning of the possibility of new, fully independent nuclear states, see Jessica Eve Stern, "Moscow Meltdown? Can Russia Survive," *International Security* 18, no. 4 (spring 1994). Fortunately, Stern's predictions of full independence from Moscow have not been borne out in reality, but some of the nuclear safety and control problems implied in her article are beginning to emerge despite the persistence of the Russian state.

10. For more information on this facility, see data provided by the International Nuclear Safety Center, operated by Argonne National Laboratory, U.S. Department of Energy <www.insc.anl.gov/neisb/neisb4/NEISB_3.1.html>.

11. The region lacks other sources of fuel and is cut off from river transport from October to May. Also, residents are not eager to return to the days when black coal smoke hung over their cities throughout the long winter months.

12. Figures drawn from the most recent Strategic Arms Reduction Treaty Memorandum of Understanding (START I MOU) from July 2001, available from the U.S. Department of State.

13. Figures drawn from *Jane's Fighting Ships 1999/2000* (Alexandria, Va.: Jane's Information Group, 1999), 558-571; Thomas Nilsen, Igor Kudrik, and Aleksandr Nikitin, "Chapter 2: Nuclear-powered vessels," The Russian Northern Fleet, Bellona Foundation website <www.bellona.no/e/russia/nfl/>; Andrey Bondarenko, "Tikhookeanskiy 'Drakon' stal 'Samaroy'," *Nezavisimaya gazeta*, May 11, 2000 <news.mosinfo.ru>; and author's correspondence with Mark Ettesvold, Pacific Northwest National Laboratory, May 2000.

14. Author's interview with a senior scientist in the Russian Academy of Sciences who works with the Pacific Fleet, October 18, 1999, Vladivostok.

15. Author's interview with a Russian economist who had recently visited the facility,

October 22, 1999, Khabarovsk.

16. Ibid.

17. Bomber figures taken from the July 2000 START I MOU.

18. Figures drawn from *Jane's Fighting Ships 1999/2000* (Alexandria, Va.: Jane's Information Group, 1999), 558-571; Thomas Nilsen, Igor Kudrik, and Aleksandr Nikitin, "Chapter 2: Nuclear-powered vessels," The Russian Northern Fleet, Bellona Foundation website <www.bellona.no/e/russia/nfl/>; Andrey Bondarenko, "Tikhookeanskiy 'Drakon' stal 'Samaroy'," *Nezavisimaya gazeta*, May 11, 2000 <news.mosinfo.ru>; and author's correspondence with Mark Ettesvold, Pacific Northwest National Laboratory, May 2000.

19. Author's interviews with U.S. contractors and Russian officials, January–February 1996, in Vladivostok and Bolshoi Kamen.

20. Author's correspondence with Lt. Col. Ron Alberto, Cooperative Threat Reduction Office, Department of Defense, January 7, 2000; also DTRA Fact Sheet, "SLBM Launchers/SSBN Elimination," December 1, 1999.

21. The author thanks Nikolai Sokov for a useful discussion of these issues during the preparation of this study.

22. For example, see Jordan Seng, "Command and Control Advantages of Minor Nuclear States," *Security Studies* 6, no. 4 (summer 1997):55.

23. Vadim Bertsov, "Bandity predlagali 'kryshu' oboronnomu zavodu," *Kommersant-Daily*, no. 44, March 19, 1999 <www.commersant.ru>. See also "Zavod i gorod lezhit na boku," *Sovetskaia Rossiia*, November 11, 1998.

24. Geoffrey York, "Unhappy Russian Workers Threaten Nuclear Disaster," *The Globe and Mail* (Toronto), July 2, 1997, A1.

25. In late May 1997, for example, the Russian military recorded 19 violent deaths in a single week, including 3 suicides and 2 instances where soldiers opened fire on their fellow servicemen. See Anna Politovskaia, "The Army is Going Out of Its Mind" (in Russian), *Obshchaia gazeta*, June 5–11, 1997 <www.or.ru>.

26. "Vkliuchite musyku i prigotovtes k smerti," *Kommersant*, June 5, 1999 <www.commersant.ru>.

27. "Voennye na Kamchatke podaiut signal bedstviia," *Izvestiia*, July 22, 1999 <www.izvestia.ru>.

28. "Russians Bust Apparent Nuclear Smuggling Ring," Reuters, September 2, 1999.

29. "American Sentenced for Exporting Speedboats to NK," *Joongang Ilbo* (Seoul), November 2, 1999; reported on the Nautilus Institute's Northeast Asian Peace and Security Network, November 8, 1999.

30. See Alexander Zhebin, "A Political History of Soviet–North Korean Nuclear Cooperation," in *The North Korean Nuclear Program: Security, Strategy, and New Perspectives from Russia*, ed. James Clay Moltz and Alexandre Y. Mansourov (New York: Routledge, 2000), 36.

31. For more on these cases, see Moltz and Robinson, "Dismantling Russia's Nuclear Subs," 11.

32. Carey Scott, "Russian Subs Face Nuclear Meltdown," *Sunday Times* (London),

February 28, 1999.

33. Mikhail Druzhinin, "Matrosy razdolbali iadernii reactor," *Kommersant*, January 29, 2000 <www.commersant.ru>.

34. Nikolai Litkovets, "I v oknakh svet zazhzhet 'Ural'," *Krasnaia Zvezda*, November 14, 1997, 2.

35. Itar-Tass, "Russian Nuclear Subs Supply Electricity to Town in Far East," November 11, 1998, in FBIS-SOV-98-316, November 12, 1999.

36. "Atomnie podvodnie lodki tikhookeanskogo flota snazhaiut elektroenergii kamchatskii gorod," *Parlamentskaia gazeta*, November 12, 1998, 2.

37. "Residents Seek to Block Nuclear Processing Plant in Primore," RFE/FL Newsline, June 16, 1997.

38. Due to a number of both technical and political problems, however, the filtration facility still has not been certified for use.

39. "Russia Seeks to Refloat a Decaying Fleet," *Jane's International Defense Review*, no. 43 (January 1, 1997):51.

40. "Na Kamchatke zatonula atomnaia podlodka," *Segodnia*, May 31, 1997, 5.

41. "Radioaktivnyi generator ne naiden," *Nezavisimaia gazeta* (Moscow), August 19, 1997, 2.

42. For more on this subject, see Katherine Burns, "Security Implications of Defense Conversion in the Russian Far East," chapter 11 in this volume.

43. Author's interview with Russian economist, October 22, 1999, Khabarovsk.

44. Author's interviews with various Russian nuclear sector and krai government officials in Vladivostok and Khabarovsk, October 1999.

45. Author's interview with a senior scientist in the Russian Academy of Sciences who works with the Pacific Fleet, October 18, 1999, Vladivostok.

46. Author's phone interview with an official from the Japanese Embassy in Washington, D.C., June 8, 2000.

11

Security Implications of Defense Conversion in the Russian Far East

Katherine G. Burns

When the Soviet Union dissolved, defense enterprises in the Russian Far East employed close to 40 percent of the regional workforce and accounted for some 20 percent of industrial production. The economies of this region—and particularly those of Primorskii and Khabarovskii krais—are therefore irrevocably tied to the fate of these industries. Successful conversion to civilian production could bring peace and stability to the region. However, conversion is progressing slowly, production has fallen sharply, and the defense sector is currently mired in an economic crisis that inflames local discontent and fosters a political instability that threatens the future of economic reform and Russia's fragile democratic institutions. The United States and other international players need to focus attention on facilitating private sector growth in the Russian Far East in order to absorb the large numbers of unemployed and disgruntled former defense employees whose social and political activities threaten instability throughout Northeast Asia.

GOVERNMENT POLICIES AND DEFENSE CONVERSION

For over 70 years, the defense industry played a critical role in the Soviet political and economic landscape. In the heyday of Soviet power, defense enterprises employed between 9 and 14 million people—between 10 and 20 percent of the Soviet workforce—in some 2,000 enterprises and their suppliers,[1] a huge number compared to America's 1990 defense employment numbers of 1.5 to 1.9 million people.[2]

Average Soviet defense spending stood at over 20 percent of gross domestic product, compared to less than 5 percent in the United States.[3] The Soviet defense sector employed the best and the brightest of the scientific community and offered the highest salaries, best social benefits, and the most prestigious work. In an economy beset by chronic shortages and delays, defense enterprises received timely delivery of high-quality inputs at vastly subsidized costs. During the Cold War, this system had phenomenal success in competing with the United States and the West in an arms and technology race.

Ultimately, however, the enormous social and economic costs required to support the defense sector undermined the entire system. By the late 1980s, the Soviet leadership under Mikhail Gorbachev recognized the untenable nature of the situation and took steps to address the problem, and conversion of the defense sector to civilian production became one of the cornerstones of reform. The first stage of the process, or the "all-union concept," lasted through the first half of 1991 and employed a top-down approach using traditional Soviet planning mechanisms. The first steps were taken in 1987 when 230 enterprises of the defunct Ministry of Machine-Building for Light and Food Industries were placed under the control of the Military-Industrial Commission. This decision was fueled by the Soviet belief that the military-industrial complex—having proven its efficiency in competition with the West—would be best equipped to handle the new burden and would effect conversion through new acquisitions. By December 1988, General Secretary Gorbachev officially endorsed defense conversion at a historic speech to the United Nations, where he launched the Soviet conversion endeavor as a component of his "new thinking" in foreign and security policy. The official Soviet conversion program was launched in December of 1989 and included a 19-percent cut in the Soviet budget for weapons procurement between 1989 and 1991. Ministries and enterprises engaged in defense production were ordered to significantly increase civilian production with little regard for their civilian production capabilities or for market forces. Disorder ensued. As Michael Costigan and William Martel illustrate: "The Ministry of Aviation Industry was given the responsibility for processing fruits and vegetables, and making starch, syrup and pasta. The ministry charged with making nuclear weapons began processing cheese-making equipment. One defense plant started producing titanium wheel-barrows."[4]

The most intractable problem facing defense conversion, however, was not poor planning or failure to grasp market principles, but rather finding the means to finance conversion. In 1992, President Yeltsin's advisor on defense conversion estimated the cost at 150 billion rubles, but that figure was later revised to 150 billion *dollars*, or the equivalent of two years of Russia's GDP. With Russian inflation rates running at 2,650 percent in 1992 and 940 percent in 1993, the Russian government was effectively incapable of providing any substantial financing for conversion. In an effort to address this problem, the new Yeltsin government—and particularly its chief economic reform strategist, Yegor Gaidar—turned its focus to the defense enterprises themselves. Under Gaidar's "shock therapy," defense enterprises would bear the brunt of the financial burden. The government removed itself from directing or supporting enterprises, slashed state orders for arms procurement by 68 percent, and effectively attempted to impose hard-budget constraints in an effort to force defense enterprises to redirect their efforts into the civilian sector.

Another tactic to which the government resorted in the effort to finance defense conversion was arms sales. Termed "economic" conversion—as opposed to the 1989–91 period of "physical" conversion—the proceeds of arms sales were to be directed to diversification to consumer products and to military activities. As Mikhail Malei, Yeltsin's advisor on conversion, explained: "The essence of economic conversion lies in orienting Russia's military-industrial complex towards exports for the next four years, and by exporting the products of the defense complex it is possible to find the necessary funds to carry out physical conversion of enterprises."[5] By August 1992, the National Industrial Policy, driven by new First Deputy Minister of Defense Andrei Kokoshin, similarly emphasized Russia's intention to develop and produce world-class weaponry. Until this point, all arms sales had been carried out through the Ministry of Defense. The move to economic conversion was particularly important for defense enterprises, because the new policy allowed them to retain a portion of the profits from arms sales themselves. In the end, however, lack of funds made it difficult for the defense sector to produce adequate quantities of weapons to substantially increase arms exports.

In 1993 the Russian government under Prime Minister Viktor Chernomyrdin turned to defense enterprise privatization in an attempt to impose hard-budget constraints and improve efficiency in the military-industrial complex. The process began in February 1993, and by March 1994 approximately 700 defense enterprises had been privatized. Privatization, it was hoped, would increase the efficiency of defense enterprises during conversion—obliging them to develop a corporate structure and making managers accountable to workers through a voting system—and offer enterprises new means to develop independent sources of finance through issuing stock, selling off parts of the enterprise, or forming joint ventures with foreign companies. To this end, defense enterprises were divided into three categories. One group was prohibited from privatizing and remained entirely in state hands. The State Committee on Defense Branches of Industry (Goskomoboronprom) handled them directly. All other defense enterprises were required to privatize. Most privatized in accordance with the "second option," in which 51 percent of shares went to enterprise workers and management; in other enterprises, privatization accorded a "gold share"—up to 20 percent of the stock—to the government, a sufficient percentage to guarantee the state veto power. A final group of defense enterprises were to be entirely private.

Alongside these efforts, the state continued its direct involvement in the defense sector. A 1998 government program to restructure the defense industry, for example, allocated 2.1 billion rubles ($339 million) from the 1998 federal budget to support defense enterprises. The program allocated 632 million rubles as credit for conversion projects, 508 million rubles to finance private projects, and approximately one billion rubles to subsidize converting enterprises. The government also took steps to eliminate defense sector debt.[6]

Unfortunately, the combination of efforts to finance and effect conversion has had only limited success in Russia and in the Russian Far East in particular.

THE DEFENSE CONVERSION EXPERIENCE
IN THE RUSSIAN FAR EAST

In the Soviet period, the defense sector played a critical role in the economy of the Far East.[7] Specializing in shipbuilding and ship repair, the region's 32 defense plants serviced the Soviet Union's mighty Pacific Fleet, and the region also boasted a large military aviation sector producing the famous Black Shark attack helicopters and Sukhoi fighter planes. Of the Russian Far East's defense production in 1989, 90 percent was concentrated in these three sectors. In 1991 defense enterprise production accounted for a sizable proportion of regional industrial output: 22.5 percent in Khabarovsk and 13.6 percent in Primorye. Urban centers were heavily militarized. For example, the region's largest city, Vladivostok, is home to 9 defense enterprises which accounted for nearly 50 percent of the city's total industrial production. The majority of the Russian Far East's defense industry is located in Khabarovskii krai, which accounts for more than 60 percent of RFE defense production, while Primorskii krai accounts for 35 percent. These two krais together account for nearly 92 percent of defense sector employment in the Russian Far East. At the time the Soviet Union collapsed, the defense sector in Primorskii and Khabarovskii krais employed over 400,000 personnel directly involved in defense production, a figure which does not take into account the sizable number of people indirectly involved in defense production—cafeteria workers, civilian parts manufacturers, dependent families, and others. The above-mentioned figures for the Russian Federation suggest that the total number of defense-related employees could be upwards of three times the official number. In addition, the defense sector in the Russian Far East is characterized by a large number of remote mono-industrial towns—dominated by one large defense enterprise that essentially supports the entire town. Primorye towns such as Arsenev (1991 population of 71,200), home to Progress, the manufacturer of Black Shark helicopters, and Bolshoi Kamen, home to the Zvezda nuclear submarine plant, which produced 99.8 percent of the town's 1991 industrial production, illustrate this phenomenon.

Common Ills

During the conversion process, defense enterprises in the Russian Far East have suffered a variety of ills common across the Russian Federation. Between 1989 and 1991, government orders to Russian Far East defense enterprises shrank by 22 percent. By 1995, the volume of defense orders in Primorskii krai was just 71 percent of the 1991 value. Enterprises for which a high percentage of production (between 70 and 90 percent dependence on state orders) was exclusively military—generally those specializing in aviation and shipbuilding—continued to rely on dwindling state orders. Narrowly specialized, such enterprises faced the most difficult conversion challenges, or have simply not been able to convert to civilian production at all. A second group of enterprises, for which 50–70 percent of production depended on state orders, found it easier to move into nonmilitary production. In addition, changes in the structure of government orders adversely affected Russian Far East enterprises. The 1995–97 Government Program on Conversion of the Defense Industry stipulated that defense orders would be awarded on a competitive basis rather than determined at an administrative level. In 1995, of the 32 Russian Far East defense enterprises, only 20 received government orders.

The drop in government orders was not the greatest challenge facing the region's defense sector. Rather, the failure of the central government to pay for these orders put the enterprises in a difficult bind. This has been particularly galling, as the state *requires* defense enterprises to fulfill orders even when the Ministry of Defense is not in a position to pay. At the federal level, for example, by March 1994, the Ministry of Defense had already placed orders for the year worth 28 trillion rubles, although the federal budget had allocated only 5 trillion rubles for this purpose.[8] By October 1996, the state owed 417.3 billion rubles to Primorye enterprises and 128 billion rubles to enterprises in Khabarovskii krai.

State insistence on fulfillment of orders and failure to pay was further compounded by the dearth of government funding for the conversion process itself. In 1992–94, for example, funds from the federal budget amounted to only 0.8 percent of estimated conversion costs in Primorskii krai, with only a very modest increase to 3.4 percent in 1995, and no federal funding for conversion whatsoever in 1996–97. In Khabarovsk, federal budget funding for conversion amounted to 15 percent of estimated conversion costs in 1992–95, but in 1996–97 the krai received no federal funding for conversion. As a result, defense enterprises across the Russian Far East have become entangled in a web of debt: they are unable to honor their debts to suppliers because they have not received payments for deliveries to the central government.

Another factor that has confounded enterprise conversion has been the general chaos in the central government as well as in the formulation of conversion policy. Indeed, while some analysts have argued that government policies are, in and of themselves, ill-conceived—pushing enterprises too hard by withdrawing credits too quickly and providing inadequate assistance in the conversion process—others have argued that it is the *inconsistency* of government policies that is to blame for the current state of affairs. The 1994 conflict with the Ministry of Defense over defense orders and the federal budget, noted above, is a case in point. Considerable wrangling in Moscow over defense policy continues. The defense industry's main advocate in Moscow is Goskomoboronprom, which is allied with the Federal Counterintelligence Committee and the Federal Procurator's office. The recently formed League for Aid to the Defense Industry similarly lobbies for increased funding and, not surprisingly, the communist-dominated State Duma has often tangled with the presidential administration on defense policy. Advocates of rapid reform in the sector include the State Committee for the Management of State Property and the Ministry of Finance. The position of the Ministry of Defense itself is elusive, changing from one pole to another depending on timing and issues.

Frequent political infighting at the federal level, as well as rapid changes in government personnel, have encouraged the defense enterprises to focus on short-term survival tactics rather than long-term conversion strategies. One tactic has been simple noncompliance, and there is considerable evidence to suggest that defense enterprise managers have actively opposed the government policies that oblige them to privatize and become self-sustaining. The chaotic atmosphere has been psychologically grating for everyone, but particularly for enterprise managers, who were accustomed to elite status and social and economic perks. For them, the transition has been devastating. Moreover, as with the case of defense conversion in the United States, the "culture" of defense enterprise—lack of regard for costs and inexperience with concepts of supply and demand, common to all Soviet enterprises, together with the elite mentality engendered by defense status under the Soviet system—is ill-suited to market conditions. In Russia, for those enterprises with a high level of military production, these problems are compounded by the traditional isolation between defense and civilian sectors that the Soviet regime maintained.

The election of President Vladimir Putin in March 2000 has spelled some relief for the defense industry, if not for the conversion process. Indeed, Putin has placed a great deal of emphasis on the defense sector. Already in the fall of 1999, he had arranged for an extra $100 million to be transferred to the defense budget, principally to support the war in Chechnya. The new president announced a 50-percent increase in defense spending and approved a 62 billion ruble defense procurement budget for 2000, with 27.3 billion to go to defense enterprises to pay for weapons systems.[9] With about half the 2000 procurement budget going to research and production of conventional weapons, the budget provided welcome relief to those beleaguered defense enterprises for which the obstacles to conversion have proved insurmountable. Efforts to prop up defense enterprises continued in 2001 with the Defense Ministry promising to pay 5 billion rubles in debts to defense industry enterprises.[10] Despite these efforts, however, the government remains some $880 million in debt to defense contractors.[11]

Unique Challenges

Besides falling government orders and a general lack of government funding—which are problems faced by the entire Russian military-industrial complex—defense enterprises in the Russian Far East face a number of unique challenges dictated by geography and the legacy of the Soviet defense production system.[12] To begin with, security objectives—not economic logic—dictated the geographical dispersion of large enterprises to the desolate regions of the Russian Far East. The remote location served to guard the secrecy of Soviet defense production and would assure continued defense production in the event of hostilities that might compromise production in the European portions of the Soviet Union. In some cases it was designed to provide a "back-up" defense production system in the event of war. This was the case in Vladivostok, where defense production was almost entirely composed of "back-up" systems designed to pick up the slack in case of failures in the factories to the west. The logic of geography also meant that, to a much greater extent than among their Siberian or European cousins, the distribution of Russian Far East defense enterprises was characterized by a preponderance of "company towns" that afforded little or no access to the diverse economies of urban settings, which facilitate the conversion process. Under the Soviet regime, enterprises were responsible not only for providing employment, but also for a myriad of social services including housing, education, health care, and recreation. This greatly increases the costs of conversion, particularly in mono-industrial towns where collapse of a defense enterprise effectively entails collapse of the entire town structure.

The dispersion of the Far Eastern defense complex among multiple company towns was further aggravated by the organizational structure of the Soviet defense system, according to which defense enterprises were vertically integrated with branch ministries delineated by sector.[13] As Kevin O'Prey has explained:

> Plants located next door to one another conceivably had absolutely no contact between them if they were subordinated to different industrial ministries. For example, an aircraft plant would not communicate with a nearby electronics manufacturer even if it were in need of microcircuits. Instead, it would look to the aviation industry branch ministry for the required supplies, even though the aviation-affiliated plant manufacturing them might be located on the other side of the country.[14]

Problems such as this built walls between the defense enterprises of the Far East and raised artificial barriers to regionally based cooperation, a particularly vexing issue in urban centers such as Vladivostok, where defense plants were attached to different ministries and traditionally maintained little contact amongst themselves.

The internal logic of the Soviet production system also has caused problems for the post-Soviet Far East. Production was organized such that research institutes, large-scale factories, and assembly plants were located in disparate regions of the former Soviet Union. Under the Soviet system, most major research centers were located in European Russia, while factory facilities and assembly plants were built across the territory of the USSR. Most were narrowly specialized in the production or assembly of a specific military part or product, and this was particularly true the farther east one went. In Vladivostok, for instance, the majority of defense enterprises consist of assembly plants, and have neither research facilities nor production capability. Assembly plant workers tend to be narrowly specialized in specific aspects of defense production, making it particularly difficult, if not impossible, to make the leap to the civilian sector. The Soviet migration policy further reinforced this tendency by offering high salaries and multiple perks designed to attract highly specialized workers to remote regions of the Russian Far East.

Such dilemmas are compounded by distance: nine time zones from Moscow and a week's journey by rail, in the post-Soviet period the Russian Far East has effectively been cut off from centers of Russian power. The situation is further compounded by the rapid rise of rail tariffs since the collapse of Soviet subsidies, causing a prohibitive increase in costs for defense inputs from the far-flung reaches of the former Soviet territory. Cities that are located along major rail lines—Vladivostok for instance—are at some advantage because they have access to rail links, however unaffordable they may be. The logic of Soviet planning dictated a transportation system focused on direct links between the regions and Moscow, with little focus on intraregional contact. In the post-Soviet period, this system has produced particular challenges for Far Eastern defense conversion because it increases the difficulty and cost of reconstructing former supply lines or of developing new intraregional support structures.

Another obstacle to conversion in the Russian Far East is related to the relatively recent industrialization in the region. In European Russia, the Soviet defense industry developed against an already industrialized background. As conversion progressed, the regional economies were able to fall back on an underlying industrial base that predated the defense sector. In the RFE, by contrast, a comparatively later industrialization was wholly predicated on the defense sector, leaving the region few industrialized resources on which to fall back in the conversion period.

Some Advantages

Some Russian Far East defense enterprises—notably those in Vladivostok—were sheltered from the early ravages of the conversion process.[15] Home to the Pacific Fleet, Vladivostok was a closed city until 1992, and, as a result, defense enterprises located in Vladivostok were unaffected by the conversion policies of the Gorbachev era. Between 1987 and 1991, the majority of Soviet defense enterprises reacted to the drawdown in government orders and chronic government nonpayments with shock. Totally unprepared for exposure to market forces, it took most enterprises five years to even begin to find their feet in the rapidly shifting eddies of Soviet and post-Soviet economic life. During this period, enterprises attempted to meet plan expectations by consuming the resources that they had accumulated during the Soviet period. As a result, they encountered the tumultuous post-Soviet era, shock therapy, and an accelerated government conversion policy with few or none of their accumulated resources.

Conversely, defense enterprises in closed cities such as Vladivostok were isolated from the chaos of the early conversion years. For them, the Gorbachev period was one of relative calm, affording an opportunity to observe the trials of the defense sector in other regions. Vladivostok enterprises used this time to observe the strategies of others and select those which proved most successful. When conversion eventually came, Vladivostok enterprises were comparatively adept at developing coping strategies and modifying those strategies as needed. When the city opened in 1992, enterprise directors, recognizing their inability to compete with Asian companies in the consumer goods market, set their sights on exports of specialized products to the Asia Pacific region. Then, when that strategy did not prove successful, they reoriented their efforts to focus on the local market, particularly modernization of regional infrastructure and the needs of the more dynamic local sectors.

In addition, Vladivostok's local economy—oriented to the fishing industry—has proven advantageous to the defense enterprises. The expansive fishing industry in particular has provided alternative employment opportunities for jobless defense employees. Compared to company towns such as Arsenev or Bolshoi Kamen, where no such opportunities exist, this is a distinct advantage.

The Vladivostok defense sector has enjoyed another advantage in the clarity of its enterprises' relations with the federal government; from the very beginning, the central ministries made it clear that Vladivostok's defense sector could not expect a continuation of government orders. The precipitous drop in government orders which ensued forced the enterprises to turn their face to the future, without harboring continued hopes of central defense contracts. This is in contrast to other areas of the Russian Far East, where the center deemed enterprise production to be more critical to the state and held out the hope of continued state orders. Enterprises subjected to central or local ambiguity have had a more difficult transition experience, with many continuing military production in the vain hope of winning future government orders. Such is the case of the Zvezda nuclear submarine facility in Bolshoi Kamen. In January 1997, the director of that enterprise promised a state order and persuaded his employees to continue working. In June, however, the Defense Ministry expressed surprise at the workers' efforts and could not confirm that state orders would be forthcoming.[16] Clearly this lack of clarity about government policy makes it particularly difficult for enterprises to cope in the new era.

Strategic Approaches

Defense enterprises in the Russian Far East have developed a series of "coping strategies" to address the challenges of the conversion period. One such strategy has been the formation of "industrial groups"—often in league with local governments—designed to preserve defense enterprise assets and lobby central government officials. While Moscow bureaucrats dictate policy, nine time zones away in the Far East, it is local governments that must cope with the devastating social consequences and costs of defense enterprise reform. Not surprisingly, many governors have become advocates for their beleaguered defense enterprises.

Primorskii krai provides a classic example of this approach. The process began in 1989 when a group of defense enterprises banded together with civilian enterprises and various branches of the regional Sberbank in an association called Red Pine. Red Pine aimed to facilitate the conversion experience for krai enterprises by reorienting them toward the local economy. By 1993, Red Pine had reinvented itself as an organization called the Primorskii Shareholding Company of Commodity Producers (PAKT), which embraced defense sector plants as well as all the large extractive industries in the krai. PAKT's stated goal was economic—to coordinate conversion projects and reorient the local economy to exports—but its primary activities were political. Within a few months of its founding, PAKT succeeded in dislodging the krai governor—a man renowned for his international outlook but out of synch with local needs—and installing their own candidate—Yevgenii Nazdratenko. PAKT members felt that Nazdratenko, the former director of a large extractive enterprise, could better understand the dire straits in which the large krai enterprises found themselves. Indeed, Nazdratenko set about vigorously lobbying Moscow and demanding that the central government honor its financial obligations to krai enterprises. Although the new governor met with minimal success in this endeavor, he quickly found blaming Moscow to be politically expedient, and by 1995 won the Primorye gubernatorial election by a landslide. Nazdratenko later developed a personal political agenda, abandoning many of his former PAKT allies and assuming personal political control of the krai. Although the personal patronage system that Nazdratenko ushered into the krai failed to produce the desired increase in central government funding, the governor was able to successfully use it to grant special privileges—amounting to local subsidies—to those defense enterprise directors who continued to support him. Thus, for example, he kept electricity prices artificially low, which contributed to an energy crisis, and granted respite from electrical bills to select defense enterprises. He also allocated local budget funding to failing defense enterprises in his political camp and granted relief from local taxes. In this way, the local government under Nazdratenko managed to support at least some of the defense enterprises in the krai, although at the cost of social and political stability and a deceleration of the economic reform process.

Links with the local government aside, a number of Far Eastern defense enterprises have developed their own strategies for coping with the hardships of conversion. Most have focused their energies on the local economy, producing refrigeration equipment for the fishing industry, constructing and repairing fishing vessels, producing equipment for the food industry, or teaming up with foreign investors to work on local infrastructure projects. In addition, privatizing defense enterprises have restructured in an effort to break their dependence on the state, diversify their clientele, and secure new sources of funding. The Vladivostok defense enterprise Dalzavod provides an interesting illustration of this process.[17] Specializing in ship repair, Dalzavod was founded in 1888 and is one of the oldest enterprises in the krai. Blessed with special status in the Soviet era, the enterprise boasts a number of affiliated facilities, including an ironworks, a smelting works, and an electricity station. By 1995, Dalzavod found that its state orders had fallen to 30 percent of Soviet-era levels. Dalzavod was obliged to fulfill these orders, which became a considerable financial burden on the enterprise, particularly in light of the government's chronic nonpayments. By 1995 the state owed Dalzavod a total of 70 billion rubles in back payments. As a result, the enterprise was obliged to finance its obligatory defense contracts through the proceeds from its civilian undertakings. In the civilian sector, Dalzavod's main client was the fishing industry, but the enterprise needed to invest in new technologies in order to keep up with the changing demands of the marine sector. To cope with this situation, Dalzavod devised a strategy that divided civilian from military production. Originally electing a privatization scheme that accorded the state a "gold share," Dalzavod subsequently transformed itself into a holding company to include the 20 factories that fell under its umbrella. These factories became legally separate entities, linked by a common development strategy. Dalzavod held the majority of shares in each of the new entities and provided its "daughter-companies" with funding to support their activities in the civilian sector. In this way, Dalzavod was able to isolate the profits from its civilian business and move more fully toward civilian production. From a legal and financial standpoint, it was no longer in a position to honor its defense orders.

Primorskii defense enterprise Variag provides another example of a "coping strategy," similarly designed to isolate civilian from military production.[18] Located on the outskirts of Vladivostok, Variag was officially declared converted in 1993, meaning that it was no longer to receive state orders. In 1996, however, some 40 percent of the enterprise's production remained in the military sector. Variag's technology, unlike Dalzavod's, was not dual-use—it produced specialized hydraulic systems and navigational instruments for military ships. The enterprise therefore lacked the ability to convert its military production to civilian use. As a result, the company was obliged to develop completely new industries geared to civilian production. In order to do this, management decided to break the enterprise down by department, increase departmental autonomy, and effect a "closed-type" privatization for its departments. Each department was to make its own separate foray into civilian production. Thus, disparate departments began to produce such civilian goods as medical instruments, banking equipment, telephones, plastic containers, and transportation equipment. Departments were responsible for finding their own clients. In some instances, Variag departments were able to forge partnerships with other former defense enterprises, bridging the Soviet-era barriers that had separated defense enterprises in different sectors. Such was the case in telephone production: a Variag department produced the plastic parts, and Radiopribor, a Vladivostok defense enterprise specializing in electrical equipment, produced the electrical components. Variag's scheme separated military from civilian production by effectively breaking up the original enterprises and handing over the civilian initiative to distinct smaller units.

Defense enterprises in the Russian Far East have thus engaged in a variety of schemes designed to cope with the shock of conversion. All have attempted, to one degree or another, to enter the civilian sector. All experienced a precipitous drop in production. In 1997, for example, production at converted enterprises in Primorskii krai fell to 11.5 percent of 1992 levels, and in Khabarovskii krai to 7 percent of 1992 levels. During this period, converted and converting enterprises turned to the civilian sector, but their efforts were often hampered by a drop in civilian production even more severe than that in military production. In 1996, military production in Primorskii krai stood at 27.5 percent of the 1992 level, while civilian production had dropped to 20.4 percent of the 1992 level. This radical drop in civilian production, due to the weakness of the domestic market as well as competition from higher-quality and lower-priced imported goods, has made it difficult for defense enterprises to engage in civilian production. The most successful are those that have set their sights on the fishing industry, the most lucrative industry in the region. But even in the fishing industry, foreign services— Korean and Chinese ship-repair facilities, for instance—offer better quality work at cheaper prices. These factors have produced enduring obstacles to the conversion process in the Russian Far East.

THREAT ASSESSMENTS

The defense conversion process in the Russian Far East has given rise to a number of security concerns. Most noted of these is the sale of arms—particularly of Sukhoi Su-27 fighter planes to the People's Republic of China. Although increasing, these sales do not yet represent a serious threat to stability in the region. Of greater import is the widespread social unrest, the consequent threats to social order, and the ensuing rise of nationalist forces which threaten the fragile fabric of Russia's young democratic institutions. A final concern lies in the environmental realm, as decaying nuclear and chemical facilities threaten to seep toxic wastes into the environment.

Arms Exports

As defense conversion in the Russian Far East failed to progress rapidly, the options for defense enterprises were increasingly those with the greatest destabilizing effects, such as layoffs or expanded military production, primarily for export into Northeast China. By the mid-1990s, this arms export option seemed to offer the line of least resistance and the greatest promise for profit. This was evidenced by Russian transfers of Pacific Fleet submarines to North Korea, diverse arms components to China, and two old Kiev-class aircraft carriers to South Korea.[19]

Particularly important for Russia's Far Eastern defense sector has been the sale to China of Su-27 fighter planes—produced at the Gagarin Aircraft Manufacturing Association in Komsomolsk-na-Amure in Khabarovskii krai.[20] The Association is one of the krai's major exporters. It is state-owned, and during his October 1999 visit, then Prime Minister Putin promised to maintain the plant's state-owned status and provide it with foreign contracts and state orders.[21] With proximate access to the northeastern region of China, the Gagarin plant has maintained commercial ties with China since the mid-1950s.[22] In 1991 China purchased an initial batch of 24 Su-27s for about $1 billion. By 1997 the total number of Chinese Su-27 purchases had risen to 72.[23] In February 1996 Moscow and Beijing reached agreement on a $2.5 billion deal for China to begin coproducing the Su-27.[24] Estimates vary widely as to the final number of Su-27s that China may purchase or coproduce, but it seems reasonable to assume that the total could exceed 100, and if China masters full coproduction, this figure could exceed several hundred. China continues to express an interest in the Gagarin plant's production. In June 1999 the deputy chairman of China's Central Military Council, Colonel General Zhang Wannian, visited the Gagarin plant and met with Khabarovsk Governor Viktor Ishaev in preparation for signing a contract to purchase Su-30 fighters.[25]

While the Gagarin plant's Su-27s constitute the largest and most visible of the Russian Far East's arms exports, other enterprises are also expanding into the arms export business, seeking to reap financial rewards and balance their abysmal accounts. For example, in 1997 the Progress aviation plant in Arsenev attempted to sell one of its trademark Ka-50 Black Shark helicopters to the Slovak Republic at the steep price of $17 million. Since the company had no license to sell abroad, it was obliged to sell through the Ministry of Defense—which takes a 25 percent cut for the favor and also charges the enterprise for transportation fees. This pushed the price of the enterprise's wares up, rendering them noncompetitive on the world market.[26] To circumvent the problem, managers facilitated the sale of the state's 51-percent controlling stock to government defense company Moscow Aviation Production Association, or MAPO, an enterprise that does have an export license. By February of 1998, things at Progress were looking up. While Dalzavod awaited government back-payments to the tune of 27.7 trillion rubles, and Zvezda almost 22 trillion, the state paid its entire outstanding debt to Progress. In addition, Progress signed a contract for the sale of a 3M-80E Moskit ship missile complex to China, and precontract preparations were underway for the export of Black Sharks and an additional Moskit complex.[27] By the middle of 2000, Progress had manufactured four times more products than the previous year, and the Russian Federation contracted to sell two destroyers equipped with Moskit complexes to China.[28]

While such moves spell good news for defense enterprise workers and managers, they have raised security concerns, especially in the United States. In particular, American military analysts point out that sales and coproduction of the Su-27 are likely to shift the balance of power in Northeast Asia by allowing China to develop greater strike capabilities vis-à-vis Taiwan. In addition, some have argued that the transfer of Su-27 technology to China will allow the Chinese to develop their own aircraft, which China would be able to sell, and thereby undercut Russian producers on the world market. This view does not resonate in at least some of Russia's defense policy circles. In 1996, for example, Foreign Minister Yevgenii Primakov argued that Russia must oppose U.S. unipolar hegemony; by this logic, Russian-Chinese cooperation could be a step toward that goal. Primakov's position does resonate with Russian Far East political leaders. Explaining the projected sale of Su-30 aircraft to China, for example, Khabarovsk Governor Ishaev stated that "the modern world should be either multi-polar or at least bi-polar, in order to oppose the powerful NATO bloc from the deterrent standpoint, because NATO is seeking to replace the UN Security Council and other UN bodies." Ishaev further stated that Colonel General Zhang supports "the policy toward creating a pole which should ensure the protection of our states against encroachment by other parties."[29]

Yet many American analysts portray the Russian defense industry as victim to a forceful Chinese militarization drive. They point to a security threat to Taiwan because of China's acquisition of Russian military technology. U.S. War College Professor Stephen J. Blank's perspective is a case in point. Blank argues that China's acquisition of large numbers of Su-27s would pose a serious challenge to U.S. air superiority. In order to sustain deterrence, Blank argues:

> Aircraft that are "good enough" or slightly superior to the Su-27 do not provide a sufficient margin of superiority to guarantee U.S. dominance in the air. The U.S. must proceed with plans to field advanced combat aircraft superior to the Su-27. Current and future aircraft must be equipped with an effective helmet-sighted missile to counter the Archer. Failure to do so risks allowing the Asian balance of power to shift dangerously in favor of China.[30]

Both the actual danger of an arms build-up posed by China's weapons acquisition and the obvious disparities in perception among Russian, Chinese, and American parties constitute security threats to the balance of power in the region.

Another concern is the lack of Russian control over the process of arms sales. In theory, arms sales are under the control of the Ministry of Defense. In the regions, however, frustrated defense enterprises are taking it upon themselves to directly arrange arms sales, even when they do not have a license to do so. The Gagarin plant is a case in point. According to one report, in 1993 "the government [had] not paid 22 billion rubles to the enterprise for ready-made products, forbidding the sale of planes abroad at the same time. True, the factory sold a batch of SU-27s to China last year."[31] Even if enterprises do have licenses for arms exports, the prohibitively high cuts taken by the Ministry of Defense—as evidenced by the Progress case—encourage enterprises to circumvent formal procedure. By one count, at least 40 percent of the revenue from Chinese purchases does not go to Russian manufacturers, while the Ministry of Defense takes a 6-percent commission on sales to China.[32] Exorbitant commissions charged by middlemen and frequent non-cash payments compound defense enterprises' financial problems. In their search for export autonomy, Far East defense enterprises have found willing supporters in local government. Local governments have lobbied central authority for reductions in arms export regulations, and when this is not forthcoming, have unilaterally decided to expand on the prescribed amounts of military exports.[33]

At times, the general disorder in the Russian Far East, coupled with the desperation of defense enterprise employees, has led to illicit arms deals, a process which constitutes a further threat to stability in Northeast Asia. In 1998, for example, Russian customs officers at the Khasan border crossing in Primorskii krai intercepted five Mi-18 military helicopters destined for North Korea. Apparently, Russian military personnel sold the helicopters at an official Moscow military sale to a Khabarovsk middleman firm, at the price of 60 thousand to 100 thousand rubles each. The helicopters were originally the property of the Far East Military District. In this way, the high costs of effecting sales through official mechanisms, together with the economic desperation of remote defense enterprises, combines to produce a proliferation of agents willing to deal in arms sales.

Social Unrest

At the heart of the defense enterprise's search for export markets lies the economic desperation of large sectors of the population in the Russian Far East struggling to adapt to a post-Soviet world in the face of multiple obstacles. That desperation has had serious consequences in the social sphere, consequences that threaten strife and endanger the fabric of the young democratic system that initiated defense conversion in the first place. It is this social unrest—and most importantly its political manifestation—that truly threatens the security of the region. Should the system implode—and give rise to new nationalist leaders who speak to the interests of a disgruntled defense workforce—Cold War tensions in Northeast Asia could arise again. For this reason, social unrest and, critically, the economic conditions that give rise to it should be the focus of any effort to achieve and maintain stability in Northeast Asia.

Economic hardship is the crux of the problem. By 1997, workers at converting defense enterprises in Primorskii krai earned an average of 906,000 rubles (equivalent to $150) a month, if they were paid at all. Of defense enterprise workers forced to leave their jobs, only 7.4 percent had found other employment.[34] Layoffs were endemic. In July 1998, 800 workers at the Amur Ship-Building Plant at Komsomolsk-na-Amure were laid off, with another 3,600 to go by the end of the year.[35] At many defense enterprises, wages were not paid for months or even years. As a result, at enterprises such as the Amur Ship-Building Plant, the number of workers fell by nearly half during the 1990s.

Public protest became a regular feature of life. In Primorskii krai, workers from the Zvezda nuclear submarine repair plant and the Progress aviation plant have been particularly vocal. In March 1997, 2,000 Zvezda workers blockaded the highway between Vladivostok and the port of Nakhodka, demanding six months back-wages.[36] In April they protested again at the Zvezda plant, demanding that the government pay the 150 billion rubles owed for completed state orders.[37] In October they joined a group of some 300,000 protesters, including workers from Progress, demanding back-pay and the provision of social services.[38] By November, workers had not received pay for fifteen months. A visit from a Defense Ministry commission ended in recriminations when the commission accused the shipyard managers of "business passivity," and left without any promise to pay its debts to the enterprise.[39] Protests over government nonpayments continued in this vein throughout 1998 and into 1999, until Zvezda eventually signed a contract with China to repair ten submarines.[40]

Protests were accompanied by strikes. In June 1997, for example, Zvezda workers went on strike and blocked the Trans-Siberian Railway. A month later, Progress workers went on strike demanding that the management find paying customers and pay fifteen months of back wages. The action brought support from defense workers across the krai.[41] Protest spread to Khabarovsk, and in July 1998, workers at the Amur Ship-Building Plant in Komsomolsk-na-Amure went on strike. They demanded back wages for the past year, exhorted the government to pay its 70 million ruble debt, and adopted a resolution demanding the resignation of President Yeltsin and the government.[42]

As noted above, discontent over economic hardship has induced some defense employees to begin illicitly selling off military wares. Defense employee tampering with production—particularly where there are nuclear or chemical hazards—poses another threat to stability in the region. In March 1997, for instance, engineers from a nuclear submarine plant in the northern town of Severodvinsk threatened to tamper with a nuclear reactor if they were not paid their wages.[43] Purposeful action aside, the risk of accidents in the current chaotic atmosphere is a constant threat. The local press is rife with accounts of accidents and explosions at arms depots. In a similar vein, in May 1999, 300,000 tons of large-caliber ammunition were discovered at a civilian pier near a densely populated area of Vladivostok.[44] Theft of military wares, threats of reprisals for nonpayments, accidents, and the possibility of terrorist action all contribute to the growing crisis in the Russian Far East, with potentially destabilizing consequences throughout Northeast Asia.

The abysmal financial situation at many defense enterprises in the Far East also has contributed to a general public health crisis, which further serves to enflame social discontent. In 1993, when Vladivostok Mayor Viktor Cherepkov uncovered the deaths from starvation of three young navy officers and accused Pacific Fleet and krai officials of negligence, the public revelation catapulted him to power in the city and set off a continuing political battle with Primorskii krai administration officials. In 1994 local government structures took over responsibility for medical services previously supported by defense enterprises. Local budgets, however, were not up to the task. As a result, illness and malnutrition have further aggravated an already volatile situation. In addition, there is evidence to suggest that drug use—particularly of opium and heroin—is on the rise in the Russian Far East, fueled by the despair and futility experienced by unemployed defense workers.

Politically, defense worker discontent has found expression in regional warlords who nurture a confrontational relationship with Moscow, and in support for nationalist policies and nationalist leaders at the federal level. Election data from 1993, 1995, and 1996, for example, show that while support for the Yeltsin leadership was strong in the Russian Far East, in those electoral districts (*raiony*) dominated by defense enterprises, 15 percent of voters marked their ballots "against all" (as compared to the national average of less than 3 percent), revealing a huge disaffection and alienation from the system among defense employees. The Far East has turned out an unusually high vote for the Communist Party, as well as in 1995 almost twice the national average vote for ultra-rightist Vladimir Zhirinovsky's Liberal Democratic Party of Russia. Support for Vladimir Putin is high, which is not surprising given the new president's emphasis on increasing arms exports and procurement.

Environmental Threats

In 1997 military journalist Grigorii Pasko was arrested and imprisoned in Primorskii krai for reporting on corruption in the Pacific Fleet and the hazards of nuclear and chemical contamination in the region. Such environmental hazards predate the collapse of the Soviet Union, but the financial crisis precipitated by economic reform and the challenge of defense conversion have aggravated the situation. Nuclear waste has received particular attention. During the Soviet period, Russia routinely dumped nuclear waste into the Sea of Japan, and this practice continued into the post-Soviet era.[45] In 1997 Pasko attempted to report on the Pacific Fleet's practice of submerging containers of liquid radioactive waste and ammunition stores in the Sea of Japan.[46] In addition, he drew attention to the disposal of chemical weapons, noting that containers holding toxic chemical agents had been submerged in the Sea of Japan during the 1950s. Similar dangers are posed by the storage of rocket fuel and, in particular, one of its most lethal components—heptyl. The fuel is in the ballistic missiles carried by the nuclear submarines produced in Primorskii krai. The current disarray of the defense sector in the region means that no financing is available to address these environmental concerns. As a result, Pasko reported, heptyl containers in the region are corroding, and there is no monitoring of chemical agent containers submerged in the Sea of Japan or of chemical weapons arsenals buried in Primorskii krai.

The disastrous ecological and health repercussions of leakage pose a threat to the health and security of the Russian Far East and its Northeast Asian neighbors. Developments since Putin's election do not bode well for the environmental security of the region. In May 2000 President Putin signed a decree abolishing the State Committee for the Environment and folding all the committee's functions into the Natural Resource Ministry—a move that effectively does away with official environmental monitoring in the Russian Federation.[47]

WHAT IS TO BE DONE?

International efforts to facilitate the defense conversion process in Russia have been largely ineffective. U.S. efforts, while generally focused in a promising direction— assisting the conversion of defense enterprises by supporting joint-venture activities with the American private sector—have been inadequate to the task. Other countries have met with similar difficulties in enticing private sector involvement in the Russian defense industry. Some foreign projects have focused on specific areas, such an environmental clean-up, and these have met with some success. If defense conversion is to proceed in the Russian Far East, a great deal more international effort must be focused on reviving local economies to allow for Russian worker mobility into new sectors.

Direct U.S. assistance to Russia has been based on the 1993 Cooperative Threat Reduction Act, also known as the Nunn-Lugar Act.[48] Originally intended to reduce military threat by dismantling nuclear weapons, the Act was later broadened to include economic assistance for defense conversion. Under the umbrella of the Defense Special Weapons Agency—later renamed the Defense Threat Reduction Agency (DTRA)—the Nunn-Lugar program was designed to provide U.S. government funding and matching private sector investment to establish joint ventures between American partners and Russian defense enterprises. In 1994 three joint ventures were formed on this basis; at their peak, they employed a total of only 260 former defense workers, and by 1999 none had begun production. Furthermore, the guidelines of DTRA programs have been a source of irritation for the U.S.-Russian relationship because they require that the bulk of money be spent on U.S. personnel, with little left over to finance the actual conversion process itself. As a result, Russians feel, they have de facto served to finance U.S. studies of Russian defense enterprises.

The Nunn-Lugar Act also established a private, not-for-profit venture capital fund—the Defense Enterprise Fund—to continue the efforts of the DTRA. By the end of 1998, the Defense Enterprise Fund managed $66.7 million in assets and had formed a total of twelve joint ventures in Russia comprising a commitment of $50 million. While Fund programs have met with greater success than DTRA programs, they have come under increasing scrutiny and criticism. A recent audit concluded that the program is "poorly managed, lacking even the most basic business plan for setting goals and measuring progress...."[49]

Because the Defense Threat Reduction Agency and Defense Enterprise Fund programs have focused on joint ventures with Russian defense research institutes and design bureaus, their impact on the Far East's defense complex—composed almost exclusively of assembly plants—has been negligible. Of greater import have been the programs established under the U.S.-Russia Investment Fund, formed in May 1995 to facilitate joint ventures with private Russian companies. In conjunction with this effort, American Business Offices have been established across the Russian Far East in Vladivostok, Khabarovsk, Sakhalin, and the Republic of Sakha-Yakutia. By providing investment stimulus to the Far Eastern economy, these programs have at least provided some minimally increased opportunity for converting defense enterprises to form joint ventures with U.S. partners. In light of the private sector's unwillingness to engage the volatile Russian market, however, much remains to be done in order to increase private sector involvement.

Japanese programs have similarly sought to increase government and private sector investment in the Russian Far East, but after an initial rush in the early 1990s, little progress has been made. Japanese efforts subsequently have focused on joint environmental clean-up programs, such as one that assists in decommissioning nuclear submarines at the Zvezda plant. In this, they have been joined by the American government, which in 1998 contracted with the Zvezda plant to dismantle two ballistic submarines decommissioned by the Pacific Fleet.[50]

Vladimir Putin's attention to the defense sector is likely to improve the lot of the beleaguered enterprises in the Russian Far East by increasing military production and opening export markets for weapons in the Asia Pacific region. In the long term, this process could give rise to security concerns, but as yet, the numbers are too small to pose any serious threat to Northeast Asian stability. The deeper problems, however, lie in the overwhelming obstacles that the defense enterprises have encountered in attempting to convert to civilian production. Any policy that seeks to effectively address Russian Far East defense conversion, therefore, must consider the broader social, economic, and political context in which conversion is taking place. It must, for instance, take into account the large number of defense facilities whose highly specialized foci render them simply nonconvertible. There must be a greater recognition of the fact that such enterprises will inevitably generate large numbers of impoverished, unemployed, and disgruntled workers, whose social and political activities will seek to bring to power a government that will once again serve their needs—namely one that will redirect the focus of Russian policy toward defense production and export. This is the crux of the security threat posed by the challenge of defense conversion in the Russian Far East. In order to effectively address this threat, the United States and other members of the international community need to focus their policy goals on stimulating private sector development and economic renewal that will redirect the energies of former defense employees into economically and politically productive channels.

NOTES

I would like to thank Charles Ziegler for his helpful comments on an earlier draft. I would also like to acknowledge the contribution of Sonia Ben Ouagrham, who generously shared with me her outstanding doctoral dissertation, *La conversion des entreprises de défense en Russie: une analyse régionale*. Her insightful examination of the regional aspect of defense conversion enriched this study immeasurably.

1. There is no concrete information on the number of defense employees in the Soviet period. Keith Bush, in "Aspects of Military Conversion in Russia," *RFE/RL Report* 3, no. 14 (April 1994):31–34, illustrates this point with a variety of figures from different sources: The ballpark figure Bush cites is 2000 enterprises with 4–5 million employed in 1994. He notes that other sources cite some 15–20 million defense employees. Such numbers probably take into account workers in civilian enterprises whose work was contingent on supplying materials to defense enterprises. Michael J. Costigan and William C. Martel in "Our Failure to Convert Russia's Arms Industry," *Orbis* 43, no. 3 (summer 1999):461–478, cite the number of defense employees as 4.8 to 5 million in 1989, but also note that the number comes to 12 million when the number of employees in "supporting jobs" is taken into account. Inexplicably, in the same article, Costigan and Martel cite a figure of 6.5 million defense employees. They cite their source as Julian Cooper, *The Soviet Defence Industry, Conversion and Economic Reform* (New York: Council on Foreign Relations Press, 1991), 21. Julian Cooper provides the estimate of 9 million for the Soviet period in "The Soviet Defence Industry Heritage and Economic Restructuring in Russia," in Lars B. Wallan, ed., *The Post-Soviet Military-Industrial Complex* (Stockholm: Swedish Nations Defence Research Establishment, 1994), 30. First Deputy Minister of Defense, Andrei Kokoshin, cites figures between 12 and 14 million in "Defense Industry Conversion in the Russian Federation," in Teresa Pelton Johnson and Steven E. Miller, eds., *Russian Security after the Cold War: Seven Views from Moscow* (McLean, Va.: Brassy's, 1994), 48. Following the lead of Cooper and Kokoshin, Kevin P. O'Prey sites the 9–14

million figures in *A Farewell to Arms? Russia's Struggles with Defense Conversion* (New York: The Twentieth Century Fund Press, 1995), 15.

2. U.S. Department of Defense, *Adjusting to the Drawdown*, Report of the Defense Conversion Commission, December 31, 1992, 17–18, cited in O'Prey, *A Farewell to Arms?*, 15.

3. These figures cited in Costigan and Martel, "Our Failure to Convert Russia's Arms Industry," 465. The authors cite Sergei V. Kortunov, "Defense Conversion in Russia: The Need for Multinational Support," in *After the Cold War: Russian-American Defense Conversion for Economic Renewal*, ed. Michael P. Claudon et al. (New York: New York University Press, 1993), 58. The authors further note that there is considerable disagreement over the exact percentage of the Russian economy devoted to military production, citing one estimate by a senior official at the Institute of Canadian-American Studies of 35–55 percent of GDP.

4. Costigan and Martel, "Our Failure to Convert Russia's Arms Industry," 467.

5. Cited in Steven Gallant, "The Failure of Russia's Defense Conversion," *Jane's Intelligence Review*, July 1994:305.

6. *RFE/RL Newsline* 2, no. 125, part I (July 1998), "Government Approves Plan to Restructure Defense Industry."

7. Unless otherwise noted, this discussion is based on Pavel A. Minakir and Gregory L. Freese, eds., *The Russian Far East: An Economic Handbook* (Armonk, N.Y.: M.E. Sharpe, 1994), 217–26; Yeveniia V. Gudkova, "Roshia oyobi Roshia kyokuto no gunmin tenkan" (Defense Conversion in Russia and the Russian Far East), *ERINA Report*, Economic Research Institute for Northeast Asia, vol. 19 (October 1997):28–34; Yevgeniia V. Gudkova, "Problemy konversii oboronnoi promyshlennosti rossiiskogo Dal'nego Vostoka" (Defense Conversion Issues in the Russian Far East), in *Perspektivy Dal'negovostochnogo regiona: nacelenie, migratsiia, rynka truda* (Perspectives of the Russian Far East: population, migration, labor market), Carnegie Moscow Center, Working Papers, issue 2, 1999; Sonia Ben Ouagrham, *La conversion des entreprises de défense en Russie: une analyse régionale* (Ph.D. diss., 1999, Faculté Économie du Développement, École des Hautes Études en Sciences Sociales, Paris); statistical reports from the various krais and oblasts of the Russian Far East; and interview materials.

8. Interfax and ITAR-TASS, March 3, 1994, cited in Bush, "Aspects of Military Conversion in Russia," 32.

9. Simon Saradzhyan, "Arms Industry to Get $960M Boon," *Moscow Times*, January 28, 2000.

10. David Hoffman, "Putin Faces Split Over Future of Russian Military," *Washington Post*, November 30, 2000.

11. Dave Montgomery and Jonathan S. Landay, Knight-Ridder, "Russia Revving Up Foreign Arms Sales: Deals Could Revive Industry, Influence," *Charlotte Observer*, March 6, 2001, CDI Russia Weekly 144, March 9, 2001.

12. This section is largely based on Sonia Ben Ouagrham's excellent analysis in *La conversion des entreprises de défense en Russie*.

13. There were nine branch ministries subject to the Military Industrial Commission (Voenno-Promyshlennaia Komissiia) and the State Planning Committee (Gosplan). They were: Aviation, Communications, Defense Industry, Electronics, General Machine-Building,

Machine-Building, Medium-Machine Building, Radio, and Shipbuilding.

14. O'Prey, *A Farewell to Arms?*, 18.

15. This section is largely based on Ben Ouagrham, *La conversion des entreprises de défense en Russie.*

16. "Zvezda workers to Strike 1 July," Radio Russia Network, June 30, 1997, in FBIS-SOV-97-181, June 30, 1997.

17. This example provided in Ben Ouagrham, *La conversion des entreprises de défense en Russie.*

18. Ibid.

19. Pavel Felgengauer, "Russkoe Oruzhie dlia Kitaia i natsional'naia bezopasnost' Rossii," in *Rossiia v mirovoi torgovle oruzhiem: Strategiia, politika, ekonomika,* Andrew J. Pierre and D. V. Trenin, eds. (Moskva: Moskovskii tsentr Karnegi, 1996).

20. Unless otherwise indicated, the discussion of Su-27 sales and security implications is based on Stephen J. Blank, "The Dynamics of Russian Arms Sales to China," Monograph of the Strategic Studies Institute, The U.S. Army War College, March 4, 1997; and David D. Fisher, "China's Purchase of Russian Fighters: A Challenge to the U.S.," *Asian Studies Backgrounder,* no. 142, The Heritage Foundation, July 31, 1996.

21. Andrei Vasenyov (U.S. Department of Commerce BISNIS Representative, Khabarovsk), *Komsomolsk-na-Amure Regional Overview* (Washington, D.C., U.S. Department of Commerce, March 2000).

22. "Russia, China discuss military cooperation in the Far East," ITAR-TASS, June 15, 1999, in FBIS-CHI-1999-0615, June 15, 1999.

23. These figures represent total Russian Federation sales of Su-27s to China, not only those from the Gagarin plant.

24. The $2.5 billion figure is given by Michael Nikoulichev, *Russian Aviation Industry,* U.S. Embassy, Moscow, January 1998.

25. "China set to buy SU-30 fighters from Russia," Radio Russia Network, June 15, 1999, in FBIS-SOV-0615, June 15, 1999; and ITAR-TASS, "Russia, China Discuss Military Cooperation in the Far East."

26. "Slovakia Hunting for Primorskii Krai Helicopters," *Vladivostok News,* no. 141 (May 1997).

27. "Progress Aviation Is Doing Better," *Vladivostok,* no. 38, February 27, 1998, 5. Moskit complexes are designed to destroy surface ships. They consist of a ship control system, a launcher, and a low-flying supersonic missile. The missiles have their own targeting and control mechanisms. Maximum range is 120 km, minimum 10 km, and the flight level below 20 meters. Interestingly, in March 1997 Progress had attempted to sell a Moskit complex but was informed that Moskit exports from the Russian Federation were prohibited. See "Nazdratenko Finds a New International Scandal," *Vladivostok,* no. 15, March 20, 1997, 10.

28. Interfax, May 15, 2000, FBIS-SOV-2000-0515, May 15, 2000.

29. Quoted in ITAR-TASS, "Russia, China Discuss Military Cooperation in the Far East."

30. Stephen J. Blank, "The Dynamics of Russian Arms Sales to China," March 4, 1997.

31. TASS, "Vice-premier Gaidar Ends Tour of the Russian Far East," October 2, 1993.

32. Stephen J. Blank, "The Dynamics of Russian Arms Sales to China," March 4, 1997.

33. See "Export Industries in Khabarovsk Krai," *Tikhookeanskaia Zvezda*, December 7, 1995, 1; and "Primorskii Krai Defense Industry Seeks Ways to Survive," ITAR-TASS, November 17, 1998, in FBIS-SOV-98-321, November 17, 1998.

34. "Primorskii Krai Defense Profits Implode," *Vladivostok News*, no. 151, October 2, 1997.

35. "Komsomolsk-na-Amure Shipbuilders Go on Strike," ITAR-TASS, July 24, 1998, in FBIS-SOV-98-205, July 24, 1998.

36. "Defense Industry Protests," *OMRI Daily Digest* 1, no. 45 (March 1997).

37. "Protest of Zvezda Submarine Repair Plant Staff for Back Wages," ITAR-TASS, April 23, 1997, in FBIS-SOV-113, April 23, 1997.

38. "More on Russia Far East Protests," ITAR-TASS, October 30, 1997, in FBIS-SOV-303, October 30, 1997.

39. "Unrest Continues at Plants in Russian Far East," Radio Russia Network, November 6, 1997, in FBIS-SOV-310, November 6, 1997.

40. "Russia Signs Contract to Refit 10 Chinese Submarines," Interfax, March 1, 1999, in FBIS-SOV-0301, March 1, 1999.

41. "Staff of Far East Aircraft Manufacturer Holds 1-day Strike," Interfax, July 28, 1997, in FBIS-SOV-97-209, July 28, 1997.

42. "Komsomolsk-na-Amure Shipbuilders Go on Strike," ITAR-TASS, July 24, 1998, in FBIS-SOV-205, July 24, 1998.

43. "Defense Industry Protests," *OMRI Daily Digest* 1, no. 45 (March 1997).

44. "Large Amounts of Ammunition Found in Vladivostok," Interfax, May 12, 1999, in FBIS-SOV-0512, May 12, 1999.

45. See Tsuneo Akaha, "Environmental Challenge in the Russian Far East," in *Politics and Economics in the Russian Far East: Changing Ties with Northeast Asia,* Tsuneo Akaha, ed., (London and New York: Routledge, 1996), 120–34.

46. The discussion of Pasko's findings is based on an article in *Literaturnaia gazeta,* no. 44 (November 4, 1998), 1, 5.

47. Anna Badkhen, "State Environmental Body Goes Way of Dodo," *St. Petersburg Times,* May 23, 2000.

48. Unless otherwise noted, the discussion of U.S. policy and its relation to Russian defense conversion is based on Costigan and Martel, "Our Failure to Convert Russia's Arms Industry," 475–78.

49. Tony Capaccio, "Pentagon's Soviet Investment Program Poorly Managed, Audit Says," *Defense Week,* August 21, 2000, in *Johnson's Russia List,* no. 4468, August 22, 2000.

50. "U.S. to Pay for Dismantling of Russian Submarines," Interfax, May 21, 1998, in FBIS-SOV-98-141, May 21, 1998.

INTERNATIONAL RELATIONS:
PERSPECTIVES FROM THE REGION

12

The Regional Dynamic in
Russia's Asia Policy in the 1990s

Elizabeth Wishnick

Russia's foreign policy concept, adopted in July 2000, calls attention to Asia's growing importance for Russian diplomacy.[1] President Vladimir Putin lost no time in putting those words into action with a series of high-profile summits—since the summer of 2000 the Russian president has met with leaders in China, Japan, and North and South Korea—and demonstrated that his government planned to put Russia on the Asian map.

These high-level meetings also gave Putin an opportunity to select the policies he planned to continue and to outline where he hoped to forge a new direction. Putin's task was to address his predecessor's mixed record in foreign policy toward Asia. Although President Boris Yeltsin fashioned the strategic partnership with China and improved the atmosphere of relations with Japan, he also downgraded the importance of North Korea, thereby reducing Russian influence on the Korean Peninsula, and promised more than might be realistically achieved in terms of a peace treaty with Japan. In his Asian debut, Putin clearly decided to maintain the partnership with China and restore relations with North Korea, while approaching Japan with greater caution.

The new Russian foreign policy concept also makes it clear that the "dynamic" economic development of the Russian Far East is a precondition for a more prominent role for Russia in Asia.[2] Artificially isolated due to the Sino-Soviet conflict and the Cold War, since the 1990s the federation subjects of the Russian Far East increasingly have viewed their Asian neighbors as essential partners in investment and trade. The development of regional economic relations in the past decade generally has had a positive impact on Russia's bilateral relations with Asian states, although since 1994 the difficult development of Sino-Russian regional relations has been in sharp contrast to the deepening strategic partnership between Moscow and Beijing.

This chapter explores the rationale for the development of regional relations between three regions of the Russian Far East—Khabarovskii krai, Primorskii krai, and Sakhalin oblast—and China, the United States, the Koreas, and Japan. Attention will focus on cooperation between these regions and their Asian neighbors in trade, transportation, and natural resources.

SINO-RUSSIAN REGIONAL RELATIONS

Russian Views of Regional Relations with China

Since 1992 China has been the centerpiece of Russia's foreign policy toward Asia. Disillusionment with the consequences of what many policymakers perceived to be Moscow's excessive subordination to the West during the first few months of the new Russian state's existence provided the initial impetus for giving China pride of place in Boris Yeltsin's Asia policy. Russian and Chinese leaders quickly found common cause in their opposition to U.S. domination of the evolving post–Cold War order and in their efforts to shape a more inclusive multipolar international system.

The Yeltsin leadership's emphasis on improving relations with China led to proclamations of deepening partnership—the two countries established a "constructive partnership" in 1994 and a "strategic partnership" in 1996. Partnership has involved regular exchanges of high-level visits, agreement on many key international issues, and far-reaching defense cooperation. Russia and China have succeeded in demarcating most of their lengthy common border and have included their Central Asian neighbors in confidence-building measures.

The new Russian president's July 2000 visit to Beijing demonstrated that the Sino-Russian partnership would continue to be an important part of the geopolitical landscape in the twenty-first century. One of the key results of the summit was the signing of a joint declaration condemning the U.S. plan to create a national missile defense (NMD) system, which the Russian and Chinese presidents argue would undermine their own security by enabling the United States to achieve unilateral military superiority.[3] In addition to restating their well-known positions on mutual respect for territorial integrity and opposition to separatist activities, Putin and Jiang Zemin also agreed to prepare a new friendship treaty, to continue to cooperate with their Central Asian neighbors, and to expand confidence-building measures in their border regions.[4]

However, unlike the Yeltsin leadership, Putin appears to view relations with China with far less idealism and is attempting to take a more hard-nosed approach to developing a truly equal partnership.[5] Indeed, there is a sense in Russian foreign policy circles that China benefited more than Russia from the partnership of the 1990s. In coming years, we can expect to see Russian policymakers make more explicit efforts to link their country's interest in gaining lucrative Chinese contracts for aircraft and energy equipment with issues of greater concern to China, such as NMD, and perhaps even with sales of military equipment to China.

In contrast to the greater harmonization of Russian and Chinese political goals in the 1990s, their economic relationship remains relatively weak. The 1996 pledge by Yeltsin and Jiang to boost Sino-Russian trade to $20 billion by 2000 has proved impossible to fulfill—in 2001 trade reached $8 billion—the largest volume since 1993, when trade peaked at $7.68 billion. Generally bilateral trade has fluctuated between $5 and $6 billion per year since 1994. Changing conditions in both countries have complicated economic cooperation, but problems in Sino-Russian regional economic relations have proved most difficult to overcome.

At first, regional economic relations seemed to be the most dynamic component of Sino-Russian relations. The volume of border trade increased steadily in the early 1990s—by 1993 trade between the border regions accounted for two-thirds of the overall Sino-Russian trade balance. The rapid expansion of regional economic relations turned out to be a temporary phenomenon, however, stimulated by short-term factors in the Russian economy. In 1991–92, the Russian Far East suddenly was cut off from traditional suppliers of food products and consumer goods in European Russia due to interrupted economic links and high transportation costs.[6] Disillusioned by inadequate federal support, the Russian Far East began viewing economic integration in the Pacific Rim as a solution to regional underdevelopment. Initially, regional leaders focused their efforts on expanding trade and joint ventures with China. Much of the trade with China during this period was barter trade, carried out by shuttle-traders from China's northeastern provinces.

The boom in border trade proved to be short-lived, however. Although Russian and Chinese policymakers emphasized the complementary nature of their economies—Russia has the natural resources and machinery that China lacks while China produces the consumer goods and food products that are in short supply in the Russian Far East—the Sino-Russian trade balance fell by 34 percent in 1994, reflecting a sharp downturn in border trade. This could be seen clearly in regions of the Russian Far East such as Amurskaia oblast, dependent on border trade for 92 percent of its foreign trade: the territory's overall trade volume plummeted from $407.6 million in 1993 to $189.5 in 1994.

Sino-Russian border trade suffered a sharp decline for a variety of interrelated reasons, including complaints about inadequate control in both countries, the imposition of new rules regulating border trade, decreased demand in China for traditional Russian exports such as construction materials, and the growing demand in Russia for higher quality consumer goods.[7] Russian customers increasingly complained about the poor quality of the Chinese goods reaching the Russian Far East and began seeking better quality, higher-priced goods from South Korea, the United States, and Japan.

Although residents of the Russian Far East depended on border trade with China for necessary goods, they soon began to fear the geo-economic consequences of an influx of Chinese migrants to once-closed provinces.[8] In their view, excessive reliance on Chinese products could lead to excessive dependence on China and possibly invite Chinese economic control over Russia's weakened peripheries. One solution was to expand the number of regional economic partners: by the mid-1990s, food products and consumer goods from other Pacific Rim countries, especially South Korea, Japan, and the United States, began competing for a share of the consumer market in the Russian Far East.

The rapid expansion of border trade with China in 1992–93 was a major adjustment for the Russian and Chinese border regions, largely closed off for security reasons for almost three decades. For example, in 1988 only 6,233 border crossings were reported in Amurskaia oblast, a land-locked region bordering on China, but in 1992 there were 287,215 crossings, and the region's imports and exports were oriented almost entirely to the Chinese market.[9] In 1992–93, traders were allowed to travel across the Sino-Russian border without visas. Initially, the regions welcomed the rapid opening of border trade to address their economic needs, but transportation, housing facilities, and administrative mechanisms needed to support it were woefully deficient. Poor regulation on both sides enabled criminals and unscrupulous businesspeople to take advantage of the sudden opening of the border. The new markets catering to the shuttle trade soon became associated with criminal activity.

Moreover, by 1994 Russia's regional leaders began to view China as the main potential challenge to the regional balance of power. Although they recognized the positive aspects of expanding regional economic relations, they argued that the largely unregulated opening of the border with China—with its large population, high unemployment, and historical claims to Russian territory—could have serious consequences for the Russian border provinces.

By 1994 it also had became apparent that the Russian Far East would not be an easy fit in the "open regionalism" involving the multidirectional flow of capital, goods, and labor which characterizes economic relations in the Pacific Rim. At the

same time that the Russian border regions were opening up to economic cooperation with Asian neighbors, Russians were moving out of these economically declining areas—from 1992–96, the population of the Russian Far East decreased by
7 percent.[10] Russians who remained faced underemployment in depressed defense
and resource industries and resented the introduction of cheap foreign labor, even
if the Chinese and North Koreans worked in areas such as agriculture where there
was a shortage of qualified workers.[11] Newly impoverished Russian residents, once
living comfortable lives on their state salaries, grumbled about having to buy cheap
goods from Chinese traders, whom they perceived as taking advantage of their
plight. By mid-1993, the local press in the Russian Far East was full of articles
condemning China's "quiet expansion" and calling for countermeasures for fear
that the continued influx of Chinese workers and traders would become tantamount
to a reassertion of de facto Chinese control over areas that China lost to the Russian
Empire in the late nineteenth century.

Concern about Asian migrants proved disproportionate to their numbers, however.[12] According to reliable data from the Institute of Economic Research in
Khabarovsk, even in the peak period of Sino-Russian border trade, 50,000–80,000
Chinese worked in the Russian Far East, including 10,000–15,000 contract workers
and 10,000–12,000 students on long-term exchanges. Police data revealed that
5,000–6,000 Chinese were in Primorskii krai and Khabarovskii krai illegally.[13] Measures to restrict the migration of Chinese and Koreans to the Russian Far East were
an early indication of the limits to the region's openness to economic cooperation
with its Asian neighbors.

Just as Moscow focused on improving relations with China, regional leaders in
the Russian Far East began advocating the need for new regulations to control
Sino-Russian regional relations. Due to mounting complaints from the Russian
border regions about unregulated shuttle trade, on January 1, 1994, Russia and
China decided to end the brief period of visa-free trade and once again require
business visas for traders. New restrictions also were imposed on the use of foreign contract labor in Russia for construction and agriculture.

In addition to the new federal rules, regional authorities in Russia began taking
steps of their own to prevent illegal Chinese immigration. Concerned that shuttle
traders would be able to circumvent new visa rules by joining fictitious tour groups
that were not subject to the new visa requirements, Primorskii krai authorities
passed an edict in April 1994 limiting the number of hotels allowed to house
foreign tourists and placing greater controls on tour groups from China. Under the
new rules, travel agencies would be responsible for ensuring that Chinese tourists
traveled only to the destinations specified and stayed only for the time allotted by
their visas.[14]

Public concern about massive numbers of Chinese living in Russia illegally prompted regional authorities in Primorskii and Khabarovskii krais to engage in police sweeps—called "Operation Foreigner"—of markets and tour companies. Conducted periodically since 1994, these campaigns have not produced evidence of large-scale violations of Russian visa rules. According to data from the Primorskii krai migration service, 2,870 Chinese were asked to leave the region in 1997 for violating visa rules. In the same year, 124 Chinese were found guilty of similar visa violations in Khabarovskii krai.[15] If caught, illegal immigrants were deported. Although regional authorities claimed that police sweeps were not directed against Chinese citizens, the majority of those apprehended have been from China.

Anyone who visits the markets outside of Khabarovsk or Vladivostok can see that these visa violation figures understate the number of Chinese residing in these cities. Since legitimate Chinese businesspeople complain of difficulties in obtaining visas, frequent document checks, and police harassment, it is likely that the Chinese traders at the market, who work there for several years at a time, find means of acquiring the necessary legal documentation to live and work in Russia. Although regional officials blame the Chinese government for encouraging illegal migration to Russia, corruption in Russia makes it possible for Chinese economic migrants to remain there.

Policymakers in Moscow have promised to make the Russian Far East open to trade and cooperation with the Pacific Rim. Yet the reality has turned out to be more complex, and the regions have had to find their way to Asian markets largely on their own. This has meant capitalizing on regional strengths—sales of oil, gas, minerals, timber, and fish—to pay for items in short supply, especially consumer goods and food products from China. Although the complementary features of the economies of the Russian Far East and Chinese Northeast make sense to economists and policymakers, in the Russian border regions the exchanges of resources for goods reinforces the reality of China's rise and Russia's decline and creates an undercurrent of nationalism, often phrased in anti-Chinese terms.

Regional political leaders, like former Governor Yevgenii Nazdratenko of Primorskii krai, have proven adept in manipulating anti-Chinese sentiment in the media to win points in their struggles with Moscow over subsidies.[16] They also have focused attention on the problems associated with border trade to strengthen local opposition to any demarcation of the eastern section of the Sino-Russian border that would require the return of territory to China. Concern about the socioeconomic consequences of a continuing influx of Asian migrants to the Russian Far East has persisted. In July 1999, Governor Viktor Ishaev of Khabarovskii krai warned then-Prime Minister Sergei Stepashin of a "peaceful invasion" by Chinese and Koreans to the Russian Far East.[17]

Efforts to restrict the presence of Asians in the Russian Far East have had a detrimental impact on the regional economy.[18] Many of the territories of the Far East face a growing labor shortage in certain sectors, particularly agriculture and construction, but hiring foreign workers from neighboring Asian countries remains controversial due to concerns that they will seek to remain in Russia beyond the terms of their employment. However, underdevelopment of local agriculture leads to a dependence on higher priced imported food products and limits opportunities to create new food processing industries, which could be a source of employment for those Russians laid off in other sectors.

Sensitivity in Russia to the social consequences of use of Chinese labor has restrained the growth of Sino-Russian regional economic cooperation, much to the distress of policymakers in Moscow and Beijing. Given the shortage of investment capital in both the Russian Far East and Northeast China, the employment of Chinese workers in Russian resource industries seemed at first to provide the best chance for mutually beneficial economic cooperation. However, many regional leaders in Russia resent becoming "Third World resource suppliers" for China and fear that substantial reliance on Chinese labor would adversely affect the demographic balance in the region.

Indeed, concern about the unfavorable regional demographic and economic balance between China and Russia has prompted leaders in Primorskii and Khabarovskii krais to broaden cooperation with other countries, especially the United States, Japan, and South Korea. At a time when leaders in Moscow and Beijing have found common cause in world affairs, in the Russian Far East regional leaders are seeking to counterbalance economic and demographic pressures from a rising China with improved relations with the United States and others in the Pacific Rim.

The Putin government has tried to address some of the concerns in the Russian Far East about Chinese intentions. The newly appointed presidential envoy for the Russian Far East, Konstantin Pulikovskii, accompanied the Russian president on his visit to Beijing. As soon as the summit meetings concluded, Pulikovskii was dispatched to Khabarovsk to reassure the krai administration that the Russian and Chinese governments agreed to maintain the status quo of the three remaining disputed islands, including the two located in the Amur River right across from the city of Khabarovsk.[19]

To find new prospects for regional cooperation, the Russian and Chinese governments have shifted their focus westward. Russia agreed to explore the possibility of participating in energy projects in China's western regions. The governors of Altaiskii krai and Chita oblast, more enthusiastic about cooperation with China than the Far Eastern regions, accompanied Putin during his visit to Beijing. Putin also adroitly neutralized the most outspoken critic of Russia's China policy—

Nazdratenko was invited to the banquet in Beijing, but not the working sessions.

Putin's level of commitment to the development of the Russian Far East remains the real test of his government's intention to improve regional economic relations with China. It remains unclear what new measures, apart from greater scrutiny of local leadership, the Russian president will adopt to stem the root causes of unease about China in the Russian Far East—economic decline and outmigration.[20]

Chinese Views of Regional Relations with Russia

Like their Russian neighbors, the Chinese border regions seized on new opportunities to expand economic relations with Russia to remedy their own economic difficulties. Heilongjiang and Jilin Provinces in China's economically depressed Northeast initially saw border trade with Russia as a means of spurring development. Policymakers in Beijing predicted that regional economic relations would flourish due to the complementary features of the economies of the Russian Far East and Northeast China.

From 1991 to 1993, enthusiasm for "opening to the north" outpaced measures to regulate border trade. Many inexperienced firms participated in the mad rush to the border, leading to the aforementioned complaints in the Russian Far East about shoddy goods and unscrupulous Chinese traders. Chinese traders also accumulated their own list of complaints about the difficulties of doing business in Russia due to the unstable economic environment and pervasive corruption.

Chinese officials in Beijing have been supportive of measures to regulate border trade. They have protested vigorously against Russian allegations that Beijing promotes illegal immigration. Indeed, criticism of provincial authorities in Heilongjiang for inadequate administration of border trade was a factor in leadership reshuffling in the province in 1996 and led to such sharp restrictions on the issuance of passports for foreign travel that businesspeople complained of difficulty in going about their work.[21] Moreover, Chinese authorities have faced similar problems of criminal activity by Russians living in China and implemented a well-publicized campaign against illegal border crossings.[22] At the same time, Chinese leaders have expressed concern that efforts to prevent illegal immigration could harm the rights of law-abiding Chinese citizens who are legitimate businesspeople or tourists in Russia.[23]

The overall weakness of Sino-Russian economic relations and the difficulties in regional relations have fueled debate in China about the long-term prospects of the Sino-Russian partnership. Some see economic relations as fundamental and stress the potential for instability when political and economic ties develop at an uneven pace. Others argue that even if economic relations grow more slowly than political ties, the strategic partnership has its own rationale and will not be affected adversely.

Indeed, the strategic partnership with Russia appears to have had little impact on Chinese economic decisions. Russia's bid to provide turbines for the Three Gorges Dam was rejected as noncompetitive, and China opted to purchase Boeing and Airbus aircraft over Tupolevs. Since Chinese officials use market criteria to make decisions about major deals, it is unclear how successful any efforts by the Putin government to link the military, political, and economic aspects of relations will be. Chinese analysts generally attribute the weakness of economic relations with Russia to the instability in the Russian economy and argue that improvement in Sino-Russian relations will have to wait for overall improvement of Russian economic conditions.[24]

China also faces stiff challenges in expanding its presence in the Russian market. In an effort to boost the prestige of its products among Russian consumers, two new Chinese department stores opened in Moscow in the fall of 1999. Yet these swanky new retail outlets may do little to change the minds of increasingly brand-conscious Russian consumers. Even in the Russian Far East, Chinese goods remain a tough sell. As the regional trade data in Table 12.1 shows, Primorskii krai prefers to buy from South Korea. Following the August 1998 financial crisis, Chinese exports to Khabarovskii krai have rebounded, and Chinese purchases of Sukhoi aircraft, produced in the krai, are reflected in export figures for 2000.

Apart from Chinese purchases of Russian weapons, energy is the most promising area for Sino-Russian economic cooperation and regional economic ties. China is interested in purchasing oil and natural gas from the Sakhalin projects and is a participant in a feasibility study for the development of the Kovyktinsk fields near Irkutsk. Nevertheless, China and Russia remain at odds over the route of the proposed pipeline from the Kovyktinsk field. The Russian side has proposed constructing the pipeline from Irkutsk via Mongolia to Beijing, the shortest route from East Siberia to China. The Chinese, however, want the gas pipeline to go directly from Russia to Daqing in Heilongjiang Province and then to Dalian in Liaoning Province.[25] The Asian financial crisis has made it even more difficult to proceed with energy cooperation due to the depressed demand for energy in Asia. The crisis also has made Asian states more reluctant to commit investment funds to costly new energy projects. As a result, there has been much more discussion than concrete progress in Sino-Russian energy cooperation.

RUSSIAN-AMERICAN REGIONAL RELATIONS

Russian Views of Regional Relations with the United States

During the first year of the new Russian state, President Yeltsin spoke of the United States as a potential ally, but initial hopes for the Russian-American

Table 12.1 Trade of Sakhalinskaia Oblast, Primorskii Krai, and Khabarovskii Krai with Major Asia Pacific Partners, 1992–98 (million U.S. dollars)

	1992	1993	1994	1995	1996	1997	1998	1999	2000
			Khabarovskii krai imports						
PRC	33.7	230.0	48.5	46.6	49.6	67.2	52.8	34.0	30.0
United States	12.3	13.1	37.4	37.4	43.7	27.6	18.4	11.5	19.3
South Korea	5.3	28.1	52.3	44.4	31.2	32.1	24.1	10.9	14.0
Japan	48.9	43.2	36.7	37.4	26.2	37.8	17.8	42.0	35.8
			Khabarovskii krai exports						
PRC	81.4	161.4	66.7	64.4	501.0	82.5	637.0	134.0	524.0
United States	32.3	0.6	8.3	24.8	42.0	57.7	17.4	14.0	21.0
South Korea	19.5	20.2	31.2	50.9	50.0	65.3	100.4	55.0	61.0
Japan	182.5	277.4	246.0	301.0	248.4	281.1	178.5	213.0	210.0
			Khabarovskii krai's trade turnover						
PRC	33.7	230.0	48.5	46.6	49.6	67.2	52.8	167.8	554.3
United States	12.3	13.1	37.4	37.4	43.7	27.6	18.4	25.6	40.3
South Korea	5.3	28.1	52.3	44.4	31.2	32.1	24.1	65.6	74.6
Japan	48.9	43.2	36.7	37.4	26.2	26.2	17.8	255.1	245.8
			Primorskii krai imports						
PRC	320.0	115.2	85.0	67.0	91.6	129.0	91.0	83.0	92.0
United States	–	2.6	95.0	114.8	128.1	148.6	79.0	41.0	26.0
South Korea	114.6	13.0	95.0	107.2	143.4	187.0	113.0	100.0	127.0
Japan	98.3	66.2	76.0	57.1	71.6	91.9	61.0	38.0	32.0
			Primorskii krai exports						
PRC	106.8	187.0	101.0	88.4	111.0	185.0	159.0	160.0	284.0
United States	–	6.0	11.0	5.2	6.6	211.2	252.0	302.0	269.0
South Korea	21.7	34.2	49.0	62.1	163.4	179.3	105.0	134.0	151.0
Japan	110.3	122.3	189.0	206.4	228.0	318.7	264.0	161.0	194.0
			Primorskii krai's trade turnover						
PRC	426.8	302.2	186.0	155.5	202.6	314.0	250.0	243.0	376.0
United States	–	8.6	106.0	120.0	134.7	359.8	331.0	343.0	295.0
South Korea	136.3	47.2	144.0	169.3	306.8	366.3	218.0	234.0	278.0
Japan	208.6	188.5	265.0	263.5	299.6	410.6	325.0	199.0	226.0

Source: A. B. Ignatiev, et al., *Investitsionnyi Atlas*, tom 1 (Khabarovsk: Far Eastern Office for the Preparation and Examination of Investment Projects, 1999), 68–71. Data compiled by the Association for the Russian Far East and Trans-Baikal, the Far Eastern Office for the Initiation and Examination of Investment Projects, and the Department of Foreign Economic Relations of the Administration of Khabarovskii krai.

partnership were not fulfilled. Russian policymakers were disappointed by the level of U.S. economic assistance and accused American officials of disregarding Russian economic and foreign policy interests. Differences over foreign policy became more obvious throughout the decade and reached a peak over NATO expansion and the crises in Bosnia and Kosovo. Russian policymakers drew closer to their Chinese counterparts as they found broad agreement in their opposition to what they perceived as U.S. unilateralism in international relations and Washington's tendency to interfere in the domestic affairs of other states. In his last summit meeting in Beijing in December 1999, Yeltsin lashed out at the United States for pressuring Russia over Chechnya. He and Jiang blamed "the negative momentum in international relations" on U.S. policies.[26] The deepening Sino-Russian partnership has provided a sharp contrast to the tensions in Russian-American and Sino-American relations.

However, unlike Sino-Russian relations, which thrive at the bilateral level and lag in the Russian Far East, Russian-American regional economic ties grew steadily until 1998. Of all the regions in the Russian Far East, the United States trades most with Primorskii krai (see Table 12.1). The krai exports minerals and fish products to the United States and imports consumer goods and food products. The devaluation of the ruble after August 1998 reduced the region's buying power. Imports from the United States fell precipitously in 1998 and have yet to recover: at their peak U.S imports to Primorskii krai reached $148.6 million in 1997, but were only $26 million in 2000.

Sakhalin's offshore oil and gas projects have attracted the largest American investments in the Russian Far East—the oblast is second only to Moscow as a destination for U.S. capital and foreign investment in general. Thus far, these energy projects have drawn in more than $1.7 billion in investment, more than 10 percent of accumulated foreign direct investment in Russia. The United States has contributed more than 80 percent of the total invested and potentially could inject more than $40 billion in Sakhalin's offshore oil and gas over the next several decades.[27]

The relative balance of power between the governor of Sakhalin, the oblast Duma, and the Yuzhno-Sakhalinsk city government leads U.S. diplomats and businesspeople based in the Russian Far East to view Sakhalin as somewhat more open to economic relations with foreign countries. Unlike neighboring Primorye and Khabarovsk, ruled by iron-fisted governors, greater give-and-take in the Sakhalin political process has decreased the propensity for excessive politicization of problems with foreign investment and encouraged a problem-solving mentality. Moreover, the September 1998 Law on Foreign Investment, passed by the oblast Duma, has shown flexibility by linking the time frame for special incentives granted to foreign investors with the length of the expected payback period for their investment.

Indeed, many Sakhalin-based businesses give credit to the Sakhalin government for doing as much as possible to promote foreign investment given the constraints established by Moscow.

This is not to say that there have not been difficulties with foreign investment on Sakhalin, including: (1) federal legislation regarding environmental standards, customs duties, and VAT; (2) conflict with oblast laws; and (3) the terms of the production-sharing agreements (PSAs). The Russian Duma has yet to pass a substantial number of laws necessary to implement the PSAs. Although most of the difficulties facing the Sakhalin oil and gas projects stem from these legislative issues, oblast officials also have been suspicious of foreign investors. The speaker of the oblast Duma called for the books of foreign oil companies to be audited, and the governor required his administration's oversight department, along with the Federal Security Bureau, to approve all contracts with foreign firms.[28] Joint ventures in Sakhalin face the same dizzying array of taxes and changeable rules of the game.[29] Local content rules have led to some bad feeling, when projects have selected foreign suppliers over Russian firms. The 70-percent local content goal established for Sakhalin-2 has not been achieved, but more than half of the suppliers for the project are Russian companies. Most Sakhalin officials view Russian participation in the projects positively and hope that in time local businesses will become more competitive when they bid for lucrative contracts.

Foreign companies that have made a commitment to Sakhalin believe that over time the potential benefits of economic cooperation will reduce local concerns about the consequences of foreign involvement and that in the long run their operations will be profitable. According to one subcontractor for Sakhalin-1, public opinion in Nogilki, the base for the project, became more supportive when the consortium, out of concern for public health, assumed the cost of replacing pipes made with asbestos. Although the local population initially was wary of foreign control and concerned about the environmental impact of the project, workers involved in the venture soon benefited by receiving well-constructed homes and lucrative jobs.

The U.S. companies also have invested in Khabarovskii and Primorskii krais, albeit with more mixed results. The Pioneer Corporation formed a joint venture with Delplast in 1994 to explore a gold deposit in the north of Khabarovskii krai. Pioneer invested $27 million in the project, which is expected to produce 2 tons of gold per year. Production has not yet begun due to delays caused by obtaining proper licensing and changes in the gold market. In 1997, the Quaker Corporation invested $2.2 million to develop coal from a deposit near Komsomolsk-na-Amure. This project is producing only one-fifth of expected output due to nonpayment by local governments and incompatibility between the type of coal produced and the specifications of local power plants.[30] In the forestry sector, foreign investors are concerned by the Khabarovskii krai administration's decision in 1999 to increase control by creating a new regulatory agency, Khabarovsk-Glavles, and current American investors (Pioneer Corporation in Forest Starma and Global Forestry Group) have been losing money.[31]

The United States was the third largest investor in Primorskii krai in 1998, accounting for 14.6 percent of all investment capital. The largest U.S. investment in the krai is a Coca-Cola bottling factory in Vladivostok. A total of $100 million has been invested in the plant. U.S. companies have made smaller investments in telecommunications, shipping, and fishing.

Nonetheless, U.S. investment in Primorskii krai has been controversial due to concern about the implications of foreign control, especially control by Western business interests. In June 1999, for example, former Governor Nazdratenko asked the Federal Security Bureau to investigate the business dealings of Andrew Fox, a British investor and the British honorary consul, who was serving on the board of the Far Eastern Shipping Company. Fox alleged that Nazdratenko threatened to put him in jail unless he turned over 7 percent of the shares owned by foreigners. Fox, whose firm, Tiger Securities, had invested $30–40 million in Primorskii krai, fled to the United Kingdom.[32] The case sparked a regional media campaign assailing foreign efforts to take over shipping companies. While the former governor earned political capital from the campaign in the months leading up to the elections in December 1999, his administration quietly reassured U.S. consular officials of the region's continued interest in attracting American investment.

U.S. Views of Regional Relations with Russia

Despite the difficulties involved in expanding economic relations with Russia, the U.S. West Coast has played an active role in expanding ties with the Russian Far East. American officials often comment that the two regions are natural partners, linked together by geography, history, culture, and economic interest. In the immediate years after the collapse of the Soviet Union, cultural and environmental exchanges helped forge new links between the West Coast and the Russian Far East. The regions share many common environmental concerns, such as depletion of fish stocks and sustainable forestry. U.S. nongovernmental organizations (NGOs), such as the Pacific Energy and Resources Center and the Initiative for Social Action and Renewal in Eurasia (ISAR), have played a key part in forging links with NGOs in the Russian Far East to protect the environment and promote women's rights. The Foundation for Russian American Economic Cooperation has developed many initiatives to facilitate commercial relations, most notably, CLEAR-PAC, a system of automated customs clearance. U.S. universities, especially the American

Russian Center at the University of Alaska, have taken the lead in providing training in business and other disciplines in many areas of the Russian Far East.

Beginning in the mid-1990s, West Coast businesses became interested in developing Russian resources, and their counterparts in the Russian Far East sought to import U.S. consumer products and machinery. Economic relations between the two regions have long roots—entrepreneurs from Alaska and California have been traveling to the Russian Far East to engage in trade and other business ventures since the mid-nineteenth century.

Alaska was the first state to play an active role in developing economic relations with the Russian Far East. Cooperation began with technical assistance, cultural exchanges, and educational programs. Russian-American centers were set up in the 1990s in several regions to assist small business development. Alaskan businesses have played a significant role in contracts for the Sakhalin oil and gas projects. The State of Washington also has been important in promoting trade and investment, especially in Primorskii krai.

In 1994 cooperation between the West Coast of the United States and the Russian Far East acquired an institutional basis under the framework of the Gore-Chernomyrdin Commission, formally called the U.S.-Russian Joint Commission on Economic and Technological Cooperation. The U.S. West Coast–Russian Far East Ad Hoc Working Group was established to coordinate the participation of five West Coast states in cooperation with the Association for the Russian Far East and Trans-Baikal, created in 1993 to represent all of the regions of the Russian Far East plus Buriatia. Regular meetings between the two organizations have helped promote regional economic ties in a wide range of sectors, including forestry, fishing, energy, and transportation. At the June 2000 annual meeting, for example, the Ad Hoc Working Group moved forward with projects to facilitate financing of oil and gas projects on Sakhalin, develop transit trade from the U.S. West Coast via Primorskii krai to Northeast China, modernize coastal fisheries infrastructure in Primorskii krai, introduce tele-medicine in Khabarovskii krai, and promote sustainable development and tourism in the Russian Far East as a whole.

As officials in Washington, D.C., began encountering difficulties with assistance programs that channeled funds through Moscow, new programs were designed to go directly to the regions. The Russian Regional Initiative, launched by the U.S. Department of State in 1997, targets the Russian Far East as a recipient of funds for a wide range of technical assistance projects, including small business development, energy efficiency programs, educational exchanges, and support for NGOs.

However, despite the Russian Far East's geographic location, U.S. government agencies and the private sector have not yet integrated economic relations in the Russian Far East with their Asian projects. Although there is some discussion of future coordination of regional environmental and fishing issues via the U.S. embassy in Tokyo, at present there is little interaction between U.S. diplomats dealing with Asia and those working on the Russian Far East, who are currently part of the State Department's European Bureau. The committees in the U.S. Congress have a similar structure: Russia is viewed exclusively in terms of Europe, and issues relating to its eastern regions are not integrated in U.S. Asia policy. American businesses tend to view Russia as a separate entity, distinct from both European and Asian operations.

RUSSIAN-KOREAN RELATIONS

Russian Views of Relations with the Koreas
In the early 1990s there were major shifts in Moscow's policy toward the Koreas. First Mikhail Gorbachev and Roh Tae Woo normalized Soviet–South Korean relations in September 1990. Optimistic about the future of economic relations, Seoul extended a $3 billion loan to the Soviet government. In November 1992, Yeltsin abandoned the 1961 treaty with North Korea in which Moscow had pledged to come to Pyongyang's aid in case of conflict. By June 1994, the transformation in Korea policy was complete—Moscow and Seoul announced their "constructive partnership."

The Yeltsin government would soon realize that the downgrading of relations with North Korea had reduced Russia's influence on the Korean Peninsula. Russia was not invited to talks in mid-1994 to resolve a crisis over North Korea's announced withdrawal from the nuclear nonproliferation treaty, and China, which maintained relations with North Korea while expanding ties with the South, became the country with the most leverage in the dispute. Foreign Minister Igor Ivanov's visit to Pyongyang in February 2000 represented an attempt to recoup some of Moscow's influence over Korean affairs. Ivanov explained that Russia wanted "its voice to be heard in the resolution of the most explosive problem in the Asia-Pacific region ... thanks to a balanced policy with respect to the two Koreas."[33] During Putin's first six months in office, Russia managed to achieve just that—during Ivanov's visit to Pyongyang, the two countries signed a new, more restricted friendship treaty, and then in July 2000, Putin paid an unprecedented visit to the North Korean capital. In March 2001, the Russian president traveled to Seoul for a summit meeting with South Korean President Kim Dae Jung. During Putin's visit, the two leaders outlined their future economic cooperation in energy projects and Russia's potential role in the construction of the inter-Korean railway.

As was the case with Russia's relationship with China, it turned out to be far easier to declare a partnership with South Korea than to implement one. Some outstanding bilateral issues—especially Seoul's demand that Moscow pay reparations for the downing of a Korean airliner in 1983—have clouded the new Russian–South Korean relationship. Economic relations proved more complex to develop than expected. Russia encountered difficulties in repaying the South Korean loan, and South Korean companies were unprepared for the problems involved in doing business in the risky Russian economic environment.

Some of the largest South Korean investments in Russia are in the Far East, a remarkable development considering Seoul's initial difficulties in the region. One of the earliest ventures, the Hyundai timber project in Svetlaia in Primorskii krai, encountered fierce local and even international opposition because of its adverse ecological impact and had to be abandoned. South Korea's participation in a technopark in Nakhodka took more than a decade to arrange. Because of wrangling over special economic zone (SEZ) legislation in the Primorye Duma, plans for the technopark languished. The project's development was complicated further by allegations of corruption and political infighting in Primorskii krai between the former governor and one of his main rivals, Sergei Dudnik, the former administrator of the zone and chairman of the krai Duma. Finally, SEZ legislation was passed in December 1998, and in May 1999 the Russian and South Korean governments signed an agreement to move the project forward. The size of the technopark has been scaled down considerably, from 330 to 20 hectares. The Korea Land Development Corporation will lease the site for 49 years to build infrastructure and facilities, which will be rented to Korean firms.

In the Russian Far East, attitudes toward the Koreas have proven complex. On the one hand, as discontent with barter trade with China grew, residents of the Russian Far East looked to South Korea as a source of higher quality consumer goods. Even after the Russian financial crisis in 1998, South Korea has retained its position as the top source of imports for Primorskii krai and Sakhalin (see Table12.1).

Approximately 100,000 Russian traders now travel regularly by ferry between Vladivostok and Pusan. A small Russian community has developed in the Tonggu district of Pusan, now called Russia Town, but most of the Russians come to Pusan on shorter visits to purchase goods to sell back home.[34] The recession in South Korea led some of the thousands of unemployed to resort to shuttle trade, too, but they mostly have focused their efforts on selling lower-priced manufactured goods in the Chinese market.[35]

The 1998 financial crisis in Russia led to a drop of more than 40 percent in South Korea's trade with Russia. Some smaller South Korean firms had to pull out of the Russian market when their partners failed to pay them for goods sent before the crisis. Despite this, the Korea Trade Investment Promotion Agency (KOTRA) continues to maintain an office in Vladivostok, and the Russian Far East remains a strong market for South Korean electronics, food products, and construction supplies.

In the late 1990s, some South Korean clothing manufacturers began purchasing controlling shares in factories in Primorskii krai to take advantage of Russia's unused textile export quotas. For example, a South Korean apparel factory employing 600 was set up in Partizansk to produce clothes for the U.S. market. Although many residents welcomed the new source of employment (where low wages were at least paid on time), some criticism of sweatshop conditions developed.

Residents of Primorskii and Khabarovskii krais increasingly have become concerned about the presence of Koreans on their territory. At first, Khabarovskii krai supported the continuation of a forestry agreement with North Korea, which provided cheap labor for the regional timber industry—against the opposition of policymakers in Moscow who were concerned about allegations of human rights abuses in forestry camps that employed workers in prison-like conditions. When North Korean timber workers were implicated in drug trafficking and their work methods were linked to environmental degradation, regional sentiment turned against the venture, and its scope has been narrowed. Smaller numbers of North Korean contract workers continue to be employed in the construction industry in Primorskii and Khabarovskii krais.

In the early 1990s, residents of these regions became concerned about the return of Korean exiles from Central Asia. As of 1991, some 15,000 Koreans lived in the Russian Far East, and approximately 400,000 remained in Kazakhstan, Uzbekistan, Tajikistan, and other regions of Russia. In early 1993, the Russian parliament recognized the illegal nature of the repression of Russian Koreans in the Stalin era and affirmed their right to national development and equal opportunity in the exercise of their political freedoms. Their rehabilitation gave them the right to return individually to their former places of residence, a decision that evoked an immediately negative reaction in Primorskii krai.

With the passage of the July 1, 1993, law on repressed peoples, Russian Koreans were entitled to some compensation, including discounted transportation and housing.[36] Since then, a few thousand Koreans have moved back to the Russian Far East to work in agriculture, although most Koreans have preferred to remain in Central Asia. Despite concern in Primorye that a growing number of resident Koreans would demand autonomy, there has been no organized effort to achieve this.

To some extent illegal Chinese immigration and Korean migration are overlapping concerns—some of the Chinese shuttle traders accused of illegally setting up residence in the Russian border regions actually are ethnically Korean and come from the Yanbian Autonomous Prefecture in Jilin Province. These Chinese citizens speak Korean and potentially could be integrated more easily into Korean communities in the Russian Far East. Even at the marketplaces in Vladivostok and Khabarovsk, smaller numbers of Chinese Koreans, primarily selling food products, stand apart from their more numerous Han compatriots, who sell consumer goods and mostly come from Heilongjiang province.

South Korean Perspectives on Regional Relations with Russia

South Korea has strategic, political, and economic interests in the Russian Far East. Seoul's investment in the region has been directed to Primorskii krai, the region bordering on North Korea. Hyundai, a major supporter of Kim Dae Jung's "sunshine policy" of reducing tensions with the North, is the largest investor. Although its timber venture failed, the corporation also has invested $90 million in a hotel and business center in Vladivostok. As a means of promoting North Korea's economic integration in Northeast Asia, South Korea has played an active role in regional development efforts in Primorskii krai. Shippers have explored a variety of transit trade projects. In the spring of 2000, three new car ferry routes and one new container route opened, linking South Korea, China, and Primorskii krai. South Korea also has supported efforts to develop infrastructure and tourism in Primorskii krai, Jilin Province in Northeast China, and the Rajin-Sonbong Economic Zone in North Korea as a part of the Tumen River Economic Development Area. The progress in inter-Korean dialogue in the summer of 2000 paved the way for new forms of cooperation involving Russia and the two Koreas. In an effort to connect the Korean Peninsula to the Trans-Siberian railroad, South Korean President Kim Dae Jung has proposed that Russia join the two Koreas in restoring the inter-Korean rail line.[37]

In the early 1990s, South Korean businesses were perhaps overly optimistic about the prospects for Korean-Russian economic cooperation. Crises in South Korea and Russia served to scale back original expectations, and many South Korean firms pulled out of the Russian Far East. However, in the summer of 2000, there were signs of recovery. For the first time since the Asian crisis, an official business delegation from South Korea paid a visit to Khabarovsk to explore new ventures in equipment leasing, mining, and printing.[38]

Over the long term, South Korea's most significant economic interest in the region is likely to be energy. The first shipment of 81,000 tons of oil from the Sakhalin-2 project went to South Korea. Seoul is a prospective market for natural gas from the Sakhalin projects, and once a pipeline connects Sakhalin to the mainland, another could be built from Primorskii krai to South Korea. Although there has been much talk about South Korea's participation in the Kovyktinsk pipeline project, it remains at the feasibility stage. Much will depend on the pace of South Korea's economic recovery and its demand for gas.

South Korea has been concerned by the fate of Korean nationals living in the Russian Far East. A program has been established to repatriate some older Koreans living on Sakhalin who had been forced into labor there by the Japanese during World War II. Seoul also has contributed financially to programs that provide farmland to Korean exiles returning from Central Asia to the Russian Far East.

RUSSIAN-JAPANESE REGIONAL RELATIONS

Russian Views of Regional Relations with Japan

Japan's economic might and clout in the Asia Pacific region reinforced Yeltsin's determination to try to reinvigorate Russian-Japanese relations during his last years in office. By the end of the 1990s, relations had improved in atmosphere but remained stalled over the Kurile Islands/Northern Territories issue. The November 1997 meeting between Yeltsin and Japanese Prime Minister Ryutaro Hashimoto in Krasnoyarsk had such a cordial and informal ambiance that it was dubbed the "meeting without ties." The new spirit in bilateral relations resulted in Japanese support for Russia's entry into the G-7 and APEC. The two countries made progress on resolving their differences over fishing issues. Military exchanges developed, and opportunities for visa-free travel for residents of the Kuriles and Hokkaido were expanded.[39]

Although Yeltsin and Hashimoto pledged to sign a peace treaty to end World War II by 2000, no agreement was reached. Most Japanese leaders argue against signing a peace treaty without any progress on the islands issue for fear that this would shelve the territorial questions indefinitely. Putin's September 2000 meeting with Prime Minister Yoshiro Mori made little headway. Although Putin reaffirmed the 1956 declaration, which stated that once a peace treaty was signed, Moscow would hand over Shikotan and Habomai, Putin made it very clear that he had no intention of handing over any islands to Japan. For the Japanese, this was tantamount to shelving the peace treaty issue indefinitely. Some Russian commentators suggested that Moscow had nothing to gain from concessions on the islands, since major Japanese investment was unlikely due to the caution of the Japanese business community about involvement in Russian projects.[40]

Despite the obstacles to closer bilateral relations, Russian-Japanese regional ties have been expanding. In an August 2, 2000, press conference, Sakhalin Governor Igor Farkhutdinov noted that regional cooperation with Japan was proceeding apace—in 1998 Sakhalin and Hokkaido prefecture signed a cooperation agreement, which the governor termed a "mini-peace treaty." Nevertheless, he lamented that without a bilateral peace agreement, Russian federal authorities were unlikely to work with their Japanese counterparts to resolve issues of concern to his region, especially joint measures to address key problems such as poaching, unlawful fishing, and circumvention of duties on fish products.[41]

Economic recession in Japan and crisis in Russia further complicated efforts to improve Russian-Japanese economic relations. In the Russian Far East, however, there is considerable interest in attracting Japanese investment, a goal frustrated to some extent by the lack of significant progress in bilateral issues. Japan is the top export destination for the Russian Far East as a whole. Although Japan was Khabarovskii krai's main export destination in 1999, a large military order made China the territory's main export market in 2000, with Japan in the number two position (see Table 12.1). Leading Russian exports to Japan include nonferrous and precious metals, timber, fish products, and fuel. While there is considerable interest in importing Japanese consumer products, their higher cost relative to South Korean and U.S. products has restrained demand. It should be noted, however, that due to illegal trade in fish and timber products, Russian-Japanese regional trade figures may be underreported.

In the Russian Far East, attracting Japanese investment is an important priority. Infrastructure development has been a key area for cooperation. Japan has participated in the renovation of airport terminals in Vladivostok, Khabarovsk, and Yuzno-Sakhalinsk. Japan also contributed $30 million to a feasibility study investigating improvements for the port of Zarubino. In May 1999, the Primorskii krai administration and the Japanese-Russian Business Committee signed an agreement according to which Japan would invest $10 million to build new facilities in Zarubino for grain storage, wood chip processing, and container transshipment.

In the aftermath of the 1997 international meeting in Kyoto on reducing greenhouse emissions, several Japanese firms, including Sumitomo, Mitsubishi, and Mitsui, began exploring the possibility of investing in renovations of power plants in Primorskii krai, Khabarovskii krai, and Sakhalinskaia oblast. Seven projects were identified, but no final decisions regarding feasibility studies have been made yet.

Japan was one of the early investors in the Sakhalin offshore oil and gas projects. The Japanese consortium Sodeco has a 30-percent share in Sakhalin-1, and Mitsui and Mitsubishi hold shares totaling 37.5 percent in Sakhalin-2. All of the options for delivery of natural gas target the Japanese market. Plans under discussion include the construction of a liquified natural gas facility on Sakhalin, which would ship the product to Japan, an underwater power grid connecting Japan to Sakhalin, and a gas pipeline from Sakhalin to Hokkaido.

Japan is the leader in terms of the number of joint ventures established on Sakhalin and also has a number of successful timber joint ventures in Primorskii and Khabarovskii krais. The Ternowood joint venture in Primorye has been described as a "miracle" due to its success in producing high-quality construction materials at Japanese standards.[42] The Tairiku timber project in Khabarovskii krai reportedly is one of most sophisticated manufacturing operations, involving the production of kiln-dried pine for the Japanese market. Mill waste from the project is used for power generation for the sawmill and nearby villages.

Japanese Views of Regional Relations with Russia

As Sino-Russian relations drew closer in the mid-1990s, Japan began to seek ways of improving relations with Russia as well. In 1997 Prime Minister Hashimoto announced a "Eurasia" policy, which would link Russian–Japanese political and economic relations. Since that policy was outlined, Japanese officials have focused on the Russian Far East in their effort to boost Russian-Japanese economic relations. Japan has established cultural centers that provide free Japanese lessons and business advice in many cities in the region. The Japanese government has provided humanitarian assistance to hospitals in the Russian Far East and undertaken a program of assistance with the dismantling of nuclear submarines.

Japanese prefectures bordering on the Sea of Japan have been pressing for greater economic cooperation with Russia.[43] Niigata has been active in establishing ties with Primorskii krai, and Hokkaido has a permanent representation office on Sakhalin. As in the case of the U.S. West Coast and the Russian Far East, the establishment of regional organizations, including the association of governors from Japan and the Russian Far East and the Russian Far East–Hokkaido association, has facilitated the growth of Russian-Japanese regional relations.

Many obstacles stand in the way of the development of economic cooperation between Japan and the Russian Far East. Japan's determination to recover the southern Kurile Islands is at the root of many Japanese efforts to become more involved economically in the Russian Far East—Japan is most involved in Sakhalin, the province that administers the Kuriles. Nonetheless, due to the continuing impasse over the islands, the Japanese government will not allow Japanese firms to invest in the Kuriles and discourages other foreign investment.

The greatest obstacle to Japanese investment in the region, however, is the high level of risk. Some high-profile failures of joint ventures in Khabarovsk and Yuzhno-Sakhalinsk have given prospective investors in Japan considerable pause. The consensus-style decision-making prevalent in Japanese firms has accentuated Japan's cautious approach to economic relations with Russia, especially compared to South Korean and U.S. companies.

Financing is another obstacle for Japanese firms with an interest in projects in the Russian Far East. Since Russia is not categorized as a developing country, it cannot receive loans from Japan's Overseas Development Agency to finance Russian–Japanese projects. Thus, Japanese firms must rely on loans from the Bank for

International Cooperation (created in 1999 by the merger of the Export-Import Bank and the Overseas Economic Cooperation Fund), which requires conditions not easily fulfilled—some sharing of risk and financing with the Russian government.

CONCLUSIONS

Despite difficulties in Russia's bilateral relations with the United States, Japan, and South Korea, regional economic relations with these countries have been developing steadily. Motivated by security, political, and economic concerns, the federation subjects of the Russian Far East have endeavored to become more integrated in the Pacific Rim economy. Regional leaders in the weakened peripheries on Russia's Asian borders have come to view China, Moscow's strategic partner, as a potential threat. This has led the regions bordering on China to avoid economic dependence on China and to diversify their economic relations. Russia's Asian neighbors have their own strategic rationales for building economic relations with the Russian Far East. All share an interest in reducing tensions in Northeast Asia, especially on the Korean Peninsula, and in engaging the Russian Far East in mutually beneficial economic cooperation, particularly in natural resources.

To some extent, the regional dynamic in Russia's Asia policy reflects the failure of Moscow's regional policy—cut off economically from European Russia by high transportation tariffs and energy costs, regions of the Russian Far East have turned to their Northeast Asian neighbors for markets for their resources and sources of consumer products.

Nonetheless, the complex investment climate in this part of Russia has made it difficult for even willing partners to cooperate. The success of the Sakhalin offshore oil and gas projects will be critical in creating a stronger economic base in the Russian Far East and providing a model for multilateral cooperation involving the United States, Japan, South Korea, and China. For this to occur, however, President Putin's commitment to the development of the Russian Far East will be essential. At this point, it is difficult to say whether his main aim is to reassert federal control over wayward governors in Russia's peripheries or to ensure that legislative and economic conditions in the Russian Far East are hospitable to economic cooperation with Asian neighbors.

NOTES

1. "Kontsepsiia vneshnei politiki Rossiiskoi Federatsii," *Nezavisimaia gazeta*, July 11, 2000, 6.

2. Ibid.

3. *Rossiiskaia gazeta*, July 19, 2000, 7.

4. Xinhua News Agency, "China-Russia Declaration," July 18, 2000.

5. The discussion of Putin's Asia policy is drawn from interviews with officials and scholars in Moscow, July 2000.

6. For more on the disruption in trade between the Russian Far East and European Russia, see Vladimir Popov, "Reform Strategies and Economic Performance: The Far East Compared to Russia's Other Regions," presented at the conference "Security Implications of Economic and Political Developments in the Russian Far East," The National Bureau of Asian Research, Washington, D.C., May 2000.

7. For a discussion of the problems facing border trade, see Lu Nanquan, "Fazhan liangguo jingmao guanxi de duice jianyi," in Xue Jundu and Lu Nanquan, eds., *Zhong-E Jingmao Guanxi* (Beijing: CASS, 1999), 255–67.

8. The discussion of the migration issue is drawn in part from my article "Russia in Asia and Asians in Russia," *SAIS Review*, winter–spring 2000, 87–101. On this question, see also Mikhail Alekseev, "Chinese Migration in the Russian Far East: Security Threats and Incentives for Cooperation in Primorskii Krai," chapter 13 in this volume.

9. Galina Vitkovskaia and Zhanna Zaonchkovskaia, "Novaia Stolypinskaia politika na Dalnem Vostoke Rossii," in Galina Vitkovskaia and Dmitrii Trenin, eds., *Perspektivy Dal'nevostochnogo regiona: Mezhstranovye vzaimosdeistviia* (Moscow: Carnegie Moscow Center, 1999), 96–97.

10. Although the northern regions of the Russian Far East lost the most people, the populations of Primorskii krai and Khabarovskii krai declined by 1.5 percent and 3.3 percent respectively. Galina Vitkovskaiia, Zhanna Zayonchkovskaia, and Kathleen Newland, "Chinese Migration into Russia," in Sherman Garnett, ed., *Rapprochement or Rivalry? Russia-China Relations in a Changing Asia* (Washington, D.C.: Carnegie Endowment for International Peace, 2000), 351.

11. With the collapse of the Soviet economy, imports of food products from western parts of the Soviet Union proved too expensive due to high rail tariffs, and the Russian Far East was obliged to revive an underdeveloped agricultural sector.

12. Vilya Gelbras, a leading economist and China specialist at Moscow State University who has interviewed more than 750 Chinese living in Moscow and several cities in the Russian Far East, attributes some of the difficulty in arriving at conclusive numbers to the varying definitions of "migrants," a term which can refer to seasonal labor as well as to permanent residents. In his view there are approximately 300,000 Chinese now living in Russia, including 20,000–25,000 in Moscow. Vilya Gelbras, "Kitaitsy v Rossii," *Ekspert*, no. 27 (July 17, 2000):17.

13. Vitkovskaia and Zaonchkovskaia, 84.

14. Nikolai Nepsha, "Kitaiskie turisty stanoviatsia rossiiskimi prestupnikami," *Vladivostok*, July 7, 1994, 2.

15. Yurii Avdeev and Sergei Pushkarev, et al., "Migratsionnaia situatsiia i rynki truda v Primorskom Krae," 67, and Stanislav Khodakov, "Immigratsiia i immigratsionnaia politika v Khabarovskom Krae," in Galina Vitkovskaia and Dmitrii Trenin, eds., *Perspektivy Dalnevostochnogo Regiona: Naselenie, Migratsiia, Rynki Truda*, Working Papers Issue 2, Carnegie Moscow Center, 1999.

16. Viktor Larin, *Kitai i Dalnyi Vostok Rossii* (Vladivostok: Dalnauka, 1998), 74.

17. Aleksandr Babakin and Aleksandr Shinkin, "Tridstat shest granits Rossii," *Rossiiskaia gazeta*, July 10, 1999, 4.

18. In a study by the Carnegie Moscow Center, several prominent scholars concluded that for the Russian Far East to develop economically, a long-term policy regulating the use of Chinese labor would be necessary. See, for example, Vitkovskaia and Zaonchkovskaia, "Novaia Stolypinskaia politika na Dalnem Vostoke Rossii," in Vitkovskaia and Trenin, eds., 117; Vilya Gelbras, "Kitaiskii vopros Rossii," in Vitkovskaia and Trenin, eds., 70; and Pavel Minakir, "Integratsiia Rossiiskogo Dalnego Vostoka v ATR i SVA: vozmozhnosti i realnosti," in Vitkovskaia and Trenin, eds., 22.

19. The two islands (Bolshoi Ussuriiskii/Heixiazi and Tarabarov/Yinlong) fall on the Chinese side of the river boundary, but Khabarovsk authorities adamantly oppose their return or even joint economic development for fear of turning their capital city into a border outpost.

20. Dmitrii Kosyrev, "Putin postavil vopros. Lingvisticheskii ili politicheskii?" *Nezavisimaia gazeta*, July 22, 2000, 1.

21. Heilongjiang Vice-Governor Wang Zongzhang, "Heilongjiang shen bianjing difang jingji maoyi shishi yu duice yanjiu," unpublished paper presented to Harbin conference, June 11, 1996, 19–20. For a detailed discussion of Chinese views of problems in regional relations, see Elizabeth Wishnick, "Chinese Perspectives on Cross-Border Relations," in Garnett, ed., 227–56.

22. Gai Jindong and Li Daijun, "Border Defense Guards Clamp Down on Illegal Border Crossing," *Renmin Ribao*, January 6, 1995, 4, in FBIS-CHI-95-012, 36.

23. Foreign Minister Qian Qichen's speech at Moscow University, Xinhua, June 28, 1994, in FBIS-CHI-94-126, June 30, 1994, 8.

24. Interviews with officials and scholars in Beijing, Harbin, and Changchun, November 1999.

25. Igor Sergeev, "Sammit reshit sudbu 'neftianogo mosta,'" *Ekspert*, no. 27 (July 17, 2000):10.

26. "Russian President Was Just Using Terms the West Can Understand," *Nezavisimaia gazeta*, December 13, 1999, in East European Press Service <www.securities.com>.

27. For more in energy developments and levels of investment in Sakhalin oblast, see Judith Thornton, "Sakhalin Energy: Problems and Prospects," chapter 7 in this volume.

28. *IEWS Russian Regional Report* 2, no. 28 (August 28, 1997).

29. Michael J. Bradshaw, "Going Global: The Political Economy of Oil and Gas Development Offshore of Sakhalin," *Cambridge Review of International Affairs*, summer–

fall 1998, 165. See also Thornton, "Sakhalin Energy," chapter 7 in this volume.

30. Carana Corporation, *Opportunities for Increasing Investment in the Minerals Sector of Khabarovsk Krai*, presented to the Department of Foreign Economic Relations, September 1999; BISNIS RFE: Mining in Khabarovsk, April 2000 <www.bisnis.doc.gov/bisnis/country/000323rfe-khab-mining.htm>.

31. Wood Resources International Ltd. and CARANA Corporation, *Investment Promotion for the Forest Product Industries of Khabarovsk Krai*, Final Outline Report to Khabarovsk Krai Administration, August 1999.

32. Russell Working, "Foreign Investors Lose a Round at Russian Ship Concern," *New York Times*, July 7, 1999, C4.

33. Igor Ivanov, "La Russie et l'Asie-Pacifique," *Politique Étrangère*, February 1999:310.

34. Shim Jae Hoon, "Trading Post," *Far Eastern Economic Review*, January 13, 2000:22.

35. Shim Jae Hoon, "Suitcase Traders," *Far Eastern Economic Review*, October 28, 1999:18.

36. Yonhap, July 6, 1993, in FBIS-SOV-93-128, July 7, 1993, 26.

37. Northeast Asian Peace and Security Network, Daily Report, August 3, 2000 <www.nautilus.org>.

38. BISNIS RFE: "Commercial Update—Khabarovsk," distributed by Tanya_Shuster@ita.org, August 2000.

39. Leszek Buszynski, "Russia and Northeast Asia: Aspirations and Reality," *The Pacific Review* 13, no. 3 (2000):408–9.

40. Aleskandr Chudodeev, "Moskva zakryla territorial'nyi vopros," *Segodnia*, January 17, 2001 <www.securities.com>.

41. Press Conference with Sakhalin oblast Governor Igor Farkhutdinov, RIA Novosti, August 2, 2000, Federal News Service <www.securities.com>.

42. Tatiana Kurochkina, "Primorskii 'Teknovud' rabotaet po-iaponskii," *Zolotoi rog*, February 8, 2000 <www.vladivostok.com>.

43. Gilbert Rozman, "Backdoor Japan: The Search for a Way Out via Regionalism and Decentralization," *Journal of Japanese Studies* 25, no. 1 (1999):16–17.

13

Chinese Migration in the Russian Far East: Security Threats and Incentives for Cooperation in Primorskii Krai

Mikhail Alexseev

The improvement of relations between Moscow and Beijing in the late 1980s and the demise of the Soviet Union lifted the political, economic, and cultural isolation of the Russian Far East from China. While creating economic incentives for cooperation, the cross-border flow of people, goods, and services has given rise to security concerns and socioeconomic grievances among political elites and the public in the Russian Far East. Many in the Russian Far East fear China's territorial designs on Russia. Scarcity of publicly available official information on this issue has been accompanied by alarmist speculations by officials, scholars, and the media on the scale of Chinese migration. Viktor Larin, director of the Vladivostok Institute of History, counted more than 150 articles in the local and national press in 1993–95 that raised the specter of the "yellow peril," or massive Chinese migration into the Russian Far East as part of China's territorial expansion. Some press articles in 1993 and 1994 claimed that up to 150,000 illegal immigrants were settling in Primorskii krai as part of the 400,000 to two million migrants from the People's Republic of China (PRC) who have infiltrated the Russian Far East.[1] As part of his 1999 election campaign in Primorye, Governor Yevgenii Nazdratenko issued a glossy promotional book entitled "And all of Russia is behind my back ... ," which warned that the Russian Far East may turn into the "Asian Balkans" as a result of cross-border Chinese migration and border disputes.[2] In July 1999 Governor Viktor Ishaev of Khabarovskii krai warned of "a peaceful invasion" of the region by ethnic Chinese.[3]

This chapter estimates the scale of Chinese migration and assesses which factors associated with Chinese migrants may increase interethnic tensions and nationalist activism or, conversely, promote cooperation and cross-border economic development. The study focuses on Primorskii krai—the most populous and economically advanced region in the Russian Far East and the one most representative of the Chinese border migration problem.[4]

CROSS-BORDER TRAVEL AND THE SCALE OF CHINESE MIGRATION IN PRIMORSKII KRAI

In the last quarter of the twentieth century, Chinese migration emerged as a global phenomenon driven by demographics and political and economic incentives. The Russian Far East is just one of several peripheral destinations for Chinese migrants, mostly from the poorer regions of China's northeastern "rust belt," few of whom can afford to pay thousands of dollars to migration entrepreneurs to be smuggled to the West. A recent study of Chinese migration by the Carnegie Endowment for International Peace concluded that in the Far East of Russia, the typical Chinese migrant is "poor, persevering, modest, hungry for earnings of any size, and brutally exploited by his own countrymen with the silent approval of the Russians."[5] It is little surprise then that official Chinese sources reported that the number of Chinese migrants in all Soviet successor states in the mid-1990s was approximately one percent of the worldwide Chinese diaspora.[6]

According to the Visa and Registration Department (OVIR) of the Ministry of Internal Affairs of Russia for Primorskii krai, the total number of Chinese nationals visiting Primorye increased from 35,000 in 1995 to 73,000 in 1998 (see Table 13.1). Most visitors and migrants from the PRC in Primorye and other border provinces (about half of PRC nationals observed in Vladivostok are ethnic Koreans, reflecting the proximity of the PRC's Korean enclaves) come from the three neighboring provinces of Heilongjiang, Jilin, and Liaoning. More than half have high school or college education and say they are driven by the opportunity to make a lot of money fast (which explains why more PRC migrants reside in Moscow than in the entire Russian Far East).[7] Whereas 34 percent (27,530) of PRC visitors to Primorye failed to return home in 1994 and 1995, the number of illegally overstaying visitors plummeted following the introduction by law enforcement agencies, starting in 1994, of tighter visa controls and spot checks in the streets, markets, and in the workplace (Operation Foreigner).

The data suggests that the flow of PRC nationals into Primorskii krai has been increasingly rule-based and controlled by the authorities. Visa-free travel—a putative cause of illegal immigration in the region—increased almost threefold from 1996 to 1998, with nearly 84 percent of all visitors to Primorye coming on tourist permits (standing in lieu of visas). At the same time, however, only 0.4 percent of registered visitors in 1998 remained illegally in the krai. The number of administrative penalties (mostly fines), deportation orders, and forced deportations decreased more than twofold from 1996 to 1998 relative to the total number of PRC visitors.

Table 13.1 Number of PRC Citizens Visiting Primorskii Krai

	PRC visitors to Primorye			Sanctions against violators		
	Total	Without visas	Failed to return	Administrative penalties	Deportation orders	Forced deportation
1994	40,000	18,500	14,400	9,500	2,700	1,500
1995	35,000	18,500	11,200	12,300	6,600	4,500
1996	35,500	21,000	1065	8,250	3,700	1,900
1997	52,000	39,000	468	8,250	4,000	2,100
1998	73,000	61,000	292	8,250	3,200	1,190
1999	80,287	n.d.	105*	n.d.	n.d.	n.d.
2000*	41,355	n.d.	n.d.	n.d.	n.d.	n.d.

* Based on data for January–March 1999 and January–June 2000. According to Lt. Col. Viktor M. Plotnikov of OVIR, in 1999 and in the first half of 2000 the administrative violations and deportation rates remained essentially the same as in 1996 to 1998, although the exact statistics were not available.

Source: Otdel viz i razreshenii Primorskogo kraia (OVIR), Spravka, Lt. Col. Viktor M. Plotnikov, deputy head of the department, Vladivostok, June 2, 1999.

Assuming that all nonreturnees from 1994 to the first quarter of 1999 stayed in Primorskii krai, their total number would still be a fraction of the earlier panic estimates. Visual observations by this author in and around Vladivostok, Ussuriisk, and Nakhodka in summer and fall 1999 indicate that even close to the areas of concentrated (and temporary) settlement, the number of Chinese migrants is likely measured in dozens, perhaps hundreds, but by no means in thousands.

A July 1999 internal report on migration and sedentarization (osedanie) of foreign nationals in Primorskii krai by the head of the Pacific regional administration of the federal border service (TORU) corroborates the OVIR data. The border service report states that 80,622 PRC nationals entered Primorye "through tourist exchange channels" from 1998 through June 1999. This border service report refers to these Chinese visitors as "tourist-businessmen," which fairly well reflects the reality of most Chinese nationals entering Primorye on tourist visas to engage in business. The TORU report also suggests the tendency toward legalization of Chinese visitations, with the number of attempted entries on forged passports declining from 230 in 1996 to 120 in 1997 and 107 in 1998.

As for entry outside border checkpoints, from November 1998 to March 1999 the border patrols intercepted just 41 PRC nationals attempting to cross the Russian border illegally. In a memorandum issued upon this author's request in May 1999, TORU stated: "The situation on the border with the PRC in recent years has been stable and predictable. It reflects the mutual aspiration of China and Russia to develop the necessary political conditions for a constructive partnership."[8]

A more alarmist report by the Primorskii krai internal affairs administration in January 1996 claimed that 415,000 PRC citizens had traveled to Primorye from 1993 through 1995, but that only 145,000 registered, while the rest moved on to other parts of Russia.[9] The alleged report was released for distribution in 1996 by the governor-controlled *Vladivostok* daily. Yet, the internal affairs public liaison office did not make the report available to local Russian scholars nor to this author, which puts into question the existence of the report. It is also unclear how the internal affairs administration physically counted nearly 300,000 unregistered Chinese migrants over three years. Moreover, if the police found and counted these illegal migrants, it is unclear why they were not deported, given that Operation Foreigner had been in effect since 1994. Finally, a substantial number of these migrants would have to be located in or around the krai's largest cities of Vladivostok, Ussuriisk, Nakhodka, and Pogranichnyi. These settlements would have to be much larger than the presently largest compact settlement area of Chinese migrants numbering around 2,000 in Ussuriisk.[10]

The number of legally employed PRC citizens in Primorye was 7,895 in 1994; 8,349 in 1995; 8,292 in 1996; 6,968 in 1997; and 7,179 in 1998, also suggesting a stable and limited flow.[11] Between 63 and 69 percent of these migrant workers are concentrated in the cities of Vladivostok, Ussuriisk, Nakhodka, Artem, Arsenev, and Partizansk. Approximately 30 percent are located in the krai's thirteen border-line districts *(raiony)*.[12] Since nearly 90 percent of these migrant laborers are employed in construction and agriculture, these migrant flows are seasonal, with about one half of the total annual number present in Primorye at any one time. In Ussuriisk, for example, I visited an enclosed area on the outskirts of the city where one is greeted by a sign, "China Town" *(Kitaiskii gorodok)*, in Russian and Chinese. Designed to house some 1,300 Chinese laborers, China Town was deserted during my visits in May and October 1999.[13]

Given the OVIR and TORU estimates, and assuming that Chinese migrant workers and "tourist businessmen" spend half their time in Russia and half in China, a maximum of approximately 15,000 PRC nationals in 1997 and 35,000 in 1998 could have been in Primorye at any given time. Chief of the federal migration service in Primorskii krai, Sergei Pushkarev, estimated in May 1999 that no more than 5,000 Chinese nationals could be found in Primorye on any given day.[14] Thus, the number of Chinese nationals present in Primorye at any given time in 1996–1998 is unlikely to have been more than 0.3 to 1.1 percent of the average krai population of 2.2 million mostly ethnic Russians and Ukrainians.

BEYOND THE NUMBERS: CORRELATES OF HOSTILITY TOWARD CHINESE MIGRANTS AND VISITORS

Despite the relatively low actual Chinese migrant presence or assimilation in Primorskii krai, theories of ethnic conflict and international relations suggest several factors that could spark anti-Chinese activism in the Russian Far East, leading potentially to a deterioration of Russia's relations with China. This would explain the disproportionately alarmist perceptions of the "Chinese factor" among politicians and the media in the Russian Far East.

First, from the viewpoint of "essentialist" theories—which emphasize the absolute power of the "congruities of blood, speech, and custom"[15]—ethnic Chinese and Koreans (most of whom are PRC nationals) in Primorye comprise a racially distinct and readily identifiable minority with a culture and history about which local Slavic residents understand little. These "essential" racial and cultural differences between the Russians and the PRC migrants would be expected to evolve inevitably into some violent confrontation over time. The continuing (and long) history of Sino-Russian territorial disputes that erupted in armed conflict over Damanskii Island as recently as 1969 would nurture deeply seated perceptions of threat to physical security and cultural traditions of ethnic Russians.[16]

Second, as constructivist theories suggest, the rise of oligarchic government (or what one scholar called "local authoritarianism") in Primorskii krai in the 1990s under Governor Yevgenii Nazdratenko[17] sets the stage for political oppression and persecution of ethnic minorities. From this perspective, distinct and readily identifiable ethnic minorities are likely to be "constructed" by nationalist Russian politicians as adversaries, competitors, scapegoats, or undesirables. The traditions of the Russian frontier, the absence of strong democratic institutions, a border dispute with China, and Nazdratenko's conflicts with both the federal government and the mayor of Vladivostok all favored a strong nationalist position in the local power struggle.[18]

Third, political realists have argued that if the ratio of nationalisms to states rises, so does the probability of violent conflict. From that perspective, cross-border migration of an ethnically distinct group creates a de facto nation-bisecting interstate border and increases demographic intermingling. As a result, societal and intergroup tensions are likely to rise since both nation-bisecting borders and demographic intermingling, as Stephen van Evera puts it, "entrap parts of nations within the boundaries of states dominated by other ethnic groups."[19] The "truncated nation" (represented by PRC nationals) thus has incentives for expansionism, and the "entrapping nation" faces a security dilemma favoring preemptive coercive action against the cross-border migrants.[20] As hostility perceptions spiral on both sides, interstate relations are prone to deteriorate without warning. And with 2.2 million ethnic Slavs in Primorye facing approximately 70 million ethnic Chinese in the neighboring Heilongjiang Province, one would expect this security dilemma to have a strong impact on Russian policymakers (both in Primorye and in Moscow). In this situation, China (the "truncated nation") would find it problematic to send credible signals of peaceful intentions to actors controlling means of violence in Russia (the "entrapping nation")—a situation known as the "commitment problem."[21]

Another major contribution of political realism is the notion of the "security dilemma," where absence of central authority (or "structural anarchy") forces actors to measure their security relative to the rise or decline of perceived capabilities of other actors.[22] Chinese migration in the Russian Far East increased when the sovereign power in Russia weakened following the collapse of the communist government. Geographical remoteness from Russia's political center adds to the sense of insecurity in Primorskii krai. Moreover, the absence of international institutions in Northeast Asia that could guarantee mutual self-restraint, the long history of Sino-Russian territorial disputes, and the fact that the 1991 border demarcation has been called into question are consistent with a classic security dilemma under structural anarchy.[23] Ethnic-based activism would then arise from perceptions of insecurity and "causal ambiguity."[24]

Fourth, an economic implication of the security dilemma is relative deprivation. This perception occurs when economic growth happens in sectors associated with a different ethnic group (e.g., Chinese migrants), which threatens to accentuate and aggravate ethnic grievances,[25] especially amidst general economic decline and scarcity, as in Russia. Groups are likely to "conclude that they can improve their welfare only at the expense of others" and opt for nationalism.[26] Russians in Primorye would thus mobilize because the Chinese, more than the local Russians, are likely to succeed economically and translate this success into political advantages.[27]

That a combination of "essentialist," "constructivist," and "realist" factors must be considered seriously is suggested by observations about disparities in long-term economic and demographic trends between Primorskii krai and the neighboring provinces of China and by a decline of Primorskii krai's capacity to finance government and law enforcement activities from 1998 to 1999. As the population and economy in the Russian Far East declined in the 1990s, the population and economy of China grew steadily. From 1996 to 1997, the population of the southern part of the Russian Far East[28] declined by 40,000 and the GDP dropped by 8 percent, while in the neighboring Chinese provinces of Heilongjiang, Jilin, and Liaoning, the population increased by one million and the GDP rose by 13 percent. From the relative deprivation perspective, the GDP in the southern part of the Russian Far East declined relative to the GDP of the neighboring Chinese provinces by 19 percent in just one year.[29]

One Russian scholar has operationalized the population differences between China and the southern part of the Russian Far East as "demographic pressure." By his indicators, this pressure amounts to 63,000 Chinese nationals per one Russian per kilometer of the Russian-Chinese border in the Far East. Population density pressure amounts to 380,000 Chinese per one Russian per kilometer of the border inside a one-kilometer band.[30]

Demographic insecurity (and negative perceptions of Chinese migration) are likely to be highest in regions with lower population size and density. By these measures, the strongest negative incentives could be associated with Chinese migration in Dalnerechenskii, Kirovskii, Pogranichnyi, Spasskii, Khankaiskii, Shkotovskii, and Ussuriiski raions (excluding the city of Ussuriisk) of Primorskii krai.[31] For example, in Dalnerechenskii raion, population declined by 7.5 percent from 1993 to 1998, and population density in 1998 was five times below average for the krai's borderline raions. Natural population growth in that raion (8.2 per 1,000 in 1990) gave way to natural decline (-3.1 per 1,000 in 1997). Not surprisingly, one of the themes recurring in street conversations and interviews with officials in Vladivostok, Ussuriisk, and Nakhodka in 1999 was that if Chinese nationals settle down in Primorye, they would gradually take over. As one taxi driver said, using a racially charged description of ethnic Chinese that is common in Russia: "We will wake up one day and find out that every other person is squint-eyed *(kosoglazyi)*."

Against this background, state capacity to regulate cross-border exchanges also declined in the late 1990s. Primorski krai budget data shows that the dollar value of budgetary spending for executive agencies and police in Primorye decreased by about one-half in the wake of the August 1998 financial crisis. The amount of spending on programs supporting environmental protection, border security, and tax inspection decreased nearly four times. Thus, budget appropriations for

Primorskii krai Directorate of Internal Affairs (police) dropped from the equivalent of $24.4 million in 1997 to $15.7 million in 1998.[32]

The inadequacy of these funding measures becomes evident in the extent of cross-border cash flows from smuggling of sensitive bioresources like timber, ginseng, and tiger parts from Primorye into China. In 1998 and 1999, Chinese smugglers generated an estimated $3 million in revenues annually for themselves and about the same amount for local Russians, according to the Office of the Prosecutor for Environmental Protection of Primorskii krai. This estimate is conservative, for it excludes revenues from illicit trade in fish, frogs, sea cucumbers, sea urchins, bear parts, and musk deer glands.[33] Thus, conservatively estimated revenues from illicit trade in sensitive bioresources amounted to nearly one-third of funding for the krai executive agencies in 1997, but more than two-thirds in 1998. Such decreasing state capacity, from the standpoint of political realism, would heighten the security dilemma and the commitment problem in Sino-Russian relations. More broadly, the security dilemma in the Russian Far East is enhanced by diminishing policing capacity (hence, increasing perception of anarchy) and by diminishing population (hence, increasing perception of a growing power disparity in China's favor).

CROSS-BORDER SECURITY:
KEY ISSUES FOR RUSSIAN OFFICIALS

Chinese migration gives rise to insecurity perceptions among government officials in Primorskii krai on four key issues. First, they are concerned not so much about the size of migration as about the lack of institutional capacity to regulate the cross-border flow of people. According to Lt. Col. Viktor Plotnikov, deputy head of Primorskii krai's Visa and Registration Department of Russia's Interior Ministry:

> We do not see "the yellow peril" rising as yet, but we do see problems. One of them, a very acute one, is lack of personnel and technical means to regulate border crossings. For example, according to the law signed on December 18, 1992, Chinese tourists are allowed to enter Russia without visas if they enter as part of a tourist group. They then may enter Russia 8 or 10 times whereas their passports are issued only for one trip. We also know cases of one person entering on different personal identification papers. We have little capacity to monitor and control all that. That is why we are concerned about illegal migration.[34]

And while taking pride in recently closing "two secret channels for Chinese migrant traffic to Europe and Japan," Plotnikov still lamented the lack of capacity to close other such channels that he believed remained operational. Former representative of President Yeltsin in Primorskii krai, Vladimir Ignatenko, who currently chairs the krai Duma committee that deals with migration issues, punctuated these fears by saying: "If we lifted border controls right now, more than half of [Primorskii] krai population would be Chinese."[35]

Second, Primorye officials have been concerned that cross-border economic exchanges, primarily barter trade, have disproportionately favored China. For example, Iurii Shevchuk, counsel to the Ussuriisk county government, complained that Chinese traders were taking advantage of Russia's economic difficulties by selling inferior manufactured goods and purchasing "strategically valuable resources" such as aluminum, copper, bronze, rare-earth metals, and timber for export outside of Russia.[36] TORU chief Tarasenko voiced a more sophisticated concern:

> [Chinese] tourists pose another threat—while on the territory of the Russian Federation, they are investing the proceeds of their commercial activities into real property, securities, and contraband…. As you realize, such activities of Chinese nationals affect the demographic, economic, military, and other aspects of Russia's national interest in this region. These activities are explicitly aimed at undermining Russia's security. [37]

Third, the sense of Russia's strategic retreat after the collapse of the Soviet Union and the perceptions of China's territorial claims on Russia gave rise to the Primorye government's opposition to border demarcation outlined in the 1991 treaty between Moscow and Beijing. In the introduction to his report, for example, Tarasenko directly attributed to the collapse of the Soviet Union the "lack of control over migration processes which now challenges us."[38] While serving as Yeltsin's representative in Primorskii krai, Vladimir Ignatenko wrote an inter-departmental memorandum in which three out of seven pages were devoted to the history of Russia-China border relations. Ignatenko stressed China's constant pressure on Russia to verify border demarcation and cataloged increasing Chinese troop concentration in border districts. Ignatenko accused the Soviet Foreign Ministry under Gorbachev of making historically unjustified concessions to China in three locations in Primorskii krai. "Here, in Primorye," he concluded, "one gets a more acute sense of the incontrovertible fact, that the Chinese seek precedent. No one can guarantee that they would be satisfied after getting those three [disputed] border areas."[39]

These interpretations suggest that under the security dilemma linked to the migration issue, Russian officials in the Far East are likely to suspect China of territorial designs on Russia no matter what position Beijing articulates. Thus, silence on or downplaying of the border problems would signal a conspiracy, whereas assertions of benign intentions would signal deception. The actual long-term intentions of Beijing on the border issue have been opaque. On the one hand, China reassured the Kremlin and the Far Eastern governments that it wants to adhere to existing treaties and agreed to tighten controls over cross-border travel.[40] On the other hand, Chinese officials interpret the nineteenth-century border treaties with Russia—that underlie current boundaries—as historical injustices, with an implication (officially denied) that they intend to right them when China gets stronger.[41]

Fourth, mistrust of China's territorial designs has colored perceptions of the UN-sponsored and Japan-financed Tumen (Tumangan) River project at the juncture of Russia, China, and North Korea. While questioning economic benefits to Primorskii krai, Ignatenko fears that the project would give China an oceanic port diverting cargo traffic away from Vladivostok, Nakhodka, and Poset, enable China to build a naval station at the mouth of the Tumen River, and increase pollution of Lake Khasan, a major local water source for Primorye. In Ignatenko's view, the Tumen River project does not have the potential to reduce interstate tensions.[42]

CORRELATES OF RESTRAINT OF ANTI-CHINESE ACTIVISM: ECONOMIC BENEFITS AND INCENTIVES FOR COOPERATION

While these factors make Primorye more prone to interethnic conflict than, for example, regions in Russia's European core, they hardly represent the full range of necessary conditions and are by no means sufficient conditions for intergroup violence. Recent studies show that latent hostilities and ethnic activism rooted in cultural differences, histories of intergroup conflict, and deficiencies in social and political systems in most cases do not engender organized interethnic violence.[43] In the spring and fall of 1999, having systematically combed miles of areas where ethnic Chinese trade, work, and reside in Primorye, I observed that interactions between ethnic Russians and Chinese nationals were predominantly peaceful.[44] Street observations suggest that these interactions are cooperative by virtue of mutual economic necessity (e.g., facing the same gangsters or the same rent-seeking officials) and by the isolation of rather small and dispersed Chinese communities from the local Slavic population.

These observations also suggest that economic incentives are likely to constrain anti-Chinese activism in the RFE, especially among the elites. Moreover, economic incentives must be potent in a political environment such as Russia's, where the rule of law and ethical norms are weak and offer few restrictions on purely instrumental behavior. Resources derived from cross-border economic activities between Primorye and China shape incentives for interethnic cooperation through a number of channels.

Trade

Domestic and foreign trade generates taxes and other payments for local, krai, and federal budgets. Businesses and traders generate income and profit taxes;

customs dues; visa or entry permit fees; bus, train, or boat fares and cargo charges; space use fees; value-added and sales taxes; environmental taxes and fees; sanitary license fees; and other officially prescribed payments. Since the provision of federal funds is routinely delayed, the economic benefits resulting from Chinese traders, who deal and make payments in cash, increase.

Since the late 1980s, Chinese "shuttle" traders in Primorye eased chronic food and consumer goods shortages endemic to the Soviet centrally planned economy. In the 1990s, this trade offset a sharp drop in output by producers of consumer goods in Primorye. In Vladivostok, Ussuriisk, Artem, and Arsenev, the decline of consumer goods production from 1990 to 1997 averaged 99 percent for shoes, garments, kitchenware, refrigerators, washing machines, and soap, thus increasing the economic incentives for cross-border trade and exchanges. The production of key food staples like milk, meat, and eggs declined in all of the borderline raions and major cities except one, raising incentives for supply from Chinese traders and growers.[45] At the same time, supplies from European Russia became too costly as a result of increased electricity and transportation tariffs. While most local residents complain that Chinese goods traded by "shuttlers" (chelnoki) are of low quality, these goods are superior to most formerly available Soviet-made products and come in a wider assortment. In addition, consumers in Primorye now can buy fresh fruits and vegetables that were unavailable when Chinese nationals were not allowed to trade there. Even a xenophobic-minded chieftain of the Ussury Cossack Army grudgingly admitted that Chinese traders deserve credit for supplying the krai with fresh vegetables.[46]

Moreover, while Chinese shuttle traders fill the gap in domestic supply, the laid-off employees of idle factories have seized the opportunity to make a living through cross-border trade. Similarly, a decline in real wages in Primorye since 1990 has driven people to secure outside sources of income and the lowest possible prices. Cross-border trade provides an escape to local Russians from deteriorating conditions in the old economic sectors. The number of Russians from Primorye visiting China (with most of these travelers engaging in cross-border trade) exceeded the number of Chinese tourists visiting Primorye by about ten times from 1992 to 1996.[47] According to Yevgenii Plaksen of the Vladivostok Institute of History who conducts opinion surveys at the numerous "Chinese markets" and regularly shops there, prices are on average one-third to one-half of those in most shops and department stores in Primorye cities.[48] In the city of Ussuriisk, the Chinese trade center has become one of the three major contributors to the city budget—a telling example of a local government receiving significant economic benefits from cross-border migration.[49]

Joint Ventures

The volume of goods produced and services rendered by Russian-Chinese joint ventures (JV) in Primorskii krai's major cities and borderline raions rose from $400,000 in 1993 to $4.8 million in 1996, but then declined to $1.4 million in 1998.[50] Only in Khankaiskii and Dalnerechenskii raions did the JV output increase during this time, whereas JV output fell to zero in four raions and declined most significantly in the big cities.

Despite low production output, these JVs have generated a large volume of domestic and cross-border trade, in most cases exceeding local tax revenues. This gives local government elites strong incentives to support economic activities with China. The higher the trade-to-taxes ratio, the larger the resources that Russian-Chinese joint ventures have to bribe local officials, and the greater the incentive for local officials to seek rent for themselves. In this sense, the ratio is an unobtrusive indicator of corruption incentives by city and raion. These incentives have stayed moderately high in Vladivostok and low in the Partizanskii district, and have increased significantly in Ussuriisk and phenomenally in Dalnerechenskii raion.

Even in large cities with diverse economies, Russian-Chinese joint ventures generated sales exceeding entire tax revenues (by 3.7 times in Vladivostok and by 8.2 times in Nakhodka in 1997). In areas with a less diverse, underdeveloped economic base, these joint ventures generated sales that outstripped locally collected tax revenues by large margins (e.g., by 30.3 times in Nadezhdinskii raion and by 64.3 times in Dalnerechenskii raion in 1996). No systematic data is available on revenues officially collected from joint-venture sources (joint venture data is collected by local agencies and tax data is collected by the federal tax service, even for local taxes). However, estimates suggest that joint-venture activities are significant sources of revenue for city budgets. As discussed later in the chapter, Mikhail Vetrik, director of the Ussuriisk Chinese trade center, estimated that his operations with Chinese traders generated 10–11 percent of the city budget (and, with a population of 160,000, Ussuriisk is the third-largest city in Primorskii krai).

Migrant Labor

At the same time, the dependence of local economies in Primorye on Chinese migrant labor has been generally low. However, since most Chinese migrant workers are employed in construction and agriculture—sectors in which Russian laborers have a reputation for incompetence—these numbers also reflect incentives for local business and government leaders to cooperate with ethnic Chinese. By this measure, these incentives have been the lowest in cities, except for Ussuriisk and Nakhodka (in 1996), and the highest in the border raions, especially in Oktiabrskii, Partizanskii, and Pogranichnyi. According to the chief of the Russian federal migration service for Primorskii krai, Sergei Pushkarev, Russian businesses hire Chinese migrant workers for three main reasons—quality, work discipline, and farming skills. PRC nationals are seen daily at main construction sites in Vladivostok. This author, for example, observed them working hard at around 7:00 p.m. in Vladivostok's central square renovating the monument in honor of the fighters for Soviet power next to the krai administration headquarters.

Illicit Trade

According to Andrei Kopaev, a senior investigator at the "Tigr" department that deals with cross-border smuggling at the State Environmental Committee for Primorskii krai, Chinese smugglers reselling tiger parts provided by Russian poachers can expect to generate around $100,000 per year. Chinese traders who buy illegally harvested ash trees in Primorye at $40 per cubic meter can resell this timber for $80–100 per cubic feet in China, generating, Kopaev estimates, over $1,000,000 a year. The chief of the "Tigr" department, Sergei Zubov, estimates that in Krasnoarmeiskii district alone, 5,000 cubic meters of ash were harvested in 1998 with Chinese traders turning up to $70 profit per cubic meter. And with approximately one ton of illegally harvested wild ginseng, Chinese resellers can expect to raise $2 million a year at the going rate of $2 a gram.[51] Overall, Kopaev estimates, about 90 percent of demand for poaching and smuggling is generated from across the Chinese border. The "Tigr" department—funded primarily by the World Wildlife Fund with smaller contributions coming from Exxon and Coca-Cola—intercepts only a portion of this illicit trade.[52]

Even subtracting the money received by smugglers for items such as fish, frogs, sea cucumbers, sea urchins, bear parts, musk deer glands, and others, Chinese traders make upwards of $3 million per year from smuggling operations (with a similar amount going to Russian poachers and sellers).[53] This rise in illicit trade has coincided with a decline in tax revenues collected by the Tax Service of the Russian Federation in the largest Primorye cities and border districts. In dollar terms, these tax revenues fell from $2 billion in 1997 to $656 million in 1998, reflecting a sharp drop in the ruble-to-dollar exchange rate after the August 1998 currency devaluation.[54] Illicit traders have increased their financial resources (mostly in ready cash) against the background of declining tax revenues, especially in remote districts such as Dalnerechenskii. This availability of illegal cash combined with a decline in legally available resources establishes a strong foundation for corruption of government officials in Primorskii krai. According to Kopaev, larger traders in key transit districts pay protection money to police captains who ensure their business is safe from both police raids and petty criminals. He added, with anger and despondency, "If only these police officers knew for how little they sell their protection."[55]

Economic Incentives for Cooperation

Cross-border travel and trade offer local businesses and individuals the opportunity to make money and create jobs, a situation that favors interdependence with Chinese counterparts. With more resources, local governments have greater opportunities to maintain infrastructure and the public sector in general (which also helps win elections), as well as have more money for sanitation and security at Chinese markets (reducing potential socioeconomic grievances on both sides). Also, since local governments have to use local funds for stop-gap measures (such as payments to the military) when federal payments fail to arrive, revenues obtained from Chinese traders and businesses increase local government capacity to control state agents of political coercion, such as the police and the military. Finally, the flow of resources from cross-border activities gives border guards, customs and immigration officials, police officers, and officials overseeing licensing, taxation, and permits the incentive to benefit personally by illegally privatizing or cashing in on a part of that flow, or by manipulating institutions to help them appropriate public revenues as a matter of legal "exceptions" from the law.

Hence, revenues from cross-border trade in Primorye enhance the local tax base and benefit the public, as well as give political and economic elites opportunities to use public office for privatizing some of these revenues. This, in turn, suggests the following interplay of political and economic incentives for suppressing anti-Chinese mobilization. Under the best-case scenario—given the economic hardship in Russia and in Primorye particularly—both the public and the elites would benefit sufficiently from cross-border exchanges to favor accommodation of ethnic Chinese traders and workers. However, if the economic benefits to the public are small, while the perception of threat from Chinese migration is large, the political elite will come under pressure to implement measures restricting Chinese migration and economic activity. In this case, those elites that have few opportunities to benefit economically from cross-border exchanges are likely to promote aggressive antimigration measures, while those who have many opportunities for personal gain would face a dilemma. Should such actors take a strong antimigration position resonating with the public opinion so as to maximize political benefits, or should they continue to promote cross-border migration and economic activity so as not to lose an important source of revenue? As for public opinion, questions remain about whether attitudes toward Chinese migrants depend in any way on what people think about the scale of Chinese migration and whether people make linkages between political security and economic benefits or treat those issues separately.

For elite actors, a balancing strategy would be one rational solution to this dilemma. The strategy would be to make symbolic statements addressing economic and security concerns of ethnic Russians arising from Chinese migration and border disputes, but at the same time restrain potential agents of ethnic mobilization and accommodate Chinese traders, investors, and businesses. However, if the economic benefits to the political elites decrease, this balancing strategy could quickly degenerate into anti-Chinese activism, with the political leaders having few incentives to restrain ethnic mobilization and numerous incentives to benefit from politicizing migration and ethnic differences.

Estimating the scale of revenues available to public officials in Primorye is especially important in determining economic incentives for ethnic activism or restraint. First, economists analyzing Russia's post-Soviet transitions generally agree that cronyism and corruption are endemic.[56] In addition, as Judith Thornton argues, corruption and cronyism have evolved into institutional traps in post-Soviet Russia in the sense that they have become "stable institutionalized norms which impose high transaction costs on an economy" and "may come to dominate other institutional arrangements." These traps emerge when policymakers "are able to block or distort changes in the rules of the game that threaten to reduce the value of their existing control rights"—which was particularly the case under the Nazdratenko administration in Primorye.[57] Political uncertainty resulting in short-term time horizons reinforces the propensity for corruption.[58] In addition, a number of studies have shown that material interests account for a larger variation in political orientation of elites than do symbolic interests.[59]

Although most people in Primorye accept it as an axiom that government officials regulating cross-border trade receive "additional revenues," systematic and specific information is lacking. However, a pilot survey of 100 Chinese migrant traders in Primorskii krai in the winter of 1999 provides circumstantial evidence supporting this popular axiom. In answer to the question, "Who do you pay for your security?" government officials were named by 62 percent, police by 80 percent, border guards by 55 percent, and transportation service providers by 60 percent of Chinese respondents.[60] In other words, without payments for "security" to officials, most Chinese nationals would not be doing business in Primorye.

The business weekly *Zolotoi Rog* reported in April 1999 that thirteen new Chinese markets and two wholesale trade bases opened in Vladivostok, operating efficiently but illegally. The same article cited sources saying that thirty Chinese families had been trading from $400,000 to $500,000 worth of fruits and vegetables at the wholesale food products base at Fadeeva Street in Vladivostok without registering their businesses or paying taxes. And in Ussuriisk, where city revenues increased threefold as a result of Chinese trade in the late 1990s, the local customs office, fearing a decrease in the customs income, blocked the city sanitation department from inspecting the quality of Chinese goods stored at the customs warehouse.[61]

SECURITY, ECONOMIC INCENTIVES, AND ATTITUDES TOWARD CHINESE NATIONALS IN PRIMORSKII KRAI, 1991–98

The data shows that the overall economic impact on Primorye of legal cross-border transactions with China increased in 1993–96, then declined in 1996–98. This decline of legally available revenues coincided with the previously mentioned decrease in public financing of government agencies in Primorye in dollar terms. These trends are likely to have contradictory effects on attitudes by Russians toward PRC migrants. On the one hand, one would expect larger numbers of Russians, both among the elites and the general public, to become disillusioned about the possibility of economic conditions improving as a result of exchanges with China. Frustrated expectations would then open the gates for more negative attitudes toward Chinese nationals, for rising nationalist activism by those seeking political power, and for increasing public hostility toward Chinese migrants. On the other hand, the same economic trends may result in public demands for greater accommodation of Chinese nationals and policies that would enhance cross-border economic opportunities. Given these contradictory motivations, the political elites could also be expected to play a two-level game by vowing to prevent an alleged "creeping Chinafication" of Primorye, yet also by increasing restraint of radical nationalist groups and promoting regulated cross-border exchanges (to maximize payoffs).

Surveys conducted by the Public Opinion Research Center at the Institute of History, Archeology, and Ethnography of the Peoples of the Far East provide descriptive statistics for evaluating shifts in attitudes of Primorye residents toward China and Chinese nationals (see Table 13.2). The surveys were based on random population sampling stratified by age, income, education, occupation, and location. Changes in public opinion from 1991–94 (when economic benefits from cross-border exchanges increased) to 1997–98 (when these benefits decreased) are summarized in the far right-hand column in Table 13.2. Scores twice exceeding the estimated average margin of error for the surveys are considered significant and displayed in bold type. The following trends appear noteworthy:

(1) Close to half of respondents expected that Russia would lose territory to Chinese expansion in the region. Asked in 1998 how this Chinese expansion would take place, 16 percent of respondents said it would result from bilateral negotiations between Moscow and Beijing, and 12 percent expected China to take Russian territory by force. The largest number (28 percent) of respondents, however, said territory would be lost due to a "peaceful infiltration" of Primorye by Chinese nationals. The questionnaire defined "peaceful infiltration" as migrant labor, trade, tourism, and marriage.

(2) The number of Primorye residents who liked the presence of Chinese nationals remained under 5 percent, and 4-percent fewer respondents (close to the single margin of error value) approved of visits by Chinese for "specific purposes," defined as migrant labor in industry and agriculture. Indirectly, this low acceptance of nonethnic Russians in Primorye is confirmed by the low number of respondents supporting restoration of historic ethnic Korean settlements.

(3) Chinese occupation of Primorye was viewed as more likely in 1998 than in 1994 by respondents with vocational-technical education (mostly blue-collar workers), high-income recipients, owners of private businesses, and the military. At the same time, fewer government employees and people with higher education believed Primorye would lose territory to China. Similarly, lower levels of education and higher levels of income translated into significantly larger opposition to Chinese presence in Primorskii krai (even for short visits). These results are consistent with the contradictory impact of changing economic trends in 1993–98 that brought about a decrease in benefits available to the general public while increasing the utility of cross-border trade to government officials (most of whom also have higher education).

(4) The significant (13-percent) increase from 1994 to 1998 in the share of respondents who opposed their relatives marrying Chinese nationals coincided with an even more sizeable (22-percent) drop in the number of respondents who considered such a decision to be their relatives' personal issue. These numbers warn about the growing racial antagonisms among Primorye residents through the growing perception of Chinese nationals as "ethnic others" vis-à-vis the Russians. This perception of "otherness," in turn, is likely to result from a combination of cross-border security dilemmas and the commitment problem.

(5) Concurrently, the number of people who considered mass deportation of ethnic minorities by Stalin as the "manifestation of the leader's wisdom" doubled, comprising one-fifth of survey respondents. Thus, latent racial antagonisms in Primorye increased from 1994 to 1998 in synch with public support for massive state violence against ethnic minorities.

(6) Perceptions of "typical characteristics" of ethnic Chinese migrants also reflect increasing potential for interethnic hostility in Primorye. From 1994 to 1998, few Russians saw Chinese migrants as honest, polite, and responsible. While viewed as increasingly hard-working and entrepreneurial, Chinese migrants were also viewed as more aggressive and sly. These trends are consistent with the logic of conflict escalation under relative economic deprivation.

Table 13.2 Attitudes toward China and Migrants from PRC
in Primorskii Krai, 1991–98 (N=number of respondents)

	1991 (N=1610)	1992 (N=1200)	1994 (N=869)	1997 (N=620)	1998 (N=522)	1991–94 vs 1997–98
Q1: Chinese expansion/loss of of territory to neighbors is likely						
Agree			45		47	2
Disagree			26		23	-3
Hard to tell			26		28	2
Q2: Attitude to presence of Chinese nationals in Primorye						
Approve			5		4	-1
Approve for specific purposes			53		49	-4
Don't approve			33		38	5
Hard to say			6		6	0
Q3: Attitude to relatives marrying Chinese nationals						
Approve			1		2	1
Don't approve			33		46	**13**
Personal issue			58		36	**-22**
Hard to say			4		9	5
Q4: Places in Primorye where ethnic Koreans settle can be considered traditionally Korean						
Yes	9			5	7	-3
No	67			60	56	**-9**
Don't know	22			34	35	**12.5**
Q5: Mass deportation of ethnic minorities (Koreans, Crimean Tatars, Chechens, Volga Germans, etc.) was:						
Act of tyranny and lawlessness	65			56	61	-6.5
Manifestation of leaders' wisdom	10			18	20	**9**
Hard to say	25			25	18	-3.5

Table 13.2 Attitudes toward China and Migrants
from PRC in Primorskii Krai, 1991–98 (continued)

	1991 (N=1610)	1992 (N=1200)	1994 (N=869)	1997 (N=620)	1998 (N=522)	1991–94 vs 1997–98
Q6: Most typical characteristics of ethnic Chinese individuals						
Hard working		50		83	70	**26.5**
Aggressive		5		20	27	**18.5**
Selfish		5		5	7	1
Entrepreneurial		17		34	33	**16.5**
Generous				1	1	0
Responsible				8	5	-3
Savers				13	16	3
Honest				4	4	0
Polite				7	4	-3
Sly				40	43	3

Source: Institute of History, Archeology, and Ethnography of the Peoples of the Far East (IHAE), "Sotstium Vladivostoka: Osen–91, 92, 94, 97, 98" (Vladivostok opinion survey results: autumn 1991, 92, 94, 97, 98), Russian Academy of Sciences, Far Eastern Branch, 1998.

Economic Incentives and Local Elites' Perceptions of the "Chinese Factor"

In interviews with political and business elites in Primorskii krai in May 1999, I observed a distinct differentiation in responses to the open-ended question: How do you assess the impact of Chinese migration in Primorskii krai? The answer depended on the person's economic incentives for cooperation with China. Those who benefited or expected to benefit economically from cross-border economic interactions focused primarily on business and trade logistics issues in their responses. Those who did not benefit or did not expect to benefit economically from cross-border interactions focused primarily on demographic issues and border security. Within the first group, responses differed depending on whether the individuals' economic incentives for cooperation were increasing, stagnant, or decreasing.

Case 1: Increasing Economic Incentives

Mikhail Vetrik, director of the Ussuriisk Chinese trade center, prefaced his response with an accusation that the United States deliberately destroyed the Soviet Union and brought Russia to its knees and with an openly expressed dislike for ethnic Chinese "infiltration" of the region. However, for most of the interview, he spoke with pride about the expansion of his Chinese trade center:

> In 1996 there was a swamp here, and now we have a twenty-hectare trading area in its place with five hostels, six residence halls, loading-unloading facilities, a maintenance service, a passport registration service, a police station, an international telephone exchange, new public restrooms, a new septic system, and Chinese, Korean, and Russian restaurants. We generate 10–11 percent of tax revenues for the city of Ussuriisk (population 160,000), somewhere between $750,000 and $1,000,000 in 1998. We expect to generate at least the same amount of taxes for the city in 1999.

Vetrik pointed out that Chinese businesspeople were beginning to trust the new trade center—evidenced by their investment in the karaoke bar, a casino, and a table tennis facility. While acknowledging the threat of potential ethnic clashes, Vetrik favored increased contacts and showed that he was ready to deal with conflicts: "About two years ago we had up to ten clashes a year, a lot of them between Chinese and Koreans, some involving local Russians. I intervened in these conflicts personally, as an arbitrator and a mediator, and I saw to it that disputed issues were resolved and the parties to the conflict shook hands in the end." With Russian factories idle and salaries unpaid, Vetrik concluded, it was time to forget about nationalism: "Our back is against the wall. We've got to help these traders."[62]

Case 2: Stagnant Economic Incentives

Yelena Moroz is deputy director of the Nakhodka-based Yuan Dong company which, owns a massive trade center known locally as the "Chinese Wall"—a two-storied white structure with a pagoda-shaped roof housing fifty-one stores and stretching for about half a mile. Born and raised in Harbin, of mixed Russian and Chinese descent, Moroz came to Nakhodka in 1991 to capitalize on trade opportunities with China. But by the time the "Chinese Wall" was opened in 1998, the Primorskii krai government had tightened regulations on border crossings and a mix of local and federal laws had imposed higher tax and registration costs on cross-border interactions. Committed to playing by the rules, Moroz was frustrated: "We had thirty-seven requests for renting store space at the beginning of 1997, but government officials have been a destructive force. Now we don't have Chinese traders in the whole shopping complex."

Nevertheless, the "Chinese Wall" center rents space to local Russian traders, many of whom purchase their inventory in the Chinese city of Suifenhe across the border—large handwritten ads for sourcing trips were posted at the entrance to several of the stores in the trade center. Moroz still sees cross-border trade as a vehicle to economic development: "Look at Suifenhe—it used to be a village, and now it's a thriving city." Moroz would like the Primorskii and Russian governments to abstain from harsh restrictions on trade and from publicizing China's past territorial claims. Speaking from the perspective of an ethnic Chinese person raised in China, she said: "Seeing a lot of articles in the local press condemning China's actions at Damanskii Island in 1969 and praising Russian troops is extremely unpleasant to Chinese nationals." Similarly, Moroz was upset by graffiti on the center's walls that reads: "Chinese are treacherous scum!" *(Kitaitsy—lokhi)*. She would like to see less nationalist rhetoric and more effort by the local and federal governments to reduce cross-border transaction costs for Chinese businesspeople.[63]

Case 3: Declining Economic Incentives

Prior to his appointment as President Yeltsin's representative in Primorye, Vladimir Ignatenko served as the mayor of Spassk-Dalnii and experienced diminishing economic incentives from cross-border cooperation with China. In 1988, just when the Soviet economy started opening up to the world, Ignatenko signed a sister city agreement with neighboring Mishan. Chinese laborers joined the local silicate brick plant and housing construction trust. Ignatenko attributes their input to an increase in housing construction in Spassk-Dalnii from 14,000 square meters in 1985 to 35,000 square meters of floor space in 1994. Local agriculture, he added, benefited a lot from Chinese farmers who started producing soy and vegetables. Official and cultural exchanges flourished. The local government made estimates for economic growth based on increasing exchanges. But things started to change after 1991: "In 1989–90, we had good business interactions, but then we gradually began to notice that protocols of intent that we had signed with Chinese counterparts were left unfulfilled. Beijing's support for our joint venture projects declined. In fact, none of the planned projects were implemented after 1991." On the Russian side, the major problem, according to Ignatenko, was rapid price liberalization that led to multiple increases in electricity prices. "City and county budgets had a meltdown. We had no capital to invest in joint projects with China. The then-newly opened border crossing at Turii Rog is still unfinished—the construction of the hotel and recreation facilities stopped. I just talked with the new official there in charge of cargo transit, and he told me that shipments had gone down almost to nothing, although the road is in good shape."[64]

While focusing primarily on economic issues, Ignatenko did not pin hopes on expanding trade with China. Unlike Vetrik, who sounded upbeat on cross-border trade, and unlike Moroz, who sounded hopeful, Ignatenko sounded cautious and concerned. Dashed expectations of economic growth resulting from trade and joint ventures led him to support tougher regulation of Chinese visits to Primorskii krai and bank on domestic producers and the Russian market. Russia's general economic decline, meanwhile, made Ignatenko think that the krai's proximity to China posed a long-term security problem: "If we let our economy deteriorate and collapse, then with Chinese migration we may end up with a problem similar to the problem of Israel. We'll be okay, as long as the proportion of Chinese nationals does not exceed one-third of the local population, but if it does, we will be in trouble." [65]

Case 4: Lack of Economic Incentives for Interacting with Chinese Nationals

Local political notables who derived no personal or organizational benefits from cross-border economic exchanges with China focused their responses to the question about Chinese migration almost exclusively on security and demographic issues. Anatolii Kolupaev, Primorskii krai spokesman for the Liberal Democratic Party of Russia of extreme nationalist Vladimir Zhirinovsky, said his constituency has no intentions to do business with China and that he was never involved in such business. The LPDR, he said, would raise anti-Chinese themes in its 1999 Russian Duma campaign, focusing on "Chinese domination of local markets," "illegal immigration," and border demarcation, "especially the threat of China getting access to the ocean at the mouth of the Tumen River." Kolupaev said he believes these issues must be publicized, "otherwise, we are going to wake up one day and everyone around us will be squint-eyed." [66]

Vladimir Tsypliaev, first secretary of the Vladivostok committee of the Communist Party of the Russian Federation, also sounded alarmist. Representing a constituency similarly lacking sizeable benefits from cross-border economic exchanges, he started his response by saying: "Ah, of course, you in America would love to see Russia and China clash, but we are not going to allow it. This is not to say that Chinese infiltration is not a problem. A lot of these tourists and traders are spies, they are out to get our military secrets and make super-precise topographical maps of Primorskii territory. They have secret settlements in the north of the krai and they intend to gradually settle here until they de facto occupy our territory and make us face a fait accompli." Tsypliaev said, however, that the communists would not push Chinese issues in their 1999 State Duma campaign—but they would support former Governor Nazdratenko's tough stand, because "it's the right thing." [67]

Vitalii Poluianov, Chieftain of the Ussuri Cossack Host, started his response with two broad claims: "The Chinese are trying to break through by hook and by crook. Chinafication will lead to the same problems here that they now have in Yugoslavia. The Asians would smile at you, but they respect only force." Poluianov then spoke with pride about Ussuri Cossacks' participation in suppressing the Boxer rebellion in China and said that his goal is to raise the number of Ussuri Cossacks from the current 5,000 to 45,000, "as we had before the [1917] revolution." He then showed me the map delineating the boundaries of his Khasan Free Economic Zone project, which he wants the Primorskii government to support. The word "free" refers to the total exclusion of Chinese nationals and reflects Poluianov's emphasis on the threat of relative deprivation: "If we don't work well, the Chinese will infiltrate the area and ultimately annex a 30–40 kilometer strip of territory along the border. The yellow peril is rising."[68]

POLICY IMPLICATIONS FOR THE UNITED STATES

Despite the nationalistic rhetoric from many quarters, Primorskii krai's key political players so far have strong incentives to restrain anti-Chinese activism. Nevertheless, if economic benefits to them from cross-border cooperation fail to increase—as appears plausible given a stalemate on projects such as the Tumen River free trade area and the incentives to boost political ratings through xenophobic campaigning—perceptions of geopolitical and demographic vulnerability are likely to grow stronger. Interviews and opinion data suggest that Russian officials and the public exaggerate the threat of Chinafication, which in turn suggests that Russian government and society are unprepared for multicultural accommodation of Chinese migrants. At the same time, long-term demographic and economic factors will continue to necessitate an increased presence of Chinese nationals in Primorye, and in the Far East in general.

The impact of Vladimir Putin's rise to power on this situation is ambiguous. On the one hand, the Putin administration has increased funding and political support for military and security agencies, moved to curtail the powers of regional governors, and emphasized Moscow's commitment to a strategic partnership with China. To the extent that these moves increase Russia's control over cross-border traffic, curtail nationalist campaigns of local politicians, and generate greater security cooperation with Beijing, perceptions of vulnerability associated with cross-border migration will be reduced. On the other hand, the conduct of the Chechen campaign and lack of measures to crack down on expressions of ethnic hatred and xenophobia directed at ethnic minorities under Putin boost a political climate that rules out large-scale measures to promote multiculturalism, diversity, and interethnic tolerance, especially in regions with disproportionately strong nationalist constituencies. Thus, while short-term improvements in security are likely, the challenges of accommodating Chinese migrants over the long-term will persist.

The U.S. government has viable instruments in place to increase Russian elites' incentives for cooperation with China and for greater accommodation of Chinese migrant workers and traders. One such instrument is the U.S. West Coast–Russian Far East Ad Hoc Working Group, currently operating within the framework of the successor to the Gore-Chernomyrdin Commission and focusing on international projects at the junction of Russia, China, Korea, and Japan. The usefulness of this policy instrument will increase if the forum engages key economic and government actors from China, Korea, and Japan. Another instrument is APEC, through which the United States can facilitate more active and broader engagement of Russian federal and regional officials and of the business community in multilateral economic development projects, including free trade zones, production sharing in natural resource extraction, and infrastructure projects. Engagement in these institutions is also likely to lessen currently strong incentives of Chinese businesses to pursue short-term rent-extraction and asset-stripping strategies in the Russian Far East.

A more active U.S. role in forging multilateral institutional collaboration among the Ad Hoc Working Group, APEC, United Nations Development Program, and other organizations would also create more opportunities for inter-elite dialogue and problem-solving in the area.

Since economic development, migration, and interethnic issues are currently at the heart of evolving relations between Russia and China, any positive role that the United States can play on these issues will enhance its political leverage in maintaining security in East Asia. Greater constructive involvement now—which can be achieved at a relatively low cost through existing institutions—will help avoid future and potentially higher costs of dealing with any destabilizing effects of interstate disputes and/or intrastate violent conflict in that region.

NOTES

Research for this chapter was partially funded by the National Council for Eurasian and East European Research. Tamara Troyakova, senior research fellow at the Institute of History, Archeology, and Ethnography of the Peoples of the Far East at the Far Eastern Branch of the Russian Academy of Sciences assisted me greatly by arranging and conducting interviews in Vladivostok in May 1999, gathering socioeconomic statistical data, collecting local newspaper articles on Chinese migration, and sharing a databank of news stories on Chinese-Russian economic interactions in the Russian Far East. Yevgenii Plaksen, director of the public opinion research center at the same institute, spent countless hours going over surveys conducted from 1991 to 1998 and selecting data on issues pivotal to this project. Jacek Wasilewski, research assistant and graduate student in public administration at Appalachian State University, provided invaluable support with library searches, news article databank management, literature reviews, and data entry. He also set up a web page on Chinese migration in the Russian Far East, where additional data and material can be located at <www.acs.appstate.edu/dept/ps-cj/faculty/russia/>. I would also like to thank Charles Zeigler and Judith Thornton for their comments on two drafts of this paper.

1. Viktor Larin, *Kitai i Dal'nii Vostok Rossii v pervoi polovine 90-kh: Problemy regional'nogo vzaimodeistviia* (Vladivostok: Dal'nauka, 1998), 72, 74–75.

2. Yevgenii Nazdratenko, *I vsia Rossiia za spinoi* ...[And all of Russia is behind my back...] (Vladivostok, 1999), 20–24.

3. *Rossiiskaia gazeta,* July 10, 1999, 4, quoted in Elizabeth Wishnick, "Russia in Asia and Asians in Russia," *SAIS Review* 20 (winter–spring 2000):98.

4. Primorskii krai's indexed economic development was estimated as the highest for the Russian Far East at 3.0 (with Kamchatka = 1.0), followed by Khabarovsk at 2.5, in Elisa Miller and Soula Stephanopoulos, eds., *The Russian Far East: A Business Reference Guide* (Seattle, Wash.: Russian Far East Update, 1997). Chinese migration levels, demographic and economic trends, cross-border trade, and perceptions of migration by local Russians in Primorye are similar to Khabarovskii krai and Amurskaia oblast, as evidenced by reports presented at the roundtable "Prospects of the Far East: The Chinese Factor," Vladivostok, Institute of History, Archeology, and Ethnography (IHAE) of the Far Eastern Branch, Russian Academy of Sciences, June 28, 1999.

5. Galina Vitkovskaya, Zhanna Zayonchkovskaya, and Kathleen Newland, "Chinese Migration into Russia," in *Rapprochement or Rivalry: Russia-China Relations in a Changing Asia,* Sherman W. Garnett, ed. (Washington, D.C.: Carnegie Endowment for International Peace, 2000), 361.

6. Tyan Czan, "Kitaitsy v immigratsii," *Rossiia i ATR,* no. 2 (1994):82–92.

7. "Prospects of the Far East: The Chinese Factor," IHAE round table. Vilya Gelbras report.

8. TORU Press Service, *Spravka o migratsii grazhdan Kitaia v Rossiiu i tret'i strany cherez ee terriroriiu v 1998–99 gg.*

9. *Vladivostok,* January 6, 1996, quoted in Larin, *Kitai i Dal'nii Vostok Rossii,* 106.

10. Sergei Pushkarev, head of the Federal Migration Service of the Russian Federation for Primorskii krai, author's interview, Vladivostok, May 20, 1999; Mikhail Vetrik, director, Chinese trade center, Ussuriisk, author's interview, Ussuriisk, May 26, 1999.

11. Goskomstat Rossiiskoi Federatsii, *Primorskii kraevoi komitet gosudarstvennoi statistiki,* no. 19, sv. 39, May 28, 1999.

12. Confirmed in Lt. Gen. P. Tarasenko, "Migratsionnye protsessy, ikh vliianie na kriminogennuiu obstanovku v krae i o dopolnitelnykh merakh po uporiadocheniiu prebyvanniia i osedaniia inostrannykh grazhdan na territorii Primorskogo kraia," report by the Pacific Regional Administration of the Russian Border Service (TORU), Vladivostok, July 1999,1–2.

13. Mikhail Vetrik, author's interview, Ussuriisk, May 26, 1999.

14. Sergei Pushkarev, author's interview, Vladivostok, May 20, 1999.

15. Clifford Geertz, *The Interpretation of Cultures,* quoted in Daniel Treisman, "Russia's 'Ethnic Revival': The Separatist Activism of Regional Leaders in a Postcommunist Order," *World Politics* 49, no. 2 (January 1997):216.

16. In this view, intellectuals are the first to realize such threats and to activate nationalist symbols that mobilize public support and lead to collective action directed at another ethnic group. See Harold R. Issacs, *Idols of the Tribe: Group Identity and Political Change* (New York: Harper and Row, 1975); and Anthony D. Smith, *The Ethnic Origins of Nations* (New York: Basil Blackwell, 1986). For a practical and politically influential exemplar of essentialism, see Robert D. Kaplan, *Balkan Ghosts: A Journey through History* (New York: St. Martin's Press, 1993).

17. Peter Kirkow, *Russia's Provinces: Authoritarian Transformation versus Local Autonomy* (New York: St. Martin's Press, 1998).

18. See Benedict Anderson, *Imagined Communities: Reflections on the Origins and Spread of Nationalism* (London: Verso, 1983). John Chipman, "Managing the Politics of Parochialism," in *Ethnic Conflict and International Security,* ed. Michael E. Brown (Princeton, N.J.: Princeton University Press, 1993), 240, argues that pathological social systems rapidly lead to "total" ethnic violence, since "everyone is automatically labeled a combatant—by the identity they possess—even if they are not."

19. Stephen van Evera, "Nationalism and the Causes of War," in *Nationalism and Nationalities in the New Europe,* Charles A. Kupchan (Ithaca, N.Y.: Cornell University Press, 1995), 146–47.

20. Barry R. Posen, "The Security Dilemma and Ethnic Conflict," in *Ethnic Conflict and International Security,* ed. Brown, 103–25.

21. James D. Fearon, "Commitment Problems and the Spread of Ethnic Conflict," in *The International Spread of Ethnic Conflict: Fear, Diffusion, and Escalation,* David Lake and Donald Rothchild, eds. (Princeton, N.J.: Princeton University Press, 1998), 107–27.

22. Stephen van Evera, "Nationalism and the Causes of War"; and Jack Snyder and Robert Jervis, "Civil War and the Security Dilemma," in *Civil Wars, Insecurity, and Intervention,* Barbara F. Walter and Jack Snyder, eds. (New York: Columbia University Press, 1999), 15–37.

23. Robert Jervis, "Cooperation under the Security Dilemma," *World Politics* 30, no. 2 (January 1978).

24. Rui J. P. Figueiredo, Jr. and Barry R. Weingast, "The Rationality of Fear: Political Opportunism and Ethnic Conflict," in *Civil Wars, Insecurity, and Intervention,* Walter and Snyder, eds., 261–302.

25. T. R. Gurr, *Why Men Rebel* (Princeton, N.J.: Princeton University Press, 1970); Edward L. Azar and John W. Burton, *International Conflict Resolution: Theory and Practice* (Lynn Reinner, 1986).

26. Lake and Rothchild, eds., *The International Spread of Ethnic Conflict: Fear, Diffusion, and Escalation*; Milica Zarkovic Bookman, *Economic Decline and Nationalism in the Balkans* (New York: St. Martin's, 1994).

27. Donald L. Horowitz, *Ethnic Groups in Conflict* (Berkeley: University of California Press, 1985).

28. Primorskii and Khabarovskii krais, Jewish autonomous oblast, and Amurskaia oblast.

29. P. Ia. Baklanov, "Geograficheskiie, sotsial'no-ekonomicheskie, i geopoliticheskiie factory migratsii kitaiskogo naseleniia na iug Dal'nego Vostoka" (paper presented at the roundtable "Prospects for the Far East Region: The Chinese Factor," IHAE, June 28, 1999, 3).

30. Ibid.

31. Goskomstat Rossii, Primorskii kraevoi komitet gosudarstvennoi statistiki, *Chislennost' naseleniia Primorskogo kraia v razreze naselennykh punktov* (Vladivostok, 1999).

32. "Zakon Primorskogo kraia o kraevom biudzhete na 1995 god," *Vedomosti Dumy Primorskogo kraia*, no. 8 (1995):4–21; "Zakon Primorskogo kraia o kraevom biudzhete na 1996 god," *Vedomosti Dumy Primorskogo kraia*, no. 23 (1996):2–25; "Zakon Primorskogo kraia o kraevom biudzhete na 1997 god," *Vedomosti Dumy Primorskogo kraia*, no. 44 (1997):2–25; "Zakon Primorskogo kraia o kraevom biudzhete na 1998 god," *Vedomosti Dumy Primorskogo kraia*, no. 13 (1998):2–37. Ruble values were converted into dollar values at half-year average exchange rate increments, with the January 1998 three-digit ruble redenomination taken into account.

33. Andrei Kopaev, senior investigator, "Tigr" department, State Environmental Committee for Primorskii krai, author's interview, Vladivostok, May 25, 1999.

34. Lt. Col. Viktor Plotnikov, deputy head of Primorskii krai's Visa and Registration Department of Russia's Interior Ministry, author's interview, Vladivostok, OVIR headquarters, June 2, 1999.

35. Vladimir Ignatenko, author's interview, Vladivostok, Primorskii krai Duma, June 1, 1999.

36. Iurii Shevchuk, counsel to the Ussuriisk oblast government, author's interview, Ussuriisk city government, May 26, 1999.

37. Lt. Gen. P. Tarasenko, "Migratsionnye protsessy," 5.

38. Ibid., 1.

39. Vladimir Ignatenko, "Spravka. K voprosu o demarkatsii Rossiisko-kitaiskoi granitsy v Primorskom krae" [Memorandum. On the issue of demarcation of the Russian-Chinese border in Primorskii krai], Office of the Plenipotentiary Representative of the President of the Russian Federation in Primorskii krai, May 1996, 4, 7.

40. Sherman W. Garnett, "Limited Partnership," in *Rapprochement or Rivalry*, ed. Garnett, 25.

41. Charles Ziegler, private communication. Gilbert Rozman, "Turning Fortresses into Free Trade Zones," in *Rapprochement or Rivalry*, ed. Garnett, 193.

42. Rozman, "Turning Fortresses into Free Trade Zones," 5–6; Vladimir Ignatenko, author's interview, Primorskii krai government, June 2, 1999.

43. David L. Laitin and James D. Fearon, "Explaining Interethnic Cooperation," *American Political Science Review* (December 1996); Carnegie Commission on Preventing Deadly Conflict, *Preventing Deadly Conflict: Final Report* (New York: Carnegie Commission on Preventing Deadly Conflict, 1997), 3.

44. Two major exceptions happened in the border town of Pogranichnyi. At the local central market, I witnessed a heated row between a Chinese trader and a Russian customer (a young male who was not sober). The Russian customer accused the trader (with numerous expletives) of selling inferior products, threw some of the wares displayed in the stand at the Chinese national, and tried to take the Chinese person's peanuts. Another Chinese trader came to help and slapped the Russian customer forcefully on the hand. The two traders removed the peanuts from the customer's hand by force. The second episode involved Russian railroad security officials who stopped a Chinese woman near the public latrines by the railway station and demanded a fine for unauthorized walking on the railroad track. The Russian officials were armed, and they removed the Chinese woman's passport. A dozen or so members of the Chinese tourist delegation (from Harbin) surrounded the security officials and passionately argued the woman's case. After a heated argument, several members of the Chinese delegation went to settle the case in a building housing the Special Security Detachment for the Protection of the Far Eastern Railways.

45. Goskomstat Rossiiskoi Federatsii, Primorskii kraevoi komitet gosudarstvennoi statistiki, *Sotsial'naia sfera gorodov i raionov Primorskogo kraia* (Vladivostok, 1998), 78, 80–81.

46. Author's interviews with Viktor Poluianov, cossack chieftain, Vladivostok, May 31, 1999.

47. Larin, *Kitai i Dal'nii Vostok Rossii,* 113.

48. Yevgenii Plaksen, author's interview, Vladivostok, May 22, 1999.

49. "Chinese Migration in Primorskii Krai: An Assessment of Its Scale, Socioeconomic Impact, and Opportunities for Corruption," Working Paper, National Council for Eurasian and East European Research, Washington, D.C., 1999.

50. Goskomstat Rossiiskoi Federatsii, Primorskii kraevoi komitet gosudarstvennoi statistiki, no. 19, sv. 39, May 28, 1999.

51. Sergei Zubov, chief of the "Tigr" department, State Environmental Committee for Primorskii krai, author's interview, Vladivostok, May 25, 1999.

52. *Rezul'taty kontrol'no-inspetsionnoi deiatel'nosti otdela "Tigr" Goskomekologii Primorskogo kraia za period s aprelia 1994 po dekabr' 1998 gg,* comp., B.I. Litvinov, Deputy head of the "Tigr" deparment, 1999.

53. Ibid. Also, author's interview, Vladivostok, May 25, 1999.

54. Goskomstat Rossiiskoi Federatsii, Primorskii kraevoi komitet gosudarstvennoi statistiki, No. 19sv-39, May 28, 1999.

55. Andrei Kopaev, author's interview, Vladivostok, May 25, 1999.

56. Anders Aslund, "Russia's Collapse," *Foreign Affairs* (September/October, 1999):64–77; Clifford G. Gaddy and Barry W. Ickes, "Russia's Virtual Economy," *Foreign Affairs* (September/October, 1998):53–67.

57. On institutional traps, see Judith Thornton, "Has Russian Reform Failed?" The National Bureau of Asian Research, working paper, 1999 (www.nbr.org/members/thornton.pdf). For a case study of political elites' ability to block or distort economic reform in Primorye, see Kirkow, *Russia's Provinces: Authoritarian Transformation versus Local Autonomy.*

58. Stephen E. Hanson, "Breaking the Vicious Cycle of Uncertainty in Postcommunist Russia," Program on New Approaches to Russian Security, Policy Memo no. 40 (1999).

59. Seymour Martin Lipset, *Political Man: The Social Bases of Politics* (Garden City, N.Y.: Doubleday Books, 1963); W. Lance Bennett, *The Political Mind and the Political Environment: An Investigation of Public Opinion and Political Consciousness* (Lexington, Mass.: D.C. Heath and Co., 1975); Horowitz, *Ethnic Groups in Conflict*, 132.

60. Institut Istorii, Arkheologii i Etnografii Narodov Dal'nego Vostoka DVO RAN, "Migratsiia inostrantsev v Primorskom krae i vo Vladivostoke. Anketa dlia kitaiskikh torgovtsev," (Vladivostok, 1999), pilot survey results, 5–6.

61. "Administration Does Not Know How to Resolve the 'Chinese Question' in Primor'e," *Zolotoi Rog*, April 1, 1999.

62. Mikhail Vetnik, author's interview, Ussuriisk, May 26, 1999.

63. Yelena Moroz, author's interview, Chinese Wall center, Nakhodka, May 27, 1999.

64. Vladimir Ignatenko, author's interview, Primorskii krai government, Vladivostok, June 2, 1999.

65. Ibid.

66. Anatollii Kolupaev, author's interview, Primorskii krai headquarters, Liberal Democratic Party of Russia, Vladivostok, June 2, 1999.

67. Vladimir Tsypliaev, author's interview, Primorskii krai headquarters, Communist Party of the Russian Federation, Vladivostok, June 2, 1999.

68. Vitalii Poluianov, author's interview, Headquarters, Ussuri Cossack Host, Vladivostok, May 31, 1999.

14

Peculiarities of the Region's Political Mentality

Sergei Chugrov

The past ten years of Russia's political development demonstrate that the process of regionalization plays an increasingly important role.[1] Among different challenges to Russia's territorial integrity, one of the most obvious is that of separatism. This is especially true for peripheral regions. It is clear that the Russian Far East has become politically more remote from the center, and its regions have acquired specific political preferences characterized by gradual movement toward stronger autonomy. Far Eastern regions have a huge potential to give birth to separatist movements based on strong territorial identity, protest against injustice, decline of the economy, and exploitation of local resources by the center.

This strong territorial identity and a feeling of being exploited by Moscow fuel such movements. The separatist trends also are nurtured by an energy crisis and wage arrears (some companies are a year overdue in paying their employees), which have made the conflict with Moscow more spectacular and even dramatic. Despite abundant forest and mineral resources, the region is on its knees. Forty percent of the population of Primorye lives below the poverty level of $36 a month.[2] These tendencies may result in the emergence of local criminal regimes supported by their own armed structures and fed by smuggling and the sale of mineral resources, land, and armaments. If Russia's leadership fails to introduce fundamental changes in economic and federal policies in regard to the Far East, the region may turn into a large zone of instability and potential turmoil spilling over into neighboring states.

The federation subjects of the Russian Far East encompass only 5.1 million voters, or about 5 percent of the electorate. In comparison, Moscow and St. Petersburg account for about 10.3 million voters, or 10 percent of the electorate; and Central Russia accounts for 16.6 million voters, or 15 percent of the electorate.[3] However, the Far East plays an especially important role in the Russian electoral process since these regions report initial results on the day of election. Since persistent patterns of voting have been formed at the RFE, one is able to predict the final results using specific coefficients.

This chapter examines the distinctive electoral patterns in the RFE—in particular the population's nonconformist mentality and difficult political choices—in light of the Russian parliamentary elections of 1993, 1995, and 1999.[4] While some researchers are inclined to speak about "apolitical" or "anti-political" sentiments of the Far Eastern population—pointing, among other things, to low voter turnout there[5]—this nonconformity is not strong enough to challenge the integrity of the Russian state. Some Far Eastern territories are deeply concerned about impending threats and are enthusiastically looking with new hope toward Moscow.

The research is based on a statistical analysis of data for three State Duma (lower house of Russia's Federal Assembly) elections, which took place by party list.[6] The analysis examined regional variation in support for parties and candidates whose platforms present alternative visions for Russia's development. For comparative reasons, the analysis embraced from 87 to 89 subjects of the Russian Federation that took part in national elections, with special emphasis on the Far East.[7]

Half of the State Duma's 450 deputies are elected by the plurality system in single-mandate districts. The remaining 225 seats are filled by a proportional voting system in which voters choose a party, not a specific candidate, to represent them. The proportional voting is carried out with Russia serving as one huge electoral district (called the "general federal district").[8] An electoral threshold of 5 percent is imposed, partly in an effort to encourage very small parties to coalesce.

The single-mandate district elections and elections to the Federation Council were omitted from the analysis, since they are not held according to party lists and do not show variations in political preferences in a way that could be compared across regions. Similar problems emerge in the case of the presidential elections for two major reasons: first, while electing a president, in whom enormous powers are concentrated, people vote on fundamental issues (surveys indicate that the general population considers these elections to be a choice between communism and democracy, the plan and the market); and second, personal qualities of presidential hopefuls may overshadow the attractiveness of their platforms and slogans.

To find a common denominator for Russia's regions, factor analysis was used for two purposes: first, to single out the key dimensions characterizing the Far Eastern political mentality using data from elections by region; and second, to use these dimensions to demonstrate the principal fault lines (i.e., the relative balance of support for or opposition to socioeconomic reforms; and centrifugal and centripetal tendencies).

THE 1993 ELECTION

On December 12, 1993, Russia held its first truly multiparty parliamentary elections, which appeared to be an important element of the effort to form a new political order to replace one that had been paralyzed by persistent conflict between the executive and legislative branches.[9] These elections, together with a referendum on a new constitution, followed President Yeltsin's September 1993 order to disband the Russian Congress of People's Deputies, the parliament's refusal to disband, the attempt by some pro-communist leaders to take control of the country, and the storming of the parliament building by military units. Adopted by a vote of 58.4 percent, the new constitution established the Federal Assembly, made up of the State Duma and the Federation Council.

The results of the election to the Federal Assembly in the Russian Far East were released immediately after polls closed in Kaliningrad. They were a shock to Russian politicians and analysts. The most shocking development was the impressive showing of the ultranationalist Liberal Democratic Party of Russia headed by Vladimir Zhirinovsky, which won more votes than any other party, and Grigory Yavlinsky's Yabloko Party. The Communists and the Democratic Choice of Russia, headed by Yegor Gaidar, were relatively less successful in the Far East. After the votes were counted in western Siberia, the Ural regions, and European Russia, the picture drastically changed. Hidden by the overall figures presented in Table 14.1 is considerable variation by federation subject in the support for parties.[10] The parties that participated in the December 1993 elections can be classified according to their political platforms. Four major groupings can be designated: "reformers," "noncommunist nationalists," "anti-reformers," and "quasicentrists."

Reformers

Reformers included Russia's Choice headed by Gaidar, the main advocate of liberal values, and Yabloko. They ardently backed a combination of a market system and Western democratic ideals with strong social policies.

Noncommunist Nationalists

Noncommunist Nationalists consisted of Zhirinovsky's LDPR. A party with ultranationalist orientation, the LDPR emphasized "great power appeal," including the restoration of the Soviet Union, during the 1993 campaign. In its domestic policy, the LDPR emphasized the need for the elimination of ethnically based administrative entities and the complete subordination of all territorial units to a Moscow-based central government.[11]

Table 14.1 Results of the 1993 Parliamentary
Elections by Party List for Four Political Parties

	Yabloko	LDPR	CPRF	DVR*
National average	7.9	22.9	12.4	15.5
RFE average	10.1	24.9	11.9	14.3

Note: DVR stands for Yegor Gaidar's Democratic Choice of Russia (Demokraticheskii Vybor Rossii), a so-called party of power.
Source: Tsentralnaia Izbiratelnaia Komissiia, *Biulleten*, no. 1 (Central Electoral Commission, Bulletin, no. 1), 1994.

Anti-reformers

Anti-reformers consisted of those who supported a continued strong role for the state in economic activity. These views were coupled with expression of virulent "great-power" Russian nationalism and even support for restoring the Soviet Union. These parties included the Communist Party of the Russian Federation (CPRF) and the Agrarian Party of Russia. Traditional Soviet values such as the paternalistic role of the state, great power status, and the powerful system of social security are embodied in the ideology of Zyuganov's Communist Party. The call of communist leaders for revising privatization implies not nationalization as such but the redistribution of property from the capitalists, who are "trading away the Motherland," to "patriotic entrepreneurs." This is the core of the antiwestern rhetoric of communist leaders.[12]

Quasicentrists

Quasicentrists deserve this name because parties and movements that occupy this niche are not genuine parties, but quasiparties, or protoparties. They are usually formed ad hoc to pursue short-term political ends. Usually, a so-called party of power dominates in this sector. But in the 1993 period of "romantic democratization," Russia's Choice was clearly in the reformers' niche. The most eminent among the quasicentrist parties was Sergei Shakhrai's Party of Unity and Accord, which had links with ethnic nationalism, since it stood out from the other reformist parties as strongly in support of Russia's regions. It viewed "the economy and all other problems though the prism of regional and provincial interests."[13]

The 1993 elections showed that the northern regions of Russia tended to support reformist positions, while the south—which can be roughly demarcated as the territory below the fifty-fifth parallel—has proven to be hostile to reform.[14] The RFE also gives a spectacular illustration of this north-south divide if one compares Kamchatskaia oblast in the north and Amurskaia oblast in the south. The communists received 26.0 percent of the vote in Amur and only 6.2 percent in Kamchatka. At the same time, the pro-reform Yabloko and Democratic Choice of Russia received, respectively, 4.7 percent and 12.5 percent in Amurskaia oblast and 17.5 and 15.5 percent in Kamchatka. It is also noteworthy that the Republic of Sakha (Yakutia) demonstrated its sympathies toward the Communist Party, while pro-reform forces failed to obtain their average result there. Though Sakha cannot be considered a southern region, this example is rather illustrative for ethnic republics, which tend to demonstrate specific patterns of political behavior. Jewish autonomous oblast, for example, is noted for its sympathies for Zhirinovsky's party and the Communist Party, whereas the percent of votes for pro-reform parties in 1993 was below the national average.

This north-south divide was notably striking in the European part of Russia. However, in Siberia, and to an even greater extent in the Far East, this clarity was partially blurred by the "Zhirinovsky factor." Thus, the Siberian provinces of Tomsk and Krasnoyarsk, with relatively small agricultural sectors and declining military industrial complexes, should have voted for pro-reform parties. However, the reformist showing in these provinces was rather mediocre. At the same time, Zhirinovsky's party, which won 22.9 of the vote nationally, won a plurality in eight Far Eastern territories. Support for the LDPR was especially strong in Sakhalinskaia oblast (36.9 percent of the vote), in Magadanskaia oblast (29.2 percent), and Jewish autonomous oblast (25.0 percent). Even in procommunist Amurskaia oblast, the LDPR received an impressive 24.9 percent of the vote.

This LDPR support appears to be a protest vote against the authorities and the old communist *nomenklatura* in Siberia and the Far East. In general, Zhirinovsky's party ran relatively well in both the northern and southern areas.[15] The most interesting detail is that the LDPR received between one-third and one-half of the vote in seven federation subjects—Sakhalin, Pskov, Belgorod, Kursk, Tambov, Stavropol, and Mordovia. Four of them are *border provinces*. It is noteworthy that Sakhalinskaia oblast is involved in a territorial dispute with Japan (the Kurile Islands are an administrative district of the oblast). Stavropolskii krai, situated in the volatile Northern Caucasus, is painfully affected by inflows of refugees from Chechnya. Pskovskaia oblast is the target of territorial demands from Estonia, which claims the western part of the *oblast.* At the same time, less than 10 percent of voters chose the nationalists in four autonomous ethnic regions—Dagestan, Kabardino-Balkaria, Ingushetia, and Tuva.

What were the sources of Zhirinovsky's remarkable success in border regions and his visibly poorer showings in a number of autonomous units? One hypothesis is that, because Zhirinovsky's program pinpoints the strengthening of unity of the country and the curtailing of special rights of ethnic republics, it would have greater appeal in the politically sensitive border regions, which are far more sensitive to the prospect of Russia's disintegration. In Zhirinovsky's view, Russia should consist uniquely of "guberniias" with equal rights.[16] Zhirinovsky threatened the autonomous units with virulent "great-power nationalism." Thus, in this sense Zhirinovsky was perceived by the general population as a protagonist of Russia's grandeur and as an ardent critic of regionalization and ethnic nationalism. Let us consider the following hypothesis.

One set of regions demonstrated a rather strong tendency for Sergei Shakhrai's Party of Unity and Accord. Though Shakhrai enjoyed close formal and informal links with the leadership of autonomous units as Minister of Nationalities, this factor alone cannot explain his success. It is logical to assume that some additional circumstances affected Shakhrai's influence, especially the fact that his platform focused on the strengthening of regionalism and privileges for ethnic republics. Whereas Zhirinovsky threatened the autonomous units with Russian "superpower nationalism," Shakhrai's regionalism (together with his vague economic program) attracted many of them as the alternative to Zhirinovsky. In this sense, Shakhrai was considered by the general population to be an antagonist to Zhirinovsky.

In the RFE, this point is illustrated by the example of the Republic of Sakha. In 1993, Zhirinovsky's showing there was far from impressive (only 15.5 percent), while Shakhrai's party was clearly more successful than in neighboring regions. The 1992 Sakha constitution places republic laws above those of the Russian federation and has a provision for the republic's "right to leave the Russian Federation." However, many Sakha residents say they would prefer not to exercise that right unless a major upheaval in the center pushes them into it.[17]

The conventional Western perception of the alignment of political forces in Russia simplistically portrayed it as one-dimensional. And until 1993 this point of view to some extent reflected Russia's main political realities. The key political conflict seemed to exist between reformers ("good guys") and anti-reformers ("bad guys"). Yet the real spectrum of political attitudes was more complicated. The trick is that sympathies for reformers and communists are interconnected, whereas Zhirinovsky's and Yavlinsky's successes hardly depended on communists' losses or reformers' victories. In other words, Zhirinovsky's performance had practically no connection with economic motives, but rather with the emotional reaction to the fear of Russia's loss of great-power status. By the same token, Yabloko's performance is connected to an idea of Russia's openness to the outside world.

A number of analysts in the Western and Russian press argued that the relative success of Zhirinovsky and the communists was due to economic hardship and a sharp deterioration in the living standards under Yeltsin's socioeconomic policies. If this were true, one could expect to find a correlation between the patterns of electoral choice shown by regions and socioeconomic conditions.

For this purpose, a number of indicators can be used, including average wages, unemployment rates, and the proportion of urban population. The distribution of regions on the reform/anti-reform dimension correlates well with several social and economic indicators. For example, for 1993 elections, data on average wages (which to some extent indicates living standards) correlates with popular support for liberal or state-controlled economic policies.

Another socioeconomic variable that correlates well with support for reform is the degree of urbanization. The more urbanized a region, the more likely its population was to support reform parties. The population in rural regions, on the other hand, was more likely to vote for parties favoring strong state control over the economy.[18] Indeed, less-urbanized Amurskaia oblast was a communist stronghold.

A different picture emerges along the "strong center" versus "strong regions" dimension. Regional economic indicators show no significant correlation in voting for the LDPR or Shakhrai's party. Rather, the distribution of regions suggests that one can explain Zhirinovsky's strong showing by psychological factors, allegedly by his vision of a "strong state." Various cohorts of voters with different levels of income sympathize with his "great-power," ultranationalist rhetoric.

It is of special interest to look at how the regions are located along both dimensions (i.e., at the crossing of the axis "strong center" versus "strong regions" and the axis "strong state control" versus "economic liberalism"). These two axes cut the space of political attitudes into four quadrants.

"Economic Liberalism" plus "Strong Regions"

Judging by the results of the 1993 elections, this quadrant was occupied by regions that benefited more from economic reforms and supported the idea of further regionalization, such as those well-endowed in natural resources as Nenets autonomous oblast (AO), Khanty-Mansi AO, and Taimyr AO. In the Far East, the most pronounced position in this quadrant belongs to Chukotka, which benefited from economic reforms and supported regionalism. Also in this sector one can find Primorskii krai, Jewish AO, Koriak AO, and Khabarovskii krai.

"Economic Liberalism" plus "Strong Center"

In this quadrant, support for radical economic reforms goes hand-in-hand with advocating Russian nationalist appeals for an end to the special privileges enjoyed by ethnically based administrative units. Here we find St. Petersburg, Murmansk, and northeastern regions like Kamchatka and Magadan.

"Strong State Control over Economy" plus "Strong Center"

This quadrant would describe the interests of regions that were the most conservative in political terms—where the local population supports subsidies and continued regulation of the economy. These regions naturally benefit by redistributing wealth through tax and budget policy from richer to poorer regions. Regions with predominately Russian populations in this quadrant would also support ultranationalists' calls for restoring a strong center. Among Far Eastern regions, Amurskaia oblast perfectly fit this niche.

"Strong Control over Economy" plus "Strong Regions"

Regions in this quadrant were marked by a combination of political and economic conservatism and support for a weak center in order to preserve a non-Russian identity or to enhance the role of local elites. There would be an antipathy to Zhirinovsky in these regions and relatively strong support for Shakhrai—perhaps as a proxy for a regional party. In the Far East, this quadrant was occupied by the Republic of Sakha.

The presence of a federation subject in a quadrant indicates the direction toward which political forces were leaning in 1993. The provinces favoring regionalism may be considered to be promoters of politically centrifugal trends. However, the danger of Russia dissipating is weakened, since the autonomous republics inclined toward decentralization and state control were scattered all over Russia. For the republics rich in natural resources, market values were far more important. Thus, they seem to counterbalance poor and procommunist republics.

THE 1995 ELECTION

In December 1995, 107,496,507 voters participated in the proportional voting. Forty-three political parties and blocs competed for seats in the State Duma. As in the previous election, half of the Duma was divided up proportionally among those parties that surpassed the 5 percent hurdle. The other half of the Duma was won district by district in 225 individual races across the country. With few exceptions, small parties had a poor showing across Russia and were excluded from the Duma.

The voting for four major political forces[19] that surpassed the 5 percent hurdle demonstrated that Far Eastern regions were consistent in their political preferences (see Table 14.2). The reformist Yabloko bloc won 6.8 percent of the vote nationwide. It received the highest support in Far Eastern Kamchatka (20.8 percent), as well as in the cities of St. Petersburg (16.2) and Moscow (15.1). In 1995 Zhirinovsky's LDPR saw its percentage of the national party list drop by half, to 11.1 percent. However, in the Far East, especially in Magadanskaia oblast (22.5), it did far better than in Moscow and St. Petersburg (2.9 percent). The anti-reform CPRF emerged victorious in 1995, with 22.3 percent of the vote. The communists only won a majority (52.6 percent) in rural North Ossetia in the North Caucasus. Support for the Communist Party was also notably strong in rural regions—over 40 percent in Altai—but just 17.5 percent throughout the Far East. In the quasicenter, Our Home Is Russia (NDR for *Nash Dom Rossiia*) deserved the name "party of power," since it was headed by then Prime Minister Viktor Chernomyrdin. As a matter of fact, it was a party of the *nomenklatura* and governors. Nevertheless, it came in third with only 10.1 percent of the vote. NDR was most successful in the Republic of Ingushetiia (35.4 percent), Kurskaia oblast (31.2 percent), and the Republics of Tatarstan (29.4 percent), Tuva (29.3 percent), and Kabardino-Balkaria (25.4 percent). In the RFE, Our Home Is Russia was not very successful.[20]

Table 14.2 Results of the 1995 Parliamentary
Elections by Party List for Four Political Parties

	Yabloko	LDPR	CPRF	NDR
National average	6.8	11.1	22.3	10.1
RFE average	8.1	14.6	17.5	7.5

Source: Tsentralnaia Izbiratelnaia Komissiia, *Biulleten,* no. 1 (Central Electoral Commission, Bulletin, no. 1), 1996.

By and large, the analysis of the 1995 election follows the trends of the previous analysis with some minor modifications. The use of factor analysis once again permitted going beyond the more obvious, one-dimensional classification of Russian regions (which divides them into "democratic" and "conservative"), revealing new patterns among the data that could then be used as a new dimension. Two major factors appear to be particularly important to an explanation of Far Eastern political preferences.

The most influential factor regarded the *attitude toward economic reform and democratization*. Russia was still divided along the fifty-fifth parallel. Nevertheless, cleavage between the more pro-reform north and relatively anti-reform south did not look exactly like the analysis of the 1993 elections. The regions with the lowest share of votes for the CPRF and LDPR tended to be regions showing the highest support for reformist Yabloko and centrist Our Home Is Russia, and vice versa.

In addition, by 1995 another political conflict had developed between *preferences for two different groups of elites*. On one side of this axis one could find Yabloko and the LDPR, while the Our Home Is Russia and CPRF were on the other side. Presumably, the common denominator here was the perception of the CPRF and the Yeltsinist Our Home Is Russia as an "old" and "new" *nomenklatura*.

On the other end of the spectrum were newly emerging elites represented by Yabloko and the LDPR. Yabloko seemed to have an agenda that would prevent it from cooperating with Zhirinovsky. If one looks at their programmatic goals, they appear to have very little in common. However, there is evidence that some regions perceived them as forces of protest. What is truly common is the lack of participation of their leaders in the top echelons of power structures in the Soviet era and during the post-communist period. In both cases we have to deal with a sort of "political modernism." Yavlinsky and Zhirinovsky were pointing at Yeltsin and the communists as forces who had already proved their ineffectiveness in power. The relatively good showing of the LDPR was also a sort of response to governmental inadequacy, but in contrast to a communist vote (a "nostalgic protest"), the LDPR vote was a challenging response.

For Yabloko's and LDPR's electorate, the second factor characterized a *vote of no confidence in the old and current governments*—"those who promised a better life, but cheated." Thus, the second motivation may be called "conformist choice versus nonconformist choice." The conformist pattern was more spectacular in European Russia (with some minor exceptions like Moscow and St. Petersburg), while the Far East tended toward the nonconformist one.

Only one indicator, degree of urbanization, demonstrates a persistent and strong (opposite) correlation in the vote for two parties, CPRF and Yabloko. The more urbanized a region is, the more likely its population voted for Yabloko. On the other hand, the population in less-urbanized, rural regions was more likely to vote for the communists. The reasons seem to be not only economic: the urban population is much more informed about the real processes that are taking place in Russia, while the rural population feels more confused and is reluctant to support changes without being sure of the possible outcomes.

Some Far Eastern federation subjects perfectly fit into this picture. In territories with a high level of urbanization, Yabloko did rather well, while the communists were far more successful in rural areas. For example, Yabloko celebrated a sweeping victory with 20.8 percent of the vote in Kamchatka, where 81.4 percent of the population lives in urban areas, and the CPRF won far below its national average, only 11.5 percent. At the same time, in Amurskaia oblast, with a 66.3 percent urban population, Yabloko received 3.4 percent of the vote compared to the communists' 35.4 percent. However, this link is far less evident in Chukotka, with a rather high level of urbanization (73.3 percent), where both Yabloko and the communists were below their averages (6.6 and 11.2 percent of the vote, respectively). Highly urbanized Sakhalin (85.3 of the population), where communists won 25 percent of the vote, and to a lesser extent Khabarovskskii krai and Magadanskaia oblast, may also be considered exceptions. Thus, the especially strong "Zhirinovsky factor" in the Far East blurred the clarity of the picture.

Far more interesting is a correlation (though a weak one) between the regional share of export production and support for Yabloko and LDPR. In short, the more export production produced in a federation subject, the more its population tended to vote for Yabloko and LDPR and the less for CPRF. However, Yabloko and LDPR received similar results for different reasons. Both parties did especially well in the provinces furthest to the east (Kamchatka, Magadan, and Primorye). Voters backed Yavlinsky's bloc most likely because they were trade-oriented provinces that would benefit from reform and would lose from protectionist constraints.

Zhirinovsky's party did well in these federation subjects for another reason—they need centralized state and protectionist import barriers to deal with the growing influence of strong neighbors, for instance, China and Japan. The examples of St. Petersburg and Pskov region may serve as a litmus test to verify this hypothesis. The former, one of the main ports oriented toward external trade, gave strong support to Yabloko (and in the June 1996 presidential election support for Yavlinsky was 15.27 percent against the 7.42 percent Russian average). By contrast, neighboring Pskov region, which has miserable export potential but may suffer from territorial claims from Estonia, largely supported Zhirinovsky's LDPR.[21]

Finally, by scaling all federation subjects through extracted political dimensions, we can demonstrate the bases for potential interregional conflict. For this purpose, the coordinates for the regions derived from the factor analysis were plotted in Figure 14.1.

There is a large group of 54 regions that is hard to classify because of the ambiguity of their attitudes toward the reforms and elites. The remaining 35 regions, which demonstrate well-articulated political attitudes, are shown in Figure 14.1. Zones of total domination of political parties occupy the corners of the

Figure 14.1 Main Dimensions of Political Conflict among Russia's Regions
(factor analysis based on support for political parties in
each region in the December 1995 parliamentary elections)

NONCONFORMISTS

LDPR		YABLOKO
		Kamchatka
Primorye	Magadan	Koriak
Kirov	Yaroslavl	
Marii El		St. Petersburg
Chita		Yamalo-Nenets
Kurgan		
Smolensk		Moscow
Briansk	Moscow obl.	
Belgorod	Kalmykia	
Amur		
Ulianovsk		
Chuvashia		
Kemerovo Ust-Orda	Bashkiria	Chechnya (?)
North Ossetia Kursk		Ingushetia
Tambov		Tatarstan
Orel Dagestan		Tuva
Adygeia		Kabardino-Balkaria
CPRF		OUR HOME IS RUSSIA

Left axis: ANTI-DEMOCRATS   Right axis: DEMOCRATS

CONFORMISTS

graph. For example, Yabloko enjoys total control only over Kamchatka, where Yavlinsky's bloc won over 20 percent of the vote, leaving behind all political adversaries. (In June 1996, Yavlinsky received strong support in this region in his campaign for president.) At the same time, Magadanskaia oblast and Primorye tend to be closer to the anti-democratic sector.

A line of political divergence has become visible between European Russia—cradle of "Russianness," stronghold of traditionalism, and therefore bastion of conformist vote—and the Russian Far East, with its nonconformist patterns of voting for Yavlinsky and Zhirinovsky.

THE 1999 PARLIAMENTARY ELECTIONS

For the December 1999 elections to the State Duma, the Central Electoral Commission registered more than 5,000 candidates, though most of them could be regarded as noncontenders in the fight for the Duma's 450 seats. In fact, 28 parties or blocs competed for 225 seats allocated by proportional voting, though only 6 of them managed to clear the 5 percent barrier. Unprecedentedly, Russia's regions played a pivotal role in the 1999 parliamentary elections. Far beyond Moscow politics, newly emerged political blocs formed for the Duma elections were grounded in the support of governors. There are many factors to consider when analyzing the results of the December 1999 elections.[22] One should keep in mind that there were multiple fraud and other violations. The communists, for instance, argued that in nine regions the results were completely falsified.

In 1999, the *pro-reform group* was represented by the Union of Right-Wing Forces (*Soiuz Pravykh Sil,* or SPS), headed by former Prime Minister Sergei Kiriyenko, liberal politicians Irina Hakamada and Boris Nemtsov, and Yabloko. Yabloko had been forecast to win between 10 and 15 percent of the vote, but only won 5.9 percent nationwide and in the Far East, its traditional stronghold. The general population in the RFE—previously attracted by Yavlinsky's refusal to trade his basic principles for power—this time seems to have assumed a more critical stance. Yavlinsky and Yabloko had staked out the moral high ground, speaking out in favor of reforms and against corruption and the painful war in Chechnya. But his most ardent critics—including many fellow liberals—say he was trying to avoid soiling his hands in government office in fear of assuming responsibility for policies that might lead to failure. Though in seven out of ten Far Eastern regions Yabloko got somewhat more than its regional and national averages, especially in Khabarovskii krai (8.7 percent), Sakhalin (8.1 percent), and Chukotka (7.0 percent), the bloc's lost positions in the region were a painful failure for Yavlinsky.

Among the *noncommunist nationalists,* Zhirinovsky's star in 1999 was clearly declining. The LDPR was registered on the ballot this time as the Zhirinovsky Bloc for legal reasons before the December 1999 election and as usual demonstrated stable showing in the Far East: in all ten regions its results were visibly higher than the national average of 6 percent. It attained the best results in Magadanskaia (11.5 percent), Amurskaia (11.3 percent), and Kamchatskaia (10.9 percent) oblasts. Noncommunist nationalists were again substantially less successful in the Jewish autonomous okrug (6.7 percent) and the Republic of Sakha (6.1 percent).

In the *anti-reformer* group, the Communist Party of the Russian Federation emerged victorious with 24.3 percent of the vote. It became clear that the CPRF had finally become a systemic part of Russia's political landscape. However, in the Far

East, its results were not overwhelmingly high. For example, in Magadan the party won only 8.9 percent and in Chukotka only 11.1 percent of the vote. These two regions are the most critically minded toward the communists. Only one small Far Eastern territory, the Jewish autonomous oblast, demonstrated special sympathies toward the Communist Party, giving the party 34 percent of its vote; and the communists' results were below average in all other regions. In Amurskaia oblast, known for its strong procommunist sympathies, in 1999 the CPRF achieved only its average level. It is noteworthy that Primorskii and Khabarovskii krais, the most heavily populated provinces in the RFE and carrying the most weight politically, now demonstrate their lack of interest in the Communist Party and in Zhirinovsky's bloc—with vote percentages close to the average.

Two major quasicentrist blocs ("parties of power")—Yevgenii Primakov's and Iurii Luzhkov's Fatherland-All Russia and Sergei Shoigu's pro-Kremlin Unity—can hardly be called full-fledged political parties. They were formed some months before the elections and were reminiscent of political quilts, eclectic agglomerations of competing forces. What was common was their attention to regional issues. They appealed to regional leaders from different angles, but with the same goal—to tighten the screws after the elections in order to reassert control from the center. Primakov called for a reassertion of central control over the regions, a measure that could turn out to be a risky game because it would pit Russia's regions against each other along economic lines. The bloc experienced a deplorable defeat (13.3 percent) with the exception of the City of Moscow and the ethnic Republics of Tatarstan and Bashkortostan. Actually, this bloc was backed by the regions that were relatively independent from central transfers. Though Fatherland's result in the Republic of Sakha was rather high (10.0 percent), in the Far East as a whole its showing appeared to be worse than the national average. For example, it won only 3.5 percent of the vote in Amurskaia oblast and 6.0 in Kamchatskaia oblast.

Table 14.3 shows that electoral attitudes in the Far East have changed substantially. Yabloko has practically lost its support there; Zhirinovsky's party and the CPRF demonstrate the same pattern as before—the former above and the latter below their national averages. The most striking change is the sweeping victory of the "party of power" in the RFE. Its result there is far above the national average. The Unity bloc has become the real winner, although it desperately lacked regional political organizations and left 35 federation subjects uncontested in the "first-past-the-post" vote. Therefore, it had to rely exclusively on regional bosses. In fact, the appeal to the regional leaders was part of a much broader attempt to reestablish the contract between Russia's center and its regions. This contract turned out to be a "one-way street": after newly elected

Putin launched administrative reforms aimed at taking control over the federation subjects, some regional bosses considered themselves to have been cheated.

The "Unity phenomenon" deserves special investigation. I argue that Unity's victory in December 1999 manifests a significant shift in the Far Eastern political mentality—from a confrontational to a more cooperative approach with the center. The strong votes against the "presidential parties" or "parties of power" (i.e., Russia's Choice in 1993, Our Home Is Russia in 1995) could be seen as a fairly clear vote of protest. The vote for Unity in 1999 and Putin in 2000 appears to manifest a striving for order and the country's integrity. What are major sources of Unity's victory in the Far East?

Table 14.3 Results of the 1999 Parliamentary
Elections by Party List for Four Political Parties

	Yabloko	LDPR	CPRF	Unity
National average	5.9	6.0	24.3	23.3
RFE average	5.9	9.3	19.8	30.5

Source: Central Electoral Commission, *Svodnaia tablitsa po federalnomu izbiratelnomu okrugu. Proekt, 1999* (Consolidated Table for Federal Electoral District. Draft, 1999), December 1999, sheets 1–15.

First, the Kremlin was rumored to be actively seeking political support among regional elites through the Unity bloc. Regional bosses of over half of Russia's 89 federation subjects were supporting Unity, and the bloc very hastily became the most influential governor-backed political bloc in the elections. For example, Governor Yevgenii Nazdratenko of Primorskii krai openly supported Unity after leaving the Luzhkov-Primakov Fatherland. Unity, a pro-Kremlin bloc, was reportedly backed by the most dependent provinces, with Putin suggesting they assume a greater role in forming the budget, and there is no secret that the RFE consists exclusively of recipient regions due to the higher cost of living.[23]

As a rule, federation subjects that challenge Moscow are more successful in squeezing transfers from the federal government than cooperative regions;[24] prodigal sons often are far luckier than challengers. In the Far East, Unity demonstrated a sweeping victory in Chukotka (43.4 percent), Magadanskaia oblast (43.0 percent), Koriakskii AO (42.5 percent), Amurskaia oblast (36.2 percent), and Kamchatka (30.0 percent). It came in second to the Communist Party in the Jewish autonomous oblast (12.1

versus 34.0 percent) and challenged the communists in Sakhalin (23.1 to 24.3 percent). In addition, Unity's success was in many respects attributable to an intensive propaganda campaign carried out by the pro-Kremlin mass media, mainly the national television channels ORT and RTR. In this part of Russia, they were the only available sources of information. In regions where the general population had alternative sources, Unity's showing was far poorer than in the RFE. Government-controlled media were openly biased during the campaign. For example, the critically minded NTV channel did not reach the Far East.

Moreover, Unity's showing was a clear tribute to the image-based and highly personalized electoral habits of the Russian people. Unity had no economic or political program at the time of the elections. Instead, it was marked by a pattern based on authoritarianism and order. Putin's backing notwithstanding, Unity was not viewed by the people as a presidential party. Putin was an integral part of Yeltsin's establishment, but he always remained in the shadows as a career secret-service officer. Therefore, Unity was associated with uncorrupted newcomers, new ideas, and upcoming changes—and the Far East has adhered to this nonconformist pattern.

The RFE demonstrated the tendency to reject old politicians. It sought someone new and looked for tough solutions. Unity's ideology, if there was any, seemed to be based uniquely on the idea of the country's unity and grandeur. Much of Putin's popularity has been built on his tough stance regarding the war in Chechnya. The president owes much of his unprecedented popularity to his image as a loyal, careful, yet tough man-of-action with nationalistic leanings, a true believer in the power of the state and an advocate of the struggle against corruption.[25] The popular perception in the Far East seems to highly evaluate this set of qualities based on a mixture of respect for authority and challenge to the status quo.

Actually, during the December 1999 elections, Far Eastern voters demonstrated their frustration about skyrocketing prices and rising crime (these were the two issues most frequently mentioned by respondents in public opinion polls asking what they considered to be the crucial issues in the elections). By and large, the vote for Unity meant that the population of the Russian Far East was willing to have a strong government to deal with the deplorable economic situation and a threat of dissipation of the Russian state. In this sense, it was no wonder that pro-Putin Unity enjoyed exceptional success in the Far East.

COMPARATIVE ANALYSIS

There are some apparent contradictions as well as persistent patterns in the 1993, 1995, and 1999 parliamentary elections in the Russian Far East, which are reflected in Table 14.4.

The table spectacularly (though a bit simplistically, since the actual percentages are not taken into account) shows three major patterns characterizing political sympathies in the federation subjects in the Russian Far East.

Table 14.4 Relative Success of Four Major
Political Forces in 1993, 1995, and 1999 Elections
(+ results higher than national average; − results below national average)

	Yabloko			LDPR			CPRF			Party of Power		
	93	95	99	93	95	99	93	95	99	93	95	99
Sakha (Yakutia)	−	−	−	−	−	+	+	−	−	−	+	+
Jewish AO	−	−	−	+	+	+	+	+	+	−	−	−
Chukotka AO	+	−	−	+	+	+	−	−	−	−	+	+
Koryak AO	+	+	+	+	+	+	−	−	−	−	−	+
Primorye	+	+	+	+	+	+	−	+	−	−	−	+
Khabarovsk	−	+	+	−	+	+	+	−	−	+	−	+
Amur	−	−	−	+	+	+	+	+	−	−	−	+
Kamchatka	+	+	+	+	+	+	−	−	−	−	+	−
Magadan	+	+	−	+	+	+	−	−	−	−	−	−
Sakhalin	−	+	+	+	+	+	−	+	−	−	−	−

A *nonconformist pattern* is represented by Chukotskii and Koriakskii autonomous okrugs, Primorskii krai, and Kamchatskaia, Magadanskaia, and Sakhalinskaia oblasts. In these regions, the results of Yabloko and Zhirinovsky's party tend to be higher than the national averages, and the results of the communists and the "party of power" tend to be lower. This pattern can be seen as a challenge to the old and new *nomenklatura*.

The Jewish autonomous oblast and Amurskaia oblast are marked examples of a *procommunist conservative pattern*. These regions tend to vote for LDPR and the communists, whereas Yabloko and "parties of power" tend to demonstrate results below their national averages. The Jewish autonomous oblast represents the sole example of outstanding stability of political preferences and "pure conservatism." In each of the three parliamentary elections, Yabloko and "parties of power" received below their national average results, while the communists and LDPR received greater endorsement from voters in the Jewish AO than in the nation overall.

Finally, the Republic of Sakha and Khabarovskii krai show an *intermediate pattern*, although the former is closer to the conservative pattern and the latter to the nonconformist one. Political preferences of voters in both regions are not very particular or stable.

Only three Far Eastern regions—Sakha, Jewish AO, and Amurskaia oblast— demonstrated a stable, critical attitude toward Yabloko: in 1993, 1995, and 1999, Yabloko's results there were poor and declining (for instance, 7.0, 3.7, and 3.4 percent in Sakha; and 4.7, 3.4, and 3.3 percent in Amurskaia oblast), while Kamchatka may be considered Yabloko's stronghold (17.5, 20.8, and 6.2 percent) in spite of a far worse showing in December 1999.

At the same time, it is noteworthy that in Primorskii and Khabarovskii krais, and to some extent in Magadanskaia oblast, gubernatorial power plays a more important role than in other Far Eastern regions. Amurskaia oblast seems to be controlled by a leftist administration. Reformist political parties have more room for maneuvering in Kamchatka, Sakhalin, and Koriak, and leftist parties do better in the Jewish autonomous oblast, and to a lesser extent in Sakha.[26]

Indicators pointing to the development of a market mentality in the Far East are associated with the demographic and generational voting patterns. One very evident correlation is that between the communist vote and relatively poor and small towns and villages. The other strong correlation is between age and the communist vote. Because of the higher rate of migration, the RFE is relatively younger than the European part of Russia. Public opinion surveys everywhere, and especially in the Far East, also indicate that younger people have a much stronger commitment to democracy than do the elderly. Thus, the communist vote is likely to decline in future elections and, assuming the economy gradually improves, the commitment to democracy could strengthen, too.

Surveys and voting behavior also demonstrate that there is a much stronger affinity with old Soviet values in areas relatively unaffected by modernization, and, as is surely inevitable given globalizing trends, when modernization takes root in these provinces, then the old values will give way to those more conducive to sustaining democracy. The RFE is deeply affected by economic crisis, and from this point of view prospects for high democratic performance are not so evident.

The above analysis shows that the Far Eastern regions are politically engaged, two parties or electoral blocs are generally successful, and voters are polarized.[27]

These postures are relatively stable. At the same time, there is one dominant political preference, which is characterized by adherence to economic reforms, a challenging position vis-à-vis Moscow on economic issues, and support for the political integrity of the country.

Why are people in the Russian Far East less conformist than in the European part of Russia? First of all, this part of Russia for three centuries accumulated different categories of people who had one common trait—they represented opposition to central power. Among them were peasants fleeing from serfdom in search of new land and freedom; several waves of criminals or, more often, political prisoners; and old believers and others escaping religious persecution. This concentration of protest potential gave life to a certain type of "pioneer mentality," which can easily be compared to the Wild West in the United States.

Two different peculiar patterns of voters' protest have been formed in the RFE: a democratic pattern represented by those who voted for Yabloko, and a conservative pattern in those who voted for Zhirinovsky's party. Pro-Putin Unity's sweeping victory in 1999 does not contradict these patterns, as this quasi-party seems to have been perceived by the electorate as an alternative option to the old and new *nomenklatura*.

The regional distinctiveness of eastern Siberia and the Russian Far East was well pronounced about 150 years ago. After the Great Reforms of the 1860s, the ideas of economic autonomy were still alien to emerging local elites, with the exception of Siberia. Up until 1917, so-called Siberian regionalism (*sibirskoe oblastnichestvo*) existed in the Far East as a sociopolitical movement. Some representatives of intellectual groups considered Siberia and the Far East to be an economic and political entity with its own distinctive path of development. Moreover, they perceived the population of the Far East as a new, specific nation—a concept that was characterized by marked separatism.[28]

Separatist trends in Siberia and the Far East have become pronounced again after the collapse of the Soviet Union. We are witnessing a process of growing consolidation of regional elites in the RFE. However, it looks like they are divided by two major political temptations—centrifugal and centripetal.

The centrifugal tendency derives from several major factors. First, the economic and political weakness of the center led to the relative independence of the governors from Moscow. Second, there is a huge problem with transport tariffs. According to economist Gavriil Popov, "current transport tariffs make [it] more profitable for Siberia to promote contacts with China, and for Kaliningrad—with Europe, than with partners in the country. This development will give birth to separatism, and in ten to twenty years may result in a new political orientation."[29] Moreover, governors, even those who proclaim their loyalty to the

Kremlin, criticize Putin's efforts to curtail the powers of the Federation Council and, more generally, to reassert control over the regions. This centrifugal tendency is fraught with the danger of turning Russia into a quilt of fiefdoms.

However, there are some important countertendencies at work: for instance, the development of financial-industrial groups that transcend particular regions, and migration flows that bring people in and out of regions.[30] Another very important circumstance from the point of view of security implications is that strong perceptions (or misperceptions) are reinforcing a general opinion that the RFE is under threat from the inflow of Chinese.[31] The RFE has few human resources (border troops, police) to control the situation without help from Moscow. This makes regional authorities and the population seek Moscow's protective umbrella (hence the electoral results in favor of Zhirinovsky and Putin). Unifying factors such as the Putin-initiated administrative reform and new budgetary rules are reducing regional politicians' ambitions and their ability to distribute subsidies. Of particular importance, great-power nationalism in the Far East is a powerful factor hampering the collapse of the Russian Federation.

To summarize, the political mentality of the Russian Far East is dynamic and generally nonconformist. It is extremely important for Russia's security in the twenty-first century that the Far Eastern regions are based on a strong territorial identity. At the same, research indicates that the current trends in political mentality are not conducive to separatism.

NOTES

This study of Russian regionalism was inspired by Harvard professors Samuel Huntington and Timothy Colton. The author also expresses his gratitude to Peter Rutland (Wesleyan University), Margot Light (London School of Economics), Archie Brown (Oxford University), Philip Hanson (Birmingham University), Richard Sakwa and Philip Boobbyer (University of Kent), and Jacques Sapir (École des Hautes Études en Sciences Sociales). Special thanks are also addressed to Anne de Tinguy and Marie Mendras (Centre des Études et de Recherches Internationales). Finally, the author thanks Vladimir Gimpelson (Institute of World Economy and International Relations), Rostislav Turovsky (Moscow University), and Nikolai Petrov (Macalister College) for program support and consultations.

1. S. Shihab, "La Russie chaotique," *Le Monde: Économie*, April 22, 1997, 1–2; J. Sapir, *Le chaos russe* (Paris: La Découverte, 1996), 14; and P. Hanson, *Regions, Local Power, and Economic Change in Russia* (London: The Royal Institute of International Affairs, Russian and CIS Programme, 1994), 40.

2. For further analysis, see T. D. Buchs, "La transition dans les régions de Fédération de Russie (1992–1995): Un aperçu de la fragmentation des marchés," in *La Russie dans tous ses états*, Frédéric Grare, ed. (Bruxelles: Bruylant, 1996), 60; R. Working, "Far East

Needs Evils of West," *Moscow Times,* December 7, 1999, 11; and R. Working, "Far East Press Losing Fight," *Moscow Times,* November 20, 1999, 11.

3. The region of Central Russia includes Briansk, Vladimir, Ivanovo, Kaluga, Kostroma, Orel, Riazan, Smolensk, Tver, Tula, Yaroslavl, and Moscow oblasts.

4. One of the best analyses of regional politics in Russia is K. Matsuzato, "Subregional'naia politika v Rossii: Metodika issledovaniia" (Subregional policies in Russia: Methodology of analysis), in *Tret'e zveno gosudarstvennogo stroitel'stva Rossii* (The third link in constructing of the state in Russia), K. Matsuzato, ed. (Sapporo: Slavic Research Center, Hokkaido University, 1998). See also one of the latest contributions to the field, V. Gelman, S. Ryzhenkov, and M. Brie, eds., *Rossiia regionov: Transformatsiia politicheskikh rezhimov* (A Russia of regions: Transformation of political regimes) (Moscow: Ves mir, 2000).

5. J. Hughes, "Régionalism économique en Sibérie," *Nouveaux mondes,* no. 7 (1997):119–20.

6. Similar methodology is used in V. Bokser, M. McFaul, and V. Ostashev, "Rossiiskii elektorat na parlamentskikh vyborakh i referendume 12.12.1993 goda: Motivatsiia vybora," in *Analiz elektorata politicheskikh sil Rossii* (Moscow: Carnegie Endowment for International Peace, 1995), 2–110; and A. Halushka, *Presidential Elections and Structure of Industry in Ukraine,* East European Series, no. 14, Institute for Advanced Studies, Vienna, December 1994.

7. In 1993 Tatarstan and Chechnya did not take part in the elections, in 1995 and 1996 Chechnya did not take part, and in 1999 and 2000, all 89 regions took part in the elections.

8. The election law was published in *Rossiiskaia gazeta,* October 8, 1993.

9. For more details, see D. Slider, V. Gimpelson, S. Chugrov, "Political Tendencies in Russia's Regions: Evidence from the 1993 Parliamentary Elections," *Slavic Review* 53, no. 3 (fall 1994):711–32.

10. The Central Electoral Commission published data on voting for party lists for each of Russia's eighty-nine territories, with the exception only of Tatarstan and Chechnya. In Tatarstan, an unofficial boycott resulted in a turnout of less than 13 percent, which was less than the required 25 percent. In Chechnya no polling stations were allowed to open because of a boycott.

11. The LDPR program was published in *Rossiiskaia gazeta,* December 3, 1993.

12. V. Solovey, "The Reluctant Capitalist," *Moscow Times,* December 2, 1995, 8.

13. *Rossiiskaia gazeta,* December 3, 1993.

14. Some researchers tend to draw this divide along the 52nd parallel. See G. Helf, "All the Russias: Center, Core, and Periphery in Soviet and Post-Soviet Russia" (Ph.D. diss., University of California, Berkeley, 1994), 19.

15. See the articles by V. Kolesov in *Segodnia,* December 21, 1993, and A. Sobianin and V. Sukhovolskii in *Segodnia,* March 10, 1994; A. Malashenko, ed., *Chego khotiat regiony Rossii?* (What do Russia's regions want?) (Moscow Carnegie Center, 1999); and A. Yusupovskii, "Federalizm: Vozmozhno li 'vtoroe dykhanie'?" (Federalism: Is a "second breath" possible?), *Politeia* 3, no. 13 (1999):5–19.

16. V. Zhirinovsky, *LDPR: Partiia svobody, spravedlivosti i patriotizma* (The LDPR is a

party of freedom, justice, and patriotism) (Moscow: LDPR, 1997), 33, 183.

17. M. Mandelstam Balzer and U. A. Vinokurova, "Nationalism, Interethnic Relations and Federalism: The Case of the Sakha Republic (Yakutia)," *Europe-Asia Studies* 48, no. 1 (1996):113.

18. The correlation coefficient between level of urbanization and statism/reformism was $r = .61$, with p less than .001.

19. For analysis of alignment of forces, also see V. Kolosov and R. Turovsky, "Kampaniia 1995 goda: Regionalnye strategii predvybornykh blokov" (The 1995 campaign: Regional strategies of electoral blocs), in *Rossiia na vyborakh: Uroki i perspektivy* (Russia in elections: Lessons and prospects), ed. V. Kolosov (Moscow: Center for Political Technologies, 1995), 141–90. In fact, the spectrum of political alignment was broader. "Reformers" in the broad sense of the word were represented by Yavlinsky's Yabloko bloc, Gaidar's Democratic Choice of Russia, Boris Fedorov's Forward, Russia! bloc, Irina Hakamada's Common Cause, the Pamfilova-Gurov-Lysenko bloc, and other minor parties. "Anti-reformers" were represented by the Communist Party of the Russian Federation headed by Gennady Zyuganov, Viktor Anpilov's hard-line Communists for the Soviet Union, Nikolai Ryzhkov's Power to the People bloc, etc. "Nationalists" were represented by the LDPR and the Congress of Russian Communities headed by Yuri Skokov and Alexander Lebed. "Centrists" were mainly pragmatists who were between the groups. They were represented by Chernomyrdin's Our Home Is Russia, the Women of Russia bloc, and some minor groups.

20. *Svodnaia tablitsa ob itogakh golosovaniia po federal'nomu izbiratel'nomu okrugu po vyboram deputatov Gosudarstvennoi Dumy Federal'nogo Sobraniia Rossiiskoi Federatsii vtorogo sozyva* (Consolidated table of the results of voting in the federal electoral district elections of the State Duma of the Federal Assembly of the Russian Federation—second convocation), (Moscow: Tsentrizbirkom, 1996), sheets 1–13.

21. N. Rozov, "Puti samoopredeleniia Rossii v kontekste geopolitiki" (Russia's self-identification in the context of geopolitics), *Rossiia i sovremennyi mir* (Russia and the modern world) 1, no. 14 (1997):76.

22. "Taking Russia Region by Region: Duma Election Preview," *Moscow Times,* November 18, 1999, 5.

23. See V. Popov, "Strategiia reform i ekonomicheskie itogi transformatsii" (Reform strategy and economic results of transformation), in *Rossiiskie regiony pered vyborom: Varianty ekonomicheskoi politiki v perekhodnyi period* (Russian regions face their choices: Variants of economic policy in the transitional period), (Ottawa: Carleton University, 1999), 50.

24. D. Treisman, "Fiscal Redistribution in a Fragile Federation: Moscow and the Regions in 1994," *British Journal of Political Science* 28 (1998):186–87.

25. S. Zemlianoi, "Problema Putina" (Putin's Problem), *Nezavisimaia gazeta*, April 14, 2000, 8.

26. An interesting analysis of the problem by Nikolai Petrov and his research team can be found at <www.pubs.carnegie.ru>.

27. "Kto proidet v Dumu?" (Who will be elected into the Duma?), *NG-Stsenarii*, no. 7 (1999):4.

28. B. Mironov, "Le gouvernement des provinces sous les tsars," *Nouveaux mondes*, no. 7 (winter 1997); and *Russie: le gouvernement des provinces*, Marie Mendras, ed., (CRES: Genève, 1997), 7.

29. G. Popov, "Transport: vopros o tarifakh—vopros o edinstve strany" (Transport: The problem of tariffs is a problem of the country's unity), *Nezavisimaia gazeta*, March 15, 2000, 8.

30. For details, see P. Hanson, "How Many Russia's? Russia's regions and Their Adjustment to Economic Change," *International Spectator* 32, no. 1 (January–March 1997):39, 52.

31. For further discussion, see Mikhail Alexseev, "Chinese Migration in the Russian Far East: Security Threats and Incentives for Cooperation in Primorskii Krai," chapter 13 in this volume.

THE BALANCE OF POWER
AND THREAT PERCEPTIONS

15

China's Threat Perceptions and
Policies toward the Russian Far East

Ni Xiaoquan

China attaches great importance to its relations with Russia. The main goal of China's foreign policy is to create a long-term peaceful and stable international environment and particularly to maintain good relations with the surrounding countries to encourage domestic economic development. Russia and China share a border of about 4,300 kilometers. Therefore, maintaining long-term, friendly relations with Russia is extremely important to China's security, especially in view of the history of Sino-Soviet relations. The economies of the two countries are complementary in many respects, and there is great potential in developing economic cooperation between them. China and Russia also hold similar views regarding the most important contemporary international issues. From China's perspective, this is of particular importance. The Chinese leadership holds that although Russia is currently experiencing tremendous difficulties at home, it still plays an important role in world affairs and, with the eventual recovery of the Russian economy, it will undoubtedly play a more important role with regard to peace and stability in the Asia Pacific region and the world as a whole. Therefore, to establish and develop a strategic partnership with Russia oriented toward the twenty-first century is not an expedient measure but a strategic decision of the Chinese government.

As China and Russia are confronted with very similar problems at home and abroad, they naturally hold similar views regarding the establishment of a multipolar world order—opposing the effort to set up a unipolar world and any interference in the internal affairs of other countries. In dealing with their mutual relations, the two countries have treated each other as equals. For these reasons, relations between China and Russia have developed smoothly and quickly since the breakup of the Soviet Union, especially in the last few years. Since Boris Yeltsin's second visit to Beijing in 1996, when the leaders of the two countries announced that China and Russia were determined to develop a "strategic cooperative partnership based on equality and trust and oriented to the twenty-first century," this strategic partnership has been constantly enriched. Cooperation has been expanded to include collaboration between the departments of frontier defense in cracking down on various kinds of cross-border criminal activities, cooperation in safeguarding and observing the 1972 ABM treaty, mutual support in safeguarding their respective national sovereignty and territorial integrity, etc.

Relations between China's northeastern provinces and the Russian Far East are a component part of Sino-Russian relations, and largely have developed in conformity with the general trends in Sino-Russian relations. After overcoming many difficulties, the two countries basically resolved the historical boundary issues between them. Since the eastern section of the shared border is nearly 4,300 kilometers long and the western section is only about 55 kilometers, and there has been no serious dispute concerning the western section of the border, the so-called boundary issues between the two countries mainly concern the border between China and the Russian Far East.

In spring 1992, the parliaments of the two countries approved the boundary agreement concerning the eastern section that had been signed by China and the Soviet Union in 1991. Five years later, on November 10, 1997, then President Boris Yeltsin and Chinese President Jiang Zemin issued a joint statement in Beijing in which it was announced that the work of demarcating the eastern section of the Sino-Russian border had been finished. While demarcating their common border, China and Russia also reached agreements on reducing troops and weapons in the border regions and on establishing military confidence-building measures, and these agreements are now being implemented earnestly by both sides. As a result of the above-mentioned progress, the border between the two countries has become a peaceful and stable area.

Problems remain concerning illegal immigration between the two countries.[1] However, there has never been any tension or confrontation between them regarding this problem. As a matter of fact, the law enforcement agencies, including border guards, have cooperated well in combating illegal immigration and other forms of cross-border criminal activity.

There has also been marked progress in economic and trade cooperation between China's border regions and the Russian Far East. In 1998 trade volume between China and the Russian Far East reached $1.13 billion, which constituted

23.8 percent of the total foreign trade of the Russian Far East that year and which surpassed the trade volume of the Russian Far East with the Republic of Korea, Japan, or the United States.[2] In 1999 the volume of cross-border trade reached $1.89 billion, which was an increase of 27.7 percent over the previous year and which constituted about one-third of the total trade volume between the two countries that same year.[3]

Contacts and exchanges between local government officials, entrepreneurs, scholars, and other people in the border regions have also been expanding, and with this, mutual understanding has grown between the peoples living in both sides of the shared border.

DIFFICULT ISSUES REMAIN

Although there has been constant development in relations between China's northeastern regions and the Russian Far East, it has lagged far behind the development of relations between the central governments of the two countries. And mutual understanding and trust between the peoples of the border regions have yet to reach the level of mutual understanding and trust between the central governments of the two countries. Since the breakup of the Soviet Union, owing to the constant development of Sino-Russian relations and the complicated domestic situation in Russia, the potential military threat to China from the north has basically disappeared. However, from China's perspective, there still exist hidden troubles and destabilizing factors in relations between China and the Russian Far East. These have negatively affected the development of a strategic partnership between China and Russia, and, if they are not removed, will become potential causes of conflict in the future. The hidden troubles and destabilizing factors are mainly reflected in the following two aspects.

Boundary Issues

In May 1991, during President Jiang Zemin's visit to Moscow, China and the Soviet Union signed an agreement on the eastern section of their shared border. According to this agreement, with the exception of three small islands including Bear (Bolshoi Ussuriiskii) Island near Khabarovsk, all the other islands to the Chinese side of the main channels of the boundary rivers were transferred to China. The agreement also stipulated that Chinese ships, including naval vessels, should be allowed to navigate from the Ussuri River to the Heilongjiang (Amur) River through the waters near Khabarovsk. In addition, three pieces of land with a total area of about 1,500 hectares in Primorskii krai that were occupied by the Soviet Union in the 1930s in violation of an existing boundary treaty (the Treaty of

Peking, signed in 1860) were to be returned to China. It was agreed that the two countries would continue negotiations over these three small islands to find a just and reasonable solution. However, after the boundary agreement was approved in spring 1992 by the Russian and Chinese parliaments, its implementation met with obstruction from some local leaders of the Russian Far East.

Although the Russian government made it clear that Russia would resolutely implement the boundary agreement and insisted that only the central government had the right to handle boundary issues, local leaders in the Russian Far East, owing to the weakening of the authority of Moscow, still played a significant role in the boundary issues. In the name of "patriotism," former Governor Yevgenii Nazdratenko of Primorskii krai and others claimed that Russia had made "unilateral concessions" to China in the boundary negotiations and demanded that the agreement be abolished or revised. Their position was supported by many in the Russian Far East, especially in Primorskii krai, and by some politicians in Moscow as well. There is no doubt that Governor Nazdratenko and others had their own political aims for opposing the boundary agreement. But because of their obstruction, progress in implementing the agreement was very slow, and it was not until November 1997 that the work of border demarcation in the eastern section was finally completed.

The border demarcation has been accepted by Nazdratenko and others in the Russian Far East. In a speech made in early March 1999, Nazdratenko said that six passages leading to the Chinese border had been opened in Primorye, which would contribute to the expansion of trade and the creation of new jobs.[4]

However, the sensitive boundary issue has not been completely resolved. The issue of Bear (Bolshoi Ussuriiskii) Island and two other islands still exists, and it will be more difficult to solve this issue than the boundary issues that have already been resolved. In late 1999, Governor Viktor Ishaev of Khabarovskii krai claimed that "the position of the Far Eastern government on this issue will never change, that is, this [Bolshoi Ussuriiskii] is our territory and we have never admitted that it is a disputed area."[5] The krai government and some religious and mass organizations have solicited contributions for building a small church on Bolshoi Ussuriiskii, which, they say, will serve as "a symbol that the island belongs to Russia."[6] The number of Russian soldiers stationed on the island has also increased from less than 60 in the early 1990s to a few hundred as of late 1999. Another noticeable event occurred on March 1, 1999, when Nazdratenko and a number of other local officials and scholars organized and participated in a memorial to the soldiers and officers who had "sacrificed their lives in defense of the Damanskii (Zhenbao) Island" on the thirtieth anniversary of the 1969 border dispute in the border city of Dalnerechensk.[7] Ownership of the three small islands could become an explosive issue jeopardizing relations between the two countries if it is not resolved properly.

The Issue of Illegal Immigration and the So-Called China Threat
Following the breakup of the Soviet Union, because of the new openness of the Sino-Russian border and lack of control, a large number of Chinese traders and other people entered the Russian Far East to make money. According to Russian newspapers, the figure ranged from a few hundred thousand to several million Chinese. The majority of these people abided by Russian rules and laws, but there were also quite a few Chinese who violated Russian rules and immigration laws or engaged in criminal activities in the Russian Far East. At the same time, the large quantities of shoddy Chinese goods that were brought into the Russian Far East aroused dissatisfaction with and aversion to the Chinese among the population. Beginning in late 1992, "illegal immigration" became a topic frequently discussed in newspapers and journals of the Russian Far East and there was a lot of rhetoric about China's "demographic expansion" or "quiet expansion." Some people, including politicians and scholars, in the Russian Far East and in Moscow claimed that the Chinese government deliberately encouraged migration to the Russian Far East so as to solve China's overpopulation and unemployment problems. For example, Yegor Gaidar, a radical liberal politician, contended that China, with population density and total population greatly surpassing Russia's, constituted a threat to Russia. He said that Russia should form a military alliance with the West and move its nuclear weapons to the Russian Far East.[8]

This anti-Chinese sentiment and propaganda have been detrimental to the enhancement of mutual understanding and trust between the peoples of China and the Russian Far East. They have also hindered to some extent the development of cooperation in various fields. It is well known that the economies of Northeast China and the Russian Far East are highly complementary, and labor flow is conducive to the economic development of both sides. However, as the local governments of the Russian Far East have taken measures to tighten their control over the Chinese and restrict the use of Chinese laborers, it has been difficult for China and the Russian Far East to bring their economic complementarity into full play. The anti-Chinese sentiment in the Russian Far East has also negatively affected contacts and exchanges in cultural, educational, and other fields, and it certainly has made it more difficult for China and Russia to completely resolve their border issues.

The anti-Chinese sentiment in the Russian Far East has also affected the attitudes of the Chinese people near the border regions. In the early 1990s many people in those regions were eager to engage in business activities in the Russian Far

East and other parts of Russia. But now, in part because of the anti-Chinese sentiment, only a small number of people want to go to Russia. Moreover, the majority of those who still choose to go to Russia prefer to go to European Russia rather than to the Russian Far East. According to one Russian source, in mid-1999 there were 40,000 Chinese in Moscow, whereas the total number of Chinese in the three border cities of Khabarovsk, Vladivostok, and Ussuriisk was less than 10,000.[9] According to several Chinese traders whom I met in Khabarovsk in October 1999, anti-Chinese sentiment in the region was widespread, and they did not feel safe there. They listed a number of cases of Chinese traders being killed, robbed, or beaten by local Russians. They also complained that Chinese traders in the Russian Far East were often subject to extortion and blackmail by Russian policemen, local tax officials, and border guards. They all said that they did not like the Russian Far East and had no intention to stay there for long. This view was confirmed in a July 1999 article published in a Russian newspaper, which stated that Chinese in Russia were afraid of Russians, and, of all the Chinese in the region, only 1.5 percent expressed a willingness to settle there.[10]

In the past several years, as strategic partnership between China and Russia has developed quickly, the demarcation of the eastern section of the Sino-Russian border has been completed, and the disorderly situation of cross-border trade has been greatly improved, anti-Chinese sentiment and statements about a "China threat" in the Russian Far East have been reduced. Interviewed by a correspondent of the Chinese weekly newspaper *The Far East Trade Herald* on January 20, 2000, then Governor Nadzdratenko said that China was one of the most important trading partners of Primorskii krai and that he would make efforts to give further impetus to the development of Sino-Russian relations.[11] In a 1998 book coauthored by Governor Ishaev and Pavel Minakir, various programs for accelerating the economic development of the Russian Far East are discussed. The authors proposed that a "China Program" be adopted, by which they meant realizing the integration of the Russian Far East with the Asia Pacific region by introducing China into its economy with a final goal of forming a unified economic space between the Russian Far East and Northeast China.[12]

However, anti-Chinese sentiment and statements about a "China threat" have not totally disappeared. An article published in *Izvestiia* in May 1999 asserted that if China continued to be strong politically, economically, and militarily and Russia still could not rid itself of the long-standing crisis, then the problem of territorial dispute would once again be on the agenda.[13] Another article carried in the Russian newspaper *Tribuna* in August 1999 said that the Chinese were not like the aggressors of Chechnya, but their "infiltration" was actually more terrible. It said that the Russian Far East would soon become a Chinese province "without our notice" and proposed that strict rules be formulated to restrict the inflow of Chinese citizens, in particular those Chinese engaging in trade in the Russian Far East.[14] There also exists discrimination against the Chinese in the Russian Far East. For instance, in July 1999 the municipal government of Nakhodka in Primorskii krai began to set a quota that limited the annual number of Chinese entering the city to 1,200. It also decided that Chinese tourists visiting the city could only stay in specially designated hotels where they had to pay $40 a day, which greatly exceeded the average charge in the area.[15]

Some politicians in Moscow are also worried about China's future policies. During a talk with a group of Chinese scholars visiting Moscow in October 1999, Aleksei Arbatov, deputy chairman of the defense committee of the State Duma, said that a large increase of Chinese citizens in the Russian Far East might bring about hidden troubles to Russia, especially as the economy and population of the Russian Far East are declining. He said that despite the existence of a border demarcation agreement, the proportion of Chinese to the local population in the Russian Far East could result in a territorial dispute. Arbatov admitted that Russia trusted the present Chinese leaders, but he had no idea what policies future Chinese leaders would pursue. He said that in fifteen years the balance of forces would be undoubtedly favorable to China, but Russia would not be willing to become a junior partner just as China had refused to act as a junior partner of Russia in the past.[16]

The relationship between China and the Russian Far East is an important component of overall Sino-Russian relations. It is obvious that without mutual understanding and trust between the peoples on both sides of the border, there will be no friendly relations between China and the Russian Far East, and, without such relations, there will be no solid foundation for the development of strategic partnership between the two countries.

New Security Issues

"New security issues" have also emerged in recent years along the Sino-Russian border. These issues have not affected Sino-Russian relations as obviously as the issues discussed above, but they are negative factors affecting the stability of the border regions of both China and Russia. Illegal border crossing has become a prominent issue along the Sino-Russian border. According to Russian media, in 1998 alone Russian border guards in the Far East repatriated about 25,000 Chinese and Koreans who had illegally entered Russia. And from January to the beginning of May 1999, frontier guards in the Russian Far East seized and repatriated more than 1,000 Chinese citizens who had crossed the Sino-Russian border illegally.[17] Many of these illegal activities were arranged jointly by Chinese and Russian criminal gangs.

Drug smuggling is another major issue affecting the stability of the Sino-Russian border regions. According to a 1997 article in the Russian newspaper *Vladivostok*, the number of drug addicts in Primorye was four times the Russian average.[18] Primorye is also one of the main distribution centers of drugs in Russia. Because of the large demand for drugs in Primorskii krai, drug (mainly ephedrine) smuggling has been rampant on the Sino-Russian border in recent years. In 1998 the law enforcement organs of the Russian Far East intercepted and captured as many as 1,108 kilograms of narcotics in the area close to the Chinese border, which was 3.5 times more than in the previous year.[19] Chinese and Russian criminals have also collaborated frequently in smuggling white spirit (a Chinese alcoholic beverage), sea cucumbers, ginseng, furs of endangered species, etc.

Even more dangerous is the spread of large amounts of weapons, especially ammunition and explosives, in the Russian Far East. Owing to the anarchic state of the Russian military forces and arsenals, weapons and ammunition have often been stolen and then sold to criminals. Some Chinese criminals also have tried to purchase weapons from Russian underground arms dealers and mafia gangs and then bring them to China for criminal use. In addition, local newspapers in the Russian Far East often carry advertisements telling Russian girls where and how to find jobs in China. It is possible that some of these advertisements were actually placed by Russian criminals engaged in providing sex service. Although no direct evidence has been found, the possibility that Chinese and Russian criminals have collaborated in this activity cannot be ruled out.

To date, these organized criminal activities have not yet posed a serious threat to the security of China. But they are growing both in number and scale, and it is possible that Chinese and Russian mafia gangs will try to establish and strengthen links with each other. Therefore, if the authorities do not respond with strong measures, they may pose a grave threat to China's security in the not-too-distant future, especially in view of the fact that a large amount of nuclear weapons and nuclear materials are deployed or stored in the Russian Far East.

CHINESE POLICIES

Comparatively speaking, the Chinese government has paid much more attention to its relations with Moscow than with the Russian Far East. This is proven by the fact that so far the Chinese government has yet to formulate a clear-cut and comprehensive policy toward the Russian Far East, and no Chinese leader has ever paid an official visit to the region. This is one of the reasons that relations between China and the Russian Far East have not developed as quickly as the overall Sino-Russian relationship. However, this does not mean that the Chinese government has totally neglected the importance of the Russian Far East to overall Sino-Russian relations. In fact, Beijing has taken many concrete measures to promote the development of friendly relations between China and the Russian Far East.

Settling Boundary Issues through Friendly Consultations

Territorial disputes were an important cause of tension and confrontation in Sino-Soviet relations. The Chinese government holds that in order to eliminate the root causes of conflicts and lay a solid foundation for enhanced trust and closer friendship, it is necessary to resolve in a fair and reasonable way the historical boundary issues between the two countries.

The Chinese government has always held that the boundary treaties signed between China and tsarist Russia in the mid-nineteenth century were unequal treaties because they were imposed upon China after the Opium War, which was launched by Britain against China in 1840, at a time when China was very weak. Tsarist Russia took advantage of China's weakness and seized more than 1.5 million square kilometers from China, including more than 600,000 square kilometers to the north of the Heilongjiang (Amur) River and about 400,000 square kilometers to the east of the Ussuri River in accordance with the Treaty of Aigun and the Treaty of Peking, respectively. Today, the Chinese government and academic circles still hold that these boundary treaties were unequal. But even in 1964, when China and the Soviet Union first began negotiations on boundary issues, the Chinese government made it clear that it was willing to resolve the boundary issue between the two countries on the basis of the existing boundary treaties and did not demand the return of the territories seized by Russia. What China insisted at the time was that the Soviet Union admit that the nineteenth-century boundary treaties were unequal and that territories invaded and occupied in violation of those boundary treaties should in principle be returned to the other side and that, in accordance with international law, the main channels in the Heilongjiang (Amur) and Ussuri Rivers should be the demarcation line between the two countries. Because the Soviet leadership refused to accept Chinese demands, negotiations between the two sides ended in failure. In 1986, Mikhail Gorbachev made a famous speech in Vladivostok in which he announced that the main channels should be the international boundary. Meanwhile, China gave up the demand that the Soviet side admit the existing boundary treaties to be unequal. As both sides took more realistic attitudes toward boundary issues, substantial progress began to be achieved in boundary negotiations, which were resumed in 1987 after a suspension of nine years.

The willingness of the Chinese government to resolve boundary issues with Russia on the basis of the existing treaties shows that it now accepts the nineteenth-century boundary treaties and does not demand the return of the territories lost to

Russia in accordance with them. The generally recognized principles of international law stipulate that the demarcation line between the two countries should be the main channels in navigable boundary rivers, central lines in nonnavigable boundary rivers, and watershed on dry land. Thus, the islands and land to the Chinese side of the demarcation line should in principle belong to China and those to the Russian side of the demarcation line should in principle belong to Russia. It should be mentioned here that the nineteenth-century treaties concerning the eastern section of the common border stipulated that the Heilongjiang (Amur) and Ussuri Rivers were the common border of the two countries, but they did not say that the boundary lines were along the Chinese banks of the rivers. It was only in the early 1930s, when Japan invaded and occupied China's northeastern provinces, that the Soviet government unilaterally moved the boundary lines to the Chinese banks—a move that China has never recognized.

Therefore, the present demarcation only means a restoration of the boundary lines stipulated in the nineteenth-century treaties. Mutual understanding and mutual accommodation means that in resolving disputes, consideration should be given to the interests of both sides, and the importance of friendship and cooperation between the two counties must be taken into account so that the boundary issues will not affect the development of bilateral relations.

Concretely speaking, while insisting that the 1991 boundary agreement concerning the eastern section of the shared border be fully implemented within a fixed period of time (i.e., before the end of 1997), the Chinese government has also given full consideration to the interests and feelings of the local population in the Russian Far East and adopted a flexible and pragmatic attitude in this respect. For instance, it has agreed to let local Russians make joint economic use with the Chinese of certain islands and the surrounding waters, which according to the principles of the agreement should be transferred to China. This agreement on joint use is almost a unilateral concession made by China to Russia. Another example of Chinese flexibility concerns about 300 hectares of land near Khasan Lake in Primorye. According to the principle of the agreement, this area should be handed over to China, but the land is considered to be sacred by the Russians living there because a cemetery where some Russian soldiers were buried after a battle between Soviet and Japanese troops in the late 1930s is located near the lake. After consultations, the Chinese government agreed to let the Russian side retain the cemetery and the surrounding land, which is about 140 hectares, and the rest of the land was to be returned to China. As for the three disputed islands, including Bear (Bolshoi Ussuriskii) Island near Khabarovsk, which are difficult to resolve at present, the Chinese government is willing to put them aside and continue to hold negotiations on them.

Owing to the joint efforts of the Chinese and Russian governments, many difficulties in implementing the 1991 boundary agreement have been gradually overcome. By the end of 1997, the surveying work related to the demarcation basically had been completed, after which the implementation of the boundary agreements concerning the eastern and western sections of the border were accelerated. In November 1998, when President Jiang Zemin visited Moscow, the two countries issued a joint statement which announced that surveying of the western section of the shared border had been finished and that, for the first time in the history of bilateral relations, the eastern and western sections of the boundary had been accurately marked.

While actively resolving the boundary issues, China has also sought to reach agreement with Russia on confidence-building measures and on reducing the military presence along the common border. In April 1996 China and Russia, together with Kazakhstan, Kyrgyzstan, and Tajikistan, signed an agreement in Shanghai on military confidence-building measures in the border areas. According to the agreement, each side has an obligation to inform the other in advance if it is going to conduct military exercises on a large scale or station new troops in the border areas. In other words, in the Sino-Russian border areas, each side should be "transparent" to the other side militarily. In April 1997 the "Shanghai Five" again signed an agreement on the reduction of military forces in the border areas, according to which the military forces of each country deployed along the common border should be reduced to the lowest levels. As a result of these agreements, military activities in the common border areas are now becoming transparent, predictable, and controllable. There are no significant forces in China today, including the military, that do not accept the boundary or other agreements that China has reached with Russia.

Opposing Illegal Immigration and Expanding Security Cooperation

The Chinese government also has paid great attention to the issue of illegal immigration, which has already affected mutual trust between the peoples of China and the Russian Far East and the development of relations between the two sides. It holds that the more quickly this issue is resolved, the more smoothly cooperation between the two countries will develop. It has declared many times that China has absolutely no intention of encouraging illegal immigration to Russia and it firmly opposes the violation of the Russian passport and visa regulations by Chinese citizens.[20] Jiang Zemin specifically mentioned this problem in a speech to the Russian public while visiting Moscow in September 1994. He emphasized that "the principled stand of the Chinese government [on the issue of immigration] is that it supports and protects orderly and lawful economic and trade activities and does not support and protect illegal and disorderly trade activities that harm the Russian consumers' interests, and the Chinese citizens engaged in such activities."[21]

As early as May 1994, when former Russian Prime Minister Chernomyrdin visited Beijing, the two countries signed an agreement on establishing a control regime along the Sino-Russian border, and this regime has since played a positive role in curbing illegal immigration. In recent years the Chinese government has intensified its efforts to curb illegal immigration of Chinese citizens to Russia. For instance, the relevant departments in the border regions have strengthened the examination of the personal histories of Chinese citizens, especially individual traders and contract laborers, who apply for visas to travel to Russia. Chinese border guards in the northeastern provinces also have strengthened cooperation with their counterparts in Russia in curbing illegal border crossing and in cracking down on other cross-border criminal activities. In September 1999, invited by the border guards of the Russian Far East, a delegation of the frontier defense bureau of China's Heilongjiang Province paid a visit to Khabarovsk. The two sides formulated a number of concrete measures with regard to information sharing, the strengthening of coordination in handling border events, etc. These efforts have produced a marked effect. For instance, from May 15 to June 15, 2000, the frontier defense forces of the two countries conducted 18 joint actions along the shared boundary rivers to examine the observance of the boundary rules and curb acts that damage ecological resources. In the first 6 months of 2000, the frontier defense forces of the 2 countries acting jointly intercepted 122 smuggling activities, and the amount of money involved in these criminal activities reached 900,000 rubles. In addition, the Chinese Foreign Ministry has cooperated with its Russian counterpart in formulating concrete measures to regulate contacts and exchanges between citizens of the two countries. During Chinese Foreign Minister Tang Jiaxuan's visit to Moscow from February 28 to March 1, 2000, he and his Russian counterpart, Igor Ivanov, signed an agreement on the exchange of visits by citizens and an accord on the exemption of visas for citizens visiting as members of tourist groups.

Personal Contacts and Trade Cooperation

The Chinese government has also made great efforts to promote cutural understanding between the Chinese people and the people of Russia, including the Russian Far East. It is obvious that for historical reasons most of the population in the Russian Far East does not know much about China's history, culture, and current situation. Local mass media, including newspapers and TV programs, report very little about neighboring China. And the little coverage that exists usually depicts China in a negative way. So it is no wonder that many people in the Russian Far East have prejudice against Chinese or fear a "China threat."

To encourage mutual understanding, the governments of both China and Russia place a high priority on the expansion of nongovernmental contacts and exchanges and are willing to work for better understanding of each other's history, culture, traditions, and current situation. Each government supports the efforts of various social bodies and news media to present true and friendly images of the other. In 1997 the Sino-Russian Committee for Friendship, Peace, and Development was set up to expand the social foundation of the Sino-Russian strategic partnership and promote mutual understanding. In 1999 and 2000, owing to the efforts of governmental and nongovernmental organizations, there was an evident increase in people-to-people exchanges between the two countries, including those between journalists, youths, writers, etc. In 1999, both China and Russia (including the Russian Far East) conducted activities on a large scale in celebration of the fiftieth anniversary of the establishment of diplomatic relations between the two countries and in commemoration of the founding of the People's Republic of China.

The Chinese government has increasingly recognized that economic cooperation is an important material foundation of the development of friendly relations, and without a solid foundation in this area, political relations between the two sides are fragile. Although there was a marked increase in China's trade volume with the Russian Far East in 1998 and 1999, the level of economic cooperation, especially in investment, production, and science and technology, is still very low. China and the Russian Far East are highly complementary economically. The Russian Far East is rich in natural resources such as oil, gas, and timber, whereas China does not have enough of these resources, and its Heilongjiang Province has an advantage in oil refining and wood processing. It costs more for the Russian Far East to import food and consumer goods from European Russia than from China, whereas China's Heilongjiang and Jilin Provinces bordering the Russian Far East produce enough grain, fruits, vegetables, consumer products, and other goods to satisfy the needs of the Russian Far East. China can produce consumer goods and various kinds of electrical household appliances in the Russian Far East, which would increase employment in the region and save the hard currency that it would have to pay to import them from abroad. At the same time, the Russian far East can provide China with advanced military technologies and other high technologies for civilian use. However, for various reasons, this economic complementarity is far from being fully exploited.

In the late 1990s, the Chinese government made new efforts to diversify economic and trade cooperation between the two countries. Priority has been given to large and medium-sized cooperation projects. Since Chinese Premier Zhu Rongji's visit to Moscow in February 1999, China and Russia have signed quite a few agreements concerning projects related to energy, forestry, technology, and other areas, nearly half of which concern the Russian Far East. Several agreements also have been reached on establishing direct economic and trade links between the provinces of the two countries. According to these agreements, Jilin Province and Primorskii krai have established an economic and trading partnership, as have Shanghai and Amurskaia oblast. In order to promote border trade, the Chinese government also has supported the establishment of border-crossing markets. So far, a number of border-crossing markets have been set up along the Chinese side of the border. The Chinese government has also taken measures to raise the prestige of Chinese goods in the Russian Far East. Local governments in northeast China have dissolved quite a number of unqualified trading companies doing business with Russia. And government departments and customs bodies have also established or strengthened quality-control systems to prevent shoddy and substandard goods from being exported to Russia. All this will undoubtedly strengthen the material foundation for further development of friendly relations.

Today, as a result of the efforts made by both sides, the issue of illegal immigration and fear of a "China threat" in the Russian Far East are no longer as serious as before. According to an article published in a Russian newspaper in July 1999, in mid-1998 about 70 percent of the people in Primorye regarded Chinese as dangerous, but one year later an opinion poll showed that the local population no longer regarded Chinese immigrants as dangerous, and their fear of the Chinese had disappeared.[22]

COOPERATION IN INTERNATIONAL AFFAIRS

Arms treaties between Russia and the United States and U.S. plans to deploy a national or theater missile defense system have great bearing on China's security interests and Sino-Russian relations. On April 18, 2000, the Russian State Duma ratified the START II arms reduction treaty. The Chinese government welcomes this move because it conforms to China's consistent policy of standing for the complete prohibition and thorough destruction of nuclear weapons. The Chinese government hopes that both Russia and the United States will put the treaty into effect as soon as possible and will continue large-scale reductions in their respective nuclear arsenals so as to create necessary conditions for other powers to join a multilateral process of nuclear arms reductions. From the Chinese perspective, the realization of global nuclear arms reduction cannot be separated from a stable global strategic balance. China, therefore, resolutely opposes the effort of the United States to develop a national missile defense system, which China believes will seriously threaten existing global strategic balance and stability, undermine trust and cooperation in the field of international arms control, and impede the process of arms reduction. The Chinese government has declared that China will not evade

its own responsibilities and obligations in nuclear arms reduction but will participate in arms control talks, particularly nuclear arms control talks, only when its two
preconditions are satisfied: that is, the talks and treaties or agreements to be reached
must not harm the global strategic balance and stability, nor should they jeopardize
China's national security.[23]

China objects to U.S. deployment of a TMD system either in Taiwan, Japan, or
South Korea because it believes that preventing possible missile attacks by North
Korea or other so-called "rogue countries" is only a pretext, and the real purpose of
the United States is to seek absolute military superiority over China and Russia.
China holds that this is unacceptable, particularly under the present circumstances.
From China's perspective, in recent years the tendency of the United States and its
allies to use force or threaten to use force has been strengthened. NATO has
adopted a new strategic concept that allows the United States and its allies to take
military actions outside of the organization's spheres of influence without the
approval of the U.N. Security Council. The United States has also strengthened its
military alliance with Japan by signing a new guideline for defense cooperation.
This new guideline, which has been approved by the Japanese parliament, has
extended the scope of U.S.-Japanese military cooperation to the entire Asia Pacific
region, including China's Taiwan. And the United States and Japan have also decided to cooperate in developing a TMD system. From China's perspective, U.S.
deployment of TMD in Japan will undermine China's national security interests,
and deployment of TMD in South Korea will spur an arms race on the Korean
Peninsula and endanger peace and stability in the region.

The Chinese government issued a white paper entitled *China's National Defense*
on July 28, 1998, which points out that "security should not rely on the increase of
armaments or military alliance. It should rely on mutual trust and the tie of common interests."[24] This means that no country should try to guarantee its own
security by threatening or undermining the security of other countries. Without the
security of other countries or regions, no country or region in the final analysis will
be able to realize its own security or maintain it for long. The white paper also
points out that "all countries should try to increase mutual understanding and
trust through dialog and cooperation and resolve differences and disputes between
each other by peaceful means. This is a realistic way of guaranteeing peace and
security."[25] The fact that China and Russia have basically resolved their boundary
and territorial issues on the basis of consultation on an equal footing and mutual
understanding and accommodation has set a good example for resolving disputes
between different countries.

China and Russia have similar views regarding U.S. deployment of TMD. They
both hold that NMD and TMD are aimed first of all at Chinese and Russian

missiles, which would upset the balance of forces and strategic stability.[26] Therefore, the deployment of missile defense systems (be it regional or national) will fundamentally undermine the arms reduction process. Besides, it will also inevitably lead to a new arms race in Asia, where both China and Russia have vital interests. The common stand of China and Russia with regard to NMD and TMD has already become an important aspect of cooperation between the two countries in the international arena, and it will also help strengthen relations between China and the Russian Far East.

PROSPECTS FOR THE PUTIN ERA

In two articles published at the end of 1999, President Putin emphasized that Russia must rid itself "in a very short period of time" of its long-standing crisis. He said that there must be a "drastic change" in Russian economic and social development within the next decade. Otherwise, Russia would "face a real danger of lagging behind the world's major powers forever."[27] These remarks show that compared with Boris Yeltsin, Putin seems to have a stronger sense of urgency in resolving Russia's economic crisis and reassuming great-power status. In an open letter to the Russian electorate published in *Izvestiia* on February 15, 2000, Putin emphasized that with regard to Russia's national interests, "internal goals should take precedence over the external ones." He said that Russia's status in the world directly depended on whether or not it could successfully resolve its own internal problems. All this indicates that: (1) Putin will attach more importance to economic interests in Russian foreign policy than Boris Yeltsin; (2) Russia under Putin will quicken its steps to improve relations with the West so as to create a more favorable external environment for its economic recovery and its integration into the world economy; and (3) the Putin government will try to avoid conflicts and confrontation with the United States and other western countries, especially on those issues in which Russia has no vital interests and which would be costly for Russia.

On the other hand, Putin has also made it clear that Russia will resolutely defend its vital interests on issues related to Russia's national sovereignty, territorial integrity, and national security. Putin's handling of the war in Chechnya has fully proved this. Putin has also declared that Russia will continue to oppose NATO's eastward expansion, especially NATO's intention to grant membership to former Soviet republics. He has expressed his determination not to allow the United States to alter the existing strategic balance and has warned that if the United States violates the ABM Treaty and deploys an NMD system, Russia will consider withdrawing from the START II and other arms reduction treaties—including those related to short- and medium-range nuclear missiles. Putin has also declared that Russia will not accept a unipolar world based on the hegemony of one country or a few countries, and it will continue to safeguard the dominant role of the U.N. and its Security Council in international security affairs. It seems, therefore, that Putin's foreign policy will be more pragmatic, stable, and predictable than was Yeltsin's.

Sino-Russian relations, which were developed smoothly and quickly in the Yeltsin era, have brought real benefits to both countries. The strategic partnership between the two countries has not only made it possible for them to resolve difficult issues in their bilateral relations, but also has strengthened their respective status in the international arena. After the leadership change in Russia, the basis of the strategic partnership between China and Russia has not changed. The two countries still have many common interests in their bilateral relations and in international affairs. Since creating a favorable external environment in order to promote domestic economic development remains the most important goal of the foreign policies of both China and Russia, the two countries still need to cooperate with and draw support from each other in safeguarding their respective national sovereignty and territorial integrity, opposing foreign interference in their internal affairs, maintaining the dominant role of the U.N. in international security affairs, promoting multipolarity, and maintaining the existing strategic stability. And they both believe that this cooperation will remain an important factor in global stability. In a telephone conversation with President Jiang Zemin immediately after his election, the new Russian president made it clear that developing and deepening a strategic partnership with China was a persistent policy of Russia, and he expressed his belief that Russian-Chinese relations would develop in a comprehensive manner in the new century.[28]

However, there are some signs of differences between Putin's China policy and Yeltsin's. The most important difference is that Putin's China policy probably will be more pragmatic than that of his predecessor. Yeltsin paid more attention to the development of political relations with China than to economic relations. In my view, this is one of the reasons that the development of economic cooperation between the two countries has lagged behind political cooperation. From 1992–2000, trade volume between the two countries, with the exception of 1993, has fluctuated around $6 billion, which is only about one-tenth of China's trade volumes with Japan or the United States. This obviously is not in conformity with the actual ability of the two countries, nor is it in their interests. In a letter to Chinese Premier Zhu Rongji in February 2000, Putin emphasized that at present the expansion of economic cooperation between the two sides had particularly important significance.[29] When meeting with Chinese Foreign Minister Tang Jiaxuan the following month, Putin said that the development of technological and economic cooperation between the two countries and regional cooperation between the two sides had good prospects.[30]

We can expect the Putin government to take more effective measures on such issues as illegal immigration and cross-border criminal activities. Putin will also strengthen cooperation with China within the framework of the "Shanghai Five." The overall situation in Central Asia remains very complicated. Religious extremism, national separatism, international terrorism, and other external factors have posed a grave threat to the security of Central Asia and the surrounding areas. Because Russia and China have common interests in maintaining peace and stability in Central Asia, the two countries will strengthen cooperation against various forms of cross-border criminal activities and prevent external forces, including Western forces, from expanding their influence in this region. China, Russia, Kazakhstan, Tajikistan, and Kyrgyzstan are determined not to allow NATO to intervene in the conflicts of Central Asia.

Like its predecessor, the Putin government will continue to support China in its stand regarding Taiwan. In the above-mentioned telephone conversation with President Jiang, Putin stated that Russia respects and supports China in its stand regarding Taiwan, and he promised that Russia would not sell weapons to Taiwan. Nevertheless, as Russia is now more eager to improve relations with the United States, it will try to avoid being directly involved in conflicts between China and the United States. In a speech at the Moscow Institute of International Relations on March 16, 2000, Sergei Ivanov, Secretary of the Russian Security Council and Russian Defense Minister, said explicitly that Russia will sell weapons to China, but it does not want them to be used to resolve the Taiwan issue.[31] At present, Russia is under pressure from the United States to stop selling sophisticated weapons to China. There are also influential forces in Russia that fear the emergence of a militarily stronger China and are opposed to selling weapons to China. Under these circumstances, it is possible that Russia will tighten its control over the export of sophisticated weapons and equipment to China. But even so, as Russia is desperately in need of hard currency, military-technological cooperation between the two countries will continue to expand.

Since the beginning of 2000, Russia and China have cooperated well in areas where Russia has vital interests, such as the maintenance of strategic stability, U.S. development of missile defense systems, and the dominant role of the U.N. in international security affairs. As the Asia Pacific region, especially Northeast Asia, is becoming more important to Russia both in economic and security terms, Russia will also continue to strengthen cooperation with China on issues related to peace and stability there. But at the same time, like the Yeltsin government, the Putin government will have no interest in forming a Russian-Chinese political and military alliance, nor will it want to give the impression that the strategic partnership between China and Russia is aimed at the United States and its allies. This is also an important reason why Putin has emphasized the comprehensive nature of the strategic partnership between Russia and China rather than concentrating on political and military cooperation.

On the whole, therefore, Putin's China policy also serves China's national interests. The fact that Putin attaches more importance to Russia's economic cooperation with China than Yeltsin entirely conforms to China's interests. For a number of reasons, the Chinese government also desires the expansion of economic and trade cooperation with Russia, and particularly with the Russian Far East. First, China has a relatively short supply of mineral resources. With the exception of coal, most of the important mineral resources that China possesses, such as oil, iron, copper, and aluminum, cannot satisfy the needs of a rapid and sustained development of China's national economy. But the Russian Far East and Siberia are very rich in these resources. Second, developing economic cooperation with Russia, especially with the Far East, is also in the interests of more balanced economic development between China's north and south. Third, strengthening economic cooperation with Russia conforms to China's policy of pluralizing its foreign economic relations. Moreover, because economic relations are increasingly becoming the foundation of political relations, the strategic partnership between China and Russia would be fragile without a closer economic link.

The fact that Putin will take more effective measures to deal with cross-border criminal activities than his predecessor is also in keeping with China's desire to maintain tranquility and stability along the Sino-Russian border. In the past few years, China's border forces have cooperated very well with their Russian counterparts in cracking down on various forms of cross-border crimes, and China hopes to strengthen this cooperation. So far, cross-border criminal activities along the Sino-Russian border have not posed a serious threat to China's security. However, if they are not curbed effectively, their threat to China's security will grow, especially in view of the fact that large amounts of Russia's nuclear weapons and materials are deployed or stored in the Russian Far East.

An important reason for the existence of the fear of a "China threat" among the population in the Russian Far East is the fact that while Russia's strength is declining sharply, China is increasingly becoming a strong world power. Putin's foreign and economic policies will definitely promote economic development of the Russian Far East. If the economy of the region develops quickly and the outmigration is curbed, then the people in the Russian Far East probably will not be as fearful of a stronger China. This, in turn, will be conducive to the further development of friendly relations between China and the Russian Far East.

As for international affairs, the Chinese government does not want to give the impression that the Sino-Russian strategic partnership is aimed at the United States or its allies. Like Russia, China has no desire to form a political or military alliance with its huge neighbor. That is mainly because both China and Russia are eager to develop constructive and friendly relations with the United States and other Western countries, and they both believe that it is in their national interests to pursue an independent and balanced foreign policy.

On the whole, these trends in Russian foreign policy will not negatively affect, but will further promote, the development of strategic partnership between China and Russia. At the June 2000 Sino-Russian summit, it was stressed in the "Beijing Declaration" that the strategic partnership established in 1996 entirely conforms to the fundamental interests of the two countries and that China and Russia are determined to make constant efforts to raise their relations to a new level. The declaration pointed out that further comprehensive development of cooperation in the fields of economics and trade, science and technology, and military technology is one of the important directions of expanding and deepening the strategic partnership. The declaration particularly mentioned that the agreement on joint economic utilization of individual islands and their surrounding waters in the boundary rivers, which was signed by the Russian and Chinese governments on December 9, 1999, is unprecedented and that the successful implementing of the agreement will constitute another important step in making Sino-Russian relations harmonious. The declaration announced that China and Russia will, in a constructive and pragmatic spirit, continue to hold negotiations regarding the sectors of the common border on which the two countries have yet to reach agreement. Therefore, after Putin's visit to Beijing, China's relations with Russia, including the Russian Far East, are likely to be raised to a new level.

NOTES

1. See Mikhail Alexseev, "Chinese Migration in the Russian Far East: Security Threats and Incentives for Cooperation in Primorskii Krai," chapter 13 in this volume.

2. Men Zhen, "Social and Economic Situation in the Russian Far East in 1998," unpublished paper presented to Beijing conference, November 9, 1999.

3. ITAR-TASS, March 23, 2000.

4. *Zolotoi Rog,* March 5, 1999.

5. Reference Materials, Xinhua, November 15, 1999.

6. Ibid.

7. *Vladivostok,* March 2, 1999.

8. Yegor Gaidar, "Rossiia XXI veka: Ne mirovoi zhandarm, a forpost demokratii v Evrasii," *Izvestiia,* May 18, 1995, 4.

9. Andrei Karachinsky, "Chinese Do Not Need Russia," *New Russia,* July 23, 1999, in Reference Materials, Xinhua, July 29, 1999.

10. Ibid.

11. Qin Xiangyuan, "Giving New Impetus to the Development of Russo-Chinese Economic and Trade Relations: An Interview with Nazdratenko, Governor of the Russian Maritime Krai," *The Far East Trade Herald*, January 31, 2000.

12. Viktor Ishaev and Pavel Minakir, *Dalnii vostok Rossii: Realnosti i vozmozhnosti ekonomicheskogo razvitiia* (Khabarovsk: DVO RAN, 1998).

13. Maxim Ukhin, "ROK and Japan May Become Russia's Ally," *Izvestiya*, May 26, 1999, in Reference Materials, Xinhua, May 28, 1999.

14. Andrei Soglin, "Gun Smoke is Emerging in Russian Border Areas: The Government Held a Special Meeting to Study the Economic Situation of Russian Border Areas," *Tribuna*, August 6, 1999, in Reference Materials, Xinhua, August 9, 1999.

15. *Vladivostok*, July 29, 1999.

16. The talk was held between Aleksey Arbatov and a Chinese delegation, of which I was a member, from the Euro-Asian Social Development Research Institute of the Development Research Center of the State Council of China on October 13, 1999.

17. *Vladivostok*, May 6, 1999.

18. *Vladivostok*, June 26, 1999.

19. *Zolotoi Rog*, March 5, 1999.

20. See, for example, a speech made by Zhu Bangzhao, spokesman of the Chinese Foreign Ministry, in a press conference held on November 24, 1998, in Moscow, reported by Xinhua, November 24, 1998.

21. *People's Daily*, September 4, 1999, 6.

22. Karachinsky, "Chinese Do Not Need Russia."

23. Speech of Sha Zukang, head of the Chinese delegation at the 2000 Meetings Reviewing "The Treaty of Nonproliferation of Nuclear Weapons," April 24, 2000, Xinhua, April 24, 2000.

24. *People's Daily*, July 28, 1998, 1.

25. Ibid.

26. Interview given by L. Iwashov, head of the Department of International Military Cooperation of the Russian Ministry of National Defense on April 13, 2000, in Xinhua, April 17, 2000.

27. "The First Ten Years of the 21st Century," Russian News Agency, December 27, 1999; and "Russia at the Turn of the Millenium," *Nezavisimaia gazeta*, December 30, 1999, in Reference Materials, Xinhua, December 28, 1999, and January 6, 2000.

28. "President Jiang and President Putin Had a Telephone Conversation," Xinhua, March 27, 2000.

29. *Izvestiia*, February 5, 2000.

30. Xinhua, March 1, 2000.

31. Xinhua, March 16, 2000.

16

The Dynamics of Russian–South Korean
Relations and Implications for the Russian Far East

Yong-Chool Ha

The year 2000 marked the tenth anniversary of normalization of relations between South Korea and the Soviet Union. Bilateral relations started with great expectations on both sides, with five presidential visits and the establishment of various committees for cooperation in areas such as science and technology, the economy, and the environment. However, both sides now acknowledge that relations failed to meet expectations, and have reached a point where a sober review is needed.

From the beginning, Soviet/Russian and South Korean approaches to each other were quite different. Russia's expectations of South Korea were definitely of an economic nature.[1] Contrary to the then prevalent view that Russia tried to play a Korea card with Japan, Russia was motivated by short-term economic interests in approaching South Korea rather than by long-term strategic considerations.

However, the enthusiasm turned out to be short-lived. The investments that Korea promised did not materialize, and the Russians became disappointed by empty Korean promises and thinly veiled attempts to cheat them. The offer to lend the Soviet Union $3 billion, made during negotiations for establishing diplomatic relations, put both parties in an awkward position. Originally it was agreed that the Korean side would provide a $3-billion loan in 1991. With the fall of the Soviet Union, only $1.47 billion was loaned, and the remaining amount has not been delivered. Disagreement over interest and principal payments contributed to the dampening of the fragile relationship. The Russians felt that the South Koreans were unusually aggressive and pressuring in rescheduling loan payments.

Korean news media played some role in flaring up the disputes by raising questions about the prospects for full repayment.

Another factor that facilitated Russian-Korean relations at the initial stage was South Korea's determined pursuit of its northern policy.[2] With the collapse of the Cold War structure, South Korea began to make assertive efforts to approach socialist countries. After South Korea normalized relations with Russia, it established diplomatic relations with China. Such an aggressive diplomatic posture, the ambiguity of Russia's policy toward Korea, economic confusion, and the needs of Russia contributed to the initial breakthrough in relations between South Korea and Russia. As a result, Russia came to support South Korea even to the extent of alienating its traditional ally, North Korea.

However, South Korea's active northern policy was not supported by delicate management of the new relations. For instance, the Russian side was very sensitive about South Korea's heavy tilt toward China.[3] South Korea's lack of diplomatic skill frequently alienated the Russians, especially as Russia went through the sudden change in international status from a superpower of the Cold War to a troubled country. It was a rare diplomatic situation in which the two status-conscious countries had to adjust their expectations. South Korea was for the first time experiencing high self-esteem and desired recognizition in the international arena for its economic development and earnest pursuit of democratization. In a strange way, South Korean foreign policy manifested a thinly veiled nationalistic tendency in the form of too much self-confidence. In contrast, Russia lost national prestige.

For the Soviets, the establishment of diplomatic relations with South Korea was a symbol of the end of the Cold War policy in Northeast Asia. Russia, based on new thinking and de-ideologization of foreign policy, distanced itself from North Korea. But as the expectations of South Korea in the economic field evaporated, a one-sided tilt toward the south was criticized not only by the opposition forces but also within the ruling establishment. At the same time, it turned out that South Korea had not overcome the Cold War structure in terms of its relationship with the United States. The Russians have realized that South Korea's political and military ties with the United States are not likely to change anytime soon. This perception was supported in discussions of weapons sales from Russia to South Korea as a way of paying back the loans. This perception was further reinforced by North Korea's nuclear diplomacy, where North Korea wanted to deal mainly with the United States, and South Korea made furious efforts not to be left out of the process, especially trying to guard against any secret deal between the United States and North Korea.

Unlike Moscow's approach to South Korea, Seoul's approach to the Soviet Union and Russia has been mainly political in nature.[4] South Korea was eager to use relations with the Soviet Union and Russia to induce North Korea into a high-level dialogue, including a North-South summit. The Russian and South Korean sides did not share a common outlook in their foreign policy orientations, except that they both sought short-term expediency.

South Korea tried to win Russia's favor by economic means. However, the Korean side soon realized that its approach was based on an overly optimistic assessment of Soviet and Russian influence on North Korea, an inadequate understanding of the character of their bilateral relations, and a face-value acceptance of the concept of new thinking. Thus South Korea, faced with the unexpected difficulty in accomplishing its objectives, was forced to change its view of Russia. The Soviet and Russian approach to South Korea, and the South Korean perspective of Russia, were both rooted in opportunistic, short-term considerations, and neither side focused on long-term prospects or the management of everyday diplomacy.

When the Soviet Union collapsed so unexpectedly and easily, the initial South Korean reaction was that of skepticism about Russia's future capabilities. As Russia became increasingly caught up in internal turmoil, this skepticism turned into concern about Russia's ability to maintain a consistent foreign policy. Russia's lack of progress in its Asian diplomacy after Gorbachev's 1986 Vladivostok speech, as well as the later, more nationalistic character of its foreign policy, were not surprising. Russia's threatening approach to South Korea, whereby it used its export of nuclear technology to North Korea as a diplomatic instrument, considerably lowered its credibility and did not help improve South Korean images of Russia, especially considering the immaturity of their relationship. In South Korea's eyes, Russia expected only short-term profit from the relationship with no specification of long-term goals. South Korea also wondered whether Russia was still giving priority to its relationship with Europe and the United States, and whether in fact it had any interest in Asia at all.

In addition, dealing with a Russia that had just lost its superpower status placed South Korea in a very puzzling and unusual situation. South Korea was accustomed to a very simplistic conception of the enemy, basically in the black-or-white lense of the Cold War, and as such it had no prior experience in dealing with a superpower with the vague pride and desire for external recognition. Similarly, Russia did not understand the specific elements of its relationship with South Korea that distinguished this relationship from Russian relations with China or with the United States.

South Korea's relations with Russia have been affected by its relations with the United States. This is not only a consequence of the country's history of dependence on the United States. North Korea's strategy has been to engage with the United States through security matters, such as nuclear and missile issues. North Korea's determined policy to engage the United States gives the whole situation a trilateral North Korea–U.S.–South Korea structure. North Korea's strategy has made it difficult for Russia to establish a role for itself, while the fast-changing diplomatic circumstances have not allowed South Korea room for a more balanced diplomacy.

Overall, relations between Russia and South Korea are not yet on a solid foundation. As one Russian diplomat remarked, South Korean–Russian relations are just past the stage of mutual recognition.[5] At the bilateral level, South Korea has been disappointed at the weakened influence of Russia in Northeast Asia, especially with North Korea. Also, South Korea has not been pleased with the complications in getting back its loans to Russia. On the Russian side, South Korean investment in Russia was less than the Russians expected, and they were humiliated with South Korea's demands for loan repayment. And the Russians feel that they have not been fully compensated for supporting South Korea— by abandoning their former ally, North Korea—in the process of resolving North Korean nuclear issues. The Russians felt displeased with their exclusion from the four-party talks involving China, the United States, and the two Koreas to resolve North Korean nuclear issues. Bilateral issues, some of which involved broader regional and peninsular issues, reached an unsatisfactory level by 1997. The economic crises in both countries in 1997 and 1998 further worsened economic relations. Worsening relations were epitomized by the 1998 expulsions of diplomats for the inappropriate gathering of information. At the same time, they provided chances for sober reevaluations of the relations between the two countries. Bilateral trade decreased considerably, and Korean direct investment also had not materialized as planned. In the meantime, inside Russia for the past few years the perception that Russia lost North Korea has been strong.

RUSSIAN–SOUTH KOREAN ECONOMIC AND MILITARY RELATIONS

Progress on trade, direct investment, and intergovernmental economic cooperation has been slow and uneven. Trade showed rapid growth up to 1996, reaching $3.8 billion in total volume. However, due to the South Korean economic crisis and a Russian moratorium, trade volume decreased significantly to $2.1 billion in 1998. South Korean direct investment in Russia is quite small. Of the 139 projects (worth $259 million) that have received Russian government permission, only 93 projects, amounting to $151 million, have been realized so far. The proportion of trade with the Russian Far East to total trade ranged from 7 to 13 percent between 1992 and 1998, but the proportion of foreign direct investment has been considerably higher: fifty-five projects received South Korean direct investment in the Far

East between 1990 and 1999 (59 percent of total South Korean investment in Russia) worth $69 million (45.7 percent of the total).[6]

During President Boris Yeltsin's visit to South Korea in 1992, the two governments agreed to construct a free economic zone, and in 1995 a basic agreement was concluded to lease land (one hundred hectares) for forty-nine years for an industrial complex. During President Kim Dae Jung's visit to Russia in May 1999, an agreement was concluded on the construction of the Nakhodka industrial complex.[7] The agreement stipulates exemptions from taxes and customs duties for construction materials for the industrial complex, and the deduction of corporate and value-added taxes for those companies that export more than 50 percent of what they manufacture in the industrial complex.

Another project on which North and South Korea and Russia are participating is the Tumen River Economic Development Area. South Korea has been interested in the project largely because of the possibility it holds for opening up relations with the North. Russia has been interested in the project but lacks financial resources. So far there have been more than twenty formal and informal meetings for the project, but no significant progress has been made.[8]

Military relations between South Korea and Russia were quite active in the 1990s. During Yelstin's 1992 visit to Korea, the two sides concluded a memorandum of understanding on military exchanges, including personnel exchanges, visits of naval vessels, and the exchange of observers for military exercises. Since then, five memoranda of understanding for military exchanges have been signed, and there have been ministerial-level meetings and four meetings of the chief commanders of the army, navy, and air force. In addition, an agreement was reached in 1997 on cooperation in the defense industry and military supplies. Korean defense officials evaluate the exchanges with Russia positively because they have accumulated defense technology and know-how by obtaining Russian military equipment as a partial payback of the previously mentioned loans.[9]

However, the exchanges were strictly bilateral and did not have any strategic implications. Moreover, it is known that purchasing Russian military equipment has aroused U.S. concerns. It is almost certain that the nature of military exchanges will change as the tension between North and South Korea begins to reduce and multilateral talks on a regional security formula become more active.

RUSSIA'S RESPONSE TO ITS LOSS OF INFLUENCE

Russian–North Korean Relations

Gorbachev's domestic political and economic reforms and new thinking in foreign policy caused the lukewarm relations with North Korea to decline precipitously. North Korea was particularly alarmed by the weakening political role of the Communist Party of the Soviet Union and the dismantling of the command economy. These reforms not only affected North Korea in ideological and political terms; they also affected economic relations between the Soviet Union/ Russia and North Korea in terms of trade and other forms of cooperation. Trade between the two countries dropped from $2.6 billion in 1990 to $65 million in 1996. Furthermore, the end of the Cold War posed a serious challenge for Kim Il Sung by changing the international environment. Gorbachev's foreign policy completely changed the nature of both Sino-Soviet relations and U.S.-Soviet relations. For Kim Il Sung, who defined the United States as his primary enemy and took advantage of the Sino-Soviet dispute, the new international order shook the basis of his regime.

On the other hand, Russia expected that more economic gains could be obtained from South Korea while at the same time North Korea was increasingly becoming a burden. Russia adopted a pro–Western posture in 1991 as it democratized and liberalized the economy. Russia was absorbed in dealing with its own domestic political, economic, and social problems. Given their domestic tasks, Russian foreign policy shifted from a pro–North Korea orientation to a pro–South Korea policy. As noted, South Korea's aggressive efforts to isolate North Korea facilitated this trend. With improving Sino-Russian relations, the value of North Korea was further lowered. In addition, Russia had no immediate political issue with South Korea, especially compared with Japan. Moreover, North Korea's adventurous nuclear policy was viewed by the Russians as threatening Northeast Asian security.

One of the signs of deteriorating relations was Russia's position on the future of the 1961 Treaty on Friendship, Cooperation, and Military Assistance. President Yeltsin, without any prior consultation with his Foreign Ministry, announced that Russia would stop providing weapons to North Korea and that the 1961 treaty needed to be overhauled, as Russia would not be willing to observe its military obligations as stipulated in the treaty. Instead, Yelstin concluded an agreement on the principles of bilateral relations, trade, and economic cooperation and a memorandum of understanding on military exchanges with South Korea.[10]

During his visit to Seoul, Yelstin also announced that Russia would stop providing nuclear technology to North Korea, and when North Korea decided to withdraw from the Nonproliferation Treaty (NPT), Russia criticized the move as adventurous. In 1995 Russia decided not to extend the 1961 treaty, and on September 10, 1996, the treaty expired.

In consequence, Russian–North Korean military relations became significantly constrained. As one scholar remarked, Russia continued a minimalist low-level military contact approach to preserve an effective channel of influencing Pyongyang and to keep a foothold in the North Korean market.[11]

However, this did not mean all military supplies were stopped. Russia continued to deliver spare parts and weapons of a defensive nature. Russia's pursuit of arms exports on a commercial basis has limited sales, as North Korea cannot meet Russian demands to pay in hard currency. It is estimated that approximately 70 percent of North Korea's $4 billion debt to Russia can be accounted for by weapons that have not been paid for. Pyongyang feels extreme animosity about the Russian policy shift. This has been manifested in the refusal to permit friendship calls by Russian naval vessels to Wonsan, the periodic expulsion of Russian diplomats, and the imposition of severe restrictions on the movement of Russians in North Korea.

Regarding economic cooperation, traditional relations between factories broke down, and trade volume plummeted from $2.5 billion (61 percent of North Korea's trade) to $83 million in 1995 (4 percent of the trade volume). The number of staff at the Russian Office of the Trade Representative in Pyongyang was reduced to 4 persons from the previous 40–50 people. Other representatives of governmental agencies closed their offices in Pyongyang, and all the correspondents except one withdrew from North Korea. As a result, Russia lost whatever influence that it had over North Korea.[12]

North Korea's New Strategies and the Isolation of Russia

In an effort to adjust to a new regional and international environment, North Korea has played security and military cards rather than opening its economy and society. Basically, North Korea tried to gain the attention of the United States by playing its nuclear card, and to translate that card into economic gains. It was an attempt to avoid direct pressure from South Korea in its efforts to open the North.

North Korea's military games started with its refusal to sign the International Atomic Energy Agency's (IAEA) nuclear safety agreement in 1991. Defying international pressure to sign the agreement, North Korea argued that it was in violation of sovereignty and interference in domestic affairs. It refused to admit IAEA inspectors to its nuclear reactors and sites. In March 1993 North Korea announced its withdrawal from the NPT. From that time on, a slow negotiation began between the United States and North Korea. Ultimately the two sides reached an agreement in Geneva in 1994—in return for North Korea staying within the NPT regime and allowing IAEA inspection, efforts to replace North Korea's plutonium-producing reactors with light-water nuclear reactors by an international consortium, normalization of North Korean–American relations, and cooperation for the security of a nuclear-free Korean Peninsula were promised.[13]

In March 1995 an international consortium, the Korean Peninsular Energy Development Organization (KEDO), was established to implement one of the Geneva agreements. Korea, Japan, the United States, and North Korea became the original members.[14] KEDO's main function was to determine the standard nuclear power plant model for the two 1,000-megawatt nuclear power plants and to divide construction costs among the members. Originally, North Korea wanted the Russian standard for a light-water reactor in an effort to avoid the South Korean standard. In the process of negotiations, Moscow made it known that it wanted the Russian standard to be adopted given the close nuclear cooperation during the Soviet period between North Korea and the Soviet Union.[15]

Negotiations on the peace and security of the Korean Peninsula also took place. North Korea took measures to endanger the armistice agreements and the system. Czech and Polish delegates to the Overseeing Committee of Neutral States were excluded in 1994 and 1995. In 1994 North Korea announced the establishment of the Office of People's Army and requested the recall of the Chinese representative to the Military Armistice Committee. In April 1996 North Korea surprised South Korea and the United States by announcing that it would no longer be responsible for maintaining and managing the demilitarized zone. A series of these measures put the 1953 Armistice Agreement in danger. Alarmed by North Korea's provocative actions, South Korea and the United States proposed four-party talks consisting of North and South Korea, China, and the United States. After turbulent preparatory meetings in early 1997, there were six main meetings through August 1999. To date, these talks have not produced any tangible results, but have gradually developed an agenda for discussion.

Russia has been persistently excluded in dealing with events occurring in and around the Korean Peninsula. When North Korea withdrew from the NPT, Russia demonstrated its firm commitment to the treaty by supporting the IAEA position. Russia decided to freeze the $4 billion project to build three light-water reactors at Sinpo on North Korea's east coast. Russia also proposed an eight-party international conference to resolve North Korean nuclear issues, but it was given the cold shoulder. However, Russia continued to support the idea of denuclearization of the Korean Peninsula.[16]

Russia was also excluded from KEDO, and Moscow's suggestion for a Russian standard nuclear reactor was not accepted. Even worse for Russia, it was singularly disregarded in North Korean–American negotiations in Geneva. Russia felt so isolated from the process that it stated that the resolution contradicted an agreement between the United States and Russia to act jointly—to work out a draft resolution jointly, not to put forward unilateral initiatives, and to address ideas regarding sanctions in an international conference.[17]

North Korea's international maneuverings and its impact on the issues related to the Korean Peninsula have preempted a Russian role. At the same time, as mentioned earlier, Russia's expectations of South Korea, especially in economic areas, failed to materialize. Further, the success of the Russian Communist Party and the Liberal Democratic Party in the 1995 Duma elections highlighted Russian humiliation and loss of status. The strong nationalist orientations of these two groups contributed to more critical views of Russia's Western-oriented foreign policy. These factors contributed to a reevaluation of Russian policies toward North Korea.[18]

Signs of Improvement in Russian–North Korean Relations

The first sign of changing Russian–North Korean relations consisted of increasing visits of high-ranking political and governmental figures to Pyongyang. Starting with Deputy Foreign Minister Gregorii Kunadze's visit in 1993, Deputy Prime Minister Vitalii Ignatenko, Duma Chairman Gennadii Seleznev, and Vladimir Lukin, Chairman of the Russian Duma's Committee on International Affairs, have visited Pyongyang since 1996. One of the agenda items was to start negotiations on a new treaty that would replace the defunct 1961 friendship treaty. In January 1995 the Director of the Asia Bureau, Yevgenii Afanasiev, visited Pyongyang to present a draft of a new treaty for friendship and economic cooperation in which the automatic military intervention clause was omitted. Negotiations began on the new treaty in January 1997. Points of contention were whether to include North Korea's Koryo confederation formula for unification. Russia's position was to solve the unification issue based on the U.N. charter and international law. In March 1999 the two sides agreed to a new Treaty of Friendship, Good Neighborliness, and Cooperation, and the treaty was signed in February 2000. The treaty does not stipulate automatic military intervention, nor is it aimed at a third country; it does comply with the demands of international law and the U.N. charter. In short, the main purpose was to move toward normalizing bilateral relations.

What is also significant about the process of negotiation of the new treaty is the fact that the two countries tried to maximize their common outlook on regional and international situations. For instance, on ways to resolve the issue of the suspected Kumchangri nuclear site, Yevgenii Afanasiev, Russian ambassador to Seoul, warned that the United States should not threaten North Korea in any way.[19] In March 1999, when North Korean Foreign Minister Paek Nam Soon explained North Korean positions on the need for a North Korean–U.S. peace treaty, the withdrawal of U.S. troops, and confederal unification, Karasin expressed Russian understanding of the North Korean positions and deep concerns about unilateral moves by the United States, military coalitions among the United States, Korea, and Japan, and U.S.-Japanese joint efforts to build TMD.[20]

During the 1990s, military relations between Russia and North Korea had been practically at a standstill following Gorbachev's decision not to sell offensive weapons and weapons of mass destruction to North Korea in 1991 and Yelstin's decision to stop supplying parts and weapons in 1994. However it appears that the supply of spare parts needed for maintenance of Russian arms in North Korea has continued. It is known that North Korea concluded a contract with Rosovooruzhenie, the Russian official arms export agency, to build a factory for Mig-29 fighter planes. North Korea also purchased military Pchela 1T spy scouter planes from Russia. Rumors have it that several hundred Russian scientists are working in North Korea, without official permission from the Russian government, apparently to help in developing missiles and other armaments.[21]

In 1996 Russia's Deputy Prime Minister Ignatenko went to Pyongyang for the first meeting of the Russian–North Korean Joint Committee for Economic, Scientific, and Technological Cooperation. During this visit, the two countries agreed to restore economic relations to the 1991 level and to establish a working group to promote North Korean–Russian Far East economic relations. In November 1996 an agreement was concluded to promote investment. Russia offered North Korea $800,000 worth of medicine and canned food. In August 1997 the two sides agreed on principles for repaying North Korea's debt to Russia. Several months later it was reported that Pyongyang had agreed that gas pipelines from the Republic of Sakha to South Korea and Japan could pass through North Korea.

In 1998 an interesting development emerged—old forms of economic cooperation revived between the Kemerovo oblast government and the North Korean metallurgy department to supply special equipment and parts to the Kimchaek steel mill. It was also agreed that Russia would supply coke to Kimchaek to facilitate its operation. In 1999 Vladivostok's Dalmore rented 20 fishing vessels from North Korea. It was reported that many North Korean production facilities built with Soviet support would start operations with Russian assistance.[22] By strengthening Russian–North Korean relations, Russia hopes to play a more active role in the peninsula and Northeast Asia.

In the midst of an awkward period in the relationship with South Korea, President Kim Dae Jung visited Russia in May 1991. The visit became a catalyst for putting relations back on a normal track. Presidents Kim and Yeltsin agreed that both countries were pursuing similar goals of promoting democracy and a market economy. Russia expressed support for South Korea's sunshine policy, which recognizes the need for neighboring powers to approach North Korea. The South Korean side recognized the importance of Russia's role in maintaining stability and security in Northeast Asia. Both sides also agreed to establish a Northeast Asia multilateral security cooperation forum involving six countries.

Russia's renewed relationship with North Korea, South Korea's sunshine policy, and the June 2000 summit between North and South Korea suddenly opened new possibilities and generated new dynamics in South Korean–Russian bilateral relations, as well as in the Northeast Asian regional environment.

RUSSIA AND THE FUTURE OF THE KOREAN PENINSULA

Russia has both short-term and long-term interests on the Korean Peninsula. First of all, Russia is interested in maintaining stability in and around the peninsula. Any unstable situations will greatly affect the security of the Russian Far East and complicate security relations with other regional countries. For this reason, Russia does not want to see a sudden collapse of North Korea. At the same time Russia is also economically interested in the peninsula. Given its proximity to the Russian Far East, economic interactions will help improve economic conditions there. Most importantly, Russia has a long-term strategic interest in the military and security posture of a unified Korea. As one Russian expert on Korea remarked:

> Regardless of the status of Russian-American relations, a unified Korea under the military influence of America will be understood as an attempt to install modern military facilities near the Russian border. We think that any changes in the Korean situation affects Russian security. It will not sound too strange if we declare the peninsula to be a special zone of interest to the Russian Far Eastern security. Russia has a wide spectrum of measures and capacity to affect the situation in the peninsula and to play a mediating role.[23]

Russia has been consistent in supporting the principle of unification of the peninsula by North and South Korea themselves. At the same time, Russia has proposed a six-party multilateral regional security formula. However, the latter approach has not received support from the countries in the region.

Russia has largely been left out of the processes on the Korean Peninsula for the following reasons: Russia's declining political and economic influence; Russia is not a legal participant in the armistice agreement; the persistent strategy of North Korea to deal solely with the United States on security matters related to the Korean Peninsula; and the low level of economic integration of the Russian Far East with the peninsula and the region as a whole.

Most important among these limitations has been North Korea's persistent strategy to isolate South Korea in dealing with security and peace issues. Conscious of South Korea's economic and political pressure, North Korea has tried to exclude the South in any negotiations involving a new peace system except where the United States is involved. As long as North Korea pursues such a strategy, there is little room for Russia to play any role.

The four-party talks formula was based on an extreme lack of trust between the two Koreas and thus was the result of a compromise between Seoul's insistence on direct dialogue with the North and Pyongyang's attempts to exclude the South. Given this context of negotiations, there is a very limited possibility for a Russian role. However, a Russian role is conceivable assuming the four-party talks evolve along the following three stages.[24]

The first stage in building a peace system on the Korean Peninsula would be for the two sets of bilateral relations (North Korea–China and South Korea–United States) to improve the situation significantly in various ways—including military confidence-building. The four-party talks can contribute to the initial stage by incorporating the North Korean demand for direct talks with the United States while the South Koreans emphasize inter-Korean dialogue. There are two essential tasks to be undertaken during the first stage of the peace process on the Korean Peninsula. One is the preparation for the legal transition of the armistice into a peace treaty regime between the four nations that participated directly in the war—the two Koreas, the United States, and China. This includes the establishment of normal foreign relations between North Korea and the West. The other task is the creation of confidence-building, and a basic arms control regime among those nations with a military presence on the peninsula—principally the two Koreas and the United States.

An important point to be made about this first stage is that the four-party format does not exclude the constructive participation of other counties, especially Russia and Japan. By definition, they are not supposed to have formal power in determining the contents of the peace talks. As long as they want to contribute positively to the facilitation of peacemaking on the Korean Peninsula, their informal participation is surely something that should be welcomed. At this stage, Russia should recognize the validity of the four-party talks and support them. However, it should be noted that Russia should not utilize the strengthening of North Korean–Russian relations as a lever for pressure on the South.

The starting point of the second phase of the peace process is the adoption of a peace treaty. It would involve a higher-level arms control regime for the region that would require the wider participation of regional states, including Russia and Japan. A Northeast Asia–wide regime of restraints in arms transfers to the Korean Peninsula and a regional agreement to make the peninsula a nuclear-free zone requires the additional involvement of the two countries. The Koreans, both in the South and the North, are highly negative about the idea of accepting the role of the Japanese government in the first stage of the peace process. However, they must be ready to engage Japan as well as Russia in the process of building a wider system of peace and security on and around the peninsula. This means that the formal framework to realize the second phase of the peace process would turn into six-party talks including Russia and Japan.

The third and final stage of the peace process may result from the successful progress of six-party talks. If the peace process is intensified, as it should be during the course of the second stage, the two Koreas will be able to enter a qualitatively higher level of inter-Korean dialogue. That may produce a basis for a political commonwealth, possibly a confederal form of political integration, between the two Koreas. At this juncture, the multilateral peace talks, which began as a specific forum for peace on the Korean Peninsula, could develop into a region-wide security forum for Northeast Asia in general. The formation of a loose political commonwealth on the peninsula should be an indication that a mature and stable peace regime has emerged in Korea. Therefore, in the third stage, a multilateral peace forum for Korea should be able to shift to the higher mission of peace for East Asia. By this time, Russia should prepare the basis to execute an active role as a significant actor in this region, and the other states should support it.

This reasoning does not sustain itself when North Korea faces a sudden collapse or when North and South Korea make direct contacts and reach some breakthrough. And the role and influence of Russia may vary accordingly. As for the first possibility, the North Korean regime has proven its resilience in enduring food shortages and economic difficulties. Also, the possibility of collapse seems remote in the near future.

As for the second possibility, a significant historic development occurred in June 2000, when President Kim Dae Jung and Chairman of the Military Defense Committee Kim Jong Il held a summit in Pyongyang. The summit came as a surprise to many people, given the North Korean track record of avoiding direct contact with South Korea. It is known that the North agreed to the meeting because of the dire economic conditions, especially the state of its infrastructure (e.g., provision of electricity is a major problem). On the part of South Korea, the summit was the result of Kim Dae Jung's sunshine policy, in which South Korea has repeatedly assured that it does not have any intention of absorbing North Korea and has encouraged major powers to establish relations with the North. President Kim's Berlin Declaration in March 2000 also must have reassured North Korea of the South's willingness to open economic relations with the North. In the declaration, President Kim reaffirmed the commitment to support North Korea's economic recovery and the need to end the Cold War on the peninsula by establishing peaceful coexistence between the two sides rather than rushing toward a hasty unification.

At the summit meeting, the two sides agreed on the principle of independent solution of the Korea problems without outside interference, further search for forms of unification, economic cooperation, and reunions of individual families.[25] Since the summit meeting, visible changes have occurred. For example, three sets of family reunions were allowed in the second half of 2000; three ministerial-level meetings were held; a working group on North-South economic cooperation was established; and the first defense ministerial meeting was held on September 25. In addition, the defense ministers agreed in principle to eliminate dangers of war and cooperate in reconnecting the Kyungui railroad, which has been disconnected for the past 50 years.[26]

Whatever the ultimate outcomes of the summit may be, implications for the regional powers, including Russia, are enormous. It is expected that regional powers will be more active in their efforts to improve relations with North Korea, since South Korea no longer feels uneasy about regional powers approaching the North. In fact, it is likely that discussions on confidence building and changing the armistice system into a peace system will be more seriously and actively pursued. It is especially in economic areas that bilateral and joint international efforts will be made to invest in North Korea. If North-South relations develop to reduce the level of tension, it will facilitate peace talks not only for the Korean Peninsula but also for general regional security.

What all this means is that Russia, now with more balanced bilateral relations with the two Koreas, can play a more active role in security and economic areas. Russian proposals for a Northeast Asian security formula may receive more support than before. In bilateral relations with North Korea, Russia can exercise more influence than before when North Korea seeks Russian support in missile and nuclear issues. President Putin already demonstrated his shrewd diplomatic skill when he visited Pyongyang in July 2000 on his way to Osaka for the G-8 summit meeting. He revealed North Korean intentions to use only foreign rockets for peaceful space research.[27] Russia now can persuade North Korea to change its nuclear and missile programs, which might help thwart U.S. rationale for pursuing NMD. Bilateral economic relations with North Korea may be facilitated. Russia can gain more influence when North Korea wants to secure stable energy sources from Russia, and joint projects among North Korea, South Korea, and Russia in the Russian Far East will proceed with more speed. Most important, reestablishing the railroad between the Koreas would open the possibility of connecting the Korean Peninsula with the Trans-Siberian Railroad. The so-called iron silk road will bring new economic opportunities among Russia and North and South Korea. Compared to the aforementioned three-stage development of the peace system where deep mistrust and suspicion between North and South Korea was assumed, direct contacts between North and South Korea will provide a more dynamic environment for Russia to play some role.

IMPLICATIONS FOR THE RUSSIAN FAR EAST

Images of the Russian Far East have not been strongly established in South Korea. Geographical proximity notwithstanding, most Koreans are barely aware of the Russian Far East. Perhaps as a consequence of the Cold War and partly due to Korea's center-oriented mentality, Russian-Korean relations revolve around Moscow. With this broad caveat in mind, a number of news articles directly and indirectly related to the Russian Far East between 1997 and 1999 can be viewed as rough indicators of the nature of Korean (including North Korean)–Russian Far East relations.[28]

From 1997 to 1999, 56 articles appeared. Among them, 10 were about political, military, and security issues; 40 about economic matters; and 6 on cultural relationships. As expected, the Russian Far East is viewed predominantly in economic terms. Economic issues ranged widely from investment and trade to negotiations on economic deals. At the same time, some negative reports have appeared regarding such issues as vodka smuggling and labor abuse by joint-ventures. Regarding political and military contacts, reports were in the context of Moscow–Seoul relations, except in two reports about a local political leader visiting Seoul and a Korean–Russian Far East Association meeting. Thus, unlike in economic areas, in political and security areas the Russian Far East has not been directly involved. As my informal conversations with military officers in Seoul confirmed, the Russian Far East has not yet emerged with an autonomous security image in the strategic thinking of South Korean military planners and the general population.

There have been some cultural contacts, though limited in scale and scope. Many people have memories of the Russian Far East as a base for the Korean independence movement. Also, long-time South Korean residents and recent relocated South Koreans in Russia are a social base for contacts. Several universities and institutes have initiated academic exchanges, including student exchanges, though the scale has been very limited.

What is also noteworthy is that, contrary to our expectations, there has been considerable contact between North Korea and the Russian Far East. Thirteen articles on political and security matters and ten articles on North Korean–Russian Far East economic relations appear in the press survey. Russian–North Korean relations in political and security areas, such as negotiations on the sale of new submarines and North Korean missile tests, have more direct relevance to the Russian Far East. Although the majority of political articles were about negotiations on renewing the Russia–North Korea friendship treaty, most of the direct interactions between North Korea and the Russian Far East were economic in nature. However, some of these articles discuss negative factors, including abuse of North Korean labor, smuggling, and environmental damage.

South Korean interest in the Russian Far East is not much different from that of other countries—South Koreans have been mainly interested in natural resources and short-term gains.[29] At the same time, the perception of South Korea is different from that of China and Japan in the Russian Far East because South Korea does not have historical or political legacies in the region. What is unique about the perception of Koreans toward the Russian Far East is that the region is becoming a locus of contention and competition between South and North Korea.[30]

Among multilateral issues, oil and gas development, gas and oil pipeline construction, sea transportation, joint economic projects like the Tumen River Economic Development Area, and environmental issues have received press coverage. In comparison with the number of issues involved, little success has been recorded. This indicates that efforts to build region-wide regimes have been slow, reflecting a low degree of community-building in Northeast Asia.

Concrete implications for the Russian Far East can be derived from bilateral relations and future developments in and around the Korean Peninsula. First of all, renewed North Korean–Russian relations facilitate economic relations between North Korea and the Russian Far East. This may take multilateral as well as bilateral forms. For instance, the Tumen River Economic Development Area can be more actively pursued if North Korea becomes more open as a result of the July 2000 North-South summit. South Korea and Russia have already agreed on developing the Nakhodka industrial complex, and consequently South Korea, North Korea, and Russia may develop cooperative economic relations inside the Special Economic Zone. Most important, the connection of the Trans-Korean Railroad with the Trans-Siberian Railroad will further facilitate economic interactions between the Russian Far East and the Korean Peninsula. Not only will transportation costs of Korean products bound for Europe and Russia be reduced by more than by one-third, it will also open new opportunities for investment by Russia and the Koreas in RFE resource extraction industries.

At the same time, active economic interactions will further contribute to opening up North Korea. Thus the Russian Far East directly and indirectly will contribute to the stabilization of the Korean Peninsula. This will change the perception that the Russian Far East is becoming the locus of contention and competition between North and South Korea.

CONCLUDING REMARKS

In the post–Cold War era, relations between South Korea and Russia have shown interesting ups and downs. Differing expectations raised high hopes for both parties that eventually turned out to be unrealistic. Coinciding with the regime changes in both South Korea and Russia, the two countries have come to terms with realism. The realism was to renew Russia's relations with North Korea and to push for new ways for Russia to play some kind of regional role. South Korea has changed its policy toward North Korea from a rigid encirclement policy toward a more open and flexible engagement policy. Russia now can play a more even-handed policy toward the two Koreas and is likely to find new ways of participating in the peace process on the Korean Peninsula, while South Korea will need a new formula for establishing a peace system, in the process of which South Korea may open new venues for Russian roles.

With the breakthrough in North-South relations, more dynamic regional relations are expected to develop in the years to come. Russia, with its redefined foreign-policy orientations, can be more active in dealing with North Korea and economic cooperation among Russia, South Korea, and North Korea, especially through energy and transportation cooperation and joint venture opportunities.

The Russian Far East is currently viewed in economic terms by both North and South Korea. But with reduced tension on the Korean Peninsula, economic interests in the Far East may take on more political significance in facilitating the peace and stability of the peninsula. In turn it is hoped that the Russian Far East will be an integral part of the Northeast Asian community.

NOTES

1. On this point, see Yong-Chool Ha, "Engaging Russia in Northeast Asia," in Koji Watanabe, ed., *Engaging Russia in Asia Pacific* (Tokyo and New York: Japan Center for International Exchange, 1999), 26, 28.

2. On Korea's northern policy, see Hakjoon Kim, "Emerging Relations between South Korea and the Soviet Union," in Yu-Nam Kim, ed., *Korea, America, and the Soviet Union in the 1990s* (Seoul: Dankook University Press, 1991), 33–49.

3. Based on author's interview with Russian Vice Foreign Minister A. Panov in Moscow in 1995.

4. Ha, "Engaging Russia in Northeast Asia," 28; and Hongchan Chun and Charles E. Ziegler, "The Russian Federation and South Korea," in Stephen J. Blank and Alvin Z. Rubinstein, eds., *Imperial Decline: Russia's Changing Role in Asia* (Durham, N.C.: Duke University Press, 1997), 186.

5. Yevgenii Afanasiev, Russian ambassador to South Korea, quoted in an interview at the Sejong Insitute, in *Policy Paper for the Development of Partnership Between South Korea and Russia* (in Korean) (Seoul: Sejong Institute, 2000), 9.

6. Russian–South Korean economic relations are dealt with in Seung-Ho Joo, "Economic Relations between Russia and South Korea," chapter 18 in this volume.

7. The Sejong Insitute, *Policy Paper for the Development of Partnership Between South Korea and Russia*, 9.

8. On the details of the Tumen River Economic Development Area, see Unchol Yang, "Rajin, sunbong Economic and Trade Zone"(in Korean), in Haksoon Paek and Changsoo Chin, eds., *Bukhanmunjeu Kujechokchaengjom* (International Dimensions of "North Korean Problems")(Seoul: Sejong Institute, 1999), 165–223.

9. On the military relations between South Korea and Russia, see Chun and Ziegler, "The Russian Federation and South Korea," 200–201. This information also comes from the author's interviews with Korean Ministry of Defense officials, April 10, 2000.

10. On the process of deteriorating relations between Russia and North Korea, see Hyun Ik Hong, "North Korean-Russian Relations: Process, Causes, and Prospects"(in Korean), in Paek and Chin, eds., *Bukhanmunjeu Kujechokchaengjom,* 291 ff.

11. Ibid., 292; and Alvin Z. Rubinstein, "Russia's Relations with North Korea," in Blank and Rubinstein, eds., *Imperial Decline: Russia's Changing Role in Asia,* 163–69.

12. Hong, "North Korean-Russian Relations," 304. On the statistics, see *Bukhan News-letter* (North Korea Newsletter), June 1999, 3; and *Tongil Kyongje* (Unification Economy), July 1998, 71.

13. On the process of the resolution of the North Korean nuclear issue, see Daewoo Lee, "North Korean-U.S. Relations: Current Issues and Prospects" (in Korean), in Paek and Chin, eds., *Bukhanmunjeu Kujechokchaengjom,* 247 ff. There are several negotiation channels operating between North Korea and the United States: the missile talks, the talks on returning remains of soldiers of the Korean War, and the Kim-Kyegwan-Katman line.

14. Membership now includes the European Union.

15. On the details of KEDO developments, see Haksoon Paek, "Hanbandoenojigaebalgigu (KEDO)," in Paek and Chin, eds., *Bukhanmunjeu Kujechokchaengjom,* 65–129.

16. Rubinstein, "Russia's Relations with North Korea," 170.

17. Ibid., 177.

18. Hong, "North Korean-Russian Relations," 308–12.

19. *Chosun Ilbo* (Chosun Daily), January 28, 1999, cited in Hong, "North Korean-Russian Relations," 297.

20. Central News Agency (North Korea), March 20, 1999.

21. *Chosun Ilbo,* May 3, 1998.

22. On the recent economic interactions between North Korea and Russia, see Hong, "North Korean-Russian Relations," 301–305.

23. V. Tkachenko, "Current Situation on the Korean Peninsula and Its Prospects," unpublished discussion paper, 5.

24. The following analysis of the three stages of the development in the Korean peninsula is from Ha, "Engaging Russia in Northeast Asia," 40–42.

25. *Hangyure Shinmun* (Hangyure Daily), June 15, 2000.

26. On the connection of the Kyungui line, see *Chosun Ilbo,* July 31, 2000. On the announcement by the Hyundai Company on developing the Kaesung industrial complex, see *Chosun Ilbo,* August 23, 2000. On the defense ministerial meeting, see *Chosun Ilbo,* September 25, 2000. On the food aid, see *Chosum Ilbo,* September 26, 2000. And

on the discussion of investment guarantees, see *Chosun Ilbo*, September 30, 2000.

27. *Chosun Ilbo*, July 20, and July 21, 2000.

28. Event data were collected from the Yonhap News Agency reporting on Russian-Korean relations.

29. Peggy Falkenheim Meyer, "The Russian Far East's Economic Integration with Northeast Asia: Problems and Prospects," *Pacific Affairs* 72, no. 2 (1999):217.

30. Ibid., 216.

INTERNATIONAL RELATIONS:
PROSPECTS FOR COOPERATION

17

The Japanese Economic
Presence in the Russian Far East

Kunio Okada

Many observers have suggested that the Japanese-Soviet, and later the Japanese-Russian, economic relationship has not been very active because of the long-standing and unresolved Northern Territories dispute between the two countries.[1] In reality, from 1945 to 1991, the volume of Japan-Soviet trade increased almost constantly. In 1970 Japan was the largest trading partner of the former Soviet Union among the Western countries, and through the 1970s was the second largest after Germany. However, in the 1980s Japan ranked fifth or sixth among the USSR's Western trading partners, and in the 1990s its ranking among Russia's trading partners was even lower.

In the 1990s Japanese exports to Russia decreased almost every year. By 1999 the volume of exports had declined to the level of the early 1970s—less than one-sixth of the peak in Japan-Soviet trade.[2] Russia's share in overall Japanese exports became very small: it declined from 1.1–1.2 percent in the 1980s to only 0.11 percent in 1999. By comparison, China's share in total Japanese exports was 5.5 percent in the same year.

COMMODITY STRUCTURE OF JAPAN-RUSSIA TRADE

The main Japanese exports to Russia are industrial products (metals, machinery, and equipment), which comprise about 80 percent of total exports to Russia. Major exports have included communications equipment, home appliances, automobiles, mining and construction machines, loading machines, and metal processing machines. Russia's share of Japanese steel exports, which was 2.3 percent in 1991, declined to around 0.1–0.3 percent at the end of the 1990s.

Furthermore, a new problem arose that might further cut down on Japan's exports to Russia. According to the Russian Federation Federal Law No. 192-20-3, signed on December 29, 1998, freight must now clear customs and be delivered to Russian users within ninety days after the initial payment. According to this "ninety-day rule," when Russian enterprises remit an advance overseas, they must deposit the same amount of money in the Central Bank. Therefore, for the Russian enterprises the amount of initial "payment" will be doubled. In addition, when goods do not reach the Russian users within ninety days, the deposited money will be confiscated. This new system was most likely introduced to counter capital-flight. But it is almost impossible to deliver production goods such as machinery and equipment, for which production usually begins once the order is received, to the vast Russian territory within ninety days. Commodities are also difficult to deliver to Russian customers within ninety days. In addition, Russian customs procedures are considered to be very complicated and unclear, thus taking a lot of time.[3]

Japanese imports from Russia consist of four main items—fish and shellfish, timber, coal, and aluminum products, which account for more than 70 percent of total imports. Imports of these items have slackened largely because of declining prices and declining demand due to the recession in Japan. Problems among the Russian suppliers also account for part of the decline. First, because of indiscriminate fishing, the quality of fish and shellfish has deteriorated. Second, because of forest fires in production areas, the supply of timber has decreased. Third, Russian coal has lost its price competitiveness compared to Australian and Chinese coal.

In the near future, Japan's imports of those four major items are likely to be influenced by several factors. First, despite poor economic performance in Japan, the demand for fish and shellfish is likely to remain because they are important food items in Japan. Second, imports of aluminum are indispensable, since there is no longer an aluminum-refining industry in Japan. Russian aluminum is competitive and is likely to maintain a considerable market share in Japan. Third, although Russian timber has been very popular in Japan in the past, the timber trade has been declining gradually, and will probably continue to decline. This trend is largely due to problems with Russian supply and the failure of the two sides to reach agreement on the so-called Fourth KS Sangyo Project.[4] As for coal, the South Yakutsk coal development project provides for imports of a certain amount of coal every year for Japanese steel mills, but the stipulated amounts have never been reached due to problems in the Russian supply system.[5] Moreover, as mentioned, Russian coal has been losing price competitiveness to Australian and

Chinese coal, so, unless there are improvements, the Russian share of the Japanese market will continue to decline.

IMPROVED POLITICAL RELATIONS AND DETERIORATED ECONOMIC RELATIONS

After World War II until the end of the 1980s, political relations between Japan and the Soviet Union were almost continually poor. After the war, severe confrontation continued over the Northern Territories, so even mutual visits of the leaders of both countries rarely took place. Mikhail Gorbachev made an official visit to Japan in April 1991, and that was the first visit of a Russian head of state to Japan throughout the long history of Japanese relations with Russia, which had started in the mid-nineteenth century. This fact alone is enough to prove how bad political relations between the two countries were.

Official Japanese policy toward Russia also has changed. The fundamental difference in political and economic systems, which used to hinder the normal development of relations, no longer exists. Almost all of the impeding factors in the development of normal neighborly relations have disappeared, except for the unresolved Northern Territories dispute. Japan does not consider Russia as a potential enemy anymore, and a package of government programs to support Russia with a total sum of $4.3 billion has been implemented—in the forms of Japanese government trade insurance, credits from the Japan Bank for International Cooperation (formerly Export-Import Bank),[6] and other measures.

Political relations between Japan and Russia received remarkable momentum when then Prime Minister Ryutaro Hashimoto announced three principles of Japan's diplomatic policy toward Russia in 1997, namely "trust, mutual benefit, and a long-term perspective."[7] The announcement was highly appreciated in Russia and followed by two unofficial summits "without ties"; one in Krasnoyarsk in November 1997 and the other in Kawana, a resort near Tokyo, in April 1998. At no time in the past have there been so few factors in Japanese-Russian relations causing hostile confrontation as there are today.

Although Japanese-Russian political relations have improved, bilateral economic relations have lagged behind. Political issues, such as the Northern Territories dispute, have not had a strong effect. Rather, the trend in Japanese-Russian economic relations is largely the result of economic factors. The deterioration of the trade environment after the Russian financial crisis in August 1998 has affected Russia's trade with other countries, but its effects on Japanese-Russian trade seem most pronounced. Russia's trade with Europe is characterized by the same pattern as its trade with Japan—the exchange of raw materials for finished goods[8]—

but there are important differences. Russian shipments of natural gas and oil, delivered to the West via pipelines that were built long ago, provide a basis for greater economic and political interdependence.[9] Improved political relations appear to have helped to maintain economic ties between Russia and Europe.[10]

On the other hand, because the major Japanese exports to Russia were production goods, poor Russian economic performance has reduced Russia's domestic production and thus its demand for Japanese machinery and equipment. In addition, the relatively weak euro compared to the Japanese yen has improved the competitiveness of European exporters. If that is the case, why do Japanese companies adhere so closely to this pattern of trade with Russia?

After World War II, special trade companies, which were established for business with the Soviet Union only, first resumed Japan-Soviet trade. Then after the 1970s, Japan's big companies started to conduct business directly with the Soviet Union and took the leading position. Chemical plant and engineering companies, construction machine manufacturers, and big steel manufacturers (mainly exporting steel pipe) were the main players. Therefore, for Japan at that time, exporting machinery and equipment was the main element in trade with the Soviet Union. Even though there were some imports of timber and coal from the Soviet Union, these imports also made it possible to set up large resource-development projects, which led to further machinery and equipment exports from Japan. From the beginning, therefore, Japanese-Russian trade was very much oriented to Japanese exports of machinery and equipment.

For instance, in the 1970s several large-scale resource-development projects were realized with the help of large Japanese bank loans. In particular, the South Yakutsk coal resource development project and the second Far East forest resource development project (the Second KS Project), to which the Japan Export-Import Bank granted loans totaling more than $1 billion, gave a big impulse for further expansion of Japanese-Russian trade. Following these projects, bank loans were given for the export of large-diameter steel pipe and of large petrochemical plants—Japanese bank loans to the Soviet Union from 1974 to 1977 totaled $3.2 billion. The intention was to develop an active trade policy with the Soviet Union because of the significant national merit in developing a new export market for Japanese industrial goods and also in securing stable sources of energy and other resource imports from Soviet Siberia and the Far East. At that time, economic and trade relations between Japan and the Soviet Union were driven strongly by pure economic and commercial factors. But after the $1-billion contract of the Third KS Project was signed in 1981, no economic cooperation project was realized between Japan and the Soviet Union until the end of the 1980s. And after the collapse of the Soviet Union, besides Sakhalin oil and gas development projects (Sakhalin-1 and Sakhalin-2), no major resource-development project has materialized.

So the economic positions of both countries and the typical patterns of Japanese-Russian economic relations can be characterized by the following pattern:

- Russia's very rich natural resource endowment;
- Japan's great need for natural resources;
- Russia's lack of financial resources to develop them;
- Japan's financial resources to do so;
- Russian financing from Japan for the purchase of Japanese machinery and equipment for resource development;
- Russian export of resources to Japan, realized with the help of Japanese financing and machinery;
- Japanese payment for imported resources; and
- Russian payment for financing.

However, as noted, exporting machinery and equipment to Russia is very difficult. Therefore, it is inevitable that Japanese-Russian trade, especially exports to Russia, have been decreasing substantially. Nonpayment by some Russian importers has discouraged Japanese trading firms from developing their business with Russia.[11] Moreover, some major projects that could be financed by the Japan Bank for International Cooperation have not materialized. For example, two major contracts that were signed in the fall of 1995 for the modernization of an oil refinery in Yaroslavl (valued at $200 million) and the supply of equipment for a new diesel motor plant at the Kama Truck Factory (valued at $150 million) have not been finalized.[12]

NEW METHODS FOR JAPANESE EXPORTS TO RUSSIA

According to official Russian statistics, Japanese-Russian trade, especially Japanese exports to Russia, seems to be no longer mutually beneficial. It looks like the old model is no longer promising, while a new model has not been created. But it is well known that sales of Japanese household appliances in Russia have exceeded by many times the amount shown in Russian customs statistics. It is said that from 1994 to 1996, two million Japanese television sets were exported annually to Russia via third countries. The annual export value was estimated at more than $2 billion. And in 1997, the number may have reached four million units.[13] Thus, in those four years, some ten million Japanese televisions were sold in Russia. Japanese automobiles were also actively sold to Russia via third countries in the same period. Consumer goods made in Japan or produced by subsidiaries in Europe and Southeast Asia were brought into Russia by many means, including so-called shuttle trade from Finland, Dubai, Singapore, and so on. Japanese cars were also sold in the same way to Russia. Since there are no official statistics on the actual results of the Japanese-Russian trade via third countries, it is difficult to evaluate its size precisely. But it can be said that this style of trade complemented the low level of Japanese exports to Russia. Russian consumers bought them with the recognition that they were Japanese goods. So in this context they may be considered Japanese exports to Russia. Japanese televisions conquered the Russian market. They were sold at department stores and shops in remote areas such as the Russian Far East and northern regions, not to mention in Moscow and St. Petersburg. Russians are, in a sense, brand freaks, and they choose the high-quality televisions manufactured by Japanese companies. The same can be said about Japanese-made cars in Russia. The new middle class in Russia was the chief generator of the boom. Japanese manufacturers had studied the Russian market, built up their own business channels and know-how, and made big profits. If we take into consideration these exports through third countries, it can be said that Japanese exports to Russia are prospering—contrary to the common impression of poor trade relations.

Following the financial crisis of August 1998, the situation changed completely. Japanese export of consumer goods via third countries suffered a significant blow. It is said that Panasonic had increased audio and video product exports to Russia to some 20 billion yen in fiscal year 1997, but in 1998, exports were cut by half. SONY as well sold some 50–60 billion-yen worth of products in 1997, but in 1999 sales were cut to the level of 10 billion yen.[14] It seems that there was no clear recovery in 1999, and a little sign of recovery in 2000. One major manufacturer closed down its warehouse in Finland, which was set up for exports to Russia. In place of audio and video products, Japanese exporters now concentrate on selling personal computer notebooks, for which there seems to be high demand in Russia. Similarly, after the August financial crisis, Japanese automobile exports were cut in half in 1998, but there was a slow recovery in 1999 and 2000.

There are several reasons why Japanese goods are exported to Russia via third countries. First, some of them are Japanese products that are made in the Japanese overseas factories and exported from that country to Russia. These are not considered to be Japanese exports to Russia. Japanese cars manufactured in Europe or Japanese appliances made in Asia are in this category. Second, Japanese goods are purchased by Russian dealers in Singapore, the United Arab Emirates, and so on, where there are duty-free systems. Russians bring them back to the country and get them through customs without paying any, or few, taxes. Although controls have become stricter, according to some Moscow-based representatives of Japanese companies, the practice of avoiding customs duties is still rampant. Therefore, high-class Japanese cars are sometimes sold for several thousands dollars less than in a normal dealer's shop in Russia. Japanese appliances are also sold for several hundred dollars less. Generally, Japanese companies prefer not to be involved in the customs procedures and domestic distribution. Japanese companies prefer to have a so-called shoreline operation, which means that they deliver goods to Russian dealers at the border with Finland, for instance. This phenomenon is not the same as when Japanese companies send their goods to Russia via a third country, for instance another former Soviet republic, in order to gain preferential customs tariffs. In addition, there are still very large volumes of unreported "shuttle trade." Many Russians go to China, Turkey, Greece, Poland, and other countries to buy cheap consumer goods and bring them back for themselves. In the Russian Far East, many Russian visitors to Japan have brought Japanese used cars and household appliances to Russia in this way. Therefore, it is difficult to calculate the scale of shuttle trade by official means.[15]

JAPANESE INVESTMENT IN RUSSIA

In 1988 the Soviet Union adopted a law on joint ventures. Even though it was impossible to expect quick returns, Japanese active in Russian business tried to establish joint ventures with the view of long-term investment trial projects and expansion of a future market. But most of the joint ventures in the Russian Far East ended in failure because of the unreasonable business practices from the Russian side.

For instance, at the beginning of 1999, of the 532 companies with foreign capital participation (CFCP) registered in Primorskii krai, only 360 were actually operating.[16] Many had ceased operations, often because of the instability of the Russian political and economic situation, taxation and legal systems, and so on. The average share of foreign capital in the CFCPs has been increasing and reached 73 percent in 1999 (see Table 17.1). This indicates that foreign companies increasingly prefer to have a majority of shares in order to control management. Among the regions of the Russian Far East, Primorskii krai has the second largest share (after Sakhalin) of foreign investment (see Table 17.2). Still, the share of foreign capital in the region is very limited, accounting for only 2.3 percent of the region's gross product in 1999. Among the 360 operating CFCPs in Primorskii krai at the end of 1999, 121 (33.6 percent) involved Chinese capital. South Korean investors were involved in 41 ventures (11.4 percent), U.S. investors in 39 (10.8 percent), and Japanese investors in 26 (7.2 percent) (see Table 17.3).[17] Although the CFCPs' share of total production in Primorskii krai is still very small, their activities have been increasing in some sectors, such as manufacturing, transportation, and communications.

Table 17.1 Companies with Foreign Capital Participation in Primorskii Krai

Basic Indicators	1992	1993	1995	1996	1997	1998	1999
Operating companies	51	88	300	320	340	303	360
Average percent of foreign capital	51	54	65	60	60	62	73
Workers	2,962	4,240	8,769	8,923	8,276	8,247	11,493
Share in the gross regional product (percent)	0.7	2.3	3.1	2.2	2.2	2.3	2.3

Source: Russian State Statistics Committee, Primorskii krai branch

The main areas in which Japanese companies participate are wood processing (e.g., STS Technowood), car repair (e.g., Autotest, Summit Motors, and Haruyama Auto), fishing (e.g., Roshinka and Rosshini), communications (Vostoktelecom), and hotels (e.g., Versailles). STS Technowood is considered one of the most successful cases of the region's joint ventures. Since 1997, the company has been producing and exporting lumber to Japan. The construction cost of the factory was $20 million, with the Japanese side providing $15 million. The company employs 250 people. The lumber processing, which includes drying, measuring, cutting, and selecting, is highly automated and managed by computers. STS Technowood was one of the largest investments in the region in 1999.

The investment environment in the RFE is not good compared to other regions of the Russian Federation. Infrastructure maintenance is well below that in European Russia. And with a small population, the retail market is small. The region's Japanese-Russian joint ventures are rather old and small in general. The reasons that many are no longer operating include: (1) various promised incentives for the joint ventures were abolished; (2) systemic changes resulted in a sharp increase in the tax burden; (3) for fishing joint ventures, securing fishing quotas became very difficult; (4) some of the Japanese-Russian joint ventures got into trouble in the RFE, and usually the joint ventures were taken over by the Russian partners; and (5) in many cases, when the initial investment was done, all the facilities were set up, and the Russian side would betray its partners. Unfortunately, territorial administrations could not help the Japanese side.

Since 1997 there has been only one major Japanese investment in the Russian Far East outside of oil-rich Sakhalin. PTS Hardwood, established in Primorskii

Table 17.2 Foreign Investment to Russian Far East, by territory, 1995–99
(millions U.S. dollars)

Territory	1995		1996		1997		1998		1999		2000*	
	Total	FDI	Total	FDI	Total	FDI	Total	FDI	Total	FDI	Total	FDI
Russia	2,983	2,020	6,970	2,440	12,295	5,333	11,773	3,360	9,560	4,260	7,888	3.2
Far East	198	127	408	243	271	196	554	250	1,258	1,097	359	136
Sakha Republic	12	5	8	8	14	10	197	0.9	86	0.4	95	0.5
Jewish AO	0.03	0.03	0.3	0.3	0.5	0.5	...	...	0.05	0.05	0.06	0.05
Primorskii krai	53	23	97	66	95	61	85	46	54	20	37	21
Khabarovskii krai	42	33	79	78	12	12	40	15	33	25	20	15
Amurskaia oblast	0.9	0.9	6	1	0.5	0.3	0.4	0.4	2.3	2.3	4.5	4.5
Kamchatskaia oblast	24	0.8	24	1.8	34	1.9	43	7.2	26	0.04	10	0.07
Magadanskaia oblast	14	14	49	45	63	62	54	49	30	27	7	2.7
Sakhalinskaia oblast	52	50	45	43	53	49	136	132	1,028	1,022	185	181

Note: Figures for 2000 are from data compiled for the first nine months of the year.
Source: Russian State Statistics Committee.

Table 17.3 Foreign Capital Participation in Primorskii Krai, by Country
(Number of Companies)

	1990	1992	1993	1994	1995	1996	1997	1998	1999
Australia	1	1	–	1	8	9	8	8	7
Austria	1	–	–	–	2	1	1	1	–
Canada	–	–	–	1	3	3	3	4	3
China	5	11	20	56	106	98	99	102	121
Finland	1	2	2	2	3	5	5	3	3
Germany	–	1	3	2	5	4	8	6	8
Hong Kong	–	3	2	3	7	7	5	7	7
Italy	–	1	2	2	1	4	3	4	3
Japan	2	6	24	27	45	48	51	27	26
Korea	1	1	2	10	34	30	40	30	41
North Korea	1	2	2	2	4	3	3	2	2
Others	3	3	5	14	14	15	24	47	79
Singapore	1	3	5	5	9	10	10	6	6
Sweden	1	1	1	1	3	2	1	2	1
Switzerland	2	2	1	1	4	3	2	2	1
Taiwan	–	–	–	1	2	4	4	2	2
United Kingdom	–	2	2	3	6	9	10	7	5
United States	3	9	16	17	39	60	59	40	39
Vietnam	2	3	1	2	5	5	4	3	6
Total	24	52	88	150	300	320	340	303	360

Source: Russian State Statistics Committee, Primorskii krai branch

krai in the field of wood processing, is the exception. This was established in April 2000 as a sister company of STS Technowood. The Japanese side has a roughly 45-percent share, and the size of the investment is some $4.2 million. The primary reason why the Japanese side chose the same Russian partner for setting up the second joint venture is the management of the Russian company. One Japanese investor said, "We had a very good and reliable partner. The Russian manager shared the same idea and aims with us and he could understand that we had to provide the goods which the customer wanted." Unfortunately, it is difficult to find partners in the RFE who understand this very basic idea of the market economy.

Joint ventures in the timber industry have benefited wood processing in Russia. Initially, the quality of Russian-made processed lumber was very bad, and it did not meet Japanese standards in many ways. Japan started to buy unprocessed wood from Russia, but since Japanese labor is very expensive, processing in Japan also is expensive. So Russian raw timber lost its price competitiveness, and eventually it became difficult to sell Russian lumber in the Japanese market. Therefore, it became necessary to process wood in Russia. Usually, the Japan-Russian joint ventures in the field of wood processing have the latest Japanese equipment and the proper management, who know the idea of quality control, on-time delivery, and so forth. Therefore, they can have both technical support and management support. This is a very good example of technology transfer to Russia.

But, there is a serious problem in this field of joint ventures as well. Joint ventures pay value-added tax for buying the materials, which are mainly the raw lumber. VAT should be refunded when the joint ventures export their processed products, but this has not been happening. Even though a federal court ruled in favor of the Japanese side, no refund has been made.

Japanese manufacturers of consumer goods, for example household appliances or automobiles, also have considered direct investment for massive local production in Russia. Unfortunately, Russian authorities have taken very few steps to encourage local production. In May 1998, for example, they enforced controls on imports by allowing the import of televisions only by licensed importers in order to foster domestic production. Some Japanese manufacturers have tried to shift to local assembly with a minimum manufacturing process because taxation on the finished goods has been exacted more strictly. On the other hand, it seems that two major Japanese household appliance manufacturers have given up on the possibility of switching to local production in Russia.

The same can be said about the Japanese automobile industry. There was a leading Japanese manufacturer seriously examining local production of minivans in 1997. Several other Japanese manufacturers were considering small-scale local assembly. By spring 1999, those plans were abandoned. Manufacturers think that assembling or producing their own automobiles in Russia is not feasible, at least in the short- or mid-term, because of the decline in purchasing power following the August 1998 financial crisis.[18]

Many Russian observers think the Japanese are too cautious and too late to arrive. In Japan it seems like a failure becomes a "scarecrow" for all other companies, and that is why they do not make the decision to enter the Russian market. For European or American companies, however, a failure of a specific "unlucky" investor does not prevent others from moving forward and earning good money. For instance, the Russian automobile industry is expected to gain a large-scale investment in the near future. The Russian automobile industry is ready for local assembly with minimal manufacturing (i.e., "screwdriver manufacturing"), and foreign automobile companies, including Fiat, BMW, Skoda, Daewoo, Ford, Renault, and others are ready to begin production. Japanese companies are conspicuous by their absence. The Japanese hardly participate in the privatization of Russian enterprises, so there is no possibility to influence processes in any sphere or branch of Russian industry. In the final analysis, Japanese companies are late in participating in the economic reform processes in Russia.[19] Such, at least, is a very typical opinion of Russians concerning Japanese investment in Russia.

In fact, Japanese investment in Russia is not very big. At the end of 2000, Japanese investment in Russia was $372 million, putting Japan in tenth place after the United States, Germany, and others. Japanese cumulative investment is only 1.1 percent of all investment in Russia. However, although Japanese automobile manufacturers may not be aggressive enough, the cautious attitude of Japanese companies is reasonable. Many projects with the participation of foreign automobile makers have not yet started. On the other hand, Japanese companies are leading the two largest investment projects in Russia, namely the Sakhalin shelf oil and gas development and the Japan Tobacco (JT) International/RJR Reynolds joint venture.

JT International's case is a bit exceptional. JTI is a major international tobacco company ranking third in the world in terms of production (450 billion cigarettes a year) and sales (over $15 billion). It is the international division of the Japanese holding company Japan Tobacco Inc., with headquarters in Tokyo. JT International was formed when Japan Tobacco Inc. acquired the international tobacco business of the U.S. company RJR Nabisco. During 2000, RJR and Japan Tobacco continued to integrate their structures, including in Russia. RJR Nabisco has been present in Russia since 1992 and is the leader in the Russian market in terms of output and sales. The first among international tobacco companies to invest in the Russian tobacco industry, it is one of the largest investors in Russia (total direct investments in the Russian economy of $500 million). The production complex Petro in St. Petersburg is the most modern tobacco facility in Russia and the largest tobacco factory in Europe (it produced 44 billion cigarettes in 1999). The company employs more than 3,000 persons in Russia. So when JT International bought out RJR Nabisco, Japan automatically became a major investor in Russia.

When Russian observers comment on the above-mentioned practices, they say that Japanese companies do not want to take any risks, so they are keeping a close watch on the West and prefer to implement large projects only together with strong Western partners.[20] As in the case of the Sakhalin oil and natural gas projects, Japanese companies work together with Americans. Japanese also prefer to buy out a smooth-working business than to go through all the stages of establishing their own enterprises, as they did in the case of RJR Nabisco. The Russian consumers are practically unaware that they are smoking "Japanese cigarettes." But one cannot say that these two cases show a very passive approach on the part of Japan. Rather, some Japanese companies, including large ones, conscientiously "conceal" their investments, or the main role of managers is given to Russians so as to avoid "raids" by the mafia, tax police, corrupt bureaucrats, etc.

Major obstacles to investing in Russia remain, and they include:

- instability of the political, social, and economic situation;
- lack of macroeconomic stability;
- lack of industrial infrastructure;
- discrimination against foreign capital;
- instability of laws and legislation; and
- a complicated and very demanding taxation system.

Of course, this phenomenon is not unique for Japanese companies, but without an improved investment climate, no further foreign investment can be expected.

To sum up, Japan-Russia trade, especially Japanese exports to Russia, has been stagnant for years. Yet even though it does not appear in the customs statistics, there is a large amount of Japanese exports via third countries. Moreover, some of the big projects with the participation of Japanese companies have started to operate. Thus, further acceleration of trade turnover can be expected. In this context, Japanese–Russian economic relations are not as stagnant as they might appear at first glance. The main import items from Russia are seafood products, timber, coal, and aluminum—all items that are produced mainly in the Russian Far East. The Russian Far East is an important supplier of specific commodities very much in demand by Japan. At the same time, economic relations with Japan are essential to the RFE.

JAPANESE TRADE WITH THE RUSSIAN FAR EAST

Japan is the largest trading partner of the Russian Far East. In 1997 the total amount of foreign trade of the Russian Far East peaked at $6.2 billion, with exports totaling $3.7 billion and imports $2.5 billion (see Figures 17.1 and 17.2). In that year, one-third of Russian Far East exports went to Japan.

It has become very important for the Russian Far East to keep close trade contacts with neighboring countries since its economic relations with Russia and other former republics and have been reduced. The countries of the Asia Pacific region are the most logical market for Far Eastern exports and the most economical source of imports of food, consumer goods, machinery, and transport equipment.

Natural resources such as a fish, lumber, coal, and petroleum occupy 60–80 percent of Far Eastern exports. This ratio is probably higher because many observers think that 90 percent of exports of fish and marine products are not being counted in Russian trade statistics. Besides natural resources, the only other goods produced in the Russian Far East that are competitive on world markets are weapons.

Consumer goods, including food and automobiles, account for a large share of Far Eastern imports. Generally speaking, agriculture and industries for production of consumer goods have not been well developed in the Russian Far East. In the RFE, the retail market share of imported consumer goods reached some 70 percent in 1995–96.[21] Furthermore, shuttle trade mainly involves imports of consumer goods from China. Approximately $1 billion worth of goods were imported just from Heilongjiang Province in 1997. It seems that in Russian Far East retail sales of consumer goods, the market share of imports should be much higher because shuttle trade is counted neither in the Russian nor Chinese customs statistics. The two major centers of shuttle trade are between the cities of Blagoveshchensk and Heihe (by ferry) and between Grodekovo and Suifenhe (by rail).

The main RFE trade partners are Japan, China, South Korea, and the United States. These four countries comprised 67 percent of total RFE trade in 1997, 76 percent in 1998, and 71 percent in 1999. In the context of Japanese-Russian trade, the Russian Far East holds a very important position. According to Russian statistics, the share of the RFE in overall Japanese-Russian trade reached 31.6 percent in 1997 (34.4 percent of exports and 23 percent of imports). This ratio is actually higher. According to Russian statistics, Russian exports of fish and marine products to Japan were valued at $92 million in 1997, while Japanese statistics showed $1.1 billion of imports of the same products. Russian fishing boats have been unloading marine products directly at Japanese fishing ports, mainly in Hokkaido. Even though Moscow considers it illegal trade, Japanese customs authorities duly record these products.[22]

Fig. 17.1 Russian Far East Exports by Partner
(million U.S. dollars)

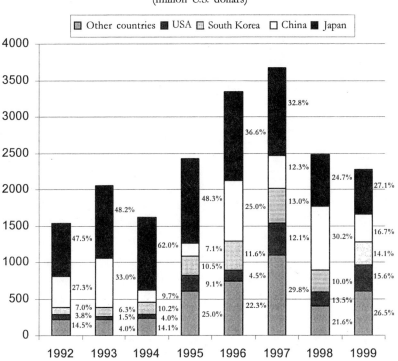

Source: Prepared from materials of the regional governments and statistical bureaus of the Russian Far East.

According to the Hokkaido Prefecture government, about 3,500 Russian vessels enter the ports in Hokkaido each year, which means that some ten Russian ships, most of them fishing vessels carrying crab and other marine products, enter Hokkaido ports every day. Japanese importers write invoices and make payments in yen. The Russian crew and fishermen then buy various Japanese products, such as used cars, refrigerators, washing machines, fresh vegetables and fruits, and other household items, and take them to Russia. Many shops in these Japanese port cities sell only to Russian customers. The number of Russian tourists visiting Hokkaido for sightseeing and shopping is also rapidly increasing. According to official statistics of the Otaru branch of the Bank of Japan, some 32,000 Russians visited the city of Otaru on Hokkaido in 1997. They exchanged 1.8 billion yen, six times more than in 1993, when the branch started to keep these statistics.[23] In Otaru, a free Russian language journal with shopping information, *Druzhba*, is published. Similarly, about 1,700 Russian vessels and 24,000 people visited the city of Nemuro on Hokkaido in 1998. In that year Russian visitors spent some 1.9 billion yen. The total impact of spending by Russian tourists and Russian imports in Nemuro is estimated to be 9.4 billion yen.[24]

Fig. 17.2 Russian Far East Imports by Partner
(million U.S. dollars)

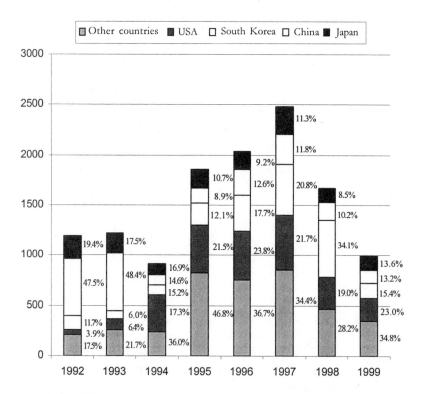

Source: Prepared from materials of the regional governments and statistical bureaus of the Russian Far East.

Automobiles (especially used cars) and household appliances are the main imports into the RFE from Japan. In Vladivostok, there are 430,000 cars registered for 800,000 inhabitants (for 8 million Muscovites—inhabitants of the richest city in Russia—there are only 1.9 million cars). More than 70 percent of the cars in Vladivostok are second-hand Japanese cars with right-wheel drive (in Moscow, only 19 percent are foreign-made cars). In Khabarovsk, the second largest city in the Russian Far East, there are four foreign-made cars for every Russian-made car. There are more than 63,000 Toyotas alone in the city. Apparently, it is difficult for the Russian central or local governments to control this form of trade.[25]

SECURITY OF NORTHEAST ASIA AND MULTINATIONAL ECONOMIC COOPERATION

The improvement in political relations between Japan and Russia has not yet been reflected in the development of bilateral economic relations. According to official statistics, trade and economic relations between Japan and Russia remain very limited. However, if unofficial trade and business activities are included in the figures, then Japanese-Russian economic relations are not so inactive. Furthermore, in terms of regional economic relations, Japan fairly consistently has been the biggest importer of RFE products. In the 1990s, some $1 billion worth of imports to Japan from the Russian Far East had a big impact on the regional economy. In addition, trade in the main export items of the region, namely fish and marine products, has a very significant economic effect on the cities of Hokkaido and the Russian Far East. Moreover, promising large-scale cooperation projects between Japan and Russia are located in the Far East. As the Russian economy recovers, Japanese-Russian economic relations should be much more active.

This scenario of the development of the Japanese economic cooperation with the Russian Far East is favorable not only for neighboring Japan and Russia but also for the economic development of Northeast Asia as a whole. With the disappearance of the Cold War confrontation and the globalization of the world economy, multilateral economic cooperation is starting to materialize in the so-called Japan Sea Rim Economic Zone, which includes the Russian Far East, China's three northeastern provinces (Heilongjiang, Jilin, and Liaoning), North and South Korea, and Japan. Some may claim that the efforts to develop this as an economic area have been a failure so far, but the Japan Sea Rim Economic Zone is not an analog of EU or ASEAN types of ecomomic cooperation units, which unite member countries in the framework of agreements or treaties. It is rather a natural economic cooperation area, which unites the neighboring countries and regions with a concept of interdependence without any agreements or treaties. As mentioned above, there have been a lot of examples of complementary economic activities among the countries and regions of the zone.

In Northeast Asia, the given economic endowments are quite different by country and region. It should be beneficial to use these differences as much as possible in the initial phases of cooperation so that a vertical international division of labor might be developed. As for the Russian Far East, the strongest economic factor must be its rich natural resources. Moreover, because of the 70-percent content requirements for Sakhalin oil and gas projects, it is possible that the Russian Far East will play a large role in the developing division of labor in Northeast Asia. But at the same time, this means that the Russian companies supplying the materials and equipment have to meet international standards for quality, price, and delivery. Since the Russian Far East machinery industries are in a very difficult situation, they will have to seek the cooperation of foreign companies in order to supply local content. Otherwise, the Sakhalin projects may not proceed. The economic development of Northeast Asia is likely to respond to and stimulate strongly the economy of the Russian Far East.

In the context of Northeast Asian security, multilateral energy-sector cooperation is very important. Big energy consuming countries of Northeast Asia—China, South Korea, and Japan—depend on energy imports from distant areas, and Russian energy resources are hardly being used. In the mid- to long-term, the demand for energy and the degree of dependence on foreign energy resources will increase in those countries. This is especially true for Japan, which has no domestic energy resources and a so-called allergy to nuclear power. In China, if high dependence on coal lasts for a prolonged period in the context of increasing energy demand, China's natural environment will be seriously damaged, and eventually there could be significant problems throughout Northeast Asia. Environmental and energy problems are closely related to security issues in Northeast Asia, so in this respect, the Sakhalin or Kovyktinsk projects are very important for the region.

Japan has not imported energy resources from its neighbor because Russia's production fields are far away—mainly on the west side of the Ural Mountains. The Soviet energy strategy had been to produce oil and gas in fields nearer to European Russia, where the population is concentrated and energy consumption is higher. Oil and gas also were transported further to the west and exported to various European countries. There were several reasons why oil and gas were not transported eastward: the small population in East Siberia and the RFE; poor relations with China; no relations at all with South Korea; and the fact that the Japanese economy was not as developed as it is today. Therefore, it was simply impossible to build pipelines to the east because of the inefficiency and cost.[26] Though the major development fields were moved to the Yamal and Tumen regions of West Siberia, the above-mentioned conditions did not change fundamentally. There was also a psychological element, which was the national security worry. Today, however, it can be said that if there is multinational economic inter-dependence in the region, it would have a positive effect on regional security.

Can Japan become one of the main importers of Russian energy resources in today's conditions? The development of these huge projects leads to Japanese machinery and equipment exports to Russia. In return, the possibility of Japan's energy import from Russia becomes greater. In particular, the plan to import gas from Sakhalin-1 by underwater pipeline becomes more realistic. The energy council of Japan's Ministry of International Trade and Industry has shown a positive atti-tude toward the plan.[27] From the fields of Sakhalin-1 to the areas of greatest con-sumption in Japan is some 2,000 km. One half of this distance is the inland por-tion of the pipeline route from the fields to Korsakov, which is at the southern end of Sakhalin Island. There are two planned routes to Japan from Korsakov. One is the Pacific route, which reaches Chiba prefecture, and the other is the Japan Sea route, which reaches Niigata prefecture. Both routes would go through Hokkaido and Aomori prefectures, and the length of each of these pipeline options is some 1,000 km each. It is said that gas pipeline transport is cheaper than importing LNG if the transport distance is shorter than 5,000 km.

But in the case of pipeline transport to Japan, a rather large fee to compensate coastal fishermen has to be considered. Furthermore, in order to export gas to Japan, a solid buyer must be secured. In the case of Japan, long-term contracts with the electric power companies are most important, since they consume 70 percent of the natural gas in Japan. In general, the big users, such as the municipal gas companies and the electric power companies, have been importing LNG from Southeast Asia, Australia, and other countries based on long-term contracts, which are normally valid for more than twenty years. As far as Sakhalin gas imports are concerned, the public relations department of Hokkaido Electric said, "The possi-bility of the introduction is being examined";[28] and the president of Tokyo Electric has stated, "As a result, if it is cheap, we will buy."[29] So it seems that they are not active enough to participate in the plan at this moment. But it is obvious that Japan has to diversify the primary energy import sources, and from the environmental point of view, demand for gas in Japan will be growing.[30] So, it is reasonable to think that natural gas imports from Russia will occur at some point.

There is no doubt that the energy sector is one of the most promising invest-ment areas in Russia, but since development costs are enormous and it takes quite a long time for realization, the stability of the region and stable relations among the parties are indispensable. In other words, the three principles of Japan's diplomatic policy toward Russia, namely, "trust, mutual benefit, and a long-term perspective" are especially important in the multinational energy projects. In this sense, coopera-tion in the energy sector prescribes Japanese–Russian relations.

NOTES

1. For more on the dispute over the Northern Territories (the islands of Etorofu, Kunashiri, Shikotan, and a group of smaller islets off Hokkaido—in Russia, called the Southern Kuriles), see Akihiro Iwashita, "Japanese Interests in the Russian Far East: Search for a New Relationship," presented at the conference "Security Implications of Economic and Political Developments in the Russian Far East," The National Bureau of Asian Research, Washington, D.C., May 2000.

2. Japanese exports to Russia began to decrease markedly right after the Russian financial crisis in 1998. Since there is a time difference between the signing of contracts and shipment, a big influence is reflected in export data for 1999.

3. See Directive of the Central Bank of Russia No. 519-U of March 22, 1999, on the Procedure for Purchase of Foreign Currencies by Resident Legal Entities at the Internal Currency Market of the Russian Federation for Rubles to Clear Payments under Contracts for Import of Goods to the Russian Federation, with Amendments and Addenda of March 24, June 28, 1999. See also the Directive of the Central Bank of Russia No. 721-U of December 30, 1999, on the Purchase by Resident Legal Entities of Foreign Currency to Make Payments for the Performance of Work, the Rendering of Services, or the Transfer of the Results of Intellectual Activity. On the peculiarities of the procedure for applying this Directive, see the Directive of the Central Bank of the Russian Federation No. 543-U of April 14, 1999.

4. The KS was the Japanese-Russian forest resources development project, which was signed in 1968 as one of the first Japanese-Soviet Siberian and Far East resource development projects. The second agreement was signed in 1974, and the third was signed in 1981. But the fourth agreement was not finalized, mainly due to the collapse of the Soviet Union.

5. The South Yakutsk coal development project, signed in 1974, was also one of the large Japan-Soviet Siberian and Far East resource development projects. With this project, the Soviet Union and then Russia continued to export some 100 million tons of coal to Japan for more than 20 years.

6. The Bank was reorganized and became the Japan Bank for International Cooperation (JBIC) in 1999.

7. Mr. Hashimoto's speech at Keizai Doyukai on July 24, 1997.

8. Some people in Russia feel that this model has eroded Russia's national interests and plundered the wealth of Russia. It is also seen as the most inefficient trade due to the growth of various expenditures, high taxes, the impact of fluctuations on the world raw materials market, and low profit margin. Many trendy Russian businessmen think that trade based on such a model has no future. At a time when the market environment is developing, the new economic order stimulates the export of goods with a higher degree of manufacture, all the more since the state has lately started bringing order to exports and imports in the "shadow economy," and "easy money" is disappearing. There can be no doubt that raw materials will always be regulated by the state in a special way. In reality, Russia does not produce many products that can compete in terms of quality in the

international market. Russian arms exports are a very exceptional case.

9. For instance, in 1997 crude oil and natural gas consisted of 66.6 percent of German imports from Russia.

10. Geographical and historical proximity with Russia, and the presence of Russian communities, are also favorable factors for Europe.

11. It is estimated that each of the nine major Japanese trading companies has at least $100 million in nonpayments for exports to the Soviet Union.

12. In early April 2000, an agreement was reached on the so-called Blue Stream project. This is a project of Russian gas giant Gazprom, which plans to build a natural gas pipeline under the Black Sea to Turkey. The total amount of the contract reached $3 billion, of which some $400 million are contracted with Japanese companies. Mitsui, Itochu, and Sumitomo will supply some 300,000 tons of steel pipe. The Japan Bank for International Cooperation and Fuji Bank will also participate in the project as financiers, so this will be a joint loan from the government and private sector. The JBIC takes some 60 percent, and private banks, including Fuji Bank, take some 40 percent of finance, which amounts to some $400 million. Then, the Ministry of International Trade and Industry applies trade insurance to some 90 percent of the contracted amount.

13. Kazuo Ogawa, "Nichiro Keizai Kankei wo Saikenntou suru"(Review of Japanese-Russian Economic Relations), *Rosia Touou Boueki Chousa Geppou* (Monthly Bulletin on Trade with Russia & East Europe), August 1998, Tokyo, ROTOBO.

14. *Nihon Keizai Shinbun,* February 5, 1999.

15. The Turkish central bank estimated that this type of unreported exports from Turkey to Russia by Russian visitors amounted to some $8.8 billion in 1996. *Nihon Keizai Shinbun,* December 23, 1997.

16. Companies with foreign capital participation refer to joint ventures with foreign capital, 100-percent foreign-owned companies, and branches and subsidiaries of foreign companies.

17. These data refer to the number of CFCPs, not to the value of investments. Many Chinese investments, for example, are very small, and the value of Chinese investments in the region is smaller than the value of investments of some of the other countries.

18. The investment tendencies of Japanese manufacturers are based on the author's interviews with the people concerned.

19. This type of argument is often written in the Russian press. See, for instance, A. Rodionov, *Overviews of the state of economic ties: The potential and its utilization: Japan's economic presence in Russia* (Moscow: Maximov Publications, 2000).

20. For instance, V. Ramzes mentioned the weakness of the Japanese management system and said it is out of date. *Vedomosti,* June 6, 2000.

21. Ogawa, "Nichiro Keizai Kankei wo Saikenntou suru."

22. For instance, former Prime Minister Kirienko mentioned that the annual damage for the Russian Far East caused by the export of illegal marine products from the region is considered to be some $2.5 billion. *The Japan Times,* June 12, 1998. For more on this issue see Tony Allison, "The Crisis of the Region's Fishing Industry: Sources, Prospects, and the Role of Foreign Interests," chapter 6 in this volume.

23. *Hokkaido Shinbun,* April 16, 1998.

24. *Hokkaido Shinbun,* January 19, 2000.

25. Rodionov, *Overviews of the state of economic ties.*

26. Actually, negotiations took place between Japan and the Soviet Union on joint energy development on Sakhalin Island already in the 1960s, but an agreement was not reached. The main reasons were: the confirmed deposit was not big enough; except for Japan, there were no customers to supply; the scale of the Japanese economy was not big enough; and Japan made an agreement to buy gas from Brunei; etc. In other words, there was not enough trust between the two countries. Ryo Kiire, *Nisso Boeki no Rekishi* (History of Japan-Soviet Trade) (Tokyo: Ningen-sya, 1983), 93–94.

27. *Asahi Shinbun,* August 22, 2000.

28. *Hokkaido Shinbun,* August 13, 2000.

29. *Asahi Shinbun,* August 22, 2000.

30. In Japan, more than 80 percent of primary energy is imported. Dependence on imports of oil, which accounts for about 55 percent of the primary energy supply in Japan, was 99.7 percent in FY1996. In FY1960, there were no imports of natural gas in Japan. In FY1975 the share of gas in Japan's primary energy imports was 1.8 percent, and its share came to 11 percent in FY1996. *Asahi Shinbun Japan Almanac 1999* (Tokyo: Asahi Sinbun, October 1998), 172. The reduction of carbon dioxide and greenhouse-gas emissions, major causes of global warming, has become a global issue. In 1988, Japan adopted "The Law Concerning the Rational Use of Energy" and "Law Concerning the Promotion of Measures to Cope with Global Warming." Both the industrial community and local government are now leading a nationwide effort to regulate greenhouse gases.

18

Economic Relations between South Korea and Russia

Seung-Ho Joo

The Cold War atmosphere and continuing Sino-Soviet conflict in Northeast Asia during the pre-Gorbachev era directed the general trends and goals of Soviet foreign policy toward the Korean Peninsula. The Soviet Union's Korea policy during this period was influenced by its ideological affinity with and the geostrategic importance of the Democratic People's Republic of Korea (DPRK or North Korea). Moscow supported the DPRK's "one Korea" policy and refused to recognize the Republic of Korea (ROK or South Korea) as a legitimate political entity. As a result, the Soviet Union did not have any contact with South Korea until the 1960s.

Although Moscow began limited economic and cultural contacts with Seoul in the early 1970s, it strictly limited its relations with Seoul to the nonpolitical, unofficial level, insisting on separating politics from economics. After Gorbachev came to power in March 1985, South Korean–Soviet relations entered a new phase. Gorbachev's foreign policy direction and behavior vis-à-vis the two Koreas moved from a pro–North Korean policy, which called for a sustained alliance relationship with Pyongyang, to a new policy that demanded the establishment of official relations with Seoul to promote the Soviet Union's national interests.[1] Subsequently, Seoul and Moscow established formal diplomatic relations in September 1990. At the same time, Moscow distanced itself from Pyongyang. When the Russian Federation became the successor to the Soviet Union and assumed all of its international rights and obligations, President Yeltsin followed his predecessor's foreign policy toward the Korean Peninsula with only minor adjustments.

At the time of Seoul-Moscow normalization, the two countries were expected to expand their economic ties rapidly and to intensify bilateral economic cooperation based on shared political goals and complementary economic structures. Bilateral economic relations, however, fell far short of initial expectations.

In 2000, the DPRK and Russia normalized bilateral relations by signing a new "Treaty of Friendship, Good Neighborliness, and Cooperation." The signing of the new friendship treaty was followed by Russian President Vladimir Putin's visit to Pyongyang in July. Moscow and Pyongyang now share a common interest in mending their damaged relations and restoring cooperative ties. The historic June 2000 summit in Pyongyang between South Korean President Kim Dae Jung and North Korean leader Kim Jong Il paved the road to reconciliation and cooperation between the two Koreas.[2] As inter-Korean relations improve dramatically and DPRK-Russian relations normalize, economic cooperation between the ROK, the DPRK, and Russia will be likely.

THE POLITICAL ECONOMY OF SEOUL-MOSCOW RELATIONS

Gorbachev's new political thinking and South Korea's *nordpolitik* (northern policy) intersected, facilitating economic cooperation and political normalization between Moscow and Seoul. Nordpolitik and the new political thinking, however, were driven by differing goals and interests. Nordpolitik was designed to establish political relations with communist countries as a prelude to peaceful unification of the two Koreas, whereas Gorbachev's new political thinking vis-à-vis South Korea was intended to induce trade, investment, and economic aid from South Korea for domestic economic development.

The prospect of mutually beneficial economic relations was not the only factor that prompted Soviet economic cooperation with Seoul. First, the stagnation in Soviet-Japanese trade contributed to Moscow's move toward closer ties with Seoul. Despite repeated requests from the Soviet Union to participate in development projects in Siberia, Japan insisted on the return of the four disputed Kurile Islands as the precondition for resuming massive economic cooperation. The Russians hoped that South Korean–Soviet economic cooperation would not only replace Japan's role, but also exert pressure on Japan to reconsider its position. Second, the Soviet Union was interested in the Chinese economic experiment and did not wish to fall behind China in tapping the potential of the booming East Asian economies, especially in South Korea. Third, the Soviets were eager to learn from South Korea's remarkable economic achievements, which were made possible by its state-led, export-oriented economic development strategy, its integration with the world economy, and the diligence and discipline of South Korean workers. Fourth, through improved economic relations with Seoul, the Soviet Union wanted to establish it-self as a major player on the Korean Peninsula and in the Asia Pacific region.

The institutional and legal basis for bilateral economic cooperation between the ROK and the USSR was laid down in December 1990 when the two countries signed an agreement on trade, investment guarantees, avoidance of double taxa-tion, and cooperation in science and technology. In January 1991 Seoul agreed to provide a $3 billion economic aid package to Moscow, which boosted bilateral trade and economic cooperation. In July 1991 the first direct sea route opened between the two countries, connecting Pusan with Vostochnyi. The new sea route facilitated transportation for tied-loan commodities to the Soviet Union, while greatly reduc-ing bilateral transport costs for cargo.[3] In September 1991, South Korea and the Soviet Union signed a fisheries agreement that allowed South Korean ships to operate in Soviet fishing zones and also led to cooperation in fishing technology.

Like Gorbachev, Boris Yeltsin focused on domestic economic development in his dealings with South Korea. He hoped to improve Russia's ailing economy with Seoul's economic cooperation and aid. Yeltsin focused on the economic development of Siberia and the Far East, believing that they held the key to the success of Russia's overall economic development. In stark contrast, political concerns continued to overshadow South Korea's Russia policy: Seoul was pri-marily interested in eliciting Moscow's support for its position on inter-Korean relations and North Korea's nuclear and missile development programs.

Bilateral economic cooperation was discussed in detail during Prime Minister Vladimir Chernomyrdin's visit to Seoul in September 1995. The two countries agreed on the development of trade as well as economic and scientific-technological cooperation. Both sides agreed to cooperate in the development of the gas fields near Irkutsk and in the Republic of Sakha (Yakutia), the creation of a South Korean industrial complex in the Nakhodka free economic zone, and the construction of a Korean trade center in Moscow. In July 1997, Deputy Chief of the Presidential Administration Oleg Sysuev led a Russian delegation to the first session of the ROK-Russian Intergovernmental Commission for Trade, Economic, Scientific-Technical Cooperation in Seoul. It was the first meeting of its kind since the commission was established in 1992. At the end of the session, Sysuev and his South Korean coun-terpart Kang Kyong Shik announced a plan to create an industrial complex for Korean plants in the Nakhodka free economic zone and other agreements. In order to help Korean agencies utilize Russia's state-of-the-art science and technology, the two sides also agreed to establish the Korea-Russia Science and Technology Infor-mation Exchange Center in Moscow.[4]

In 1998, Seoul-Moscow relations experienced their worst diplomatic crisis since the two countries had opened diplomatic relations. In July 1998 Cho Sung

Woo, a political counselor at the South Korean embassy in Moscow, was expelled from Russia on espionage charges. In retaliation, the ROK expelled Oleg Abramkin, a Russian councilor in Seoul. The expelled diplomats were career intelligence officers operating under diplomatic cover. In the wake of this incident, bilateral political relations quickly deteriorated. The diplomatic crisis eventually calmed down, but the spy scandal left a bitter taste in the mouths of both countries. The fact that this scandal quickly escalated into a diplomatic crisis testified to a widening gap in perception and interests between the two countries.

The frozen relationship began to thaw in 1999. Shortly before President Kim Dae Jung's trip to Moscow, the second session of the ROK-Russian Intergovernmental Commission for Trade, Economic, and Scientific-Technical Cooperation was held on May 11–12, 1999, in Moscow. ROK Minister of Finance and Economics Lee Kyu Sung and his Russian counterpart Georgii Boos agreed to enhance cooperation in the mobile telecommunication sector and signed a memorandum of understanding to set up a Korean industrial complex in Nakhodka.[5]

President Kim Dae Jung's state visit to Moscow on May 27–30, 1999, offered an opportunity for the two countries to restore estranged relations. He became the second South Korean president to visit Russia after Kim Young Sam in 1994. Kim Dae Jung's main goal was to elicit Russia's support for his "sunshine policy" (constructive engagement policy) toward North Korea. Yeltsin expressed support for the "sunshine policy" and promised to play a constructive role in improving inter-Korean ties. Moscow was most interested in enhancing bilateral economic cooperation and trade with Seoul. Primarily, Moscow wanted Seoul to implement the South Korean industrial complex project as early as possible. During Kim's visit, Seoul and Moscow signed a number of agreements relating to an industrial complex in Nakhodka, mutual criminal and judiciary cooperation, and nuclear power and industrial cooperation.

In 2000, Putin succeeded Yeltsin as Russian president. In the same year, the Russian Federation and the DPRK signed a new friendship treaty, the two Koreas held their first summit meeting, and Putin paid an official visit to Pyongyang. These dramatic events led to normalization of DPRK-Russian relations and a remarkable improvement in inter-Korean relations. The rise of a new leader in the Kremlin, the conclusion of the new friendship treaty, and improved inter-Korean relations combined to provide favorable circumstances for Russia's active and energetic involvement in the Korean affairs.

Putin's Pyongyang trip in July 2000 amply demonstrated Russia's eagerness to become an important player on the Korean Peninsula. This trip was significant in three ways. First, it symbolized the beginning of a new era in Moscow-Pyongyang relations as normal neighbors. Putin's visit marked the formal closure of uncomfortable relations and the onset of a new relationship. This trip sent a clear message that Russia wished to forge new ties with North Korea from a clean slate. Second, it was part of Russia's diplomatic offensive designed to enhance its influence and prestige in the Korean Peninsula and Northeast Asia. Following the July summit, Russia has sought with renewed energy and persistence to cultivate its image as an honest broker (or mediator) for peace and stability in the Korean Peninsula. Third, Putin used the occasion to push for economic cooperation with the two Koreas in both bilateral and multilateral settings. During this trip, Putin expressed a strong interest in trilateral economic cooperation with both Koreas. He stated that Russia was ready to modernize DPRK plants and power stations with ROK's capital. He also discussed multilateral economic projects, including the proposal to link the inter-Korean railway to the Trans-Siberian railroad.

The main difference between Yeltsin's and Putin's foreign policy is that the latter has been pursuing pragmatic and realistic policies with determination and vigor and has followed the new foreign policy principles in words and deeds. Unresolved problems at home (economic and political), however, continue to constrain Putin's foreign policy choices and undermine his efforts to enhance Russia's stature on the world stage.

TRADE AND INVESTMENT

Trade

After South Korea's nordpolitik was announced in the early 1970s, economic and cultural contacts at the private level increased steadily between Seoul and Moscow. Trade relations between Seoul and Moscow began in the late 1970s as individual South Korean businessmen, in pursuit of their own economic interests, energetically cultivated economic exchanges with the Soviet Union and other socialist countries. Initially, trade was conducted unofficially and indirectly through third countries.

In 1979 two-way trade stood at $11.6 million. In the 1980s, trade increased steadily, reaching $289.9 million in 1988. Soviet trade with North Korea was still greater than that with South Korea, but the gap was narrowing rapidly. As the political relationship between Seoul and Moscow improved rapidly in 1988–89, bilateral trade increased accordingly. Trade in 1989 reached $599.4 million, a hefty 107-percent increase over 1988. Overall, the trade volume increased more than four times between 1988 and 1991, exceeding one billion dollars in 1991. Trade increased on an average of 60 percent annually between 1992 and 1996 (see Table 18.1).

Table 18.1 South Korea's Trade with the Soviet Union/Russia, 1979–2000
(thousand U.S. dollars)

	Exports	Imports	Total	Increase (percent)	Balance
1979	7,400	4,200	11,600	–	3,200
1984	3,400	41,500	44,900	–	-38,100
1985	16,200	42,200	58,400	30	-26,000
1986	49,900	67,800	117,700	101	-17,900
1987	67,200	133,100	200,300	70	-65,900
1988	111,600	178,300	289,900	45	-66,700
1989	207,700	391,700	599,400	107	-183,954
1990	519,100	369,700	888,800	48	149,495
1991	641,800	581,500	1,223,300	38	60,275
1992	118,000	75,000	193,000	-86	43,000
1993	601,200	974,800	1,576,000	817	-373,647
1994	961,900	1,229,700	2,191,600	39	-267,741
1995	1,415,900	1,892,900	3,308,800	51	-476,999
1996	1,967,500	1,810,300	3,777,800	14	147,268
1997	1,767,900	1,534,800	3,302,700	-13	233,150
1998	1,113,800	998,600	2,112,400	-37	1,013,989
1999	637,000	1,590,500	2,227,500	5	-953,500
2000 (Jan–June)	350,400	849,400	1,199,800		-499,000

Sources: Korea International Trade Association (KOTIS) at <www.kita.or.kr>.

However, the combination of the Asian financial crisis in 1997 and Russia's devaluation of the ruble and imposition of a ninety-day moratorium on its international debt in August 1998 had a chilling effect on Moscow-Seoul trade.[6] In 1997–98, trade decreased sharply. In 1999 trade gained 5 percent over 1998 at $2.2 billion. Still, this trade volume was a 41-percent drop from 1997. In the first half of 2000, trade increased modestly—South Korean exports to Russia increased by 25 percent and its imports from Russia rose 3 percent compared with the same period of the previous year (see Table 18.1). Seoul-Moscow economic cooperation in 1988–2000 did not rebound as rapidly as initially expected due to many obstacles. The Russian system lacked the legal and institutional infrastructure for external economic transactions and needed a more efficient cost-accounting system, price reforms, and a freely convertible ruble. The red tape in the Russian bureaucracy meant additional difficulties for economic cooperation. Cultural dissimilarity between the two countries, lack of information about Russia among South Koreans, and absence of South Korean experts in the Russian economy also contributed to the sluggish pace of economic cooperation between Russia and the ROK. The proportion of the bilateral trade in the two countries' overall trade is insignificant. Russia's share in South Korea's total trade is about 1 percent, and South Korea's share in Russia's total trade is around 2 percent. As of 1998, Russia was the twenty-fourth largest trading partner of South Korea.

With the exception of modern weaponry, the terms of trade remain the same as in the Soviet era. Major Russian exports to South Korea are raw materials, including steel and metal products (40 percent), food and fishery products (20 percent), and chemical products (16 percent). The major items exported by South Korea to Russia include manufactured goods, consisting of clothes and textiles (31 percent), electronics and electrical products (16 percent), chemical goods (14 percent), and machinery and vehicles (10 percent). The trade pattern between Seoul and Moscow is similar to that between a developed and less-developed country, and Moscow is eager to change this unfavorable pattern. It wants to assemble and manufacture products domestically that are currently supplied by South Korea, including household appliances and cars. It also wants to increase Russian processing of raw and other materials supplied to Korea.[7]

Trade through Russian shuttle traders (*chelnoki*) also constitutes a significant component of the bilateral trade. The number of shuttle traders visiting South Korea increased from 40,000 in 1993 to 50,000 in 1994, and jumped to 70,000 in 1995. Beginning in 1996, the number began to dwindle—to 30,000 in 1997. In 1998, 40,000–50,000 Russian shuttle traders were estimated to have visited South Korea to buy cheap Korean clothing, home appliances, and other items.[8] Each trader purchases $5,000–$10,000 worth of Korean commodities. Their purchases of Korean commodities were valued at $300–400 million in 1996, $250 million in 1997, and $400 in 1998.[9]

It is noteworthy that seven major South Korea corporations—Hyundai, Samsung, Daewoo, LG, Sunkyong, Kohap, and Jindo—account for 90 percent of total ROK-Russia trade. This relationship is in sharp contrast to ROK-China trade, in which small and medium-sized Korean companies are as active and successful as major companies. The near monopoly of ROK-Russia trade by South Korean conglomerates is attributable to a few factors. First, Russia's economy is dependent on abundant energy resources and large-scale industries, and consequently, economic cooperation with Russia requires a large-scale investment. Second, the center of Russia's economic activities is located in European Russia, far away from Korea. Large companies possessing capital, information, and management skills are in a much better position to conduct business in Russia. Third, Russian culture and customs are unfamiliar to Koreans and pose an additional obstacle for Korean businessmen. Fourth, political instability and economic volatility in Russia make economic activity in the country much more risky and unpredictable. Such an unfavorable business environment further deters small- and medium-sized companies from entering the market.

Investment

South Korean business firms began direct foreign investment in the Soviet Union through third countries in 1989 mostly in the services, electronics, and natural resource sectors. After normalizing relations, the Soviet Union and South Korea laid down the legal basis for direct investment by signing agreements on investment protection and avoidance of double taxation in December 1990.

Prior to and shortly after the establishment of diplomatic relations, a number of South Korean businessmen proposed several large-scale investment projects. The major projects outlined by South Korean conglomerates between 1988 and 1991 were valued at $5.6 billion.[10] Many of these investment projects focused on Siberia and the Soviet Far East and concentrated on manufacturing, construction, and resource development. Also planned were several projects involving food processing and fisheries, production of chemical raw materials, communications, and transportation.

Actual South Korean investment in Russia has fallen far short of expectations. South Korea's investment in Russia is limited and increasing slowly. Within the total volume of investment in Russia, the mining sectors, metallurgy, the hotel business, and the food industry, including the fishing industry, constitute the lion's share. Geographically, South Korea's investments in Russia are concentrated in the Far East, Moscow, and East Siberia in order of importance. Within the Russian Far

East, Primorskii krai dominates South Korea's investment. Primorskii krai received over $33 million from South Korean investors through the mid-1990s. Geographical proximity[11] and the presence of roughly 60,000 ethnic Koreans living in the Russian Far East provide favorable conditions for South Korean investment.

In 1989 Hyundai, South Korea's largest business corporation, concluded contracts on joint projects in fisheries and forest, natural gas, and mineral resources in the Soviet Far East. The Russian–South Korean timber-processing joint venture Svetlaia in Primorskii krai has been operating at a loss. The Hyundai Corporation owns 50 percent of the authorized capital of the venture, with Russia's Primorsklesprom and Terneiles each holding 25 percent. Svetlaia is a "headache" for Hyundai. Difficulties include extremely high taxes on timber and property, large contributions to the pension fund required by the Russian government, and the interaction difficulties with Russian partners and with central and local authorities. Protests by environmental organizations have also impeded the company's activities. As a result, instead of 1 million cubic meters of timber per year as expected, only about 100,000 cubic meters can be produced. In July 1997 Hyundai also opened a 12-story, 250-room office-hotel complex in Vladivostok. Hyundai invested $102 million on the building, which houses offices, an international communications center, conference rooms, cafes, restaurants, a nightclub, and shops.[12]

Samsung is active in high technologies, oil production, and marine product processing. Samsung Electronics invested $2.85 million in Samsung-Crosna, a manufacturing business formed in 1995. Russia's Crosna owns 29 percent of the company's shares and 71 percent belong to Samsung. The joint venture develops projects, assembles and services communications equipment, and provides consulting and training of Russian personnel. Samsung-Crosna began assembling digital telephone stations using Samsung parts in March 1998.[13] Korea's Jinro Group has $3.59 million invested in the manufacturing of bread and cakes, and LG Electronics produces 500,000 to 600,000 color television sets a year at its assembly plant in Russia. In 2000, Kia Motor began producing cars at its automobile assembly plant in Kaliningrad, but Daewoo's automobile assembly factory in Rostov-na-Donu stopped rolling out cars due to internal difficulties.[14] In 1997, Lotte Hotel agreed to a joint venture with a Russian corporation to build a multipurpose building in Moscow that would include a 700-room hotel, a department store, and a theme park. This building is expected to be completed by late 2001.[15]

South Korean investment in Russia has increased modestly over the years. The cumulative value of South Korean investment in Russia was $480,000 (two projects) in 1989 and increased to $17.7 million (seven projects) in 1991 (see Table 18.2). The annual investment in 1992 dropped sharply, recording $3.2 million as a result of the collapse of the USSR and subsequent economic turmoil in Russia. The figure for 1993 dropped further to $3 million. In 1994–96, investment increased remarkably, reaching $41 million in 1996. In 1997, investment plunged to $8 million. By the end of 1999, cumulative investment stood at $154 million in 100 projects. In contrast, South Korea's cumulative investment in China at the end of 1999 recorded $4.33 billion in 4,254 projects.[16]

Table 18.2 South Korean Investment in the Soviet Union/Russia, 1980–99
(thousand U.S. dollars)

	Planned		Actual	
	Projects	Dollars	Projects	Dollars
1980	0	0	0	0
1989	2	480	2	480
1990	3	8,782	0	0
1991	5	9,541	5	17,244
1992	12	7,387	7	3,247
1993	23	4,945	12	3,042
1994	29	35,927	20	11,925
1995	21	51,618	24	30,808
1996	22	72,038	12	41,357
1997	16	33,642	6	8,175
1998	7	34,656	5	35,137
1999	6	2,307	7	714
Total	146	261,323	100	153,744

Source: The Export-Import Bank of Korea at <www.koreaexim.go.kr/>.

Under the impact of the 1997 Asian financial crisis and Russia's announcement of a moratorium on debt repayment in August 1998, South Korea's direct capital investments in Russia dropped sharply from 1997 to 1999. The reduction of direct investment in Russia reflects the weakness of the South Korean economy in the midst of the domestic financial crisis and economic restructuring. Overseas direct investment by South Korean companies slid from $5.1 billion in 1998 to $4.4 billion in 1999.[17] Total foreign direct investment in Russia plummeted in 1998, dropping to $2.2 billion from $6.2 billion in 1997. The lack of new privatization measures and the economic collapse in the second half of 1998 in Russia were responsible for the sharp reduction.[18] The proportion of South Korean investment in Russia was small for both economies. In 1997, South Korean investment in Russia accounted for only 1.4 percent of South Korean FDI;[19] and amounted to 0.5 percent of the total foreign investments in Russia in 1998.[20]

The Russian Far East

Economic cooperation between South Korea and the Russian Far East has been most remarkable. In 1991, only one enterprise with Korean investment was operating in Primorskii krai, but in 1997 the number exceeded seventy, and total Korean investment in the territory topped $6 million (or 232 billion rubles).[21] In early 2000, a total of eight Korean businesses and associations were engaged in agricultural production and cooperation in Primorskii krai.[22] Since March 1995, the Kohap Group has been engaged in agricultural production on the Kremovskii state-owned farm in the Ussuriskii raion.[23] In 1999, Saemaul Undong Chungang Hyopuihoe (Saemaul Movement Association) began agricultural cooperation on the Petrovitch and Shivakovka farms in Khorolskii.[24] South Korean companies intend to produce rice, corns, beans, and other crops by combining South Korea's capital and farming technology and equipment, Russia's land, and North Korea's labor. To date, ROK agricultural investment in the Russian Far East is limited, and all South Korean companies involved are operating at a loss. A growing number of South Korean companies, using cheap Russian labor and easy access to the U.S. market, are producing clothes in the Russian Far East. South Korean textile companies, long constrained by U.S. quotas, now export clothes manufactured in Russian factories. The U.S.-Korean-owned S. H. International, for example, makes T-shirts and sweatshirts in the Russian Far East and sells them in U.S. stores like the Gap. The Seoul-based Seishin Apparel Company bought a bankrupt Soviet-era clothing factory in Vladivostok in 1997 for $760,000 to expand sales in the United States. Seishin's Russian subsidiary, Koruss, sold $1.68 million worth of sweatshirts, dresses, and polo shirts to the Gap in 1998. Similar factories have sprung up in ten cities in the Russian Far East, including Partizansk and Vladivostok.[25]

The construction of the Korean industrial complex in the Nakhodka Free Economic Zone in Primorskii krai will be a major economic project between South

Korea and Russia. First discussed during the ROK-Russia summit meeting in November 1992, agreement on the creation of the industrial complex in Nakhodka was reached during President Kim Young Sam's state visit to Moscow in 1994. The Korea Land Corporation (a government-run organization) and the Nakhodka Administrative Committee signed a memorandum of understanding on the project in 1995. The final agreement was signed during President Kim Dae Jung's May 1999 visit to Moscow.

The agreement initially called for the lease of 3.3 million square meters of land in the Nakhodka Free Economic Zone by the Korea Land Corporation for forty-nine years. More than 100 South Korean firms were expected to rent lots from the corporation and participate in the construction of a "technology park," which would produce electronic goods, foodstuffs, and light-industrial products, as well as process lumber. The zone, located close to Russia's deep-water port of Vostochnyi, was expected to eventually produce goods worth two billion dollars each year. In light of the economic difficulties facing the two countries, South Korea plans to build an industrial complex of just 200,000 square meters instead of 3.3 million square meters and complete the construction within six years instead of the three-year schedule. South Korean manufacturing companies in the technopark will be given a 50-percent tax holiday on the value-added tax from the day of their registration until the date of their declaration of the first profit. Korean companies, however, will be obliged to export 50 percent of the output.[26]

This economic project would be mutually complementary. Moscow needs Seoul's investment for the development of the Far East. Seoul wants to help its small and mid-sized companies advance into the Nakhodka Free Economic Zone and then use it as a springboard to advance into other parts of Russia and Central Asia. However, only a limited number of South Korean companies are interested in the Nakhodka project due to economic difficulties at home and bleak prospects for immediate profits.

Russian Debts to South Korea

South Korea's $3 billion loan package to the Soviet Union acted as a catalyst for Moscow-Seoul normalization in September 1990. However, Moscow's debt repayment became a thorny issue between the two countries. Consequently, this impeded progress toward improved economic relations.

Although Seoul agreed to provide "a few" billion dollars in aid to Moscow in exchange for diplomatic normalization in 1990, the amount and terms of aid were not finalized until January 1991, when Seoul agreed to grant a $3 billion loan package to the Soviet Union. The aid package included $1.5 billion for the purchase of South Korean consumer goods, $1 billion as bank credit to be used without condition, and $500 million for the purchase of South Korean capital goods. Because it did not have sufficient funds, Seoul delivered the loan package after borrowing internationally.

South Korea's economic aid to the Soviet Union was temporarily suspended during the August 1991 coup attempt. Shortly thereafter, the South Korean government decided to fulfill its pledge of $3 billion in economic aid to the Soviet Union as planned. By that time, Seoul had already sent $500 million in cash loans. After the coup, Seoul decided to send the remaining $500 million in cash loans and deliver $800 million worth of consumer goods as scheduled.[27] By 1992 Seoul provided $1.47 billion in loans—$1.0 billion in cash from nine Korean banks and $470 million in tied loans by the Korea Export-Import Bank. In May 1992 Russia guaranteed that it would take on the former Soviet Union's debts to South Korea.[28] After Moscow failed to repay the principal and interest on time, Seoul stopped payment on the remainder of the loans. In August 1994, the two sides finally compromised on a repayment solution and agreed in principle that Russia should repay half of the debts with military hardware and the remaining half with raw materials.[29] In April 1995, Seoul agreed to accept $450 million in arms, raw materials, and civilian helicopters from Moscow over a period of three years as partial repayment of Russian debts. However, even after Russia agreed on the debt rescheduling, it only paid intermittently and has failed to repay any of the $1 billion cash loan. The overall debt swelled to $1.7 billion by late 1999.

In November 1998, Russia requested that South Korea write off a significant portion of its outstanding debt and allow repayment of the remainder to be made over twenty-five years rather than eight years as previously agreed. South Korea rejected this suggestion. Then in October 1999, Russia agreed to repay $1.7 billion owed to South Korea over the next fifteen years. The repayment would be made in goods as agreed in 1995; one half would be defense materiel/technology and the other would be raw materials.[30] Debt repayment discussion continues.

NATURAL GAS DEVELOPMENT

Russia has actively promoted large-scale investment projects to develop natural gas and to construct international gas pipelines in Siberia and the Far East. Proposals have been made to supply gas by international pipeline from the gas fields of North Sakhalin, the Republic of Sakha (Yakutia), and Irkutsk to China, Japan, and Korea.

South Korea has shown a keen interest in the Siberian gas project. As early as January 1989, Chung Ju Young, founder of the Hyundai Group, proposed running a gas pipeline from Yakutsk to South Korea through North Korea.[31] Following a November 1992 summit between Presidents Yeltsin and Roh Tae Woo, a South

Korean consortium was established, and the Korean Gas Corporation (KOGAS) was authorized by the South Korean government to negotiate the project on its behalf.[32] At the end of 1995, both Russia and Korea finished a preliminary study of the technical and economic feasibility of Sakha gas development. Under the agreement, a 6,600 km (4,125 miles) natural gas pipeline would extend from the territory of Yakutia through Khabarovskii and Primorskii krais. It was expected that the annual output of gas would total 30 to 45 billion cubic meters, 15 to 28 bcm of which would be exported to the Korean Peninsula. Total cost of the project was estimated at $17 billion to $23 billion, with supplies to last for fifty years. The Russian side would receive 70 percent of the profit and foreign investors would receive 30 percent. The North Korean government approved transit of the gas pipeline through its territory as it considered the project economically beneficial.[33] The South Korean side, however, decided against pursuing a full feasibility study due to the project's low rate of profitability. Subsequently, South Korea's main interest shifted to the Kovyktinsk gas field near Irkutsk.

Kovyktinsk gas-condensate field, discovered in 1987 in Zhigalovskii raion, 350 km northeast of Irkutsk, contains an estimated 870 billion cubic meters of natural gas and 400 million barrels of gas condensate. The exploration and development rights to both giant fields belong to RUSIA Petroleum, of which the Russian company Sidanko is the main shareholder. Other major shareholders are Irkutsk oblast, Irkutskenergo, Angarsk Refinery, and East Asia Gas Company (EAGC).[34]

In July 1996, EAGC, a subsidiary of the Hanbo Group, announced that it had purchased 27.5 percent ($25 million) of RUSIA Petroleum's equity shares and that it would promote early development of East Siberia's oil and gas reserves.[35] After the Hanbo Group went bankrupt, it sold off a large part of its equity share in RUSIA Petroleum to Sidanko, which then sold it to British Petroleum as part of a deal between BP, Sidanko, and Oneximbank. Consequently, EAGC interests now have just a 7.5-percent share of a potential project to deliver natural gas from Siberia to China.[36]

The ROK consortium conducted a feasibility study on the Kovyktinsk gas fields for eight months starting in December 1996. The study proved that its development would be economically profitable to South Korea.[37] In December 1997, Korea, Russia, China, Japan, and Mongolia agreed to advance the development of natural gas fields in Siberia. In February 1999, RUSIA Petroleum and the Chinese National Petroleum Corporation (CNPC) signed a general agreement on carrying out a feasibility study of the Kovyktinsk project. In November 1999, KOGAS, which had already completed a preliminary study, joined the basic agreement between Russia and China on feasibility studies. While China is likely to benefit most from the gas project, Korea and Japan are expected to shoulder major financial burdens.

If it proves feasible to develop the natural gas fields, then the development of the fields and construction of a 4,100 km (2,560 miles) pipeline will take about 5–6 years. The pipeline would link Irkutsk, Ulaanbaator in Mongolia, Beijing, and possibly Pyongtaek near Seoul. A total of $11 billion would be poured into the project. When completed, the gas field would provide a total of twenty million tons of natural gas to China, Russia, and Korea annually for thirty years beginning in 2006. If it provides seven million tons of gas annually to Korea, it would satisfy one-third of the country's total gas demands. With the pipeline's construction, Korea will be able to acquire natural gas at a price 22–25 percent lower than the import price of liquefied petroleum gas (LPG) or liquefied natural gas (LNG).

COOPERATION IN SCIENCE AND TECHNOLOGY

South Korea wishes to acquire Russian scientific knowledge and technology. In particular, South Korea is interested in Russian studies in aerospace research, integrated circuit design, software, communications technologies and equipment (satellites, light and mobile communications), shipbuilding, new industrial materials, metal processing, and engineering products.[38] Russia, in turn, is interested in developing applied technologies for domestic industrial production and converting defense industries to consumer production facilities with the help of South Korea. The Korean Institute of Science and Technology (KIST) is actively involved in cooperative research with Russia in core technology development and technology transfers. Other cooperative activities include exchange of specialists and sales of information and licenses.

The December 1990 intergovernmental agreement on science and technology cooperation between the Soviet Union and South Korea was followed by a June 1991 agreement regarding the details of technology transfer, commercialization, and exchanges of personnel. The science and technology ministers of the two countries agreed to start the transfer and commercialization of 9 technologies of the 48 selected for joint research and commercialization.[39]

Cooperation in the fields of aviation and aerospace started as early as 1992. In January 1992, Daewoo Heavy Industries imported Russian technology to build pilotless helicopters for agricultural purposes. In the same year, Daewoo was engaged in joint production of aircraft brake disks with the Niigrafit Research Institute and was working on high-performance training planes with the Mikoyan Avionics Research Institute. Samsung Aerospace Industries was involved in the joint development of composite materials for aircraft with the Central Aero-Hydrodynamic Institute.[40] In cooperation with a Russian research institute,

Daewoo Heavy Industries developed an unmanned deep-sea vehicle in 1996 that can submerge up to 6,000 meters. This vehicle resulted from a total investment of 2 billion won (about $2.5 million) and three years of research efforts.[41]

As of late 1997, Russia and South Korea were engaged in 79 joint research projects and 24 projects involving institutions of both countries. Four projects, including a diamond video tape recorder head, have been commercialized, and over ten projects, including shape memory alloys, are being prepared for commercialization.[42] There are five joint scientific and technical centers in Russia. About 1,500 South Korean students are studying in Russia, and Russian and Korean scientists and experts are participating in exchange programs.[43]

South Korea's myopic approach to acquiring Russian technology is a source of friction. Korean companies and research institutes often seek to obtain Russian technologies at a low cost and for immediate gains. In the process, they tend to disregard Russian conditions and needs. This approach stokes Russia's resentment and hampers long-term cooperative efforts. Russians are particularly critical of South Korea's practice of importing a small number of Russian engineers and scientists for quick results. To build a broad and solid basis for science and technology development, South Korea needs to pursue cooperative programs for long-term mutual benefits.

South Korea has also actively pursued military technology cooperation with Russia through KIST and the Agency for Defense Development. Russo-Korean technology cooperation in this field began with dual-use technology and later expanded into military technology. Acquiring core military technologies necessary for high-tech weapons is a top priority for the ROK, and Russia is more open to technology transfer than other arms suppliers.

Russia's severe economic problems force Russian military producers and research institutes to search for customers abroad. The level of Russian government funding for military research and development (R&D) has dwindled drastically since the Soviet era, and Russian R&D institutes are struggling to sustain a military technology base. According to the Stockholm International Peace Research Institute, "Russian design bureaus [are] encouraged to sell their services directly to foreign firms, offering either technology transfer or simply modification of arms produced in Russia for export."[44] In fact, export of armaments and military technology is directly linked to the survival of the Russian military-industrial complex. Part of the income from arms exports and technology transfer has been used for R&D and for procurement by the Russian military of advanced weapons such as the Su-30, Su-35, and Su-37 aircraft.[45]

South Korea's missile development programs will benefit immensely if the ROK can enlist Russia's technological help. The ROK's indigenous missile development program started in the mid-1970s with the help of the United States. The 1990 diplomatic note signed by Washington and Seoul stipulates that South Korea should not develop missiles with a range longer than 180 km. In exchange, the United States provided technology support for South Korea's NHK-2 (Hyunmu) missile program. The NHK-2, the longest missile South Korea possesses, has a striking range of 180 km. As the last batch of U.S.-made high-tech parts for the NHK-2 was delivered in 1999, the diplomatic note lost binding force. In 1998, South Korea requested that the United States allow it to develop missiles with a range up to 300 km, which is permitted by the Missile Technology Control Regime. In response, Washington attached an unusual condition: the United States would allow a maximum range of 300 km for South Korean missiles, but South Korea must open its missile development programs to U.S. inspections.[46] This condition is unacceptable to South Koreans because U.S. inspection of Korean missile programs would be a serious violation of Korea's national sovereignty. During his visit to Washington in July 1999, President Kim Dae Jung demanded the right to develop and deploy military missiles with a maximum range of 500 km and to develop private rockets for scientific purposes without range limits.[47]

Seoul is strongly motivated to develop medium-range missiles in the wake of Pyongyang's test of the Taepodong-1 (TD-1) missile. On August 31, 1998, Pyongyang tested a three-stage TD-1 missile, which flew 1,500 km over Japan. Although the third stage of the missile failed to work, the test proved that the DPRK had acquired a medium-range missile capability. After the test, the United States, Japan, and South Korea intensified pressures on North Korea to discontinue its missile program. North Korea has maintained that it will continue the program as a matter of sovereign right. North Korea is also believed to be working on a more advanced two-stage missile, the Taepodong-2, which could deliver larger payloads as far as Alaska and Hawaii, and smaller payloads to the continental United States.

U.S. inflexibility about the ROK's development of medium-range missiles is driving it toward Russia, which is willing to sell missile technologies and components for cash. As of January 1999, South Korea was considering the purchase of military and industrial high technology from Russia worth $200 million as a partial repayment of Russia's debt. The ROK Defense Ministry, for example, was interested in radar, missile guidance, and other electronic technology.[48] South Korea's sudden decision in August 1998 to include the Russian Kilo-class submarine as a candidate for its new KSS2 submarine program is likely to have been influenced by Russia's offer to provide advanced technology. During his 1998 trip to Moscow, Admiral Yu Sam Nam, Chief of ROK Naval Operations, was offered a complete Russian submarine package, including submarine-building technologies. Russia even offered to provide onboard vertical launcher technology.[49]

RUSSIAN ARMS SALES TO SOUTH KOREA

Russia's outstanding debt to South Korea, Russia's need to earn cash through arms export, and South Korea's desire to diversify sources of high-technology weapons and core military technologies have intertwined to boost mutual interest in arms sales.[50] Russian arms exports to South Korea are closely related to the repayment of Russia's debt.

As mentioned above, in August 1994 Seoul and Moscow agreed in principle that Russia should repay half its 1.47 billion in debt with military hardware and the remaining half with raw materials. Since Russia was incapable of paying cash to settle the debts, South Korea was forced to accept whatever Russia had to offer, including armaments and military equipment.

In the 1990s, South Korea embarked on a number of military procurement projects to upgrade its existing armaments and to acquire high-technology weapons and military equipment. Russia has persistently promoted its military products for the ROK's military force improvement programs.

Russia's primary interest in arms trade is commercial: it wants to pay off its debt to Seoul with weapons and to provide additional weapons and spare parts for cash. Arms trade is extremely profitable, and military products are the only Russian manufactured items that can effectively compete on the world market. Arms sales to South Korea also would have the effect of strengthening bilateral military ties. Acquiring core military technologies is a top priority for the ROK, and Russian openness to technology transfer is an advantage over other arms suppliers. This pursuit of core technologies and key weapons components is a driving force behind military cooperation with Russia. However, arms trade with Russia may have a lasting impact on South Korea's military capability and may affect South Korea's security relations in Northeast Asia.

The first shipment of Russian weapons arrived in South Korea in September 1996. In October, South Korea inaugurated its first mechanized infantry battalion armed with Russian-made BMP-3 (the Russian version of the U.S. Army's Bradley fighting vehicle).[51] As of 2000, South Korea accepted arms and military hardware from Russia worth $240 million, including 33 T-80U tanks, 33 BMP-3 armored personnel carriers, 70 MEITS-M portable tactical rocket systems, and 50 IGLA portable air defense systems. In addition, South Korea received a total of 28 civilian helicopters from Russia as part of the debt repayment scheme.

Missile Systems

Russian armaments have been a strong contender for South Korea's SAM-X missile defense system, FX fighter aircraft, and KSS2 submarine projects. Seoul possesses the Nike Hercules surface-to-air missile that was developed by the United States in 1954. The ROK program to upgrade its surface-to-air missile system, code-named SAM-X, is an ambitious and expensive undertaking. South Korea launched an estimated $1-billion weapons procurement project to defend against possible attacks from North Korea's Scud-type missiles. The Korean Defense Ministry chose the U.S. Patriot air defense system and the Russian S-300 missile system as the final candidates for the project and has been carefully weighing the two systems.

The S-300 has advantages over the Patriot in price and technology transfer. The price of the S-300 is about 30 percent less than that of the Patriot. Moreover, purchasing the S-300 is appealing to South Korea because it can partially pay for the missile system by using Russia's debt. Furthermore, Moscow is more willing to transfer core technology than is Washington. The Fakel Design Bureau, which produces the S-300, even offered an upgradeable system, providing some assurance of continued improvement. The Patriot, on the other hand, is more compatible with South Korea's existing weapons systems, since 80 percent of South Korea's weapons imports are from the United States. Preliminary plans for the SAM-X project called for implementation before the year 2000. However, the target year has now been set for 2003. This delay was due mainly to a lack of sufficient financial resources.

Pyongyang's test firing of the Taepodong-1 missile caused a stir in the international community and strongly motivated Seoul to accelerate its own missile program. In November 1998, the ROK Defense Ministry announced that it had initiated a program the preceding January to develop a medium-range surface-to-air missile, code-named M-SAM. M-SAM, with a range of 40 km, is designed to intercept invading North Korean military aircraft and Scud-type missiles. This system aims to replace the aging anti-aircraft Hawk missiles that South Korea currently employs. The missiles are expected to be operational in 2008. The ROK plans to acquire technological help from Russia in areas such as electronic guidance in developing the M-SAM, which is reportedly modeled after the S-300.[52]

Fighter Aircraft

Russia's S-35 fighter aircraft has been competing for South Korea's FX next-generation fighter program. As the ROK Air Force completes the $5 billion Korea Fighter Program[53] to replace its aging F-4 Phantoms and F-5 Freedom Fighters with 120 KF-16s, it is searching for candidates for Korea's next-generation fighter program, code-named FX, worth about $8 billion. Seoul has planned for some time to acquire new-generation military aircraft. The Rafale of French Dassault, Boeing's F-15E, Russia's Su-35, and the Eurofighter Typhoon jointly developed by Germany, the United Kingdom, Spain, and Italy are considered the top candidates for the FX program.

At the 1996 Seoul Air Show, Moscow offered South Korea heavily modified Su-35s or Su-37s to meet ROK Air Force requirements.[54] The Su-35 will be equipped with phased grid radar and multifunctional color displays and AL-31FP variable jet direction engines.[55] The Russian proposal included the assembly of Su-35s in South Korea, 100-percent servicing, and technology transfers. Russia suggested that South Korea pay partly in cash and partly with the Russian debt owed to South Korea.

Submarines

In 1987, the ROK launched its first submarine program to produce nine 1,200- ton 209-class diesel submarines. Daewoo teamed up with Germany's HDW for this project. As of 1998, Daewoo had produced seven 209-class submarines and was building two more. As the first submarine program nears completion, the ROK Navy is pushing for the KSS2 submarine program to acquire 1,500–2,000- ton advanced submarines by the early 2000s. In the long run, the ROK Navy plans to use its own technology to build 3,000-ton submarines that are capable of launching missiles and staying under water for an extended period of time. Daewoo, with HDW's technology, Hyundai with the French company DSN's technology, and Russian submarines are final candidates for the KSS2 project.

Russia has been lobbying hard to sell its submarines (2,500-ton Kilo-class or 1,900-ton Amur-class diesel submarines) to South Korea. During his visit to Seoul in March 1998, Russian Vice Defense Minister Nikolai Mikhailov officially requested that the ROK purchase Russian-made submarines and S-300 missiles.[56] On May 20, 1999, the Korean Defense Ministry expressed its interest in purchasing three Kilo-class diesel submarines from Russia.[57] The $1 billion deal would be paid half with cash and half as debt repayment. Obviously, the controversial announcement was made out of political considerations. In the wake of the spy scandal in 1998, the relationship between South Korea and Russia reached its lowest point. President Kim looked into the possibility of purchasing Russian submarines in the hopes that Russia-Korea relations would improve. The ROK Navy is opposed to the purchase of the Kilo submarine on the grounds that it has less operational ability than South Korea's own 209-class.[58] Naval officers point out that the storage battery of a Kilo-class submarine lasts about 18–24 months, whereas the German-made batteries of the 209-class submarines last 5 years longer. They also note that the submarines offered by Germany's HDW and France's DCN will have the capability to stay submerged longer with their advanced Air Independent Propulsion systems. South Korean Navy officers also maintain that the Kilo-class submarine is an outdated model and that there will be problems with spare parts.[59] Reversing its earlier decision, the Ministry of National Defense announced in July 1999 that the final decision on the KSS2 project would be postponed for one year. In October 2000, South Korea decided not to purchase Russian diesel submarines due to its failure to meet the minimum requirements in telecommunications systems, logistics abilities, battery capacity and continued operation. South Korea instead chose the German 214-class submarine for the next generation submarine project.[60]

Russia is pitching hard to sell its weapons to South Korea. Rosvoorouzhenie, Russia's state-run weapons exporting firm, has stationed two representatives permanently in Korea. Russia is interested in selling weapons to South Korea mostly for commercial reasons: it wants to pay off debts to Seoul and to provide additional weapons and parts for cash. Arms sales would also have the effect of strengthening Russian–South Korean bilateral military cooperation.

For Seoul, arms purchases from Moscow are attractive in three ways. First, by diversifying its sources of arms imports, Seoul can reduce its excessive dependence on the United States for military hardware. Second, Russian military hardware is relatively inexpensive. The T-80U, the latest version of Russia's main battle tank, is priced at two-thirds the cost of Korea's self-developed K1 and half that of the U.S. M1A1 Abrams.[61] Third, transfer of military technology from Russia is much easier than from the United States, and Seoul needs sophisticated military technology to produce modern weaponry for military self-sufficiency and for exports. Given the importance of the U.S.-Korean alliance to Korean security, however, South Koreans will not easily ignore U.S. pressure concerning arms sales. Nevertheless, South Korea has repeatedly demonstrated its readiness to purchase weapons from countries that offer generous military technology transfer and superior products.

COOPERATION THROUGH THE TUMEN RIVER AREA DEVELOPMENT PROGRAM

Russia-Korean economic cooperation may proceed as part of a multinational project such as the Tumen River Area Development Program (TRADP), a project initiated by the United Nations Development Program (UNDP) and designed to develop the area near the Tumen River into a hub for transportation, tourism, and manufacturing in Northeast Asia.[62] The Tumen River delta region is situated at the juncture of China, Russia, and the DPRK, with Japan to the east across the sea. To the west is access to the markets of Europe via the Trans-Siberian railway. If this economic zone is completed, goods in Jilin can be sent down the Tumen River to seaports in Russia or the DPRK, saving five to seven days compared with the route via the port in Dalian.

The Tumen River delta program promises to be the best place in Northeast Asia for international cooperation. The area has reserves of gold and coal as well as cheap and abundant land and fresh water. In the hinterland, there are the rich reserves of Siberian timber, coal, oil, and other minerals, and cheap labor is plentiful in Manchuria and North Korea. South Korea and Japan have capital and technological advantages. Through international cooperation and development, the region may become a hub for the transshipment of international commodities and one of the key processing areas for trade in the twenty-first century.

The UNDP has sponsored and coordinated TRADP, and five nations—China, North Korea, Russia, South Korea, and Mongolia—have been participating in the project since 1992. The five countries will start a six-month survey on the investment climate in four areas of the Tumen River delta, including the Rajin-Sonbong free economic and trade zone in North Korea. According to some estimates, this project will take over twenty years to complete and cost $30 billion.

In recent years, governments of the countries around the Tumen River basin have taken a number of concrete actions to further the development of the Tumen region. China proclaimed Hunchun as a class-A city open to the outside world; Russia announced that Vladivostok would be opened to the outside world and unveiled a huge plan to use $700 million to develop the port in Zarubino; and the DPRK also declared Chongjin and Rajin to be economic development zones. In particular, the Chinese city of Hunchun has become an area where the flow of international commodities and foreign investment are brisk.

However, the three riparian countries are concentrating on their own economic development programs—North Korea in the Rajin-Sonbong free trade zone, China in the Hunchun special economic zone, and Russia in development of the Vladivostok area—and are at this point reluctant to pursue the TRADP as a joint program. North Korea's development of the Rajin-Sonbong area conflicts with the PRC's development plans for Hunchun, and Russia is less interested in the Tumen River development project than the Greater Vladivostok Free Economic Zone comprising Vladivostok, Nakhodka Free Economic Zone, and Khasan. The institutional framework for cooperation and sufficient funding are also lacking.

Northeast Asia needs to create regional cooperative mechanisms that can make authoritative decisions regarding TRADP before they embark on the program in earnest. In addition, financing the program (to develop a network of roads, railways, ports and airports, education facilities, power, water, telecommunications, and waste disposal plants) is a formidable problem. So far more than $900 million has been invested on the project, but raising $30 billion will prove difficult.

Both Russia and South Korea stand to benefit from this multinational project. In addition to economic benefits, Russia will share capital, technology, and know-how with Asia Pacific countries, and South Korea will have an opportunity to boost its ties with North Korea through multinational economic cooperation.

IMPLICATIONS OF SEOUL-MOSCOW ECONOMIC COOPERATION

South Korean–Russian economic relations are in flux as they are subject to multiple influences. Russia's internal conditions relating to political instability, economic uncertainty, high tax rates, changing rules and regulations, corruption, lack of foreign currency, and inadequate infrastructure are detrimental to Seoul-Moscow economic relations. Korea's internal conditions—insufficient knowledge about Russian culture and business practices, unsettled credit relations, and difficulties with export settlement—also restrict bilateral economic ties. International conditions such as oil prices, economic embargoes, and the Asian financial crisis influence the bilateral economic relationship.

Before Seoul and Moscow normalized relations in September 1990, the major obstacle to improved economic cooperation was lack of a basic legal and institutional foundation. In the 1990s, however, Russia's political and economic instability were the main problems. Unless Russia gains some semblance of an effective central authority and a functioning market economy, economic cooperation between Seoul and Moscow will remain limited.

South Korea experienced an economic crisis in 1997 as a result of the Asian financial crisis, mismanagement of foreign debt, and other structural problems at home. To avoid a default on its foreign debt, South Korea received a $57 billion rescue package led by the International Monetary Fund (IMF). Despite this package, the Korean currency continued to weaken and interest rates soared. In the wake of the economic crisis, the ROK government has taken a number of measures to open capital markets, restructure the financial system, strengthen supervision over illegal business practices, increase labor flexibility, and urge corporate restructuring. Subsequently, the number of bankruptcies doubled and the unemployment rate reached a peak not seen for decades.[63] Russia's declaration of a moratorium on debt repayment in August 1998 further damaged bilateral economic cooperation. Following the moratorium announcement, Korean companies halted shipments to Russia while they determined the credit-worthiness of Russian buyers and reviewed their contracts with Russian companies. In 2000, bilateral trade was only about 60 percent of the 1996 level, and South Korea's investment in Russia remained low. Economic problems forced many of the South Korean companies operating in Russia to withdraw completely or cut personnel.

South Korean–Russian economic cooperation may alter political relations. The geostrategic importance of the Korean Peninsula to the Russian Far East motivates Moscow to cultivate a friendly and cooperative relationship with Seoul. Economic relations (particularly, arms sales and military technology transfer) with South Korea may offer opportunities for Russia to increase its influence in Korea.

ROK-Russia cooperation in multinational development projects such as the Russian natural gas pipeline project and the TRADP is likely to involve North Korea, and cooperative economic endeavors between Moscow, Seoul, and Pyongyang will help North Korea out of self-imposed isolation, facilitate Russia–North Korea rapprochement, and contribute to the creation of a peace regime on the Korean Peninsula.

Bilateral economic developments have security implications. Russia considers a unified Korea a long-term strategic partner. It is in Russia's interests to prevent any country, particularly Japan and China, from attaining a position of dominance in the region. In this context, South Korea (more likely a unified Korea) may become Russia's strategic partner (or coalition partner). Strong economic ties combined with shared political interests between Moscow and Seoul may breed common strategic outlooks.

Russian arms sales and military technology transfer to South Korea have the potential to affect political and security relations in Northeast Asia. As exchanges of military personnel between Seoul and Moscow continue into the twenty-first century, mutual confidence and trust between the South Korean and Russian militaries will grow. Russia has already provided modern military hardware to South Korea, yet large-scale arms sales to South Korea are problematic since the bulk of South Korea's military hardware and equipment are U.S.-made, and Russian armaments may be incompatible with South Korea's existing weapons systems. It would be too risky and costly to operate two different weapons systems. The purchase and operation of Russian advanced weapons will require a long-term political commitment from South Korea—a commitment for which Seoul is not ready yet.

More promising are the prospects for joint research and development of high-tech weapons and military components for domestic use and export. Moscow badly needs foreign currency to develop cutting-edge military technologies and to maintain its military-industrial capability. Seoul, on the other hand, needs to acquire core technologies and components for its military modernization. Thus, military technology cooperation between Seoul and Moscow is mutually beneficial. Russia's technology transfer to South Korea, however, will be limited without a South Korean commitment to purchase high-tech weapons. Still, South Korea needs to focus on the acquisition of core military technologies and limited hardware from Russia to enhance military independence.

Russia's debt to South Korea has been a thorny issue in the bilateral relationship, and South Korea is eager to settle the matter as early as possible—the debt does not have to be a major obstacle. Given Russia's deplorable economic situation, South Korea needs to reschedule Russia's debt while seeking to resolve the issue gradually and on a long-term basis. North Korea owes about $3.6 billion to

Russia from the Soviet era; in the event the two Koreas unify voluntarily, the unified Korean government will have a legal obligation to assume this debt from Russia.

The impact of Korean-Russian economic relations on political and security relations in Northeast Asia will vary depending on the nature of the newly emerging power structure in Northeast Asia, the relative economic capability of Northeast Asian countries, the timing and method of Korean unification, and the continuation of U.S. engagement in the region. Russo–North Korean relations will have an impact on Northeast Asian security relations. In February 2000, Moscow and Pyongyang normalized their relationship after signing a new friendship treaty. In July 2000, President Putin flew to Pyongyang to hold the summit meeting with Kim Jong Il. During this trip, Putin expressed a strong interest in economic cooperation between Russia and North Korea. Particularly, he stated Russia's willingness to modernize North Korean plants and power stations by providing new equipment and specialists. He also discussed a proposal to link the inter-Korean railway to a Trans-Siberia system. Following the historic inter-Korean summit of June 2000, Seoul and Pyongyang agreed to re-link a railway severed by the division of the nation. As the inter-Korean railway (the Kyungui line linking Seoul and Shinuiju) is restored, a Trans-Siberian railroad system will be connected to an inter-Korean railroad system. Should this happen, trilateral economic cooperation including Russia, the ROK, and the DPRK would gain momentum.

Following the Moscow-Pyongyang rapprochement, Russia will seek to maintain a balanced relationship (or evenhanded approach) with the two Koreas, while separating politics and economics. In other words, Russia will maintain a neutral position between the ROK and the DPRK as regards political issues particularly relating to inter-Korean affairs. On certain international matters, such as U.S.-led U.N. sanctions against North Korea over nuclear weapons and missile issues, Russia may exercise a veto power. Russia, however, will continue to support unequivocally nuclear non-proliferation on the Korean Peninsula, while championing a peaceful and diplomatic solution to the Korean question and North Korea's nuclear and missile development issues.

As far as economic (trade and investment) and military relations (arms sales and technology cooperation) are concerned, Seoul is by far a more important partner to Russia than Pyongyang is. Moscow thus will continue to lean heavily toward Seoul in economic and military cooperation, hoping that Seoul will play a central role in the development of the Russian Far East. Moscow's economic relations with Pyongyang are insignificant compared with Moscow-Seoul relations. Trade between Pyongyang and Moscow in 1999 stood at a meager $100 million, while that between Seoul and Moscow recorded over $2 billion in the same year. Barring Russia's massive economic aid to North Korea, bilateral economic cooperation will not increase drastically. Given Russia's economic difficulties and North Korea's inability to repay its debt owed to Russia, we cannot expect a breakthrough in the economic relationship in the near future.

Therefore, Russia's evenhanded approach toward the two Koreas will be most visible in political relations. By separating political issues from economic benefits, Moscow will try to enhance its influence and prestige in Korean affairs and at the same time continue to intensify economic cooperation with Seoul, particularly in connection with the Korean industrial complex in Nakhodka and the Kovyktinsk gas pipeline project.

Moscow wants to enhance its influence in Korea and Northeast Asia by serving as a mediator between the two Koreas and by playing a leading role in a multilateral conference on the Korean question. South Korea hopes that Russia contributes to inter-Korean reconciliation by conveying Seoul's messages to Pyongyang as an impartial broker. But for now Moscow does not have a crucial leverage over Pyongyang, and Russians have yet to earn the trust of North Koreans. Russia's internal problems and limited diplomatic resources will continue to constrain its latitude in the international arena.

NOTES

1. On Gorbachev's Korea policy, see Seung-Ho Joo, *Gorbachev's Foreign Policy Toward the Korean Peninsula, 1985–1991: Power and Reform* (Lewiston, N.Y.: Edwin Mellen, 2000).

2. For more on developments in DPRK-ROK relations and its impact on Russian policy, see Yong-Chool Ha, "The Dynamics of Russian–South Korean Relations and Implications for the Russian Far East," chapter 16 in this volume. On the inter-Korean summit, see Cameron W. Barr and Lienne R. Prusher, "The Last Cold-War Frontier Thaws," *Christian Science Monitor*, June 15, 2000; Howard W. French, "Koreas Reach Accord Seeking Reconciliation After 50 Years," *New York Times*, June 15, 2000.

3. *Korean Times*, July 10, 1991, 9, in FBIS-EAS-91-132.

4. "Russia Promises Attractive Tax Incentives to ROK Companies in Nakhodaka," *Korea Times*, July 9, 1997; Leonid Vinogradov, "Korea to Create Free Economic Zone in Nakhodka," ITAR-TASS, July 9, 1997, in FBIS-SOV-97-190.

5. Yonhap, May 12, 1999, in FBIS-EAS-1999-0512.

6. For example, Daewoo Corporation, Korea's largest exporter to Russia, completely stopped all shipments to Russia pending an evaluation of its Russian trading partners. LG Electronics decided to sell its home electronics products on a 100-percent cash basis, and Samwon Trading of Pusan considered demanding down payments of 30–50 percent of the value of goods. *Korea Times*, August 18, 1998, in FBIS-EAS-98-230.

7. "Developing Links with South Korea," *Asian Review of Business and Technology*, November 1997:16.

8. Korea Trade Investment Promotion Agency (KOTRA), *Rusia pottari changsa siltae mit uri ui hwalyong bang'an* (Russian Shuttle Traders) (Seoul, February 1998), 9.

9. Ibid., 10.

10. Chongbae Lee and Michael J. Bradshaw, "South Korean Economic Relations with Russia," *Post-Soviet Geography and Economics* 38, no. 8 (1997):463–64.

11. The distance from Seoul to Vladivostok is 750 km (470 miles), whereas Seoul and Moscow are 10,000 km (6,250 miles) apart.

12. Construction costs exceeded the initial estimate by $30 million, and the total included some $12 million to cover federal tax and customs payments. "Mixed prospects for investment," *Asian Review of Business and Technology*, November 1997:15.

13. *INTERFAX Communications and Electronics Report* 2, no. 12 (March 18–24, 1998), in FBIS-SOV-98-082.

14. Kia Motor went bankrupt and was taken over by Hyundai Motor in 1998. In 1998, Daewoo Motor went bankrupt under heavy debts, and, as of summer 2001, talks for the sale of Daewoo Motor to General Motors were in the final stages. (Don Kirk, "Company News; GM-Daewoo Talks in Final Stage, Korean Official Says," *New York Times*, July 13, 2001.) Daewoo provided commodity loans worth $150 million for the automobile assembly plant in Rostov-na-Donu (Yonhap, November 4, 1999).

15. Author's interview with Lotte's Northern Business Team, August 1, 2000. South Korea's earlier proposal to invest $400 million—the largest South Korean investment project in Russia—to construct a hotel complex, including a department store and an office building, in the Arbat area in Moscow was withdrawn because neither side could agree on the terms of contract.

16. Korea International Trade Association (KOTIS) website at <www.kita.or.kr>.

17. *Korea Herald*, February 4, 2000.

18. "Foreign Direct Investment in Russia Falls Sharply," *Financial Times* (London), June 3, 1999.

19. South Korea's total foreign direct investment (cumulative) in 1997 amounted to $16.44 trillion. Export-Import Bank of Korea website at <www.koreaexim.go.kr/>.

20. The total foreign investment in Russia in 1998 reached $3.4 billion. Moscow Interfax, May 28, 1999, in FBIS-SOV-1999-0528.

21. Yevgeniya Lents, "Details of South Korean Investment in Maritime Territory," ITAR-TASS, August 21, 1997, in FBIS-SOV-97-233.

22. They include Saemaul Undong Chungang Hyopuihoe, Taehan Chutaekgonsul Saup hoephoe, Nongchon chidoja Chungang Hyopuiheo, Hannong Pokkuhoe, Daegyung, Da-A Industry, Hohap, and Namyang Aloe. Yonhap, January 20, 2000.

23. Kohap's web site at <www.kohap.co.kr/get.html>; Yevgeniya Lents, "Details of South Korean Investment in Maritime Territory."

24. For the Saemaul Movement Association's agricultural cooperation in Primorskii krai, see the Association's web site at <www.saemaul.or.kr>.

25. Russell Working, "Russia's Patchwork Economy; Korean Companies, Chinese Workers and U.S. Entrée," *New York Times*, March 18, 1999.

26. Yonhap, March 27, 1999, in FBIS-EAS-1999-0327; Yonhap, July 24, 2000, in FBIS-EAS-2000-0724.

27. Yonhap, December 18, 1991, in FBIS-EAS-91-243.

28. *Choson Ilbo,* May 26, 1992, 23.

29. *Choson Ilbo,* August 4, 1994.

30. *Korea Times,* October 25, 1999, in FBIS-EAS-1999-1025.

31. Keun Wook Paik, "Japan, Korea, and the Development of Russian Far Eastern Energy Resources," *The Journal of Energy and Development* 16, no. 2 (1992):238.

32. The consortium led by KOGAS includes nine corporations—KOGAS, Korea Petroleum Development Corporation (PEDCO), Daewoo, LG, Hyundai, Daesung, Hanhwa, Hohap, and Hyosung. Sansung and East Asia Gas (Dong-A Gas) are not participating in the consortium. Author's interview with Professor Yun Lee, Economics Department, Inchon University, February 13, 2000.

33. Rossiyskaia gazeta, Ekonomicheskii Soyuz Supplement, March 30, 1996, 11, in FBIS-SOV-96-084-S.

34. Keun Wook Paik and Jae Yong Choi, "Pipeline Gas Trade between Asian Russia, Northeast Asia Gets Fresh Look," *Oil and Gas Journal,* August 18, 1997, 41–45.

35. Ibid., 41.

36. Choongbae and Bradshaw, "South Korean Economic Relations with Russia," 475.

37. KOGAS, "Rusia irkutsk chunyongas kaebalsaup chuyonaeyong" (The Irkutsk Natural Gas Project), at <www.kogas.html> (January 2000) in Yonhap, October 8, 1999, in FBIS-EAS-1999-1008.

38. Sun Hon Kim, "Present Trends and Priorities in Economic Cooperation between Russia and the Republic of Korea," *Far Eastern Affairs* (Moscow), no. 4 (1996), 53.

39. Yonhap, June 5, 1991, in FBIS-EAS-91-108.

40. Yonhap, September 2, 1992, in FBIS-EAS-92-178.

41. "Daewoo Heavy Industries Develops Unmanned Deep-Sea Vehicle," *Korea Herald,* February 23, 1996.

42. *Hanguk Kyongje Sinmun,* December 22, 1997, 20, in FBIS-EAS-98-121.

43. Nadezhda Anisimova, ITAR-TASS, May 16, 1997, in FBIS-SOV-97-136.

44. Stockholm International Peace Research Institute, *SIPRI Yearbook 1998* (London: Oxford University Press, 1999), 271–72.

45. Ibid., 296.

46. *Korea Herald,* August 11, 1998, 1.

47. *Chosun Ilbo,* July 4, 1999.

48. "ROK to Receive $200 Million High Tech Military Transfer from Russia," *Korea Times,* January 25, 1999.

49. *Korea Times,* August 18, 1998, 3, in FBIS-EAS-98-230.

50. For military relations between Seoul and Moscow, see Tae Hwan Kwak and Seung Ho Joo, "Military Cooperation between Russia and South Korea," *International Journal of Korean Unification Studies* 8 (1999):147–77.

51. "ROK Army Activates Russian Arms-Equipped Infantry Battalion," *Korean Herald,* October 2, and October 3, 1996, in FBIS-EAS-96-192.

52. "ROK to Develop Missile Interceptor," *Korea Times,* September 4, 1998. Nikolai Poliashev, director of the Almaz bureau, announced in July 1999 that his bureau was developing parts of air defense systems for South Korea. Interfax, July 20, 1999, quoted

in *RFE/RL Newsline*, July 21, 1999.

53. Under the Korea Fighter Program that started in 1994, 12 F-16s were purchased from Lockheed Martin, and Samsung has assembled 36. Samsung is producing an additional 72 under a license agreement with Lockheed Martin.

54. Nicolai Novichkov, "Desperate for Sales, Moscow Courts Seoul," *Aviation Week & Space Technology*, November 18, 1996:31.

55. *Nezavisimoe voennoe obozrenie*, October 16–22, 1998, 113.

56. *Korea Times*, "Russia Pushing for Weapons Sale to Korea," May 30, 1998.

57. *Korea Herald*, May 20, 1999.

58. The Kilo-class submarine has 6 torpedo tubes for 18 torpedoes and mines and a launcher for 8 surface-to-air missiles. It can stay at sea for 45 days and dive up to 300 meters. Its top speed under water is 10 knots.

59. *Korea Times*, June 4, 1999, 9, in FBIS-EAS-1999-0604.

60. "ROK Daily Views 'Diplomatic War' for Weapons Sales," *Dong-a Ilbo*, February 1, 2001, in FBIS-EAS-2001-0219.

61. "Defense Ministry Considering Purchasing Weapons from Russia," *Korea Times*, September 8, 1996, 3.

62. In terms of the geographic scope of development for TRADP, three options are considered: the Tumen River Economic Development Area (TREDA), the Tumen River Economic Zone (TREZ), and the Northeast Asia Regional Development Area (NEARDA). TREDA includes a 10,000-square km triangular area that connects DPRK's Chonjin to Russia's Vladivostok and China's Yanji. Within the TRADP is a 1,000-square km area called TREZ, which centers on the delta region connecting China's Hunchun, Russa's Zarubino, and DPRK's Rajin-Sonbong. The NEARDA includes a broad area encompassing the Korean Peninsula, Mongolia, China's three Northeast provinces, and the Russian Far East. TRADP's primary interest now lies with TREDA. <www/ec21.net/oros/content>.

63. Jennifer Veale, "Is This Recovery for Real?" *Business Week*, January 25, 1999, 54; and *OECD Economic Outlook*, June 1998, no. 63, 104.

Index

labor strikes, 282, 283
privatization, 269, 272
productivity, 20, 89, 91, 117, 225, 226,
　229, 267, 268, 270, 271, 274, 278-
　79, 280-81, 283, 287n1, 287n3
shipbuilding, 270
social services, 273, 283-84
Soviet legacy, 4-8, 20, 267-68, 273-74
state orders, 269, 271, 273, 275, 276,
　280
transportation costs, 274
wage arrears, 255, 283
Ministry of Agriculture, 206-07
Ministry for Atomic Energy (Minatom),
　248, 254
Ministry of Defense, 248, 253, 269, 280-
　81
Ministry of Economic Development, 142
Ministry of Energy, 174
Ministry of Fisheries
　See State Fisheries Committee
Ministry of Interior (MVD), 19, 238
Ministry of Natural Resources, 285
Ministry of Oil and Gas, 170
Mitsubishi, 170, 172, 174, 312
Mitsui, 170, 172, 174, 312, 439n12
Molikpaq, 174, 180-81
Mori, Yoshiro, 311
Moscow Aviation Production Association
　(MAPO), 280
Moskit antiship missiles, 231, 280,
　289n27

N

Nakhodka Free Economic Zone, 44, 308,
　401, 412, 443, 444, 451-52, 462, 466
narcotics
　See drugs
national missile defense (United States),
　21, 22, 23, 24, 30, 31, 230, 240, 388-
　90, 392, 405, 410
National Industrial Policy, 269
National Pipeline Research Society, 185
nationalism, 22, 36, 38, 45, 46, 47, 48,
　50, 51, 298, 299, 320, 323, 334,

338, 342, 352-53, 368, 405
　See also migration
natural gas, 11, 12, 15, 25-26, 27, 28,
　127, 131, 132
pipelines, 13, 15, 127, 185
natural resources industries, 11, 12, 15,
　20, 25-27, 35, 85, 87, 91, 93, 108,
　110, 118, 119, 120, 130, 131, 132,
　133, 349
competitiveness in Northeast Asian
　markets, 117-135, 436, 438n8
productivity, 106, 131, 133, 166
as share of gross regional product,
　118, 128
See also individual sectors
Nazdratenko, Yevgenii, 19, 23, 35, 45,
　46, 55n22, 228, 242, 246n32, 276-
　77, 299-300, 305, 308, 323, 333
and Association of Businesses, 45, 46
and China threat, 46, 298, 319, 323,
　378, 380
and fisheries, 150-51, 157, 159,
　164n26, 246n32
and foreign investment, 305, 308
and military-industrial complex, 228,
　236, 276-77
and separatism, 46
and Unity, 363
Nemtsov, Boris, 361
Nonproliferation Treaty (NPT), 402, 403
Norota, Hosei, 232
North Atlantic Treaty Organization
　(NATO), 30, 31, 39, 234, 237, 281,
　303, 389, 390, 392
Northeast Asian Development Bank, 47
Northeast Asian Regional Development
　Area, 469n62
North Korea, 3, 7, 33, 34, 42
defense, 279, 398, 402-03, 404, 457,
　459
energy, 124
drug trafficking, 50, 255-56, 309
relations with China, 40-41, 307
relations with Russia, 7, 32, 33, 307-
　311, 398, 399-400, 401-03, 404,
　407, 413, 442-43, 444, 465-66

About the Editors and Contributors

Dr. Judith Thornton is professor of economics at the University of Washington, specializing in the transition of Russia and other post-communist economies. Dr. Thornton is a member of the International Advisory Board (and founding Head of Board) for the Eurasia Foundation Program on Economics Education and Research in Russia and member of the Board of Directors of the Foundation for Russian-American Economic Cooperation. Dr. Thornton's extensive publications on the economy of the Far East include: "Committing to an Energy Project in Russia; Is There a Successful Strategy?" *Comparative Economic Studies* (2001); "The Exercise of Rights to Resources," in Michael Bradshaw, ed., *The Russian Far East and Pacific Asia: Unfulfilled Potential* (2001); "Economic Reform in the Russian Far East; the Implications for Russian-Chinese Economic Cooperation," in Sherman Garnett, ed., *Rapprochement or Rivalry? Russia-Chinese Relations in a Changing Asia* (2000); "Economic Reform in the Russian Far East: The Implications for Russian-Chinese Economic Cooperation" in *The Future of Russian-Chinese Relations* (1998); "Restructuring Production without Market Infrastructure" in D. North, ed., *Transforming Post-Communist Political Economies* (1998); and "The Strategies of Foreign and Foreign-Assisted Firms in the Russian Far East: Alternatives to Missing Infrastructure," with N. Mikheeva, *Comparative Economic Studies* (1996).

Dr. Charles E. Ziegler is professor and chair of the department of political science at the University of Louisville. His research and teaching interests include democracy and democratization, foreign relations and policy, and Russia and East Asia. He is also Executive Director of the Louisville Committee on Foreign Relations. In 1995, Dr. Ziegler was a Fulbright Lecturer and Research Fellow in Pusan, Korea. Dr. Ziegler is the author of numerous scholarly publications, including: "Russia and Northeast Asia," in *The Lost Equilibrium* (2001); "Soviet Union: Environment," in *The International Encyclopedia of the Social and Behavioral Sciences* (2001); "Transitioning from Delegative Democracy: The Russian Federation and South Korea," *International Politics* (1999); *The History of Russia*, (1999); and "Russo-Japanese Relations: A New Start for the 21st Century?" *Problems of Post-Communism* (1999).

Dr. Mikhail A. Alexseev is assistant professor of political science at San Diego State University. He specializes in threat assessment of interstate and internal wars, with emphasis on ethno-political conflict and the political economy of center-periphery relations in post-communist Russia. Dr. Alexseev is the author of *Without Warning: Threat Assessment, Intelligence, and Global Struggle* (1997); and is editor of *A Federation Imperiled: Center-Periphery Conflict in Post-Soviet Russia* (1999). Dr. Alexseev has published his research in *The Journal of Peace Research*, *The Journal of Post-Soviet Geography and Economics*, *Political Communication*, *Europe-Asia Studies*, *Nationalities Papers*, *The Fletcher Forum of World Affairs*, and *Pacific Focus*.

Mr. Tony Allison served until recently as the CEO of Marine Resources Company International (MRCI), a Seattle-based international seafood company owned jointly by Russian and American interests. Prior to heading MRCI, Mr. Allison served as Director of International Trade for the State of Oregon. Mr. Allison received an executive MBA from the University of Washington in 1995. Previously, he completed an M.A. in International Studies (Russian history) and Marine Studies (Russian maritime policy) at the University of Washington. Mr. Allison has published articles in professional journals on Siberian regional history and on the Russian position toward the Law of the Sea, as well as book reviews on topics relating to the history of Siberia and the Russian Far East.

Ms. Katherine G. Burns is a doctoral candidate in political science at the Massachusetts Institute of Technology. Her research interests focus on economic and security issues in Northeast Asia with particular emphasis on Russia, China, and Japan. Her publications include "China and Japan: Economic Partnership to Political Ends," in *Economic Confidence-Building and Regional Security*, The Henry L. Stimson Center (October 2000); "Primor'e: Local Politics and a Coalition for Reform" in Timothy Colton and Jerry Hough, eds., *Russia's Protodemocracy in Action: Perspectives on the Election of 1993* (1998); and "Battling for Foreign Capital in Primorskii Krai," *Transition* (September 1995).

Dr. Sergei Chugrov is deputy editor-in-chief of *The World Economy and International Relations Journal* at the Institute of World Economy and International Relations, Moscow. In 1994, Dr. Chugrov was a visiting scholar at Harvard University's Program on U.S.-Japan Relations. His research articles have been published widely and include "Political Tendencies in Russia's Regions: Evidence from the 1993 Parliamentary Elections," *Slavic Review* (fall 1994) with Vladimir Gimpelson and Darrell Slider; and *Rossiia i Zapad: Metamorfozy Vzaimovospriiatiia* (1993).

Ms. Jennifer Duncan, at the time this chapter was prepared, was an attorney at the Rural Development Institute in Seattle, Washington. Ms. Duncan has extensive research, legal, and policy experience on land tenure reform, land market development, and farm reorganization issues. Ms. Duncan received her J.D. from the University of Washington School of Law in 1996 and has extensive field and research experience in China, Russia, Romania, Mongolia, the Kyrgyz Republic, Tajikistan, the Republic of Moldova, and the Republic of Georgia.

Dr. Yong-Chool Ha is associate dean of the college of social sciences and professor of international relations at Seoul National University. He is also director of international affairs of the Korea Association of Political Science. Dr. Ha received his Ph.D. in Soviet politics at the University of California-Berkeley. His recent publications include *Colonialism, Neo-Familism and Rationality: Perspectives of Korean Issues* (1995) and *Economic Reforms in the Socialist World,* edited with S. Gomulka and C. Kim (1989).

Dr. Seung-Ho Joo is assistant professor of political science at the University of Minnesota-Morris. Dr. Joo received his Ph.D. from The Pennsylvania State University. His research focuses on Russian foreign and security policy, Russian-Korean relations, and Korean foreign relations. Dr. Joo is the author of *Gorbachev's Foreign Policy Toward the Two Koreas, 1985-1991* (2000); and co-editor of *Korea in the Twenty-First Century* (2001). He has authored over twenty journal articles and book chapters.

Dr. Victor D. Kalashnikov is head of the fuel-energy complex at the Economic Research Institute of the Far Eastern Branch of the Russian Academy of Sciences in Khabarovsk. Dr. Kalashnikov specializes in energy economics, including regional energy policy and the development of energy resources in the Russian Far East. His most recent publications include: "The Russian Far East: Economic Potential," in P. Minakir and N. Mikheeva, eds. (1999); "Far Eastern Economics: Five Years of Reform," in P. Minakir and N. Mikheeva, eds. (1998); and "Natural Resources of the Russian Far East and Northeast Asia," in A. Sheingauz, ed. (1997).

Dr. Natalia V. Lomakina is a senior researcher at the Economic Research Institute of the Far Eastern Branch of the Russian Academy of Sciences in Khabarovsk. She has been a visiting scholar to Washington State University, Osaka University of Economics and Law, and the Institute of Developing Economies of the Japan External Trade Organization. Dr. Lomakina's research interests focus on mineral economy, especially mineral resource use and sustainable development of the Russian Far East. Her most recent publications include: "Russian Far East Mining

Industry and Its Opportunities for Cooperation in the Asia-Pacific Region" (2001); "The Russian Far East," in *Asian Mining Yearbook and Suppliers Source* (1999 and 2000); "Natural Resources Use of the Russian Far East and Northeast Asia," in A. Sheingauz, ed. (1997).

Dr. Rajan Menon is Monroe J. Rathbone Professor of International Relations at Lehigh University and director of the Eurasia Policy Studies Program at The National Bureau of Asian Research. He has served as Academic Fellow and Senior Advisor for the Carnegie Corporation of New York and is a member of the Council on Foreign Relations. Professor Menon is author and editor of numerous publications on international relations and security in Russia and the independent states of the former Soviet Union, including, most recently: *Energy and Conflict in Central Asia and the Caucasus*, ed. with R. Ebel (2000); and *Russia, The South Caucasus, and Central Asia: The Emerging 21st Century Security Environment*, ed. with Y. Fyodorov and G. Nodia (1999). His recent articles have appeared in *International Security, Survival, The Review of International Studies, Foreign Affairs*, and *The National Interest*.

Dr. Nadezhda N. Mikheeva is deputy director of the Economic Research Institute at the Far Eastern Branch of the Russian Academy of Sciences in Khabarovsk. Her current research interests include regional economy, economic development, and trade and economic relations. Dr. Mikheeva's recent publications include: "Production Dynamics in the Russian Far East During Reform," *Journal of Econometric Study of Northeast Asia* (1999); "The Use of Regional Accounts in Analysis of Development of the Russian Far East," *ERINA REPORT* (1997); "The Strategies of Foreign-Assisted Firms in the Russian Far East: Alternatives to Missing Infrastructure," with J. Thornton, *Comparative Economic Studies* (1996); and *The Russian Far East: An Economic Outlook*, coauthor (1995, 2nd edition).

Dr. Pavel Minakir is executive director of the Economic Research Institute at the Far Eastern Branch of the Russian Academy of Sciences in Khabarovsk. His research interests include macroeconomics and regional comparative economics. Dr. Minakir is the author of "System Transformations in Economy" *Dal'nauka* (2001); "Economic Stabilization in China: Comparative Steps," *Economic Reforms in Russia and China: Problems and Perspectives* (2000); "Foreign Economic Partnerships in the Russian Far East: Problems and Perspectives," *Ekonomika and Sociologika* (2000); and "Regional Economic Politics and Federalism in Russia," in *Banks of the Far East and Siberia: History, Modernity, Problems of Development* (1999).

Dr. James Clay Moltz is associate director and research professor at the Center for Nonproliferation Studies at the Monterey Institute of International Studies, where he directs the Newly Independent States Nonproliferation Program. Dr. Moltz's research interests include arms control, international implications of weapons proliferation, and Northeast Asian security issues. His recent publications include: "The Strategic-Military Implications of NMD Deployment," *International Perspectives on Missile Proliferation and Defenses*, CNS Occasional Paper No. 5, March 2001; "National Missile Defense and Nonproliferation Regimes," *Nonproliferation Review* (2000); "Russian Nuclear Submarine Dismantlement and the Naval Fuel Cycle," *Nonproliferation Review* (2000); and *The North Korean Nuclear Program: Security, Strategy, and New Perspectives from Russia*, edited with A. Mansourov (2000).

Dr. Ni Xiaoquan is professor of international relations at the Institute of East European, Russian and Central Asian Studies, Chinese Academy of Social Sciences in Beijing. He specializes in Russian foreign and security policy, with emphasis on Russian relations with China and the United States. Professor Ni is coauthor of *Russia in the Yeltsin Era: Foreign Policy* (2001); *The New Russia: Politics, Economics and Diplomacy* (1997); *The Newly Independent States* (2001); and co-editor of *The Strategic Triangle: U.S.-Soviet-PRC Interactions since 1971* (1993). Professor Ni has published his research in many Chinese academic journals.

Mr. Kunio Okada is deputy director of the Economic Cooperation Department and deputy director of the Institute for Russian and East European Economic Studies of the Japan Association for Trade with Russia and Central-Eastern Europe (ROTOBO), a nonprofit organization in Japan engaged in promotion of trade and business cooperation between Japan and Russia and other countries. He received an M.A. from the Soka University in Tokyo. Trained as an economist, Mr. Okada has coauthored *Politics and Economics in the Russian Far East: Changing Ties with Asia-Pacific* (1997), and published a wide range of scholarly and popular articles.

Ms. Michelle Ruetschle is an attorney at the Rural Development Institute in Seattle, Washington, where she coordinates the Women and Land Program. Ms. Ruetschle has extensive research, legal, and policy advisory experience on land reform and land market development issues. Ms. Ruetschle received her J.D. from the University of Washington School of Law in 1999. She has contributed to numerous published reports, and her fieldwork experience includes China, Indonesia, the Kyrgyz Republic, and Russia.

Dr. Sergey Sevastyanov is associate professor of political science and director of the International Studies Center at the Vladivostok State University of Economics. Dr. Sevastyanov is an expert in Asia Pacific international relations, specializing in multilateral cooperation processes in security and economics in Northeast Asia. Dr. Sevastyanov participates in American and Canadian research projects and international conferences on Northeast Asia and the Russian Far East. Among his most recent publications are: "Naval Cooperation in the Asia Pacific," *Sea Bulletin* (1999); "Russian Reforms: Implications for Security Policy in the Russian Far East," *NBR Analysis* (2000); and "The Russian Far East and New Regional Development Cooperative Plans," *NIRA Policy Research* (2000).

Dr. Alexander S. Sheingauz is professor of economics and director of the department of natural resources and infrastructure at the Economic Research Institute at the Far Eastern Branch of the Russian Academy of Sciences in Khabarovsk. Dr. Sheingauz has been a visiting scholar to Osaka Economics and Law University, University of British Columbia, and Harvard University. His research interests include the economics of natural resources, especially forests. Dr. Sheingauz's extensive publications include: *Problems and Perspectives of Potential Natural Resource Use and Industry Development in Khabarovskii Krai* (2000); *Natural Resources of the Russian Far East and Northeast Asia* (1997); and *Natural Resources and Environment in Northeast Asia: Status and Challenges*, ed. with H. Ono (1995).

Dr. Grigoriy I. Sukhomirov is a researcher at the Economic Research Institute of the Far Eastern Branch of the Russian Academy of Sciences in Khabarovsk. His economic interests include wildlife management, especially hunting and fishing, and traditional natural resource use of native and minority peoples. Recent publications include *Wildlife Management of Khabarovskii Krai: Development and Perspectives* (2000); and "Natural Resources of the Russian Far East and Northeast Asia," in A. Sheingauz, ed. (1997).

Dr. Elizabeth Wishnick is the author of *Mending Fences: The Evolution of Moscow's China Policy from Brezhnev to Yeltsin* (2001) and numerous articles about international relations and regional development in Asia, including "The East by West Trade Corridor: Myth and Reality," *ERINA Report* (August 2000); "Russia in Asia and Asians in Russia," *SAIS Review* (winter-spring 2000); and "Chinese Perspectives on Cross-Border Relations" in S. Garnett, ed., *Rapprochement or Rivalry? Russia-Chinese Relations in a Changing Asia* (2000). She has served as research associate and visiting lecturer at the department of political science at Columbia University's Barnard College and visiting lecturer at the department of political science at Yale College.